Becky Walters

FORTRAN 77 Principles of PROGRAMMING

FORTRAN 77

Principles of PROGRAMMING

Jerrold L. Wagener

Computer Science
State University of New York, Brockport

JOHN WILEY & SONS

New York • Chichester • Brisbane • Toronto • Singapore

Library of Congress Cataloging in Publication Data:

Wagener, Jerrold L
  Fortran 77 Principles Of
  Programming
  Includes indexes.
  1. FORTRAN (Computer program language) I. Title.
QA76.73.F25W32 001.6′424 79-17421
ISBN 0-471-04474-1

Printed in the United States of America

10 9 8 7

PREFACE

This book is a comprehensive text/reference on Fortran programming, and completely describes the new standard Fortran language—Fortran 77. In general it presents, in a Fortran 77 context, the important principles of contemporary computer programming practice. In particular it presents structured programming by application as the normal way to program.

Fortran 77 has many features, not contained in the previous Fortran standard, that contribute significantly to its suitability as a modern general-purpose computer language. Among these features are the CHARACTER data type (which provides a good fixed-length string facility), the block-IF control structure (which provides if-then-else and general n-way selection control), and extensive I/O facilities (which include format-free READ and PRINT statements, file connection control, and provisions for I/O error recovery). There are a number of others, and I have tried to show that the resulting Fortran 77 is indeed an excellent general-purpose language for modern software development.

I have treated Fortran 77 as an entirely new and versatile language, with the presentation unencumbered by references to and comparisons with previous versions of Fortran. Experienced Fortran programmers are assured, however, that their old Fortran programs will function unchanged as Fortran 77 programs, almost without exception. Experienced and novice programmers alike will benefit from the emphasis on effective modern use of the features of Fortran 77. Concepts and techniques pertaining to well-structured programs, program modularization, numeric and nonnumeric processing, program correctness, data files, data types and structures, and recursion are discussed in detail.

An important feature of this book is the presentation of a large number of example computer programs, usually complete with output. These examples systematically progress from extremely simple ones in the first chapters to quite sophisticated ones later on, with each new example (in most cases) illustrating one additional feature of Fortran 77. The example programs are all written in the same consistent style, a style that I believe to be in the spirit of contemporary practice and highly effective in impressing on the reader the virtues of well-structured, readable, well-documented programs. One benefit of this, I hope, is that the example programs are so complete and lucid that they are, by themselves, sufficient to initially acquaint the reader with the essence of Fortran 77. They are easily distinguished from the rest of the text by the shading along the left margin.

The book is divided into three major parts. Part 1 (''Fortran Fundamentals'') contains six chapters of material basic to Fortran programming. It includes simple I/O, the declaration and use of data elements in problem solving, selection and repetition control structures, and ends with an introduction to program modularization (subroutines). Preceding Part 1 is an introductory chapter (Chapter 0) supplying background material on the structure of computing machinery and the nature of computer programming. After Part 1 the chapters are largely independent and self-contained, and their order is not especially critical.

Part 2 (''Program Structure'') deals with the structuring of programs and related aspects of programming and program development. This part begins with two chapters on procedures (subroutines and functions), examining—in detail—argument passing and association, local and global data element facilities and their uses, and guidelines pertaining to procedure design and use. A chapter is then devoted to an in-depth examination of control structures and corresponding Fortran 77 facilities, with particular attention paid to loop exits. One application of these concepts occurs in Chapter 10, which deals with program correctness and proofs of correctness. This chapter contains an introduction to proving programs correct, and, to my knowledge, contains the first reasonably general treatment of proving Fortran programs correct. Chapter 11, on recursive procedures, completes Part 2, and discusses another important programming technique largely ignored (in the literature, but increasingly implemented) in the context of Fortran.

Part 3 (''Data Structure'') deals with data elements and Fortran's facilities for representing and processing data. The intrinsic data types of DOUBLEPRECISION and COMPLEX are introduced, and illustrated with program examples using each. Techniques are developed for utilizing either INTEGER or CHARACTER data types for simulating bit strings, enumerated data types, lists, trees, and records, and program examples illustrate the use of each of these kinds of data elements. The major focus in this part, however, is on data files and the Fortran 77 provisions for opening, closing, reading, writing, and inquiring about sequential, direct, and internal data files. Appendices B and C illustrate typical ways in which Fortran's data elements are implemented on computing machinery.

Several computer courses could use this book as a text. No prerequisites are necessary, and each course should include all six chapters of Part 1. A minimal introductory course in Fortran programming could reasonably terminate at this point. A very ambitious course in Fortran programming or introductory computer science could include most of the material in the book, as could a more leisurely two-course sequence. Most courses in Fortran programming will include, in addition to Part 1, Chapters 7 and 8 (''Subroutines'' and ''Functions'') from Part 2 and then an appropriate selection from the last seven chapters (9–15). For example, a course emphasizing business applications of computing would also include Chapters 14 and 15 (''Data Files'' and ''File I/O''); a course emphasizing scientific/engineering applications would include Chapters 12 and 13 (sophisticated use of data elements). The end-of-chapter programming exercises constitute an unusually large and diversified set of problems. An instructor's manual, containing solutions to many of these exercises, is available from Wiley.

Programming-oriented courses in computer science fundamentals, for which this book would be an excellent text or language supplement, normally include all of those topics in Part 2 and some of those in Part 3. In general the choice of which chapters to include from the last seven should be governed by the interests and objectives of the class and the time available. Whichever chapters are chosen will be useful for future reference, since the programming practitioner will most assuredly eventually encounter these areas. Experienced programmers will need only to quickly review Part 1 (perhaps glancing mostly at the example programs and Appendix A), and then concentrate on those chapters of interest in Parts 2 and 3.

The example programs have all been processed with a commercially available Fortran 77 compiler, and I thank the Prime Computer Co., Framingham, MA, for making an early version of their Fortran 77 compiler available to me. Most commercial compilers contain useful extensions to the standard language. I have carefully avoided any such extensions so that the material in this book will apply directly to any implementation of Fortran 77 that conforms to the standard language. The official description of the Fortran 77 standard may be obtained from American National Standards Institute, Inc., 1430 Broadway, New York, NY, 10018, as document ANSI X3.9-1978 Programming Language Fortran.

As previously indicated, I believe that Fortran 77 is an excellent general-purpose language. For the most part I have endured its deficiencies, often developing alternative techniques that can be used to advantage by the programmer. Fortran 77 has one deficiency, however, although it is easily remedied: it does not have a general loop control structure with exiting. Therefore toward the end of Chapter 5 (''Loop Control'') I define a simple do-repeat-exit loop control structure with a single-level exit facility. Thenceforth I use do-repeat-exit when describing loops. When this nonstandard feature appears in a program it is clearly identified as such, and the conversion to standard Fortran 77 is simple. In fact subroutine DOREPX in Chapter 8 (and program F PLUS in Chapter 15) performs this conversion automatically (and has been tested on all of the program examples containing do-repeat-exit). This program (which works for do-repeat-exit in either lower- or upper-case letters) may be used in lieu of the given manual conversion technique.

I am indebted to a number of individuals who reviewed the original manuscript and made suggestions for improvement. I especially thank Anthony Ralston for his many valuable suggestions. Others deserving special thanks for their suggestions are Harry Gross, Charles Hughes, Larry Humm, Charles Pfleeger, and Jean Wagener. These individuals, and others, deserve much credit for spotting errors and recommending an occasional different tack. Any remaining deficiencies in the finished product are, of course, solely my responsibility.

Jerrold L. Wagener

Brockport, New York
September 1979

CONTENTS

PART II PROGRAM STRUCTURE 157

PART III DATA STRUCTURE 249

FORTRAN 77 Principles of PROGRAMMING

Chapter Programming Fundamentals

This book describes completely the elements of the Fortran computer programming language, and in considerable detail, illustrates effective, contemporary use of Fortran. While the treatment of Fortran is comprehensive, and many aspects of contemporary programming technology are described, no prior knowledge of programming is assumed. Because of the comprehensive nature of this book, and the resulting inclusion in places of somewhat specialized material, the presentation of Fortran is organized into three parts. Part 1 (Fortan Fundamentals) describes a minimal subset of Fortran that is useful for writing programs. All six chapters of Part 1 are fundamental, and these chapters contain only general material, important to all programmers. Parts 2 and 3 contain more specialized material, and the chapters in these two parts will be of varying relevance, depending on the interests and objectives of the reader. For this reason the chapters in Parts 2 and 3 have been designed so that their order is not critical and the interdependence among these chapters is minimal.

The reader who is already familiar with the fundamental concepts of computer programming, and wants to turn immediately to the description and use of Fortran, may proceed directly to Part 1. This chapter provides the background concerning computers and the nature of programming necessary to prepare the reader for the art and science of Fortran programming.

0.1 Computing Systems

The principal elements of a typical computing system are shown schematically in Figure 0.1. (Large computing systems are often considerably more complex than shown in Figure 0.1, but even in such systems the following fundamental concepts are still valid.)

These elements fall into three general categories:

1 Processing units (the CPU box).

2 Memory units (the elements labeled "Main memory" and "Secondary memory").

3 Input/output units (the "Line printer", "Card reader", and "Terminals").

In general, the CPU (Central Processing Unit) performs the actual computations and data processing, and controls the interaction of the various parts of the system. The memory units are those devices that "hold" the data that is to be processed. The arrows in Figure 0.1 represent possible paths over which data can move. Thus data can be moved between the CPU and main memory (MM). Input/output units provide the interface for the flow of information between the computer and the outside world (e.g., humans). In the following sections each of these three categories of computer system elements are described in greater detail.

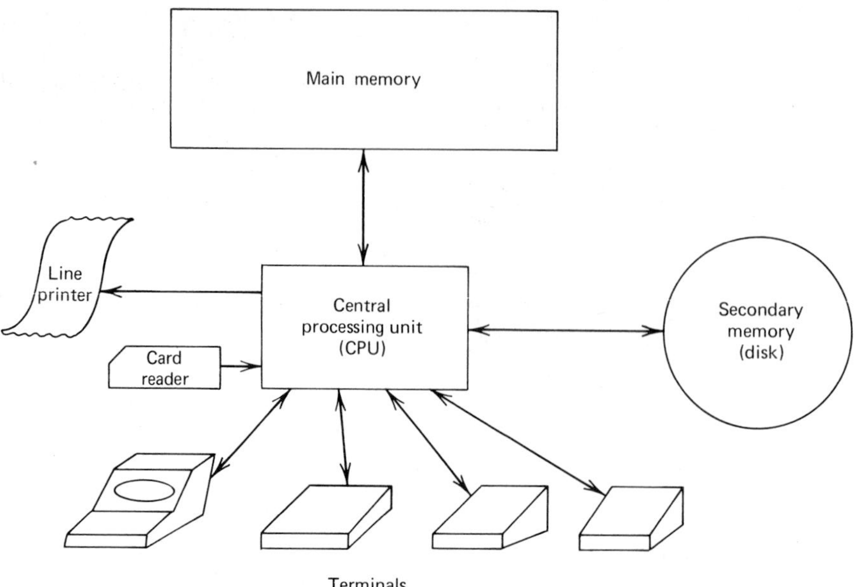

Figure 0.1. Elements of a computing system.

0.1.1 Processing Units

All of the elements of a computer system are important to its functioning, but the CPU is the "heart" of the system. It is an intricate electrical structure, composed of large numbers of electronic components, which provides the electrical control for the movement of data between the CPU and any other part of the computing system. Note from Figure 0.1 that all data flow goes through the CPU (which—at least partially—accounts for the word "Central" in the term Central Processing Unit).

In the computer all data is actually represented as series of pulses of electricity. The presence of a pulse can be thought of as a "1", and the absence of a pulse as a "0". Thus the data can be thought of as packets of 1's and 0's. All numeric information (e.g., integer numbers) is coded in 1's and 0's for the purposes of processing by the computer. The nature of such coding is shown in Appendix C, although the Fortran programmer normally need not be concerned with the details of this coding. Similarly, nonnumeric information (e.g., character symbols, English text, etc.) is coded in "bits" (as the 1's and 0's are called) and Appendix B shows the most common forms this coding takes. Thus the transmission of data performed by the CPU is the transmission of 1's and 0's in the form of electrical pulses. Such transmission can occur at the very high rates typical of electrical/electronic phenomena.

The other function of the CPU is the modification of data. Certain electronic parts of the CPU, called "registers," can accept the bits of data and the CPU can modify data in its registers. For example, suppose that the bits in two different registers represent two numeric values. The CPU is capable of adding these two values and placing the resulting pattern of bits in a register. This (newly obtained) data may then be transmitted to another part of the system (such as one of the Input/Output units). Figure 0.2 illustrates schematically two registers containing bits that represent integers (5 and 9) to be added and the sum placed in a third register. The CPU in most computing systems is capable of a large variety of data modification operations, so that virtually any desired processing of data can be readily accomplished. Such processing occurs at very high electrical/electronic speeds.

The CPU is the only place in the computing system where data can be modified. Thus the CPU really is central to the functioning of the computer—it's where the action is. It's where data is processed, and/or transferred to some other part of the system. The registers of the CPU are where the data are when it's being processed (modified) or in the process of being transferred. Although the number of registers, and size of each register, vary tremendously from computer to computer, typically a

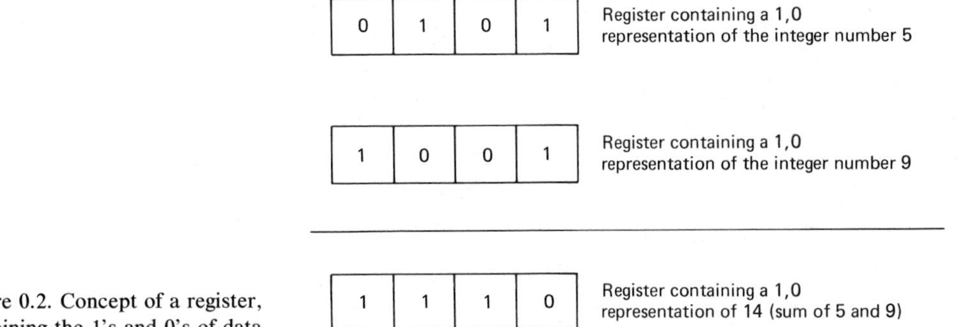

Figure 0.2. Concept of a register, containing the 1's and 0's of data.

CPU has perhaps 20 registers with 16 bits in each register (other typical register sizes are 8, 32, and 60).

0.1.2 Memory Units The CPU is a beehive of activity and volatility. It cannot hold much data at any one time (because there aren't a great many registers), and what data it does have is probably in the process of being changed or moved (or both). A typical computer application involves the processing of a great deal of data. Provision must be made to store this mass of data, and make it available a little bit at a time to the CPU for processing. Memory units are used for this purpose. Memory units are places where large amounts of data can await their turn for processing in the CPU. No changes of data take place in memory. In order for a piece of data in memory to change, it must be transferred to the CPU, changed in the CPU, and then transferred back to the memory.

A memory unit can be thought of as merely a large collection of registers, with provision for transferring the contents of any register, or cell, to and from the CPU (see Figure 0.3).

Figure 0.1 shows two memory units, called Main Memory and Secondary Memory. The reason for this situation, which is typical in contemporary computing systems, is a limitation of present-day technology—high-speed memories are very expensive and low-speed memories are, in comparison, cheap. Thus a small amount (often less than 1,000,000 cells) of high-speed memory (Main Memory) is used for most of the CPU-Memory data transfers, and a large amount of low-speed memory (Secondary Memory) is used to hold data that are not currently being processed.

The individual cells in a Main Memory unit may be processed in a random fashion. That is, the cells may be accessed in any order. For example, immediately after main memory cell number 478,256 is accessed, cell number 93,401 may be accessed. In order to make such random access possible, each memory cell must have a unique identification, and this identification must be given when that cell is to be accessed. Such identification is called the cell "address", and in Figure 0.3 the cell addresses are given as 1, 2, 3, 4, . . ., n-1, n. The bits in the cell representing data, are called the cell "contents."

Thus each memory cell has two items associated with it—its address and its contents. When the CPU needs to access a certain memory cell it specifies the address of that cell; when the CPU transfers data to or from a cell it is the contents of the cell that are moved. The address of a cell always remains the same, and constitutes the unique identification of that cell. The contents of a cell may be any pattern of bits (which represent data), may change from time to time (under the control of the CPU), and has no relation to that cell's address. Memory cell addresses and contents are very important aspects of computer programming. Fortran's provisions concerning these aspects of programming are introduced in Chapter 2.

0.1.3 Input/ Output Units A CPU and a memory unit constitutes a "complete" computing system, in the sense that if the original data is somehow placed in the memory, virtually any processing of

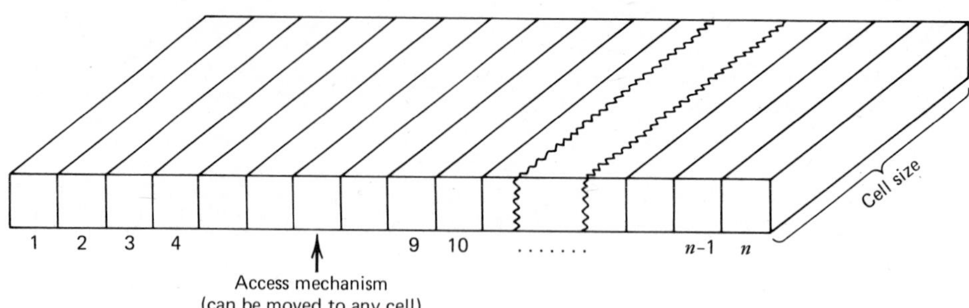

Figure 0.3. The structure of a memory unit. Each cell (register) contains a set of bits (e.g., 8, 16, 32, 60) representing bit-coded data. The value of n for main memory units can vary considerably, from computer to computer, from about 10,000 for very small systems to about 10,000,000 for large ones. Secondary memory units are much longer (have many times more cells). The access mechanism is capable of rapidly accessing individual cells, one after the other, usually in any order, for the purpose of transferring data between the cells and the CPU.

that data may be performed. In order to be practical, however, results of the processing must be communicated to the outside world (i.e., outside of the CPU-memory combination). Moreover, practical means must be available for placing the initial data in the memory. Thus communication links are needed between humans and the CPU-memory combination. These links are provided by the input/output units.

A typical computing system has (or may have provisions for) a number of input/output units by which humans can communicate with the system. Three different such units are shown in Figure 0.1. The line printer is a high-speed printing device that can be used to display the data contents of (any group of) memory cells. The card reader is a high-speed reading device that can be used to input data into memory cells (the data is first placed, by humans, on punched cards, and the punched cards are then placed in the card reader). An increasingly used input/output unit is the *terminal*, four of which are shown in Figure 0.1. This device has a keyboard, similar to that of a typewriter, for inputting data into the computer, and either a typewriter printing mechanism or a television-type screen for displaying output from the computer. The human user can use any or all of these devices for communicating with the computer.

When a human depresses a key on the terminal, for example, a group of bits, representing that character, is generated and transmitted to the CPU. The action that the CPU takes then depends on what the computer is currently *programmed* to do—often the data bits are simply moved to a cell in memory to await further processing. Similarly, when data from memory is to be displayed on a device (e.g., the line printer or a terminal), the bits representing the data are first transferred by the CPU from the memory cell(s) in which they reside to the CPU. From there they are transferred to the output device, where they are converted from bit packets to the corresponding characters, and printed. That is, the input/output units not only provide communication links between human users and the computing system, but they also provide the necessary conversion of the communicated data between the human-oriented forms and the bit-coded forms.

0.2 Computer Programs

In order for data to be processed in the desired manner, the CPU must transfer data between its parts and make the appropriate modifications of data in its registers, all in a proper sequence. However, the CPU does not automatically know which actions to take next—it must be *instructed* each step of the way. One of the properties of the CPU is its ability to accept, and obey, certain *instructions*. Each of these instructions results in the modification of the data within a register of the CPU or the transfer of data from or to the CPU. Each instruction must be one selected from a predefined set, called the *instruction set*, associated with that CPU.

A particular data processing task is accomplished when the CPU follows, or *executes*, a sequence of instructions. The human desiring such processing must specify an appropriate sequence of instructions. Such a sequence is called a *computer program*, and the process of designing a computer program is called *programming*. This section introduces instructions, programs, programming, and related concepts. Programming is the topic of the next section also, and indeed is the major concern of this book.

0.2.1 Concept of an Instruction

Whatever the data processing task, the computer cannot do it all at once. It is done in tiny steps, one after the other. Each step is an extremely simple one, such as adding 1 to a number in a CPU register, or transferring one piece of data from the CPU to the main memory. Not only is each individual step very simple and limited, the CPU is capable of performing only a limited number of different kinds of such simple steps. Moreover, the CPU performs one of these steps only when it is instructed to do so.

For each individual step or action that the computer is capable of there is a corresponding instruction that can be used to cause that action to occur. In considering the kinds of actions that the computer is capable of, one must think in terms of the various instructions associated with (supplied with) that computer. Examples of such instructions are shown in Figure 0.4.

In Figure 0.4 the <things in pointed brackets> indicate a choice of options. For example <register id> refers to the identification of any one of the registers in the CPU. Suppose that a certain computer has three CPU registers, identified respectively as R1, R2, and R3. Then the specific instruction

ADD REGISTER R3 TO REGISTER R1

could be used to cause the current contents of register R3 to be added to the current contents of R1, with the result replacing the original value in R1.

There are three general classes of instructions represented in Figure 0.4. Instructions (*a*) and (*b*) specify the transfer of data between the CPU and other parts of the system. The first of these transfers data from <source id> to one of the CPU registers; the second transfers data from a CPU register to <destination id>. The <source id> may be a memory cell, I/O device, or another CPU register, for example:

MEMORY CELL M27
I/O DEVICE D4
REGISTER R2

Similarly, <destination id> may be a memory cell, I/O device, or another CPU register.

Instructions (*c*) and (*d*) of Figure 0.4 specify the modification of contents in CPU registers. The ADD instruction in (*c*) is typical of the several instructions available to perform simple arithmetic. The COMPLEMENT instruction in (*d*) is typical of the several "logic" instructions usually available. Logic instructions involve modification of a

1 MOVE <source id> TO REGISTER <register id>

2 MOVE REGISTER <register id> TO <destination id>

3 ADD REGISTER <register id> TO REGISTER <register id>

4 COMPLEMENT REGISTER <register id>

5 GOTO <instruction id>

6 IF REGISTER <register id> ALL ZEROS, GOTO <instruction id>

Figure 0.4. Examples of instructions.

register's bits in ways that are often quite useful but not easily achieved with arithmetic operations. The COMPLEMENT instruction, for example, "flips" all the bits (changes 0's to 1's and 1's to 0's) in the specified register. If register R2 contains the bits 01101000 before execution of the instruction

COMPLEMENT REGISTER R2

it contains 10010111 afterward.

Instructions (*e*) and (*f*) are examples of "branching" instructions, and will be discussed in the next section. The three classes of instructions—data transfer, data modification, and branching—represent the principal actions that any computer can take. A specific computer usually has many variations of instructions in each of these classes, rather than just the two shown in Figure 0.4, including some quite specialized instructions and even instructions combining some aspect of two or more of these classes. The total size of a typical actual instruction set is in the vicinity of 100, and often more. While each computer has instructions falling into these three general classes, and has instructions equivalent to those in Figure 0.4, the number of instructions and nature of each instruction vary considerably from computer to computer.

0.2.2 Instruction Sequences

The processing accomplished by executing any one instruction is really quite small. A practical data processing task can be accomplished only by the execution of a great many individual instructions. Moreover the order in which various instructions are executed determines what processing is actually done. Therefore any practical computer task requires the specification of a sequence of instructions to be executed—that is, requires a computer program. The programmer (person designing the sequence of instructions) writes down a list of instructions in the order that the instructions are to be executed.

Suppose, for example, that a number representing the PRICE of an item is stored in memory cell M146, that the sales TAX is stored in memory cell M23, and that the total COST of the item (PRICE + TAX) is to be stored in memory cell M5914. The following sequence of instructions, executed in the order shown, will accomplish this:

1 MOVE MEMORY CELL M146 TO REGISTER R1

2 MOVE MEMORY CELL M23 TO REGISTER R2

3 ADD REGISTER R2 TO REGISTER R1

4 MOVE REGISTER R1 TO MEMORY CELL M5914

Actually a more abbreviated form of each instruction is used, such as the following:

1 MOVE M146, R1

2 MOVE M23, R2

3 ADD R2, R1

4 MOVE R1, M5914

This sequence of four instructions constitutes a simple computer program.

The normal sequence of instruction execution in a program is the order in which the instructions are listed. Departure from this normal sequence is often needed, however, and the purpose of the branching instructions is to specify such departure. Consider, for example, the task of inputting a series of numbers from a terminal (I/O DEVICE D2), adding them together, and transferring the sum back out to the terminal. An input value of zero is to signify the end of the input values. The following program accomplishes this (assume that register R3 initially contains the value zero):

```
1 MOVE D2, R2
2 IF R2 IS 0, GOTO 5
3 ADD R2, R3
4 GOTO 1
5 MOVE R3, D2
```

In this program instruction (1) represents the inputting of the next number, instruction (5) represents the outputting of the sum, and instruction (3) adds the next number to the sum. Instructions (2) and (4) are branching instructions, and specify which instruction is to be executed next. After instruction (3) is executed, instruction (4) is encountered. Instruction (4)'s action is to cause instruction execution to resume at instruction (1)—instruction (4) is called an *unconditional branch*. Instruction (2) is also a branch instruction, but the branch occurs only if the value of register R2 is zero at the time of execution of instruction (2), otherwise execution continues with instruction (3). Instruction (2) is an example of a *conditional branch*.

Note that instructions (1), (2), (3), and (4) of the preceding example are executed repetitively—perhaps many, many times—until R2 contains the value zero when instruction (2) is executed. Most computer programs involve branching instructions to help achieve the desired processing. When branching is used to specify reexecution of a group of instructions, then execution of even a very short program can result in the execution of a great many—perhaps millions or billions—individual instruction steps. Whereas many individual instructions may be executed for a certain task, each instruction takes perhaps only a millionth of a second to execute. Therefore processing by computer may proceed very rapidly, even for complex tasks requiring millions of steps.

0.2.3 Programming Languages

It should be clear from the preceding sections that computers are basically very simple-minded devices, capable only of performing a few very simple operations, and then only as instructed. To achieve any sort of practical processing, a human must devise a sequence of instructions which, when executed by the machine, will result in the desired processsing. Because each instruction is so simple, and so limited in its actions, a practical program typically consists of a very long sequence of individual instructions. Devising such a program usually is no simple task and is susceptible to errors because the programmer must think in terms of the capabilities (and limitations) of the machine's primitive instruction set rather than in the high-level logic terms of the problem. In terms of the first example of the previous section, for example, the programmer must devise the following sequence of instructions

```
1 MOVE M146, R1
2 MOVE M23, R2
3 ADD R2, R1
4 MOVE R1, M5914
```

when what is wanted is simply PRICE = COST + TAX.

In the mid-1950s it was recognized that a (very complex) computer program could accept (as input) a statement such as PRICE = COST + TAX, analyze its sequence of characters, and subsequently generate (as output) the corresponding four machine instructions shown above. When such a program was available, programmers could then write sequences of statements in a high-level language, more like the mathematics and natural language they were familiar with, and in terms of which the data processing problem of interest could be more easily stated. The computer itself could then be used to translate the high-level language program into an equivalent sequence of machine instructions; this sequence of machine instructions could then be executed to perform the desired processing. The process of converting the high-level statements to sequences of machine instructions was known as formula translation, and that original high-level language was therefore called Fortran. Warily at first, not fully trusting the translation process, programmers began writing their programs in Fortran.

Quickly Fortran became a roaring success. Programmers found that they could write programs more quickly and reliably in Fortran than in machine language, and found the use of Fortran more interesting and satisfying. And, while that first translator program was far from perfect, a development had occurred that would change the nature of programming dramatically and permanently—large-scale programming in a high-level language had been born. In the succeeding decades hundreds of high-level languages have been devised, each having its own translator; most, however, are conceptually similar to Fortran in most respects. And today, the vast majority of programs are written in Fortran and other high-level languages, rather than in machine-level instructions. That initial Fortran result has been confirmed many times over—that programs can be written more quickly and reliably in a high-level language.

In the days since that first Fortran translating program, a very great deal has occurred in the field of computing. Knowledge about the translating process, and the writing of translating programs, has increased tremendously. In the early days of Fortran all of the computations were of a numerical nature—solving complex numerical problems of science and engineering. Steadily nonnumerical processing applications, such as text analysis and process automation, have increased, to the point where they now account for more computer usage than numerical processing. And computing systems themselves have undergone a tremendous series of developments. New since those first days of Fortran, for example, are the major developments of disk storage systems and time sharing.

That first Fortran, known subsequently as Fortran I (vintage about 1955), soon became inadequate in the face of the rapid development within the computing field. Fortran therefore underwent several stages of evolution until, in 1966, a version, known as Fortran IV, was standardized by the American National Standards Institute. Thus Fortran IV became the first officially standardized language, and translators for this language appeared on virtually every computer model manufactured. The computing field continued to develop rapidly, and so, too, did Fortran continue to evolve. Today, the 1966 Fortran standard has been superceded by a more modern version, called Fortran 77 (it was completed in 1977). While Fortran 77 is a much more sophisticated language than the 1955 version, most of the programs written in the 1955, 1966, and other versions will work properly in the 1977 version.

Today the computing world teems with high-level languages. Very few, however, have been as successful and as venerable as Fortran. And it remains, in Fortran 77, a good language in which to program. It will no doubt continue to be a good language—continuing its evolution to correct any deficiences that it might still have, and adapting to the ever-changing scene in computing.

0.2.4 Program Translation

A program written in a high-level language, such as Fortran, is not directly *machine readable*. That is, the machine does not directly "understand" Fortran statements. A Fortran program must first be converted to an equivalent sequence of machine instructions before that program can be executed. This conversion—the translation from Fortran to machine instructions—is usually called *compiling*, or *compilation*, and the program that does the translating is called the *compiler*. Thus, before a Fortran program can be executed it must be compiled.

Compilation is therefore an important phase in the processing of a Fortran program. Much will be said in this book about the compilation phase and some of the actions taking place during program compilation. The most important of these actions, of course, is the generation of sequences of machine language instructions that correspond to the Fortran statements. Another important action is that of allocating main memory storage for data used in the program, such as for COST and TAX of a preceding example. In fact, some of the statements in a high-level language program specify some action, such as some specific storage allocation, to take place during program compilation, rather than cause machine instructions to be generated. At the appropriate places in the following chapters the various forms and natures of such statements, as they appear in Fortran, are described. In particular Chapter 2 is devoted almost entirely to such Fortran statements.

0.2.5. Program Execution

The result (output) of compilation is a sequence of machine instructions, or a machine-language program. It is this machine-language program that is actually executed. During execution of the machine-language program (the *execution phase* of processing a Fortran program) the machine instructions are executed in sequence, from the beginning, with branches taking place as encountered. In this manner execution of instructions continues until a STOP instruction (not included in Figure 0.4, but part of every machine instruction set) is encountered.

The Fortran programmer need not know which machine language instructions are generated by the compilation of a Fortran statement. In fact the Fortran programmer need not ever know what machine instructions are available. The compiler takes care of all the necessary details as far as the machine language is concerned. The Fortran programmer does, however, need to know that there are two distinct phases to running a Fortran program—the compilation and execution phases—and during the execution phase the machine-language program generated during the compilation phase is executed. Much reference will be made in subsequent chapters to the execution phase.

0.3 Programming

The term "programming" refers to the process of thinking, writing, and development that takes place between the statement of a problem (to be solved on a computer) and the existence of a program that solves the problem. It is the programmer's ultimate goal to write a program (assumed here to be a high-level language program) that, when compiled and executed, solves the given problem—that is, performs the desired data processing.

As indicated in the preceding sections, a program is a sequence of very specific instructions to the computer, specifying the sequence of actions the computer is to take. This is just as true for high-level language programs as it is for sequences of machine language instructions. As a result, nothing rules the programmer's life more than the following statement:

In order to successfully write a computer program, the programmer must devise, in exact detail, a step-by-step set of actions that, when taken, will solve the given problem.

Thus the programmer must solve the problem—the program merely communicates the solution to the computer so that the steps of the solution can be carried out by the computer, at computer speeds.

This means that there is more to programming than learning the rules of a programming language such as Fortran. In fact there are four general aspects of programming:

Problem definition
Determination of data requirements
Algorithm design
Coding

and each of these four topics is described briefly here. The first three are difficult to teach, since they involve creative efforts and problem-solving skills. As a result they are learned best by example and practice. There are many programming examples throughout this book, and they have been designed to provide good illustrations of all four aspects of programming.

0.3.1. Problem Definition

Problems are often vaguely stated and hence ill-defined for computer solution. Just as programs involve a detailed sequence of instructions, so problem statements must be sharp and well-defined in order that computer solutions may be devised for them. The programmer's first job is to turn an ill-defined problem into a suitably defined problem.

For example, suppose that the given problem is:

"Write a program to generate a paycheck."

Now this seems clear enough—a program is desired to compute the take-home pay for an employee, given all the necessary data such as gross pay, tax rates, number of dependents, etc. But, is a check stub to be generated also (that's normal, but the problem doesn't specify it)? Should the amount appearing on the check be "protected" (e.g., asterisks in the empty leading digit places)? How is the written-out amount (if there is to be a written-out part) to appear? The problem as stated, is, in fact, not well defined. All of these questions, and others, must be answered before a program can be successfully written to solve this problem.

Or consider this problem:

"Write a computer program to find a root of the equation $5x^5 + 2x^4 - 2x^2 + x - 7$."

Again, at first glance, the problem seems clear enough. But there are five roots to this equation, and one, three, or all five of them are real roots. Is a real root desired, or will one of the complex roots (if there is a complex root) suffice? Moreover, it is not likely that any of the roots is an integer; how many places of accuracy should the answer contain? Again the problem is not specified well enough to allow a computer solution.

Every problem is different, and no rule can be given as to when a problem is defined well enough for a program to be written to solve it. But, in general, the programmer can expect to be given an ill-defined problem, and the first task is to refine the problem definition. The skill to do this normally comes primarily from experience in writing programs and in reading others' programs.

0.3.2 Determination of Data Requirements

The second aspect of programming is to determine, quite explicitly, what data is involved in solving the given problem. Some of this data will, normally, be input data—that is, data that are made available at the beginning of the processing, that with which the processing begins. Usually there is also output data—the results of the processing. And often there is intermediate, temporary data, which are the intermediate results of the computation. Since in developing the program provision must be made in storage units for the various *data elements*, the programmer must, at an early stage, have a concrete and detailed idea of what data elements the program will involve.

Consider the paycheck problem of the previous section, for example. Some of the more obvious data elements in this problem are

1 The employee's name (both input and output data).

2 The gross pay, before deductions (input data).

3 The net take-home pay (output data).

Some other data elements needed in order to perform the required processing are:

4 The withholding tax tables (input data).

5 Number of exemptions (input data).

6 Total gross pay for the year (for Social Security tax calculations).

7 Retirement deduction information (input, and possibly output, data).

8 Health and other deduction information (input, and possibly output data).

9 Withholding tax(es) (intermediate, and possibly output, data).

10 Social security tax (intermediate, and possibly output, data).

11 Date (input and output data).

There are usually many different ways to solve a given problem. And the data elements required in one solution are generally somewhat different from the data elements required in a different solution. As will be illustrated a number of times in subsequent chapters, the choice of data elements, and the corresponding solution (program), can have a dramatic effect on the ease of programming and/or efficiency of the processing. In any event, it is not possible to write a program unless the programmer has determined which principal data elements are involved. Thus data element determination is a vital and early phase of the programming process. And, as with problem definition, it is not possible to give rules on how to determine the data element requirements. Instead, studying examples, and especially practice, are what develop this skill.

0.3.3 Algorithm Design

The third aspect of programming, simultaneously the most challenging and intriguing aspect, is *algorithm design*. Algorithm design involves the development of a logical blueprint for solving the problem—determining an explicit, detailed step-by-step set of actions which, when performed, will solve the problem. These actions involve specific processing of data elements, beginning with input data, to produce intermediate results and the desired output data.

An algorithm is a finite sequence of well-defined, executable actions or instructions. That is, each instruction of an algorithm must be meaningful, with its action being unambiguously performable in a finite amount of time. Two examples follow, to illustrate the concept of an algorithm.

Brewing a Fresh Pot of "Perked" Coffee

1 Make sure that all parts of the percolator are clean.

2 Determine the number of cups, N, of coffee to make.

3 Place $N + (½)$ cups of water in the percolator pot. (The ½ cup to provide for water trapped in the grounds and lost in steam.)

4 Place the stem and coffee grounds basket in position in the pot, and measure $N + ½$ scoops of coffee into the basket.

5 Put grounds basket lid in place, and put percolator top on pot.

6 Turn percolator setting to desired coffee strength, and turn on power.

7 Wait until perking action has subsided (5–10 minutes), then serve fresh coffee.

Determining If a Given Positive Odd Integer Is a Prime Number

(evenly divisible only by 1 and itself)

(Note—let $r(A/B)$ stand for the remainder of A divided by B.
Thus $r(47/3) = 2$, and $r(28/7) = 0$)

1 Let N be the given positive integer (greater than 2).

2 Let $K = 1$ (start the value of K at 1).

3 Let $K = K + 2$ (add 2 to the value of K).

4 *If* $K > \sqrt{N}$ *then* stop (N is not prime).

5 *If* $r(N/K) = 0$ *then* stop (N is not prime).

6 Go to step 3 (repeat steps 4 and 5 with a new value of K).

Algorithms are a lot like recipes; in fact, unambiguous recipes *are* algorithms. One can think of an algorithm as being a recipe for solving a given problem—an unambiguous step-by-step set of actions for performing the desired processing. Algorithm design is the process of developing an algorithm.

Algorithms may be expressed in any form that the programmer finds most helpful to the design process. The step-by-step listing, with appropriate explanations of each step, as illustrated in the above examples, is one form that has proven useful. It not only is easy to read and write, but is also close to the form that the subsequent resulting computer program will take. It is the form in which algorithms are expressed in the following chapters.

Complex problems tend to result in long and complex algorithms. Such algorithms often are difficult to develop, completely comprehend, and successfully modify. In such cases it is easy to introduce errors, which later are difficult to find. The usual defense against these phenomena is to separate a complex problem into a set of simpler, more or less self-contained, constituent parts whenever possible. The details of the organization of the parts, without concern for the details of any part, is then a much simpler, and less error prone, task than developing a detailed algorithm for the entire problem. An algorithm for each part can then be developed separately, without concern for the details of any other part. Thus in place of developing one long complicated algorithm, one designs several, shorter, relatively independent algorithms. The accumulated knowledge about programming clearly shows that this modular approach to program design is quicker and more reliable than the single, complicated algorithm approach.

Consider the following simple example to illustrate separating a problem into simpler parts. Suppose that for some positive integer P we want to find the first P prime numbers. The following algorithm solves the problem:

1 Obtain the value for P (assume P is a positive integer).

2 Let $N = 1$ (N will be the next number to check for being prime).

3 Let $Q = 1$; print 2 (2 is the first prime number).

4 Let $Q = Q + 1$ (add 1 to the value of Q).

5 If $Q > P$ then stop (the first P primes have been found).

6 Let $N = N + 2$ (add 2 to N, for the next possible prime).

7 Check N for prime (use algorithm given above).

8 If N is prime then print N and go to (4) else go to (6).

Note in particular step 7 of this algorithm. It says "the details of determining whether N is prime or not go here, but let's not worry about those details just now, and concentrate on how this determination fits into the overall problem." The algorithm for making this determination was given earlier, and could simply be inserted at step 7. The problem of finding the first P primes has been divided into two (approximately equal size) simpler problems. Since these two are rather simple algorithms, the likelihood of an error in either one is considerably less than if one longer algorithm had been developed to solve the problem all at once.

The programmer must develop skills in doing such modular design. Again, the ways that such skills are developed are by watching and doing rather than by following a list of rules. Much emphasis has been devoted in this book to illustrating effective modular design techniques. These will be found starting as early as Chapter 3.

Algorithms are normally developed in a relatively informal language familiar and natural to the programmer—a language in which the programmer "thinks" best. And the form that the algorithm takes is usually best if it follows the logical pattern of the problem being solved; that is, in developing the algorithm the programmer should deform the logical structure of the problem as little as possible or not at all. The essence of the logical structure of the problem should be reflected in the algorithm design. Then when modifications to the algorithm are needed (e.g., because of a minor change in the problem or because an error is discovered in the algorithm) they will be relatively easy to make.

The effectiveness of a computer program is completely dependent on the quality of the algorithm design that preceded the program. Thus the importance of algorithm design to computer programs cannot be over estimated. For this reason this book contains many program examples. All are the result of careful algorithm design, and hopefully illustrate the techniques and results of such design.

0.3.4 Coding

The easy part of the programming process is the last part—the coding. It is the easiest because one can follow well-defined rules for the coding. Coding is the mechanics of converting an algorithm into a computer program, such as a Fortran program. For this, one needs to learn the details of the Fortran language—all of its capabilities and limitations. With this knowledge, converting an algorithm into a Fortran program is largely a mechanical procedure and can be done quickly and easily.

An important feature of this book is to present and thoroughly illustrate the use of the features of Fortran. In the numerous example programs care has been taken to illustrate good coding style. A well-written program is a work of art, in addition to being a practical tool for processing data and making computations.

0.4 Applications of Programming

As mentioned earlier, computers were originally used solely for making complex scientific/engineering numerical calculations. Then came major applications in business data processing followed closely by applications in industrial automation and other significant uses of computing. Today few areas indeed exist without major reliance on computers, and many are totally dependent on them. Applications of computers and programming now come in every conceivable form. This section discusses a few of the major application areas of programming.

0.4.1 Numerical Calculations

Making complex numerical calculations is still a major application of computer programming. This book contains, at various places, examples of simple numerical calculations. It does not contain complex ones, however, since the mathematical sophistication needed to understand such examples is not a prerequisite for this book.

Be that as it may, if anything, numerical calculations are increasingly important applications of computing. Engineering calculations of all types are requiring more precision, and tend to be more intricate as technology advances. Scientific theories, from subnuclear structure to the mysteries of astronomical black holes, increasingly involve models requiring enormous amounts of sophisticated numerical calculations. And, more and more, common modern technological society depends on complex numerical calculations—in applications as diverse as air traffic control to space craft stabilization to the scheduling of college classes.

Fortran is still the preeminent computer language for numerical calculations. And indeed, it is an indispensable tool these days for those occasionally needing more computing capability than provided by an electronic calculator. While this book does not contain much in the way of specific examples of Fortran programs for performing numerical calculations, it does present all of the aspects of Fortran needed for such applications. It therefore should be of great value to anyone wishing to apply Fortran 77 to the solution of numerical problems.

0.4.2 Data Processing

When business data processing became a popular application of computing, it quickly exceeded numerical calculation applications in volume. And, perhaps until recently, it accounted for the majority of all applications of programming. Business data processing is certain to continue to be a major user of computers. Enterprise of all types is becoming increasingly dependent on computerized data processing.

Data processing is characterized by the processing of huge files, or "banks", of data. Typical of such files, for example, are files of employee personnel data (for payroll generation, for example), product inventory data, customer charge account data, insurance account data, and so on. In processing such a file of data, typically one portion of the data, such as inventory data for one product, or charge account data for one customer, is moved into the CPU-MM part of the computer for processing. Then the processing (under the control of the program, of course) takes place, which might be updating the inventory information for that product and possibly generating an order to restock that product, or generating the monthly bill for that charge account customer. This process is then repeated for the next product, or the next customer, or the next whatever, in the file, and this repetitive processing continues until the entire file has been processed.

Files are extremely important data structures, therefore, in business data processing, and indeed files are important in many other kinds of applications, also. Until Fortran 77, however, Fortran did not have adequate file features, and therefore was not universally used for data processing applications. Other languages, most notably Cobol, were developed primarily for file processing applications, and have become the most popular for such work. Data processing programmers will need to become familiar with these languages.

Nevertheless, Fortran is used extensively for data processing, and the features of Fortran 77 make it quite good for such applications. Data processing programmers and managers should know Fortran 77. Program examples relevant to data processing are scattered throughout the book, but file processing and related topics are concentrated mainly in Part 3. Those interested in Fortran primarily for Data Processing applications will find the Fundamentals of Part 1, followed by the file processing of Part 3, to be a most useful portion of this book.

0.4.3 Systems Software

A Fortran compiler is a program. It is a program that makes it practical for a programmer to write in Fortran rather than in machine language. It is a program that makes it easier for computer users to use their computers. Such programs are often called *systems programs*, or *systems software*.

In the days since that first Fortran compiler, systems software has become a major application of programming. Every computer nowadays must have Fortran compilers, Cobol compilers, and, typically, compilers for a number of other languages. In addition most of the larger modern computing systems have various versions of time sharing—in which a number of people, perhaps 100, can all sit down at terminals and simultaneously, apparently, run their programs on a single computer. Such users are making use of another set of systems software programs—the programs providing the time-sharing facility. These programs are even more complex than compilers, and some systems software programs are among the most complex programs ever devised. In addition to compilers and time sharing, a typical modern computing system includes much more systems software, all designed to make the computing facilities conveniently available to a wide range of users, and safe and easy to use.

Each different computer model must have its systems software written from scratch. And currently, new computing models, especially ones based on the computer-on-a-chip microprocessors, are appearing at a rapid rate. Moreover each year new advances are made in the state-of-the-art of systems software technology, and so existing systems software facilities are continually being updated and augmented. For the foreseeable future, apparently, systems software will be a major application area for programming.

Systems programming, as this area of programming is often called, is quite unlike either numerical calculations or data processing. First, it is distinctly nonnumerical in nature, having little to do with making arithmetic computations. It is more nearly characterized by the processing and interpretation of "character" data, such as English words. And the various systems applications are much more varied in scope and detail than the data processing applications tend to be. As with data processing, Fortran is not the ideal language for systems applications. On the other hand, it's not bad either, especially Fortran 77, and much systems software is written in Fortran. From the very beginning this book treats character processing on an equal basis with numerical processing, and thus develops Fortran well as a systems programming language. Many of the program examples are of this persuasion.

0.4.4 Control and Automation

Early in the history of modern computing it was realized that the input devices could actually be sensors of various sorts: temperature, position, weight, light intensity, voltage, etc., and that the output devices could be instrument control panel controls. And thus a number of industrial processes and other highly mechanized operations were converted to computer automation. Of course, the automatic control provided was the result of the program continuously operating on the computer.

In those early days of automation computers were very expensive, in comparison with today's prices, and this limited severely the extent to which computer automation was employed. Today the situation is completely different. Powerful microprocessor computing systems, with many times more capability and reliability than those old computers, are now available for no more than several hundred dollars. Everyone can afford one, and these computers are now being widely used for dedicated control automation. Every such application is different, and requires its own program to achieve the desired control. The boom in this application is just really beginning, and process control and automation is certain to be a major application of programming for a long, long time.

Today most process control programs are still written in machine language. But increasingly the necessary facilities are finding their way into high-level languages, and as a result high-level languages are being used increasingly for these applications.

Fortran does not yet have a complete set of facilities for process control programming. However, Fortran is used widely for such applications, and Fortran 77 can be used quite effectively in this regard. Various examples throughout the book contain features relevant to process control technology, and Chapter 12 in particular addresses many of the issues of importance to this field.

0.4.5 Other Applications

There are, of course, many other important areas of application of programming. These include text analysis, artificial intelligence, computer graphics, statistical analyses, simulation, information retrieval, and others. The categories described in greater detail above, however, should serve to illustrate the enormous diversity and applicability of contemporary programming.

But despite this staggering diversity, programming is a discipline having certain principles, techniques, and characteristics independent of the area of application. Programmers who master these fundamental principles and techniques will feel comfortable, as far as programming is concerned, in virtually any applications area. Readers of this book should be rewarded with an understanding of these principles.

Fortran 77 is a good general-purpose high-level language. Few, if any, languages are as effective as Fortran for practical use in a wide diversity of applications. This book is dedicated to a thorough and rigorous presentation of the features of Fortran 77, and to a comprehensive description of the fundamental principles of Fortran programming.

Part

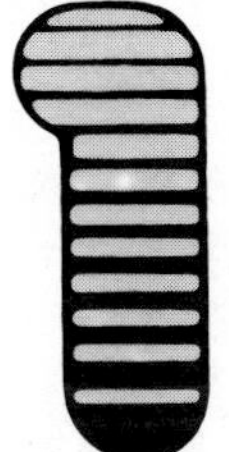

FORTRAN FUNDAMENTALS

In a systematic manner the six chapters of this part present a subset of standard Fortran (informally known as "Fortran 77", and hereafter called Fortran) sufficient for much general programming use. A number of complete program examples are given, beginning with very simple ones and progressing to fairly sophisticated ones that exhibit many of the features of Fortran. These examples not only demonstrate the mechanical features of Fortran, but also suggest effective, well-structured, programming methods.

As a pioneer among high-level programming languages, Fortran has been evolving for more than 20 years. As a result there are some archaic features present in the language that normally should no longer be used. The six chapters of this part contain none of those features. Although this book describes all of Fortran (see, for example, Appendix A) the chapters in Part 1 describe a judiciously selected set of highly useful standard features for constructing Fortran programs. Since Fortran is a standardized language, almost all computing systems should have these features; however, various implementations of Fortran include extensions to, or slight departures from, the standard language. Consult the manuals accompanying such implementations for the details of these dialects of Fortran.

One of the simplest Fortran programs possible is:

```
*....:-----------------------------------------------------------------
      PROGRAM  NULL
*              by <author's-name>   (and possibly date, etc.)
*                     ..This program illustrates the Fortran
*                          PROGRAM statement,
*                          END  statement, and
*                          comment lines.
*                     The PROGRAM statement serves to begin the
*                     program and to give the program a name.
*                     Every program must end with an END statement.
*                     Comment lines are blank lines and lines with
*                     "*" (or "C") in column 1 (the left-most position of
*                     the line).  Comment lines are ignored by the
*                     computer, and may be freely used throughout
*                     the program as explanation ("documentation")
*                     to human readers..
      END
=================================================================
```

(All example programs will be separated from the other text by the leading "*. . . .: ----" line of characters and the trailing "==========" line of characters; these lines are not part of the Fortran program.)

Even though it is a trivial program (the only function it performs is to assign itself a name), NULL does illustrate several features of Fortran. First, all Fortran programs end with an END statement; there is one and only one END statement in a program and it must physically be the last statement. Its purpose is to mark the end of the program and to terminate execution of the program. The form of the END statement is always just as shown in the example—the word END (in capital letters) with no other characters allowed before or after the END.

Second, the program begins with a PROGRAM statement. Unlike the END statement, the PROGRAM statement is optional, but its use is recommended and it will appear in all of the program examples. Its purpose is to provide program identification. The PROGRAM statement, if used, must be the first statement, and it must specify a name (NULL in the above example) that becomes the name of the program. A name is composed of from one to six alphanumeric characters, the first of which must be a letter. An alphanumeric character in Fortran is considered to be either a capital letter (A–Z) or a decimal digit (0-9). A more formal way of describing the PROGRAM statement is:

PROGRAM <name>

The capital letters PROGRAM must appear exactly as shown, while the lower case item in pointed brackets, <name>, indicates something the programmer must provide. In this case the rules for providing <name> have just been given above. It is best to choose a program name that describes the nature of the program.

Third, although it isn't too obvious, NULL exhibits the fundamental line requirement for Fortran program statements—only one statement may be on a line, and it must be contained in positions (columns) 7–72 of that line. (Occasionally a statement is longer than 66 characters and must be continued on a second line. The provision for continuing a Fortran line is described in Section 1.3.) Blank characters (spaces) are completely ignored in Fortran (except in string constants—again see Chapter 1) and may be used freely in any statement to achieve the desired readability characteristics in the program listing. This includes using spaces to visually separate elements of a statement (such as PROGRAM and NULL in the above example) and to indent statements to the right of column 7. When the "transparency" of blanks is combined wisely with the various statement features of Fortran much can be done to produce attractive and highly readable programs. In turn this facilitates the writing of error-free programs, and greatly aids the debugging process when errors do occur. Thus such structuring should always be used, and the example programs illustrate one possible style.

And finally, a program is rarely completely self-explanatory to a human reader. Therefore it is highly desirable to be able to incorporate explanatory notes into the program—notes that do not affect the function of the program but make it more understandable to a human reader. Often a short paragraph of explanation at the beginning of the program, and at key points in the body of the program, are very effective in providing such documentation. Comment lines may be used for this purpose, as illustrated in program NULL. An entire line is ignored by the computer if there is an "*" in column 1, and therefore a comment line cannot contain a Fortran statement (a comment is not considered to be a statement); conversely, lines containing program statements cannot also contain a comment. Completely blank lines are treated as comment lines, as are lines with "C" (in place of "*") in column 1. Comment lines may occur anywhere throughout the program, including preceding the PROGRAM statement, but may not follow the END statement. Any character available on the computing system may appear in comment lines. In particular lower-case letters may appear in comment lines, whereas most elements of program statements are restricted to capital letters, digits, and a few special characters. In constructing comment lines in a program, care should be taken to design them so that they maximally enhance the reader's understanding of the program without interfering visually with the program statements. The example programs illustrate an effective style for using comments. Although the example programs do not contain an <author's-name>, it is good practice to always include such a comment at the beginning of the program, as suggested in NULL.

The typical context in which a Fortran program might be processed on a particular computer is:

```
*....:------------------------------------------------------------------
.LOGIN  <identification>
.FORTRAN
      PROGRAM  <name>
        --}
        --}  Fortran
        --}  program
        --}
      END
.EXECUTE  <name>
.LOGOUT
========================================================================
```

The .LOGIN, .FORTRAN, .EXECUTE, and .LOGOUT lines are not part of Fortran but are job control language (JCL) commands needed to provide the necessary control for processing the Fortran program. Whereas Fortran itself is standard and very nearly the same for all computers, the JCL typically varies considerably among different computers and among different uses (e.g., "batch" and "timesharing") on the same computer. Many JCL forms and options are normally allowed, and the manual for the particular computer used must be consulted for the JCL details. In the example JCL above the .LOGIN and .LOGOUT commands are used to initiate and terminate, respectively, a session in which a program is compiled (the .FORTRAN command) and executed (the .EXECUTE command).

The .FORTRAN command tells the computer that the following lines (down to and including the END statement) constitute a Fortran program that is to be translated into machine-readable form. This translation (called compilation) is then performed and, if no errors are detected, the compiled program—machine readable and "ready-to-go"—is stored under the name specified in the PROGRAM statement. (Or some other name—consult the manual for the particular system being used.) If errors in the Fortran program are detected during compilation, such as misspellings (e.g., PR0GRAM instead of PROGRAM—zero instead of the letter "O") or a forgotten "*" in a comment line, then these errors will be described and no compiled program will be stored. In short, the .FORTRAN command initiates the compilation phase, which results in either a ready-to-go program or a list of errors that the programmer must correct before the program can be successfully compiled.

Compilation is merely the translation of the Fortran program into machine-readable form, and does not include running the program so that it may perform its function; compilation only gets the program ready to run. The .EXECUTE command initiates the execution phase, in which the compiled program is run on the computer, and in which the functions specified in the program's statements are performed. Thus processing a Fortran program involves two distinct phases—compilation and execution. A previously compiled program may be executed without a compilation phase; similarly, a Fortran program may be compiled (and saved) and not executed.

Some Fortran statements cause certain preparations to take place during the compilation phase, and have no effect during execution. Such statements are called specification statements in Fortran, and some of these are introduced in Chapter 2. The second class of Fortran statements are called "executable statements." These are the statements that cause action during execution of the program. The PROGRAM statement is a specification statement—it causes a name to be assigned to the program during the compilation phase and has no other function. The END statement is an executable statement—it terminates execution of the program. In so doing the END statement represents the logical end of the program (however it is also used during compilation to mark the physical end of the program). The following six chapters introduce many additional features of Fortran.

Chapter 1 Printing

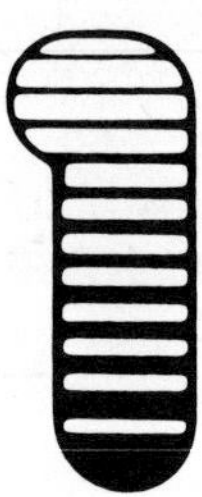

It is a curious phenomenon of programming that virtually every practical program must provide for communication of data to and from the program, yet such provision is among the more technically sophisticated of all aspects of programming. This is so for two reasons. First, most "real world" programs use several of the many devices that a typical computing system has for communicating data to and from the program, including user terminals, magnetic disk units, magnetic tape units, printers, plotters, card readers, etc. And second, the form of the communicated data must be carefully tailored so that it is intelligible to the intended reader (a human, the program itself, or some other program). Communicating data to/from a program is called input/output (I/O), and writing program statements specifying all aspects of I/O can involve some of the most complicated and critical coding in the program. Fortran has very extensive input/output capabilities, and these are described in detail in Part 3 (Data Structure).

And yet, some I/O, especially output, is needed for all of the programs described prior to Part 3. Fortran has, included in its rich assortment of I/O features, a simple PRINT statement, which allows convenient printing of output on the user's terminal or line printer. This chapter is devoted to describing the use of the PRINT statement.

1.1 Printing Literal and Numeric Data

A simple example of the PRINT statement is:

```
*....:-----------------------------------------------------------------
      PROGRAM  MYNAME
*                        ..This program illustrates the use of the
*                        PRINT statement, which is an executable
*                        statement that causes output to be generated.
*                        The command to execute this program, and the
*                        resulting output generated by the PRINT
*                        statements, is shown following the program
*                        listing..

      PRINT *,  'My name is Jerry Wagener.'
      PRINT *,  'I am a Fortran programmer.'
      END
=======================================================================
.EXECUTE  MYNAME

My name is Jerry Wagener.
I am a Fortran programmer.
=======================================================================
```

Note that each PRINT statement produces a separate line of output, and that, starting from the left (first position) of the output line, characters enclosed in single-quote (apostrophe) marks are printed exactly as they appear in the PRINT statement, but without the enclosing quotes.

A sequence of characters enclosed in single quotes is called a *string* (more accurately, a *string constant*, and a string may contain any characters available on the computer being used except the single-quote character itself. The two quotes are called the opening and closing *delimiters* of the string, and are not considered to be part of the string; the first quote begins the string and the next quote terminates the string. Since sometimes a single-quote character is desired as one of the characters in the string, the following exception is provided: after the opening quote two single-quote characters in succession (without any intervening spaces or other characters) are not considered to be string delimiters but are treated as a single quote in the string. For example, if the second PRINT statement in program MYNAME is changed to

```
PRINT *, 'I' 'm a Fortran programmer.'
```

the output contains a single-quote as follows:

```
My name is Jerry Wagener.
I'm a Fortran programmer.
```

The double-quote character may be freely used in a string; it is treated by Fortran as a different character from the single-quote, and from two single-quotes in succession, and has no delimiting significance. In addition, blank characters are treated exactly the same as any other characters in strings—that is, spaces are valid string characters. This is the only instance where spaces are significant, and not ignored, in Fortran. For example EN D, END, and E N D are equivalent, whereas 'EN D', 'END' and 'E N D' are different. Strings may be any length (i.e., have any number of characters in them). A string too long for the printing device being used will be automatically printed on two lines (or more if necessary).

A certain amount of graphic output can be generated with PRINT statements, as the next two program examples illustrate. In each case the output is left for the reader to supply.

```
*....:-----------------------------------------------------------------------
      PROGRAM  BLOCK
*                                        ..This program prints a block "+"
      PRINT *,   '     XXXXXX     '
      PRINT *,   '     XXXXXX     '
      PRINT *,   '     XXXXXX     '
      PRINT *,   'XXXXXXXXXXXXXXXX'
      PRINT *,   'XXXXXXXXXXXXXXXX'
      PRINT *,   'XXXXXXXXXXXXXXXX'
      PRINT *,   '     XXXXXX     '
      PRINT *,   '     XXXXXX     '
      PRINT *,   '     XXXXXX     '
      END
=============================================================================
```

```
*....:-----------------------------------------------------------------------
      PROGRAM  HOUSE
*                                          ..This program prints
*                                          the likeness of a house..
*                                          Try it -- you'll like it!
      PRINT *,   '            *'
      PRINT *,   '          =   ='
      PRINT *,   '        = ..... ='
      PRINT *,   '      =   :   :   ='
      PRINT *,   '    =     :...:     ='
      PRINT *,   '  =                   ='
      PRINT *,   '=..                   ..='
      PRINT *,   '  :  ......  .......  :'
      PRINT *,   '  :  :    :  :  :  :  :'
      PRINT *,   '  :  :    :  :..:..:  :'
      PRINT *,   '  :  :   *:  :  :  :  :'
      PRINT *,   '  :  :    :  :..:..:  :'
      PRINT *,   '  :  :    :           :'
      PRINT *,   '  :..:....:...........:'
      END
=============================================================================
```

The "*" following PRINT serves to indicate computer-generated (as opposed to programmer-specified) formatting of the printed line. In most situations the "*" form of PRINT is adequate, but the programmer does have the option of replacing the "*" with specifications for the form of the output. Methods of doing this will be described in Section 1.2. Assuming for now its "*" form, the PRINT statement can be described more formally, and completely, by:

PRINT* [, <list of output quantities>]

Anything in square brackets [. . . .] is an optional part of the statement. Therefore the simplest form of the PRINT statement is

PRINT *

which simply results in the "printing" of a blank line (handy for the vertical spacing of output).

The <list of output quantities> hints that more can be printed by a PRINT statement than just a single string, and such is indeed the case. The results of numerical calculations may also be printed. Strings in a PRINT statement specify the literal printing of the sequence of characters enclosed by the quotes. Arithmetic expressions (including numerical constants) in a PRINT statement specify the printing of numerical values. Arithmetic expressions are composed of numbers and the ordinary numerical operations of addition, subtraction, multiplication, and division. The next program example illustrates the printing of numeric data.

```
*....:-----------------------------------------------------------------
      PROGRAM CIRCLE
*                    ..This program uses PRINT * to output two
*                    numeric values.  (These values may represent
*                    the diameter and circumference of a circle.)
*                    Quote delimiters are not used in specifying
*                    numeric output, and commas are used to
*                    separate (delimit) output quantities..

      PRINT *, 8, 3.14159*8
      END
=======================================================================
.EXECUTE  CIRCLE

           8        25.132720
=======================================================================
```

Arithmetic expressions are formed in the familiar manner, for the most part, with "+" for addition, "−" for subtraction, "*" for multiplication, and "/" for division. A comprehensive description of Fortran's arithmetic features is given in Chapter 3 (Computations).

The output of program CIRCLE demonstrates that upon execution of a PRINT statement containing an arithmetic expression the expression is evaluated and the resulting numerical value is printed. The form that the numerical output takes may differ from computer to computer, since the form is built into the implementation of Fortran. Usually integer values (i.e., numerical values without a fractional part) are printed in a different form than real values (i.e., numerical values with a fractional part). In the above example the integer value (8) is printed in column 12, which is the rightmost column of the first group of 12 columns in the output line. The value 8 is said to be "right-justified" in the first 12 output positions. The real value (25.132720) is right-justified in the next 16 positions, with six decimal places displayed. This format will be assumed in all subsequent examples involving numerical output generated by PRINT *.

Any number of strings and numeric quantities, in any order and separated by commas, may appear in a PRINT statement for the purpose of generating output. A typical application of this is illustrated in the next example, CIRCL2, in which the <list of output quantities> contains four items—two strings and two numerical quantities.

```
*....:--------------------------------------------------------------
      PROGRAM  CIRCL2
*                       ..The PRINT statement in this program
*                       specifies the printing of four values --
*                       two strings and two numeric values..

      PRINT *,' For diameter', 8, '     the circumference is', 3.14159*8
      END
====================================================================
.EXECUTE  CIRCL2

For diameter            8    the circumference is        25.132720
====================================================================
```

The values of output quantities are printed in the same left-to-right order that they appear in the PRINT statement. Printing begins in the first (leftmost) column of the output line with the value of the first output quantity. The number of output positions required by a string is the same as the number of characters in the string (i.e., the length of the string); the number of output positions required to print an integer value is 12 and to print a real value is 16. Within the output line the second value is placed immediately following (i.e., to the right of) the last (rightmost) position required by the first value. Subsequent output is similarly "tacked on" to the last position of the preceding output. If a PRINT statement requires more columns of output than are available on one line of the output device (typical device widths: 80 columns, 120 columns), the printing is automatically continued on the next line.

Since each PRINT statement begins a new output line, and any number of blanks may be printed as a string (or part of a string), the programmer using the PRINT * feature of Fortran has considerable control over the design of computer output. The fixed form in which numerical values are printed somewhat limits the flexibility with which output can be made to appear. The next section describes the means by which the programmer can circumvent this limitation of PRINT *.

1.2 Formatting Printed Data

On occasion more control is required over output format than is possible with PRINT *. In these cases the "*" can be replaced by a *format specification*, in which the programmer dictates precisely the form of the output. The next example is a modification of program CIRCLE that specifies the exact forms in which the two numeric values are to be printed.

```
*....:--------------------------------------------------------------
      PROGRAM  CIRCL3
*                       ..A modification of program CIRCLE, in which
*                       the "*" is replaced by specifications for the
*                       printed forms of the two values.  The
*                       integer will be printed in three columns
*                       (instead of 12) and the real in eight
*                       columns with two decimal places (instead of
*                       16 and 6, respectively)..

      PRINT '(I3,F8.2)',  8, 3.14159*8
      END
====================================================================
.EXECUTE  CIRCL3

  8   25.13
====================================================================
```

The I3 means "right-justify the integer numeric value in the first three positions of the printed line", and the F8.2 means "right-justify the real numeric value in the next eight print positions, rounding off the fractional part to two decimal places." A PRINT statement using a format specification is called a "formatted PRINT".

The I and F "data descriptors" (as they are called) always have the forms

I<field width>
F<field width>.<decimal places>

where <field width> is an integer value and specifies the number of print positions to be used for printing this quantity, and <decimal places> is also an integer value and specifies the number of decimal places to be displayed in printing a real quantity. Numeric values (both integer and real) are always printed right-justified in their fields. In the fixed format cases using PRINT *, a data descriptor of I12 was assumed for each integer quantity, and F16.6 for each real quantity.

The data descriptors in a format specification are separated by commas, and constitute a left-to-right list of descriptors. The number of data descriptors is normally the same as the number of items in the <list of output quantities>, with the first (leftmost) descriptor associated with the first (leftmost) output quantity, the second descriptor with the second output quantity, and so on. In each instance the output quantity tells WHAT data is to be output and the data descriptor tells HOW that data is to be placed on the printed line.

I descriptors must always be used with, and only with, integer numeric quantities, and F descriptors with real numeric quantities. Strings can be printed with a formatted PRINT statement by using an "A" for the data descriptor, as illustrated by program CIRCL4.

```
*....:----------------------------------------------------------------
      PROGRAM  CIRCL4
*                      ..A modification of program CIRCL2, in
*                      which a formatted PRINT statement is used
*                      instead of PRINT *..

      PRINT'(A,I3,A,F8.2)',' Diameter=',8,'     Circumference=',3.14159*8
      END
======================================================================
.EXECUTE  CIRCL4

Diameter=  8     Circumference=     25.13
======================================================================
```

If the number of data descriptors in a PRINT statement is greater than the number of items in the <list of output quantities> then the extra descriptors are ignored; if the number of data descriptors is less than the number of items in the output list then the descriptors are used again, starting with the leftmost one, until the entire <list of output quantities> has been printed. Fortran provides considerably more data descriptor features, but the ones described here are sufficient for all output until the more specialized I/O needs arise in Part 3.

When one goes to the trouble of formatting the printed output it is often desirable to specify tabulation—that is, to explicitly specify the print position in which the next printing is to begin, or to specify skipping over a desired number of print positions before printing the next quantity. The position descriptors provide such capability:

T <print position>	means tabulate to specified position
<number of positions>X	means skip specified <number of positions> to the right from current position

where <print position> and <number of positions> are (unsigned, positive) integer values. In addition to these a "/" may be used to tab to the beginning of the next line. The T and X position descriptors may be mixed with the data descriptors (and separated from them with commas) in the format specification to achieve the desired column alignment, spacing, etc. in the printed output. Blanks are printed in positions skipped using the T and X descriptors. One or more consecutive slashes (which need not be separated from the descriptors with commas) make "vertical spacing" easy to control. Another version of program CIRCLE illustrates such positioning techniques.

```
*....:-----------------------------------------------------------------
      PROGRAM  CIRCL5
*                   ..This program demonstrates a formatted
*                   PRINT statement which uses the T descriptor
*                   to achieve column alignment and the / to
*                   "skip" lines..

      PRINT '(//T20,A,I3/T20,A,F8.2///)','Diam=',8,'Circum=',8*3.14159
      END
=======================================================================
.EXECUTE  CIRCL5


                  Diam=  8
                  Circum=    25.13


=======================================================================
```

The printed data starts in column 20 on each of two consecutive lines. The // at the beginning of the format specification causes two blank lines to precede the program output, and the /// at the end causes three blank lines after the values are printed. Note that n slashes at the beginning or end of the format cause n blank lines, whereas n slashes in the interior of the format cause $n - 1$ blank lines.

The PRINT statement may now be described more completely as

PRINT <format specification>[,<list of output quantities>]

where "*" is one of the options for <format specification>. With the "*" option the data descriptors for integer and real numeric values are fixed implementation-defined formats, and the position descriptors cannot be used. In a formatted PRINT the <format specification> contains the desired position and data descriptors enclosed by '(and)'. Figure 1.1 summarizes the descriptors that may be used in the <format specification>.

The careful reader may have noticed a systematic phenomenon in the output of the three previous programs (CIRCL3, CIRCL4, CIRCL5) using formatted PRINT—the

data descriptors:	A	for strings of characters
	I<field–width>	for integer numeric data
	F<field–width>.<decimal–places>	for real numeric data
position descriptors:	T<print–position>	for tabulating to a specific column
	<number–of–positions>X	for skipping to the right
	/	for line termination (i.e., begins new line)

Figure 1.1. Format specifications descriptors. (All of the <. . .> represent integer values.)

first character (a blank in each of these cases) is missing from the printout. The reason is that Fortran uses the first character of each printed line to control vertical spacing of the printing device, and doesn't print that character. The other characters are all shifted one place left for printing. The PRINT * statement automatically inserts a blank at the beginning of each print line so that single spacing is produced (this blank, of course, isn't printed). In formatted printing a character is not automatically inserted, so that the programmer is required to explicitly insert the desired character. The standard characters which are used in the first print position for line placement are summarized in Figure 1.2.

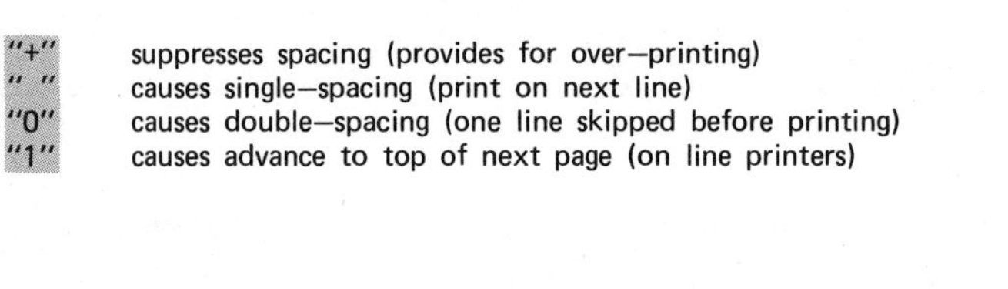

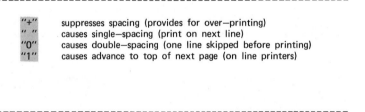

"+"	suppresses spacing (provides for over–printing)
" "	causes single–spacing (print on next line)
"0"	causes double–spacing (one line skipped before printing)
"1"	causes advance to top of next page (on line printers)

Figure 1.2. Functions of characters in position 1 of print line.

The most frequent need is for single spacing, and any method of making the first character a blank will result in single spacing. The following are all equivalent—they each output the phrase "single space" beginning in the first column of the next output line:

```
PRINT *, 'single space'
PRINT '(A)', ' single space'
PRINT '(A,A)', ' ','single space'
PRINT '(T2,A)', 'single space'
PRINT '(X,A)', 'single space'
```

Interesting applications of the use of "+" in the first position include (1) underlining, and (2) overprinting to achieve special effects (e.g., darker characters) for graphic purposes. Program OVER illustrates how two or more characters can be superimposed for such purposes.

```
*....:------------------------------------------------------------------
      PROGRAM  OVER
*                     ..This program uses the "+" in print
*                     position 1 to achieve over-printing.
*                     The first "new" character is super-
*                     position of the "I" and "H" characters;
*                     the darkest one has an additional "X"
*                     superimposed..

      PRINT '(A,A)', ' ', 'I X H H H'
      PRINT '(A,A)', '+', '       I I'
      PRINT '(A,A)', '+', '         X'
      END
========================================================================
.EXECUTE  OVER

I X H █ █
========================================================================
```

1.3 Continuing Fortran Statements

Occasionally a Fortran statement is too long for one line and must be continued on the next line. This can easily happen in PRINT statements, primarily because of the likelihood of having long strings for output quantities. Column 6 of a Fortran statement is reserved for continuation. When the compiler finds a nonblank, nonzero character in column 6 of a program line it treats that line as a continuation of the preceding line. It's as if 7–72 of the continued line were simply tacked on to column 72 of the preceding line, effectively lengthening the preceding line by 66 additional positions. A statement may be continued on more than one additional line—the limit is 19 continued lines per statement. A statement may be "broken" at any place and continued on the next line. Caution must be exercised when breaking in the middle of a string, however, since any trailing blanks up to column 72 on the initial line will be treated as part of the (continued) string. It is best to avoid continuation in the middle of a string.

A good programming habit is to always use the same character in column 6 for all instances of continuation, and to indent the continued lines a few spaces. A visually effective character to use for continuations is the ".", as is the ":". The latter is illustrated in program CIRCL6, which is functionally identical to CIRCL5 except that, by using continuation, the long PRINT statement is packaged more effectively on three lines.

```
*....:------------------------------------------------------------------
      PROGRAM  CIRCL6
*                     ..A modification of program CIRCL5 in which the
*                     PRINT statement is spread over 3 lines
*                     rather than "crammed" onto one line..
      PRINT '(//T20,A,I3/T20,A,F8.2///)',
     :      'Diameter =', 8,
     :      'Circumference =', 3.14159*8
      END
========================================================================
.EXECUTE  CIRCL6


                   Diameter =  8
                   Circumference =    25.13


========================================================================
```

Computer generated reports often involve the printing of lengthy headings and other material to enhance their appearance and usefulness. For example, suppose that a monthly sales report is to be generated, consisting of the three columns of data: salesperson identification, current month's sales, and annual sales to date. The effectiveness of such a report depends greatly on the explanations provided by appropriate headings. Program SALES demonstrates the use of the Fortran PRINT statement to generate such output.

```
*....:-----------------------------------------------------------------
      PROGRAM  SALES
*                                   ..This program generates a sales
*                                   report heading; the three columns
*                                   of data are aligned at positions
*                                   1, 24, and 44.  Note that Fortran
*                                   allows 3(T2,A,T25,A,T45,A/) for
*                                   T2,A,T25,A,T45,A/T2,A,T25,A,T45,A/
*                                   T2,A,T25,A,T45,A/

      PRINT '(////T2,A,A,A,I5///3(T2,A,T25,A,T45,A/))',
     :      'SUPER LUMBER CO.','   Monthly Sales Report   ','Oct', 1980,
     :      'SALESPERSON'    , 'CURRENT' , 'ANNUAL',
     :      'IDENTIFICATION', 'SALES'   , 'SALES' ,
     :      '--------------', '-------' , '------'
*                                    (The program statements that
*                                     determine and print the sales
*                                     data would be inserted here.)
      END
=====================================================================
.EXECUTE  SALES




SUPER LUMBER CO.   Monthly Sales Report   Oct 1980


SALESPERSON           CURRENT             ANNUAL
IDENTIFICATION        SALES               SALES
--------------        -------             ------

=====================================================================
```

Eleven lines of output (some blank) are produced by program SALES in the course of generating the headings. Exactly the same output could be achieved with 11 appropriately formed PRINT * statements, if it weren't for the integer value (1980) printed in the I5 format.

In practice, a program like SALES would be made more general so that it could be used by different companies and in any month and year, without modifying the program. The Fortran provisions for doing this are introduced in Chapter 2.

1.4 Summary

In this chapter three features of Fortran have been introduced:

1 The PRINT * statement for convenient printing of string and numeric data.

2 The formatted PRINT statement for greater control over the form of printed numeric data, and over the positioning of the output.

3 Continuing a PRINT (or any Fortran) statement over two or more lines, either because the statement is too long for a single line or because it looks better on multiple lines.

The form of the PRINT * statement is

```
PRINT * [,<list of output quantities>]
```

where the <list of output quantities> may contain any number of strings and arithmetic expressions, separated by commas. The form of the formatted PRINT statement is

PRINT '(<list of descriptors>)'[,<list of output quantities>]

where the <list of descriptors> contains descriptor elements (summarized in Figure 1.1), and includes data descriptors matching the number, type, and order of elements in the <list of output quantities>. Continuation is specified by placing a character such as ":" in column 6 of the line that is a continuation of the preceding line.

An output line may be thought of as a set of print positions numbered 1,2,3, . . ., starting at the left, with the PRINT statement causing characters (including blanks) to be printed in these positions. Each PRINT statement constructs a line (or more) of output, beginning in position 1 and progressing to the right, with values specified in the <list of output quantities>. The formatting of numeric data is fixed, and always the same, with PRINT *. In the formatted PRINT the number of print positions, and, for real values, the number of decimal places, are specified by the programmer. In addition the programmer may specify various kinds of tabulation in the formatted print, thereby overriding the normal start-in-position-1, progress-smoothly-right pattern of output construction.

Programming Exercises

1.1 Write a Fortran program that prints your initials in block letters (see program BLOCK).
Use the "*" character for constructing each block letter. Repeat using for each block letter only that capital letter in its construction (e.g., use only the character "L" for constructing a block-L).

1.2 Write a Fortran program that prints a "happy face".

1.3 Write a Fortran program that prints the likeness of an American flag (or any other flag).

1.4 Write a Fortran program that prints the dimensions and area of a square with side length 4.7182:
(a) using PRINT * and labeling each value in the output
(b) displaying only three decimal places for the area

1.5 Write a Fortran program to print the sum of 17 and its reciprocal, to
(a) two decimal places
(b) five decimal places

1.6 A table of numbers, their reciprocals, and their squares is to be computer generated. Write a Fortran program to print an appropriate set of headings for such a table, which consists of three aligned columns of values.
(a) use a sequence of PRINT * statements
(b) use a single PRINT statement
(Note—an appropriate heading will require at least four lines. See, for example, the output of program SALES.)

1.7 Repeat Problem 1.3, using only one PRINT statement.

1.8 Write a program that calculates the sales tax (7 percent) on a pair of shoes priced at $26.69, and prints the price, tax, and total cost of the shoes. All output should be nicely formatted and labeled, with the numeric data in the normal dollar and cents style with the dollar signs printed.

1.9 Repeat Problem 1.2 using overprinted "0" and "*" for the characters making the face outline, and overprinted "H" and "I" for the eyes and mouth.

Chapter 2 Data Elements

Among the various kinds of data are integer numeric values, real numeric values, and character strings. The term *data type* refers to one of these classes of data, and (some of) the data types of Fortran are INTEGER, REAL, and CHARACTER. Whereas a data type is a general class of data, a *data element* is a particular piece of data. In Fortran each data element has a unique data type. For example, any given string is a data element of type CHARACTER, and the numeric value 25.13 is a data element of type REAL. In PRINT statements, such as in the preceding chapter, each item in the output list specifies a data element; when formatting is specified in a PRINT statement each data descriptor must conform to the type of its associated element—A for CHARACTER, I for INTEGER, and F for REAL. Actually Fortran has more data types than these three; additional types will be discussed in later chapters.

As described in Chapter 0, problem solving with a computer involves three general steps:

1 Problem definition.

2 Determination of the data quantities involved.

3 Development of an algorithm.

prior to coding the problem solution into some computer language such as Fortran. Step 2 effectively says that an important phase in programming is to identify and provide for the data elements in the program. This is important for all programs, but is especially so for complex ones. Identifying an appropriate set of data elements is a highly subjective and creative endeavor, and is largely a function of the problem and the individual attacking it (for each of the many approaches to solving a given problem there is (usually) a different set of data elements involved). Once the data elements have been identified, the nature of the programming language being used governs how these data elements are accommodated. The Fortran features for providing CHARACTER, INTEGER, and REAL data elements are described in this chapter.

2.1 Declaring INTEGER, REAL and CHARACTER Data Elements

Computer memory locations can represent data elements and store data element values. Since such values can be accessed and used at will and usually can be changed, the use of memory locations for data elements is an extremely important aspect (perhaps even the essence) of programming. Remember that a memory location has a name (address) and a value (contents). Similarly, a Fortran data element has a name and a value:

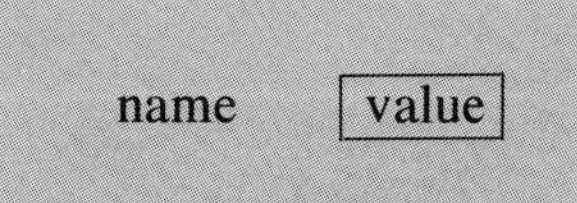

And a set of data elements can be depicted as a set of "boxes", each with its own name and value:

```
name1   | value 1 |
name2   | value2  |
name3   | value3  |
name4   | value4  |
name5   | value5  |
   :
nameN   | valueN  |
```

Of course each of these data elements has a data type, and different data types may require boxes of different kinds (or sizes).

Fortran allows the programmer to define and use any number of INTEGER, REAL, and CHARACTER data elements, with (virtually) any desired names. The programmer must specify two things for each data element—the desired name and the type. Both of these must be specified so that the compiler will be able to allocate memory space for the data element. The program statements in which this information is provided are called *declaration statements*, or *type statements*, and all named data elements used in the program should appear in such statements. Program TYPES illustrate the declaring of INTEGER, REAL and CHARACTER data elements.

```
*....:-----------------------------------------------------------------
      PROGRAM  TYPES
*                                ..This program demonstrates the use of
*                                  INTEGER, REAL and CHARACTER
*                                  declaration statements to name and
*                                  allocate space for data elements of
*                                  these types.  The rules for forming
*                                  data element names are the same as
*                                  for forming program names..
*     ....data elements....
      INTEGER  NUMBER, COUNT, TOTAL, BALL1, BALL2

      REAL  SIDE1, SIDE2, AMT,
     :      PI, THETA, LAMBDA, AREA,
     :      SPEED, TEMP

      CHARACTER  NAME*20, LETTER*26,
     :           WINNER*6, CITY*15, CODE*100

*                                ..The *<integer> following each
*                                  CHARACTER name specifies the
*                                  length (number of characters) of
*                                  that data element..
      END
=======================================================================
```

Note that, like program names, data element names are composed of from one to six characters selected from A–Z and 0–9, and the first must be a letter. The data elements provided by program TYPES are summarized graphically in Figure 2.1.

Declaration statements are all in the class of specification statements, rather than executable statements, and hence "do" things during compilation rather than during execution of the program. The only executable statement in program TYPES is the END statement, so the execution phase of this program is not very interesting. The actions that take place during the compilation phase allocate appropriate memory space for each of the (data element) names listed in the declaration statements. These important actions are "transparent" to (i.e., require no further attention from) the programmer, and do not generate any output themselves.

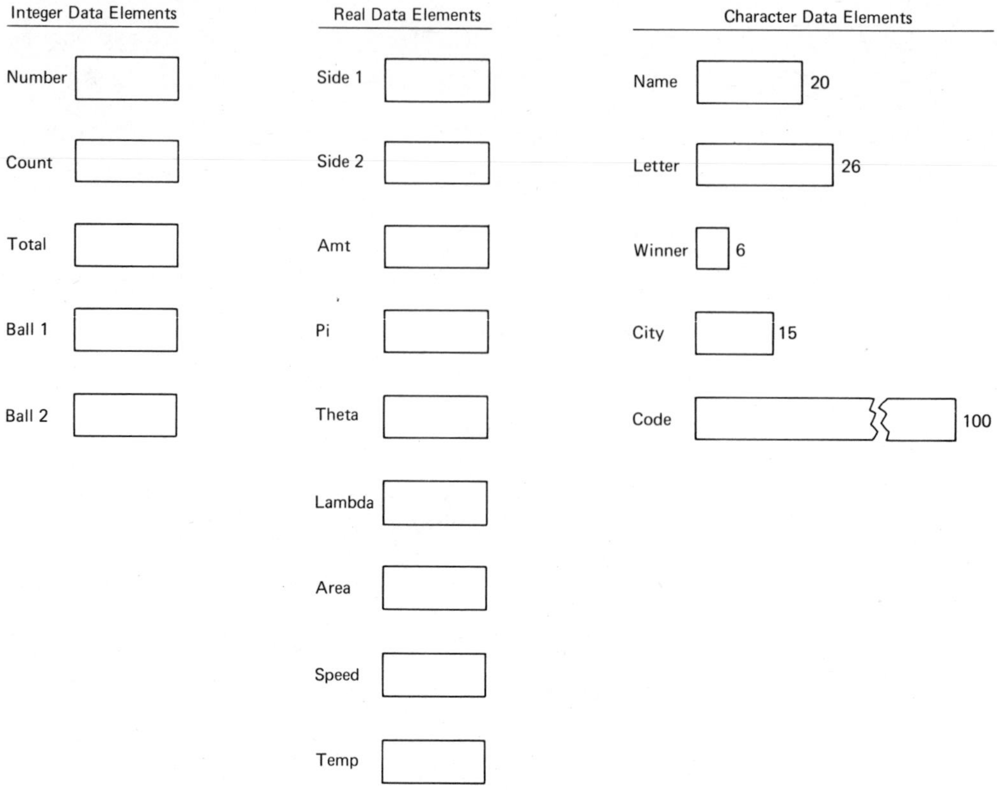

Integer Data Elements	Real Data Elements	Character Data Elements
Number	Side 1	Name 20
Count	Side 2	Letter 26
Total	Amt	Winner 6
Ball 1	Pi	City 15
Ball 2	Theta	Code 100
	Lambda	
	Area	
	Speed	
	Temp	

Figure 2.1. The data elements of program TYPES.

The form of a declaration statement is:

<typename> <list of names>

where <typename> is the word INTEGER or REAL or CHARACTER. The <list of names> is a sequence of programmer-defined names (or in the case of CHARACTER types, names followed by length specifications) separated by commas. Any name declared as a data element name in a program may thereafter be used only to refer to that data element (i.e., all names must be unique). If the length specification is omitted from any name in a CHARACTER statement then that data element is taken to be just a single character. An alternative form of the CHARACTER statement is allowed—if all of the CHARACTER data elements have the same length then the length specification can be omitted from each name, and appended insteaded to CHARACTER. Example: CHARACTER*20 NAME, STREET, CITY is equivalent to CHARACTER NAME*20, STREET*20, CITY*20.

All of the integer data elements used by the program may be declared in a single INTEGER statement, and similarly for REAL and CHARACTER types. Additional declaration statements may be used, however, if desired. For example, the REAL statement in program TYPES could be replaced by

```
REAL SIDE1, SIDE2, AMT
REAL PI, THETA, LAMDA, AREA
REAL SPEED, TEMP
```

to achieve the same REAL allocations. Most of the examples in this book will use the style illustrated in program TYPES—a single declaration statement for each type, using continuation as needed. A program may have any number of declaration statements.

If a program does not use variables of a certain type, say REAL, then that program does not need a REAL statement. Typing and declaring data elements normally come immediately after the PROGRAM statement (except for possible comment lines). The declaration statements may be in any order; however, all declaration statements must precede all executable statements of the program.

2.2 Initializing Data Element Values

The INTEGER, REAL, and CHARACTER declaration statements "build" data element boxes and give them names, but these statements do not place any data values in the boxes. Immediately after declaration, the values of the declared data elements are *undefined*, to put it properly, or *garbage* in the vernacular. It is often desirable to give a newly allocated element an initial value at compilation time, so that the element's value is already defined at the beginning of execution. A data element need not have its value initialized at compilation time, however, if a value is assigned to it during execution prior to its use. Fortran has two specification statements for the purpose of specifying initial values for data elements during compilation, the DATA statement and the PARAMETER statement, and these statements are described in this section. An executable statement that is often used to assign initial values to data elements is the Fortran READ statement, which is also described in this section. Value initializations caused by the READ statement take place during program execution rather than during compilation.

2.2.1 The DATA Statement

The DATA statement is the means by which variable data elements (i.e., those whose values may be changed during execution) can be given initial values at compilation time. In this statement a list of names of data elements is given, followed by a list of desired initial values. The data element corresponding to the first (i.e., leftmost) name in the name list is initialized to the first value in the value list, the second data element is initialized to the second value, and so on. The number of names must be equal to the number of values, and the type of each value must be appropriate for the data element to which it is assigned. The simplest form of the DATA statement is

> DATA <list of names> / <list of values> /

A more general form allows extending the statement to include additional <list of names> / <list of values> / initialization specifications. Program INIT illustrates the use of the DATA statement.

```
*....:-----------------------------------------------------------------
      PROGRAM  INIT
*                                ..This program demonstrates the use of the
*                                DATA statement to initialize data element
*                                values.  It also contains examples of
*                                declaration and PRINT statements..
*     ....data elements....
      INTEGER  COUNT, NUMBER, TOTAL
      REAL  XVAL, YVAL, AVE, PI, AMOUNT
      CHARACTER  NAME*20, CODE*15

*     ....initializations....
      DATA     COUNT ,  TOTAL ,     XVAL ,     CODE       /
     :           0   ,   100  ,     0.25 ,    'TURKEY'    /

*     ....printing....
      PRINT *,  CODE, ' is the code-name for this operation.'
      PRINT *
      PRINT *,  'The initial TOTAL is', TOTAL
      END
=====================================================================
.EXECUTE  INIT

TURKEY          is the code-name for this operation.

The initial TOTAL is         100
=====================================================================
```

Actually the DATA statement in program INIT could be crammed onto one line:

DATA COUNT,TOTAL,XVAL,CODE/0,100,0.25,'TURKEY'/

but the double-line method more clearly communicates (to a human reader) the initializations specified. If more data elements are to be initialized than will conveniently fit on a double line, the DATA statement can be continued, after a comma, with another <list of names>/<list of values>/ on a second double line, or a second DATA statement can be used. The normal placement of the DATA statement is immediately after the declaration statements, and before any executable statements. A Fortran program may have any number of DATA statements.

Note that INTEGER data elements are initialized with integer numeric constants (numbers that do not contain decimal points). REAL data elements are initialized with real numeric constants (numbers containing decimal points), or with integer numeric constants. Chapter 3 (Computations) describes various numeric constants and their use more fully. CHARACTER data elements are initialized with string constants; the single-quotes are not part of the character data element value, but simply delimit the string. If the number of characters in the initial value string is less than the number of characters declared for the data element, then the value string is automatically extended on the right with enough blank characters to just fill the data element; if the value string contains more characters than the data element can hold, then the extra rightmost characters of the value string are ignored.

And finally, note the appearance of data element names as output list quantities in the PRINT statements in program INIT. The meaning here is to print the values of the data elements associated with the names. Therefore the appearance of a data element name in a PRINT statement is acceptable only if that element has been given a value prior to execution of the PRINT statement.

2.2.2 The READ Statement

The DATA statement allows initial values of data elements to appear explicitly in the program. This is useful if these initial values are not to change for different executions of the program—the initialization takes place at compilation and is the same for every subsequent execution of the compiled program. Moreover, the programmer can see the values in the program listing. If the initial values are to change for different executions of the program, however, changing the DATA statements is inconvenient because it means recompiling the program and executing it rather than simply reexecuting the previously compiled program. Therefore Fortran provides for initial values to be supplied from an external device during program execution as an alternative to having these values written explicitly into the program. Program INPUT shows how the READ statement can be used for this purpose.

```
*....:-----------------------------------------------------------------
      PROGRAM  INPUT
                                  ..This program illustrates the use of
                                    the READ statement for
                                    initializing data element values..
*     ....data elements....
      INTEGER  COUNT, NUMBER, TOTAL
      CHARACTER  NAME*20, CODE*15

*     ....reading and printing....
      READ *,  NUMBER, CODE
      PRINT *
      PRINT *,  'The initial value for NUMBER is:', NUMBER
      PRINT *,  'The initial value for  CODE  is:     ', CODE

*                                 ..The technique of printing the values
*                                   of elements after inputting values
*                                   for them is called "echo-checking",
*                                   and is useful for catching errors..
      END
=======================================================================
.EXECUTE INPUT

The initial value for NUMBER is:          2001
The initial value for  CODE  is:      FORTRAN
=======================================================================
```

Obviously program INPUT obtained the values 2001 for NUMBER and 'FORTRAN' for CODE. Where did they come from? That depends on whether the program was executed from an interactive terminal or by submitting a card deck to be run in "batch mode". In batch mode the READ * statement assumes the data values are on cards following the .EXECUTE command. If the user is running the job from a terminal the computer expects the data values to be typed on the terminal. In either case the

READ *, NUMBER, CODE

statement expects values for NUMBER and CODE to be supplied, separated by commas or blanks; an integer value is expected for NUMBER and a string value for CODE. These may be placed on one line (or card), such as

2001, 'FORTRAN'

or on two lines:

2001
'FORTRAN'

Actually, if the user is at a terminal the appearance of the output would be a bit different from that shown in program INPUT. Since the terminal is both the input device and the output device, the typing of the data would result in the input data appearing with the program output. In batch mode the input device and output device are generally different (the former typically a card reader and the latter a line printer) so that the input data does not appear in the program output unless it is explicitly output with PRINT statements.

As a practical matter, the user at a terminal does not know when the program expects input unless a "prompt" is given (i.e., something printed on the terminal as a signal that the computer is ready for input). A well-designed PRINT statement preceding the READ statement serves in most cases as a meaningful prompt, as the following modification of program INPUT demonstrates.

```
*....:-----------------------------------------------------------------
      PROGRAM INPUT2
*                                  ..This program is identical to program
*                                    INPUT, except that it assumes the user
*                                    is at a terminal and therefore an
                                     "input prompt" is provided..
*     ....data elements....
      INTEGER  COUNT, NUMBER, TOTAL
      CHARACTER  NAME*20, CODE*15

*     ....reading and printing....
      PRINT *,  'Please supply initial values for NUMBER and CODE  :'
      PRINT *,  '                            <an integer> , ''<a string>'' '
      READ *,  NUMBER, CODE
      PRINT *
      PRINT *,  'The initial value for NUMBER is:', NUMBER
      PRINT *,  'The initial value for  CODE  is:     ', CODE

*                                  ..The first two print statements
*                                    constitute the prompt.  The last two
*                                    are the echo-checking..
      END
=====================================================================
.EXECUTE INPUT2

Please supply the initial values for NUMBER and CODE  :
                            <an integer> , '<a string>'
> 2001, 'FORTRAN '

The initial value for NUMBER is:        2001
The initial value for  CODE  is:     FORTRAN
=====================================================================
```

The ">" in column 1 of the third line of output is assumed to be the computer supplied input prompt, and thus this line is the input line and not part of the program output; in a batch mode this line would not appear in the output. (The ">" prompt character used here is implementation-dependent, and will be different from computer to computer.)

Since it is an executable statement, the READ statements can also be used to give subsequent values to data elements. Program INPUT3 illustrates this.

```
*....:-----------------------------------------------------------------------
      PROGRAM  INPUT3
*                                ..This program illustrates the use
*                                  of the READ statement to change the
*                                  value of a data element..
*     ....data elements....
      INTEGER  COUNT, NUMBER, TOTAL
      CHARACTER  NAME*20, CODE*15

*     ....reading and printing....
      PRINT *,  'Please supply initial values for NUMBER and CODE  :  '
      PRINT *,  '                            <an integer> , ''<a string>'' '
      READ *, NUMBER, CODE
      PRINT *
      PRINT *,  'The initial value for NUMBER is:', NUMBER
      PRINT *,  'The initial value for  CODE  is:    ', CODE
      PRINT *
      PRINT *,  'Try another value for CODE.'
      READ *, CODE
*                  ..here the value of CODE is redefined..
      PRINT *
      PRINT *,  'The new value for  CODE  is:     ',CODE
      END
=============================================================================
.EXECUTE INPUT3

Please supply initial values for NUMBER and CODE  :
                            <an integer> , '<a string>'
> 2001, 'FORTRAN'

The initial value for NUMBER is:        2001
The initial value for  CODE  is:    FORTRAN

Try another value for CODE.
> 'I love computing'

The new value for  CODE  is:     I love computin
=============================================================================
```

Note that when inputting strings the string-delimiting quotes must be supplied, but the delimiting quotes are not printed when character data elements are output. Also note the loss of the "g" in "computing" in the above example—the string 'I love computing' has 16 characters, whereas CODE has a limit of 15.

The general form of the READ * statement is

> READ *, <list of input names>

The data element having the first (leftmost) name in the input list gets the first input data value supplied, the second element gets the second value, and so on until data is acquired for each name in the input list. The type of each input value supplied must be the same as the associated data element in the input list, except that integer values may be supplied for real data elements. If a value is supplied that is inappropriate for the targeted data element, the consequences are implementation dependent, but often an error message is printed and execution of the program is terminated.

The READ statement may contain a format specification, in place of the "*" (i.e.,

READ statements may be formatted). This allows the programmer to specify the columns in which the various input values are to be placed, rather than using free-format input with the values placed in any columns and separated by commas or blanks. Free-format input is convenient for numeric data, but it requires that the quotes be used when inputting string data (otherwise the computer wouldn't know where a string starts or stops since blanks and commas are valid string characters), and using the quotes is sometimes inconvenient. When a formatted READ is used, string data is supplied without the enclosing quotes—there is no need for them because the computer knows which columns of input contain the string data. In most of these chapters free-format READs will be used whenever possible, but formatted READs are occasionally used when the input consists of a single string. This is convenient since the enclosing quotes are then omitted, and the READ statement for this special case is very easy to construct. Except for this case, formatted READs will not be described until Part 3.

When inputting a value for just a single string (named TEXT, say) the following READ can be used.

```
READ '(A)', TEXT
```

This is the same A format as that used with the PRINT statement, and it causes the next L characters of input to become the value of TEXT, where L is the declared length of TEXT. At a terminal this is the next L characters typed; in batch it is the first L characters on the next data card. (Remember that in batch the data cards follow the .EXECUTE command.) The quotes are not needed; and, in fact, if they are used they are treated as part of the string value and not as delimiters. Thus, when reading a string with

READ *, TEXT . . . . put quotes aound the input data for TEXT

READ '(A)', TEXT . . . . do not put quotes around the data for TEXT

2.2.3 The PARAMETER Statement

Any data element initialized by a DATA or READ statement may have its value changed by subsequent program computations or input. There are instances, however, when the initial value given to a data element is not to be changed. This kind of initialization can be achieved, and enforced, in Fortran with the PARAMETER statement. The use of the PARAMETER statement is similar to that of the DATA statement (except the format is a bit different), but any subsequent attempt in the program to change the value assigned in a PARAMETER statement is not allowed. Thus the values of data elements initialized by the PARAMETER statement remain constant throughout execution of the program. Such data elements are called *named constants*, whereas data elements whose values may be changed are called *variables*. The function of the PARAMETER statement is to assign the desired values to named constants. Program CIRCL7 illustrates the use of the PARAMETER statement.

A named constant may be used anywhere in the program that the constant value itself could be used, except in format specifications. If a certain constant value appears many times in a program it is often advisable to use the PARAMETER statement to associate a name with that value, and to use the name for each subsequent appearance of the constant. This feature is extremely useful, as will be demonstrated by many other examples.

Numeric constants (such as PI, count limits, etc.) are perhaps the most obvious use of the PARAMETER statement. Character constants are equally useful, however, and program SALES2 demonstrates that one such use is to give meaningful names to format specifications. (The format specifications of Chapter 1 are string constants, but named string constants and string variables are also allowed as format specifications.)

```
*....:-----------------------------------------------------------------
      PROGRAM  CIRCL7
*                               ..This program illustrates the use of
*                                 the PARAMETER statement to associate
*                                 names with constant values.  Note that
*                                 different declaration statements are
*                                 used in this program for named
*                                 constants and variables; this distinction
*                                 is recommended, but Fortran does not
*                                 require it, and the same statement
*                                 may be used to declare constant
*                                 names and variable names..
*     ....constant....
      REAL  PI
      PARAMETER  ( PI = 3.14159 )

*     ....variable....
      REAL  DIAM

*     ....execute....
      READ *, DIAM
      PRINT '(T20,A,F7.2/T20,A,F8.3/)',  'Diameter = ', DIAM,
     :                                   'Circumference = ', PI*DIAM
      END
=======================================================================
.EXECUTE  CIRCL7

> 8
                   Diameter =     8.00
                   Circumference =   25.133

=======================================================================
```

```
*....:-----------------------------------------------------------------
      PROGRAM  SALES2
*                               ..This is a version of program SALES of
*                                 section 1.3 in which the format
*                                 specification is given in the form of a
*                                 constant name that conveys more meaning
*                                 to a person reading the PRINT statement.
*     ....constants....
      CHARACTER  HEADER*60, STRING*5
      PARAMETER  ( STRING = '(A)'  ,
     :             HEADER = '(////T2,A,A,A,I5/3(T2,A,T25,A,T45,A/))'

*     ....printing....
      PRINT  HEADER,
     :       'SUPER LUMBER CO.','   Monthly Sales Report   ','OCT',1980,
     :       'SALESPERSON'   , 'CURRENT', 'ANNUAL' ,
     :       'IDENTIFICATION', 'SALES'  , 'SALES'  ,
     :       '--------------', '-------', '------'

*                                  ..Note that HEADER can be used as the
*                                    format specification with exactly the
*                                    same result as in the program SALES.
*                                    In SALES2 the word HEADER makes the
*                                    function of the PRINT statement much
*                                    clearer than in SALES, and the
*                                    PARAMETER statement insures that
*                                    HEADER will not get inadvertently
*                                    changed..
      READSTRING, HEADER
*                          ..will cause a compilation error because HEADER
*                            is a constant and therefore cannot be given
*                            another value. This READSTRING statement is a
*                            "clever" one though. Since a space does not
*                            separate READ and STRING it doesn't look
*                            like the ordinary READ statement that it is
*                            (a formatted READ for a single string, to be
*                            precise). For all practical purposes
*                            it can be used as a new and special
*                            purpose statement -- to read a single string,
*                            without needing the quote delimiters.
*                            Any program that defines STRING as a
*                            string constant with value '(A)' can use this
*                            "new" statement..
      END
=======================================================================
```

The format of the PARAMETER statement is

```
PARAMETER ( <list of constant assignments> )
```

Each element in the <list of constant assignments> is separated from the others by commas, and each has the form

```
<name> = <constant value>
```

The main rules for placement of the PARAMETER statement in a program are:

1 Any <name> used in a PARAMETER statement must be declared in a type statement prior to the PARAMETER statement in which its value is defined.

2 The assignment of a constant value in a PARAMETER statement must precede any other use of that named constant.

Figure 2.2 shows a good choice for systematic placement of named constant and variable declarations, PARAMETER statements, and DATA statements.

2.3 Arrays

The data elements discussed thus far have been "simple" ones—one box (i.e., one data value) associated with a name. A most useful extension to this concept is to associate a single name with a sequence of boxes all of which hold data values of the same type. Such a *compound* data element (or *data structure*) is called an *array*, and is depicted in Figure 2.3.

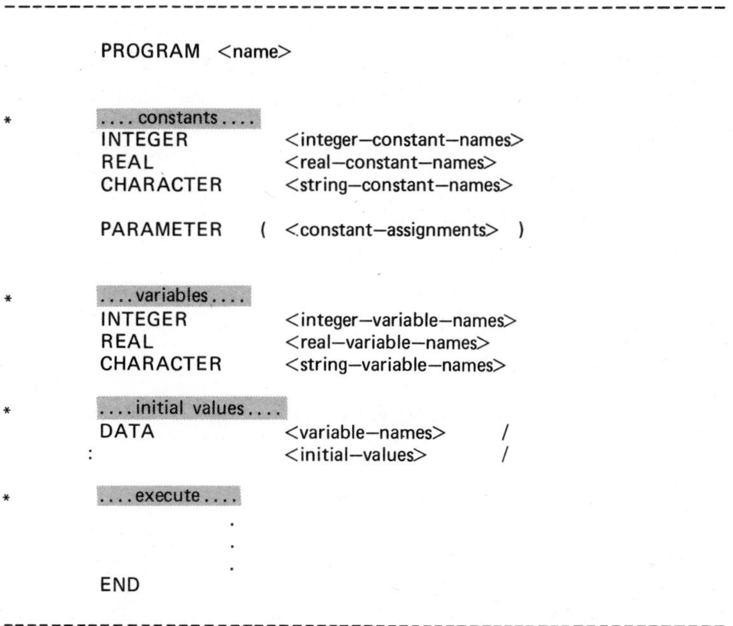

```
      PROGRAM  <name>

*     .... constants ....
      INTEGER          <integer-constant-names>
      REAL             <real-constant-names>
      CHARACTER        <string-constant-names>

      PARAMETER    (  <constant-assignments>  )

*     .... variables ....
      INTEGER          <integer-variable-names>
      REAL             <real-variable-names>
      CHARACTER        <string-variable-names>

*     .... initial values ....
      DATA             <variable-names>       /
     :                 <initial-values>       /

*     .... execute ....
                  .
                  .
                  .
      END
```

Figure 2.2. Recommended placement of declaration, PARAMETER, and DATA statements.

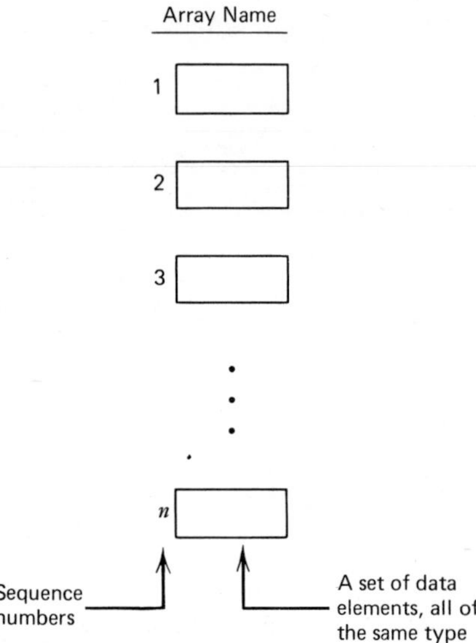

Figure 2.3. Structure of an array.

The array name refers to the entire set of elements and sequence numbers for these elements. An individual member of this set is called an *array element*, and any array element may be selected by giving the array name and the sequence number of that element. The form such a reference takes is

<array name> (<sequence number>)

Thus if TEMP is the name of an array of 24 elements (for example representing the temperatures after one-hour intervals throughout a 24-hour period, starting at noon) then TEMP(4) is the fourth element of the array (the temperature at 4 P.M.), TEMP(17) is the seventeenth element of the array, and so on. The array may be of any data type, meaning the elements of an array may be all of type INTEGER, all REAL, or all CHARACTER; but the <sequence number>, usually called the *subscript*, must be an integer expression (since the sequence numbers are integers). If K is a variable of type INTEGER, and currently has the value 7 for instance, then TEMP(K+2) specifies the same array element as TEMP(9).

Whenever a program uses an array, the programmer must supply three things to describe the nature of the array structure so that appropriate storage may be allocated:

1 The name of the array.

2 The type of the array (and element length for type CHARACTER).

3 The number of elements in the array (or, alternatively, the upper and lower subscript bounds for that array).

The first two of these three items are the same as the information contained in a declaration of any other data element, and therefore an array can be declared in an ordinary type statement if its size (number of elements or subscript bounds) is also specified. Program ARRAY illustrates the Fortran techniques for declaring, initializing, and printing arrays.

```
*....:-----------------------------------------------------------------
      PROGRAM  ARRAY
*                                ..This program demonstrates the declar-
*                                  ation of arrays. The subscript range is
*                                  specified in the declaration statements
*                                  by
*                                         (<lower>:<upper>)
*                                  and gives the range of integer values
*                                  allowable as subscripts for that array.
*                                  Note that <lower> need not be 1, but may
*                                  be any integer value, including 0 or
*                                  negative; <upper> must not be less
*                                  than <lower>. Any integer expression
*                                  involving constants (including
*                                  named constants) may be used for
*                                  <lower> and <upper>..
*     ....variables and arrays....
      INTEGER  HOUR, PN, LIMIT
      REAL  TEMP(0:24)
      CHARACTER  PERSON(201:299)*20
*                                ..The length of 20 characters specified
*                                  for PERSON means that each of the 99
*                                  elements of PERSON is 20 characters
*                                  long..
*     ....initializations....
      DATA    HOUR ,      TEMP                                      /
     :          0  ,      6*0.0, 50.0, 8*0.0, -30.0, 9*0.0          /,

*                                ..PN is used as a subscript for PERSON

     :        (PERSON(PN), PN=201,210)                              /
     :            'BROWN     ,  J. M.'    ,
     :            'FREIBURG  ,  A. L.'    ,
     :            'GREEN     ,  W. R.'    ,
     :            'GRUNE     ,  J. D.'    ,
     :            'JONES     ,  R. N.'    ,
     :            'LADMAN    ,  H. L.'    ,
     :            'RICE      ,  K. K.'    ,
     :            'THOMSON   ,  M. P.'    ,
     :            'WODLEY    ,  M. L.'    ,
     :            'WORTH     ,  K. N.'                             /

*                                ..This DATA statement illustrates the
*                                very powerful initialization
*                                capabilities of Fortran. The unsubscripted
*                                TEMP means that all 25 elements of TEMP
*                                are to receive initial values; the first
*                                6 are 0.0, the next one is 50.0, the
*                                next 8 are 0.0, the next one is -30.0,
*                                and the remaining 9 are 0.0.  However,
*                                not all 99 elements of PERSON are to be
*                                initialized, but only the first 10.
*                                Notice how these 10 are explicitly
*                                specified, with PN taking on the
*                                successive values of 201,202,203,..,210
*     ....execute....
      PRINT *, 'At hour ',HOUR,'           the temperature values are:'
      PRINT *,  TEMP
      PRINT *
      PRINT *, 'Input the value for LIMIT , in 201..210 range.'
      READ *, LIMIT
      PRINT *, 'Person',LIMIT,'          is     ',PERSON(LIMIT)

*                                ..In the second PRINT statement the array
*                                  name TEMP occurs without a subscript --
*                                  this specifies all 25 elements of the
*                                  array to be printed. In the fifth PRINT
*                                  statement a subscript is given with the
*                                  array name, so only this one element of
*                                  the array will be printed.

*                                  The PRINT below causes all of the
*                                  names up through the LIMIT one to be
*                                  printed, as PN takes on the values
*                                  201,202,....,LIMIT  ..

      PRINT '(A/)', (PERSON(PN), PN=201,LIMIT)

      END
=======================================================================
```

```
===========================================================================
.EXECUTE  ARRAY

At hour             0           the temperature values are:
          0.000000        0.000000        0.000000        0.000000
          0.000000        0.000000       60.000000        0.000000
          0.000000        0.000000        0.000000        0.000000
          0.000000        0.000000        0.000000      -30.000000
          0.000000        0.000000        0.000000        0.000000
          0.000000        0.000000        0.000000        0.000000
          0.000000

Input the value for LIMIT , in 201..210 range.
> 206
Person         206        is     LADMAN     , H. L.
BROWN     , J. M.
FREIBURG  , A. L.
GREEN     , W. R.
GRUNE     , J. D.
JONES     , R. N.
LADMAN    , H. L.
===========================================================================
```

In program ARRAY the structure of the arrays used is more general than that indicated in Figure 2.3. Figure 2.4 shows the structure of arrays TEMP and PERSON of program ARRAY, and indicates the kinds of array structures possible in Fortran. The <list of output quantities> of PRINT statements, <list of names> of DATA statements, and <list of input names> of READ statements all may include array names and array subset specifications. The first of these (array names) is equivalent to listing every array element, in order from the smallest subscript value to the largest. A subset of an array may be specified as illustrated in program ARRAY, with the general form

(<array name>(<integer var>),<integer var>=<low value>,<high value>)

where <low value> and <high value> may be any expressions having integer values within the declared subscript limits of <array name>. The value of <high value> must not be lower than the value of <low value>.

The arrays described here are called one-dimensional arrays. These are extremely useful data elements, and are used extensively in the following chapters. Arrays may

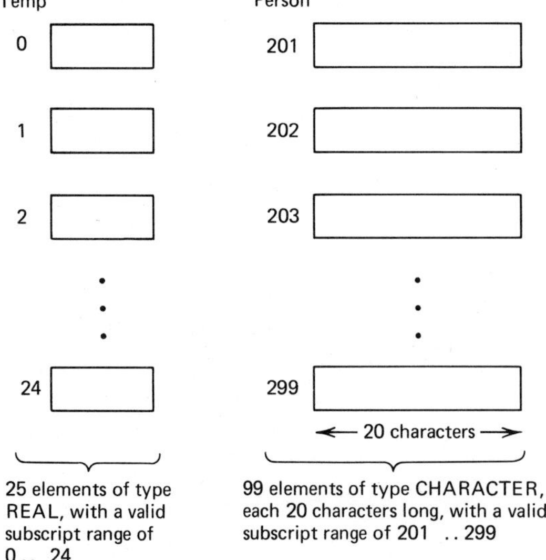

Figure 2.4. Sketch of array elements declared in program ARRAY.

be higher order than one-dimensional, and two-dimensional arrays in particular are occasionally very useful data elements. Higher-order arrays are discussed in Section 13.1, and the first few pages of that section (up to program PLANET) may be included here.

2.4 Summary

Several important concepts concerning data elements in Fortran have been introduced in this chapter. The main ones are as follows.

1 Data element attributes—name, type, and value.

2 Simple variable data elements.

3 Constant data elements.

4 Array data elements.

5 Declaration of data elements.

6 Types INTEGER, REAL, and CHARACTER.

7 Initializing the values of data elements: DATA, READ, and PARAMETER statements.

The INTEGER, REAL, CHARACTER, PARAMETER, and DATA statements are specification statements and only specify the existence and initial state of the program's data ele-

```
      PROGRAM      <name>
*                  by <author>, and other pertinent information.
*                    . .Make use of appropriate comments
*                      in appropriate places.
*                      Use continuation as desired.
*     . . . .constants. . . .
      INTEGER      <integer-constant-name-list>
      REAL         <real-constant-name-list>
      CHARACTER    <character-constant-name-list>
      PARAMETER    <list-of-constant-assignments>

*     . . . .variables and arrays. . . .
      INTEGER      <integer-data-element-list>
      REAL         <real-data-element-list>
      CHARACTER    <character-data-element-list>

*     . . . .initializations. . . .
      DATA         <list-of-data-element-names>      /
     :             <list-of-initial-values>          /

*     . . . .execute. . . .
      READ *,      <list-of-input-names>
      READ '(A)',  <string-name>
      PRINT <format-specification> , <list-of-output-quantities>
*                    . .Note that the <format-specification>
*                      may be either "*", or a string constant,
*                      or a character data element name. .

*     . . . .and other executable statements, to be described later. . . .

      END
```

Figure 2.5. Summary of the structure of a Fortran program.

ments. They do not have any function during the execution of the program. The executable statements cause changes in the state of the program (e.g., cause data element values to change, or output to be generated during program execution). The READ statement is an executable statement and allows values to be input for data elements during program execution; it has no function during compilation. The specification statements should be in the order shown in Figure 2.5, preceding all of the executable statements.

Thus far all variable names, constant names and array names have been declared in type statements. This practice will be steadfastly maintained throughout this book, and is strongly urged as common practice in Fortran programs. However, Fortran does not require names to be declared in type statements. Any name that is used and not declared is automatically a simple integer data element if its beginning letter is in the range I . . N; and it is automatically a simple real data element otherwise. This is called "implicit" typing, and, besides not providing for type CHARACTER, is an error-prone feature of Fortran. Misspelling names, for example, is a common error in writing programs, and because of implicit typing many such errors go undetected by the compiler, often causing puzzlingly incorrect program results. Most of these errors would be detected by the compiler if explicit typing were required.

If explicit typing (using type statements) is to be encouraged then it is desirable to have the implicit typing turned off. This can't be done in Fortran, but a "trick" can accomplish very nearly the same thing. Implicit typing can be changed, but not "turned off", in Fortran by inserting an IMPLICIT statement immediately following the PROGRAM statement so that the IMPLICIT statement precedes all other statements in the program. The trick is to use the statement

```
IMPLICIT LOGICAL (A-Z)
```

If this statement precedes all declarations, then any names not explicitly declared (e.g., misspellings) are taken to be of type LOGICAL (more about this and the IMPLICIT statement later), and are virtually guaranteed to be detected as errors by the compiler. Program TRICKY illustrates the trick.

```
*....:----------------------------------------------------------------
      PROGRAM  TRICKY
*                                    ..This program illustrates the trick for
*                                      "turning off" implicit typing:

                                       IMPLICIT LOGICAL(A-Z)
*     ....constants....
      INTEGER  HOUR, PN
      PARAMETER  ( HOUR = 0,  NP = 202)
*                                    ..Note the misspelling of PN in the
*                                      PARAMETER statement. Without the
*                                      IMPLICIT statement the error would
*                                      go undetected; with the IMPLICIT
*                                      statement NP is taken as a logical data
*                                      element (to be discussed later) and 202
*                                      is not a valid LOGICAL value -- hence
*                                      the error is detected immediately by
*                                      the compiler..
      END
=====================================================================
```

Programming Exercises

2.1 Write specification statements to provide named constants ONE and ZERO for a program, with integer values 1 and 0, respectively.

2.2 Write specification statements to allocate an INTEGER array with subscripts ranging from −10 to +10, and with an initial value for each element equal to its subscript value.

2.3 One way of representing pictorial data is to superimpose a grid over the picture, and to represent the predominant state or color of each grid square with a certain character. Such a picture is said to be "digitized", since it is represented by a finite number of values. Suppose a character array is to be used to represent a digitized picture of N rows and M columns. Each element of the array is to represent one of the rows. Write specification statements declaring such an array. Include statements adequate for making N and M named constants, and use these in the array declaration.

Chapter 3 Computations

This chapter describes the Fortran features for formulating arbitrary data values, and for modifying data element values. A problem is typically solved on a computer by manipulating the values of various data elements in the program until the solution is obtained. In this chapter these manipulations are referred to as computations, and the mechanics of these computations are discussed here.

3.1 Assignment Statements

The process of giving a value to a data element during program execution is called *assignment*, and the executable statements in which value assignment is specified are called *assignment statements*. This process is shown in Figure 3.1.

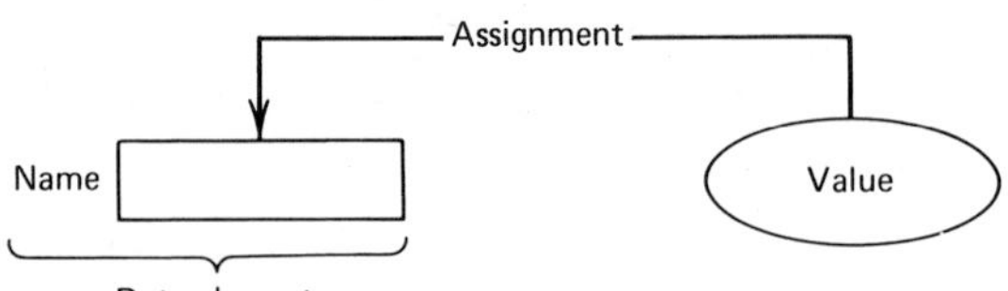

Figure 3.1. The concept of assignment.

Normally in assignment the value must be of the same type as the data element. The DATA and PARAMETER statements described in the preceding chapter, cause value assignment at compile time. The assignment statement, on the other hand, like the READ statement, provides for arbitrary redefinition (i.e., changing the value) of data elements during program execution.

Execution of an assignment statement results in one data element being given a value; the value may be the initial value for that data element (if a previous initialization had not occurred for that element), it may be equal to the element's current value, or it may be (and this is usually the case) a different value. In an assignment statement precisely two things must be specified:

1 The name of the data element that is to receive the value.

2 The value itself that is to be assigned.

The form of a Fortran assignment statement is

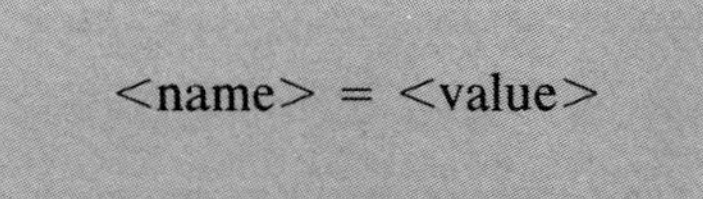

<name> = <value>

and the meaning is "assign the specified <value> to the data element with the specified <name>". In Fortran the "=" character in the assignment statement is called the assignment operator and merely separates the <name> and the <value> and signifies the assignment process. The assignment operator does not represent equality between two objects, in the mathematical sense, but rather the assignment of a value to a single object. Several examples of assignment statements are given in program ASSIGN, in which areas for certain geometrical shapes are computed. Figure 3.2 shows the four shapes involved and gives the formula for the area of each.

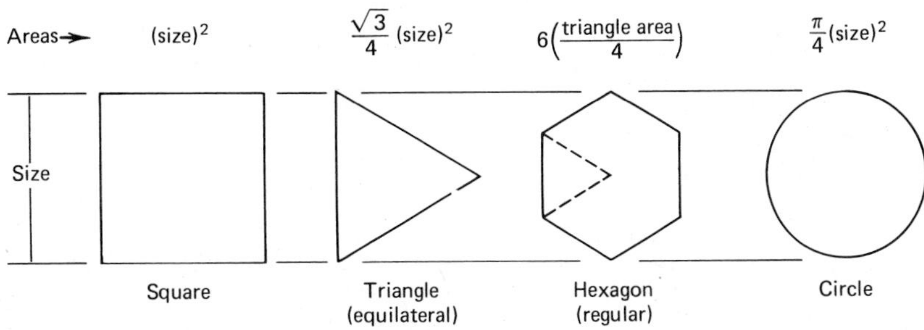

Figure 3.2. The shapes for program ASSIGN.

Program ASSIGN first computes the areas of the four shapes, for a given SIZE and prints the results. The value of SIZE is then changed and the computations are repeated.

Program ASSIGN illustrates the two forms that <name> can have for numeric (REAL and INTEGER) assignments—a simple variable name or an array element name. Respective examples from the program are:

```
SIZE2 = SIZE*SIZE
AREA(4) = (PI/4)*SIZE2
```

Variable names assigned values via the PARAMETER statement (i.e., constants) are not allowed on the left of an assignment statement, nor are array names without subscripts allowed (individual array elements are legal, but not the whole array).

The <value>s on the right of the assignment operator are specified by *expressions*, which may be quite complex. When the assignment statement is executed the expression is evaluated to yield the <value> that is assigned to <name>. For example, in the statement

```
SIZE2 = SIZE*SIZE
```

the expression (SIZE*SIZE) is evaluated by:

1 Obtaining the current value of SIZE.

2 Multiplying this value by itself.

The resulting value is assigned to (becomes the value of) the data element named SIZE2. In the statement

```
SIZE = 1.5*SIZE
```

the expression (1.5*SIZE) is evaluated by:

1 Obtaining the current value of SIZE.

2 Multiplying it by 1.5.

```
*....:-----------------------------------------------------------------
      PROGRAM  ASSIGN
*                                 ..This program illustrates the use
*                                 of the assignment statement by
*                                 computing the areas of various
*                                 (four) geometrical shapes.  SIZE
*                                 is the shapes' size, as defined
*                                 in figure 3.2; SIZE2 is SIZE
*                                 squared.  An array AREA is used
*                                 for the four areas, with AREA(1),
*                                 AREA(2), AREA(3), and AREA(4) used,
*                                 respectively, for the square,
*                                 triangle, hexagon, and circle.  The
*                                 CHARACTER variable RESULT is used
*                                 to contain the format for printing
*                                 the results of the calculations..
*     ....constants....
      REAL  PI
      CHARACTER  TITLE*25
      PARAMETER  ( PI = 3.14159,
     :            TITLE = 'Areas for figures of size' )

*      ....variables....
      REAL SIZE, SIZE2, AREA(1:4)
      CHARACTER SHAPE (1:4)*8, RESULT*20
      DATA  SIZE  /2.45/,
     :      SHAPE /'  SQUARE','TRIANGLE', ' HEXAGON', '  CIRCLE'/
*                               ..The initial size is specified (2.45) --
*                                 now for the computations:
*                                       * means multiply
*                                       / means divide
*                                   SQRT means square root of ..
*     ....execute....
      SIZE2 = SIZE*SIZE
      AREA(1) = SIZE2
      AREA(2) = (SQRT(3.0)/4)*SIZE2
      AREA(3) = 6*(AREA(2)/4)
      AREA(4) = (PI/4)*SIZE2
      RESULT = '(/4A10/4F10.2////)'
      PRINT *, TITLE, SIZE
      PRINT RESULT,
     :      SHAPE, AREA
*                               ..Now redefine the value of SIZE,
*                                 and repeat the calculations;
*                                 also redefine the format of the
*                                 printed results..
      SIZE = 1.5*SIZE
      SIZE2 = SIZE*SIZE
      AREA(1) = SIZE2
      AREA(2) = (SQRT(3.0)/4)*SIZE2
      AREA(3) = 6*(AREA(2)/4)
      AREA(4) = (PI/4)*SIZE2
      RESULT(5:6) = '16'
      RESULT(10:13) = '16.4'
*                               ..RESULT is now '(/4A16/4F16.4////)'
      PRINT *,  TITLE, SIZE
      PRINT RESULT,
     :      SHAPE, AREA
      END
======================================================================
.EXECUTE  ASSIGN

Areas for figures of size        2.450000

    SQUARE  TRIANGLE   HEXAGON    CIRCLE
      6.00      2.60      3.90      4.71




Areas for figures of size        3.675000

          SQUARE          TRIANGLE          HEXAGON           CIRCLE
         13.5056            5.8481           8.7722          10.6073



======================================================================
```

The resulting value is assigned to SIZE, thereby causing SIZE to take on a new value (note that the old value of SIZE was used in evaluating the expression). The rules governing construction and evaluation of such expressions in Fortran are described in Section 3.2.

For CHARACTER assignments the <name> can also be a simple variable or array element, as in numeric assignments, but one additional form for <name> is allowed in CHARACTER assignments. That form is a *substring* <name>. A substring is a contiguous (i.e., adjacent) subset of individual characters of a CHARACTER data element. For example in the string

'the moon is made of bleu cheese',

'the moon'	is a substring,
'cheese'	is a substring,
'bleu chee'	is a substring,
'oon is mad'	is a substring,
'bleu moon'	is not a substring,
'the moon is cheese'	is not a substring.

If the leftmost character of a string, or data element of type CHARACTER, is defined to be in position 1 of the string, the next character to the right to be in position 2, and so on, then a position number is defined for each character in the string. A substring is composed of the characters from a set of consecutive positions of the original string, and can be specified by giving the position numbers of the leftmost and rightmost characters of the substring. In Fortran a substring has the form

<name>([<left position>]:[<right position>])

where <name> is the name of a variable or array element of type CHARACTER, and <left position > and <right position> are integer values (or expressions having integer values). If, for example, the CHARACTER variable LUNA has the value 'the moon is made of bleu cheese' then

LUNA(1:8) is	'the moon'
LUNA(21:29) is	'bleu chee'
LUNA(6:15) is	'oon is mad'

Note that <left position> may be omitted, as may <right position> in a substring. If <left position> is omitted then the value 1 is assumed, and if <right position> is omitted the right-hand end of the string is assumed. Thus

LUNA(23:) is 'eu cheese' . . . . same as LUNA(23:31)
LUNA(:7) is 'the moo' . . . . same as LUNA(1:7)
LUNA(:) is the same as LUNA(1:31)—which is just LUNA

The integer values for <left position> and <right position> must satisfy the relations:

1 ≤ <left position> ≤ <right position> ≤ <string length>

An important special case is when <left-position> has the same value as <right position>. Such a substring is just a single character. For example LUNA(5:5) is the character 'm' and LUNA(K:K) is the character 'b' if K has the value 19.

Substrings may be freely used as the <name> portion of assignment statements. In these cases only the specified substring gets a value assigned, and the rest of the string (CHARACTER data element) remains unchanged. Thus in program ASSIGN the statements

```
RESULT(5:6) = '16'
RESULT(10:13) = '16.4'
```

redefine just the indicated portions of the string value of RESULT. If the <name> portion of an assignment statement is a CHARACTER data element or substring then the <value> portion must be an expression of type CHARACTER. The rules governing construction and evaluation of such expressions are described in Section 3.3.

The Fortran assignment statement may therefore be described as having one of the following two forms:

<name of numeric data element> = <arithmetic expression>
<name of CHARACTER data element> = <CHARACTER expression>

(Later, when additional data types of Fortran are described this list will be expanded.) In each case the execution of the assignment statement proceeds as follows.

1 The expression on the right of the "=" is evaluated, and a value results.
2 The resulting value is assigned to the data-element identified on the left of the "=", thereby replacing the original value (if any) of the data element.

After execution of an assignment statement the data-element named on the left of the "=" has a new value. The old value (if there was one) is lost. No other data element values are affected.

3.2 Arithmetic Expressions

Arithmetic expressions are familiar everyday constructs, and Fortran's arithmetic expressions are pretty much like those found in ordinary arithmetic. That is, they involve addition, subtraction, multiplication, division, and exponentiation of numerical values. A key thing to remember is that, no matter how complicated an expression might appear, each element in the expression represents a numerical value that is involved in the calculation, and a few simple rules govern the process of expression construction and evaluation. This section describes these rules.

3.2.1 Rules for Arithmetic Expression Formation

The valid forms for an arithmetic expression are listed in Figure 3.3. The characters +, −, *, /, and ** are called *arithmetic operators*, and signify the arithmetic operations of addition, subtraction, multiplication, division, and exponentiation (the + and − operators may also be used in the normal manner as identity and negation operators), respectively. The only restriction imposed on the formation of expressions using the forms shown in Figure 3.3 is that no two arithmetic operators may be adjacent (consecutive) in a legal arithmetic expression. For example the valid expression

```
AREA(3)*(-17)
```

cannot legally be written as AREA(3)*−17 [although −17*AREA(3) is legal and, in this case, yields the same numeric value as the original expression].

Form	example 1	example 2	example 3
1 A numerical constant	17	43.7	62E4
2 A numerical variable name	XVAL	COUNT	SSNUM
3 A numerical array element	AREA(2)	TEMP(7)	TEMP(K+2)
4 A numerical function call (see Section 3.4)	SQRT(3.0)	EXP(XVAL)	LEN(TITLE)
5 Arithmetic operations given by:			
+ (addition)	XVAL + TEMP(7)		
− (subtraction)	COUNT − 17		
* (multiplicaion)	AREA(2) * SQRT(3.0)		
/ (division)	XVAL / COUNT		
** (exponentiation)	SSNUM ** 4		
6 Grouping—any of these 7 forms enclosed in parentheses		XVAL / (COUNT − 2)	
7 Identity, negation—any of the above 6 forms preceded by			
+ (identity)		+43.7	
− (negation)		− (COUNT + 17)*LEN(TITLE)	

Figure 3.3. Legal arithmetic expressions in Fortran.

The names of named numerical constants are also valid in arithmetic expressions, and may be freely used whenever a numerical constant [form(1) of Figure 3.3] is valid [note that named constants appear similar to variables (form(2))]. Functions are discussed in Section 3.4 and in Part 2; suffice it here to say that the value of SQRT(3.0) is the square root of 3.0, and that the value of LEN(TITLE) is the length (number of characters) in the character string TITLE. [Note that function calls—form(4)—may appear the same as array element names—form(3). This apparently confusing situation will be clarified in Section 3.4.]

Integer numerical constants are simply a sequence of decimal digits (to be denoted by <digits> hereafter), without a decimal point or an exponent, and optionally preceded by a sign ("+" or "−"). Such constants are interpreted by the compiler as ordinary decimal (base 10) integer numbers. Unsigned, or "+" signed, integer constants are assumed to be positive; "−" signed integer constants are negative. A real numeric constant may take any one of several forms:

<digits>.
.<digits>
<digits>.<digits>
any of the above three forms followed by E<digits>
<digits>E<digits>

The first three of these forms represent a real constant in ordinary decimal form. The E<digits> represents a power-of-10 exponent (the E stands for Exponent). The exponent may have an optional sign (+ or − immediately following the E), and the constant itself may be signed (+ or − preceding it). An exponent unsigned or with a "+" means a positive power of 10 and a "−" signed exponent means a negative power of 10. Similarly if the entire real constant is unsigned or has a "+" sign then its value is positive; a "−" sign indicates a negative value. Some examples of valid real constants in Fortran are:

Real constants	Numeric value
43.7	43.7
−16.	−16.
.92	0.92
2.1E2	210
67E-4	0.0067

Type REAL in Fortran is an attempt to represent in a computer the real numbers of mathematics. Because there are an infinite number of real numbers in any mathematical interval, and because computers are finite objects, it is not possible in a computer to represent all real numbers precisely. Thus the values of type REAL in Fortran programs are really approximations (although usually very good ones) to the actual intended real numbers. The difference between the actual values and the computer approximations is called *round-off-error*, and is a source of some concern in programs where very accurate calculations are desired.

Type INTEGER values, on the other hand, are completely accurately represented in the computer and involve no approximating error to the intended value. When specifying subscripts, substring bounds, and other distinctly integer quantities, it is important that no error be possible in the computer representation of these quantities. And, as a practical matter, numerical calculations involving only type INTEGER quantities are faster than the same calculations involving type REAL quantities. For these reasons, and others to appear later, Fortran provides both INTEGER and REAL data types, even though mathematically the integer numbers are a subset of the real numbers. There is a largest integer value that can be represented by type INTEGER and a largest real value that can be represented by type REAL, again due to the finiteness of computers (and these limiting values may be different for different computers). Program A C EXPR at the end of this chapter contains a number of examples of valid arithmetic expressions.

3.2.2 Rules for Arithmetic Expression Evaluation

When the arithmetic operators +, −, *, /, or ** are present in an arithmetic expression then the numeric operations of addition, subtraction, multiplication, division, or exponentiation are to be performed in the process of obtaining the value of the expression. In order to perform a numeric operation the values of the *operands* must be known (i.e., the values to be used in performing the operation must be known). Sometimes (part of) an expression must be evaluated in order to determine the value of an operand in a given operation. To deal with this situation Fortran has a hierarchy of operations governing the order in which operations are performed if an expression has more than one operation in it. This hierarchy is shown in Figure 3.4, in the order of "done first" to "done last". For operators at the same hierarchy level the evaluation is left to right, except for exponentiation, which is right to left.

The following examples illustrate these hierarchical principles:

Example Expressions	*Evaluated the Same as*
A+B*C	A+(B*C)
A/B*C	(A/B)*C
A**B**C	A**(B**C)
A−B+C	(A−B)+C
A/B/C	(A/B)/C
A−B/C+D	(A−(B/C))+D
(A−B)/C+D	((A−B)/C)+D
A−B**(C+(D))	A−(B**(C+D))
−A+B**C*D	(−A)+((B**C)*D)
−A*B	−(A*B)
−A−B	(−A)−B (not − (A−B)!)

Figure 3.4 provides systematic rules for the order in which arithmetic operations are performed in an arithmetic expression, with parentheses allowing the programmer to

1	Operands in parentheses—innermost ones first
2	** (exponentiation)—in right-to-left order.
3	*, / (multiplication, division)—in left-to-right order.
4	+,− (addition, subtraction, etc.)—in left-to-right order.

Figure 3.4. Hierarchy of numeric operations in Fortran.

specify any desired order. Parentheses can be used effectively to override any of the hierarchy rules; so when in doubt about evaluation order, use parentheses.

Each operand in a numerical operation is either a numeric constant, variable, array element, function call, or itself an arithmetic expression. In any event the value of that operand must be obtained before the operation can be performed. The value of a constant is, of course, just the constant itself; the value of a variable or array element is the value contained in the location with the variable (or array element) name; the value of a function call is the value returned by executing the function (see Section 3.4); and the value of an expression is, of course, the value obtained by evaluating the expression. In this manner and in accordance with the hierarchy rules, an expression is systematically evaluated.

There is no prohibition in Fortran against both integer and real quantities appearing in the same expression, and this possibility raises the question as to the type of the resulting value of such a mixed expression. The answer is that if all of the quantities in the expression are of type INTEGER then the result is of type INTEGER; if any one of the quantities in the expression is of type REAL then the result is of type REAL. An expression is evaluated by performing operations between pairs of operands (in the order described above) until only one quantity is left and its value is then the value of the expression. In performing an arithmetic operation (involving two operands) if both operands are of type INTEGER then *integer arithmetic* is performed and the result of that operation is of type INTEGER; if both operands are of type REAL then *real arithmetic* is performed and the result of the operation is of type REAL. If, however, one of the two operands is of type INTEGER and the other is of type REAL then the INTEGER quantity value is automatically (and temporarily) converted to the equivalent REAL value, real arithmetic is performed, and the result of the operation is of type REAL. Everything works out as one might expect with such mixed calculations, with the possible exception of integer division.

Addition, subtraction, and multiplication involving integer operands always give integer results. Division with two integer operands, however, may not, mathematically speaking, give an integer result—for example 8/3 has the mathematical value 2.6666. . . . Since, in Fortran, an arithmetic operation between two integer operands must result in an integer, there must be a rule for which integer is to be used in the case of division. The Fortran rule is "take the integer part, ignoring the fraction, of the mathematical result." Thus, for example, in Fortran:

Expression	*Value (resulting from integer arithmetic)*
8/3	2
12/2	6
−14/4	−3
2/5	0

whereas

Expression	*Value (resulting from real arithmetic)*
8/3.	2.6666 . . .
12.0/2	6.0
−14./4.0	−3.5
2/5.	0.4

Note especially that the value of 2/5 is 0—this phenomenon is sometimes the subtle source of wrong answers.

Ignoring the fractional part of a real value is known as truncating to an integer—the fractional part is truncated, leaving only the integer part. A similar (in fact, identical) action occurs in the assignment

<name> = <value>

when <name> happens to be a variable or array element of type INTEGER and <value> is REAL; the REAL value is truncated and the integer part of it becomes the value <name>. If <name> is REAL and <value> is INTEGER then the equivalent REAL value is assigned to <name>. Program A C EXPR also illustrates the values of a number of arithmetic expressions.

3.3 Character Expressions

The <name> portion of an assignment statement may be either a CHARACTER variable name, a CHARACTER array element name, or a substring of a CHARACTER variable or array element. In this event, <value> must be the value of a character expression, and the valid forms for character expressions, which result in character string values, are given in Figure 3.5.

Form	Example 1	Example 2
1 A character constant (string)	'Fortran 77'	'bleu cheese'
2 A character variable name	TITLE	CODE
3 A character array element	SHAPE(3)	STMT(NSSS+1)
4 A substring	NAME(1:3)	STMT(N)(7:72)
5 A character function call (see Section 3.4)	CHAR(7)	CHAR(NUM−2)
6 Concatenation—any two of these six forms separated by //	TITLE // 'Fortran 77' CODE // STMT(1)(7:10)	

Figure 3.5. Legal character expressions in Fortran.

The two slashes in succession (//) are called the concatenation operator. (Concatenation is the connection of two separate strings into a single longer string.) Unless concatenation is specified, the value of the character expression is just the character value of the quantity appearing in the expression. If concatenation is specified then this operation is performed and the resulting character string becomes the value of the expression. For example if STRNG1 has the value 'Fortran is fantastic' and STRNG2 has the value 'I like bleu cheese,' then

STRNG1 // STRNG2

has the value 'Fortran is fantasticI like bleu cheese,'. Other examples of concatenation are: STRNG1(1:11)//STRNG2(3:18), which has the value 'Fortran is like bleu cheese' whereas STRNG2(3:19)//STRNG1 has the value 'like bleu cheese,Fortran is fantastic'. Still another example demonstrates multiple concatenations in a single-character expression:

STRNG1(1:11)//STRNG2(3:18)//'—both robust.'

has the value

'Fortran is like bleu cheese—both robust.'

As the last example suggests, and as provided for in Figure 3.5, a character expression can contain any number of concatenations. For two or more concatenations, parentheses may be used, as in arithmetic expressions, to specify the order in which the concatenation operations are to take place. Parentheses are never needed, or useful, in such expressions, however, since the resulting expression value is always the same regardless of the order of performing the concatenations. A mathematician would say that the concatenation operation is associative, that is,

(A//B)//C gives exactly the same result as A//(B//C).

Note, however, that concatenation is not commutative:

A//B is not equivalent to B//A

Although concatenation is the only character string operation provided in character expressions, it gives Fortran considerable power and flexibility for processing character string data, especially when combined with the use of substrings.

The character expression in an assignment statement may result in a character string value of any number of characters in length. The CHARACTER data element represented by the <name> portion of the assignment statement is a fixed, predetermined length, as specified in the type statement in which it was declared, and must remain at that length. The question arises, therefore, as to what happens in a character assignment statement when these two lengths (of the <name> and the <value>) are not the same. Fortran requires all of the characters of the <name> data element to be redefined upon execution of a character assignment statement. If the length of the expression value is greater than the length of the <name> element then the extra rightmost characters of the expression value are ignored and the appropriate number of leftmost characters become the new character string value for the <name> element. If the length of the expression value is less than the length of the <name> element then the expression value is extended to the right with blank characters until it is the same length as the <name> element (i.e., the appropriate number of blanks are automatically concatenated onto the right end of the expression value) prior to being assigned as the value of the <name> element. In particular, it should be noted, these rules apply to assignment to substrings. Assume, for example, that STRNG2 has the value given in the examples above. Then the assignment

```
STRNG2(8:11) = 'green'
```

results in STRNG2 having the value 'I like gree cheese,' and

```
STRNG2(8:11) = 'no'
```

results in STRNG2 having the value 'I like no   cheese,' (note the three spaces between "no" and "cheese").

Character string assignments have one major restriction—none of the character positions included in <name> may be referenced in <value>. For example, if a character variable STR is to have its seventh character deleted, the statement

```
STR = STR(1:6)//STR(8:)
```

is the logical approach. However, since both sides of this assignment statement reference a common character data element (in fact, many such elements) it is not allowed. Another character variable may be used temporarily:

```
TEMP = STR(1:6)//STR(8:)
STR = TEMP
```

On the other hand, something like

```
STR(1:4) = STR(7:9)
```

is allowed.

3.4 Intrinsic Functions

A function is a prewritten program that performs a certain computation and makes available to an expression the result of that computation. Each function has a name and a type, and normally has one or more *arguments* that are values the function uses to make its calculations. Take the square-root function, for instance, as it appeared in examples above:

```
SQRT(3.0)
```

The appearance of this construct in an arithmetic expression constitutes a *call* on the square root function to calculate the square root of 3.0. Since the square root of 3.0 is 1.732..., the effect in the expression is the same as if 1.732...had been written instead of SQRT(3.0); that is, as far as the evaluation of the expression is concerned a function call is replaced by the value computed by the function. SQRT is the name of this function that computes square roots, its type is REAL since the value it computes is a real value, and it has one argument (3.0 in the above example) which constitutes the value for which the square root is to be computed. The form of a function call is always

<function name>(<list of arguments>)

and the location of a function call is always as one of the operands in an expression.

Provision is made in Fortran for the programmer to write any functions desired (see Chapter 8), but a number of functions for making commonly needed computations are automatically available as an integral part of Fortran. These *intrinsic* functions, as they are called, are summarized in this section. The programmer may call any of these intrinsic functions in the course of constructing expressions in the program. In the listings of Figures 3.6, 3.7, and 3.8 the "arguments" column lists the number, type, and order of arguments required by each function. When calling a function, any legal expression that has the proper type for its value may be used as an argument. In particular, variables and array elements may be used as arguments, and in making its computation an intrinsic function does not change the value of any such arguments. Figure 3.6 describes 10 of the Fortran intrinsic functions whose values are integers; Figure 3.7 describes the 19 intrinsic functions whose values are real; and Figure 3.8 describes the single intrinsic function whose value is a character.

Note that in most cases the values of an intrinsic function is the same type as the type of its arguments. Exceptions are INT, NINT, REAL, CHAR, ICHAR, and LEN, all of which have a single argument and a computed value of a different type. Such functions are called *transfer functions*, and facilitate a conversion from a value of one type to a corresponding value of a different type.

Function Name	Arguments	Purpose of Function
INT	<real>	Determines the integer part of the argument value, by truncating it
NINT	<real>	Determines the nearest integer to the argument value (i.e., rounding)
ABS	<integer>	Determines the absolute value (magnitude) of the argument value
MOD	<integer1>, <integer2>	Computes the remainder of <integer1> divided by <integer2>
DIM	<integer1>, <integer2>	Computes <integer1> − <integer2> if <integer1> is greater than <integer2>; 0 otherwise
MAX	2 or more <integer>s	Chooses the (algebraic) largest of the argument values
MIN	2 or more <integer>s	Chooses the (algebraic) smallest of the argument values
ICHAR	<character>	Argument value must be a single character; ICHAR determines the position of that character in the processor's collating sequence (see also Figure 3.8)
LEN	<character>	Determines the length (number of characters) of the argument string value
INDEX	<character1>, <character2>	Searches <character1> to see if it contains a substring identical to <character2>, if not (including the case where <character2> is longer than <character1>) the value of INDEX is zero; if a match is found then the position in <character1> of the first (leftmost) character of the matched substring is the value of INDEX; if <character2> occurs more than once in <character1> then the leftmost match is used

Figure 3.6. Fortran intrinsic functions of type INTEGER.

When making function calls care must be taken to insure that the type of each argument supplied in each call matches the type specified in Figures 3.6, 3.7, and 3.8; otherwise incorrect computations may result. For example, the purpose of SQRT(3.0) is clear—to compute the square root of 3.0; but note that SQRT(3) is incorrect since the argument for SQRT must be an expression whose value is real. Converting 3 to 3.0 for use in the SQRT function is simple; but suppose that the square root of the value of COUNT is desired, where COUNT is an INTEGER variable (whose value may be 3). Either of the following uses of SQRT will work, and give the desired result:

```
SQRT(REAL(COUNT))
SQRT(1.0*COUNT)
```

In both of these cases expressions whose values are real—REAL(COUNT)and 1.0*COUNT—are used as arguments to SQRT.

Intrinsic functions can be enormously useful in writing programs since a simple function call can effectively take the place of a quite complex program (or portion of a program). Among the most widely used numeric functions are SQRT, INT, NINT, REAL, and ABS. When making scientific calculations the trigonometric and exponential functions are indispensable. In character string processing LEN and INDEX are extremely useful. For example, the simple function call

```
INDEX(TITLE,'FORTRAN')
```

Function Name	Arguments	Purpose of Function
REAL	<integer>	Determines equivalent real value of the argument value
ABS	<real>	Determines the absolute value (magnitude) of the argument value
MOD	<real1>, <real2>	Same as MOD in Figure 3.6, but using real arguments
DIM	<real1>, <real2>	Same as DIM in Figure 3.6, but using real arguments
MAX	2 or more <real>s	Same as MAX in Figure 3.6, but using real arguments
MIN	2 or more <real>s	Same as MIN in Figure 3.6, but using real arguments
SQRT	<real>	Computes the square-root of the argument value (argument value must not be negative)
EXP	<real>	Computes E**<argument value>, where E is the base of the natural logarithms (2.718...)
LOG	<real>	Computes the natural logarithm of the argument value (argument value must be greater than zero)
LOG10	<real>	Computes the logarithm to the base-10 of the argument value (argument value must be greater than zero)
SIN COS TAN	<real>	Computes the sine, cosine, and tangent of the argument value, assuming the argument is in radians
ASIN ACOS ATAN	<real>	Computes the arc-sine, arc-cosine, and arc-tangent of the argument value; the range for the values of ASIN and ATAN is −PI/2 to PI/2, and for ACOS is 0 to PI; (the absolute value of the ASIN or ACOS argument must not exceed 1.0)
SINH COSH TANH	<real>	Computes the hyperbolic-sine, -cosine, -tangent of the argument value

Figure 3.7. Fortran intrinsic functions of type REAL.

Function Name	Argument	Purpose of Function
CHAR	<integer>	The inverse of ICHAR (see Figure 3.6)—the character in the <integer>th position of the processor's character collating sequence is the value of CHAR. Each implementation of Fortran defines a "collating sequence" for all N of the characters that it recognizes. This is an ordering of the N characters, and association of the elements of this ordering with the integers 0, 1, 2, . . ., N−1 ICHAR determines this associated integer number for the specified argument character; CHAR determines the character associated with the specified argument integer, which must be in the 0 . . N−1 range. Always: CHAR(ICHAR(<character>)) has the value <character>, and ICHAR(CHAR(<integer>)) has the value <integer>.

Figure 3.8. Fortran intrinsic functions of type CHARACTER.

searches the entire character string value of TITLE to see if it contains the substring 'FORTRAN' in it somewhere, and, if so, tells where. Additional examples of function calls:

Function Call	*What It Accomplishes*
INT(XVAL+4)	computes XVAL+4 and then truncates it
NINT(SQRT(AREA(2)))	determines the nearest integer value of the square root of the value of the data element named AREA(2)
SIN(PI/6)	computes the sine of PI/6 (which is 0.500 if PI has previously been given the π value of 3.14159 . . .)
LEN(CODE//'That' 's all!')	concatenates the value of CODE and That's all! and determines the number of characters in the result
ABS(NUMBER/2.)	determines the magnitude of half the value of NUMBER
INDEX(NAME,ALIAS(1:3))	searches the value of NAME to see if it contains three consecutive characters that are identical to the first three characters of the value of ALIAS—if found, gives match position in NAME
MAX(COUNT,K+20,100)	choose the maximum of the values of COUNT, K+20, and 100

Function calls may be, at first glance, indistinguishable from array elements since the forms

<function name>(<argument>)
<array name>(<subscript>)

are identical. If the form

<name>(<expression>)

appears in the executable portion of a Fortran program then the compiler proceeds as follows. First it checks to see if <name> has been declared in the specifications as an arrray; if so then <name>(<expression>) is taken to be an array element and the statement containing <name>(expression>) is compiled accordingly. If <name> has not been declared as an array name then <name>(<expression>) is assumed to be a function call, and then <name> is checked to see if it is one of the legal function names. Therefore the programmer should be careful not to select an array name that is the same as the name of a function that is called in the program.

3.5 Summary

Assignment statements have the form

<name> = <expression>

and are the principal means by which the values of data elements are changed in Fortran programs. The <name> must be a variable, array element, or substring, and identifies the data element to which a value is to be assigned. In execution of an assignment statement the <expression> is evaluated, and the resulting value is the value assigned to <name>. During evaluation of the expression no data element values are changed (but see Section 8.4 for possible exceptions to this rule). If <name> identifies a numeric data element then <expression> must be an arithmetic expression

```
*....:-----------------------------------------------------------------------
      PROGRAM  A C EXPR
*                             ..this program illustrates the formation
*                             and use of arithmetic and character
*                             expressions. Most emphasis in this example
*                             is upon the more error-prone aspects of
*                             arithmetic expressions, such as integer
*                             division and real-to-integer conversion..
*     ....numeric constants....
      INTEGER  I1, I2
      REAL  R1, R2
      PARAMETER  ( I1 = -5, I2 = 17,
     :              R1 = 43.7, R2 = 2.5E-3 )

*     ....string values....
      CHARACTER  STRNG1*20, STRNG2*20
      DATA    STRNG1  / 'Fortran is fantastic' /,
     :        STRNG2  / 'I like bleu cheese, ' /

*     ....variables....
      INTEGER  IE1, IE2, IE3, IE4
      REAL  RE1, RE2, RE3, RE4
      CHARACTER*40  CE1, CE2, CE3, CE4

*     ....execute....

      IE1 = 2 * (I1 + I2)
      IE2 = I2 / 3
      IE3 = I1 / I2
      IE4 = MAX(R1,R2,1.1)

      RE1 = 2 * R1
      RE2 = SQRT(I2*R2)
      RE3 = I1
      RE4 = ABS(R1*(I1+3.14159))

      CE1 = STRNG2(8:18)
      CE2 = STRNG2(3:) // STRNG1
      CE3 = STRNG2(1:2) // 'don''t' // STRNG2(2:18)
      CE4 = STRNG1(:8) // STRNG1(:8)  // STRNG1(:8) // '...'

      PRINT *,  'IE1 =', IE1
      PRINT *,  'IE2 =', IE2
      PRINT *,  'IE3 =', IE3
      PRINT *,  'IE4 =', IE4
      PRINT *
      PRINT *,  'RE1 =', RE1
      PRINT *,  'RE2 =', RE2
      PRINT *,  'RE3 =', RE3
      PRINT *,  'RE4 =', RE4
      PRINT *
      PRINT *,  'CE1 =  ', CE1
      PRINT *,  'CE2 =  ', CE2
      PRINT *,  'CE3 =  ', CE3
      PRINT *,  'CE4 =  ', CE4
      PRINT *
      END
=============================================================================
.EXECUTE  A C EXPR

IE1 =          24
IE2 =           5
IE3 =           0
IE4 =          43

RE1 =      87.400000
RE2 =       0.206155
RE3 =      -5.000000
RE4 =      81.212517

CE1 =  bleu cheese
CE2 =  like bleu cheese, Fortran is fantastic
CE3 =  I don't like bleu cheese
CE4 =  Fortran Fortran Fortran ...

=============================================================================
```

(see Section 3.2); if <name> identifies a character data element then <expression> must be a character expression (see Section 3.3). Expressions may contain constants, references to variables and array elements, function calls, and arbitrarily many operations involving such quantities.

Expressions are ubiquitous in Fortran. Any output-list quantity in a PRINT statement may be an arbitrary expression. Subscripts and substring positions may be arbitrary expressions that evaluate to INTEGER values. Array bounds and character lengths in declaration statements may be arbitrary expressions involving only integer constants. Values in PARAMETER statements can be arbitrary expressions involving only constants (of the proper type). (Initial values in DATA statements, however, must be only constants, and not expressions involving operators.) And, of course, arbitrary expressions may be used in assignment statements and as function arguments. As additional features of Fortran are described, it will be seen that expressions are used in many more places.

The use of expressions contributes significantly to the power and convenience of Fortran. In return for this power and convenience it is the programmer's responsibility to see that improper or undefined expressions are not written; these include things like dividing by zero and taking the square root of a negative number. Subscript values must be within bounds, as must substring positions. Character constants must not be "empty" (i.e., must have at least one character—although that one may be a blank). Clearly expressions are an important part of Fortran, and the programmer must be well versed in their uses.

This chapter ends with program A C EXPR (for Arithmetic and Character EXPRessions), which demonstrates a number of Fortran assignment statements, corresponding expressions, and resulting values.

Programming Exercises

3.1 Construct an expression to compute the total cost of an item with LIST list price, TAX sales tax, and DSCNT discount. TAX is the sales tax rate in percent, and DSCNT is the percent (of list price) that is to be discounted.

3.2 Write a sequence of assignment statements that transpose the two halves of a string. For example 'C3P7' would become 'P7C3'.

3.3 Making use of intrinsic functions, construct one or more assignment statements that extracts the Nth digit left of the decimal point, of the real VALUE. For example, if VALUE is 479.6 and N is 2, your statement(s) should compute the value 7. (N may be negative, in which case a digit to the right of the decimal point is extracted.)

3.4 Write a sequence of Fortran statements which will locate the blank character in the string ZING and replace it with the character '*'. If the value of ZING were 'more than   1   blank', how would it appear after execution of these statements?

3.5 The current value of the character variable STATE is 'NEW YORK'. Write a sequence of Fortran statements to assign the value 'NY' to STATE, using the 'N' and 'Y' found in the first and fifth positions of STATE. (Hint: temporarily use a character data element ABBREV.)

3.6 Write a Fortran expression to compute the value of

½ + (½)**2 + (½)**3 + (½)**4 + (½)**5

(What is the Fortran value of 1/2?)

3.7 Write a Fortran expression to compute the grade point average (GPA) for a student receiving these grades in five three-hour courses:

2 A's, 2 B's, 1 C

(A = 4, B = 3, C = 2 quality points.
GPA = total quality points/number of hours.)
The value of the GPA should be real; show at least two different methods of obtaining a real-valued expression for the GPA.

3.8 Give the value of each of these Fortran expressions.

```
9/10
9/10.
0.9/10
REAL (9/10)
LEN('9/10.')
MAX(9,10)
DIM(10,9)
MOD(10,9)
NINT(9./10.)
INT(9./10.)
```

Chapter 4 Selection Control

The output (PRINT), input (READ), and assignment statements are the basic executable statements in Fortran that cause data element values to be transferred or modified, that is, these are the statements that perform the actual data processing. Such statements are therefore called *processing* statements. Processing statements are executed in the order that they appear in the program, and this is called the normal execution sequence. An important aspect of programing involves specifying changes to this normal execution sequence when necessary. The programmer may specify that one or more statements be "skipped" during execution (selection control), or that execution resume at some previously executed statement (repetition control). The statements that provide such control are called *control* statements (or control structures), and they provide execution control rather than data manipulation. This chapter describes the primary method of achieving selection control in Fortran programs.

4.1 The IF-ENDIF Statement

Program CHANGE demonstrates the most fundamental form of selection control, that of conditionally executing a group of statements.

```
*....:-----------------------------------------------------------------
      PROGRAM  CHANGE
*                                 ..This program demonstrates conditional
*                                   execution of statements. It checks to
*                                   see if a Fortran statement (supplied
*                                   as a string of data) contains the
*                                   character "C" in column 1,
*                                   and if it does, changes the "C"
*                                   to an "*" and prints a message that
*                                   it has done so. The .EQ. (for EQual)
*                                   causes a comparison of the first
*                                   character of STMT with the character "C"
*                                   to see if they are the same..
*     ....variable....
      CHARACTER  STMT*72

*     ....execute....
      PRINT *,  'Input any Fortran statement:'
      READ '(A)',  STMT
      PRINT *

      IF  (STMT(1:1) .EQ. 'C')  THEN
*                          ..change "C" to an "*"
            STMT(1:1) = '*'
            PRINT *,  '"C" in column 1 has been changed to "*"'
            PRINT *
      ENDIF

      PRINT *,  'The statement is:'
      PRINT *,  STMT
      END
=====================================================================
```

```
.EXECUTE  CHANGE

Input any Fortran statement:
>       AREA = PI * RADIUS**2

The statement is:
      AREA = PI * RADIUS**2
==========================================================================
.EXECUTE  CHANGE

Input any Fortran statement:
> C          This is a comment, with a "C".

"C" in column 1 has been changed to "*"

The statement is:
*          This is a comment, with a "C".
==========================================================================
.EXECUTE  CHANGE

Input any Fortran statement:
> *          This one has an "*" in column 1.

The statement is:
*          This one has an "*" in column 1.
==========================================================================
```

The expression enclosed in parentheses between the IF and the THEN is called a *condition* or *logical expression*, and when evaluated is (i.e., must have a logical value of) either "true" or "false". When the IF statement is encountered during execution of the program the first thing that happens is that the logical expression is evaluated. If the resulting value is "true" then the statements between the IF and the ENDIF are executed, and execution then continues with the statement following ENDIF; if the value of the logical expression is "false" then all of the statements between IF and ENDIF are ignored (not executed) and execution continues with the statement following ENDIF. The situation is described graphically in Figure 4.1.

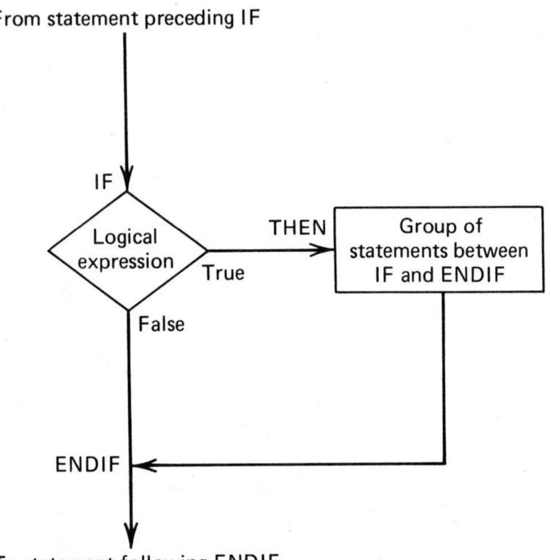

Figure 4.1. The "flow of control" in the execution of an IF-ENDIF statement.

The form of an IF-ENDIF statement is

```
IF (<logical expression>) THEN
          --}
          --}
          --}  statement group
          --}
          --}
ENDIF
```

The IF (<logical expression>) THEN must be on a line by itself, as must be the ENDIF. The statement group between the IF and ENDIF may have any number of executable statements in it, including none or one (although usually there is at least one). Although Fortran does not require that the statement group between an IF-ENDIF be indented, it is important for the appearance and readability of the program that these statements be indented. In all of the example programs they are indented eight spaces to the right of IF, and in the examples the ENDIF is always aligned with the IF.

Every IF requires a matching ENDIF somewhere in the program following the IF. All intervening statements are taken as part of the conditionally executed group of statements. There may be any number of IF-ENDIF statements in a program, and they may appear anywhere among the executable statements. The IF-ENDIF construct is, in a sense, an extended statement in that it is composed of at least two parts. The whole is greater than the sum of its parts in this case, since neither the IF statement nor the ENDIF statement has any meaning without the other. The entire construct takes at least two (and usually more) lines, and the term IF-ENDIF *structure* is therefore probably more appropriate than the term IF-ENDIF statement.

4.2 The ELSE Statement

The IF-ENDIF statement described above provides for the conditional execution of a group of statements. That is, if the condition is true the statements are executed, if the condition is false the statements are not executed, and in either case control ultimately flows to the statement following the ENDIF. It often happens that if the condition is true a group of statements is to be executed, if the condition is false a different group of statements is to be executed, and in either case control then flows to yet a third group of statements. This can be achieved with the IF-ENDIF statement in the following manner:

```
IF (<condition>) THEN
        --}
        --}  statement group 1
        --}
ENDIF
IF (<opposite condition>) THEN
        --}
        --}  statement group 2
        --}
ENDIF
--}
--}  statement group 3
--}
```

Here either statement group 1 or statement group 2 will be executed, but not both, and in either case statement group 3 will be executed. Fortran provides a superior way of achieving the same effect, however, with the ELSE option in the IF-ENDIF structure. Program CHILLY illustrates the technique.

```
*....:-----------------------------------------------------------------------
      PROGRAM  CHILLY
*                                    ..This program illustrates the use of the
*                                      ELSE option in the IF-ENDIF statement.
*                                      The effective temperature (chill-factor)
*                                      is calculated for any given wind-speed.
*                                      The formula is a good approximation to
*                                      the chill-factor if the air temperature
*                                      is in the -35 to +15 degrees Celsius
*                                      (-31 to +59 degrees Fahrenheit) range.
*     ....variables....
      REAL  TEMP, SPEED, CHILL, MPS

*                                    ..MPS is the  speed in meters per second.
*                                      SPEED is input in kilometers per hour.
*                                      TEMP is input in degrees Celsius.
*     ....execute....
      PRINT *,  'Chill-factor determination, given temp & wind-speed.'
      PRINT *,  'Input:  <degrees Celsius> , <kilometers per hour>'
      READ *,  TEMP, SPEED
*                                    ..Temperature must be in the -35 to +15
*                                      degree Celsius range. The .GT. (for
*                                      Greater Than) causes the absolute value
*                                      of (TEMP+10) to be compared with 25.
*                                      If it is greater than 25 then TEMP is
*                                      not in the -35 to +15 range.
      PRINT *

      IF  (ABS(TEMP+10) .GT. 25)  THEN
              PRINT *,  'Invalid Data:',NINT(TEMP),' given as temp.'
              PRINT *,  'Temperature must be in the range -35 to +15'

          ELSE
*                                    ..calculate chill-factor..
*                                      8 KPH assumed for speeds less than 8
*                                     90 KPH assumed for speeds greater than 90
              MPS = MAX(8.0,MIN(90.0,ABS(SPEED)))/3.6
              CHILL = 33-(33-TEMP)*(10*SQRT(MPS)-MPS+10.45)/23.165
              PRINT *, 'For',NINT(TEMP),' degrees C',NINT(1.8*TEMP+32),
     :                                                  ' degrees F'
              PRINT *, 'and',NINT(ABS(SPEED)),' KM per hr',
     :                     NINT(ABS(SPEED)/1.61),' Mi per hr'
              PRINT *
              PRINT *, 'The chill-factor is',NINT(CHILL),' degrees C',
     :                              NINT(1.8*CHILL+32),' degrees F'
      ENDIF

      END
=============================================================================
.EXECUTE  CHILLY

Chill-factor determination, given temp & wind-speed.
Input:  <degrees Celsius> , <kilometers per hour>
> -5, 30

For           -5 degrees C           23 degrees F
and           30 KM per hr           19 Mi per hr

The chill-factor is         -18 degrees C            0 degrees F
=============================================================================
.EXECUTE  CHILLY

Chill-factor determination, given temp & wind-speed.
Input:  <degrees Celsius> , <kilometers per hour>
> 20, 20

Invalid data:          20 degrees given as temp.
Temperature must be in the range -35 to +15
=============================================================================
```

The form of the IF-ENDIF structure using the ELSE option is

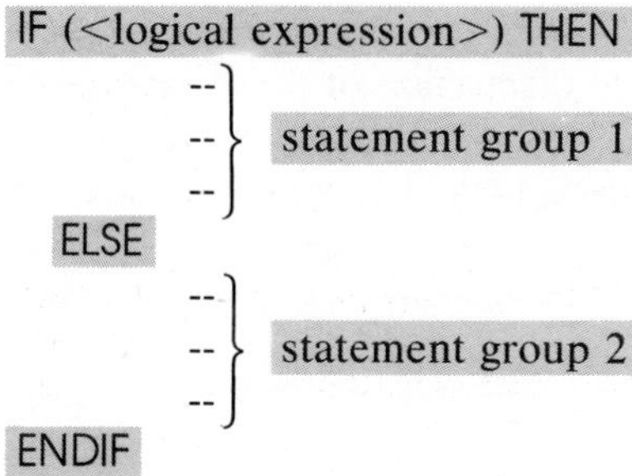

```
IF (<logical expression>) THEN
        --
        --  statement group 1
        --
  ELSE
        --
        --  statement group 2
        --
ENDIF
```

If the <logical expression> is true then statement group 1 is executed and then control flows to the statement following ENDIF; if the <logical expression> is false then statement group 2 is executed and then control flows to the statement following ENDIF. This situation is graphically depicted in Figure 4.2.

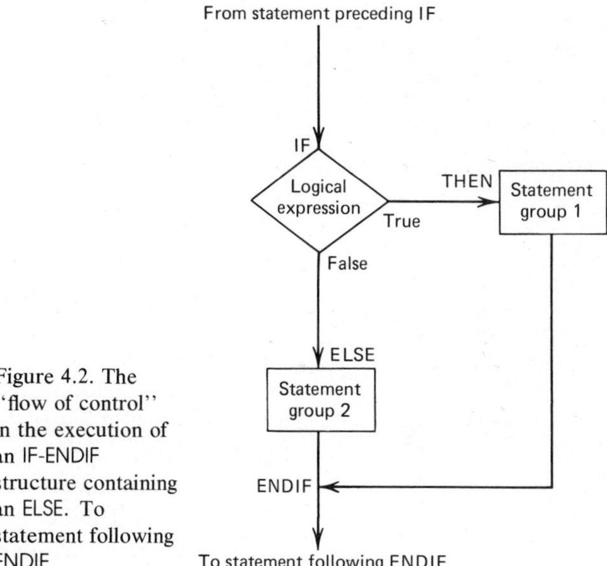

Figure 4.2. The "flow of control" in the execution of an IF-ENDIF structure containing an ELSE. To statement following ENDIF

The ELSE is considered to be a separate statement and must be on a line by itself. The ELSE block (statement group 2), like the THEN block (statement group 1), may contain any executable statements. If the programmer wishes the THEN and the ELSE to be aligned, for esthetic reasons, this can be accomplished as follows by continuing the IF statement.

```
 IF (<logical expression>)
:    THEN
        --
        --  THEN block
        --
     ELSE
        --
        --  ELSE block
        --
 ENDIF
```

4.3 Logical Expressions

Using the IF-ENDIF structure requires the programmer to construct appropriate logical expressions to achieve the desired control. Fortran has extensive facilities for constructing logical expressions, and these give the programmer great flexibility in specifying the desired conditions for selective execution of statement groups. This section is devoted to a detailed discussion of these facilities.

4.3.1 Relational Expressions

The most commonly used logical expressions have one of the two forms:

1 <arithmetic expr> <relational operator> <arithmetic expr>

2 <character expr> <relational operator> <character expr>

These forms of logical expressions are called *relational expressions* because they compare the values of two arithmetic expressions or two character expressions. There are six <relational operator>s in Fortran:

Relational Operator	*Meaning: Compare the Values of the Two Expressions to see if*
.EQ.	they are equal
.NE.	they are not equal (opposite of .EQ.)
.LT.	the left one is less than the right one
.GT.	the left one is greater than the right one
.LE.	the left one is less than or equal to the right one (opposite of .GT.)
.GE.	the left one is greater than or equal to the right one (opposite of .LT.)

The result (value) of any one of these comparisons is either true or false. No data elements have their values changed during the evaluation of a logical expression.

In the case of a relational expression involving arithmetic expressions, only one question arises: How is the comparison made if the value of one expression is of type REAL and the value of the other is of type INTEGER? The integer value is temporarily converted to the equivalent real value and the comparison is then made between the two real values. For relational expressions involving character expressions, two questions arise. First, just what is meant by comparing two character string values? Second, what happens if the two character string values are not the same length?

Character strings are compared, character by corresponding character, starting from the left (position 1) of each string and progressing to the right as long as the corresponding characters are the same. If all of the corresponding characters are the same then the two strings are equal; if the corresponding characters in any position are different then the strings are not equal. If the two strings are not equal then there will be a leftmost position in which the corresponding characters differ (the differing position). The lesser of the two strings is the one whose character in the differing position comes first in the processor's collating sequence for characters (i.e., has the smallest ICHAR value—see Section 3.4). This collating sequence may differ from processor to processor, but in all cases 'A' < 'B' < 'C' < 'D' <. . . .< 'Z' and '0' < '1' < '2' <. . . .< '9', so that the normal alphabetic and digit ordering is in effect. (Examples of widely used collating sequences are given in Appendix B.) If the two character strings have different lengths then the shorter one is extended with additional blank characters to the length of the longer string and then the comparison is made.

4.3.2 Logical Data Types

The two values "true" and "false" may be thought of as defining a data type. Each variable, constant, or expression of this type may have one of only two values—"true" or "false". Fortran provides for this data type, in addition to the types INTEGER, REAL, and CHARACTER, and calls it type LOGICAL. There are two logical constants (.TRUE. and .FALSE.), and the programmer may declare LOGICAL variables and LOGICAL arrays. There are four intrinsic logical functions in Fortran and logical expressions may be constructed, and assignments made to logical variables and array elements. LOGICAL declarations are similar in form to INTEGER declarations, except the word LOGICAL is used instead of the word INTEGER.

The forms that a general logical expression may take are:

Form	*Example 1*	*Example 2*
1 Logical constant	.TRUE.	.FALSE.
2 Logical variable	DONE	OK
3 Logical array element	TEST(3)	FLAG(COUNT)
4 Logical function call	LGT(LIST1,LIST2)	LLE(NAME(N),NAM3)
5 Relational expression	CODE .EQ. 'FINISHED'	XVAL .GT. 100.0
6 The logical operators		
.AND.	OK .AND. CODE .EQ. 'FINISHED'	
.OR.	LGT(LIST1,LIST2) .OR. XVAL .GT. 100	
.EQV.	BIT(1) .EQ. 1 .EQV. BIT(K) .EQ. 0	
.NEQV.	TEST(3) .NEQV. OK	
between any two of these eight forms		
7 The logical operator		
.NOT.	.NOT. DONE	.NOT. TEST(3)
preceding any of the other 7 of these forms		
8 Any of these eight forms enclosed in parentheses	((DONE .EQV. FLAG(COUNT)) .AND.(OK.OR.DONE))	

The hierarchy of the various logical forms is (in the order of done first to done last):

1 Expressions in parentheses

2 .NOT.

3 .AND.

4 .OR.

5 .EQV. and .NEQV.

All operations of equal hierarchy level are performed left to right. In a logical expression each operand associated with the logical operators .NOT., .AND., .OR., .EQV., and .NEQV. have logical values (i.e., are either .TRUE. or .FALSE.). Figure 4.3 shows how each of the logical operations is evaluated. Figure 4.4 describes the four intrinsic logical

L1	L2	.NOT. L1	L1 .AND. L2	L1 .OR. L2	L1 .EQV. L2	L1 .NEQV. L2
.TRUE.	.TRUE.	.FALSE.	.TRUE.	.TRUE.	.TRUE.	.FALSE.
.TRUE.	.FALSE.	.FALSE.	.FALSE.	.TRUE.	.FALSE.	.TRUE.
.FALSE.	.TRUE.	.TRUE.	.FALSE.	.TRUE.	.FALSE.	.TRUE.
.FALSE.	.FALSE.	.TRUE.	.FALSE.	.FALSE.	.TRUE.	.FALSE.

Figure 4.3. The meaning of the various logical operations (L1 and L2 represent logical operands).

Function Name	Arguments	Same as
LGT	<character>,<character>	.GT.
LGE	<character>,<character>	.GE.
LLT	<character>,<character>	.LT.
LLE	<character>,<character>	.LE.

Figure 4.4. The Fortran intrinsic functions having logical values. These functions provide string comparisons based on the ASCII collating sequence, and have the same values as the "same as" column, with the two arguments as operands, if the processor uses the ASCII collating sequence. Therefore LGT, LGE, LLT, and LLE are useful only with processors having a collating sequence different from the ASCII code, and ASCII comparisons are desired between values. (See appendix B for a description of ASCII.)

functions. Program L EXPR illustrates the declaration of logical data elements, and the values of some logical expressions. Do not confuse the <relational operators>s, which are used for comparisons (relational expressions) between numeric and character values, with the <logical operator>s, which are used to form compound logical expressions involving logical operands. Relational expressions are logical operands, as are logical variables, logical function calls, etc.

```
*....:-----------------------------------------------------------------
      PROGRAM  L EXPR
*                                   ..This program illustrates the declaration
*                                     of data elements of type LOGICAL, the
*                                     formation of various logical expressions
*                                     and the resulting values of those
*                                     logical expressions.
*     ....constants....
      INTEGER  I1, I2
      CHARACTER  C1*10, C2*20
      LOGICAL  L1, L2, L3, L4
      PARAMETER  ( I1 = 47, I2 = -634,
     :             C1 = 'FINISHED', C2 = 'Fundamental Concepts',
     :             L1 = .FALSE., L2 = .TRUE., L3 = .TRUE., L4 = .FALSE.)

*     ....variables....
      LOGICAL  LE1, LE2, LE3, LE4, LE5, LE6, LE7, LE8

*     ....execute....

      LE1 = .FALSE.
      LE2 = L1  .OR.  (I2 .LT. 0)
      LE3 = L3  .NEQV.  L2  .AND.  L1
      LE4 = (L3  .NEQV.  L2)  .AND.  L1
      LE5 = INDEX(C2,'Fun') .EQ. 0
      LE6 = I1 .GT. I2  .OR.  C1 .EQ. C2  .AND.  L4
      LE7 = .NOT. (L1 .EQV. L4 .AND. L2 .OR. L3)
      LE8 = (.NOT. (L1 .AND. L2) .NEQV. (.NOT. L3 .OR. L4))

      PRINT *,  'LE1 = ', LE1
      PRINT *,  'LE2 = ', LE2
      PRINT *,  'LE3 = ', LE3
      PRINT *,  'LE4 = ', LE4
      PRINT *,  'LE5 = ', LE5
      PRINT *,  'LE6 = ', LE6
      PRINT *,  'LE7 = ', LE7
      PRINT *,  'LE8 = ', LE8
*                                  ..note that PRINT outputs
*                                    "T" or "F" for logical values..
      END
=======================================================================
.EXECUTE  L EXPR

LE1 = F
LE2 = T
LE3 = T
LE4 = F
LE5 = F
LE6 = T
LE7 = T
LE8 = T
=======================================================================
```

Note that logical expressions may be arbitrarily complex, and in particular several relational expressions may occur in a single logical expression. For example, if A, B, and C are numeric quantities, and it is desired to see if all three have the same value (i.e., mathematically, A = B = C?), the Fortran logical expression

```
A .EQ. B .AND. B .EQ. C
```

is true if they are all the same and false otherwise. Note that

```
A .EQ. B .AND. C
```

is not legal; nor is

```
A .EQ. B .EQ. C
```

Note also that

```
A .EQ. B .AND. B .EQ. C
```

must be evaluated as

```
(A .EQ. B) .AND. (B .EQ. C)
```

A word of caution is in order concerning comparison of real values, because round-off errors can cause such comparisons to result in unexpected values. For example,

```
SQRT(2.0)**2 .EQ. 2.0
```

may be .FALSE. because of round-off error introduced during evaluation of SQRT(2.0). A much more satisfactory relation in these kinds of situations is

```
ABS(SQRT(2.0)**2 - 2.0) .LT. EPS
```

where EPS is a real variable having a small positive value somewhat larger than the likely round-off error (for example: 0.000001). Restructuring the relational expression by using EPS effectively allows for a certain amount of uncertainty to be present in the real values being compared. This is discussed more in Part 3.

4.4 The ELSEIF Statement

The IF-ENDIF control structure with the ELSE option effectively allows for convenient selection between two possible paths of execution. There often are times, however, when one choice must be selected from several (more than two) possible cases. Typical of this situation is that in which there are several conditions, each of which has associated with it a set of actions to be taken (i.e., statements to be executed) if that condition is met (is .TRUE.). Thus the concept of two-way selection provided by the ELSE may be generalized to *n*-way selection (for any positive integer *n*) among *n* different paths of execution. The ELSEIF option provided by Fortran with the IF-ENDIF control structure is a powerful programming tool for this kind of general selection, and is illustrated in program LOT. This program is based on one of the payoff schemes (see Figure 4.5) that has been used in the New York State weekly lottery, in which lottery ticket numbers are six-digit numbers and certain digit patterns that match the winning ticket digits win certain amounts of money.

All 6 digits correct	1	2	3	4	5	6	you win $50,000.
First 5 digits correct	1	2	3	4	5		you win $2,000.
Last 5 digits correct		2	3	4	5	6	you win $2,000.
First 4 digits correct	1	2	3	4			you win $125.
Last 4 digits correct			3	4	5	6	you win $125.
First 3 digits correct	1	2	3				you win $25.
Last 3 digits correct				4	5	6	you win $25.
First 2 digits and Last 2 digits correct	1	2			5	6	you win $5.
First 2 digits correct	1	2					you win $2.
Last 2 digits correct					5	6	you win $2.

Figure 4.5. New York lottery payoff system.

The ELSEIF statement is identical to the IF statement except that it starts with ELSEIF instead of IF:

ELSEIF (<logical expression>) THEN

and an IF-ENDIF structure may contain any number of ELSEIF statements. Here is the form of an IF-ENDIF structure containing three ELSEIF statements:

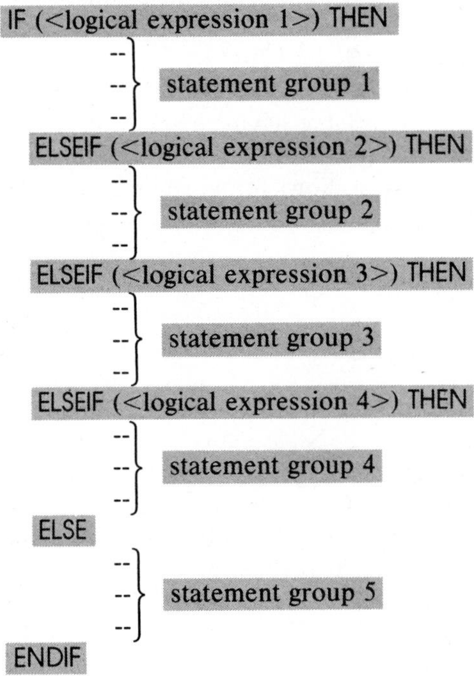

IF (<logical expression 1>) THEN
statement group 1
ELSEIF (<logical expression 2>) THEN
statement group 2
ELSEIF (<logical expression 3>) THEN
statement group 3
ELSEIF (<logical expression 4>) THEN
statement group 4
ELSE
statement group 5
ENDIF

In this structure, statement group 1 is associated with <logical expression 1>, statement group 2 is associated with <logical expression 2>, statement group 3 is associated with <logical expression 3>, statement group 4 is associated with <logical expression 4>, and statement group 5 is the ELSE block. When this structure is encountered during execution <logical expression 1> is evaluated first; if its value is .TRUE. then statement

```
*....:-----------------------------------------------------------------
      PROGRAM  LOT
*                                 ..This program calculates the amount won
*                                   by any given ticket in one version of
*                                   the New York State lottery (see figure
*                                   4.5). The winning number and the
*                                   ticket number to be checked are both
*                                   6-character strings containing the 6
*                                   digits of the number.
*     ....variables....
      INTEGER  PAYOFF
      CHARACTER  WINNER*6, TICKET*6

      DATA    WINNER  / '417059' /

*     ....execute....
      PRINT *,  'Input ticket number:    <6 digits>'
      READ '(A)',  TICKET

      IF  (TICKET .EQ. WINNER)  THEN
              PAYOFF = 25000

          ELSEIF (TICKET(1:5) .EQ. WINNER(1:5)  .OR.
     :            TICKET(2:6) .EQ. WINNER(2:6)        )  THEN
              PAYOFF = 2000

          ELSEIF (TICKET(1:4) .EQ. WINNER(1:4)  .OR.
     :            TICKET(3:6) .EQ. WINNER(3:6)        )  THEN
              PAYOFF = 125

          ELSEIF (TICKET(1:3) .EQ. WINNER(1:3)  .OR.
     :            TICKET(4:6) .EQ. WINNER(4:6)        )  THEN
              PAYOFF = 25

          ELSEIF (TICKET(1:2) .EQ. WINNER(1:2)  .AND.
     :            TICKET(5:6) .EQ. WINNER(5:6)        )  THEN
              PAYOFF= 5

          ELSEIF (TICKET(1:2) .EQ. WINNER(1:2)  .OR.
     :            TICKET(5:6) .EQ. WINNER(5:6)        )  THEN
              PAYOFF = 2

          ELSE
              PAYOFF = 0
      ENDIF

      PRINT *
      PRINT *,  'Ticket  number    ', TICKET
      PRINT *,  'Winning number    ', WINNER
      PRINT *,  'Amount this ticket wins is', PAYOFF, '  dollars.'
      END
=======================================================================
.EXECUTE  LOT

Input ticket number:    <6 digits>
> 803159

Ticket  number    803159
Winning number    417059
Amount this ticket wins is          2  dollars.
=======================================================================
.EXECUTE  LOT

Input ticket number:    <6 digits>
> 217054

Ticket  number    217054
Winning number    417059
Amount this ticket wins is          0  dollars.
=======================================================================
```

group 1 is executed after which control passes to the (statement following) ENDIF. If the value of <logical expression 1> is .FALSE. then statement group 1 is ignored and <logical expression 2> is evaluated; if its value is .TRUE. then statement group 2 is executed, after which control passes to the ENDIF. If the value of <logical expression 2> is .FALSE. then statement group 2 is also ignored and <logical expression 3> is evaluated. Continuing in this manner the statement group executed is that one associated with the first .TRUE. condition; all other statement groups in the structure are ignored. If none of the conditions are true then the ELSE block is executed. In any event no more than one of the statement groups in the structure is executed. Since the ELSE and its associated block of statements is optional, in an IF-ENDIF structure with no ELSE option and no true conditions, none of the statement blocks are executed. If an IF-ENDIF structure has more than one true condition only the statement group associated with the first true condition gets executed. Because of this last fact the programmer must take great care in designing the order of the ELSEIF statements when the conditions are not mutually exclusive (i.e., when more than one may be true). In practice often more than one of the conditions may be true, as program LOT suggests.

The flow of control concepts associated with the general IF-ENDIF structure are shown graphically in Figure 4.6. Program TRIANG is another example of an application of the ELSEIF. Program TRIANG accepts data for the three sides of a triangle, and identifies certain properties of the triangle.

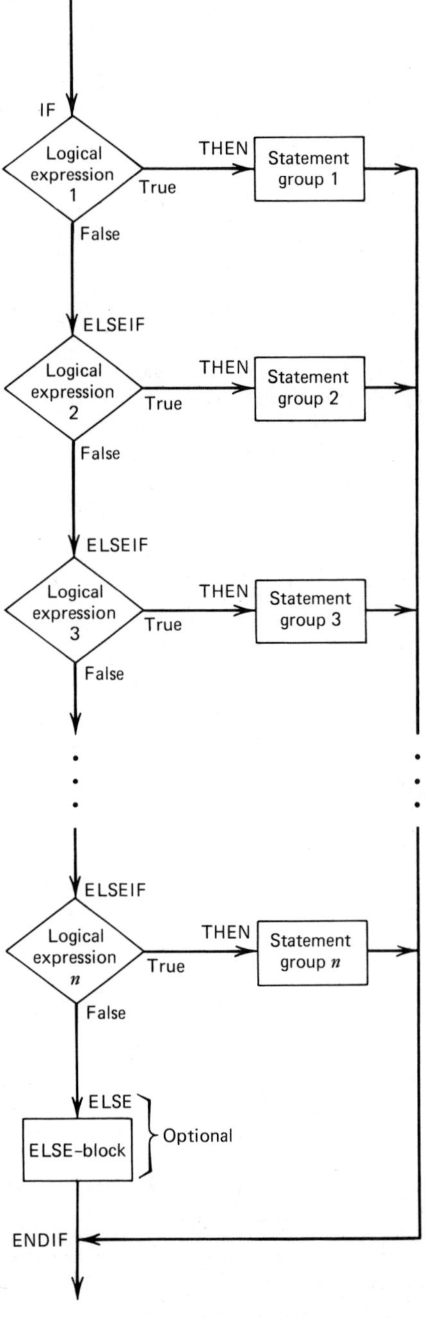

Figure 4.6. The "flow of control" in the execution of a general IF-ENDIF structure (n may be any positive integer).

```
*....:-----------------------------------------------------------------
      PROGRAM  TRIANG
*                                 ..This program calls for data for the 3
*                                   sides of a triangle. It checks the data
*                                   for validity and if the data is valid it
*                                   identifies whether the triangle is
*                                   acute, obtuse, or right, and in each
*                                   case calculates some desired property of
*                                   the triangle.
*     ....variables....
      REAL  SIDE1, SIDE2, SIDE3,
     :      LARGE, SMALL, MID, LARGSQ, SUMSQ,
     :      ANGLE, AREA, H

*     ....execute....
      PRINT *,  'Input lengths for the 3 sides of a triangle.'
      READ *,  SIDE1, SIDE2, SIDE3
      LARGE = MAX(SIDE1,SIDE2,SIDE3)
      SMALL = MIN(SIDE1,SIDE2,SIDE3)
      MID = SIDE1+SIDE2+SIDE3-LARGE-SMALL
      LARGSQ = LARGE * LARGE
      SUMSQ = SMALL * SMALL + MID * MID
      PRINT *

      IF  (SMALL .LT. 0.0)  THEN
              PRINT *, 'The length of a side may not be negative.'
              PRINT *, SIDE1,SIDE2,SIDE3,'  are not legal values.'

          ELSEIF  (LARGE .GT. SMALL+MID)  THEN
              PRINT *, 'The sum of 2 sides must not exceed the third.'
              PRINT *, SIDE1,SIDE2,SIDE3,'  can''t form a triangle.'

          ELSEIF  (LARGSQ .GT. 1.01*SUMSQ)  THEN
              PRINT *, SIDE1,SIDE2,SIDE3,'  .. an obtuse triangle.'
              ANGLE = ACOS((SUMSQ-LARGSQ)/(2*SMALL*MID))
              H = MID*SMALL*SIN(ANGLE)/LARGE
              PRINT *, 'The height of its shortest altitude is',H

          ELSEIF  (LARGSQ .LT. 0.99*SUMSQ)  THEN
              PRINT *, SIDE1,SIDE2,SIDE3,'  .. an acute triangle.'
              ANGLE = ACOS((SUMSQ-LARGSQ)/(2*SMALL*MID))
              PRINT *, 'Its largest angle is',ANGLE*180/3.14159,
     :                                               '  degrees.'
          ELSE
              PRINT *, 'The triangle formed by ',SIDE1,SIDE2,SIDE3
              PRINT *, 'is very close to being a right triangle.'
              PRINT *
              H = (SIDE1+SIDE2+SIDE3)/2.0
              AREA = SQRT(H*(H-SIDE1)*(H-SIDE2)*(H-SIDE3))
              PRINT *, 'Its area is', AREA
              PRINT *, 'The area of a right triangle with the same ',
     :                                    'legs is',MID*SMALL/2
      ENDIF

      END
=======================================================================
```

```
.EXECUTE  TRIANG

Input lengths for the 3 sides of a triangle.
> 4,4,4

        4.000000        4.000000        4.000000  .. an acute triangle.
Its largest angle is       60.000000  degrees.
=========================================================================
.EXECUTE  TRIANG

Input lengths for the 3 sides of a triangle.
> 2,4,8

The sum of 2 sides must not exceed the third.
        2.000000        4.000000        8.000000  can't form a triangle.
=========================================================================
.EXECUTE  TRIANG

Input lengths for the 3 sides of a triangle.
> 3.5, 6.6, 9.0

        3.500000        6.600000        9.000000  .. an obtuse triangle.
The height of its shortest altitude is       2.566667
=========================================================================
.EXECUTE  TRIANG

Input lengths for the 3 sides of a triangle.
> 7.5, 3.5, 6.6

The triangle formed by        7.500000        3.500000        6.600000
is very close to being a right triangle.

Its area is       11.549526
The area of a right triangle with the same legs is       11.550000
=========================================================================
```

4.5 Nesting IF-ENDIF Structures

A statement group within a selection structure may specify additional selection control. That is, a statement group within an IF-ENDIF structure may itself contain an IF-ENDIF structure. This second IF-ENDIF is said to be *nested* within the first, and is considered to be the inner structure of the two. Nested IF-ENDIF structures have the appearance

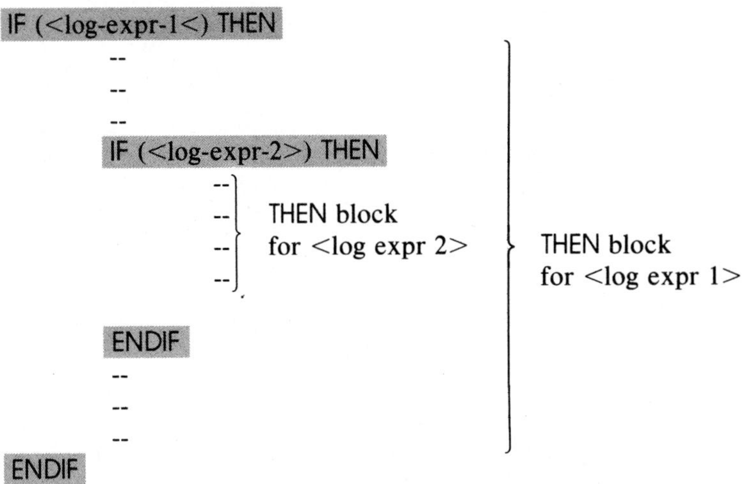

A properly nested IF-ENDIF is wholly contained within one of the statement groups of the outer IF-ENDIF structure, that is, both the IF and its matching ENDIF of the nested IF-ENDIF must be in the same statement group. Any of the statement groups of a general

IF-ENDIF structure may contain any number of arbitrary IF-ENDIF structures. IF-ENDIF structures that follow one another, such as

```
IF (<log expr 1>) THEN
        --
        --
        --
ENDIF
--
--
--
IF (<log expr 2>) THEN
        --
        --
        --
ENDIF
```

are, of course, not nested, and are said to be on the same level. A nested IF-ENDIF is said to be at the next level from the containing IF-ENDIF. A statement group may contain any number of IF-ENDIF structures at the same level, and IF-ENDIF structures may be nested to any level. Nesting more than about three levels deep is not recommended, however, since the deeper the nesting the more difficult is it for a human reader to follow the logic of the program (but the compiler has no problem at all, no matter how deep the nesting). At all times it is of paramount importance that IF statements be properly matched with ENDIF statements (for the sake of both human readers and the compiler), but this is especially important for nested IF-ENDIF structures. A single misplaced, missing, or extra ENDIF completely alters the intended meaning of the program, sometimes drastically so. The programmer must always be alert to prevent such errors when writing the program, as they can be difficult to find and correct later. Wise use of indenting can certainly improve the readability of a program having nested selection. The example programs illustrate one style of (what the author believes to be) effective indentation.

This section concludes with three program examples illustrating nested IF-ENDIF structures. The first, program ROLL, simulates the two rolls of the ball in a frame of bowling. All 10 pins on the first roll is a "STRIKE !!" and the ball is not rolled the second time; all 10 pins with both rolls is a "SPARE !", and less than 10 pins with both rolls is "NOMARK". In program ROLL it is assumed that no errors are made on input values (0. .10 on first roll, 0. .(10-BALL1) on second roll). This assumption is removed in a later example.

The next example is a sequel to program ROLL. There are two major components to a frame of bowling. The first is the rolling of the balls (program ROLL), and the second is to update the scoring of the game (program SCORE). If the MARK in the current frame is SPARE or STRIKE then this frame cannot be scored at this time. However if the MARK in the previous frame was a spare then it (the previous frame) can be scored at this time (add 10 + BALL1 to the score); if the MARK in the previous frame was a STRIKE then the scoring is more complicated. If you understand bowling then you should be able to follow program score without trouble; if you don't understand bowling but do understand IF-ENDIF then you can learn something about bowling by reading program SCORE. (If you don't understand either bowling or IF-ENDIF then either learn bowling or reread this chapter up to this point before tackling program SCORE.)

```
*....:------------------------------------------------------------------
      PROGRAM  ROLL
*                               ..This program simulates the ball rolling
*                                 in a frame of bowling. Strikes, spares,
*                                 and no-marks are identified. This
*                                 program assumes valid input data.
*     ....constants....
      INTEGER  NOMARK, SPARE, STRIKE
      PARAMETER  ( NOMARK = 0,  SPARE = 1,  STRIKE = 2  )

*                               ..Note the use of constants
*                                 named  NOMARK,  SPARE  and  STRIKE
*     ....variables....
      INTEGER  BALL1, BALL2, MARK

*     ....execute....
      PRINT *, 'Roll first ball.'
      READ *, BALL1

      IF  (BALL1 .EQ. 10)  THEN
              PRINT *, '          STRIKE !!'
              MARK = STRIKE
              BALL2 = 0

          ELSE
*             ..need to roll the second ball..
              IF  (BALL1 .EQ. 0)  THEN
                      PRINT *, 'Gutterball, roll second ball.'
                  ELSE
                      PRINT *, 'Roll second ball.'
              ENDIF

              READ *,  BALL2

              IF  (BALL1+BALL2 .EQ. 10)  THEN
                      PRINT *,  '          SPARE !'
                      MARK = SPARE
                  ELSE
                      MARK = NOMARK
                      PRINT *,  BALL1+BALL2, '  pins in this frame.'
              ENDIF
      ENDIF
*                       Note -- MARK is determined in this program because
*                               it is used in the next example.

      END
=========================================================================
.EXECUTE  ROLL

Roll first ball.
> 8
Roll second ball.
> 2
          SPARE !
=========================================================================
.EXECUTE  ROLL

Roll first ball.
> 0
Gutterball, roll second ball.
> 9
            9  pins in this frame.
=========================================================================
.EXECUTE  ROLL

Roll first ball.
> 10
          STRIKE !!
=========================================================================
```

```
*....:---------------------------------------------------------------
      PROGRAM  SCORE
*                               ..This program simulates the scoring in a
*                                 frame of bowling. It assumes that the
*                                 current score (TOTAL) is known, as are
*                                 the marks of the past two frames.
*                                 Program ROLL is to be inserted in this
*                                 program to provide the ball rolling.
*     ....constants....
      INTEGER  NOMARK, SPARE, STRIKE
      PARAMETER  ( NOMARK = 0,  SPARE = 1,  STRIKE = 2  )

*     ....variables....
      INTEGER  BALL1, BALL2, TOTAL
     :         MARK, MARKP, MARKP2

      DATA     TOTAL,     MARKP,     MARKP2     /
     :          118 ,    STRIKE,     STRIKE     /

*                               ..At this point in the game the score is
*                                 118, with strikes in the last 2 frames
*                                 (MARKP is mark for previous frame,
*                                  MARKP2 is mark for two frames back)..
*     ....execute....

*                ..insert here the    ....execute....
*                  portion of program ROLL..

*                ..first, update scoring of previous marks..

      IF  (MARKP .EQ. STRIKE)  THEN
             IF  (MARKP2 .EQ. STRIKE)  THEN
                    TOTAL = TOTAL+20+BALL1
             ENDIF
             IF  (MARK .NE. STRIKE)  THEN
                    TOTAL = TOTAL+10+BALL1+BALL2
             ENDIF

         ELSEIF (MARKP .EQ. SPARE)  THEN
             TOTAL = TOTAL+10+BALL1
      ENDIF

      PRINT *
*                ..then determine score in this frame, if
*                  possible, and print the current status..

      IF  (MARK .EQ. STRIKE)  THEN
             IF  (MARKP .EQ. STRIKE)  THEN
                    PRINT *, 'Score is',TOTAL,'  and working on',
     :                                             ' 2 strikes.'
                ELSE
                    PRINT *, 'Score is',TOTAL,'  and working on',
     :                                             ' 1 strike.'
             ENDIF

         ELSEIF (MARK .EQ. SPARE)  THEN
             PRINT *, 'Score is',TOTAL,'  and working on a spare.'

         ELSE
             TOTAL = TOTAL+BALL1+BALL2
             PRINT *, 'Score in this frame is',TOTAL
      ENDIF

      MARKP2 = MARKP
      MARKP = MARK
*                               ..The last two statements are not really
*                                 necessary, but illustrate how MARKP2
*                                 and MARKP would be updated if the
*                                 program were to go on to the next frame
      END
=====================================================================
```

```
.EXECUTE  SCORE

Roll first ball.
> 10
          STRIKE !!

Score is          148  and working on 2 strikes.
=========================================================================
.EXECUTE  SCORE

Roll first ball.
> 3
Roll second ball.
> 6
           9  pins in this frame.

Score in this frame is         169
=========================================================================
.EXECUTE  SCORE

Roll first ball.
> 8
Roll second ball.
> 2
          SPARE !

Score is          166  and working on a spare.
=========================================================================
```

The DATA statement can be changed in program SCORE if results are desired for different initial values for the score (TOTAL) and the mark status of the previous frames. A later example (in Chapter 6) will extend program SCORE so that it simulates an entire game of bowling (10 frames) rather than just a single frame.

Several comments are appropriate following examples ROLL and SCORE. First, both programs assume error-free input data. In actual practice this assumption should rarely be made, and most programs should make reasonable checks on the validity of input data. In ROLL and SCORE, for example, the input values for BALL1 and BALL2 certainly aren't valid if either is negative or greater than 10, and the programs could at least check for these particular errors. Second, SCORE is a rather nice example of a simple "real-time" calculation—certain values cannot be calculated (the score in previous frames, in this case) until additional data is acquired (the ball values in the current frame). Adequate history must be maintained (MARKP and MARKP2) until enough data are acquired to complete the calculation. (Program SCORE could be much simpler if a "look ahead" were allowed, that is, if in each frame the values for the balls rolled in later frames were known.) And finally, program SCORE, which contains program ROLL, is beginning to become somewhat large and unwieldy. It is not difficult to imagine programs so large and logically complex that they are difficult to understand [and even more difficult to correct (debug) when something goes wrong]. Usually such programs can be structured as coordinated groups of smaller, simpler, self-contained *modules*, making the entire programming process more tractable and reliable. Such techniques are introduced in Chapter 6, and treated in detail in Part 2. The final example of this section involves a problem in which there are a number of quite different approaches to the solution, and so the programmer must select among these various methods of attack. In such cases the organization of the data involved in the problem can significantly affect the complexity and/or the efficiency of the resulting program.

Program MORSE illustrates that using care in structuring the data can result in better programs. (More sophisticated data structuring than in program MORSE can lead to even better programs for the same problem—see Chapter 12.) The problem is to decode a set of dots "." and dashes "-" of Morse code. If CODE is a string of length 6 then it can hold the Morse code for one character (capital letter or decimal digit), in the form of a sequence of the "." and "-" characters followed by one or more blank characters. Morse code characters are one to five dots and dashes long, and if these are left-justified in CODE then the statement

```
LENGTH = INDEX(CODE, ' ')
```

will result in LENGTH being one more than the number of dots and dashes in that code character; that is, LENGTH will include the blank following the dots and dashes. (Recall that the INDEX function determines the starting position of a substring in a string—in this case the first blank character in CODE.) If there are not dots and dashes and CODE begins with a blank then the decoded character (called the CLEAR) is to be a blank; if there is no blank in CODE then the CLEAR is to be a "!"; and if some other error occurs in CODE then the CLEAR is to be a "?". A straightforward "brute force" way of determining the character CLEAR corresponding to CODE is as follows.

```
     IF (LENGTH .EQ. 0) THEN
*                                                    . .no blank in CODE. .
                     CLEAR = '!'
       ELSEIF (LENGTH .EQ. 1) THEN
*                                          . .blank is first character in CODE. .
                     CLEAR = ' '
       ELSE
*                              . .search for the Morse code pattern. .
                IF       (CODE .EQ. '.-') THEN
                               CLEAR = 'A'
                  ELSEIF (CODE. EQ. '-. . .') THEN
                               CLEAR = 'B'
                  ELSEIF (CODE .EQ.'-.-.') THEN
                               CLEAR = 'C'
*                                . . . .and so on, 32 more times. . . .
                  ELSEIF (CODE .EQ. '----.') THEN
                                CLEAR = '9'
                  ELSE
*                                    . .illegal code pattern. .
                                          CLEAR = '?'
                ENDIF
     ENDIF
```

This program code is clear (pun intended) but is very wasteful of the programmer's time (less than a quarter of the program is shown). By placing the Morse code patterns and the corresponding clear characters in auxiliary strings, the search for the code patterns can be done by the INDEX function rather than by explicit individual testing. Once this approach is chosen, as illustrated by program MORSE, the program becomes much shorter, structurally simpler, and (probably) less likely to contain errors than the "brute force" approach. (It is not more efficient in execution, however, but about the same.)

```
*....:-----------------------------------------------------------------
      PROGRAM  MORSE
*                                  ..This program decodes Morse Code
*                                    characters that are input to string
*                                    CODE. All of the Morse Code patterns are
*                                    placed in the constant MC, the shortest
*                                    patterns first, and a "parallel"
*                                    constant contains the corresponding
*                                    clear characters.  The function INDEX is
*                                    used to do the actual searching of MC
*                                    for a CODE pattern.
*
*                                    If there is no blank in CODE then the
*                                    CLEAR character is a "!";
*                                    if the first character in CODE is a
*                                    blank then CLEAR is a blank; and if any
*                                    other error occurs then CLEAR is a "?".
*     ....MC data....
      CHARACTER  MC*200, LETTER*200
      DATA          MC / '. - .. .- -. -- --- ..- ... -.- .-. -.. --. .--
     :   .... .-.. ..-. .--. ...- -... -.-. -.-- .--- --.- -..- --..
     :  ----- .---- ..--- ...-- ....- ..... -.... --... ---.. ----. '/,

     :          LETTER / 'E T I  A  N  M  O   U   S   K   R   D   G   W
     :   H     L    F    P    V    B    C    Y    J    Q    X    Z
     :  0?    1?    2     3?    4     5     6     7     8     9?     ' /

*                                  ..note that each clear character is lined
*                                    up directly under the beginning of its
*                                    code pattern, and has the same relative
*                                    position in its string -- the "?"  cor-
*                                    responds to an illegal code group of 4
*     ....variables....
      INTEGER  LENGTH, L
      CHARACTER  CODE*6, CLEAR

*     ....execute....
      PRINT *, 'Input Morse Code for a character (1-5 dots and dashes).'
      READ '(A)', CODE
      LENGTH = INDEX(CODE, ' ')
*                                   ..LENGTH is the number of dots and
*                                     dashes, plus one (for the blank)..
      IF  (LENGTH .EQ. 0)  THEN
*                                   ..no blank in CODE..
          CLEAR = '!'

        ELSE
*            ..search MC for Morse Code pattern..
*                                     note that this includes the case for
*                                     LENGTH .EQ. 1, and will correctly
*                                     result in CLEAR = ' ' for this case
          L = INDEX(MC,CODE(1:LENGTH))

          IF  (L .EQ. 0)  THEN
*                                      ..illegal code pattern..
              CLEAR = '?'

            ELSE
              CLEAR = LETTER(L:L)
*                                          ..because of the carefully
*                                            constructed correspondence
*                                            between MC and LETTER..
            ENDIF
      ENDIF

      PRINT *, 'The CODE    ',CODE,'        has CLEAR    ',CLEAR
      END
=======================================================================
```

```
.EXECUTE  MORSE

Input Morse Code for a character (1-5 dots and dashes).
> .-.
The CODE    .-.            has CLEAR    R
==========================================================================
.EXECUTE  MORSE

Input Morse Code for a character (1-5 dots and dashes).
> .+-/
The CODE    .+-/           has CLEAR    ?
==========================================================================
.EXECUTE  MORSE

Input Morse Code for a character (1-5 dots and dashes).
> -..-
The CODE    -..-           has CLEAR    X
==========================================================================
```

4.6 Summary

Selection control is achieved in Fortran with the IF-ENDIF structure. The basic form is:

```
IF (<condition>) THEN
          --
          --  } statements to be executed if <condition> is .TRUE.
          --
   ELSE
          --
          --  } statements to be executed if <condition> is .FALSE.
          --
ENDIF
```

The ELSE portion is optional, and may be omitted if no statements are to be executed if the <condition> is false. The two statement groups in the IF-ENDIF structure may each contain any number of Fortran statements, including none or one. Each statement group may itself contain IF-ENDIF structures, that is, IF-ENDIF structures may be nested.

The two-way selection of IF-THEN-ELSE-ENDIF may be extended to arbitrary n-way selection. The general form for this is

```
IF (<condition>) THEN
          <statement group 1>
   ELSE IF (<condition 2>) THEN
          <statement group 2>
   ELSEIF  (<condition 3>) THEN
          <statement group 3>
      .
      .
      .
   ELSEIF  (<condition n>) THEN
          <statement group n>
   ELSE
          <all false statement group>
ENDIF
```

Here the conditions are checked in order until the first "true" one is found, and then the associated statement group is executed. Control then passes to the ENDIF, and any intervening statement groups are ignored regardless of the values of their associated <condition>s. The ELSE group, which is optional, is executed only if all of the preceding <condition>s are false.

The <condition>s are logical expressions, which can only have values "true" (.TRUE.) and "false" (.FALSE.). These are expressions of type LOGICAL, and the most common forms of logical expressions are:

Relational expressions (comparisons)

Logical variable

.NOT. logical expression (logical complement)

Logical expression .AND. logical expression (logical conjunction)

Logical expression .OR. logical expression (logical disjunction)

Logical expression .EQV. logical expression (logical equivalence)

Relational expressions compare two numeric or character quantities, and have the following form:

quantity <relation> quantity

where <relation> is .EQ. (equal to), .NE. (not equal to), .LT. (less than), .GT. (greater than), .LE. (less than or equal to), .GE. (greater than or equal to). The result of any such comparison is either .TRUE. or .FALSE.. Data elements may be of type LOGICAL, declared in LOGICAL type statements, and may be assigned logical values such as in assignment statements:

<logical variable> = <logical expression>

Combined with the expressive power of logical expressions for stating conditions, the IF-ENDIF structure is an extremely useful feature of Fortran for describing and achieving the selective processing needed in a program.

Programming Exercises

4.1 Write a sequence of Fortran statements that use the INDEX function to determine whether the character variable MONTH (value to be read as data) contains the letter 'r'. Folklore tells us that oysters should be eaten only in months containing the letter 'r'—appropriate output may be designed with this in mind.

4.2 Determine which of the vowels a, e, i, o, u are contained in a given string (use the INDEX function).

4.3 What would be the values of the integer variables X, Y, and Z after execution of these statements if the initial values of X and Y are (a) 2 and 7, (b) 25 and 8, (c) 15 and 15, (d) −3 and 3.

```
Z = X
IF  (X .EQ. Y)  THEN
        X = X**2
        Y = (X+Y)/2
    ELSEIF  (X .LT. Y)  THEN
        Y = Y**2
        Z = Y-X
    ELSE
        IF  (X .GT. 0)  THEN
            Z = X/Y
        ENDIF
        Y = 200
ENDIF
```

4.4 Many banks offer special saving plans designed to encourage weekly or monthly savings for a specific purpose. County Commercial has just instituted a Vacation Savings Plan for checking account customers. A monthly deposit, VSP, is made to this special savings on June 15, and on the 15th of subsequent months, with the annual payoff made to the customer on June 1. The program, which generates the monthly checking account reports, must now be modified to include information relative to the account owner's status with regard to the Vacation Savings Plan. The report is to show the contributions made to the Vacation Savings Plan during the current month and the total saved in the plan since the previous June. Write Fortran statements that could be incorporated into the report-generating program, which use the data MONTH (value 1, 2, . . . or 12) and VSP (amount of monthly contribution to the savings plan, value zero for those not enrolled in the plan) and which will produce appropriate easy-to-understand output. Incorporate any error checking that you deem desirable in this program segment.

4.5 Write Fortran statements, which could be used as a part of a program, which generates a bank's monthly checking account reports, to process one transaction. Assume that the current balance, BAL, and the number of transactions processed thus far, NTRAN, have previously been assigned values, and that the data necessary for this transaction are: date (day of the month), amount of the transaction, and a code ('D' to indicate a deposit and 'C' to indicate a check). Processing the transaction requires updating the balance and counting the transaction. The service charge, normally based on the number of transactions processed during the month, is waived if the balance always remains above $350.00. Use a logical variable to indicate whether the balance has dropped below $350.00. No processing should take place if the transaction code is neither 'D' nor 'C'.

4.6 Each sales person employed by the Terrific Terminals for Today company is strongly encouraged to meet a minimum level of sales of $10,000 in terminal systems each month. The person who meets this minimum level is paid a base monthly salary of $1000, plus a 7 percent commission on all sales exceeding $10,000. Those who do not meet this minimum are paid $300 plus 5 percent of his/her sales for the month. The outstanding salespeople who sell more than $15,000 worth of terminal systems are paid an additional bonus of 3 percent on all sales over $15,000. Write an IF-ENDIF structure (no nesting) in which the SALARY is correctly computed for a person having sales totaling SALES for the month. Write a nested IF-ENDIF structure to accomplish the same task.

4.7 Each adult patient at the Middleview Group Health Clinic is counseled with respect to his/her level of risk of contracting heart disease. Each patient is (1) categorized as a smoker/nonsmoker, (2) judged to be a good/fair/poor risk due to heredity, and (3) is judged to be obtaining adequate/inadequate exercise. The patients exhibiting these combinations or characteristics are thought to be in the 'high-risk' category:

nonsmokers/poor heredity/inadequate exercise
smokers/poor heredity/adequate exercise
smokers/fair heredity/inadequate exercise

The ones thought to be 'moderate-risks' are those who exhibit these characteristics:

smokers/fair heredity/adequate exercise
nonsmokers/good heredity/inadequate exercise
nonsmokers/fair heredity/inadequate exercise
nonsmokers/poor heredity/adequate exercise
smokers/good heredity/adequate exercise
smokers/good heredity/adequate exercise

Those in the 'low-risk' category:

nonsmokers/good heredity/adequate exercise
nonsmokers/fair heredity/adequate exercise

Write a nested IF-ENDIF structure to check these three items of data and provide appropriate categorization as to risk. Use the outermost structure to determine whether the patient is a smoker; do not use more than three levels of nesting.

4.8 The quadratic equation has the form

$$ax + bx + c = 0$$

where x is the unknown and a, b, c are given real constants. There are two solutions to (values of x that satisfy) the quadratic equation:

$$x = \frac{-b \pm \sqrt{b^2 - 4ac}}{2a}$$

If $b^2 < 4ac$ then the square-root term contributes an imaginary value, and the two values of x are complex conjugates. Otherwise the values for x are two real numbers. Design an IF-ENDIF structure that, given the values for A, B, and C, correctly computes the two values for X. Use X1 and X2 for the two solutions if they are real; if the solutions are complex, use X1 for the real part and X2 for the magnitude of the imaginary part.

4.9 Based on discussion of the LOGICAL data type given in this chapter, explain fully why the

IMPLICIT LOGICAL (A-Z)

trick described at the end of Chapter 2 works. In what circumstances will this technique fail to detect misspellings?

4.10 In using a computer program to simulate the behavior of some system, a common technique is to identify the various events that can possibly happen in the system. The system can then be simulated by tracking in time the events as they occur, and performing the operations associated with each event as that event occurs. Suppose that a variable EVENT is used to contain the identification of the next event to occur in the simulation, and that the possible values for EVENT are EVT1, EVT2, EVT3, . . ., EVT17. How could an IF-ENDIF selection control structure be used to provide the desired control for event processing in this case?

4.11 A Fortran program is to be written that is to accept a character string, and output the message "continued" or "not continued." Only in the following cases is "continued" to be output:

(a) The last nonblank character in the string is a ","
(b) The last nonblank character in the string is a "+"
(c) The last nonblank character in the string is a "−"
(d) The last two nonblank characters in the string are "**"
(e) The last two nonblank characters in the string are "//"
(f) The last nonblank character is a "."
and it is preceded by either a "R"
a "D"
or a "V"

Assume that the position, P, of the last nonblank character in the given string is known, and that, the value of P is greater than 1. Design an IF-ENDIF structure that will result in the printing of the correct message.

4.12 A given string is to be searched for a given substring, using the INDEX function. If the string contains zero or one copy of the substring it is to remain unchanged. If it contains exactly two copies of the substring the second copy is to be removed (e.g., if the substring is 'PQR', then 'ABCPQRXPQRY' would become 'ABCPQRXY'). If there are three or more copies of the substring then the entire string is to be blanked out. Design an IF-ENDIF structure that will provide such processing. What will your design do to the string 'ABJJJJYZ' if the substring is 'JJ'?

Chapter 5 Loop Control

Most interesting and useful programs involve not only conditional execution (selection) of statement groups, but also repetitive execution of certain statement groups. Thus the means of achieving repetition control are vitally needed items in the programmer's tool kit. This chapter describes the most important Fortran features for providing such control.

Figure 5.1 illustrates the general concept of repetition in a program: at some point in the program execution control is to flow not to the next statement but back to some previously executed statement. This circuitous path of control is normally called a *loop*, and the intent (generally) is to reexecute the sequence of statements between the top of the loop and the bottom of the loop (i.e., those statements in the *body* of the loop). Figure 5.1(*b*) indicates that under certain conditions control may *exit* the loop during execution of the loop body, with execution continuing outside the loop. The examples of this chapter illustrate the various looping situations the programmer may encounter.

5.1 The CONTINUE and GOTO Statements

Any statement in the executable portion of a Fortran program may be given a *label* to identify (or name) that point. A label can then be used to cause execution to continue at that point, regardless of which statement in the program has just been executed. Thus the programmer may specify a departure from the normal "execute the next statement" sequence of execution, or override the normal flow of control in an IF-ENDIF structure. The CONTINUE statement may be used to provide the label and the GOTO statement specifies the change in flow of control.

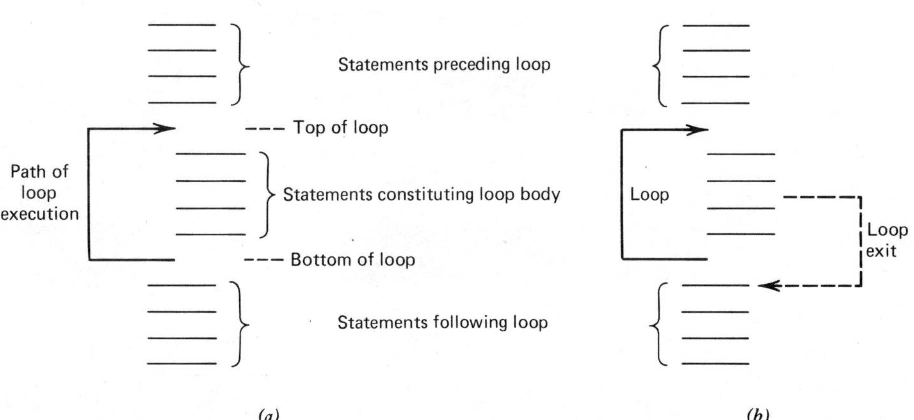

Figure 5.1. The concept of looping. (*a*) Basic loop structure. (*b*) Loop structure with exit.

The labeled CONTINUE statement has the form:

```
<label> CONTINUE
```

It may be thought of as an executable statement that does nothing, with execution simply passing to the statement following the CONTINUE. The <label> is a sequence of one to five decimal digits anywhere in columns 1–5 of the line of the CONTINUE statement. Each label in a program must be different from any other label in that program (i.e., must have a unique label value), and blank characters and leading zeros are insignificant in determining a label's value. A program may have any number of CONTINUE statements with unique labels.

The form of the GOTO statement is:

```
GOTO <label>
```

The <label> in a GOTO statement must be the same as one of the labels in columns 1–5 of the program (e.g., the same as the label defined in a CONTINUE statement). The effect of executing a GOTO statement is to cause execution to resume at the statement with the specified label. Loops may be constructed in Fortran by using a labeled CONTINUE statement at the top of the loop (call this the "top label") and a GOTO statement at the bottom of the loop that passes control back to the top label. This is shown in Figure 5.2*a* for any <label> value, and in (*b*) of the figure for the specific <label> value of 100.

Program POLY is an example of such a loop. Figure 5.3 shows an equilateral (regular) hexagon inscribed in a circle, and an inscribed equilateral triangle, and is illustrative of an equilateral polygon of any number of sides inscribed in a circle. Program POLY calculates the area of an equilateral polygon of N sides inscribed in a unit (radius = 1) circle, for N = 3, 4, 5, ...

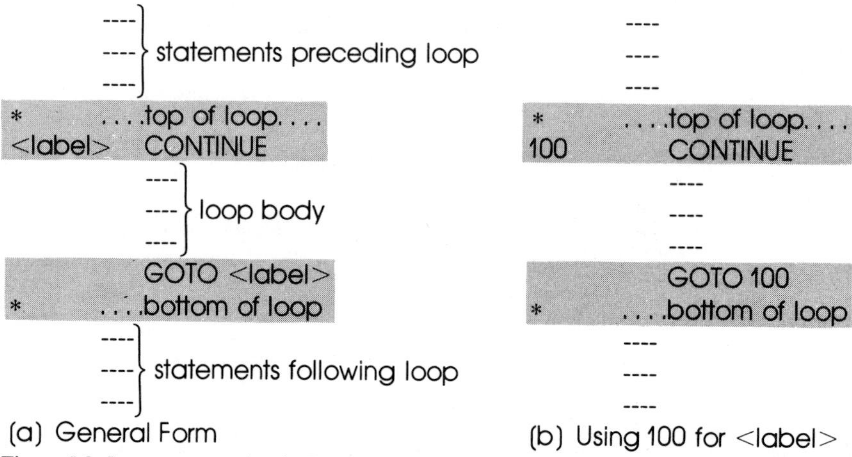

Figure 5.2. Loop construction in Fortran. (*a*) General form. (*b*) Using 100 for <label>.

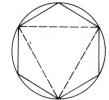

Figure 5.3. An inscribed regular hexagon (solid) and triangle (dotted). See program POLY.

Program POLY contains an *infinite loop*, and its execution will continue to generate output until some external agent interrupts it. This external agent is generally the computer's operating system, which aborts any job that takes longer than the time allotted, but sometimes it is the user causing the abort from the terminal, or the computer operator on duty observing the infinite loop output. In any event program POLY is not a "good" program since there is no compelling reason for the infinite loop, and it thus constitutes a wasteful use of computing resources. An important responsibility of the programmer is to guard against writing unnecessary or unintentional infinite loops.

```
*....:-----------------------------------------------------------------
      PROGRAM  POLY
*                           ..this program computes and prints the areas
*                           of regular polygons inscribed in a unit circle..
*     ....constant....
      REAL  PI
      PARAMETER  ( PI = 3.14159 )

*     ....variable....
      INTEGER  N

*     ...execute....
      PRINT *, 'Polygon of N sides inscribed in a unit circle ',
     :                      '(circle area 3.14159)'
      PRINT *
      PRINT *, '           N         AREA    '
      PRINT *, '           -         ----    '
      N = 3
*     ....top of POLY loop
100     CONTINUE
        PRINT *, N, N*COS(PI/N)*SIN(PI/N)
        N = N+1
        GOTO 100
*     ....bottom of POLY loop
      END
=======================================================================
.EXECUTE  POLY

Polygon of N sides inscribed in a unit circle (circle area 3.14159)

           N         AREA
           -         ----
           3         1.299040
           4         2.000000
           5         2.377639
           6         2.598073
           7         2.736407
           8         2.828424

           :
           :

....until "somebody shuts it off"....

=======================================================================
```

Program POLY can be somewhat salvaged by replacing the GOTO statement with something like

```
IF (N.LE.40) THEN
  GOTO 100
ENDIF
```

if the areas for N up to a value of 40 are sufficient, but this is not the best way to limit the number of times this loop is executed. A better way is described in a subsequent section. This section concentrates on the construction of infinite loops in a simple, efficient way, since there is an increasingly important class of computer applications in which infinite loops are appropriate. This class includes a subset of applications known as process control, some of which involve repeating the same computing function indefinitely, from the time the computer is turned on until it is turned off. Since execution never "gets beyond" an infinite loop in a program, programs legitimately containing an infinite loop contain only some initial processing followed by the loop—in many such cases essentially the entire (executable part of the) program is the body of the infinite loop.

A good example (although it is somewhat contrived) is an extension to program LOT of the last chapter. In that program the payoff for a given lottery ticket was determined. Suppose, however, that it is desired to have the program running in real time, awaiting ticket buyers to inquire about the possible winnings of their tickets. This may be accomplished by placing the main part of program LOT in an infinite loop so that it is essentially always waiting to accept and process the next ticket number, whenever that might happen to be. One way of doing this is by preceding the second PRINT statement of LOT with a label, 100 say, and placing the following statements just before the END statement.

```
PRINT *,'----------------------------------------------'
PRINT *
GOTO 100
```

The program now appears as shown in LOT2.

Despite the fact that infinite loops are appropriate for some applications, normally the programmer doesn't use such control structures and should be extremely careful not to inadvertently construct an infinite loop. The ease with which an infinite loop can be constructed with a single statement label and a single GOTO statement should be sufficient warning to the prudent programmer that great caution must be exercised when using these programming features. In the discussion to follow certain guidelines for using labels and GOTOs will be presented; consistent adherence to these guidelines will greatly reduce the likelihood of misuse of these features.

In most cases looping is terminated after a finite (although perhaps initially unknown) number of repetitions, and execution continues with the statement following the bottom of the loop. One of the two major methods of loop termination is conditional termination, the topic of the next section.

5.2 Conditional Termination of Loop Execution

In each of the examples of the preceding section there were no statements, other than END, following the loop. This is because those loops never terminate, so that no statements following them could be executed. Normally execution of loops terminate and statements following the loops are executed. One way to terminate looping is to transfer execution control, with a GOTO statement, to the statement immediately following the loop. This implies two things:

1 A statement label must follow the GOTO statement at the bottom of the loop.

```
*....:------------------------------------------------------------------
      PROGRAM  LOT2
*                           This program is the same as  program
*                           LOT in section 4.4, except that it
*                           contains a loop to repetitively
*                           determine the winnings of a given ticket
*                           (i.e., after finishing with one ticket
*                           it is ready to accept the digits of
*                           the next ticket).
*     ....variables....
      INTEGER  PAYOFF
      CHARACTER  TICKET*6, WINNER*6
      DATA  WINNER / '417059' /

*     ....execute....
      PRINT *, 'Determination of Lottery Ticket winnings.'

*     ....begin processing next ticket....
100       CONTINUE
*                        ....insert the rest of program LOT here --
*                        that part between PRINT *,'Determine...' and END

          PRINT *, '---------------------------------------------'
          PRINT *
          GOTO 100
*     ....processing finished for this ticket....
*                           ..Note that IF-ENDIF structures are legal
*                           inside loops.  Also note that the loop
*                           body is indented to the right so that it is
*                           easily spotted.
      END
=====================================================================
.EXECUTE  LOT2

Determination of Lottery Ticket winnings.
Input ticket number:  <6-digits>
> 246975

Ticket  Number    246975
Winning Number    417059
Amount this ticket wins is          0  dollars.
----------------------------------------------
Input ticket number:  <6-digits>
> 417079

Ticket  Number    417079
Winning Number    417059
Amount this ticket wins is       2000  dollars.
----------------------------------------------
Input ticket number:  <6-digits>
> 136059

Ticket  Number    136059
Winning Number    417059
Amount this ticket wins is        125  dollars.
----------------------------------------------
Input ticket number:  <6-digits>
> 555182

Ticket  Number    555182
Winning Number    417059
Amount this ticket wins is          0  dollars.
----------------------------------------------
Input ticket number:  <6-digits>
>


                    ....and on, and on....

=====================================================================
```

2 The condition(s) for terminating the looping must appear at the appropriate place(s) inside the loop.

The first of these is easily supplied with a labeled CONTINUE statement (call this the "exit label"). The second may be achieved by making the loop terminating condition the logical expression (call this the "exit condition") of an IF-ENDIF statement, with the corresponding action selected being that of transferring control to the exit label. This has the form

```
IF (<exit condition>) THEN
  GOTO <exit label>
ENDIF
```

A more general, and often very useful, form is

```
IF (<exit condition>) THEN
    ----⎫ statements to be executed
    ----⎬ just prior to leaving the
    ----⎭ loop at this point.
    GOTO <exit label>
ENDIF
```

since sometimes a loop has more than one exit condition and unique end-of-the-loop processing is needed at each exit (see Figure 5.4).

In practice loops having only one exit are most common, and hence the first of the above two forms of loop exit is the most used. This form (three lines of code) is

```
      ----
      ----
      ----
      ----
*     ....  top of loop
100         CONTINUE
            ----
            ----
            ----
            ----
            IF (<exit-condition>) GOTO 199
            ----
            ----
            ----
            ----
            GOTO 100
*     ....  bottom of loop
199   CONTINUE
      ----
      ----
      ----
      ----
```

(a)

```
      ----
      ----
      ----
      ----
*     ....  top of loop
100         CONTINUE
            ----
            ----
            ----
            ----
            IF (<exit-condition-1>) THEN
                  ----
                  ----
                  ----
                  ----
                  GOTO 199
           ENDIF
            ----
            ----
            ----
            ----
            IF (<exit-condition-2>) THEN
                  ----
                  ----
                  ----
                  ----
                  GOTO 199
           ENDIF
            ----
            ----
            ----
            ----
            GOTO 100
*           bottom of loop
199   CONTINUE
```

(b)

Figure 5.4. Typical loop structures with exit conditions. (*a*) A loop with a single exit. (*b*) A loop with two exits.

somewhat inelegant to use, however, when what is meant is simply "exit if <exit condition> is true". Fortran has another form of IF statement, called the logical IF, that allows the three-line IF-ENDIF version of loop exit to be replaced by a single line:

```
IF (<exit condition>) GOTO <exit label>
```

In this statement, which will be called the exit-IF, and used only for simple loop exits, the GOTO statement replaces the THEN and no ENDIF is used.

Figure 5.4 illustrates the two Fortran techniques for terminating looping. In both instances 100 is used as the top label and 199 as the exit label. Part (*a*) of the figure shows simple loop termination using the exit-IF statement, and part (*b*) depicts a loop with two exits and unique end-of-the-loop processing at each exit. Figure 5.5 shows a straightforward way of terminating the loop in program POLY when N exceeds 40 (although this still isn't the best way to terminate the POLY loop).

Exit points may be anywhere in the loop, and normally appear at the places where they best fit the logic of the loop. A common place for handling loop termination is at the beginning of the loop body, such as in Figure 5.5. The end of the loop body is another common exit point.

The next example, program MCMESS (for Morse Code MESSage), uses conditional loop termination in a more complicated, and realistic, problem. This example extends program MORSE of Section 4.5 from a single character of message to an arbitrarily long line (any number of characters) of coded message. Program MCMESS depends heavily on use of Fortran's intrinsic function INDEX, as does program MORSE. In fact, the use of INDEX in programs MCMESS and MORSE illustrates well the tremendous benefit that the programmer can derive from application of the intrinsic functions. In both programs simple calls to INDEX effectively do the hardest part of the problem, allowing the programmer to concentrate upon developing the overall structure of the program without being distracted by the details of the searching process that INDEX performs. Since the behavior of INDEX itself can be described as a simple, conditionally terminated loop, explaining the functioning of INDEX makes an interesting subexample prior to presenting MCMESS.

The INDEX function is typically used in the form

```
L=INDEX(STRING,SUBSTR)
```

where L is an integer variable, and STRING and SUBSTR are character variables (or, more generally, character expressions). INDEX searches the value of STRING for an occurrence of the value of SUBSTR, and if such a match is found then the value of

```
      N=3
*     ....top of finite POLY loop....
100      CONTINUE
         IF  (N .GT. 40)  GOTO 199
         PRINT *, N, N*COS(PI/N)*SIN(PI/N)
         N = N+1
         GOTO 100
*     ....bottom of finite POLY loop
199   CONTINUE
      END
```

Figure 5.5. Loop in program POLY terminated after N=40.

INDEX (and consequently also of L) is the position in STRING where the match begins. If no match is found then INDEX has the value 0. This searching process could proceed in the following manner: the value of SUBSTR, which has K characters say, is compared to

STRING(1:K), then to
STRING(2:K+1), then to
STRING(3:K+2),
 :

and so on until either a match is found or all of STRING has been searched. Figure 5.6 shows how this searching process, known as the linear search, may be accomplished in Fortran. The linear search is a widely used technique for searching a sequence of elements (the successive substrings of length K in EXTEND in Figure 5.6) for a particular value (the value of SUBSTR in Figure 5.6). Searching an array for a certain element value is a common application of the linear search. The linear search normally proceeds by comparing the desired value with the first element in the sequence, then with the second, then the third, and so on until a match is found. A match is guaranteed in this searching process if the sequence of elements is extended by the addition of the searched-for value, as illustrated by the use of EXTEND in Figure 5.6. Then a test can be made, after the match is found, to see if the match occurred with this appended value—if so then the original sequence of elements does not contain the searched for value.

The algorithm of Figure 5.6 is a very efficient one for the linear search (the technique of appending the searched-for value reduces the number of exit conditions needed in the loop). Although the Fortran implementor is free to implement the INDEX function in any way desired, as long as it performs the specified computation, it is likely that the algorithm of Figure 5.6 is often employed. Figure 5.6 also illustrates the typical extraloop processing associated with many practical loops. Three loop initializations (on K, L, and EXTEND) precede the loop, and some clean-up processing (adjusting the value of L, if needed) takes place following the loop. Such before and/or after processing can be expected to be associated with any loop.

Now back to program MCMESS. Program MCMESS decodes a given Morse code message, which is supplied as the string value of MCLINE (for Morse Code LINE) character by character, and places the decoded characters in string variable CLEAR. One

```
---------------------------------------------------------------------------
      K = LEN(SUBSTR)
      L = 1
      EXTEND  =  STRING//SUBSTR
*                             ..EXTEND is an additional string variable..
*                             ..concatenating SUBSTR to STRING insures
*                             a match..
*     ....top of linear search loop
110      CONTINUE
         IF  (EXTEND(L:L+K-1) .EQ. SUBSTR)  GOTO 119
*                                                ..match found..
         L = L+1
         GOTO 110
*     ....bottom of linear search loop
119   CONTINUE
*                         ..at this point a match has been found and L is
*                         the desired INDEX value, unless the match was with
*                         the copy of SUBSTR appended to STRING..

      IF  (L .GT. LEN(STRING)+1-K)  THEN
            L = 0
      ENDIF

          Figure 5.6 -- The behavior of INDEX as a linear search.
---------------------------------------------------------------------------
```

Figure 5.6. The behavior of INDEX as a linear search.

execution of a loop extracts one CLEAR character, and the loop is terminated when there are no more characters left to be decoded; there may be any number of CLEAR characters in the message. Informally, program MCMESS has the structure:

1 Input coded message and perform loop initializations.

2 Top of loop to decode next character.
  2.1 Exit loop if no more characters to decode.
  2.2 Get next coded character from MCLINE.
  2.3 Decode character, using algorithm of program MORSE, placing decoded character in CLEAR.

3 Bottom of loop to decode next character (GOTO 2).

4 Print MCLINE and CLEAR.

The two central data elements of program MCMESS, other than the Morse code constants, are the string variables MCLINE and CLEAR; examples of them are shown in Figure 5.7. An integer variable, PLACE, has initial value 1 and represents the starting position in MCLINE of the next coded character to be decoded. The integer variable NEXT, initialized to 0, is the number of characters thus far decoded (i.e., the number of characters placed in CLEAR). The next coded character to be decoded is placed in the string variable CODE, which is used in the decoding process of program MORSE.

Single blank characters separate the coded characters in MCLINE and multiple (two or more successive) blanks separate words. The last (rightmost) character of MCLINE is a blank. For n successive blanks in MCLINE n-1 blanks are placed in CLEAR. And, as in program MORSE, for each illegal code pattern of four or five dots-dashes a "?" is generated for the CLEAR character, and "!" is the CLEAR character for each CODE pattern containing more than five dots-dashes.

Figure 5.8 illustrates schematically the flow of control in loops with single exits. Parts (*a*) and (*b*) of that figure are in some sense logically equivalent—the only difference being that loops with bottom exits are always executed at least once whereas loops with top exits may not be executed at all. Of course, part (*c*) is the most general situation for single exit loops, and includes parts (*a*) and (*b*) as special cases if either of the groups of statements (parts of the loop body) can be empty. Figure 5.9 shows the flow of control in loop structures with two exits, with and without unique end-of-loop-processing at each exit. The concepts of Figure 5.9 may be extended to loops with any number of exits. Two additional example programs will close this discussion of conditional termination of loops. The first, program RBALL, keeps score in a racquetball game and employs a loop with two exits. The second, program CHARGE, prepares monthly statements for customer accounts and illustrates the practical use of exits in the "middle" of the loop body.

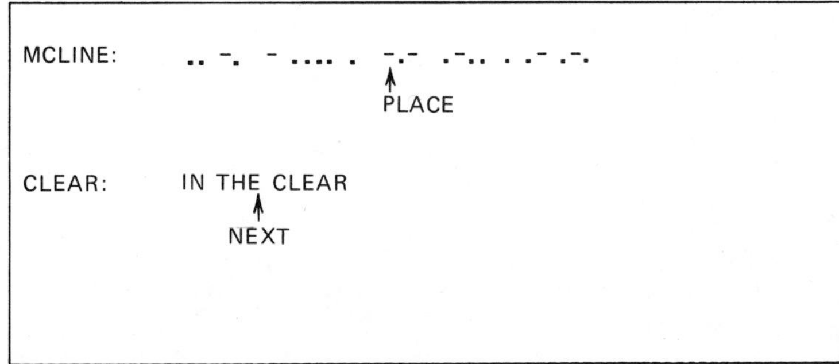

Figure 5.7. Examples for MCLINE and CLEAR in program MCMESS. (Corresponding values for PLACE and NEXT are indicated.)

```
*....:-------------------------------------------------------------------
      PROGRAM  MCMESS
*                          ..this program decodes an arbitrarily long line
*                          of Morse Code. The Morse Code is supplied in
*                          string MCLINE, and the decoded characters are
*                          placed in string CLEAR. The algorithm involves
*                          a loop, in which one execution results in the
*                          decoding of one character of message. The body
*                          of the loop is essentially the algorithm of
*                          program MORSE of the last chapter..

*     ....MC data....     (same as in PROGRAM MORSE)
     CHARACTER  MC*200, LETTER*200
     DATA        MC / '. - .. .- -. -- --- ..- ... -.- .-. -.. --. .--
     :  .... .-.. ..-. .--. ...- -... -.-. -.-- .--- --.- -..- --..
     : ----- .---- ..--- ...-- ....- ..... -.... --... ---.. ----. '/,

     :         LETTER / 'E T I  A  N  M  O   U   S   K   R   D   G   W
     :  H    L    F    P    V    B    C    Y    J    Q    X    Z
     : 0?   1?   2    3?   4    5    6    7    8    9?    ' /

*     ....variables....
      INTEGER  PLACE, NEXT, LENGTH, L
      CHARACTER  MCLINE*70, CLEAR*70, CODE*6

*     ....execute....
      PRINT *,'Input a line of Morse Code, with a blank after each '
      PRINT *,'       character, and another blank after each word.'
      READ '(A)', MCLINE
      MCLINE(LEN(MCLINE):) = ' '
*                                ..insures last character is ' '..
*     ....loop initializations....
      PLACE = 1
      NEXT = 0
*     ....top of loop to decode next character
*                           Note that LENGTH is the position of the next
*                           blank in the substring MCLINE(PLACE:), and not
*                           the position in MCLINE. Thus 1, not the value
*                           of PLACE, is the minimum value for LENGTH.
100       CONTINUE
          IF  (PLACE .GT. LEN(MCLINE))  GOTO 199
*                             ..exit if no more characters to decode..
          LENGTH = INDEX(MCLINE(PLACE:),' ')
          CODE = MCLINE(PLACE:PLACE+LENGTH-1)
          PLACE = PLACE+LENGTH
          NEXT = NEXT+1
          LENGTH = INDEX(CODE,' ')
*                                        ..PLACE and NEXT updated --
*                                          now decode CODE..

*                         ..insert here the entire IF-ENDIF structure of
*                         program MORSE, replacing CLEAR with CLEAR(NEXT:)

          GOTO 100
*     ....bottom of loop to decode character
199   CONTINUE
      PRINT *
      PRINT *, MCLINE
      PRINT *, CLEAR
      END
=====================================================================
.EXECUTE  MCMESS

Input a line of Morse Code, with a blank after each
       character, and another blank after each word.
> .. -.  - .... .  -.-. .-.. . .- .-.

.. -.  - .... .  -.-. .-.. . .- .-.
IN THE CLEAR
=====================================================================
.EXECUTE  MCMESS

Input a line of Morse Code, with a blank after each
       character, and another blank after each word.
> - .... ...... ----    ..--.. ...  .- -- . ... ..--

- .... ...... ----    ..--.. ...--.- -- . ... ..--
TH!?  !S AMES?
=====================================================================
```

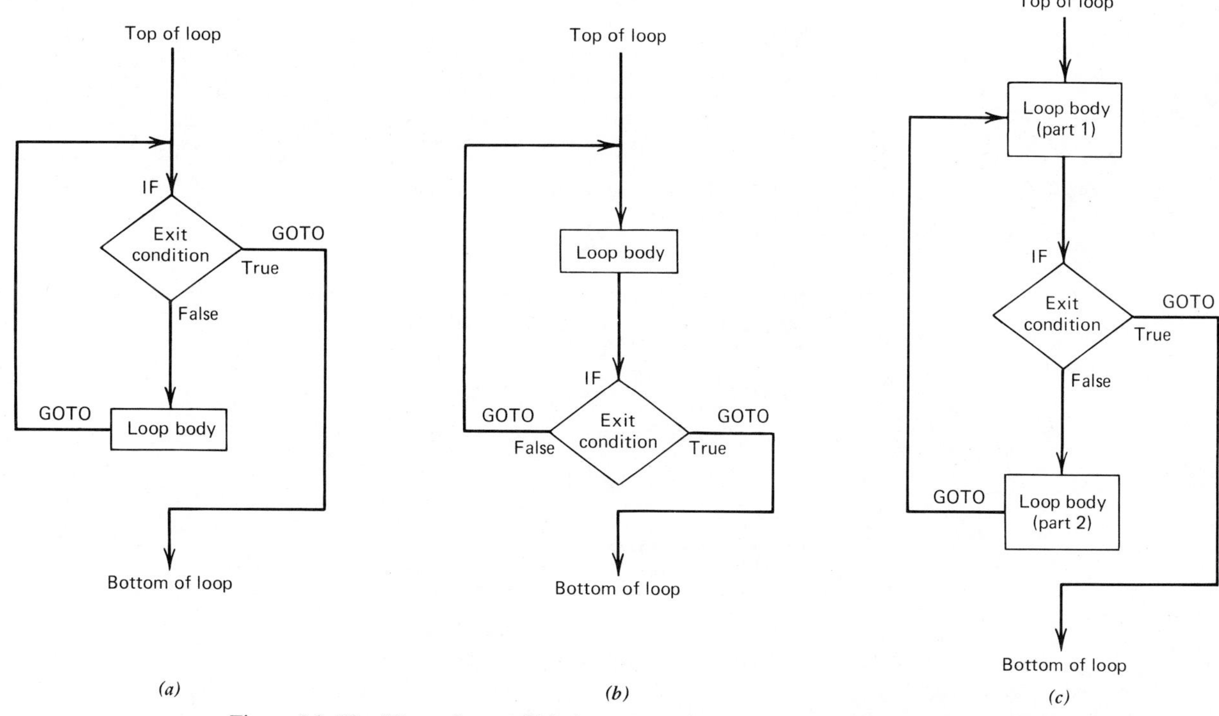

Figure 5.8. The "flow of control" in loop structures with single exits. (*a*) Exit at top of loop. (*b*) Exit at bottom of loop. (*c*) Exit in middle of loop.

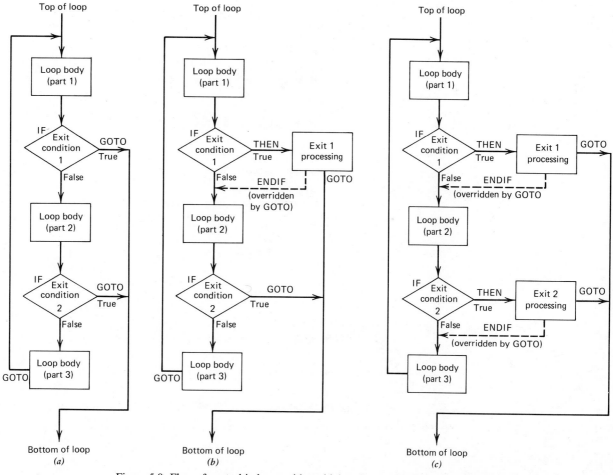

Figure 5.9. Flow of control in loops with multiple exits. (*a*) No unique end-of-loop processing. (*b*) Unique end-of-loop processing at one exit. (*c*) Unique end-of-loop processing at both exits.

```
*....:-----------------------------------------------------------------
      PROGRAM  RBALL
*                        ..this program simulates a game of racquet-ball,
*                        and keeps the score. Each execution of the loop
*                        processes one volley. The loop has two exits,
*                        one each for the possibilities that each of the
*                        two players might win..
*
*     ....constant....(value of the winning score)
      INTEGER  WSCORE
      PARAMETER  ( WSCORE = 21 )

*     ....variables....
      INTEGER  SCORE1,SCORE2,COIN
      CHARACTER*10  PLAYR1,PLAYR2,SERVER,WINNER
      DATA  SCORE1,SCORE2  / 0,0 /

*     ....execute....
      PRINT *, 'START GAME'
      PRINT *, 'Input: ''<player-name>'', ''<player-name>'',',
     :                   ' <flip-coin -- any integer>'
      READ *, PLAYR1,PLAYR2,COIN
*                                      ..now print output headings
*                                      and determine initial server..
      PRINT '(//T27,A,T43,A/T27,A,T43,A,T57,A/A)',
     :      PLAYR1,PLAYR2,'Score','Score','Server',' <volley-winner> ?'
*                                      .."randomly" generate 1 or 2,
*                                      to simulate "flipping the coin"
*                                      to select first server..
      IF  (MOD(ABS(COIN)/3,2) .EQ. 1)  THEN
              SERVER = PLAYR1
          ELSE
              SERVER = PLAYR2
      ENDIF
*     ....top of volley loop, first print current status,
*                                        then determine volley-winner....
100       CONTINUE
          PRINT '(I29,I16,T57,A)', SCORE1, SCORE2, SERVER
          READ '(A)', WINNER
          IF  (WINNER .EQ. PLAYR1)  THEN
                  IF  (PLAYR1 .EQ. SERVER)  THEN
*                                           ..increment PLAYR1's score
                          SCORE1 = SCORE1+1
                          IF  (SCORE1 .EQ. WSCORE)  GOTO 199
*                                                ..exit, PLAYR1 has won
                      ELSE
*                                          ..PLAYER1 becomes the server
                          SERVER = PLAYR1
                  ENDIF

              ELSEIF  (WINNER .EQ. PLAYR2)  THEN
                  IF  (PLAYR2 .EQ. SERVER)  THEN
*                                            ..increment PLAYR2's score
                          SCORE2 = SCORE2+1
                          IF  (SCORE2 .EQ. WSCORE)  THEN
*                                      ..PLAYR2 has won, exit after using
*                                          SCORE2 to hold loser's score..
                                  SCORE2 = SCORE1
                                  GOTO 199
                          ENDIF
                      ELSE
*                                           ..PLAYR2 becomes the SERVER
                          SERVER = PLAYR2
                  ENDIF

              ELSE
                  PRINT *, WINNER, '  is NOT in this game !?!'
          ENDIF
          GOTO 100
*     ....bottom of volley loop, after exit SCORE2 is loser's score
199   CONTINUE
      PRINT  '(//T2,A,A,I2,A,I2//)',
     :   WINNER, '    is the winner,        ', WSCORE, '  to  ', SCORE2
      END
=======================================================================
```

```
.EXECUTE  RBALL

START GAME
Input:  '<player,name>', '<player-name>', <flip-coin -- any integer>
> 'RED', 'BLUE', -913

                          RED           BLUE
                          Score         Score         Server
<volley-winner> ?
                            0             0           BLUE
> BLUE
                            0             1           BLUE
> RED
                            0             1           RED
> BLUE
                            0             1           BLUE
> BLUE
                            0             2           BLUE
> RED
                            0             2           RED
> GREEN
GREEN       is NOT in this game !?!
> RED
                            1             2           RED

      :
      :

> RED
                           19            18           RED
> RED
                           20            18           RED
> BLUE
                           20            18           BLUE
> BLUE
                           20            19           BLUE
> RED
                           20            19           RED
> BLUE
                           20            19           BLUE
> RED
                           20            19           RED
> RED

RED          is the winner,        21  to  19

=====================================================================
```

Program RBALL keeps score in a two-person (or two-team) game of racquetball (or handball or paddleball or volleyball) and announces the winner when one of the players reaches the winning score (usually 21). In a racquetball game the server initiates a volley, and the resulting play produces a volley winner. If the volley winner is the server, then 1 point is added to the server's score (and the server keeps the serve). If the volley winner is not the server then the score remains unchanged and the volley winner becomes the server. The initial scores are zero, and the initial server is chosen at random. In program RBALL each execution of a loop processes one volley, and the loop structure has the form of Figure 5.9*b*. The structure of RBALL is as follows:

1 Print headings and "flip coin" to establish initial server.

2 Top of loop to process the next volley.
- **2.1** Print score and name of server.
- **2.2** Determine volley winner (input).
- **2.3** If player 1 is the volley winner then adjust score if player 1 is server, and check to see if winning score has been reached (exit loop is so); player 1 becomes (or remains) the server.

2.4 If player 2 is the volley winner then adjust score if player 2 is server, and check to see if winning score has been reached (exit loop if so); player 2 becomes (or remains) the server.

3 Bottom of loop to process volley (GOTO 2).

4 Print name of winner.

There are, of course, many other ways to solve this problem, and some of them require only one exit from the loop. Moreover, the loop can be structured so that this single exit can be either at the top or the bottom of the loop. All of these modifications, however, require additional calculations inside the loop, which decreases the execution efficiency—and probably also the readability—of the loop.

Program CHARGE is typical of the read-test-process type of application, in which the logical structure of the problem involves a test in the middle of the loop. The SUPER LUMBER CO. allows customers to charge their purchases, and sends monthly statements to customers having balances to be paid. Program CHARGE accepts any number of lines of input representing a customer's payments and purchases during the month, calculates finance charges, sales taxes, and the new account balance, and outputs a neatly formatted monthly statement containing all of this information. Most of the input will be the payment and purchase data, and each of these items has the respective form:

'PAY', '<data of payment>', <amount of payment>

'PUR', '<date and description of purchase>', <cost of purchase>

```
*....:---------------------------------------------------------------------
      PROGRAM  CHARGE
*                              This program generates monthly statements for
*                              customers with charge accounts at the SUPER
*                              LUMBER CO. It is an example of the READ-TEST-
*                              PROCESS loop, with the condition for loop
*                              termination in the interior of the loop..
*     ....constants....
      INTEGER  SIZE
      REAL  TXRATE, FCRATE
      CHARACTER  FIRM*20
      PARAMETER  ( SIZE = 20, TXRATE = 0.07, FCRATE = 0.015,
     :             FIRM = 'SUPER LUMBER CO.' )

*                            TXRATE is the sales tax rate
*                            FCRATE is the monthly finance charge rate
*                            SIZE is the maximum number of payments,
*                            purchases displayed on the monthly statement.
*     ....variables....
      INTEGER  NPAY, NPUR, N
      REAL  AMT, OLDBAL, NEWBAL, FC, TAX, APAY(1:SIZE), APUR(1:SIZE)
      CHARACTER  CODE*3, DESC*40, CUST*20, DATE*8,
     :           DPAY(1:SIZE)*7, DPUR(1:SIZE)*40

*        NPAY, NPUR are the numbers of payments, purchases.
*        APAY, APUR are the lists of payment, purchase amounts.
*        DPAY, DPUR are the corresponding lists of dates & descriptions.
*        FC is the finance charge for this month.
*        TAX is the sales tax on a purchase.

*     ....execute....
      PRINT *,'Input: ''<month-of-statement>'', ''<customer''s-name>'',',
     :                                           ' <old-balance>'
      READ *, DATE, CUST, OLDBAL
      PRINT *, 'Transactions:  ''PAY'' or ''PUR'' or ''/$'', ',
     :                        '''<date,descr.>'', <amount>'
      NPAY = 0
      NPUR = 0
*                        a positive old balance means customer owes SUPER
*                        ....the finance charge cannot be negative

      FC = MAX(0.0,OLDBAL*FCRATE)
      NEWBAL = OLDBAL + FC
```

```
*       ....top of transaction processing loop....
100         CONTINUE
            READ *, CODE, DESC, AMT
            IF  (CODE .EQ. '/$')  GOTO 199
*                                          ..exit at end of transactions..
            IF  (CODE .EQ. 'PAY')  THEN
*                                        ..process a payment..
                NEWBAL = NEWBAL-AMT
                IF  (NPAY .LT. SIZE)  THEN
*                                              ..remember this payment..
                    NPAY = NPAY+1
                    DPAY(NPAY) = DESC
                    APAY(NPAY) = AMT
                ENDIF

            ELSEIF  (CODE .EQ. 'PUR')  THEN
*                                               ..process a purchase..
                TAX = AMT*TXRATE
                NEWBAL = NEWBAL+AMT+TAX
                IF  (NPUR .LT. SIZE)  THEN
*                                              ..remember this purchase..
                    NPUR = NPUR+1
                    DPUR(NPUR) = DESC
                    APUR(NPUR) = AMT+TAX
                ENDIF

            ELSE
                PRINT *, CODE, ' is transaction type error -- ',
     :                         're-input this transaction.'
            ENDIF
            GOTO 100
*       ....bottom of transaction processing loop....
199     CONTINUE
*                          ..transaction processing completed..
*                          now print the monthly statement if balance due
*                          is greater than the finance charge

        IF  (NEWBAL .GT. FC)  THEN
              PRINT '(//T2,A,T60,A//A,A/A,F10.2/A,F4.1,A,F10.2//)',
     :               CUST, DATE,
     :               ' Statement of Account at  ', FIRM,
     :               ' Balance from last month', OLDBAL,
     :               ' Finance charge (', 100*FCRATE, '%)', FC
              PRINT '(A/(T2,A,F10.2/))',
     :               ' Payments Received:',
     :               (DPAY(N),APAY(N),N = 1,NPAY)
              PRINT '(//A,F4.1,A//(T2,A,F10.2))',
     :               ' Purchases (including ', 100*TXRATE,'% sales tax)',
     :               (DPUR(N),APUR(N),N = 1,NPUR)
              PRINT '(///A,F10.2/A,A//)',
     :               ' Current Balance', NEWBAL,
     :               ' Due  ', FIRM
        ENDIF
        END
=========================================================================
```

After all 'PAY' and 'PUR' entries are supplied the following should be input:

'/$', ' ', 0 to signify the end of transactions for this account

Each execution of the loop in program CHARGE processes one transaction. The overall structure of the program is:

1 Obtain information pertaining to account—customer's name, old balance, etc.

2 Calculate finance charge on old balance and initialize new balance.

3 Top of transaction processing loop.
   - **3.1** Read data pertaining to next transaction.
   - **3.2** If transaction code is '/$' then exit (end of transactions).
   - **3.3** If transaction code is 'PAY' then process a payment.
   - **3.4** If transaction code is 'PUR' then process a purchase.
   - **3.5** (Anything else is an illegal transaction.)

4 Bottom of transaction processing loop (GOTO 3).

5 Print monthly statement if new balance due the company.

Program CHARGE uses string and real arrays, DPAY, DPUR, APAY and APUR, to remember all descriptive and numeric data pertaining to each transaction (up to a certain number of transactions), so that all of this data may be reorganized and displayed on the monthly statement.

In actual practice the customer's name, OLDBAL, etc., would come from a tape or disk file, and after processing this customer's account the value of NEWBAL would be stored back in this file for use in processing next month's statement. Other information, such as APAY, DPAY, etc., might also be saved in such files. The Fortran provisions for file processing are discussed in detail in Part 3. Account processing programs such as these also usually are much more thorough than program CHARGE in checking for errors in data. For example, checks are normally included to detect unreasonably large values for payment and/or purchase amounts, negative purchase amounts, and the like.

5.3 The DO Statement (Indexed Looping)

Often loops are of the form shown in Figure 5.5: a certain variable (N in that figure) is initialized before the loop, systematically modified each time through the loop, used as the basis for loop exit, and (usually) plays an important role in the processing done in the loop. Since this variable plays such an important part in the control of the loop it is called the control variable, or index variable, and such looping is called indexed looping. Figure 5.10 shows the general form for indexed looping.

This is such a common looping structure that Fortran has a special statement that consolidates all of the indexed loop control into one statement at the beginning of the loop (shown in Figure 5.11). Part (*a*) of the figure indicates that the <increment> part of the DO statement is optional—if omitted then the increment is automatically taken to be +1. The first three statements of Figure 5.10

```
     <index variable> = <initial value>
100 CONTINUE
     IF (<index value> .GT. <final value>) GOTO 199
```

have all been replaced by the DO statement of Figure 5.11*a*, as have the last three

```
      <index variable> = <index variable> + <increment>
      GOTO 100
199   CONTINUE
```

```
          <index-variable> = <initial-value>
*         ....top of indexed loop....
100          CONTINUE
             IF  (<index-variable>  .GT.  <final-value>)  GOTO 199
             ----|
             ----|  loop statements
             ----|
             <index-variable> = <index-variable> + <increment>
             GOTO 100
*         ....bottom of indexed loop
199       CONTINUE
```

Figure 5.10. General structure for indexed looping.

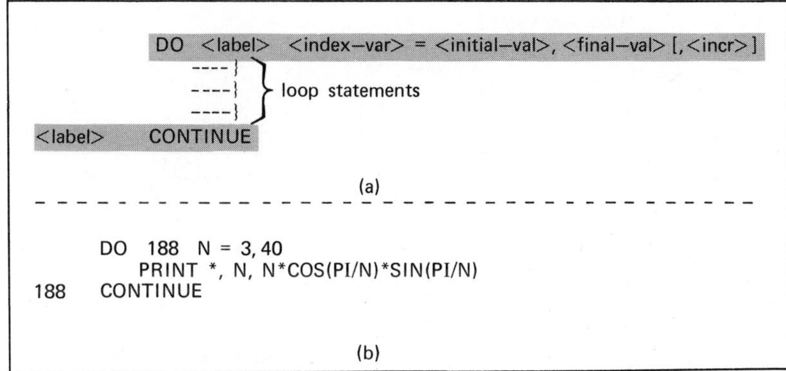

Figure 5.11. The DO statement. (*a*) General form. (*b*) Program POLY loop as an indexed loop.

The statement

<label> CONTINUE

in Figure 5.11*a* simply marks the bottom of the loop with a <label> (call this the "bottom" label) so that the extent of the loop can be specified in the DO statement.

The way to read a DO-loop is to first realize that the DO statement marks the top of the loop and the bottom label marks the bottom of the loop. Then note that the index variable is assigned the specified <initial value> and the loop body is executed; then the index variable is incremented, the loop body executed again, and this cycle is repeated until the exit condition of Figure 5.10 is met. Thus it should be clear that in Figure 5.11*b* the PRINT statement is executed exactly 38 times—for N having the values 3, 4, 5, 6, . . ., 39, 40 in succession.

In a properly constructed indexed loop, none of the statements in the loop body should assign values to the index variable, the increment, or the final value. The <index variable> may be either an integer or a real variable name, and the <initial value>, <final value>, and <increment> may be any arithmetic expressions. If the value of <increment> is positive then the exit condition used is as shown in Figure 5.10, and if the value of <increment> is negative then

(<index variable> .LT. <final value>)

is used as the exit condition. The number of times that the loop is executed is completely specified by the values of <initial value>, <final value>, and <increment> at the beginning of execution of the loop, and this number may be zero. For example the statement

```
DO 188 N=3,2
```

would result in no execution of the loop, but

```
DO 188 N=3,2,-1
```

would cause the loop to be executed twice—the first time N would have the value 3 and the second time 2.

Program CHILL2 further illustrates the use of indexed looping. It produces a table of chill factors, for any given wind speed, over a wide temperature range (the range for which the formula is valid—+15 to −35 degrees Celsius). The input to the program is (1) the desired wind speed, in kilometers (km) per hour, and (2) the interval, in degrees Celsius (C), between the different temperatures for which the chill factors are to be calculated.

```
*....:-----------------------------------------------------------------
      PROGRAM  CHILL2
*                            ..This program uses the Fortran DO-loop to
*                          generate a table of chill-factors at a given
*                          wind speed and over a wide ambient temperature
*                          range.  It is an extension of program CHILLY in
*                          section 4.2.  TEMP is an integer variable
*                          (in CHILLY it was real) because it is the
*                          index variable in the loop.  Fortran permits
*                          the index variable to be real, but generally
*                          it should be integer to prevent problems
*                          with round-off error.
*     ....constants...
      INTEGER  ITEMP, FTEMP
      PARAMETER  ( ITEMP = 15, FTEMP = -35 )
*                           ..ITEMP and FTEMP are the temperature limits
*                           over which the chill-factor formula is valid..
*     ....variables....
      INTEGER  TEMP, TINCR
      REAL  SPEED, MPS, CHILL
*                            ..TINCR is the increment between temperatures
*                            in the table..
*     ....execute....
      PRINT *, 'Chill-factor Table..'
      PRINT *, 'Input wind speed and temperature increment: ',
     :              '<KM per hour>, <degrees C>'
      READ *, SPEED, TINCR
*                              ..now insure that TINCR is negative, print
*                              heading, and then generate table..
      TINCR = -ABS(TINCR)
      PRINT '(//A,T30,A,F7.2,A/)',
     :      ' Temperature (degrees C)', 'Chill-factor with wind at',
     :      SPEED, '  KM per hour'

      DO  188  TEMP = ITEMP,FTEMP,TINCR
          MPS = MAX(8.0,MIN(90.0,ABS(SPEED)))/3.6
          CHILL = 33-(33-TEMP)*(10*SQRT(MPS)-MPS+10.45)/23.165
          PRINT '(I8,T40,I8)',TEMP, NINT(CHILL)
188   CONTINUE
      END
=======================================================================
.EXECUTE  CHILL2

Chill-factor Table..
Input wind speed and temperature increment:  <KM per hour>, <degrees C>
> 20,5


Temperature (degrees C)      Chill-factor with wind at  20.00 KM per hour

      15                                      10
      10                                       4
       5                                      -1
       0                                      -7
      -5                                     -13
     -10                                     -19
     -15                                     -25
     -20                                     -32
     -25                                     -38
     -30                                     -44
     -35                                     -50
=======================================================================
```

The indexing in the DO statement

<index variable> = <initial value>, <final value> [, <increment>]

serves to specify a sequence of values for <index variable>. In earlier examples (programs CHARGE in Section 5.2 and ARRAY in Section 2.3) a similar Fortran feature, structurally and logically, was used to specify a sequence of array elements. The simplest example of this feature has the form

(<array name>(<iv>), <iv>=<initial value>,<final value>)

with <iv> being an integer variable; this represents the list of all <array name> elements with subscripts between <initial value> and <final value>, inclusive. Here <iv> is behaving as an <index variable>, but instead of controlling the execution of a loop it is controlling the specification of a list of array elements. A more general form of implied-DO list, as this feature is called, is

(<expression list>, <index var> = <init val>, <final val> [,<incr>])

where <expression list> can be a list of any expressions (separated from each other by commas) legal in Fortran. Each expression of <expression list> is specified for each value of <index var>. In most practical cases each expression involves the <index var>, and in the overwhelming majority of cases the expressions are simply array names. An example of an implied-DO list containing more than one element appears in program CHARGE. As already seen, implied-DO lists are extremely useful for specifying a sequence of array elements in READ, PRINT, and DATA statements. Even more general forms of implied-DO lists, useful for inputting, outputting, and initializing array elements, are described in Part 3.

5.4 Nested Loops

A loop body may itself contain a loop, and such nesting may be arbitrarily deep. As with selection structures, however, it is usually not good programming technique to nest loops beyond two or three levels because the logic (flow of control) in deeply nested structures is difficult to follow. The primary rule for nesting loops is the same as for nesting selection structures: the top and bottom of a nested loop must both be within the body of the outer loop. That is, the top of the inner loop must come after the top of the outer loop, and the bottom of the inner loop must come before the bottom of the outer loop. The correct structure is shown in Figure 5.12.

Program BUBBLE illustrates the use of nested loops to arrange (sort) an array of names into alphabetical order. The algorithm is the "bubble sort," which is one of the simplest (but least efficient) of sorting algorithms. An execution of the outer loop of BUBBLE constitutes one pass through the unsorted portion of the array, and each such pass causes the largest (last in alphabetical order) of the remaining unsorted elements to be bubbled into its correct position. (This example has "lead bubbles"—they sink rather than rise!) Hence NE-1 passes are necessary, where NE is the number of elements to be sorted. After the first pass the largest element is in the last position; after the second pass the next largest element is in the next to last position; after the third pass the third largest element is in the third to last position, and so on until the entire array is sorted. The outer loop therefore could be

```
    DO 188 NPASS = 1, NE-1
         ----}  statements to implement one pass
         ----}  (i.e., to bubble one element
         ----}  into place)
188 CONTINUE
```

(a)

```
*       ....top of outer loop
100     CONTINUE
        ----
        ----
        ----
*       ....top of nested loop
110         CONTINUE
            ----}
            ----}  body of
            ----}  nested loop
            ----}
            GOTO 110
*       ....bottom of nested loop
119     CONTINUE
        ----
        ----
        ----
        GOTO 100
*     ....bottom of outer loop
199   CONTINUE
```

(b)

```
      DO 188 <outer-loop-indexing>
        ----
        ----
        ----
        DO 118 <nested-loop-indexing>
            ----}
            ----}  body of
            ----}  nested loop
            ----}
118     CONTINUE
        ----
        ----
        ----
188   CONTINUE
```

Figure 5.12. Nested loops. (*a*) General structure. (*b*) Indexed loops.

The details of the bubbling process are achieved by a second (nested) loop in which adjacent elements in the unsorted portion of the array are compared and exchanged if not in alphabetical order. If this comparison is done on successive pairs of elements, starting with the first and second, then the largest one is bubbled down the array to its proper position. The details of this are:

```
      DO 118 N=1, NE-NPASS
          IF (NAME(N) .GT. NAME(N+1)) THEN
*                                           . .switch these two names
              TEMP=NAME(N)
              NAME(N)=NAME(N+1)
              NAME(N+1)=TEMP
          ENDIF
118   CONTINUE
```

TEMP is a character variable that is used as temporary storage during the switching process, and NE-NPASS comparisons are necessary on pass number NPASS. Putting this all together gives program BUBBLE.

```
*....:-----------------------------------------------------------------
      PROGRAM  BUBBLE
*                    ..This program illustrates nested loops using the
*                    bubble sort to arrange an array of NE names in
*                    alphabetical order.  The idea behind the algorithm
*                    is, starting at the beginning of the array, to
*                    drag the largest value to its proper location at
*                    the end of the array.  This process is repeated on
*                    the next-to-largest value, then the next, and so on
*                    until the entire array is sorted.

*     ....constant....(Number of Names)
      INTEGER  NE
      PARAMETER  ( NE = 20 )

*     ....variables....
      INTEGER  N, NPASS
      CHARACTER  NAME(1:1000)*20, TEMP*20
*                                  ..there are two indexed loops, and N and
*                                    NPASS are the two indexed variables..
      DATA  (NAME(N), N = 1, NE)                    /
     :        'BOB', 'LOU', 'MARY', 'JOE', 'JEFF', 'O. J.', 'PETE', 'ED',
     :        'JOAN', 'MARK', 'CHRIS', 'FRAN', 'KAY', 'PEG', 'SUE', 'AL',
     :        'SANDY', 'JIM', 'JON', 'JOHN'         /

*     ....execute....
      DO  188  NPASS = 1,NE-1
         DO  118  N = 1,NE-NPASS
            IF  (NAME(N) .GT. NAME(N+1))  THEN
*                                              ..switch these two names..
                  TEMP = NAME(N)
                  NAME(N) = NAME(N+1)
                  NAME(N+1) = TEMP
            ENDIF
118      CONTINUE
188   CONTINUE
      PRINT '(A/)', (NAME(N), N = 1,NE)
      END
=======================================================================
.EXECUTE  BUBBLE

AL
BOB
CHRIS
ED
FRAN
JEFF
JIM
JOAN
JOE
JOHN
JON
KAY
LOU
MARK
MARY
O. J.
PEG
PETE
SANDY
SUE

=======================================================================
```

Program BUBBLE illustrates the two most common uses for indexed loops:

1. When the number of times the loop is to be executed is known (this is the case with the outer loop in BUBBLE).
2. In processing a number of elements of an array (as illustrated by the inner loop of BUBBLE).

The second use (processing an array) commonly involves using the index variable in subscript expressions for selecting the array element(s) to be processed. Specifying a subscript is sometimes referred to as indexing an array, and is a reason for the term "indexed looping."

As already noted, and illustrated again in program BUBBLE, selection (IF-ENDIF) structures may be nested inside loops. Conversely loops may be nested inside IF-ENDIFs. Thus repetition and selection structures may be mixed and nested as desired, as long as proper nesting is observed—that is, as long as the nested structure is wholly contained in a statement group, or body, of the outer structure.

The next example also illustrates the nesting of loops, and involves both indexed and conditionally terminated loops. Moreover, it is very interesting since it deals with numbers that are far too large to be handled routinely on a computer. For any positive integer N a value called N-factorial (usually written N!) may be computed by the product

1*2*3*4. . .*(N−1)*N

For a given N this is a very simple (and not very interesting) calculation to make. What makes it interesting is the rate at which N! grows as N increases. At first it looks fairly manageable:

N	N!
1	1
2	2
3	6
4	24
5	120
6	720
7	5040

but it doesn't stay that way for long, and 15! is already too large a number for integer variables on most computers to hold. 30! has 33 digits in its decimal representation (and over 100 binary digits), and is far beyond the capacity of a mere computer integer variable.

Program FACT, however, allows factorials for large values of N to be computed and printed. It does this by using several integer data elements, not just one, to represent the value of N!—in fact, an integer array is used, each element representing one decimal digit of the factorial value. The size (number of digits) in the factorial is then limited only by the array size, which may be many thousands of elements. The array, named FAC in program FACT, is shown schematically in Figure 5.13, with its elements numbered 1, 2, 3, . . ., LIMIT. FAC(LIMIT) is used for the least significant digit (units digit) of the factorial, FAC(LIMIT-1) for the next (tens) digits, and so on. The values for the elements of FAC are shown in Figure 5.13 for 6!.

Program FACT prints the factorial values for all of the (positive) integers up to the specified N. Assume that FAC currently holds the digits for a factorial value for some value of N. The next factorial value (i.e., for the next value of N) may be found by multiplying each element of FAC by N—by 7, for Figure 5.13—which would result in 0 49 14 0. Then the element values of FAC are adjusted to be in the 0–9 range, with a carry increasing the value of the next left digit (thus 0 49 14 0 becomes 0 50 4 0, which in turn becomes 5 0 4 0). Both the multiplication and carry adjusting can be done simultaneously, starting from the right (units digit) and progressing to the left.

```
                    Array  FAC

0   0   0   0   0  . . .   0   7   2   0   <— array values
1   2   3                          LIMIT   <— subscripts

              Element values for 6!
```

Figure 5.13. Example of the integer array used in program FACT to represent the individual decimal digits of factorial values.

```
*....:-----------------------------------------------------------------
      PROGRAM  FACT
*                     ..This program uses nested loops to compute the
*                     digits of arbitrarily large factorial values.  An
*                     integer array is used to hold the digits of the
*                     factorial value, and all factorials up to that for
*                     a specified integer are printed.  The individual
*                     digits are transferred to a string for printing,
*                     so that the list of factorials is printed nicely
*                     aligned on the right.  See figure 5.13 for  the
*                     use of the array, and the preceding discussion
*                     for a description of the algorithm used..

*     ....constant....
      INTEGER  LIMIT
      PARAMETER  ( LIMIT = 60 )
*                        ..factorial values can be up to 60 digits long..
*     ....variables....
      INTEGER  K, L, D, N, CARRY, FAC(1:LIMIT)
      CHARACTER  FACSTR*(LIMIT), DIGITS*10
      DATA  FAC  / LIMIT * 0 /,
     :      DIGITS  / '0123456789' /
*                          ..K and L are index variables
*                          D is used to select a digit from DIGITS
*                          N! is the largest factorial value computed and
*                          FACSTR is used to output the factorial value..
*     ....execute....
      READ *, N
      FAC(LIMIT) = 1
*                         ..now, generate and print the Kth factorial..
      DO  188  K = 1,N
          CARRY = 0
          DO  118  L = LIMIT,1,-1
*                                        ..multiply FAC by K, adjusting each
*                                          digit to be in the 0..9 range
              FAC(L) = FAC(L)*K+CARRY
              CARRY = INT(FAC(L)/10)
              FAC(L) = FAC(L)-10*CARRY
118       CONTINUE
*                     ..This completes the calculation of the next
*                     factorial value.  Note that the INT function is
*                     not necessary in the calculation of CARRY (since
*                     both FAC(L) and 10 are integers).  Now, so that
*                     leading zeros won't be printed, generate FACSTR
*                     from FAC, replacing all leading zeros with blanks..
          L = 1
*         ....top of loop to replace leading zeros with blanks....
120           CONTINUE
              IF (FAC(L).NE.0) GOTO 129
              FACSTR(L:L) =  ' '
              L = L+1
              GOTO 120
*         ....bottom of loop to replace leading zeros with blanks....
129       CONTINUE
*                           ..now put the digit characters into FACSTR..
          DO  138  L = L,LIMIT
              D = FAC(L)+1
              FACSTR(L:L) = DIGITS(D:D)
138       CONTINUE
*                 ..now print this factorial, then compute the next one..
          PRINT *, FACSTR, K
188   CONTINUE
      END
=======================================================================
```

```
.EXECUTE  FACT

> 45
                                                         1           1
                                                         2           2
                                                         6           3
                                                        24           4
                                                       120           5
                                                       720           6
                                                      5040           7
                                                     40320           8
                                                    362880           9
                                                   3628800          10
                                                  39916800          11
                                                 479001600          12
                                                6227020800          13
                                               87178291200          14
                                             1307674368000          15
                                            20922789888000          16
                                           355687428096000          17
                                          6402373705728000          18
                                        121645100408832000          19
                                       2432902008176640000          20
                                      51090942171709440000          21
                                    1124000727777607680000          22
                                   25852016738884976640000          23
                                  620448401733239439360000          24
                                15511210043330985984000000          25
                               403291461126605635584000000          26
                             10888869450418352160768000000          27
                            304888344611713860501504000000          28
                           8841761993739701954543616000000          29
                         265252859812191058636308480000000          30
                        8222838654177922817725562880000000          31
                      263130836933693530167218012160000000          32
                     8683317618811886495518194401280000000          33
                   295232799039604140847618609643520000000          34
                 10333147966386144929666651337523200000000          35
                371993326789901217467999448150835200000000          36
              13763753091226345046315979581580902400000000          37
             523022617466601111760007224100074291200000000          38
           20397882081197443358640281739902897356800000000          39
          815915283247897734345611269596115894272000000000          40
        33452526613163807108170062053440751665152000000000          41
      1405006117752879898543142606244511569936384000000000          42
     60415263063373835637355132068513997507264512000000000          43
   2658271574788448768043625811014615890319638528000000000          44
 119622220865480194561963161495657715064383733760000000000          45

========================================================================
```

5.5 Systematic Loop Construction

Several types of loops have been described in this chapter: conditionally terminated loops, indexed loops, loops with multiple exits, etc. Despite this variety, looping basically involves the repetitive execution of a well-defined contiguous set of statements, and when looping is terminated, execution continues with the statement following the bottom of the loop. The structure and functioning of a single-exit loop, for example, can be clearly described as follows:

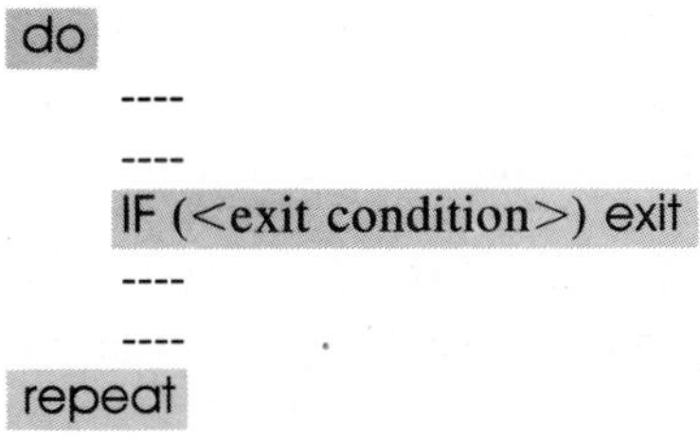

```
do
      ----
      ----
      IF (<exit condition>) exit
      ----
      ----
repeat
```

Here the do and repeat unmistakably identify the top and bottom of the loop, respectively, and the exit is an extremely clear way of indicating loop termination and continuing execution with the statement following repeat. Moreover, the repeat emphasizes the repetitive nature (''go back and do it again'') of loop execution.

Because all loops have this basic form, and since the do, repeat, and exit depict the loop structure so well, henceforth all example programs will show loops in this form. The lower case do, repeat and exit are not standard Fortran themselves, but in all cases represent standard Fortran as shown in Figure 5.14. Note that the use of do, repeat, and exit results in simplification and convenience analogous to that of the Fortran DO statement.

Using do, repeat, and exit makes the program design process conceptually simpler, and hence less error prone, since statement label selection and management may be ignored during this process. Thus despite the fact that the labels and GOTOs must be added, in the fashion of Figure 5.14, before the program is submitted for compilation, using do, repeat, and exit makes programming faster, more pleasant, and less error prone. (An example program, DOREPX, in Chapter 8 illustrates how a program can be devised to perform the Figure 5.14 conversions automatically.) In many respects the do-repeat forms a structural framework for loop control analogous to the IF-ENDIF

```
          do-repeat form              equivalent standard Fortran
          --------------              -------------------------

non-indexed loops
-----------------

          do                          *               do
                                      <top-label>        CONTINUE

          repeat                                         GOTO <top-label>
                                      *               repeat
                                      <exit-label>    CONTINUE

indexed loops
-------------

          do  <index-control>                         DO  <bottom-label>  <index-control>

          repeat                      <bottom-label>  CONTINUE
                                      *               repeat
                                      <exit-label>    CONTINUE

all loops
---------

          exit                                 GOTO <exit-label>
```

Figure 5.14. The standard Fortran equivalents of do, repeat, and exit.

for selection control, since do and repeat mark the beginning and end of the control structure, and each do must have a matching repeat somewhere in the program below it. An exit is meaningful only inside a loop (i.e., only inside a do-repeat structure), and causes exiting from the loop containing it. In nested loops just one level of looping is exited.

When adding the labels and GOTOs to a do-repeat structure a systematic choice of label values aids in preventing mistakes and in making the resulting program readable. Managing statement labels and GOTO statements are among the most error-prone aspects of programming, and following GOTOs is among the greatest detractors from program readability. In all of the above examples the <top label> ended with zero(s), the <exit label> with nine(s), and the <bottom label> with eight(s). With this scheme GOTO 100 is clearly the repeat branch back to the top of the loop, whereas GOTO 199, is clearly a loop exit. The leading digit(s) of the top, bottom, and exit labels for a given loop are always the same. Thus the first digit(s) of the label can be used to identify the loop with which the label is associated, and the last digit(s) indicate which part of the loop that label marks. Using this scheme, only two digits are needed for loop labels if the program contains no nested loops (and a total of fewer than 10 loops in succession). For nested loops (one level of nesting) three-digit labels can be used—the first to identify the outer loop, the second identifying the inner loop, and the last being the zero, eight, or nine. For nesting loops deeper, either labels with more digits are necessary (if this labeling scheme is to be followed), or some departure from this labeling scheme is necessary. Figure 5.15 illustrates this labeling scheme for a program with a single loop. Figure 5.15*a* is the do-repeat form, and (*b*) is the labeled form. Figure 5.12 and program FACT, of the previous section, also illustrate this labeling scheme, and involve nested loops.

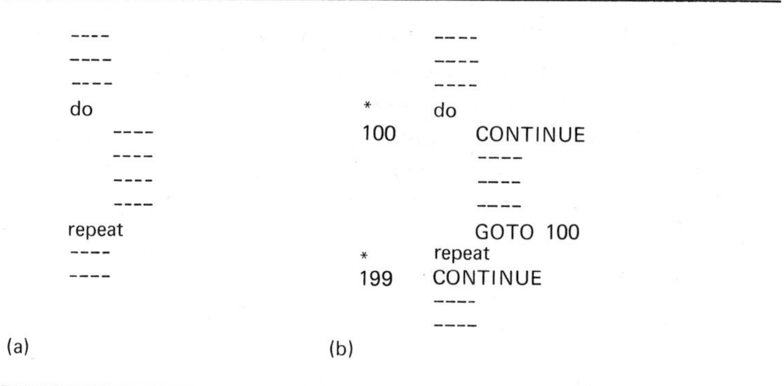
(a)

```
      ----
      ----
      ----
      do
          ----
          ----
          ----
          ----
      repeat
      ----
      ----
```

(b)

```
      ----
      ----
      ----
*     do
100       CONTINUE
          ----
          ----
          ----
          GOTO 100
*     repeat
199   CONTINUE
      ----
      ----
```

Figure 5.15. Example form of general do-repeat loops, with conversion to standard Fortran. (*a*) A do-repeat loop. (*b*) Do-repeat converted to standard Fortran.

As is apparent from Figure 5.12, and from program FACT, this labeling scheme also results in all labels being in numerical order from beginning to end of the program, which facilitates the finding of labels when reading the program. Figure 5.16 summarizes the recommended style for three-digit statement labels.

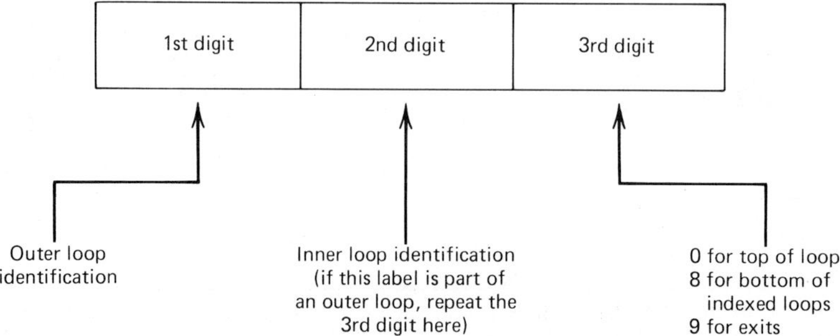

Figure 5.16. Recommended structure for three-digit labels when constructing loops.

```
*....:-----------------------------------------------------------------
      PROGRAM  PAL
*                ..This program uses the do-repeat form of loop design
*                to check an arbitrary string to see if
*                it is a palindrome (reads the same backward as
*                forward). Certain punctuation characters are ignored,
*                and if the string is not a palindrome, the
*                "mis-matched" positions are identified..

*     ....punctuation....
      CHARACTER  PUNC*20
      PARAMETER  ( PUNC = ' ,.":;-?!''' )

*     ....variables....
      INTEGER  K, L, N, LENGTH
      CHARACTER  PHRASE*70, ANALYZ*70

*     ....execute....
      PRINT *, 'Checking phrases for palindromes (input DONE to stop)'
      PRINT *
      do
*         ..loop processes a phrase -- exit when PHRASE eq 'DONE'
          PRINT *, 'Input a phrase to be checked.'
          READ '(A)', PHRASE
          IF  (PHRASE .EQ. 'DONE')  exit
          LENGTH = INDEX(PHRASE//'    ','    ') - 1
*                         ..assume no more than 3 consecutive blanks
*                         are imbedded in PHRASE; LENGTH is number of
*                         characters in PHRASE..

*                         ..now, de-punctuate PHRASE..
          K = 1
          ANALYZ = ' '
          do  L = 1,LENGTH
              N = INDEX(PUNC,PHRASE(L:L))
              IF  (N .EQ. 0)  THEN
                     ANALYZ(K:K) = PHRASE(L:L)
                     K = K+1
              ENDIF
          repeat
          PHRASE = ANALYZ
          LENGTH = K-1
          PRINT *
          PRINT *, PHRASE
          IF  (LENGTH .EQ. 0)  THEN
                  PRINT *, '....empty phrase....'
              ELSE
*                                  ..perform palindrome check --
*                                  ANALYZ is used to "flag" positions
*                                  having mis-matches..
                  ANALYZ = ' '
                  do  L = 1,LENGTH/2
                      K = LENGTH-L+1
                      IF  (PHRASE(L:L) .NE. PHRASE(K:K))  THEN
*                                              ..not a palindrome --
*                                              flag these positions..
                            ANALYZ(L:L) = ':'
                            ANALYZ(K:K) = '.'
                      ENDIF
                  repeat
*                        ..check completed, now print results..
                  IF  (ANALYZ .EQ. ' ')  THEN
                          PRINT *, '....is a palindrome..',
     :                             '..emordnilap a si....'
                      ELSE
                          PRINT *, ANALYZ
                          PRINT *, '....is NOT a palindrome....',
     :                             'mismatched positions are indicated'
                  ENDIF
          ENDIF
          PRINT *, '--------------------------------------------------',
     :                   '-------------------------'
      repeat
      END
=====================================================================
```

```
.EXECUTE  PAL

Checking phrases for palindromes (input DONE to stop)

Input a phrase to be checked.
> a man, a plan, a canal, panama

amanaplanacanalpanama
....is a palindrome....emordnilap a si....
--------------------------------------------------------------------------
Input a phrase to be checked.
> Madam, I'm Adam.

MadamImAdam
: :   . .
....is NOT a palindrome....mis-matched positions are indicated
--------------------------------------------------------------------------
Input a phrase to be checked.
> KAY, a red nude, peeped under a YAK!

KAYarednudepeepedunderaYAK
....is a palindrome....emordnilap a si....
--------------------------------------------------------------------------
Input a phrase to be checked.
> DONE
==========================================================================
```

Program PAL illustrates the use of do-repeat in writing programs (it has three loops, two of them nested inside the third, all written with do-repeat). PAL checks an input string to see if it's a palindrome—a palindrome reads the same backward as it does forward. For example, the word "level" is a palindrome; if punctuation (blanks, commas, etc.) are ignored, then phrases like "too hot to hoot" are palindromes. Program PAL removes punctuation from a string and then checks to see if it is a palindrome. The general structure of PAL is:

do
 1 Read a string (PHRASE); exit if PHRASE is 'DONE'.
 2 Depunctuate PHRASE (requires a loop).
 3 Check the value of PHRASE for a palindrome (requires a loop).
 4 Print results of check.
repeat

An auxiliary string named ANALYZ is used in PAL to "flag" those positions, if any, in PHRASE where the characters cause the value of PHRASE not to be a palindrome.

Of course, the conversions of Figure 5.14 must be made in program PAL before submitting it for compilation.

5.6 Debugging

Although careful program design is the best way to get a program to work correctly, even the most careful programmer is occasionally faced with the prospect of debugging. When a program compiles correctly but produces incorrect execution results it is said to contain logic errors, or *bugs*. Bugs are errors of program logic design, and the process of locating and correcting such errors is called *debugging*. Chapter 10 addresses the preventing and correcting of program errors. At this point, however, it is appropriate to introduce the simplest and possibly most useful of all debugging techniques—that of using PRINT statements to have the program itself provide information adequate to track down bugs.

Programs without loops are usually easy to debug since only a small amount of computation is performed prior to outputting the results. In such a case, the nature of the incorrect results is often sufficient to identify the source of error. The situation is different with loops. Much processing may be done in loops prior to outputting any results, and in such cases bugs may not be at all easy to find simply by inspecting the (incorrect) program results. At certain points inside loops, key variables are changed and/or computations made. One of the most effective debugging techniques is to obtain a "snapshot" of these key values during execution. A complete sequence of such snapshots can be extremely useful in combating bugs. These snapshots may be achieved by placing appropriate PRINT statements before and/or after the statements that change key values. If this happens to be inside a loop (which is usually the case) then detailed output will be generated that can be "traced" to see if the desired processing is in fact taking place. After the bugs are found then these bug-PRINTs may be removed from the program, so that the debugging information does not "mess up the appearance" of the program output.

Program BASE is supposed to convert integer values in one base (radix system) to another base. The string of characters (NUM1) representing the integer in BASE1 is

```
*....:------------------------------------------------------------------------
      PROGRAM  BASE
*                       ..This program supposedly converts an integer
*                       from one base to another.  The algorithm is to
*                       compute the value of the given integer, and then
*                       to generate the digits for representing this value
*                       in the new base.  The algorithm seems simple
*                       enough -- but there's a bug somewhere.  The
*                       program assumes error-free input data..

*     ....digits....(will handle up to base-20)
      CHARACTER  DIGITS*20
      DATA     DIGITS / '0123456789ABCDEFGHIJ' /

*     ....variables....
      INTEGER  BASE1, BASE2, VALUE, K, Q, D
      CHARACTER*20  NUM1, NUM2, TEMP

*     ....execute....
      PRINT *, 'Input decimal integer values for <base1>, <base2> ',
     :         'in the 2..20 range.'
      PRINT *, '          (A smaller value will terminate the program.)'
      PRINT *, 'Then input the digits of the base1 integer ',
     :          'to be converted.'

      do
         PRINT *, '-----------------------------------------',
     :              '--------------------'
         READ *, BASE1, BASE2
         IF  (BASE1 .LT. 2  .OR.  BASE2 .LT. 2)  exit
         READ '(A)', NUM1
         VALUE = 0
         NUM2 = ' '
*                 ..now construct the value of the integer, digit by
*                 digit starting with the most significant digit
*                 (assume all digits are valid)

         do  K = 1,INDEX(NUM1,' ')-1
            VALUE = VALUE*BASE1 + INDEX(DIGITS,NUM1(K:K))
         repeat
*                 ..value determined -- now convert this to the base2
*                 digits, starting with the least significant digit
         do
            Q = INT(VALUE/BASE2)
            D = VALUE-Q*BASE2
            TEMP = DIGITS(D:D)//NUM2
            NUM2 = TEMP
            VALUE = Q
            IF  (VALUE .EQ. 0)  exit
         repeat
*                 ..now print results..
         PRINT *
         PRINT *, NUM1, '    BASE', BASE1, '          is'
         PRINT *, NUM2, '    BASE', BASE2
      repeat
      END
==========================================================================
```

```
.EXECUTE  BASE

Input decimal integer values for <base1>, <base2>  in the 2..20 range.
        (A smaller value will terminate the program.)
Then input the digits of the base1 integer to be converted.
-----------------------------------------------------------------------
> 10, 8
> 6

6                BASE       10        is
6                BASE        8
-----------------------------------------------------------------------
> 10,10
> 348

348              BASE       10        is
348              BASE       10
-----------------------------------------------------------------------
> 17, 4
> 2

2                BASE       17        is
2                BASE        4
-----------------------------------------------------------------------
> 14, 18
> B

B                BASE       14        is
B                BASE       18
-----------------------------------------------------------------------
> 8, 11
> 11

11               BASE        8        is
6                BASE       11
-----------------------------------------------------------------------
> 7, 3
> 24

24               BASE        7         is
111              BASE        3
-----------------------------------------------------------------------
> 14,18
> AC

AC               BASE       14        is
84               BASE       18
-----------------------------------------------------------------------
> 17, 7
> 217

217              BASE       17        is
1325             BASE        7


        :
        :

==============================the last 4 examples are incorrect========
```

input, as are the values of BASE1 and BASE2 themselves (program BASE assumes no errors are made in supplying this input). BASE consists of two simple loops:

1 Determine the numeric value of the integer input.

2 Determine the digits for this value in the new base.

The program seems to be straightforward, but some of the output is correct and some is incorrect.

Program BASE appears to work properly for single-digit numbers, and most of the time the most significant digit of the converted number is correct. Careful examination of the converted numbers will show that they are wrong by the amount (BASE1-BASE2) for the two-digit numbers. This, however, doesn't provide much of a clue as to the source(s) of the error, and three-digit numbers exhibit a different error pattern. The bug has to be in either the loop to determine the numeric value or the loop to generate the BASE2 digits (or both). The first step is to introduce a bug-PRINT into the value-determination loop to see if the value is being calculated correctly. Therefore, insert the statement

```
PRINT *, 'VALUE = ', VALUES
```

between the VALUE = . . . and repeat statements of that loop. Then execution of base produces:

```
==========================================================================
.EXECUTE  BASE

Input decimal integer values for <base1>, <base2>  in the 2..20 range.
        (A smaller value will terminate the program.)
Then input the digits of the base1 integer to be converted.
--------------------------------------------------------------------------
> 10, 10
> 27
VALUE =            3
VALUE =           38

27                  BASE          10          is
27                  BASE          10
--------------------------------------------------------------------------
> 14, 18
> AC
VALUE =           11
VALUE =          167

AC                  BASE          14          is
84                  BASE          18
--------------------------------------------------------------------------
> 17, 7
> 217
VALUE =            3
VALUE =           53
VALUE =          909

217                 BASE          17          is
1325                BASE           7

         :
         :
==========================================================================
```

It's obvious from this output that there is a serious, but systematic, error in the value-determination loop. The value obtained for each digit is off by 1 (1 too large). This observation immediately pinpoints the source of the error—in the determination of the digit value. That is performed by the call to INDEX, which searches the string DIGITS for the digit. In DIGITS, '0' is in position 1, '1' is in position 2, '2' is in position 3, and so on, and now it's clear what the error is: the digit value is not the value returned by INDEX but one less than that. The correct statement, therefore, is obtained by subtracting 1 from the value returned by INDEX:

```
VALUE = VALUE*BASE1 + INDEX(DIGITS,NUM1(K:K)) - 1
```

Without this correction every value is wrong. But the conversion was correct in some instances. Therefore there must be another error in the program—this one in the loop to determine the BASE2 digits. This can be easily verified by executing BASE with the value-determination loop corrected: all of the conversions come out wrong now. The programmer, being "off by one" in the design of the value-determination loop, was probably consistent and made the corresponding error in the digits-determination loop. This could be investigated with a bug-PRINT in this loop, printing out the value of D, which is the digit value. However, since the source of the error is now strongly suspected, inspection of the statements in that loop may reveal the error. And sure enough, the use of DIGIT is "off by one" again (this time in the opposite direction). The error is corrected by

```
TEMP = DIGITS(D+1:D+1)//NUM2
```

(or, by adding 1 to the expression in the previous statement).

The error in BASE is a rather subtle one, compounded, and partially hidden, by a similar error. These can be very difficult errors to find by just inspecting the program—especially since the programmer, having made the same error consistently, is likely to continue in the same thought pattern and miss "seeing" the error many times. The bug-PRINT immediately cuts through this curtain of confusion and uncovers the error. (The error in BASE, by the way, is the source of potential trouble, which is not apparent from the output given above. See Problem 5.21.)

5.7 Summary

Techniques for achieving repetitive execution of statement groups (looping) have now been added to the executable features of Fortran described thus far. (The other executable features include input, output, assignment, and selection control.) These form a set of programming tools that can be used to solve a wide variety of problems. The ability to construct loops is very important in this set, since most interesting programs involve one or more loops.

The basic form of a loop is:

```
do
    ----  \
    ----   | loop
    ----   | body
    ----  /
repeat
```

where the loop body consists of any sequence of executable Fortran statements. Execution of the loop body is repeated until an exit statement is executed, at which time control flows to the statement following repeat. An exit may be the last statement of a statement group in an IF-ENDIF structure, or specified in an exit-IF statement which has the form

```
IF (<exit condition>) exit
```

A loop may have any number of exits within the loop body.

An important special case of looping involves executing the loop a known number of times, changing a certain variable—called the index variable—each time. Such indexed looping may be specified by

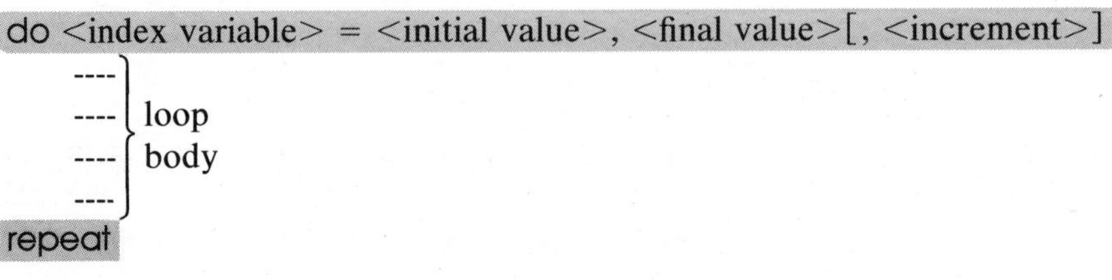

where the meaning is "execute the loop first for <index variable> = <initial value>, then for <initial value> + <increment>, then incremented again, and so on until the value of <index variable> has "gone past" <final value>. Indexed loops need no other exits within the loop body, but may have them.

Loops should be designed using do, repeat, and exit, but since these constructs are just convenient abbreviations for the standard Fortran features that they represent they should be modified as shown in Figures 5.14 and 5.16 before the program is submitted for compilation. A few dos and don'ts for constructing loops are as follows:

1 Do design loops carefully, for efficient execution and high readability.

2 Don't inadvertently construct infinite loops.

3 Do handle loop exits consistently.

4 Do use indexed loops where appropriate.

5 Don't use indexed loops where the number of repetitions is unknown.

6 Do use do-repeat and exit when designing loops.

7 Don't worry about statement labels when designing loops.

8 Do design statement labels systematically (see Figure 5.16).

9 Don't nest loops more than about three levels, unless absolutely necessary.

Programming Exercises

5.1 The exponential function, EXP(X), may be computed with the infinite series:
1 + X + X**2/2! + X**3/3! + . . . + X**n/n! + . . .
Write a Fortran program to compute this value for any given value of X. Compare your value with that obtained from a call to the intrinsic function EXP. How many terms from this series are needed to get a good approximation to EXP(X)?

5.2 Write a Fortran program that prints a table of integers, their squares, their square roots, and their reciprocals, for all integer values between 1 and 100.

5.3 Small computers are often used on "assembly lines," where the same process, and nothing else, is performed over and over. Should infinite loops be considered appropriate programming technique for such applications?

5.4 Extend program MCMESS so that it will decode a message with any number of coded lines in it. Use the CLEAR value of 'DONE' as the condition for termination.

5.5 Write a Fortran program that performs a linear search on a sequence of elements that may or may not contain the searched-for value, without appending the value to the end of the sequence.

5.6 Modify program RBALL so that it has only one exit, at the bottom of the loop, but performs precisely the same function (i.e., produces identical output). Identify, and try to minimize, the additional computation this modified program makes.

5.7 Suppose that, in program CHARGE an additional type of transaction is desired, that allows corrections to be made to an account balance (if errors had occurred). The new transaction type code could be 'CDR'. Modify program CHARGE to provide for this new feature.

5.8 In data processing applications such as program CHARGE, the standard practice is to have the program do as much "validity checking" on the transaction data as possible. Incorporate such checking into program CHARGE. Such checks could include:
(a) No payment amount should be negative
(b) No purchase amount should be negative
(c) No payment amount should be greater than a specified amount (say 10,000) without producing a certain message

5.9 Many data processing applications are structurally similar to program CHARGE. Suppose that a small plumbing firm purchases computing services to process their weekly accounting data. Transactions include purchases of pipe, tools and other materials, and payments from customers. Write a Fortran program to produce a weekly accounting statement for this company.

5.10 Extend program CHILL2 so that it prints a bigger table, a whole chart, of wind-chill factors for ranges of both wind speeds and temperatures. The chart should have 10 columns: one each for wind speeds of 0, 10, 20, . . ., 80, 90 kilometers per hour (KPH) and 11 rows: one each for temperatures of 15, 10, 5, . . ., −30, −35 degrees Celsius (C).

5.11 Repeat Problem 5.10 but use the English units of miles per hour (MPH) and degrees Fahrenheit (F). The conversion factors are
C = (F−32)*5/9.
and KPH = MPH*1.61

5.12 Rewrite program BUBBLE so that small values are "bubbled up" rather than having large values "bubbling down."

5.13 The *insertion sort* is similar to the bubble sort in that a "bubbling" takes place during the sorting process. Starting with the second, then the third, then the fourth, and so on until the last, in the insertion sort each element is transferred to its sorted position relative to all of the elements preceding the starting place. (Thus after the first such pass the first two elements are in sorted order, after the second pass the first three elements are in sorted order, and so on until the entire list is sorted.) Write a Fortran program to perform the insertion sort. Test it with the list of names used in program BUBBLE.

5.14 An interesting sequence of rapidly growing integers is the *Fibonacci sequence*, which (like factorials) starts slowly:
1, 1, 2, 3, 5, 8, 13, 21, . . .
Each number in the Fibonacci sequence (after the first two) is the sum of the two preceding it. Write a Fortran program to compute and print all of the digits of any specified element of the Fibonacci sequence. (Note: three integer arrays could be used—two for the previous two numbers and one for the sum (next number)).

5.15 Repeat Problem 5.14 using only two integer arrays.

5.16 Repeat Problem 5.14 using no arrays (only character strings and simple integer variables).

5.17 Modify program FACT so that it does not use the integer array (just character strings and simple integer variables).

5.18 Write a Fortran program that "reverses" a string (not including the trailing blanks). For example the string for 'do-repeat' would become 'taeper-od'. Use this program to check a string for being a palindrome.

5.19 Repeat program BASE (without the bug) for fractions—for example, .74BD3 (base 16, suppose)

This program can be pretty much like BASE, with the following changes:
(a) Divide the final VALUE by BASE1 until it becomes less than 1.
(b) Generate the BASE2 values starting with the most significant digit:
(i) Q=VALUE*BASE2
(ii) D=INT(Q)
(iii) VALUE=Q−D

5.20 Combine program BASE and Problem 5.19 into a single program that will convert any number between any two bases.

5.21 (a) Build "protection" into program BASE that detects invalid input data, either in the values for two bases or in the string of digits to be converted. (b) In the original version of BASE (the one that contained the bugs) the second loop is an additional source of trouble. What is this trouble?

5.22 Write an "arbitrary precision" Fortran program that adds two positive integer numbers (base 10) and prints the sum. Each of the two numbers can have any number of digits in it (up to a limit, say, of 1000) and is to be input as a string of digits.

5.23 Repeat Problem 5.22 but for arbitrary real numbers—numbers having decimal points and fractional parts.

5.24 Repeat Problem 5.23, but allow either (or both) numbers to be negative. A negative number should be preceded with a minus sign (−), and a positive number may be optionally preceded with a plus sign (+).

5.25 Repeat Problem 5.22, but multiply the two numbers rather than add them.

5.26 An interesting message coding scheme is to convert each character of the message into a number, add adjacent pairs of numbers, and then convert the sums back into characters to form the code. Suppose, for example, that the sequence
'eghiknorstw! '
defines a numbering scheme for these 13 characters (e = 1, g = 2, ! = 12, etc.). Then coding of a message is illustrated by:

w	e		s	t	r	i	k	e		t	o	n	i	g	h	t		!
11	1	13	9	10	8	4	5	1	13	10	7	6	4	2	3	10	13	12
!	e	s	n	k	!	s	n	e	t	i		t	n	k		t	!	

Write a Fortran program to code any given message in this way. (Note that the coded message has one less character in it than the original message, and sums greater than 13 have 13 subtracted from them.)

5.27 Write a Fortran program to decode a message generated by the scheme of Problem 5.26. In order to do this one of the original message characters must be known, say the last one. The next to last character of the original message can then be determined from the combination of this knowledge and the last character of the coded message. In this manner the coded message can be decoded, character by character, starting from the last one and ending with the first one. In the example in Problem 5.26 the last clear character is a "!" (assumed known)—value 12—and the last coded character (by coincidence) is a "!". Therefore since 12 is the value (possibly adjusted by subtracting 13) of 12 plus "something," where "something" is in the range 1. .13, the next to the last character of the original message must have number 13. Similarly 10 is the "sum" of "something" plus 13—giving 10 for the next character of the original. And then 13 is the sum of 10 plus "something," giving 3 as the nummer for yet the next character of the original message. Proceeding in this manner, the entire message can be decoded. In the decoding program, assume that the last character of the original message is known.

5.28 Write a Fortran program to determine the reciprocal of an integer (any positive integer) to an arbitrary number of decimal places. (Hint: use an integer array, each element of which represents one of the digits of the reciprocal value.)

5.29 One of the ways to compute the (approximate) value of PI is by the infinite series:
PI = 4 * (1 − 1/3 + 1/5 − 1/7 + 1/9 − 1/11 + ...)
Write a Fortran program to compute PI accurate to a specified (but arbitrary) number of decimal places. The program of Problem 5.28 could be useful here.

5.30 A state legislator commissions a pollster to conduct a poll among the voters, in order to estimate the sentiment for each of 15 issues likely to be important in the upcoming election. For each of the 15 issues each voter contacted in the poll is asked to check one of the following:

Strongly support
Don't really care (issue not important)
Strongly oppose
Don't know (no opinion on the issue at this time)

The legislator wants a summary of the percentage of voters choosing each response, for each issue, and also the percentage not choosing any of the four possible responses. Write a Fortran program that accepts the raw response data and generates the desired summary. The raw data consists of 15 integers for each voter polled, each integer being 1, 2, 3, 4, 5 and corresponding to strongly support, don't care, strongly oppose, don't know, and no response for each of the 15 issues.

Chapter 6 Program Modules

The example programs have progressed from very simple ones to not-so-simple ones, and, as mentioned earlier, it is not difficult to imagine considerably more complex programs. As the problems to be solved become more complex it is common that the resulting programs become longer, have more data elements, and involve more intricate logical structure. All of this combines to cause the programming process to increase in difficulty at least as fast as (and probably faster than) the problem complexity. The use of program modules allows the programmer to ''divide and conquer''—to break a complex problem up into a set of smaller problems, each of which is far simpler to solve than the original, composite problem.

Fortunately, most complex problems can be easily broken up into self-contained *modules*. Each module can be programmed separately, during which time little attention need be paid toward the other modules. When all of the modules have been completed they form a system of coordinated programs that solves the original complex problem. This technique, sometimes called *modular programming*, is widely regarded as good programming technique and is nearly universally used in practice. Modular programming is in some respects like an industrial assembly line—a complex product (program) is assembled in a series of specialized stages (modules); the entire process benefits from the simplicity and efficiency of specialization.

Program SCORE (Chapter 4) is a simple but good example of the attractiveness of modularization. Program ROLL, programmed independently of program SCORE, is used as an important part of SCORE (that of simulating the ball rolling in a game of bowling). The structure of a well-designed program to simulate a complete game of bowling might be:

```
<initializations>
do FRAME = 1, 10
    <ball rolling module>
    <score updating module>
repeat
<extra balls module>
```

This outline clearly describes the components, and their interrelation, of the bowling program. Another good candidate for modularization is program MCMESS of Chapter 5—in fact, it has already been somewhat modularized by inclusion of the heart of program MORSE in it. Program MCMESS could itself be a module to decode one line of message, and could be used in a more general program to decode a message of any length (any number of lines):

```
do
    <input next line of message>
    IF (<message> .EQ. 'DONE') exit
    <module to decode message line>
repeat
```

In fact, most of the programs of the last chapter are good candidates for modularization. Program PAL, for instance, is perhaps best structured as

```
<input a string>
<module for depunctuating>
<palindrome check module>
```

In Fortran a module may be formed as a *subroutine*, a separate, complete Fortran program that can be *called* by the *main* program, or mainline. The main program normally contains the initializations (although these may be done in a subroutine) and the program structure in which calls to the various modules are embedded. This chapter describes how subroutines are constructed and used in Fortran. This discussion cannot describe which modules to use in a given problem, however. The choice of modules is a design rather than a coding problem, and it therefore constitutes a set of creative rather than mechanical decisions. The example problems of this section illustrate modular program design, and may be used as models in developing skill at modularization. Practice is what counts, however, and every program tackled should be carefully analyzed and designed in terms of its modular structure. A model for program development might be summarized as follows:

1 Define clearly the problem to be solved.

2 Design the modular structure of the program.

3 Determine the data elements and logical structure of each module.

4 Repeat steps 2 and 3 for each module (i.e., a module may itself be modularized).

5 Code the entire system in Fortran.

6.1 The SUBROUTINE and CALL Statements

A Fortran module (subroutine) is a complete program. Its structure is virtually identical to the structure of "ordinary" Fortran programs. The simplest form of this structure is

```
SUBROUTINE <name>
    <specification statements>
    <executable statements>
END
```

Note that SUBROUTINE has replaced PROGRAM, and otherwise such a Fortran module has precisely the same structure as a Fortran program. Each module is given a unique name that is constructed using the same rules as for program and data element names.

A complete system of programs consists of one PROGRAM (the main program) and several SUBROUTINEs. The main program controls the execution of the subroutines by use of the CALL statement, which has the form

```
CALL <subroutine name>
```

The effect of executing the CALL statement is to suspend temporarily execution of the program while the specified subroutine is executed in its entirety; then execution of the program resumes with the execution of the statement following the CALL. Any number of CALL statements may appear anywhere among the executable statements of a program.

To illustrate these concepts the examples used in the introduction to this section are configured in this format. First, suppose that program BOWL simulates an entire game of bowling and employs subroutines ROLL, SCORE, and EXTRA (for the extra balls, if any, after the tenth frame); then BOWL has the form

```
PROGRAM BOWL
    <specification statements>
    <initializations>
    do FRAME=1, 10
        PRINT *, 'Frame Number', FRAME
        CALL ROLL
        CALL SCORE
        PRINT *
    repeat
    CALL EXTRA
    <print final score>
END
```

Program BOWL can be (just has been!) designed without concern for the details of the various modules (ROLL, SCORE, and EXTRA) that play important roles in it.

Second, let program DECODE be the main program for the Morse code decoding system. If MCMESS is the subroutine for decoding a line of message, then program DECODE could take the following form:

```
PROGRAM DECODE
<specification statements>
do
    READ '(A)', MCLINE
    IF (MCLINE.EQ.'DONE') exit
    CALL MCMESS
    PRINT *, MCLINE
    PRINT *, CLEAR
repeat
END
```

This design for DECODE has all of the input and output in the main program, along with the high-level logic of the system. Just the details of decoding a line (which is the most complicated part of the system) are relegated to subroutine MCMESS. Any initializations needed for decoding a line are assumed to be provided in MCMESS. In the third example let PDROME be the main program for identifying palindromes, which uses subroutines DEPUNC for depunctuating and PCHECK for the actual checking for a palindrome. Then program PDROME could be

```
PROGRAM PDROME
    <specification statements>
    <initializations>
    READ '(A)', TEXT
    CALL DEPUNC
    CALL PCHECK
END
```

In program PDROME it is assumed that the printout concerning whether TEXT is a palindrome is in subroutine PCHECK.

The discussion and examples of this section should serve to indicate how a Fortran program is modularized using subroutines, and how the CALL statement is used to cause modules to be executed. The examples have not been written as "ready-to-be-run" programs, however, since an important detail has been ignored. Fortran subroutines are complete, separate programs—separately compiled and stored in the computing system. Data from a module, or from the main program, is not automatically known in another module. For example in program DECODE, subroutine MCMESS does not automatically know the value for MCLINE that was read into the main program. In program PDROME, subroutine DEPUNC does not automatically know the value for TEXT that it must depunctuate. Therefore these examples, while illustrating the conceptual use of modules, are incomplete because of the neglect to "pass" necessary data into a subroutine when the subroutine is called. In general not only does a program need to pass data into a subroutine when a call is made, provision usually is needed for the program to obtain results from the subroutine. For example, subroutine MCMESS in program DECODE must pass the value of CLEAR (the message decoded from in MCLINE) back to DECODE in order that it may be printed. Similarly, in program BOWL subroutine ROLL must provide program BOWL with the two ball values so that these can be made available to subroutine SCORE. Providing for the passing of data between programs and subroutines is the topic of the next section.

6.2 Subroutine Arguments

Data to be passed into or back from a subroutine are represented by *arguments* of the subroutine. In making a call to a subroutine the arguments are specified by listing them in the CALL statement. The form is

```
CALL <subroutine name > (<list of arguments>)
```

As in all Fortran lists, each argument in the <list of arguments> is separated from its neighbors by commas. An argument in a CALL statement may be (virtually) any legal Fortran expression (including a constant, a variable name, and array element) or an array name. Any of these can be used to pass data into the subroutine (input arguments) and variable names, array elements, or array names may be used to receive results from the subroutine (output arguments).

Some examples may serve to explain these concepts more concretely. In program DECODE of the previous section, subroutine MCMESS requires the value of MCLINE as input data and returns (in the official jargon) the value of CLEAR. Therefore the CALL statement

```
CALL MCMESS (MCLINE, CLEAR)
```

will provide adequate "lines of communication" between program DECODE and subroutine MCMESS. The complete program is as shown at the top of the next page.

In program BOWL, subroutine ROLL must return the ball values for the current frame, and the corresponding mark value, and hence a call to ROLL might take the form

```
CALL ROLL (BALL1, BALL2, MARK)
```

```
*....!-----------------------------------------------------------------
      PROGRAM  DECODE
*                   Program to decode a Morse Code message
*                   of any number of lines.  MCMESS is the
*                   same as in chapter 5, except that it is now
*                   a subroutine, and no longer contains the
*                   inputting of MCLINE.

*     ....constant....(the terminating message)
      CHARACTER*10  DONE
      PARAMETER  ( DONE = 'STOP' )

*     ....variables....
      CHARACTER  MCLINE*200, CLEAR*80
*     ....execute....
*                             ..loop to read and decode a line of
*                               Morse Code -- one exit: when the
*                               input line is the same as DONE..
      do
         READ '(A)',  MCLINE
         IF  (MCLINE .EQ. DONE)  exit
         PRINT *,  MCLINE
         CALL  MCMESS (MCLINE, CLEAR)
         PRINT *,  CLEAR
         PRINT *
      repeat
      END
=====================================================================
.EXECUTE  DECODE

> .. ..-.  -... ..- --. ...  -.-. .-. . . .--.  .. -.
IF BUGS CREEP IN

> .- -. -..  -- .- -.- .  -.-- --- ..-  .-- .. -. -.-. .
AND MAKE YOU WINCE

> - .-. .- -.-. -.-  - .... . --  -.. --- .-- -.  -... -.--
TRACK THEM DOWN BY

> ..-. --- .-.. .-.. --- .-- .. -. --.  - .... . .. .-.  .--. .-. .. -. - ...
FOLLOWING THEIR PRINTS

>STOP
=====================================================================
```

All three of these arguments are the results that ROLL returns to BOWL (ROLL doesn't need any input data). Subroutine SCORE will need values for BALL1, BALL2, MARK, MARKP, MARKP2, and TOTAL (the current score) and will update (return a new value for) TOTAL, MARKP, and MARKP2 (MARKP and MARKP2 contain the mark status of the previous two frames). Thus a call to SCORE might appear as

CALL SCORE (TOTAL, BALL1, BALL2, MARK, MARKP, MARKP2)

And finally, subroutine EXTRA will need the value for TOTAL and the previous marks, and therefore

CALL EXTRA (TOTAL, MARKP, MARKP2)

is an appropriate call on EXTRA. The complete program for BOWL is shown at the top of the next page.

Note that there may be any number of arguments in a CALL statement, with any mix of input and output arguments in any order. An argument may be both an input and output argument, as illustrated by the argument TOTAL in program BOWL. In the above examples only variable names were used as CALL arguments, which demonstrates that this is a common form for arguments. Examples of other forms for arguments will appear in subsequent programs.

```
*....:-----------------------------------------------------------------
      PROGRAM  BOWL
*                     ..simulation of a complete game of bowling;
*                     this program calls 3 subroutines, with up to
*                     six arguments per call..

*     ....constants....
      INTEGER  NOMARK, SPARE, STRIKE
      PARAMETER  ( NOMARK=0, SPARE=1, STRIKE=2 )

*     ....variables....
      INTEGER  FRAME, TOTAL, BALL1, BALL2, MARK, MARKP, MARKP2

*     ....initializations....
      DATA    TOTAL, MARKP , MARKP2      /
     :          0  , NOMARK, NOMARK      /

*     ....execute....
      do  FRAME = 1,10
*                        ..indexed loop for 10 frames..
          PRINT *, 'FRAME NUMBER', FRAME
          CALL  ROLL (BALL1, BALL2, MARK)
          CALL  SCORE (TOTAL, BALL1, BALL2, MARK, MARKP, MARKP2)
          PRINT *
      repeat
*                     ..now roll extra ball(s) if strike or spare
*                                                 in tenth frame..
      IF  (MARK .NE. NOMARK)  THEN
              CALL  EXTRA (TOTAL, MARKP, MARKP2)
      ENDIF
      PRINT *,'FINAL SCORE IS', TOTAL
      END
=======================================================================
```

6.2.1 Dummy Arguments

When a module in a system of programs is designed the input/output arguments for that module must be identified. This is done in Fortran by placing a list of names (in parentheses) in the SUBROUTINE statement. The number of names in this list specifies the number of arguments in a CALL to this subroutine. Upon execution of the CALL statement each of the names in the SUBROUTINE statement list is "paired" (associated) with the corresponding argument in the CALL statement (in left-to-right order). The names in the SUBROUTINE statement are called *dummy arguments*, and are used in the subroutine to represent the arguments specified in the CALL statement. In other words, the dummy arguments are the names by which the subroutine knows the arguments appearing in the CALL statement, and these names may be either the same as or different from names appearing in the CALL. Each dummy argument must be declared to be the same type as the type of the argument in the CALL, but declarations of dummy arguments serve only to type these names and do not cause allocation of actual data elements.

Consider again the above examples. In program DECODE two arguments are included in the CALL on subroutine MCMESS. This means that the SUBROUTINE statement in subroutine MCMESS must have a list of two arguments (say MCODE and CLEAR) and then these names are declared to be of type CHARACTER, as follows.

```
SUBROUTINE MCMESS (MCODE, CLEAR)
                    CHARACTER*(*) MCODE, CLEAR
  . . . .rest of subroutine program. . . .
END
```

Now when subroutine MCMESS is called with the statement

```
CALL MCMESS (MCLINE, CLEAR)
```

then MCODE is associated with MCLINE (and CLEAR with CLEAR), and any reference to MCODE in the subroutine is the same as a reference to MCLINE—MCODE is the "alias" by which MCLINE is known in the subroutine. The subroutine does not know the name MCLINE. Note (as in the case of the second argument, CLEAR) that the "alias" may be the same as the "actual" name. The asterisk in parentheses for the lengths of MCODE and CLEAR are valid for dummy arguments, and means that the length of each is to be the same as the length of the corresponding data element in the CALL statement.

In program BOWL three arguments of type INTEGER are used in the CALL on subroutine ROLL. Therefore

```
SUBROUTINE ROLL (B1, B2, M)
                INTEGER B1, B2, M
      :
      :
END
```

would be a valid way to specify the dummy arguments for subroutine ROLL. For the execution of

```
CALL ROLL (BALL1, BALL2, MARK)
```

B1 is the alias for BALL1, B2 the alias for BALL2, and M the alias for MARK. B1, B2 and M are meaningful names in the subroutine; BALL1, BALL2, and MARK are not meaningful in ROLL, and their use would give erroneous results.

6.2.2 Actual Arguments

The CALL statement supplies the actual values that the subroutine uses as input data, and the actual variables that are to receive results from the subroutine. These are therefore called the *actual arguments*. The dummy arguments are the names by which the subroutine knows these input values and output destinations for a given CALL. Since the association of dummy arguments with actual arguments is by position in the argument lists, care must be taken to insure that the number of arguments in each list is the same, and that corresponding arguments have the same type. Otherwise the passing of informaion between programs is not properly specified and results will be unpredictable.

Note that the entire introductory portion of this section is a discussion of the concept and use of actual arguments. There is much more to the story of actual and dummy arguments and their association. Indeed, this is a major aspect of programming and sophisticated programmers need to know all of this story. It will be treated in detail in Chapter 7. The concepts introduced in the current chapter are adequate, however, to allow programmers to make considerable use of modular programming.

6.3 Local Variables

All Fortran programs and subprograms (referred to collectively as "program units") are separate, complete programs, and the only communication among them is through argument lists. (But see the next chapter for an additional kind of argument list known as COMMON.) No other data elements in one program unit are known to any other program unit. Such data elements are considered to be "local" to (not known outside of) their program unit. Except for arguments, all data elements used in a program unit are local to that program unit. A program unit may therefore use any variables (or constants, or arrays), with any desired names, without concern about effects upon, or from, other program units. Consider the following situation:

```
PROGRAM PNAME           SUBROUTINE SNAME(. . . .)
    :                           :
    INTEGER TEMP            CHARACTER*20 TEMP
    :                           :
    CALL SNAME(. . . .)         :
    :                   END
END
```

Assuming that TEMP is neither an actual nor dummy argument in either of these program units, if TEMP is modified in subroutine SNAME this would have no effect on any data elements, including TEMP, known to program PNAME. The two TEMPs are completely different data elements, with different storage locations in main memory, and, indeed, they even have different types. In SNAME, TEMP refers to the element of type CHARACTER named TEMP, and in PNAME, TEMP refers to the element of type INTEGER named TEMP. Even if the type of TEMP in PNAME was the same as its type in SNAME, they would still represent different data elements.

Variables are important in a program unit to help perform the processing that unit does, and this is true whether the unit is a main program or a subroutine. Constants, variables, and arrays may be declared in a subroutine as may be needed to accomplish the processing of that module. As long as these data elements are not used as arguments they will not interfere with processing in any other program unit, even if the names are the same as the names of local data elements in other program units. Figure 6.1 depicts the situation graphically.

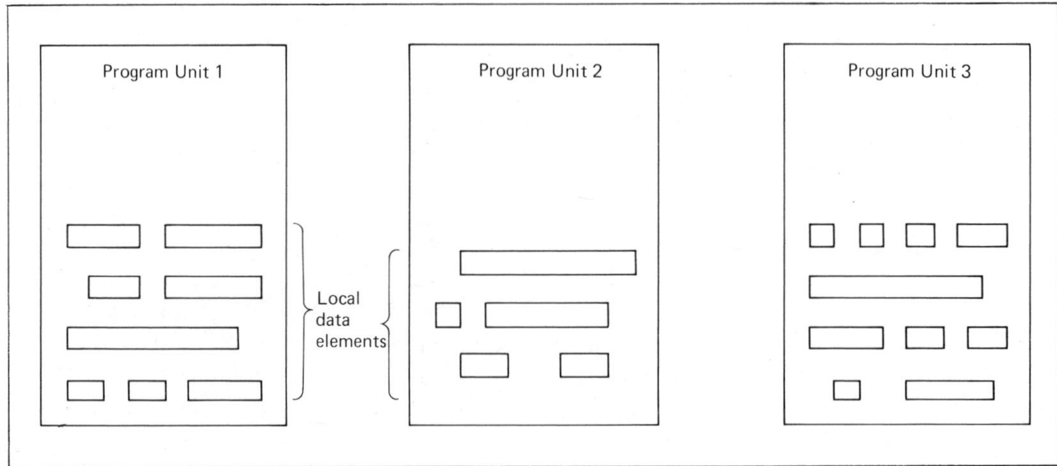

Figure 6.1. Diagram depicting the local data elements of three different program units.

When any of the program units of Figure 6.1 is executing it "knows" only about its own local data elements and no other program unit's local data elements (except those that may have been accessed as arguments). The following subroutine, SQUEEZ, illustrates the use of local variables. This subroutine takes a line of text and replaces all sets of contiguous blanks (except trailing blanks) with a single blank character; it also removes any blanks preceding punctuation characters (such as "," "." and ";"). For example SQUEEZ will change the text

```
'a man,  a plan, a  canal, panama  .'
```

to

```
'a man, a plan, a canal, panama.     '
```

Two points can be made about subroutine SQUEEZ, one of which is obvious from the program and one which is not. First, as with any main program, both constants and variables may be declared in a subroutine, and all of these data elements are local to the program unit in which they are declared. A second observation concerns the definition status (undefined, or having some valid value) of the local variables in a program unit. Typically, a subroutine is executed (CALLed) several times during the execution of a main program (subroutine ROLL, for example, is executed 10 different times during execution of program BOWL). At the beginning of the first execution of

```
*....:----------------------------------------------------------------------
      SUBROUTINE  SQUEEZ (TEXT)
                            CHARACTER*(*)  TEXT

*                                    ..this program (subroutine) uses
*                                    several local data elements: PUNC,
*                                    K, L, and CHAR.  TEXT is an argument
*                                    and therefore not a local data
*                                    element.  The subroutine replaces
*                                    groups of blanks with a single
*                                    blank, and removes blanks preceding
*                                    punctuation characters..

*     ....(local) constant....
      CHARACTER  PUNC*8
      PARAMETER  ( PUNC = ' ,.;:''"-' )

*     ....(local) variables....
      INTEGER  K, L
      CHARACTER  CHAR

*     ....execute....
      K = 1
      CHAR = TEXT(1:1)
*                                     ..loop on each TEXT character;
*                                            no additional exits..
      do  L = 2, LEN(TEXT)
*                                    ..if CHAR is a blank ignore it if
*                                    the next character (TEXT(L:L)) is a
*                                    blank or punctuation character..

         IF  (CHAR .NE. ' '  .OR.  INDEX(PUNC,TEXT(L:L)) .EQ. 0)  THEN
                TEXT(K:K) = CHAR
                K = K+1
         ENDIF
         CHAR = TEXT(L:L)
      repeat
*                                     ..put last CHAR in proper position,
*                                       and "blank" rest of TEXT..
      TEXT(K:) = CHAR
      END
===========================================================================
```

a subroutine, all of the local data elements are undefined, except those given values by PARAMETER or DATA statements; during execution local variables may become defined (given values). What is the definition status of the local variables at the beginning of the next execution of the subroutine? (In the meantime, after the previous execution of the subroutine was completed, control returned to the main program, and the subroutine has become "dormant" again until the main program issues the next CALL to it.) The answer is that initially defined local data elements whose values are not changed during execution of the subroutine remain defined with their original values; all other local data elements are undefined at the beginning of reexecution of a subroutine.

There are two major implications of this local variable definition situation. The first is that local constants (data elements defined via the PARAMETER statement) retain their values between subroutine executions, but local variable values are lost between subroutine executions. The second is that the DATA statement is not as useful in subroutines as in main programs, since DATA statement initializations are in effect only at the beginning of the <u>first</u> execution of the subroutine and not on any subsequent executions of the subroutine. Programmers must therefore be careful in initializing local variables in subroutines: if an initialization is to be done at the beginning of each execution of the subroutine then it must be done by assignment statements (or other executable statements that will accomplish the desired initialization) rather than by DATA statements.

The reason that local variables become undefined between executions of a subroutine is that Fortran is designed to allow efficient use of the computer's storage facility (main memory). Two subroutines, such as ROLL and SCORE in program BOWL, are not executed simultaneously. When ROLL is being executed, SCORE is dormant and its local variables are not being used; similarly when SCORE is being executed, ROLL is dormant and its local variables are not being used. For this reason, and contrary to the impression given by Figure 6.1, the same physical space in memory may be used for (shared by) the local variables of the subroutines ROLL and SCORE. The values left in this space by ROLL may be overwritten by SCORE, resulting in meaningless values as far as the next execution of ROLL is concerned. Therefore local variables are assumed to become undefined in Fortran between executions of a subroutine. With local constants, however, the situation is different. Space for constants is not shared among subroutines, the picture in Figure 6.1 is accurate, and constants retain their values between subroutine executions.

Returning to subroutine SQUEEZ, it is now clear that PUNC, since it is not changed by SQUEEZ, can be assumed to be defined with the same value for each execution of SQUEEZ. But K, L, and CHAR all must be initialized by executable statements each time SQUEEZ is executed.

6.4 Calling and Called Programs

Fortran subroutines may themselves call subroutines (but may not call themselves!). That is, modules may themselves be modularized. Thus the concept of the main program as a program unit that issues calls and the subroutine as a program unit that is called, while correct, is not quite complete. A *calling program* is a program unit that issues calls to other program units, and may be either a main program or a subroutine; a *called program* is a program unit that is called by another program unit, and includes subroutines and intrinsic functions. In Chapter 8 *external* functions will join subroutines as examples of program units that, in general, may be either called or calling programs.

When subroutine calls are nested (i.e., when a called program calls another program unit) then the picture of Figure 6.1 is accurate—separate data areas are needed since all of the program units involved in the nested call are still in the process of (i.e., haven't finished) being executed. Furthermore, the local nature of variables is still the same, with the local variables of the calling program not accessible to the called program, and the local variables of the called program not accessible to the calling program. Communication between calling and called programs is only via arguments. A calling program may make any data it knows about available to any program it calls as actual arguments in the CALL. These actual arguments may include constants, expressions, local variables, and dummy arguments. This last case (where a calling program uses its own dummy arguments as actual arguments in making a CALL) is a means of passing data through more than one level of modularization.

Several complete examples should help to illustrate all of these various concepts and techniques. The first example is to (at long last) complete the bowling simulation. Its main program (BOWL) is given above in Section 6.2, and it calls the three subroutimes ROLL, SCORE, and EXTRA, which are as shown below.

The great contributions that modularization makes to program comprehensibility is one of the main advantages of the use of subroutines. Another is demonstrated by subroutine BALL. Two calls to BALL appear in subroutine ROLL, and three such calls appear in subroutine EXTRA. By making BALL a subroutine, as above, the code comprising BALL need be written only once; otherwise the execute body of BALL would have to be supplied in its entirety in place of each call to BALL (i.e., the do-repeat loop of BALL would have to appear in each of the five places where input data is supplied). Rewriting such a code is wasteful of the programmer's time, boring, inelegant, and subject to errors. Writing the code once, as a subroutine, and calling it whenever needed, is a superior way of programming in such instances.

A related advantage of subroutines is that they make possible the availability of program "libraries" to programmers. Since a Fortran subroutine is written and compiled separately from any other program unit, a computing center may have (and most do) a set of prewritten subroutines that are of general use. Fortran's set of intrinsic

```
*....:-------------------------------------------------------------
      SUBROUTINE  ROLL (BALL1, BALL2, MARK)
                        INTEGER  BALL1, BALL2, MARK

*                               ..similar to program ROLL in chapter 4,
*                               but the READ statements of program ROLL
*                               are replaced by CALL BALL. Subroutine
*                               BALL performs the input and checks the
*                               data for validity. The second argument in
*                               CALL BALL argument list is the maximum
*                               number of pins allowed on this ball..

*     ....constants....
      INTEGER  NOMARK, SPARE, STRIKE
*     PARAMETER  ( NOMARK=0, SPARE=1, STRIKE=2 )

*     ....execute....
      PRINT *,  'Roll first ball.'
      CALL  BALL (BALL1, 10)
      IF  (BALL1 .EQ. 10)  THEN
              PRINT *,  '.........STRIKE !!'
              MARK = STRIKE
              BALL2 = 0
          ELSE
*                     ..need to roll second ball..
              IF  (BALL1 .EQ. 0)  THEN
                      PRINT *, 'Gutterball, roll second ball.'
                  ELSE
                      PRINT *, 'Roll second ball.'
              ENDIF
              CALL  BALL (BALL2, 10-BALL1)
              IF  (BALL1+BALL2 .EQ. 10)  THEN
                      PRINT *, '..........SPARE !'
                      MARK = SPARE
                  ELSE
                      MARK = NOMARK
                      PRINT *, BALL1+BALL2, ' pins in this frame.'
              ENDIF
      ENDIF
      END
===================================================================
```

```
*....:-------------------------------------------------------------
      SUBROUTINE  SCORE (T, B1, B2, M, MP, MP2)
                         INTEGER  T, B1, B2, M, MP, MP2

*                               ..precisely the same as the corresponding
*                               portion of program SCORE in chapter 4.
*                               Note the use of different names for the
*                               dummy arguments than used for the
*                               corresponding actual arguments. This
*                               subroutine knows these data elements only
*                               by the dummy argument names!
*     ....constants....
      INTEGER  NOMARK, SPARE, STRIKE
      PARAMETER  ( NOMARK=0, SPARE=1, STRIKE=2 )

*     ....execute....
      IF  (MP .EQ. STRIKE)  THEN
              IF  (MP2 .EQ. STRIKE)  THEN
                      T = T+20+B1
              ENDIF
              IF  (M .NE. STRIKE)  THEN
                      T = T+10+B1+B2
              ENDIF

          ELSEIF  (MP .EQ. SPARE)  THEN
              T = T+10+B1
      ENDIF
      PRINT *
      IF  (M .EQ. STRIKE)  THEN
              IF  (MP .EQ. STRIKE)  THEN
                      PRINT *, 'Score is', T,
     :                         ' and working on 2 strikes.'
                  ELSE
                      PRINT *, 'Score is', T,
     :                         ' and working on 1 strike.'
              ENDIF
          ELSEIF  (M .EQ. SPARE)  THEN
              PRINT *, 'Score is', T, ' and working on a spare.'
          ELSE
              T = T+B1+B2
              PRINT *, 'Score in this frame is', T
      ENDIF
      MP2 = MP
      MP = M
      END
===================================================================
```

```
*....:-------------------------------------------------------------------
      SUBROUTINE  EXTRA (T, MP, MP2)
                        INTEGER  T, MP, MP2
*
*                               ..this subroutine provides for one extra
*                               ball if the mark in the 10th frame was
*                               a spare, and two extra balls if the
*                               mark in the 10th frame was a strike..
*
*     ....constants....(marks)
      INTEGER  NOMARK, SPARE, STRIKE
      PARAMETER  ( NOMARK=0, SPARE=1, STRIKE=2 )
*
*     ....(local) variables....
      INTEGER  BALL1, BALL2
*
*     ....execute....
      IF  (MP .EQ. SPARE)  THEN
              PRINT *, 'Roll extra ball.'
              CALL  BALL (BALL1, 10)
              T = T+10+BALL1
          ELSE
*                     ..had a strike in the 10th frame..
              PRINT *, 'You get two extra balls -- roll the first one.'
              CALL  BALL (BALL1, 10)
              IF  (BALL1 .EQ. 10)  THEN
                      PRINT *, 'All pins are reset --',
     :                         'roll the last ball.'
                      CALL  BALL (BALL2, 10)
                  ELSE
                      PRINT *, 'Roll last ball.'
                      CALL  BALL (BALL2, 10-BALL1)
              ENDIF
              IF  (MP2 .EQ. STRIKE)  THEN
                      T = T+20+BALL1
              ENDIF
              T =T+10+BALL1+BALL2
      ENDIF
      END
=========================================================================

*....:-------------------------------------------------------------------
      SUBROUTINE  BALL (B, P)
                       INTEGER  B, P
*
*                               ..subroutine to simulate rolling of a
*                               bowling ball. The value of P is the
*                               maximum value that B can have
*                               (zero is the minimum)..
*
*     ....execute....(exit from loop when ball value is valid)
      do
          READ *, B
          IF  (B .GE. 0  .AND.  B .LE. P)  exit
          PRINT *, 'Value must be between 0 and', P
          PRINT *, 'Roll ball again, within these limits.'
      repeat
      END
=========================================================================
```

functions is an example of such a library of commonly useful program units. The subroutine feature means that there is no limit to the nature and extent of such libraries. To use a library program (subroutine) the user need only know the name and function of the program (subroutine) and the number and nature of the actual arguments needed in the CALL. Each computing center normally has a manual that lists all of the library programs available and how to use them.

Subroutine ALIGN is an example of a program that would be widely used if it were available to the users of a computing facility. (Many centers have such subroutines, and more sophisticated related ones, available to the users.) This program takes any desired text, in the form of an array of strings (each array element being one line of input text), and reformats it so that, when printed, the left and right margins are both aligned (as in a book, such as this one). Subroutine ALIGN will not alter the input data, but will generate a new array of strings that constitute the desired reformatted output. The width (number of character positions between the left and right margins) may be any specified integer value between certain limits (such as 20..120). Subroutine ALIGN is used by making the call

CALL ALIGN (TEXT, OUTPUT, WIDTH)

where TEXT is the name of the input array, OUTPUT is the name of the output array, and WIDTH is an integer expression specifying the output line width.

Now that the function of ALIGN has been specified, the program itself must be designed. The alignment will be accomplished by taking the longest sequence of as-yet-unaligned text words that does not exceed WIDTH, and systematically lengthening it by inserting extra blanks between words until it has the desired width. In alternate lines of OUTPUT the extra blanks will be inserted from right to left, and in the intervening lines from left to right. To prepare for this process subroutine NXTEXT is called to transfer the next portion of the text to be processed into the string variable LINE; extra blanks are removed from LINE by a call to SQUEEZ. Subroutine EXPAND will then be called to insert the proper number of blanks in LINE to produce the next formatted line. A '/$' value for a TEXT element terminates the processing.

Thus the general structure of ALIGN is:

```
initializations
do
        call NXTEXT, which obtains sufficient
            text from the input to be
            aligned; extra blanks are
            removed from this text.
        if DONE (determined in NXTEXT) exit
        call EXPAND, which inserts the blanks
            needed for alignment.
repeat
```

Subroutine NXTEXT may have to put several elements of TEXT together to form a LINE long enough to be formatted (if, for example, WIDTH is large and TEXT elements are short). Conversely, if WIDTH is small, subroutine EXPAND may be able to produce several OUTPUT elements from a single instance of LINE.

In most such processed text, certain special effects are occasionally desired. Two of the most important of these are paragraphing and occasional unformatted ("as is") lines. A TEXT element can be specified to be the first line of a new paragraph by "flagging" it in the first position with special characters, say '/+'. Similarly, as-is lines can be flagged, for example, with '/ ' (slash, space). Subroutine NXTEXT can take care of such special effects by testing the first columns of each line of text as it is processed. Thus NXTEXT will have to look for '/$', '/+', '/ ' at the beginning of each element of TEXT, and if any of these is present then the remaining un-expanded preceding text is output (without expansion), followed by the appropriate treatment of the "special" line. Therefore, subroutine NXTEXT will, in addition to calling SQUEEZ, also call subroutine FINISH for generating the proper OUTPUT prior to processing one of the special lines. Because NXTEXT must check for end of TEXT, paragraphing, and as-is mode, and initiate the appropriate processing in each case, it is the most complicated of the modules. Its structure is:

do

1 Examine first two characters of next TEXT line (CODE).

2 If CODE eq '/$' (end of TEXT) then:
- **2.1** Call FINISH (to OUTPUT remaining text).
- **2.2** Set DONE=.TRUE. and exit.

3 If CODE eq '/' (as-is mode) then:
- **3.1** Call FINISH.
- **3.2** Output as-is line.

4 If CODE eq "/ + " (begin new paragraph) then:
   4.1 Call FINISH.
   4.2 Output a blank line.
   4.3 Begin LINE with new paragraph TEXT.
   4.4 Set flag for inserting blanks from the right.

5 If CODE is anything else then:
   5.1 Append next TEXT to LINE.

6 Remove excess blanks from line, and determine SL (size of line).

7 If SL is greater than output width then exit.
repeat

Subroutine EXPAND, which generates one or more elements of OUTPUT from a given LINE, will call on subroutine INSERT to actually insert the extra blanks. The algorithm is:

do
 1 Find, and record, positions of blanks in LINE.

 2 Call INSERT (if alignment is possible by inserting blanks) for alignment of one line of output.

 3 Adjust LINE by eliminating the part just used in (2).

 4 If size of LINE is less than width then exit.
repeat

The module structure of ALIGN is therefore as shown in Figure 6.2.

The next step in the design of this system is to determine the data elements needed by each module, and the data communication needed between modules. The details of the various modules cannot be developed, of course, until these data elements have been determined. On the other hand, the need for some data elements (e.g., control variables, various "auxiliary" variables, etc.) may not become apparent until this development is well under way. Therefore to some extent the process of program development and the perceived need for data elements occur interleaved and are simultaneously refined. However, the major data elements, both local and shared, should be determined at the outset. In this case module NXTEXT will need access to:

1 The array TEXT, and its "next" element.	(TEXT, NT)
2 The array OUTPUT, and its next element.	(OUTPUT, NO)
3 The string LINE, and its size.	(LINE, SL)
4 The width of an output line.	(W)
5 Two "flags."	(DONE,MODE)

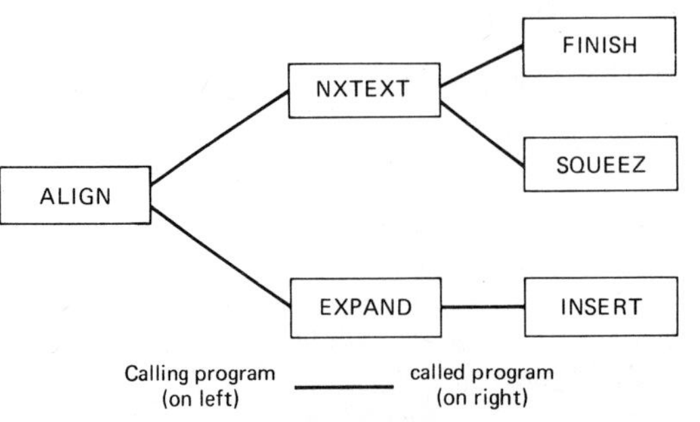

Figure 6.2. The modular structure of ALIGN.

DONE is set to .TRUE. at end-of-TEXT. MODE indicates right-to-left, or left-to-right blank expansion.

NXTEXT will need to pass to FINISH:

1 OUTPUT and NO

2 LINE and SL

and must pass LINE into SQUEEZ. EXPAND will need access to:

1 OUTPUT and NO

2 LINE and SL

3 W

4 MODE

and will pass to INSERT:

1 OUTPUT(NO)

2 Part of LINE

3 W

4 MODE

5 An array telling the position of the blanks in LINE (BLANKS).

Figure 6.3 depicts these arguments, and identifies which arguments are used as inputs to called programs, which are used as outputs (returning values to calling programs), and which are used as both.

The ALIGN system of programs has turned out to be more complex than might have been expected, since the problem is conceptually quite simple. However, reflection upon the various aspects of the problem—any number of blanks in any positions, paragraphing, arbitrary output width, as-is mode, and so on—tends to make this complexity seem reasonable. This sort of situation is, of course, ideal for modularization,

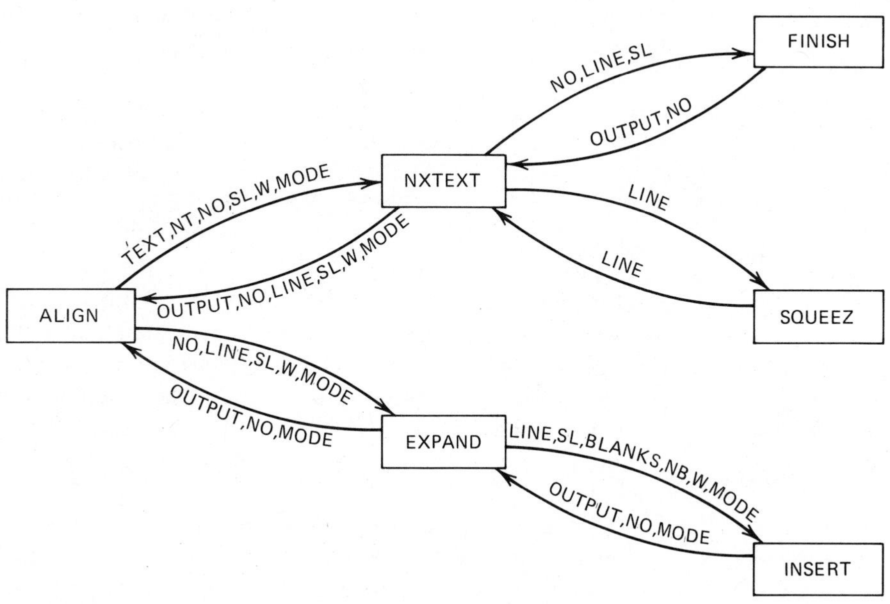

Figure 6.3. The "data flow" between the modules of ALIGN.

```
*....:-----------------------------------------------------------------
      SUBROUTINE  ALIGN (TEXT, OUTPUT, WIDTH)
                          INTEGER  WIDTH
                          CHARACTER  TEXT(1:*)*(*), OUTPUT(1:*)*(*)

*                          ..subroutine for aligning both
*                          the left and right margins of textual
*                          material. The "raw" text is in the array
*                          TEXT, and the "aligned" text is in the array
*                          OUTPUT. NT specifies the Next Text element
*                          to use, NO specifies the Next Output element..
*     ....constants....
      INTEGER  LOWER, UPPER
      PARAMETER  ( LOWER=20, UPPER=120 )

*     ....variables....
      INTEGER  NT, NO ,SL, W, MODE
      CHARACTER  LINE*240
      LOGICAL  DONE

*     ....execute....
      W = MAX(LOWER,MIN(WIDTH,UPPER))
      NT = 0
      NO = 0
      SL = 0
      MODE = 0
      DONE = .FALSE.
*                          ..DONE is used as loop exit condition..
      do
         CALL  NXTEXT (TEXT,NT,OUTPUT,NO,LINE,SL,W,MODE,DONE)
         IF  (DONE)  exit
         CALL EXPAND (OUTPUT,NO,LINE,SL,W,MODE)
      repeat
      END
=======================================================================
```

and the various modules of the ALIGN system illustrate quite nicely how such a problem can be decomposed into relatively independent modules. None of the modules of ALIGN is very long, and each can be analyzed rather easily.

The ALIGN system of programs illustrates two additional details pertaining to the use of Fortran subroutines. The first is the mechanism for passing arrays. In the ALIGN system three different arrays are passed at one time or another: TEXT, OUTPUT, and BLANKS. In each case the array bounds on the dummy arguments are (1:*). The asterisk for the upper bound signifies that the dummy array size (number of array elements) is the same as that of the associated actual argument array. This is the most common method of passing arrays in Fortran, although two other alternatives for specifying dummy array bounds are provided and these are discussed in the next chapter. The second observation is that subroutine INSERT receives access to only one element of array OUTPUT, not the whole array, and similarly only part of LINE is passed into INSERT. Thus, in INSERT, OUTPUT is a simple string variable associated with element OUTPUT(NO) in EXPAND, and has the same length (number of characters) as OUTPUT(NO); the length of LINE in INSERT is the value of BLANKS(1)−1, and is less than or equal to W.

Because of the nature of OUTPUT and LINE in INSERT, you should be especially careful that you completely understand everything about subroutine INSERT. In fact, this example was designed largely to present a subroutine like INSERT in a realistic setting. Not only does INSERT demonstrate some very fundamental things about argument associations, but it involves some data elements passed through several levels of CALLs. One way in which to study subroutine INSERT, and the behavior of its arguments, is to add some well-selected PRINT statements to it and then execute it for several sets of TEXT and WIDTH.

The last example of this section is the two-way merge sort, which is an efficient sorting algorithm for large data files (it sorts much faster than the bubble sort—but is a more complicated algorithm). Normally the merge sort is performed on a tape or disk-based data file, but for this example the data to be sorted will be an array of real numeric values. (In Part 3, where file processing is discussed, the merge-sort will be

```
*....:-----------------------------------------------------------------
      SUBROUTINE  NXTEXT (TEXT,NT,OUTPUT,NO,LINE,SL,W,MODE,DONE)
                      INTEGER  NT, NO, SL, W, MODE
                      CHARACTER  TEXT(1:*)*(*), OUTPUT(1:*)*(*), LINE*(*)
                      LOGICAL  DONE

*                               ..subroutine to obtain next data from
*                               TEXT sufficient for another line of OUTPUT.
*                               This subroutine also checks for end-of-TEXT
*                               (EOT), start of a paragraph (PARA), and
*                               unaligned mode (ASIS). Basically NXTEXT
*                               builds LINE from TEXT, and LINE is used
*                               in EXPAND. SL is the length of LINE..
*     ....constants....
      CHARACTER*2  EOT, PARA, ASIS
      PARAMETER  ( EOT='/$', PARA='/+', ASIS='/ ' )

*     ....variables....
      CHARACTER  TEMP*240, CODE*2

*     ....execute....(a loop to obtain enough TEXT for a line)
*                    two exits: one for end-of-TEXT (DONE set equal
*                    to .TRUE.), and one when enough text is
*                    obtained for another OUTPUT line
      do
          NT = NT+1
          CODE = TEXT(NT)(1:2)
          IF  (CODE .EQ. EOT)  THEN
*                              ..processing of TEXT finished..
              CALL  FINISH (OUTPUT,NO,LINE,SL)
              DONE = .TRUE.
              exit

          ELSEIF  (CODE .EQ. ASIS)  THEN
*                              ..process an "as-is" line
              CALL  FINISH (OUTPUT,NO,LINE,SL)
              NO = NO+1
              OUTPUT(NO) = TEXT(NT)(3:)

          ELSE
              IF  (CODE .EQ. PARA)  THEN
*                              ..paragraph by inserting a
*                              blank line (but no indenting)..
                          CALL  FINISH (OUTPUT,NO,LINE,SL)
                          NO = NO+1
                          OUTPUT(NO) = ' '
                          LINE = TEXT(NT)(3:)
                          MODE = 0
                  ELSE
*                              ..process a "regular" line of TEXT
                          LINE(SL+1:) = TEXT(NT)
              ENDIF
              CALL  SQUEEZ (LINE)
              IF  (LINE(1:1) .EQ. ' ')  THEN
                          TEMP = LINE(2:)
                          LINE = TEMP
              ENDIF
              SL = INDEX(LINE//'  ','  ')
          ENDIF
          IF  (SL .GT. W)  exit
      repeat
      END
=======================================================================

*....:-----------------------------------------------------------------
      SUBROUTINE  FINISH (OUTPUT,NO,LINE,SL)
                          INTEGER  NO, SL
                          CHARACTER  OUTPUT(1:*)*(*), LINE*(*)

*                               ..this subroutine outputs the remainder of
*                               LINE, without aligning the right margin.
*                               It is used at the end of TEXT, before a new
*                               paragraph, and before "as-is" text..
*     ....execute....
      IF  (SL .GT. 0)  THEN
              NO = NO+1
              OUTPUT(NO) = LINE
              SL = 0
      ENDIF
      END
=======================================================================
```

```
*....:------------------------------------------------------------------
      SUBROUTINE  EXPAND (OUTPUT,NO,LINE,SL,W,MODE)
                          INTEGER  NO, SL, W, MODE
                          CHARACTER  OUTPUT(1:*)*(*), LINE*(*)
*                               ..this subroutine generates as many
*                               expanded OUTPUT lines from LINE as
*                               possible. Prior to expanding a line,
*                               the positions of the blank characters
*                               in LINE are determined, and stored
*                               in the integer array BLANKS. Expansion
*                               is actually performed by a call to
*                               INSERT..
*     ....variables....
      INTEGER  L, BLANKS(1:60), NB
      CHARACTER  TEMP*240
*     ....execute....
      NB = 0
*                       ..main loop generates one line of OUTPUT..
*                       a single exit -- when the size of LINE is
*                       no longer greater than the OUTPUT width
      do
          do  L = W+1,1,-1
*                               ..this loop locates the positions of the
*                                                        blanks in LINE..
              IF  (LINE(L:L) .EQ. ' ')  THEN
                      NB = NB+1
                      BLANKS(NB) = L
              ENDIF
          repeat
          NO = NO+1
          IF  (NB .GT. 1)  THEN
                  L = BLANKS(1)
                  CALL  INSERT (OUTPUT(NO),LINE(1:L-1),BLANKS,NB,W,MODE)
              ELSE
*                           ..line can't be expanded..
                  L = W
                  OUTPUT(NO) = LINE(1:W)
          ENDIF
          TEMP = LINE(L+1:)
          LINE = TEMP
          SL = SL-L
          IF  (SL .LE. W)  exit
      repeat
      END
========================================================================
```

extended to the file environment.) The two-way merge sort is based on identifying the "runs" in the sequence of values to be sorted, and then the systematic coalescing of runs into ever-longer, and fewer, runs until the entire sequence is just one run and hence is sorted. A "run" is a sequence of nondecreasing values, that is, no value in a run is less than the preceding value. For example, in the sequence of values

32.8
77.7
19.3
6.5
12.7
29.9
83.1
55.9

there are four runs. The first has two elements (32.8 and 77.7), the second has just one element (19.3), the third has four elements (6.5 through 83.1), and the fourth is the last element (55.9). The merge sort "merges" (sorts) adjacent pairs of runs into single runs, thereby decreasing the number of runs in the data by half. After such an operation on the above data, the values would be in the order

```
*....:------------------------------------------------------------------
      SUBROUTINE  INSERT (OUTPUT,LINE,BLANKS,NB,W,MODE)
                                 INTEGER  W, MODE, BLANKS(1:*), NB
                                 CHARACTER  LINE*(*), OUTPUT*(*)
*                                    ..this subroutine determines the number
*                                    of additional spaces to add between each
*                                    pair of words and inserts these spaces as
*                                    OUTPUT is being generated from LINE..
*     ....variables....
      INTEGER  K, L, S, INSBLK(1:60), NBADD, NBPER, NBLEFT
*                        ..NBADD is the total number of blanks to add,
*                          NBPER is the number of extra blanks per word,
*                          INSBLK is an integer array containing the
*                          number of blanks to be inserted between
*                          words, and corresponds to the inter-word
*                          positions contained in BLANKS..
*     ....execute....
      NBADD = W-LEN(LINE)
      NBPER = INT(NBADD/NB)
      NBLEFT = NBADD-NB*NBPER
      do  S = 1,NB
          INSBLK(S) = NBPER+1
      repeat
      IF  (MODE .EQ. 0)  THEN
*                                    ..extra blanks inserted on right..
            L = 1
            K = NBLEFT
          ELSE
*                                    ..extra blanks inserted on left..
            L = NB-NBLEFT+1
            K = NB
      ENDIF
      do  S = L,K
          INSBLK(S) = INSBLK(S)+1
      repeat
      K = 0
      L = 0
      OUTPUT = ' '
*                      ..each execution of this loop places one word
*                        in OUTPUT, followed by the appropriate
*                        number of blanks..
      do  S = NB,1,-1
          do
*                   ..this loop transfers one word from LINE to OUTPUT..
            L = L+1
            IF  (L .EQ. BLANKS(S))  exit
            K = K+1
            OUTPUT(K:K) = LINE(L:L)
          repeat
          K = K+INSBLK(S)
      repeat
      OUTPUT(K+1:) = LINE(L+1:)
      MODE = 1-MODE
      END
========================================================================
```

19.3
32.8
77.7
6.5
12.7
29.9
55.9
83.1

There are only two runs in this sequence of values (of lengths 3 and 5), and merging them will complete the sort.

The two phases of the merge sort are (1) the identification of the runs, and (2) the merging of pairs of runs. The first phase, run identification, is normally achieved by using two auxiliary arrays (or files), the first to temporarily hold the odd-numbered

```
*....:------------------------------------------------------------------
      SUBROUTINE  TWOWAY (FILE, SIZE)
                        INTEGER  SIZE
                        REAL  FILE(1:*)

*                        ..this subroutine uses the two-way-merge-sort
*                        to sort the array of real numbers FILE.
*                        There are SIZE numbers in FILE to be sorted..
*     ....variables....
      INTEGER  SIZE1, SIZE2
      REAL  AUX1(1:10000), AUX2(1:10000)

*     ....execute....(repeats the SPLIT-MERGE combination until sort
*                                                      completed)
      do
          CALL  SPLIT (FILE,SIZE,AUX1,SIZE1,AUX2,SIZE2)
          IF  (SIZE2 .EQ. 0)  exit
          CALL  MERGE (FILE,AUX1,SIZE1,AUX2,SIZE2)
      repeat
      END
========================================================================

*....:------------------------------------------------------------------
      SUBROUTINE  SPLIT (FILE,SIZE,AUX1,SIZE1,AUX2,SIZE2)
                       INTEGER  SIZE, SIZE1, SIZE2
                       REAL  FILE(1:*), AUX1(1:*), AUX2(1:*)

*                           ..this subroutine implements the SPLIT
*                           phase of the two-way-merge-sort..
*     ....variables....
      INTEGER  N
      REAL  LAST, NEXT
      LOGICAL  DONE

*     ....execute....
      SIZE1 = 0
      SIZE2 = 0
      N = 1
      NEXT = FILE(1)
      DONE = .FALSE.
*                   ..one execution of the following loop causes a run
*                   to be placed in AUX1, and the next run in AUX2.
*                   This loop is exited when DONE becomes .TRUE.,
*                   which occurs when the end of FILE is reached..
      do
*         ........put next run in AUX1........
          do
              SIZE = SIZE1+1
              AUX1(SIZE1) = NEXT
              LAST = NEXT
              N = N+1
              IF  (N .GT. SIZE)  THEN
*                                 ..end of FILE..
                      DONE = .TRUE.
                      exit
              ENDIF
              NEXT = FILE(N)
              IF  (NEXT .LT. LAST)  exit
*                                    ..end of run..
          repeat
          IF  (DONE)  exit
*         ........put next run in AUX2........
          do
              SIZE2 = SIZE2+1
              AUX2(SIZE2) = NEXT
              LAST = NEXT
              N = N+1
              IF  (N .GT. SIZE)  THEN
*                                 ..end of FILE..
                      DONE = .TRUE.
                      exit
              ENDIF
              NEXT = FILE(N)
              IF  (NEXT .LT. LAST)  exit
*                                    ..end of run..
          repeat
          IF  (DONE)  exit
*         ..................................
      repeat
      END
========================================================================
```

runs (first, third, fifth, etc.) of the original array, and the second to temporarily hold the even-numbered runs. The second phase merges the first runs of the two auxiliary arrays (which merges runs 1 and 2 of the original array), then merges the second runs of the two auxiliary arrays (which merges runs 3 and 4 of the original array), and so on until all pairs of runs have been merged and the resulting sequence of values placed back into the original array. This two-phase process is repeated until only one run remains. (The term "two-way" merge sort is not due to the fact that there are two phases in the process but because the basic operation is that two runs are merged into one. It is possible to merge three runs into one, rather than two into one; that is the three-way merge sort. In general there is the *N*-way-merge sort, where *N* can be 2, 3, 4,. . . .)

The two phases of the two-way merge sort are to be implemented as subroutines called SPLIT and MERGE, and subroutine TWOWAY performs the sort by calling SPLIT and MERGE in the proper sequence. In this program FILE is the original array of data, SIZE is the number of elements of FILE to be sorted, AUX1 and SIZE1 are the first auxiliary array and its size (number of elements after SPLIT), and AUX2 and SIZE2 are the second auxiliary array and its size. Subroutine TWOWAY is quite self-explanatory. Subroutine SPLIT is also fairly simple.

Subroutine MERGE is also conceptually simple, but, because a number of possibilities must be provided for, this module turns out to be the most complicated in the TWOWAY system. The function of this module is fundamentally to merge two runs, one from AUX1 and one from AUX2, into a single run that is placed in FILE. One of the following four situations will ultimately occur during this fundamental process:

1 The end of the run in AUX1 is encountered, requiring the rest of the run in AUX2 to be transferred to FILE before processing the next pair of runs.

2 The end of the run in AUX2 is encountered, requiring the rest of the run in AUX1 to be transferred to FILE before processing the next pair of runs.

3 The end of AUX1 is encountered, requiring the rest of AUX2 to be transferred to FILE.

4 The end of AUX2 is encountered, requiring the rest of AUX1 to be transferred to FILE.

Any one of these four possibilities may occur at any time during the merging of AUX1 and AUX2. Moreover, while case 1 is being handled case 4 might occur, and, while handling case 2, case 3 might occur.

Thus the logic of MERGE has to correctly provide for all of these possibilities. Two additional modules are called by MERGE: FINRUN to take care of cases 1 and 2, and FINAUX to take care of cases 3 and 4. The structure of MERGE is then:

<initializations>
do

1 If next value in AUX2 is less than next value in AUX1 then:
- **1.1** Move AUX2 element to FILE.
- **1.2** If end of AUX2 then:
  - **1.2.1** Call FINAUX on AUX1.
  - **1.2.2** Set DONE=.TRUE.
- **1.3** If end of run in AUX2 then:
  - **1.3.1** Call FINRUN on AUX1 (which may encounter end of AUX1) and set DONE=.TRUE.
  - **1.3.2** If DONE then call FINAUX on AUX2.

2 If next value in AUX2 is not less than next value in AUX1 then:
- **2.1** Move AUX1 element to FILE.

```
*....:-----------------------------------------------------------------
      SUBROUTINE  MERGE (FILE,AUX1,SIZE1,AUX2,SIZE2)
                       INTEGER  SIZE1, SIZE2
                       REAL  FILE(1:*), AUX1(1:*), AUX2(1:*)

*                      ..this subroutine implements the MERGE phase
*                      of the two-way-merge-sort. It calls subroutines
*                      FINRUN and FINAUX when end-of-run and
*                      end-of-file situations are encountered..
*     ....variables....
      INTEGER  N1, N2, N
      REAL  LAST1, NEXT1, LAST2, NEXT2
      LOGICAL  DONE

*     ....execute....
      NEXT1 = AUX1(1)
      NEXT2 = AUX2(1)
      N1 = 1
      N2 = 1
      N = 0
      DONE = .FALSE.
*                    ..this loop merges the next run in AUX1 with
*                    the next run in AUX2. Merging is finished
*                    when DONE becomes .TRUE.
      do
          IF  (NEXT2 .LT. NEXT1)  THEN
*                                     ..take next value from AUX2..
                FILE(N) = NEXT2
                LAST2 = NEXT2
                N2 = N2+1
                IF  (N2 .GT. SIZE2)  THEN
*                                         ..merging finished..
                    CALL  FINAUX (AUX1,SIZE1,N1,FILE,N)
                    DONE = .TRUE.
                ELSE
                    NEXT2 = AUX2(N2)
                    IF (NEXT2 .LT. LAST2)  THEN
*                                                ..run finished..
                      CALL FINRUN(AUX1,SIZE1,N1,NEXT1,FILE,N,DONE)
                      IF  (DONE)  THEN
                              CALL  FINAUX (AUX2,SIZE2,N2,FILE,N)
                      ENDIF
                    ENDIF
                ENDIF
            ELSE
*                               ..take next value from AUX1..
                FILE(N) = NEXT1
                LAST1 = NEXT1
                N1 = N1+1
                IF  (N1 .GT. SIZE1)  THEN
*                                         ..merging finished..
                    CALL  FINAUX (AUX2,SIZE2,N2,FILE,N)
                    DONE = .TRUE.
                ELSE
                    NEXT1 = AUX1(N1)
                    IF (NEXT1 .LT. LAST1)  THEN
*                                                ..run finished..
                      CALL FINRUN(AUX2,SIZE2,N2,NEXT2,FILE,N,DONE)
                      IF  (DONE)  THEN
                              CALL  FINAUX (AUX1,SIZE1,N1,FILE,N)
                      ENDIF
                    ENDIF
                ENDIF
          ENDIF
          IF  (DONE)  exit
      repeat
      END
=======================================================================
```

```
*....:-----------------------------------------------------------------
      SUBROUTINE  FINRUN (AUX,SIZE,NA,NX,FILE,N,DONE)
                            INTEGER  SIZE, NA, N
                            REAL  AUX(1:*), NX, FILE(1:*)
                            LOGICAL  DONE

*                             ..this subroutine transfers the rest of
*                             the current run from AUX into FILE..
*     ....variable....
      REAL  LAST

*     ....execute....
      do
         N = N+1
         FILE(N) = NX
         NA = NA+1
         IF  (NA .GT. SIZE)  THEN
                DONE = .TRUE.
                exit
            ELSE
                LAST = NX
                NX = AUX(NA)
                IF  (NX .LT. LAST)  exit
         ENDIF
      repeat
      END
=======================================================================
```

```
*....:-----------------------------------------------------------------
      SUBROUTINE  FINAUX (AUX,SIZE,NA,FILE,N)
                            INTEGER  SIZE, NA, N
                            REAL  AUX(1:*), FILE(1:*)

*                             ..this subroutine transfers
*                             the rest of AUX into FILE..
*     ....execute....
      do  NA = NA,SIZE
         N = N+1
         FILE(N) = AUX(NA)
      repeat
      END
=======================================================================
```

- **2.2** If end of AUX1 then:
  - **2.2.1** Call FINAUX on AUX2.
  - **2.2.2** Set DONE=.TRUE.
- **2.3** If end of run in AUX2 then:
  - **2.3.1** Call FINRUN on AUX2 (which may encounter end of AUX2) and set DONE=.TRUE.
  - **2.3.2** If DONE then call FINAUX on AUX1.

3 If DONE then exit.

repeat

Figure 6.4 illustrates the module structure for system TWOWAY and Figure 6.5 diagrams the flow of data between these modules.

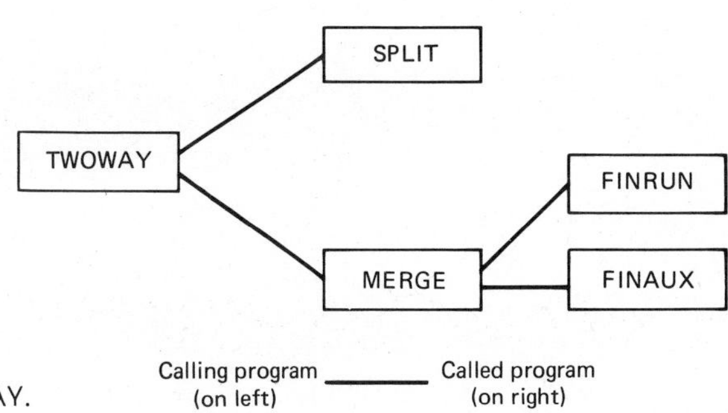

Figure 6.4. The module structure of TWOWAY.

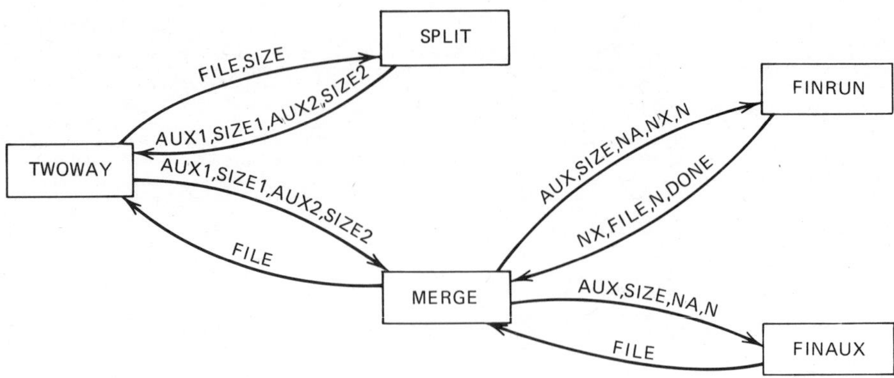

Figure 6.5. The "data flow" between the modules of TWOWAY.

These two examples, ALIGN and TWOWAY, complete this section on calling and called programs. These are good examples of practical, realistic programs, yet are reasonably short. They quite nicely illustrate both the rationale for modularization and the basic Fortran techniques for implementing modularization. Both involve more than one level of modularization and nontrivial passing of data between modules. Therefore, thorough understanding of these two examples represents considerable understanding of modularization, the calling of program units, and the passing of data between program units. Actually executing these programs for various sets of input data, with appropriate mainline programs and the addition of occasional PRINT statements, can be a very effective way of acquiring such understandings.

6.5 Summary

Programs may be organized into a main program and several subroutines. Each of these modules is a separate program unit, and may be developed quite independently of the others. A complex problem may be divided into a series of subproblems, each of which is relatively simple to solve and may be implemented as a subroutine. Such subdivision greatly facilitates the programming process since it facilitates concentrating upon just one aspect of the problem at a time.

Subroutines are complete Fortran programs, and have the form:

```
SUBROUTINE <subroutine name> (<dummy argument list>)
      <specification statements>
      <executable statements>
END
```

The only difference between this form and that of a main program is that the SUBROUTINE statement replaces the PROGRAM statement. The dummy arguments, although typed in declaration statements, do not represent actual data elements but are simply the names used in the subroutine for the actual data elements passed into the subroutine from the calling program.

A subroutine is executed upon execution of a CALL statement:

```
CALL <subroutine name> (<actual argument list>)
```

When a CALL statement is encountered during execution of a program, the specified subroutine is then executed in its entirety. Upon termination of execution of the subroutine, program execution resumes with the statement following the CALL statement. The <actual argument list> specifies the data elements being made available ("passed") to the subroutine. These may be constants, variables, array names (entire arrays), array elements, or (the value of) any legal Fortran expression.

Program modules may contain any data elements, specified in declaration statements. All such elements, not including those appearing in argument lists, are local to the module in which they are defined. Local data elements, unless passed in argument lists, are in no way known to, nor in any way affect, any other module, regardless of the names and types of such local elements. This insures the independence of modules and facilitates the independent development of each module.

Programming Exercises

6.1 Write a Fortran subroutine that accepts an array of integers and, without altering the array, determines the following:
(a) Location of the largest value.
(b) Location of the smallest value.
(c) Location of the first negative value (if any).
(d) Average value of the array values.
(e) Average magnitude of the deviation from the average value.

6.2 Write a Fortran subroutine that will accept an address (in the form of a simple character string) and prints out only those addresses having a certain zip code, say '41402'. The zip code will be the last nonblank characters of the string. For example, of the two addresses

```
'41402 Elm Plaza, Denver, CO 81420     '
'36 Park Pl., Apt. 2, Skokie, IL 41402 '
```

this routine should print out only the second.

6.3 Write a Fortran subroutine that makes change for a purchase for payment with a $20 bill. That is, the program computes the number of $10, $5, and $1 bills, and 50¢, 25¢, 10¢, 5¢, and 1¢ pieces to make the correct change from the twenty. The pattern of change pieces should be the "standard" one, which minimizes the number of pieces of change. For example, a purchase of $7.32 has change from a $20 bill of:

1—$10 bill	0—quarters
0—$5 bill	1—dime
2—$1 bills	1—nickel
1—50¢ piece	3—pennies

The input to the subroutine consists of the purchase amount.

6.4 Repeat problem 6.3, with the following three changes:
(a) There are no 50¢ pieces.
(b) There are $2 bills.
(c) The paid amount (which is to be another input to the subroutine) may be any amount (not just $20) greater than the purchase amount.

6.5 Electric power rates from a certain utility company are:
10¢/kwh for first 100 kwh
8¢/kwh for next 300 kwh
6¢/kwh for next 600 kwh
4¢/kwh for more than 1000 kwh
Write a Fortran subroutine that accepts a number of kwh consumed by a customer, and determines the cost of this energy and also the average cost per kwh in this case.

6.6 For the electric rates of Problem 6.5, write a Fortran subroutine that produces a table showing the average cost per kwh of electric energy, as a function of amount of consumption. For consumption amounts use multiples of 100 kwh. (Example points in this table: 200 kwh—9.0¢/kwh; 1000 kwh—7.0¢/kwh; 2000 kwh—5.5¢/kwh.)

6.7 Write a Fortran subroutine that determines if the value of a given character string is a legal Fortran identifier (must start with a letter, contain only letters and digits, and have no more than six nonblank characters). Note that blanks may be freely interspersed within a Fortran identifier.

6.8 A simple stock market model uses only three consecutive values of a stock, representing two intervals of activity of the stock. The model says that if in both intervals the stock value increased, and the second increase is greater than the first, then BUY (the stock is turning up). If in both intervals the stock value decreased, and the second decrease is greater than the first, then SELL (the stock is turning down). In all other cases WAIT—neither buy nor sell the stock. Write a Fortran subroutine that accepts three consecutive stock values and determines from this model whether to BUY, SELL, or WAIT on that stock.

6.9 A given character string is to be checked to see if it could possibly represent a legal Fortran assignment statement. A string is such a candidate if it contains an "=" character, and if the "=" is not:
(a) The first or last nonblank character in the string.
(b) Between the delimiting quotes of a string constant.
(c) Between matching left and right parentheses.
Write a Fortran subroutine that performs the required checking.

6.10 A real estate company has 40 salespersons, each of which is on monthly commission. Thus it is important to have a summary of total sales for each salesperson for each month. Write a Fortran subroutine that, given the number of salespersons, prints a nicely formatted summary of total sales for each. The subroutine should provide for the user to input all the individual sales data, one after the other, by supplying the salesperson number and the amount of that sale. These individual sales transactions may be supplied in any order.

6.11 Write a Fortran subroutine named CENSOR that will censor given text (the text is supplied as a character expression, and may be quite long). A list of forbidden words, supplied as an array of character strings, specifies the text words whose characters are to be replaced by a string of dots ('....' for a four-letter word, for example). Subroutine CENSOR should return the censored text.

6.12 A subroutine is desired to write "personalized" form letters. Such a subroutine could be primarily a series of PRINT statements containing the elements of the letter. However, the addressee, and the greeting part of the letter are to be specified by the user. Before producing the letter the subroutine should request the addressee information (four lines for name and address) and the desired greeting. Write such a subroutine, named LETTER. A typical output from LETTER might look like the following.

Reliable Computing, Inc.
Littleton, Ohio 48884
July 14, 1998

Louis W. Sowle, M.D.
16 Professional Plaza
Center Street, N.W.
Lockhall, NY 14617

Dear Dr. Sowle:

Sincerely,

B. William Lanton
President

6.13 Two numeric arrays, X and Y, contain a series of data points to be plotted on a graph. The X and Y coordinates of the *i*th data point are X(i) and Y(i), respectively. These points are to be *scaled* into a plot *window*. That is, the coordinates of the boundaries of the plot are given as the four values of XL, XR, YT, YB, which are the left X-value, right X-value, top Y-value, and bottom Y-value, respectively. The minimum value of X(i) should scale into XL and the maximum value into XR. Similarly, the maximum value of Y(i) should scale into YT, and the minimum value into YB. Write a Fortran subroutine that, given XL, XR, YT, YB and i returns XVAL and YVAL, which are the correct window values for the X(i), Y(i) data point. (Hint:

$$\frac{\mathrm{XVAL} - \mathrm{XL}}{\mathrm{X(i)} - \mathrm{XMIN}} = \frac{\mathrm{XR} - \mathrm{XL}}{\mathrm{XMAX} - \mathrm{XMIN}}$$

where XMIN and XMAX are the minimum and maximun values for X(i), respectively. Similar formulas hold for YVAL.)

6.14 Write a Fortran subroutine that accepts a long string of text, and outputs a list of the different words in the text and the number of times each word appears in the text.

6.15 Repeat Problem 6.14, but output the list in alphabetical (dictionary) order.

6.16 Suppose that an array of values is organized into exactly two runs. Simplify subroutine TWOWAY of this chapter and use it for this special case. (Considerable simplification is possible.)

6.17 Merge the two runs of Problem 6.16 without using any auxiliary storage. That is, your resulting subroutine should not use auxiliary arrays such as FILE1 and FILE2 in subroutine TWOWAY.

6.18 An especially simple case of merging two runs is the inserting of a single item into a sorted list. Write a subroutine that does this, in the spirit of Problem 6.17, without using auxiliary storage.

6.19 A carefully focused high-intensity microwave beam 10 meters in diameter is supposed to remain aimed at a stationary spot. To guard against the beam moving off target a circle of microwave sensors, each 1 centimeter wide, are tightly packed so that they form a circle 20 meters in diameter with the beam in the center. A warning is to be issued if any 10 contiguous (adjacent) sensors are activated. Write a Fortran subroutine that issues such a warning. Assume that each sensor governs the value of a numeric array element, that is used as input to the subroutine, in which 0 or less means the sensor is not activated and a positive value means the sensor is activated.

6.20 Two common methods of depreciating capital equipment is the straight-line (SL) method (equal depreciation each year) and the double-declining (DD) method (faster than SL). The annual SL depreciation is the life of the equipment (in years) divided into its original value. DD depreciation is a different amount each year, and is computed by dividing the remaining life (in years) into twice the current value (the current value is the original value minus all depreciation taken so far). Write a Fortran subroutine that, given the original value of an item of capital equipment, and its assumed life in years, will output a table showing the depreciation and value each year for both the SL and DD depreciating methods.

6.21 Write a Fortran subroutine that converts an array of numerical values (each in the integer range (0..100) to a corresponding array of letter values, according to the scale

91–100	A
81–90	B
66–80	C
61–65	D
0–60	E

6.22 Write a Fortran subroutine to compute the average value of an array of N given values. Each given value is one of the following:
A^+, A, A^-, B^+, B, B^-, C^+, C, C^-, D^+, D, D^-, E. In computing the average the single letter values correspond to numerical values

A → 4.0
B → 3.0
C → 2.0
D → 1.0
E → 0

A "+" on a letter makes its corresponding numerical value 0.3 higher, and a "−" makes it 0.3 lower. The numerical average is then converted as follows:

3.8–4.2 → A
2.8–3.2 → B
1.8–2.2 → C
0.8–1.2 → D
0–0.5 → E

The resulting average value has a "+" or "−" attached, as appropriate, if the numerical average is outside these ranges.

6.23 Write a Fortran subroutine that accepts an integer value and converts it to a corresponding character string of digits.

6.24 Repeat Problem 6.23, but for a given real value. An additional input value should be the number of decimal places to generate in the string.

6.25 Do Problems 6.23 and 6.24 "in reverse." That is, given a character string of digits, and possible decimal point, generate the corresponding numeric value.

6.26 The three major television networks, ABC, CBS, and NBC, compete intensely for the viewing market. And each year each network loses a percentage of its ratings to each of the other two networks. Suppose that these six percentages are known, along with each network's original share of the market. Write a Fortran subroutine that, given this information, will produce a chart showing each network's projected share of the market each year over the next decade. (Assume the six percentages stay constant over this period.)

6.27 Repeat Problem 6.26 but with the loss-percentages changing in the following manner from year to year. During a given year the loss-percentages of the network having the *highest* share of the market *increase* by twenty percent (e.g., a loss-percentage of 25 percent becomes 30 percent next year), whereas the loss-percentages of the network having the *lowest* share of the market *decreases* by 20 percent (e.g., 25 percent becomes 20 percent). The "middle" network's loss-percentages remain unchanged.

6.28 Write a Fortran subroutine INTER that returns the *intersection* of two given sets. A call to this subroutine would take the form
CALL INTER (SETA, NA, SETB, NB, RESULT, NR)
where SETA and SETB are two arrays containing the two given set elements, NA is the number of elements in SETA and NB is the number of elements in SETB. RESULT is an array to contain the elements of the intersection of SETA and SETB, and NB is the number of elements in the intersection. (The intersection of two sets are those elements that appear in both.)

6.29 Repeat Problem 6.28, but for the UNION of two given sets. The union of two sets is the collection of all elements that apear in either of the two; however those elements appearing in both of the given sets should appear only once in the union, not twice.

6.30 Write a Fortran subroutine that makes a frequency count of characters in a given long character string.

6.31 Write a Fortran subroutine, given a letter of the alphabet and any other character, prints a large block letter for the given letter using the other given character in the printing.

6.32 The following table shows the federal income tax rates for the various taxable income brackets.

Taxable Income (dollars)	Percent Tax within Bracket
0–500	14
500–1000	15
1000–1500	16
1500–2000	17
2000–4000	19
4000–6000	21
6000–8000	24
8000–10000	25
10000–12000	27
12000–14000	29
14000–16000	31
16000–18000	34
18000–20000	36
20000–22000	38
22000–26000	40
26000–32000	45
32000–38000	50
38000–44000	55
44000–50000	60
50000–60000	62
60000–70000	64
70000–80000	66
80000–90000	68
90000–100000	69
Over 100000	70

For example, on a taxable income of $15,000 the actual income tax would be $3520 (*not* .31*15000=$4650). Write a Fortran subroutine that prints a table, in increments of $2000 of taxable income up to $40,000, that shows the actual tax as a true percentage of income (for $15,000, this would be 23.4 percent).

6.33 A proposal to simplify income tax formulas, and eliminate welfare programs at the same time, calls for the income tax to be

```
(INCOME-BASE)/2
```

where INCOME is the taxable income and BASE is some fixed amount. BASE is the amount of income at which there is no tax due the government, and if INCOME is less than BASE then the formula determines the amount the government pays (rather than collects). Write a Fortran subroutine that prints a table, in INCOME increments of $2000 up to $40,000, showing the tax for each income value and the percentage this is of the income value. For a BASE value of $10,000 (for a family of four), compare this table with that of Problem 6.32.

6.34 Write a Fortran subroutine to "transpose" an array of strings. That is, replace the contents of the first array element with the sequence of first characters from each array element, the second array element gets the original second characters of each array element, and so on.

6.35 Write a Fortran subroutine that prints a calendar month in standard form. The input to the subroutine should consist of the day of the week on which the month starts, the number of days in the month, and some sort of month identification (name).

6.36 A Fortran subroutine, given an array of daily high temperatures for a month, returns another array giving the dates on which the highs were higher than a certain amount ("target" high). (This target high is also supplied as input to the subroutine.) Write such a subroutine, that also returns the number of days the target high was exceeded.

6.37 Each week Ryekoo Realty prepares a list of the weekly sales of each of their salespeople. Write a Fortran subroutine that, given this list of sales figures, returns the percentage of sales due to each salesperson, and also prints a listing of the sales amounts and corresponding percentages in order from largest amount to smallest.

6.38 In LineLand the inhabitants all live along a straight line, which is divided into equally spaced segments called LineLinks. LineLanders are an unpredictable bunch, with a random tendency, during the next LineTime interval, to move to the adjoining LineLink (either one, but never more than one LineLink away in one LineTime). Suppose that there is a 10 percent chance that a LineLander will move to one of its adjoining LineLinks during a LineTime, and 10 percent chance of moving to the other adjoining LineLink. And this is characteristic of every LineLander. In a little LineLand that is 1001 LineLinks long, that is initially empty of LineLanders except for an initial concentration of 10,010,000 in the center LineLink, approximately how many LineTime intervals are necessary before the population in any LineLink is no greater than twice the equilibrium value of 10000 LineLanders per LineLink. (Assume that LineLanders do not fall off of the ends of a finite LineLand.) Write a Fortran subroutine to simulate this behavior and determine the answer.

6.39 In a presidential candidate preference poll respondents are asked to indicate their preferences pertaining to a certain presidential candidate. This is to be done by giving integer scores according to:

5 — like enormously
4
3
2
1 — dislike intensely

These scores are collected and the total number of 5's, 4's, etc. are tabulated. This tabulation (five numbers) is given to a Fortran subroutine that prints this data in histogram form. On the histogram the average value of the data is also to be indicated. Write such a Fortran subroutine.

6.40 Write a Fortran subroutine which accepts an integer value in the range 1–99 and returns two character strings, one representing the integer value in binary (1 and 0 characters) and the other representing the integer as a Roman numeral.

6.41 Often large amounts of data is collected in which each "data point" consists of two values (the X-value and the corresponding Y-value). For example the data might consist of a large amount of observed cancer rates (Y-values) as a function of radiation level (X-values). Often there is an apparent relationship between the X-values and Y-values of a set of data, and a straight line through a plot of the data may be used to approximate and summarize this relationship. Such straight lines have the form

```
Y = A * X + B
```

where A and B are constants. The problem is to determine A and B, given a large number of data points (X,Y value pairs). Suppose that there are N such data points supplied with the X-values in an array X and the Y-values in an array Y. Furthermore, let

Σ(X) be "shorthand" for the resulting SUMX in:

```
SUMX=0
do I=1,N
      SUMX=SUMX+X(I)
repeat
```

Similarly for $\Sigma(Y)$, $\Sigma(X*X)$ and $\Sigma(X*Y)$

Then B is given by: $$\frac{N*\Sigma(X*Y) - (\Sigma(X))*(\Sigma(Y))}{N*\Sigma(X*X) - (\Sigma(X))^2}$$

and A is given by: $(\Sigma(Y) - B*\Sigma(X))/N$

Write a Fortran subroutine that, given N and the arrays X and Y, returns the corresponding values for A and B.

6.42 A nifty message coding method (but, alas, it's easy to break) is to "pair" the letters in the alphabet and to use the opposite letter of the pair in the coded message. The heart of an algorithm to perform such coding on the character string MESSAG is

```
IF (MESSAG(M) .EQ. LETTER (L)) THEN
      L = L+1
      L = L+2*(L/2*2-L)
      CODE(M) = LETTER(L)
ENDIF
```

Write a Fortran subroutine to perform such coding. One of the neat things about this code is that exactly the same subroutine, if given the coded message, will perform the decoding.

6.43 A loan is made in the amount BAL at a monthly interest rate of R, to be paid off with N equal monthly payments of amount PAY. The formula for determining what the amount PAY should be in this case is:

$$PAY = \frac{R*BAL*(1+R)**N}{(1+R)**N-1}$$

It is further stipulated in the loan contract that the unpaid balance may be paid in full at any time. Therefore a table is desired that lists the unpaid balance after each payment. Assuming payments are made regularly each month, the new balance after the next payment is related to the current balance by the formula:

BAL = BAL*(1+R) − PAY

That is, the new balance is the current balance, plus the interest for the month, minus the payment. Write a Fortran subroutine which, given R, N, and the initial BAL, prints the desired table. (Note that if *yearly* values are given for interest rate and loan duration, the appropriate value for R is one-twelfth the yearly rate, and the value for N is 12 times the number of years.)

6.44 Extend Problem 6.43 so that the table also shows the total amount of interest paid after each payment. The total interest paid is the total amount paid so far (number of payments times PAY) minus the amount of initial balance thus far retired (initial balance minus the current balance). Compare the interest paid on a 10 percent (yearly interest rate) $50,000 loan for loan durations of 10, 20, and 30 years.

6.45 A certain population model takes into account the approximate age of each individual by dividing the total population into age groups of equal time spans. Associated with each age group are the latest mortality (death rate) and fecundity (birthrate) data. Suppose that these data are given in three arrays, POP (elements are age-group population values), DEATH (age-group mortality values), and BIRTH (age-group fecundity values). Write a Fortran subroutine that uses these data to determine values for the array NEWPOP, the population distribution after such a time that each individual is (or would have been) in the next age group.

6.46 Repeat Problem 6.45 but with the population further divided into MALE and FEMALE groupings.

6.47 A rocket is moving through free space, without external forces acting upon it. It has main thrusters that can be fired to increase its forward velocity, and it has rotational thrusters that can be used to change its orientation in space. When a certain (stationary) destination is determined (such as docking with a space station) these rotational and main thrusters must be fired in proper sequence and amount in order to successfully approach that destination. Sensors are aboard the rocket that continually monitor the magnitude of the rocket's velocity (V), its direction (positive angle) with respect to the destination (A), and the distance to the destination (D). The desired velocity toward the destination has magnitude D, and therefore this component of the rocket's velocity must be changed by an amount DRV = D−V∗COS(A). If DRV is positive then the rocket must be rotated through an angle of A+ATAN(V∗SIN(A)/DRV); if DRV is negative then the rotation must be A+π−ATAN(−V∗SIN(A)/DRV); if DRV is zero then the rotation must be A+π/2. In each case the main thrusters must, after the rotation, be fired long enough to change the velocity by SQRT((V∗SIN(A))∗∗2+DRV∗∗2). Write a Fortran subroutine that, given V, A, and D, computes the proper values of ROTATE and THRUST. In actual practice this routine would be called repeatedly in order to continuously control the approach of the rocket to its destination.

6.48 *The Shell Sort.* The "Shell sort" is similar to the bubble sort in that the basic operation is to compare two values in the list and exchange them if necessary. However, unlike the bubble sort the compared values are not adjacent in the list (except on the last pass), and because of the clever selection of the compared elements much of the wasteful comparisons of the bubble sort are avoided. Thus the Shell sort is much more efficient, for long lists, than is the bubble sort, being comparable in efficiency to TWOWAY.

First of all, imagine the list to be sorted to have exactly 2^n elements, for some positive integer value of n (this is not strictly necessary—see Problem 6.50—but makes the problem somewhat conceptually simpler). Now divide the list exactly in two, and compare (and exchange if necessary) the corresponding two elements in each half. After this, elements 1 and HALF + 1 are in the correct order, elements 2 and HALF + 2 are in the correct order, and in general elements I and HALF + I are in the correct order. You now have 2^{n-1} sorted lists, each of length 2 and all "intermingled" with one another.

Now subdivide the list again, dividing each half in two so that you have four equal quarters of the original list, and sort each list of four corresponding elements (i.e., the first elements of each quarter form one four-element list, the second element of each quarter form another four-element list, and so on). Because each four-element list contains two sorted two-element lists, these can be efficiently merged to sort the four-element list. After m such subdivisions you have 2^m equal-sized blocks of the original list; you also have 2^{n-m} intertwined lists of 2^m elements each and each such list is composed of two sorted lists of 2^{m-1} elements each. An algorithm to merge the two parts of such a list of 2^m elements is:

```
*     N = 2** n is the total number of elements in the list
*     I = 2**(n−m)
      do   J = I+1, N
           do   K = J−I, 1, −I
                L = K+I
                IF  ⎧ (LIST(K) .LE. LIST(L)) THEN
                    ⎪           exit
                    ⎨ ELSE
*                   ⎩           exchange elements L & K
                ENDIF
           repeat
      repeat
```

An example of the application of the Shell sort algorithm is shown below.

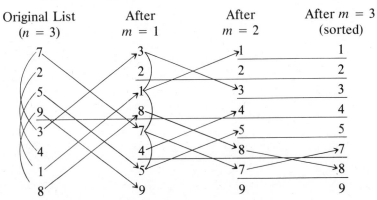

Original List ($n = 3$)	After $m = 1$	After $m = 2$	After $m = 3$ (sorted)
7	3	1	1
2	2	2	2
5	1	3	3
9	8	4	4
3	7	5	5
4	4	8	7
1	5	7	8
8	9	9	9

Write a Fortran subroutine SHELL (LIST, N) that performs the Shell sort on the LIST of N elements (assume $N = 2^n$).

6.49 How does the algorithm given in the preceding problem take advantage of the partially sorted nature of LIST?

6.50 What changes could be made in your SHELL subroutine (Problem 6.48) in order that it will work for any N (i.e., N not necessarily a power of 2). Verify your answer experimentally by executing your proposed subroutine on some test data.

Part

PROGRAM STRUCTURE

It is one thing to throw a program together and tinker with it until it ''works''; it is quite another to design and build a program that combines functionality with ''vitality.'' The former are the tar-paper shacks of programming—ugly, of limited use and little value, and often hazardous to users. The latter can be creations of esthetic value, providing versatile, reliable service, and having relatively high value and long-term usefulness. Programming is very much like architecture—an appropriate structure must be created that serves a specific purpose. A good programmer, like a good architect, thoroughly understands the problem at hand, knows what ''materials'' are available from which to construct, and has developed the ability to create an effective design.

In Part 1 (some of) the materials available to the Fortran programmer (features of the Fortran language) were introduced along with examples of their use in good program design. Emphasis was on effective design principles and use of language features, rather than upon a detailed analysis of every capability and limitation of every language feature introduced. In Parts 2 and 3 design principles will continue to be emphasized, and examples will continue to be used to illustrate effective Fortran programming. In addition, however, the features of Fortran will be more exhaustively examined, so that the Fortran programmer will know precisely the nature and limitations of the programming tools available.

To benefit most from this and Part 3, programming maturity at least to the Part 1 level is necessary. This includes firm understanding of the concepts and relevant Fortran provisions for data elements and their manipulations, specification versus executable statements, processing versus control statements, and program design and modularization. Successful well-structured completion of a representative set of programs similar to the programming exercises in Part 1 should signify adequate maturity.

Part 2 is concerned with *program structure*, and treats in considerable detail the Fortran provisions for achieving good program design and organization. The main tools here are Fortran's facilities for subroutines and functions, which are considerably more extensive than those described in Part 1. Other control structures are revisited or introduced, and concepts related to control structures are summarized. Special attention is given to the handling of ''pathological'' situations in the flow of control.

Certainly a major (and elusive) goal of programming is to produce ''correct'' computer programs—programs that do precisely what they are ''supposed'' to do, neither more nor less. The relationship between program structure and correctness is discussed briefly in the context of Fortran. One point is that the structure of a program should, in most instances, reflect the structural properties of the problem that is being solved by the program. Recursion is an important concept in this regard, and associated programming techniques are developed even though Fortran does not support recursion directly.

In short, therefore, Part 2 is a rather comprehensive treatment of concepts related to the structure of Fortran programs.

Chapter 7 Subroutines

The introductory treatment of subroutines in Chapter 6 leaves much unsaid about subroutines, particularly about subroutine arguments. There are provisions in Fortran to save local variable values between calls, other means exist for communication between calling and called programs beside actual and dummy argument lists, and associations between actual and dummy arguments need more explanation than given in Chapter 6. This chapter presents a comprehensive discussion of such subroutine features in Fortran.

7.1 Argument Association

When a subroutine execution is initiated, an "association" takes place between each subroutine dummy argument and its corresponding actual argument in the CALL. The actual argument is then used during that call wherever the dummy argument appears in the subroutine. Figure 7.1 illustrates the two principal techniques for passing arguments between separate program units.

In *call by value*, a copy of the actual argument (AA) value is used to initialize the value of the dummy argument (DA); the actual argument and dummy argument are two different data elements and the only connection between them is this initialization of the dummy argument value at the beginning of execution of the subroutine. In call by value, the value of the actual argument remains unchanged during execution of the subroutine, even though the value of the associated dummy argument may be changed.

In *call by address* (or call by reference, as it is sometimes known) the address of the dummy argument becomes the same as the address of the actual argument (i.e., the address of the actual argument, not its value, is passed into the subroutine). The

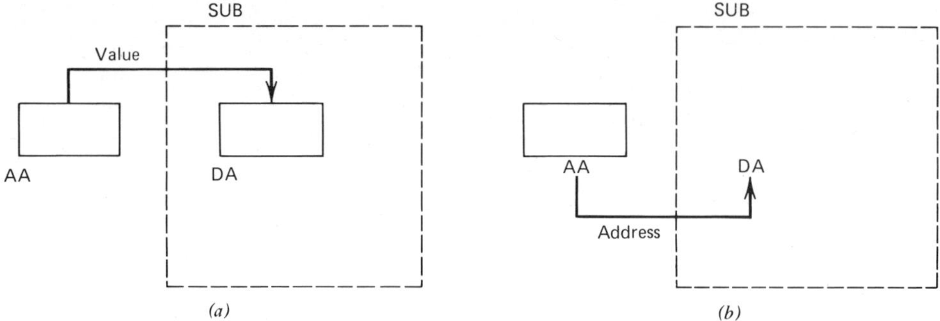

Figure 7.1. Argument passing techniques. (*a*) Call by value—the value of the actual argument (AA) is transferred, at the beginning of the call, to a different location accessed by the dummy argument (DA). The value of AA remains unchanged throughout execution of the subroutine, even though the value of DA might change. (*b*) Call by address—the address of AA becomes the address of DA. DA therefore references the same location as AA, and there is no "second" data element and the transferring of values. If the subroutine changes the value of DA, the same change occurs in AA since the two are precisely the same data element.

actual argument and the dummy argument therefore refer to precisely the same data element, and any changes the subroutine makes in the dummy argument are, of course, reflected as precisely the same changes in the actual argument. Therefore changes in the values of dummy arguments are "felt" back in the calling program as changes in the associated actual arguments passed by address. With call by value, such changes are not transmitted back to the calling program. If both call by value and call by address are available, then call by address would have to be used for all output arguments, otherwise the results of the call would not be available to the calling program. Call by value could be used for input arguments where the values of actual arguments are not to be changed—call by value will guarantee that these values remain unchanged. Of course, call by address can be used for input arguments also, but then the programmer must be especially careful to insure that unwanted changes do not take place in those actual argument values.

Fortran uses call by address exclusively, although in some instances the effect is the same as call by value. Dummy arguments may be variable names, but not any other form of expression. An actual argument, on the other hand, may be any expression legal in Fortran. If an actual argument is a variable name, an array element, or a substring then the call is by address. If an actual argument is any other form of expression, including a constant, then the call is effectively by value because Fortran does not allow the associated dummy argument in such instances to be assigned a value by the subroutine. (It is difficult for the processor to test for conformance to this rule; however, any program that does not conform to this rule is not consistent with standard Fortran, and the results of executing such a program may be unpredictable.) Figure 7.2*a* illustrates a typical way of implementing calls involving arbitrary expressions as actual arguments. At the beginning of the call each actual argument expression is evaluated and its value placed in a *temporary internal* location different from any data elements known to any program units. The address of this temporary internal is then passed to the subroutine and becomes the address of the associated dummy argument. Since the temporary internal location is in no way related to the data elements known to the calling program, any change in its value does not affect the calling program. Standard Fortran, however, prohibits the programmer from writing (standard conforming) subroutines that change the values of temporary internals for the reason sketched in Figure 7.2*b*. Values of constants may reside in locations that are equivalent to the temporary internals and whose addresses are passed into subroutines when the constants appear as actual arguments in the call. Changing such elements in the subroutine is obviously disastrous (since "constants" in the calling program could have different values before and after execution of the call).

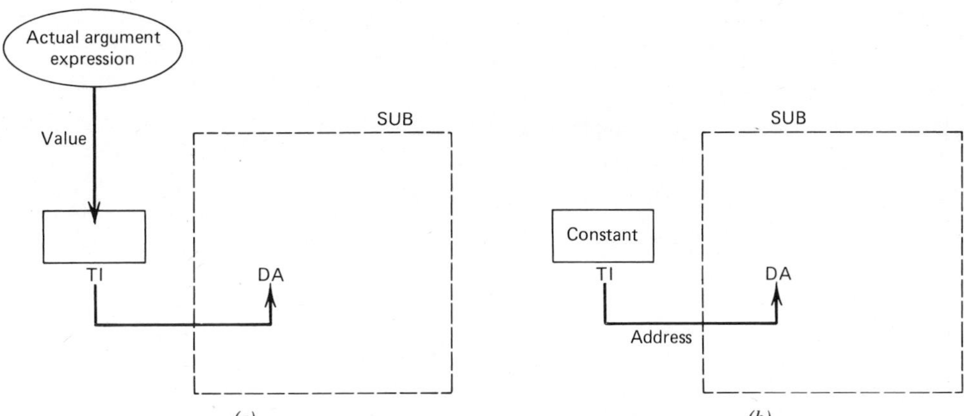

Figure 7.2. The use of temporary internal (TI) locations in argument handling. (*a*) Use of temporary internal locations for the passing of actual argument expressions. Even though what is passed is an address, the effect is that of call by value. (*b*) The passing of constants as actual arguments into a subroutine. Since changing constants must be prevented, Fortran allows values to be assigned to dummy arguments only for certain appropriate forms of actual arguments. (See text.)

Thus actual arguments other than variable names, array elements, and substrings are effectively passed by value and are therefore "protected," if the rules of standard Fortran are observed in writing the called program, from being changed by the subroutine.

In many Fortran implementations a simple technique can be used by the programmer to "force" call by value and its attendant protection of actual argument values. Variables, array elements and substrings used as actual arguments may individually be enclosed in parentheses, which causes them to be evaluated as expressions and the values passed accordingly. Thus CALL SUB (A, B, C) causes A, B, and C to all be passed by address. However, CALL SUB (A, (B), C) uses the expression (B) as an actual argument rather than the variable B, and hence B will in this case be effectively passed by value. (A and C will still be passed by address.) This technique can be used wherever the parentheses result in a legal Fortran expression (which is always the case if the argument is a variable, array element, or substring) and call by value is desired (which is usually the case for input arguments).

The Fortran programmer must thoroughly understand these association and argument passing mechanisms in order to use subroutines effectively. The normal call by address leaves data elements in the calling program "unprotected" and subject to change by the subroutine. Call by value protects such elements from such change. An inadvertently changed input argument could be the source of a very difficult-to-find bug. And since such mistakes do occur, a good rule of thumb is to use call by value whenever possible.

Achieving call by value is not possible when passing arrays, however, since "array expressions" are not legal in Fortran. The association of dummy and actual arrays adds a whole new dimension to the subject of argument association, and this is the topic of the next section.

7.2 Passing Arrays

Dummy arguments may be array names; the corresponding actual arguments may be either array names or array elements. In the first case the two arrays are associated by address, with the first (lowest subscripted) element of the actual array being that referenced by the first (lowest subscripted) element of the dummy array, the second element of the actual array corresponding to the second element of the dummy array, and so on. Figure 7.3 illustrates the nature of array association.

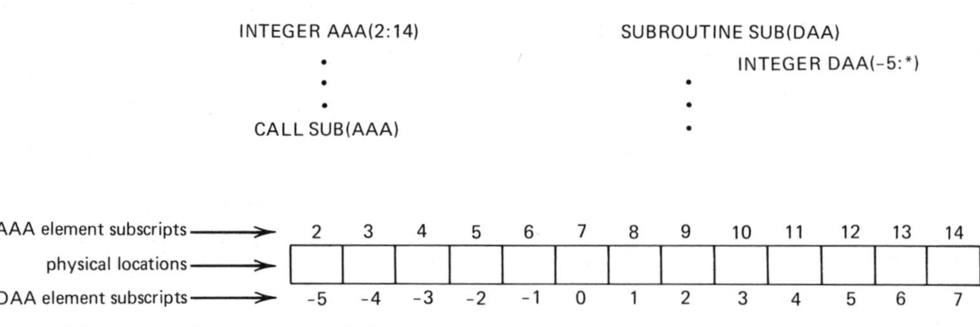

Figure 7.3. An example of array association.

The asterisk as the upper array bound of a dummy array argument (such as in Figure 7.3) makes the dummy array an *assumed size* array; that is, the number of elements in an assumed size array is the same as the number of elements in the actual array. Only dummy arrays may be assumed size arrays. If a dummy array is not an assumed size array then the specified size (number of elements) of the dummy array must not be greater than the size of the associated actual array.

The foregoing holds for character arrays when the length of the dummy array element is the same as the length of the associated actual array element. Although the data types of corresponding actual and dummy arguments (whether or not they are arrays) must be the same, in the case of character arrays the dummy array element length need not be the same as the element length of the associated actual array. If these lengths are not the same there is no one-to-one association between actual and dummy array elements; the nature of the association in these cases is shown in Figure 7.4. The limit on the size of the dummy array is that the total number of characters in the dummy array must not be greater than the total number of characters in the actual array.

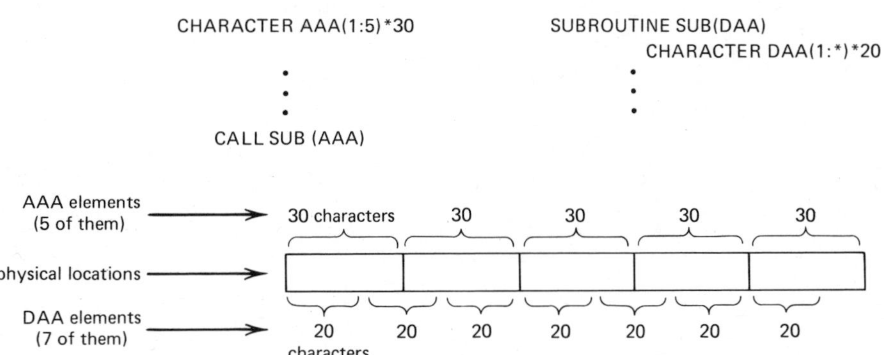

Figure 7.4. Association of character arrays with different element lengths.

If a dummy argument of type CHARACTER has an asumed length (an "*" in parentheses for the length) then the number of characters in the dummy argument is the same as the number of characters in the actual argument, and if the arguments are arrays then this rule applies to the array element sizes. A common (and recommended) method of passing arrays is to use the assumed-size feature of Fortran for the dummy argument arrays, and to use assumed length for the length of the character dummy arguments, whenever these features result in the desired association (which is most of the time). Subroutine ALIGN of Chapter 6, and the subroutines it calls, illustrate nicely the use of assumed-size (and assumed-length) dummy arguments.

When a dummy argument array is associated with an actual argument that is an array element (rather than an array name), the address of the specified array element is passed to the subprogram. An association is established between the actual and dummy arrays, but the "pairing" begins with the array element specified as the actual argument. That is, the first (lowest subscripted) element of the dummy array is associated with the actual argument array element, the second dummy array element is associated with the next actual array element, and so on. The dummy array cannot extend past the upper bound of the actual array, and if the dummy array is an assumed-size array this constraint is automatically observed. Figure 7.5 illustrates the association between arrays when the actual argument is an array element.

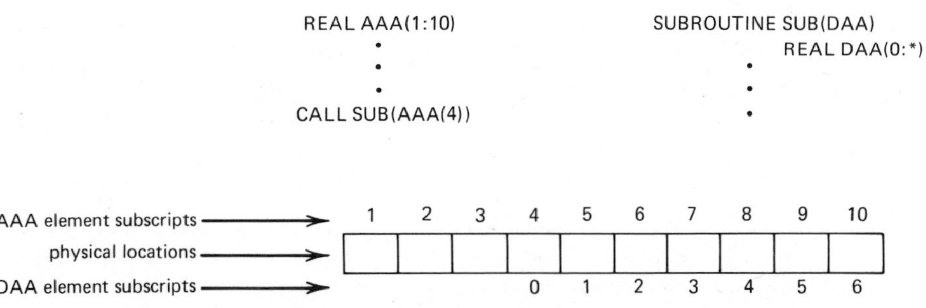

Figure 7.5. Example of array association when the actual argument is an array element.

In addition, in the case of character arrays, the actual argument may be a substring (of an array element). The association in this case is just like that shown in Figure 7.5, except that the association begins in the actual array at the substring specified in the actual argument.

Fortran has one final provision for passing arrays—dummy arrays may be *adjustable-size* arrays. In adjustable-size arrays the subscript bounds are explicitly specified, but with expressions containing integer variables instead of (or in addition to) integer constants. The integer variable(s) used to specify bounds on an adjustable-size dummy array must be variables of type INTEGER, which are dummy arguments in the same program unit. The adjustable-size provision allows the programmer to dynamically limit the bounds of dummy arrays, which is useful in connection with Fortran's requirement that all subscript values must be within the specified bounds. Figure 7.6 shows the use of adjustable-size dummy arrays.

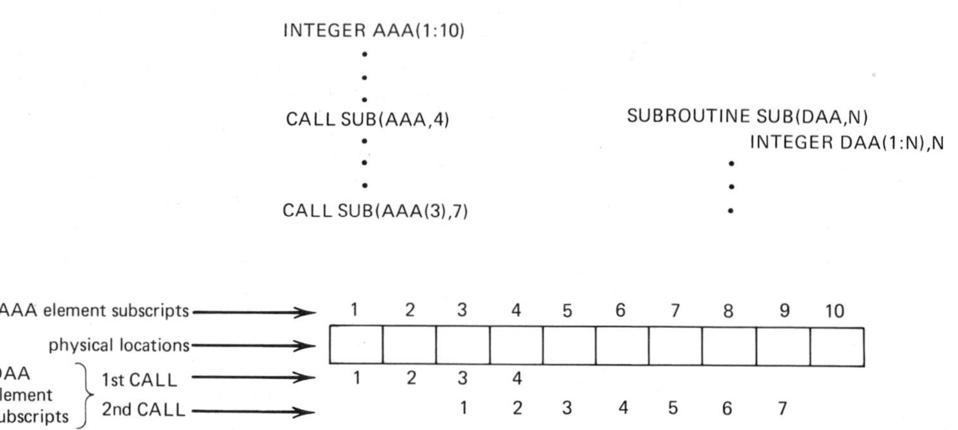

Figure 7.6. Examples of the use of adjustable-size arrays.

Of course, an adjustable-size array must not extend beyond the upper bound of the associated actual array, and it is the programmer's responsibility to see that this limitation is observed.

Local arrays may not be either assumed-size or adjustable-size arrays; local arrays must always be declared with constant bounds. Dummy arrays, and dummy arrays only, may, in addition to constant-size (like local arrays), be either assumed size (with the asterisk), or adjustable size. In Fortran, arrays can only be passed by address (as illustrated by the figures of this section) and therefore any changes that a subroutine makes in a dummy array is reflected in the associated actual array of the calling program. Another point for programmers to keep in mind is that standard Fortran prohibits subscripts from being outside the subscript range specified, and this applies to dummy arrays as well as local arrays, regardless of which of the three allowable methods (constant, assumed, or adjustable size) is used to establish the dummy array bounds.

7.3 The SAVE Statement

The SAVE statement has no connection with subroutine arguments, but it does provide for making additional input data available to a subroutine. The SAVE statement affects the definition status of local variables between executions of a subroutine and, in particular, on beginning the next execution of a subroutine.

Normally the values of local arrays and variables "disappear" on termination of an execution of a subroutine, and these values are not "saved" nor available on reexecution of the subroutine. The space used by these local data elements may, in fact, have been used by different local data elements, in different subroutines, between executions of this subroutine. The SAVE statement may be used to override this normal behavior, and to specify that values of local data elements be retained between executions of the subroutine and be available at the beginning of the next execution of the subroutine.

The form of the SAVE statement is

SAVE [<list of local variable and array names>]

All of the data elements identified in the list of the SAVE statement will be SAVEd between executions of the subroutine, and on reexecution of the subroutine they will have the same values that they had at the end of the previous execution of the subroutine. The list is optional, and if omitted (i.e., if just the word SAVE appears) then the values of all local data elements in that program unit are SAVEd. The SAVE statement is a specification statement, and its most logical location in the program is immediately following the declaration of the local variables. Also, since SAVEd data elements are defined at the beginning of each reexecution of the subroutine, initialization of such data elements for the first execution is usually needed. The DATA statement is an appropriate mechanism for such initializations. Therefore a logical sequence of specification statements in a subroutine containing SAVEd data elements is

```
. . . .local variables and arrays. . . .
<declaration of all local data elements>
SAVE <list of local data elements to be saved>
DATA <list of local data elements to be saved>       /
:     <initial values of data elements to be saved>  /
```

Although the programmer need not be concerned about the details of how the SAVE feature is implemented in a compiler, it is clear that SAVEd data elements must have their own unshared memory locations (like constants). Being local data elements, SAVEd values may not be available to any other program unit, even though the values are intact somewhere in memory. Conversely, SAVEd data elements may be actual arguments in calls to other program units, and if the call is by address then of course called programs may affect the SAVEd values. Dummy arguments are meaningful only by association with actual arguments, and therefore dummy arguments cannot be SAVEd.

A good example of the use of the SAVE statement would be in subroutine NXTEXT of the ALIGN example in Chapter 6. The integer variable NT is used in that program to specify which element of TEXT is the next one to process. Since the value NT must not be lost between executions of NXTEXT it was defined in the program calling NXTEXT (which is ALIGN) and passed into NXTEXT as an argument. Thus NT is local to ALIGN (not NXTEXT) and therefore is defined as long as ALIGN is in the process of being executed. However, the only use of NT is in NXTEXT, and hence it could be local to NXTEXT if its value is saved between executions of NXTEXT. Thus adding the statements

```
INTEGER NT
SAVE NT
DATA NT / 0 /
```

to the specifications of NXTEXT, and completely removing NT from ALIGN and the two argument lists, would give the same results as the form for ALIGN given in Chapter 6. Additional examples of the use of the SAVE statement will be given in subsequent chapters.

7.4 Passing Program Names

Occasionally a program unit name must be passed as an actual argument, and the associated dummy argument then used in a subroutine (or function) call. Thus Fortran allows

```
SUBROUTINE SUB1 (. . ., SUB2, . . .)
:
:
CALL SUB2 (. . .)
:
```

In such a case the actual parameter for SUB2, when SUB1 is called, must be either a dummy argument of the calling program or a name that has been identified in the calling program as a program name instead of a variable name. If this program name is the name of an intrinsic function then it must appear in an INTRINSIC statement in the program calling SUB1; if it is the name of an external program (subroutine or external function) then it must appear in an EXTERNAL statement. INTRINSIC and EXTERNAL statements are both specification statements (in a sense they are type statements, as they identify names as program names rather than as variable names) and have the forms

```
INTRINSIC <list of intrinsic function names used as actual arguments>
EXTERNAL <list of external program names used as actual arguments>
```

For example, suppose that subroutine AVE (for average) is to be designed to compute an approximation to the average of any given function, between any two specified limits. The structure of AVE could be:

```
      SUBROUTINE AVE (F, LEFT, RIGHT, RESULT)
                        REAL LEFT, RIGHT, RESULT
*     . . . .local variables. . . .
          .
          .
          .
*     . . . .execute. . . .
          .
          .
          .
        SUM = SUM + F(X)
          .
          .
          .
        RESULT = SUM/N

      END
```

Here F is the name of the function to be used, LEFT and RIGHT define the interval for the argument of F over which the (approximate) average of F is to be computed, and the resulting average is to be returned as the value of RESULT. (SUM, X, and N are assumed to be local variables.) The program calling AVE might contain:

```
.
.
.
INTRINSIC SIN, COS, EXP
.
.
.
CALL AVE (SIN, 0.0, PI/2, SINAVE)
.
.
.
CALL AVE (COS, PI/4, PI/3, COSAVE)
.
.
.
CALL AVE (EXP, 0.0,2.0, EXPAVE)
.
.
.
```

In this case the intrinsic functions SIN, COS, and EXP, respectively, will be used for F in the three successive executions of AVE.

If programmer-defined functions (see Chapter 8) are to be passed, then their names would be declared as EXTERNAL names (rather than INTRINSIC names) in the calling program. Subroutine names can also be passed as actual arguments. Since all subroutines are programmer defined (there are no intrinsic subroutines in standard Fortran), passed subroutine names must be declared in EXTERNAL statements.

7.5 COMMON and BLOCK DATA

Another method of communicating data between program units, in addition to argument lists, is provided in Fortran. *Global* data areas, called *common blocks* and defined by COMMON statements, may be used for such communication instead of (or in addition to) argument lists. A common block may be declared for a program unit with the specification statement

```
COMMON [/<name>/] <list of variable and array names>
```

Then the global data area identified by <name> is accessible to that program unit, and the data elements of that common block are known in that program unit by the names in the list. In the case of a called program, the effect is very much as if the <list of variable and array names> had been included in the dummy argument list, passed by address.

A common block can be thought of as a sequence of data element storage units (see Chapter 13) or memory locations. It is this sequence that is made accessible to the program unit when the COMMON statement is used. The COMMON <name>s are not local to a program unit, but are recognized by all program units in (i.e., are global to) a system of programs. A unique <name> is associated with each common block, and serves as the identification for that block, except that one such block may remain unnamed and is referred to as "blank" COMMON. The programmer may choose any desired names for the COMMON blocks.

One difference between passing data via COMMON and via argument lists is that with COMMON the associated data names in the calling and called programs do not have to be of the same type. Thus, for example, with COMMON a given storage location may be treated as an integer data element in one program unit and as a real data element in another program unit. Normally such "cross-type association" is to be carefully avoided, and it is the programmer's responsibility to see that the types of associated names match when using COMMON, just as they must match in actual and dummy argument lists. One restriction placed on COMMON, in order to avoid disastrous cross-type-association, is that a common block containing any elements of type CHARACTER must contain elements only of type CHARACTER. The <list of variable and array names> in a COMMON declaration must not contain any of that program unit's dummy argument names. It may freely contain array names, however, in which case the arrays, in their entirety, are located in the common block in the sequence specified.

Elements specified to be in COMMON must not also be initialized in that program unit in DATA (or PARAMETER) statements. The BLOCK DATA subprogram is provided to initialize COMMON variables at compile time. Normally the BLOCK DATA subprogram contains only COMMON statements (declaring the common blocks that are to be initialized), type statements (declaring the types of the names, and dimensions of arrays, appearing in the COMMON lists), and DATA statements (specifying the initial values of common block elements). This is the only instance (in BLOCK DATA subprograms) where common block elements may be initialized via DATA statements. The following example illustrates the use of common blocks in calling and called program units, and the use of BLOCK DATA to initialize common block elements.

```
      PROGRAM COMEX
         .
         .
         .
      REAL A, B, C
      INTEGER P, Q, R, S
      COMMON A, B, C
      COMMON /LIMITS/ P, Q, R, S
*     using two common blocks—one blank and the other named "LIMITS"
         .
         .
      CALL COMSUB
         .
         .
         .
      CALL COMSUB
         .
         .
         .
      END

      BLOCK DATA
*     . .all common block variables are given initial
*       values at compile time, except
*       the second element in blank COMMON
*       and the fourth element in the
*       COMMON block labeled /LIMITS/
      REAL A, B, D
      INTEGER N, O, P, Q
      COMMON A, B, D
      COMMON /LIMITS/ N, O, P
      DATA N, O, P /40,0,-10/,
     :      A, D /-1.0,2.718/
      END
```

```
      SUBROUTINE COMSUB
         REAL X, Y, Z
         INTEGER I, J, K, L
         COMMON X, Y, Z
         COMMON /LIMITS/ I, J, K, L
              .
              .
              .
*     . .all variables shown are passed through the two
*       common blocks, with the associations: A-X
*                                             B-Y
*                                             C-Z
*                                             P-I
*                                             Q-J
*                                             R-K
*                                             S-L
              .
              .
              .
      END
```

There are two principal uses of COMMON. One is in those rare cases when cross-type association is desired. Such association is not illustrated in the above example. The other, which is illustrated above, is when a program issues two or more calls to a subprogram. If argument lists are used to translate data between the calling and called programs, then each call would need an actual argument list. With COMMON, the list may need to be written only once, as a COMMON statement. This is especially useful if the argument list is very long, and identical for each call. In all other cases the use of argument lists, rather than COMMON, is the preferred way to transmit data between program units.

7.6 EQUIVALENCE

Fortran allows two (or more) data element names within the same program unit to be associated. This association is in many respects like that for COMMON association, and therefore is discussed here even though it has nothing to do with association between program units. Association of names within a program unit is called *equivalencing*, that is, one storage location is known in the program unit by two (or more) different names.

The EQUIVALENCE statement is used to cause equivalencing of two or more names in a program unit. For example the statements

```
INTEGER I, J, K
REAL X, Y
EQUIVALENCE (X, Y), (I, J, K)
```

in a program unit cause exactly two data elements to be allocated. One is an element of type REAL, and is known by either of the names X or Y. The other data element is of type INTEGER, and simultaneously has three different names, I, J, and K. The general form of the EQUIVALANCE statement is:

EQUIVALENCE (<list of names>) [,(<list of names>), . . .]

The main use of EQUIVALENCE is to "overlay" two large arrays, thereby reducing the storage requirements of the program. For example, the statements

```
REAL A(1:1000), B(1:1000)
EQUIVALENCE (A, B)
```

cause the arrays A and B to refer to exactly the same locations, with A(1) being the same data element as B(1), A(2) the same element as B(2), and so on. By specifying specific array elements, rather than unsubscripted array names, in the EQUIVALENCE list, two arrays can be associated but "offset." For example, if the above EQUIVALENCE statement were changed to

```
EQUIVALENCE (A(7), B(2))
```

then A(7) and B(2) would refer to the same data element, A(6) would be associated with B(1), A(8) would be associated with B(3), and so on.

The names of the elements in an EQUIVALENCE list need not be of the same type, although CHARACTER names cannot be equivalenced with names of numeric or logical types. But an integer array and a real array, for instance, may share the same storage. The statements

```
INTEGER P(1:1000)
REAL Q(1:1000)
EQUIVALENCE (P,Q)
```

cause arrays P and Q to share the same storage locations. If storage is in short supply, and arrays P and Q aren't needed at the same time in the program, then using EQUIVALENCE in this way to make storage do "double duty" may be warranted. Note, however, that arrays so equivalenced cannot exist with meaningful values simultaneously. When P is being used, the values of Q are meaningless, and vice-versa.

In these days of relatively abundant physical storage facilities and virtual memory systems, the need for saving storage by overlapping arrays is much less than in earlier times when the equivalencing feature was incorporated in Fortran. When sufficient memory is available, which it almost always is now, it is best to use completely separate storage for different arrays. Then errors due to (inadvertent) misuse of equivalenced elements (such as assigning a value to an element of P, when Q is "active") are avoided. Moreover, using two different names for the same (size and type) array is rarely now considered to be good programming practice. Therefore, EQUIVALENCE is rarely used now in well-structured programs, unless very large arrays are involved, storage is in short supply, and the greatest possible execution efficiency is required.

7.7 Multiple Entry, Alternate Return

A subroutine (or function) may have more than one *entry point*, each with a unique name. Ordinarily entry into a subroutine is "through the top" (i.e., the SUBROUTINE statement) of the subroutine, and the entire body of the subroutine is executed. The ENTRY statement provides for alternate entry points, which allows execution of a program unit to begin at (almost) any desired executable statement. The ENTRY statement appears just before the executable statement where execution is to begin for that particular entry. The form of the ENTRY statement is precisely the same as for a subroutine statement (complete with entry point name and dummy argument list) except that the word ENTRY is used in place of the word SUBROUTINE. All entry point names (including the subroutine name) must be unique, and the dummy argument lists may be different for each entry point. CALL statements may use ENTRY names, and the actual argument list must correspond to the dummy argument list associated with the specified entry name. Entry points must not occur in the middle of IF-ENDIF structures or DO-loops, and dummy arguments must not be used in executable statements prior to their appearance in dummy argument lists. Because of this plethora of rules and restrictions regarding multiple entries, the use of alternate entry points is discouraged as a general practice. However, there are occasional times when an application involves closely related routines that employ similar data elements and/or processing; in such instances having separate entry points into a single subroutine may be justified over having separate subroutines with much duplicated code.

Analogous (but unrelated) to multiple entry into a subroutine is alternate return from a subroutine. An alternate return from a subroutine is a return point in the calling program different from the statement following the call to the subroutine. Any labeled executable statement in the calling program may serve as an alternate return point. The labels of such points are passed as actual arguments in the CALL statement by having them appear as elements of the argument list in the form

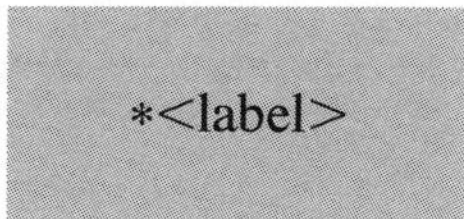

Any number of such labels may appear in an actual argument list. The associated dummy argument for each is simply an asterisk ("*"). An alternate return is processed by executing the RETURN statement, which has the form

RETURN <integer expression>

The value of the <integer expression>, which must be positive and not greater than the number of * dummy arguments, specifies which alternate return is to be taken. The leftmost * dummy argument corresponds to RETURN 1, the next * to the right corresponds to RETURN 2, and so on. The return point is the actual argument label associated with the * dummy argument specified in the RETURN statement. The use of alternate returns is not recommended. In instances where selective processing is needed upon return from a CALL, the superior method is to pass information back to the calling program so that an IF-ENDIF structure following the CALL can be used to control the processing.

7.8 Summary

This chapter treats subroutines in detail and together with the preceding chapter constitutes a thorough introduction to the characteristics and use of the Fortran subroutine facilities. The basic concept of program modularization is quite straightforward and uncomplicated. However, the technical "heart" of subroutines is in the handling of subroutine data elements, and the association of data elements between program units. Therefore this chapter has concentrated principally upon these aspects of subroutine design and application.

The concept of argument association is the main topic of this chapter. This involves associating the dummy argument names with the actual argument data elements. Dummy arguments normally do not represent their own data elements, but are merely the names by which the corresponding actual argument elements are known in the subroutine. In argument lists the type of a dummy argument name must be the same as the type of the associated actual argument. Association through COMMON is similar in many respects to association through argument lists, except that the association in COMMON is between storage sequences, rather than individual actual argument–dummy argument pairs, and hence COMMON allows association between different types. However, COMMON association between type CHARACTER and any other type is prohibited. COMMON lists may contain only CHARACTER types, as or only non-CHARACTER types. Argument lists may contain any mix of CHARACTER and non-CHARACTER types, as long as the associated list has the same mix of types. Arrays may be freely used in argument lists and in COMMON.

In Fortran actual arguments are always passed by address. For nonarray arguments, however, the characteristics of pass by value may be achieved by enclosing the actual argument in parentheses, or by forming any legal expression other than just a simple variable name. Since Fortran does not have array expressions, arrays must always be passed by address. Since the subroutine can arbitrarily modify the value of any data element passed by address, the programmer must take care to insure against any unwanted such modification.

Eight Fortran statements have been introduced in this chapter. They are the

SAVE
INTRINSIC
EXTERNAL
COMMON
BLOCK DATA
EQUIVALENCE
ENTRY
RETURN

statements. The SAVE statement allows the programmer to specify that data elements local to a subroutine remain defined between executions of the subroutine. The INTRINSIC (EXTERNAL) statement is used to declare names as intrinsic functions (programmer-written subprograms) when these names are used as actual arguments in that program unit and refer to procedures rather than data elements. The COMMON statement defines the COMMON data area(s) for that program unit, and BLOCK DATA is a subprogram whose only function is to provide compile-time initializations to data elements in COMMON blocks. the EQUIVALENCE statement allows the programmer to assign two or more names, in the same program unit, to a data element, and is used principally to overlay large arrays to save storage space. The ENTRY statement allows the programmer to provide additional entry points into a subroutine. The ENTRY statement is exactly like the SUBROUTINE statement, including a dummy argument list (which may be different from the SUBROUTINE statement argument list), but the word ENTRY is used in place of the word SUBROUTINE, and the ENTRY statement is located in the executable part of the program at the desired entry point. And, finally, Fortran provides for alternate return points from a CALL, and the RETURN statement is used to specify return to such a point rather than to the statement following the CALL.

Programming Exercises

7.1 Write a subroutine SUBV that has three dummy arguments, X, Y, and Z, of type INTEGER, in which values are assigned to all three during execution of the subroutine. Then write a calling program, with integer variables J, K, and L, and make the call
CALL SUBV(J,K,L)
Run test programs to:
(a) Verify that the changes specified in the SUBV are in fact transmitted back to J, K, and L.
(b) See whether J, K, and L can be used as both input and output arguments (i.e., the values given in SUBV may depend on the original values of J, K, and L).

7.2 Change the CALL of problem 7.1 to
CALL SUBV(J,(K),J+L)
(a) Will your computing system allow SUBV to change the values of Y and Z, even though this violates the Fortran rules?
(b) If the answer to (a) is "yes" (as it probably is), what changes made in SUBV are in fact transmitted back to the calling program?

7.3 In Problem 7.1, change K and L to be REAL variables, leaving everything else the same as specified in Problem 7.1.
(a) When the program is executed, are the values of K and L changed by the subroutine?
(b) If the answer to (a) is "yes," are the values received by K and L the ones assigned in SUBV?

7.4 Write a subroutine SUBA that has a single dummy argument that is an assumed-size integer array P, and that assigns values to the first 10 elements of P. Write a program calling SUBA that has an integer array B whose subscripts range from −5 to 27. If the call to SUBA has the form
CALL SUBA(B)
which elements of B are affected by the assignments to P in SUBA? Executing your program should clearly show this association.

7.5 Repeat Problem 7.4 with the call
(a) CALL SUBA (B(1))
(b) CALL SUBA (B(15))
(c) CALL SUBA (B(−5))

7.6 Modify the ALIGN system, as suggested in the text of this chapter, to incorporate NT as a local SAVEd variable in NXTEXT. Then test the new version of ALIGN to verify that it still works properly.

7.7 Repeat Problem 7.6, but omit the statement
SAVE NT
from subroutine NXTEXT. Does ALIGN still work on your computing system? (In general it shouldn't, but on some systems some local variables may continue to exist between subroutine executions even though saving them was not specified in SAVE statements.)

7.8 In the TWOWAY example of Chapter 6, and especially in subroutine MERGE, a number of calls are made to subroutines in which the argument lists are identical, or nearly so. Modify the TWOWAY system to utilize COMMON in order that the duplication in argument lists is eliminated, and that the argument lists contain only those elements that are different in the various calls.

7.9 Use EQUIVALENCE between a LOGICAL variable and an INTEGER variable to determine the integer equivalent of the machine form in which .TRUE. and .FALSE. are implemented on your computing system.

7.10 Repeat Problem 7.9, but use COMMON to establish the association rather than EQUIVALENCE. That is, using COMMON and two program units, associate a LOGICAL variable and an INTEGER variable—for example, assign .TRUE. to a logical variable, then call a subroutine in which an integer variable occupies the same COMMON location, and in the subroutine print the value of the integer variable.

7.11 Repeat Problem 7.10 using argument lists instead of COMMON. Does this work on your system?

Chapter 8 Functions

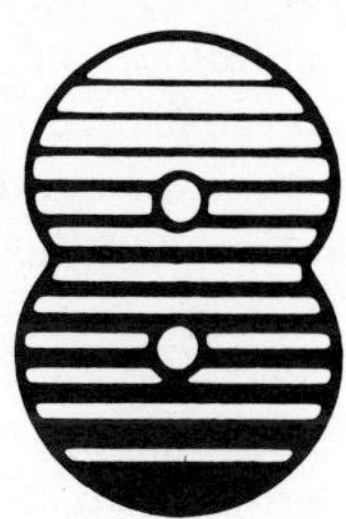

In addition to subroutines, Fortran provides a second form of program unit, the external function, that can be called from another program unit. Whereas the subroutine is simply a mechanism for modularizing programs, the function is a program module with a value associated with it. Functions are most often used when a single value is to be returned to the calling program. This concept is a familiar one, since intrinsic functions (which are simply prewritten external functions that are "built in") are used for precisely this purpose. Thus, for example, INDEX returns the location of a matched substring, and INT returns the integer part of a real value.

The only differences between functions and subroutines are due to the fact that a value is associated with a function name and not with a subroutine name. First, since a function has a value it must also have a data type; therefore the type of an external function must be specified in the function definition and in the program unit calling the function. Second, upon execution of a function, the desired value must be assigned to the name of the function before returning to the calling program. And third, a function is called not by using a CALL statement but by referencing the function name in an expression; the effect is the same as if the associated function value appeared in the expression in place of the function name.

This chapter describes these aspects of function definition and use, and contains illustrative examples of the application of Fortran functions.

8.1 The FUNCTION Statement

The form of a Fortran function is precisely the same as that of a subroutine, except that it begins with a FUNCTION statement rather than a SUBROUTINE statement, and the desired value (the resulting function value) is assigned to the function name (as if the function name were a simple variable) before returning from the function. The form of the function statement is

> [<type>] FUNCTION <name> ([<dummy argument list>])

The argument list may be empty, or may contain any of the same elements as a subroutine argument list except asterisks for alternate return specifiers. The function name may be any unique Fortran name, and the type may be any Fortran type (e.g., INTEGER, REAL, CHARACTER, LOGICAL). Type CHARACTER must include a length specification (otherwise the length is 1) with the word CHARACTER. These lengths may not involve the symbolic names of constants, but otherwise may be any legal form of length specification, including "(*)". If CHARACTER*(*) FUNCTION is specified then the length of the returned value will be the length of the (last) character value assigned to the function name during its execution.

The FUNCTION statement is the first one in the program unit, and, of course, identifies the program unit as an external function. Function names are global (i.e., known to all program units in the system) and must be unique. A function name may not be chosen that is identical to the name of an intrinsic function. An external function may optionally have one or more entry points, identified by ENTRY statements as described in Chapter 7.

Three kinds of program units have been described —PROGRAMs, SUBROUTINESs, and FUNCTIONs (four, if BLOCK DATA subprograms are included). PROGRAMs are main program units, capable of being executed by issuing a suitable command (e.g., .EXECUTE <name>) to the computing system. SUBROUTINEs and FUNCTIONs must be called by other program units and thus are called *subprograms*, or *procedures*. A system of programs that is used to solve a given problem contains exactly one main program and any number of subprograms. Typically the procedures are the modules into which the problem has been divided, each module representing one logical segment of the problem, and the main program simply establishes the proper execution pattern of the modules (procedures).

8.2 Function Arguments

Functions may be used in place of subroutines; that is, a function may have any number of input arguments, and any number of output arguments in addition to the function value itself. Function argument lists play exactly the same role, therefore, as subroutine argument lists, and are constructed in precisely the same way. Everything described about subroutine arguments (COMMON, etc., in the preceding chapter) applies to function arguments, except that alternate return points are not allowed in function argument lists.

In particular, the pass-by-value, pass-by-address rules for function arguments are the same as for subroutine arguments. To reiterate (since this is extremely important) these are as follows:

1 If an actual argument is a variable name, array name, array element or a substring then it is passed by address and its value may be changed during execution of the function.

2 If the actual argument is any other expression (including a constant) then it is effectively passed by value since its value may not be changed during execution of the function.

Arrays are always passed by address.

The external function is therefore a powerful tool indeed since it can be used simply to return a value (like an intrinsic function) or to perform any desired processing and return arbitrarily many values in the form of output arguments.

If the Fortran function provision is so powerful, why then is the subroutine facility also provided? There are several reasons. First, a value must always be associated with a function and returned to the calling program. There are times when a module need not return a value to the calling program, and in these instances requiring a return value detracts from the efficiency and (more importantly) the logical structure of the program. Second, the method of calling subroutines (the CALL statement) depicts much more clearly the modular structure of the system than does the method of calling functions (to be discussed in the next section). Third, *side effects* (to be discussed in Section 8.4) are possible with functions that can have disastrous consequences. And, finally, the primary purpose of a function is to conveniently return a single value, and using a function to "sneak back" additional results is likely to cause confusion and be a source of errors.

Some guidelines are therefore in order as to when (and how) to use functions and when not to use them. The general rule is very simple: if a module is to return a single value to the calling program then a function normally should be used and none of the actual argument values should be changed by the function; in all other cases modules should be implemented as subroutines. This rule, if observed, satisfactorily resolves every issue raised in the preceding paragraph.

Since function calls should leave the values of all actual arguments unchanged, according to the above rule, it would be desirable if function arguments were all passed by value. But since Fortran uses pass by address in functions, another rule is needed to achieve the desired effect. This rule, too, is simple: dummy arguments in function subprograms should not be assigned values (e.g., by READ or assignment statements) nor used as actual arguments in CALL statements. (The same applies to data elements in COMMON, if COMMON is used.) Strict adherence to this rule will insure that the only effect a function call will have on the calling program is the return of the function value.

8.3 Function Calls

There is not a special statement to call an external function, as there is for subroutine calls. Instead, the name of the function, together with its actual argument list, is used in an expression (see Chapter 3), and such an appearance constitutes a function call. During evaluation of an expression containing a function call, when the function call is encountered the evaluation of the expression is "temporarily suspended" and the function is executed. Upon completion of execution of the function, evaluation of the expression resumes using the just-obtained function value in place of the function call. Calls to external functions therefore appear and are used precisely like calls to intrinsic functions. Thus the form is

<function name> ([<actual argument list>])

and occurs within an expression in some Fortran statement. The program unit containing a call to an external function must contain a declaration of the type of that function, in order for the compiler to correctly process the expression containing the function call.

An example should help to explain the use of functions. Often in programs a source of random numbers is needed (see, for example, program RBALL in Chapter 5 where a coin is "flipped" to select the beginning server). Many practical programs require a source of random numbers, equivalent to flipping coins or rolling dice, in which the next number to be used cannot be predicted. The libraries of many large computing centers have functions to supply suitably random numbers (usually called *pseudo-random*, since they are not truly random but only "appear" so). Random number generators (as such functions are usually called) are not included in Fortran's list of intrinsic functions, and so must be user supplied if not available from the computing system's library. Functions RANDI and RANDU given below will serve in many instances where random numbers are needed (but RANDI and RANDU are not as satisfactory as typical modern systems library random number procedures). Function RANDI (I for integer) has two arguments, LOWER and UPPER, both integer, and returns a random integer value between (and including) these two limits. Function RANDI makes use of (i.e., calls) RANDU, which returns a real random number equal to or greater than zero, and less than 1. The RANDU (U for uniform) value is uniformly distributed in the 0..1 range, which means it is equally likely to be in any region of this range. RANDS (S for start) is exactly like RANDU except that it also provides control over the starting point in the sequence of random numbers generated.

```
*....:-----------------------------------------------------------------
      INTEGER FUNCTION  RANDI (LOWER,UPPER)
                                INTEGER  LOWER,UPPER

*                    ..Function to return a random integer
*                      between LOWER and UPPER. Note the call to
*                      another external function, RANDU, and the calls
*                      to two intrinsic function, MIN and MAX..

*     ....external function called....
      REAL  RANDU

*     ....execute....
      RANDI = L+INT(RANDU()*(MAX(LOWER,UPPER)-MIN(LOWER,UPPER)+1))
      END
=======================================================================
```

```
*....:-----------------------------------------------------------------
      REAL FUNCTION  RANDS (START)
                             INTEGER  START

*                    ..Function to return a uniform
*                      random number in the range 0..1

*     ....entry name....
      REAL  RANDU

*     ....constants....
      INTEGER  L,C,M
      PARAMETER  ( L = 29, C = 217, M = 1024 )

*     ....local variables....
      INTEGER  SEED
      SAVE  SEED
      DATA  SEED  / 0 /

*     ....execute....
*                     ..entry point for RANDS
*                       START initializes SEED value..
      SEED = MOD(ABS(START),M)

*     ....entry point for RANDU....
*                     ..determine next random number..
      ENTRY  RANDU( )
      SEED = MOD(SEED*L+C,M)
      RANDU = REAL(SEED)/M
*                     ..note how the function value is
*                       established -- with an assignment..
      END
=======================================================================
```

Besides being practical tools to add to the programmer's kit, these random number generator functions illustrate several things about using functions in Fortran. First, as befits a function, each serves a unique and separate purpose (although these purposes are all closely related), which involves the determination of a single value (the desired random number). Second, none of the functions changes any argument values. Thus the coin toss of program RBALL could be achieved by

COIN = RANDI(1,2)   (or COIN = RANDI(2,1))

rather than by inputting some "random" number. The formula for RANDI merely converts the 0..1 range of RANDU to the range LOWER. .UPPER+1 and takes the integer part of the resulting real value, giving a uniformly distributed pseudo-random integer in the LOWER. .UPPER range.

Functions RANDS and RANDU are more interesting than RANDI (from both a programming and a number-theoretic standpoint). RANDU needs no arguments—its purpose is to fetch the next (pseudo-) random number in the 0..1 range. It does this primarily via the formula for SEED (more about this formula in a minute). When a call is issued to RANDU the execution begins with the statement following the ENTRY

RANDU( ) statement. RANDU is one of those instances in which an additional entry point is warranted, since both RANDS and RANDU need exactly the same set of data elements. Moreover, if RANDU were a separate function, rather than an additional entry point to RANDS, it would need at least one argument (SEED). In the form given for RANDS all of the specification statements apply to RANDU. Note that the type of RANDU is specified in a type statement since, unlike the FUNCTION statement, the ETNRY statement may not designate the function type for that entry point. Different entry points may correspond to different types in a function, except that if one entry point is type CHARACTER then they all must be of type CHARACTER. A good practice, however, is to use multiple entry points in a function only when the corresponding function values have exactly the same type, and in fact are very closely related. Otherwise completely separate functions should be used.

Function RANDS has one argument (an integer) that is used to reinitialize the value of SEED. Otherwise RANDS is precisely the same as RANDU (another justification for the multiple entry). Initially SEED has the value zero, and so RANDS need not ever be called. Since (as it turns out) the sequence of random numbers is completely determined by the initial value of SEED, the programmer may wish to change this sequence by specifying a different initial value for SEED for different applications of the random number generators. Any integer value (other than zero and multiples of 1024) as the argument in a call on RANDS will result in such a change. And at any point in the program RANDS may be called again to establish another starting point for SEED. Note, however, that no value is assigned to RANDS; this is not necessary in this case because all entry names in a Fortran function (in this case RANDS and RANDU) refer to the same data element (i.e., are associated by address)—thus assigning a value to RANDU causes RANDS to assume the same value since both names refer to the same memory location.

From a programming point of view by far the most interesting thing about RANDS (and RANDU) is the use of SEED. This is a SAVEd local variable and its value remains intact throughout execution of the system of programs that uses RANDS (and/or RANDU). Each time RANDS or RANDU is called a new value is given to SEED—a value that depends on its previous value and the fomula involving L, C, and M. Because of the nature of the formula the sequence of SEED values is "suitably random" (if the values of L, C, and M are properly chosen), which, when scaled into the 0..1 range, serves as a sequence of uniform random numbers. Maintaining the value of SEED between calls for a random number is necessary for this method to work and the SAVE feature accommodates this nicely without the need to bother about SEED in the calling program and passing it as an argument into the function. In other words, the programmer using this random number generator need only call for and concentrate on using the desired random numbers, and not be concerned with how these numbers are provided, or the passing of arguments needed to implement the generation of random numbers.

From a number-theoretic point of view, random number generators are very interesting, and much work has been done on designing good ones. The linear congruential method (LCM) is one of the most effective of such, and has become a very popular type of random number generator. This method involves the use of three constants (L, C, and M in RANDU), and the formula in RANDU involving them, to generate a sequence of integer values. These integer values will be between 0 and M−1 (inclusive) and will be "suitably random" for proper choices of the constant values. The values of 29, 217, and 1024 for L, C, and M, respectively, as in RANDU, define a decent (but not "the best") LCM random number generator. With these values RANDU will generate 1024 reasonably random numbers between 0 and 1 before it repeats (generates the same sequence all over again). This random number generator will work well (e.g., not cause "overflow") on most minicomputers where Fortran's integer data elements are implemented in 16 bits.

Implementation of Fortran integers more commonly utilize 32 bits, in which case values of 1029, 221591, and 1048576 could be used for L, C, and M, respectively. The numbers from this generator are even more random than from the previous one, and it may be called more than a million times before the cycle starts to repeat. As the number of bits implementing an integer variable increases, better and better random number generators are possible. The trick is to get M to be as large a power of 2 as possible; then C should be any odd number such that C is approximately M*(3-SQRT(3.0))/6; and finally L should be chosen so that MOD (L, 8) has the value 5 and L is greater than the square root of M, if possible, but less than M-SQRT(M). (For additional information about random number generators see Knuth, *The Art of Computer Programming*, Vol. 2, Chap. 3, Addison-Wesley, 1969.)

Section 8.6 contains two substantial examples of practical applications of external functions. In one of these, program QUESIM, random numbers play an important role.

8.4 Function Side Effects

The use of external functions in Fortran poses a serious hazard which the programmer must be aware of and avoid. Function calls may have undesirable *side effects*, which cause puzzling and unpredictable errors. Fortunately such side effects may be prevented entirely by disciplined function design—if a function does not change the value of any actual argument (or elements in COMMON), i.e., if all communication with the function is effectively by value, then that function will not have side effects. Side effects may be thought of as changes in data element values in the calling program other than determination of the function value. Since function argument passing is normally by address in Fortran, such side effects may occur unexpectedly unless the function is written with care.

Consider the following situation, where FUN is an integer function (and K and N are integer variables):

```
IF (FUN(M,N).EQ.5 .OR. K.GT.20) THEN
     ----
     ----
ENDIF
```

Furthermore, assume the following four conditions:

1 K has the value 21.

2 N has the value 10 prior to executing the IF statement.

3 FUN will return the value 5.

4 In executing FUN the value of N will be changed to 11 (this is the side effect).

Question: Under these circumstances, what is the value of N at the beginning of execution of the THEN block?

Answer: It could be either 10 or 11, depending on the characteristics of the compiler.

What is going on here? The reason for the unpredictable behavior in this case is due to the fact that Fortran permits side effects to occur in functions and also provides for the implementor to *optimize* the compiler. One source of optimization possible is to not evaluate an entire expression if the value is completely determined after only partial evaluation. In the above case, a determination of .TRUE. for either operand in (FUN(M,N).EQ.5, .OR. K.GT.0) causes .TRUE. to be known for the value of the entire expression, regardless of the value of the other operand. Another source of optimization is, given the first option of partial evaluation, and a binary expression to evaluate, to evaluate the "simplest" of the two operands first. The combination of all of these valid possibilities is that the operand FUN(M,N) may or may not be called. If it is then the answer to the original question as to the value of N is 11; if FUN is not called then the value of N remains 10.

There are three possibilities in this particular case: (1) no optimization (all operands evaluated), which results in N having value 11; (2) partial evaluation, but with operands evaluated from left to right, which results in N having value 11; and (3) optimization with respect to both partial expression evaluation and order of operand evaluation, which results in N having value 10. Since the nature of optimization affects the value of N, this program may produce different results when used with different compilers.

In general the programmer will not know the nature of the optimization built into the compiler nor the order in which operands are evaluated. Therefore, the only sensible approach is to write Fortran code so that these implementation factors are immaterial. The way to do this is to eliminate all function side effects, and this is easy to do. The recommended way is to consistently and uncompromizingly write functions so that function side effects never occur—function calls should change nothing in the calling program except to return the function value itself. In other words, a function should not change the values of *any* of its dummy arguments, or any of its data elements in COMMON.

8.5 Statement Functions

In addition to intrinsic (built in) functions and external (programmer provided) functions Fortran provides for a third kind of function, the statement function. Statement functions are similar to external functions in that they are programmer written, but unlike external functions (which are separate complete programs) statement functions are defined within a program unit and are callable only from within that program unit—that is, statement functions are local to the program unit in which they are defined. Statement functions are so-named because they are "one-liners"—a single statement comprises the entire function definition. Any function requiring more than a single statement must be implemented as an external function.

Statement function definitions appear in the form of assignment statements, but are considered to be specification statements rather than executable statements. Therefore all statement function definitions must precede all executable statements, and should follow all data element declaration and initialization specification statements. The data types of statement functions and their dummy arguments are declared in ordinary type statements in the program. Figure 8.1 illustrates the definition and use of statement functions.

Note that statement functions are called in precisely the same way as intrinsic and external functions. (In fact, it is impossible to tell from the nature of a function call whether the function is an intrinsic function, an external function, or a statement function.) There is an important difference between the syntax of a statement function definition and that of an external function, however. In the assignment of the value to the function, which is the only statement in the definition of a statement function, the left-hand side of the assignment includes the function name and the dummy argument list (the corresponding statement in an external function definition does not include the dummy argument list). The definition of the function LENGTH in Figure 8.1 illustrates that the expression on the right of the "=" in a statement function definition may contain, in addition to dummy arguments, reference to any data elements of the program unit.

The form of a statement function definition is

<function name> ([<dummy argument list>]) = <expression>

where the types of all names are declared in ordinary type statements. The <expression> may be virtually any legal Fortran expression obeying the rules of Fortran

```
      PROGRAM SFUN
*                        . .Program illustrating
*                          statement functions. .
*     . . . .constants. . . .
      INTEGER SIZE
      CHARACTER SUBSTR
      PARAMETER ( SIZE = 80, SUBSTR = '                        ')
*     . . . .variables and arrays. . . .
      INTEGER L
      REAL C
      CHARACTER TEXT(1:100)*(SIZE)
*     . . . .local functions. . . .HYPOT and LENGTH. . . .
*                        . .LEG1 and LEG2 are dummy arguments for HYPOT
*                          and STRING is dummy argument for LENGTH. .
      REAL HYPOT,LEG1,LEG 2
      INTEGER LENGTH
      CHARACTER STRING*(SIZE)
      HYPOT(LEG1,LEG2) = SQRT(LEG1**2+LEG2**2)
      LENGTH(STRING) = INDEX(STRING//SUBSTR,SUBSTR)-1
*     . . . .execute. . . .
         ---
         ---
         ---
         ---
      C = HYPOT (A,B)
         ---
         ---
         ---
         ---
      do L = 1,LENGTH(TEXT(K))
         ---
         ---
         ---
         ---
      repeat
         ---
         ---
         ---
      END
```

Figure 8.1 Examples of the definition and use of statement functions.

assignment statements. The only exception to this is that the <expression> may not call other statement functions defined later in the list of statement function definitions (although reference to previously defined statement functions is allowed). Note that the form of a statement function definition that involves a dummy argument is exactly the same as an array element assignment. The compiler can tell that it is not an array element assignment, however, since the <function name> is not declared as an array (i.e., subscript bounds are not declared in connection with this name). Naturally a name identical to a <function name> cannot be used for an array, or for any other purpose, in the same program unit.

A statement function can be handy if a single assignment suffices to define it, and it is needed only in the program unit in which it is defined. Often a statement function is a convenient "abbreviation" for a complex expression, especially if the expression

```
      SUBROUTINE CHILL3 (SPEED)
                       REAL SPEED
*                    . .This figure illustrates the further
*                    use of statement functions, and in particular
*                    illustrates a statement function calling a
*                    previously defined statement function. .
*     . . . .constants. . . .
      REAL ITEMP,FTEMP,TINCR
      PARAMETER ( ITEMP = 15, FTEMP = -35, TINCR = -5)
*     . . . .variable. . . .
      REAL TEMP
*     . . . .local functions. . . .MPS and CHILL
      REAL MPS,CHILL,V,T
      MPS(V) = MAX(8.0,MIN(90.0,ABS(V)))
      CHILL(T,V) = 33-(33-T)*(10+SQRT(MPS(V))-MPS(V)+10.45)/23.165
*     . . . .execute. . . .
*     PRINT------------heading--------, SPEED
      do TEMP = ITEMP,FTEMP,TINCR
         PRINT *, CHILL(TEMP,SPEED), CHILL(TEMP,2*SPEED)
      repeat
      END
```

Figure 8.2 More examples of Fortran statement functions.

appears in more than one place in the program. Figure 8.2 suggests a modification of program CHILL2 of Chapter 5, and illustrates the use of statement functions to represent the value of large expressions. In Figure 8.2 MPS and CHILL are the names of real (statement) functions rather than real variables as in program CHILL2. The program in Figure 8.2 determines the chill factor for a fixed range of air temperatures and a specified wind speed (SPEED) and twice this wind speed. SPEED is used as an input argument to the program of Figure 8.2.

8.6 External Function Examples

This section contains two examples that use external functions in practical and effective ways. The first, program QUESIM, illustrates a class of applications known as "discrete-event simulations," and employs several functions, including a random number generator function (RANDU) described in Section 8.3. The second example, subroutine DOREPX, involves functions of type CHARACTER, in an application typical of systems software.

8.6.1 Program QUESIM

Program QUESIM is a simulation of a queue (waiting line). Queues are very common in modern society (people waiting in line at the grocery store checkout counter, cars waiting in line at a toll booth, programs waiting to be run on a computer, etc.), and making queues "more efficient" is a worthwhile endeavor. Program QUESIM determines the average length of and average waiting time in a given queue. Such a program can be used as a tool to investigate, for example, the effects that changing certain parameters (e.g., minimum service time) have on things like average waiting time in a queue. Figure 8.3 illustrates the fundamental concepts of a queuing situation. Entities await their turns to be processed at the "service station." At random times a new entity will arrive and be added to the "tail" of the queue. At other times, also largely unpredictable, service of an entity (the one at the "head" of the queue) will be completed and then that entity will leave the queue, allowing the queue to "move up."

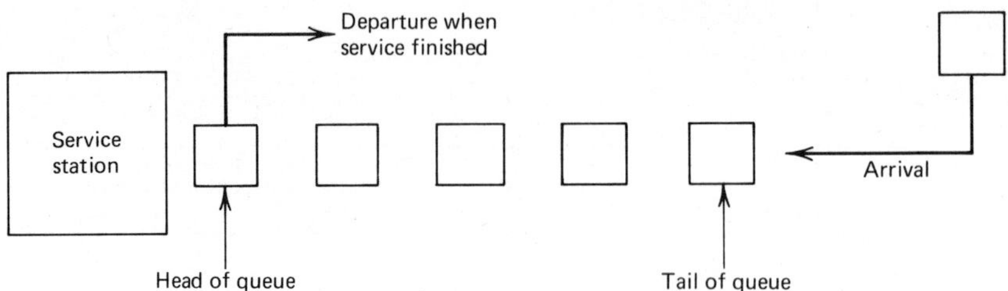

Figure 8.3. Elements of a QUEUE.

As far as QUESIM is concerned, only two things of interest occur in the behavior of a queue: arrivals (which cause the queue to increase in length), and departures (which cause the queue to decrease). QUESIM "follows" these events in the order in which they occur in time. That is, QUESIM "jumps" from one of these events to the next, in chronological order, adjusting the queue size and making other appropriate calculations. In this manner, the behavior of the queuing system is simulated, from beginning to end, and if the proper calculations are made along the way then at the end of the simulation things like average waiting time in the queue and the (time-weighted) average queue length can be determined.

What sorts of calculations must QUESIM make? Average waiting time in the queue (AVEWT) can be determined by dividing total waiting hours in the queue (QTIME) by total number serviced (NSERVE)—thus QTIME and NSERVE are determined during execution of QUESIM. Average queue length (AVEQL) is the total QTIME divided by the (simulated) duration of the study. QUESIM keeps running track of the simulated current time (TIME) and the queue size (QSIZE), in addition to NSERVE and QTIME. One way of terminating a simulation is to specify the maximum time it is to run. This is the method QUESIM uses (with MAXTIM) by checking at each departure to see if TIME exceeds this limit.

The key elements of QUESIM, however, are the event times—the time of the next arrival (ATIME), and the time of the next departure (DTIME). With these two times known the simulation is very simple to write, and QUESIM is written assuming that these values are known and that new values for ATIME and DTIME are "magically" provided at appropriate points. The "magic", of course, is the two functions, IATIME and STIME for providing the interarrival and service times, respectively. The programmer writing QUESIM need not be concerned at all about the details of how the values for IATIME and STIME are determined—these details are the concern of the writer of IATIME and STIME. All the writer of QUESIM need know is that appropriate values are returned by these two functions and may be used in QUESIM. How complex IATIME and STIME may, or may not, be is immaterial to the QUESIM programmer.

As it turns out, the really meaty concepts involved in queuing concern the determination of IATIME and STIME, and QUESIM could have been a correspondingly difficult program to write. Wise modularization saved the day, however, and QUESIM turned out to be a relatively simple program. The most difficult details are left entirely to modules—functions IATIME and STIME—that QUESIM calls. QUESIM itself can be understood, used, and modified, assuming knowledge only about the values returned by IATIME and STIME and the roles of the arguments, and without knowing about the details internal to IATIME and STIME.

STIME stands for service time, and it is a value of type REAL representing the time required to process (service) the entity (e.g., car) currently in the service station. Note in QUESIM that each time a service is completed, and a departure occurs, the next service time is obtained (by a call to STIME). The next departure time is then the current time plus the service time (or, in the case that a departure leaves an empty queue, the departure time is the next arrival time plus the service time). The real function IATIME stands for interarrival time and represents the time between arrivals. Each time an arrival occurs in QUESIM, IATIME is called to provide the time interval to the next

```
*....:------------------------------------------------------------------
      PROGRAM  QUESIM
*                     ..This program simulates a queuing situation.
*                     The main variables are:
*                         AVEIAT -- average inter-arrival time
*                         AVEST  -- average service time
*                         MINST  -- minimum service time
*                         QSIZE  -- length of queue
*                         NSERVE -- number serviced
*                         TIME   -- simulated time
*                         ATIME  -- time of next arrival
*                         DTIME  -- time of next departure
*                         QTIME  -- total waiting time in queue
*                         AVEWT  -- average waiting time in queue
*                         AVEQL  -- average queue length
*                     Two functions are called: STIME and IATIME.
*                     The arguments of these functions, AVEIAT,
*                     AVEST, and MINST, may be changed for
*                     different executions of QUESIM, in order to
*                     "experimentally" determine the effects of
*                     changing these values. (If these parameters
*                     aren't to be experimented with, then they
*                     probably should be in their respective
*                     functions rather than in PROGRAM  QUESIM.)

*     ....constants....
      REAL  AVEIAT,AVEST,MINST
      PARAMETER  ( AVEIAT = 4.0, AVEST = 3.0, MINST = 1.0 )

*     ....variables....
      INTEGER  QSIZE,NSERVE
      REAL  TIME,QTIME,ATIME,DTIME,MAXTIM,AVEWT,AVEQL

*     ....initializations....
      DATA  QSIZE, TIME, QTIME, NSERVE, MAXTIM  /
     :        0  ,  0  ,   0  ,   0   ,   600   /

*     ....external functions called....
*     REAL IATIME, STIME

*     ....execute....
*                         ..start with empty service station
*                           and generate first arrival..
      ATIME = IATIME(AVEIAT)/2
      DTIME = ATIME+STIME(AVEST,MINST)
      do
*                         ..process next event (arrival or departure);
*                           exit when TIME exceeds MAXTIM..

          IF  (DTIME .LT. ATIME)  THEN
*                                   ..process a departure
                NSERVE = NSERVE+1
                QTIME = QTIME+QSIZE*(DTIME-TIME)
                TIME = DTIME
                QSIZE = QSIZE-1
                IF  (TIME .GT. MAXTIM)  exit
                IF  (QSIZE .GT. 0)  THEN
*                                         ..begin servicing next in line
                     DTIME = TIME+STIME(AVEST,MINST)
                  ELSE
*                                     ..line is now empty --
*                                       begin service upon next arrival..
                     IF  (ATIME .GT. MAXTIM)  exit
                     DTIME = ATIME+STIME(AVEST,MINST)
                ENDIF
             ELSE
*                              ..process an arrival (put at end of line)
                QTIME = QTIME+QSIZE*(ATIME-TIME)
                TIME = ATIME
                QSIZE = QSIZE+1
                ATIME = TIME+IATIME(AVEIAT)
*                                      ..determine time of next arrival
          ENDIF
      repeat
      AVEWT = QTIME/(NSERVE+QSIZE)
      AVEQL = QTIME/TIME
      PRINT *, NSERVE, TIME, AVEWT, AVEQL
      END
========================================================================
```

arrival; the new ATIME is then the current time (the time of the current arrival) plus the interarrival time.

In order that QUESIM simulate a real-life queuing situation, the values returned by IATIME and STIME must be similar in "spread" and "unpredictableness" to those found in reality. The unpredictableness is achieved by using a random number generator, and achieving the spread involves knowing (or assuming) something about the frequencies of actual service times and interarrival times. The interesting subject of the nature of interarrival and service times is sketched here, and the final result given for use in this example, but the details are left for the interested reader to pursue in some source devoted to an exhaustive treatment of random variables (the Knuth reference cited above, for instance).

Figure 8.4 illustrates the relative distributions typically found in actual practice for interarrival times and service times. (These general shapes are easy to verify by collecting some data at the local supermarket.)

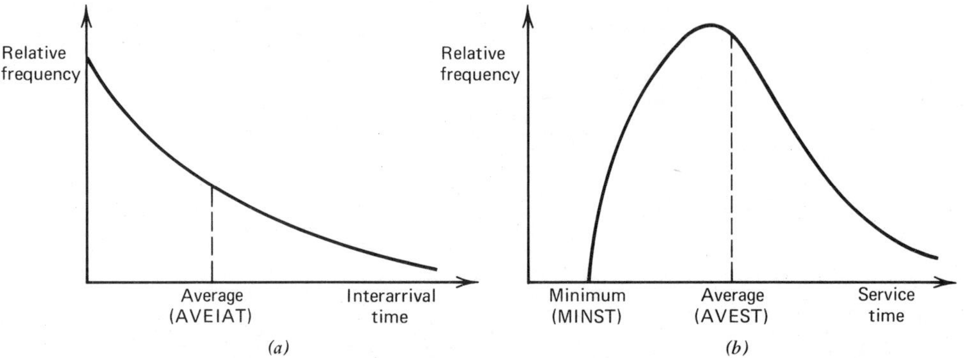

Figure 8.4. Distributions of "real-life" interarrival and service times. (*a*) Distribution of the relative frequency of observed times between arrivals in a typical queuing situation. (*b*) Distribution of the relative frequency of observed service times for a typical service function.

Both of the distributions in Figure 8.4 are nonuniform (a given time is not equally as likely as every other time), and so simple application of a uniform random number generator (RANDU) will not suffice. A set of uniform random numbers may be converted into a set of nonuniform random numbers with the desired distribution, however, and a number of means have been developed to do this. The simplest (or at least the quickest) way to do this is to closely approximate a distribution with a certain mathematical function, which then allows a formula to be applied to a uniform random number to convert it to the corresponding nonuniform value. For the distributions in Figure 8.4 exponential functions are usually adequate, and allow the imposing formulas

```
IATIME = AVEIAT*LOG(1/(1-RANDU()))/LOG(2.0)
```

and

```
STIME = MINST+(AVEST-MINST)*SQRT(LOG(1/(1-RANDU())))/SQRT(LOG(2.0))
```

to be used for IATIME and STIME, where AVEIAT is the average interarrival time (dotted line in Figure 8.4*a*), AVEST is the average service time (dotted line in Figure 8.4*b*), and MINST is the minimum service time. These three values, AVEIAT, AVEST, and MINST, must be supplied as data or constants in the respective functions (and usually are easily obtained for a given queuing situation). Armed with this knowledge, functions IATIME and STIME can be written.

The distributions in Figure 8.4 may appear puzzling (or even counterintuitive) at first, but are reasonable on reflection. Low values of interarrival time (near zero) represent near-simultaneous arrivals (everybody heads for the checkout counter at once!). Arbitrarily long interarrival times are possible, but the longer the time, the less

```
*....:-----------------------------------------------------------------
      REAL FUNCTION  STIME (AVE,MIN)
                             REAL  AVE,MIN

*                    ..function to determine
*                      the next service time..

*     ....external function called....
      REAL RANDU

*     ....execute....
      STIME = MIN + (AVE-MIN) * SQRT(LOG(1/(1-RANDU()))) / SQRT(LOG(2.))
      END
=======================================================================
```

```
*....:-----------------------------------------------------------------
      REAL FUNCTION  IATIME (AVE)
                             REAL  AVE

*                    ..function to determine the
*                      next inter-arrival time..

*     ....external function called....
      REAL RANDU

*     ....execute....
      IATIME = AVE * LOG(1/(1-RANDU())) / LOG(2.0)
      END
=======================================================================
```

likely it is because somebody may come in the meantime. The average interarrival time occurs where the area under the curve to the left equals the area under the curve to the right. Service times are also characterized by an average service time, and most of the service times are close to this average. Service times do not drop below some minimum threshold (i.e., all servicing takes some time) but arbitrarily long service times are possible. The minimum and average service times depend, of course, on the nature of the service.

8.6.2 Subroutine DOREPX

A final example in this chapter illustrates the use of non-numeric external functions. Subroutine DOREPX (for DO REPeat eXit) accepts an array of strings, each string assumed to represent a Fortran statement (the entire array is assumed to be a Fortran program), and converts each occurrence of do, repeat, and exit statements to the correct Fortran constructs (statement labels, CONTINUE statements and GOTO statements) as described in Chapter 5 (Figure 5.14). (The Fortran program in the array is assumed to be syntactically correct, except that do and repeat—in either lower-case or upper-case letters—may be used to define loops and exit may be used to terminate looping. Moreover, the numbers and nesting levels of do-repeat loops are assumed to be limited so that the three-digit statement labeling scheme of Chapter 5 is sufficient (i.e., no more than three consecutive loops at level 3, no more than seven consecutive loops at level 2, and no more than nine loops at level 1), and that no statement labels so generated duplicate any other labels that may be in the program.)

Figure 8.5 (which is similar to Figure 5.14) illustrates the processing that DOREPX is to perform. Figure 8.5*a* shows the conversions generated for a nonindexed do-repeat; in this case a labeled CONTINUE statement is inserted at the top of the loop, a GOTO statement and a labeled CONTINUE statement are inserted at the bottom of the loop, and the do and repeat are retained as comments. Similarly, Figure 8.5*b* shows the conversions generated for an indexed do-repeat; the do statement is converted to a DO statement, and two CONTINUE statements (the first to terminate the DO and the second to provide a target for possible exit statements) are inserted at the bottom of the loop. And, finally, Figure 8.5*c* shows that all exit statements are converted to the

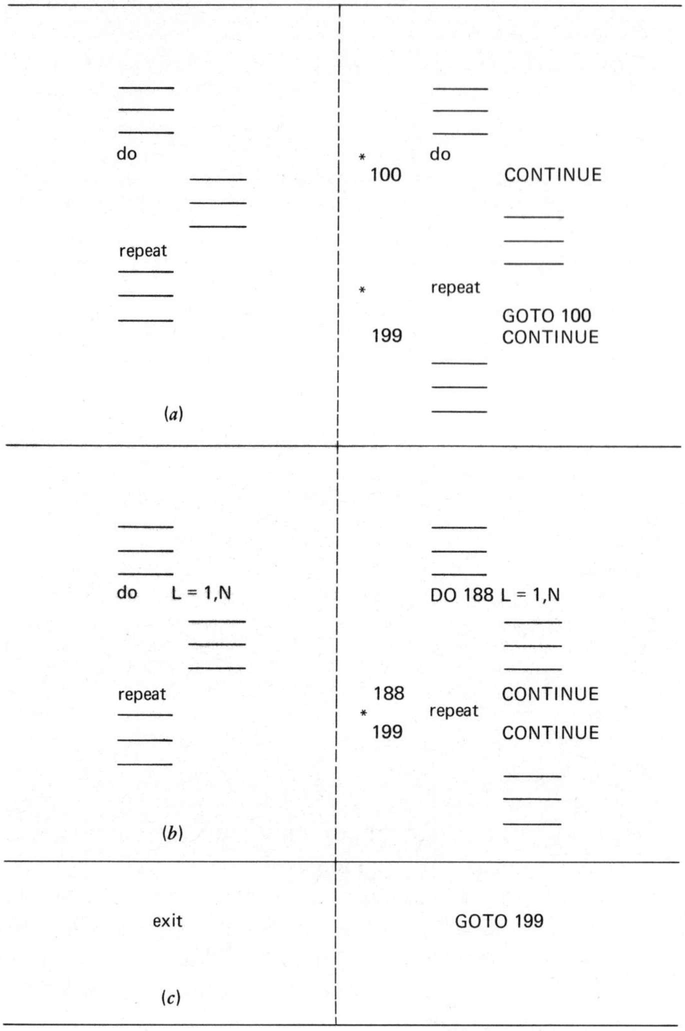

do-repeat version	standard Fortran version
do	* do
	100 CONTINUE
repeat	* repeat
	GOTO 100
	199 CONTINUE
(a)	
do L = 1,N	DO 188 L = 1,N
repeat	188 CONTINUE
	* repeat
	199 CONTINUE
(b)	
exit	GOTO 199
(c)	

Figure 8.5. The conversion performed by program DOREPX (do-repeat version on left—standard Fortran version on right). (*a*) Nonindexed loops. (*b*) Indexed loops. (*c*) Exits.

appropriate GOTO statements. Subroutine DOREPX does not change the input array, but prints the entire program in its converted form.

The most complex part of this problem is the generation of the various statement labels. There are "top", "bottom", and "exit" labels that have certain forms, and DOREPX must generate a unique and proper label in each case, regardless of the loop structure of the program. Since this involves careful design it will be relegated to a string function LABEL, which will return the correct three digits (a three-character string) when called. Function LABEL will have two arguments, the first of which will have the value 'TOP..' (nonindexed do encountered), 'TOP.X' (indexed do encountered), 'BOTTOM' (repeat encountered), or 'EXIT' (exit encountered), so that it will know which label to generate; the second argument (LEVEL) conveys the nesting level to the function. The design of DOREPX is relatively simple since it merely makes a call to LABEL when it needs a statement label. Note that DOREPX also calls subroutine CKTYPE, which checks the type of the statement (i.e., to see if it is a "do," "repeat," or "exit" statement). CKTYPE calls function CKDO to check for "do" in either lower-case or upper-case letters.

Program F PLUS in Chapter 15 is a conversion of DOREPX to a file environment (where the Fortran program is in a file rather than an array), and thus constitutes a practical mechanism for automatic conversion of do, repeat, and exit to standard Fortran.

```
*....:------------------------------------------------------------------
      SUBROUTINE  DOREPX (PROG)
                       CHARACTER  PROG(1:*)*(*)

*                 ..This program converts "do", "repeat", and "exit"
*                   to standard Fortran. PROG is an array of Fortran
*                   statements. This routine calls CKTYPE, which
*                   returns TYPE = 'do', 'repeat', 'exit' (or blank)
*                   and LOC as the keyword beginning position in
*                   STMT. INDXED tells whether or not a loop is
*                   indexed. This routine assumes that "do",
*                   "repeat", "exit", and END statements are not
*                   labelled, and it will work for "do", "repeat",
*                   and "exit" in either lower- or upper-case.
*                   in STMT, INDXED tells whether or not (this level
*                   of) the loop is indexed. This routine assumes
*                   that "do" and "repeat" statements are not
*                   labelled, and that strings are not continued.
*                   This routine calls function LABEL to supply the
*                   necessary statement labels for the conversion.

*     ....local variables....
      INTEGER  LOC, LEVEL, NEXT
      CHARACTER  STMT*72, TEMP*72, TYPE*6
      LOGICAL  INDXED(1:3)

*     ....external function called....
      CHARACTER*3  LABEL

*     ....execute....
      LEVEL = 0
      NEXT = 1
      do
          STMT = PROG(NEXT)
*                 ..now search for keywords "do", "repeat", "exit"
*                                      (or "DO", "REPEAT", "EXIT")
          CALL CKTYPE(STMT,LOC,TYPE)
          IF  (TYPE .EQ. 'do')  THEN
*                            ..process a "do"
                  LEVEL = LEVEL+1
                  IF  (STMT(LOC+2:) .EQ. ' ')  THEN
*                                         ..it is not an indexed-do
                          INDXED(LEVEL) = .FALSE.
                          STMT(1:1) = '*'
                          PRINT *, STMT
                          STMT = ' ' // LABEL('TOP..',LEVEL)
                          STMT(LOC+4:) = 'CONTINUE'
                      ELSE
*                                         ..it is an indexed-do
                          INDXED(LEVEL) = .TRUE.
                          TEMP = STMT(LOC+2:)
                          STMT(LOC:) = 'DO  ' // LABEL('TOP.X',LEVEL)
                          STMT(LOC+7:) = TEMP
                  ENDIF

              ELSEIF  (TYPE .EQ. 'repeat')  THEN
*                                         ..process a "repeat"
                  IF  (INDXED(LEVEL))  THEN
*                            ..insert bottom label for indexed-do
                          TEMP = ' ' // LABEL('BOTTOM',LEVEL)
                          TEMP(LOC+4:) = 'CONTINUE'
                      ELSE
*                         ..insert branch to top of (non-indexed) loop
                          TEMP = ' '
                          TEMP(LOC+4:) = 'GOTO '// LABEL('REPEAT',LEVEL)
                  ENDIF
                  PRINT *, TEMP
                  STMT(1:1) = '*'
                  PRINT *, STMT
*                                      ..now insert exit-label..
                  STMT = ' ' // LABEL('EXIT',LEVEL)
                  STMT(LOC:) = 'CONTINUE'
                  LEVEL = LEVEL-1

              ELSEIF  (TYPE .EQ. 'exit')  THEN
*                                         ..process an "exit"
                  STMT(LOC:) = 'GOTO ' // LABEL('EXIT',LEVEL)
          ENDIF
          PRINT *, STMT
          LOC = INDEX(STMT,'END')
          IF  (LOC .GT. 0)  THEN
*                         ..stop when  END  encountered..
                  STMT(LOC:LOC+2) = ' '
                  IF  (STMT .EQ. ' ')  exit
          ENDIF
          NEXT = NEXT+1
      repeat
      END
========================================================================
```

```
*....:------------------------------------------------------------------
      CHARACTER*3 FUNCTION  LABEL (TYPE,LEVEL)
                                 CHARACTER  TYPE*(*)
                                 INTEGER  LEVEL

*                           ..function to determine and return
*                             loop-related statement labels..
*     ....label digits....
      CHARACTER DIGIT*9
      DATA    DIGIT / '123456789' /

*     ....local variables....(the 3 digit values)
      INTEGER  NEST(1:3), N
      SAVE  NEST
      DATA  NEST(1)  / 0 /

*     ....execute....
*                    ..adjust nest number --
*                      necessary only upon entry into a loop..
      IF  (TYPE .EQ. 'TOP..' .OR. TYPE .EQ. 'TOP.X')  THEN
              NEST(LEVEL) = NEST(LEVEL)+1
              IF  (LEVEL .EQ. 1)  THEN
                   NEST(2) = 0
                ELSEIF  (LEVEL .EQ. 2)  THEN
                   NEST(3) = -2
                ELSE
                   NEST(3) = NEST(3)+2
              ENDIF
      ENDIF
*                        ..now, generate the 3 digits of the label..
      LABEL = DIGIT(NEST(1):NEST(1))
      IF  (LEVEL .EQ. 1)  THEN
              LABEL(2:2) = '0'
          ELSE
              LABEL(2:2) = DIGIT(NEST(2):NEST(2))
      ENDIF

      IF  (TYPE .EQ. 'TOP..'  .OR.  TYPE .EQ. 'REPEAT')  THEN
*                                           ..generate "top" label..
              IF  (LEVEL .LT. 3)  THE"LLABEL(3:3) = '0'
                ELSE
                   LABEL (3:3) = DIGIT(NEST(3):NEST(3))
              ENDIF

          ELSEIF  (TYPE .EQ. 'BOTTOM' .OR. TYPE .EQ. 'TOP.X')  THEN
*                                           ..generate "bottom" label..
              IF  (LEVEL .LT. 3)  THEN
                   LABEL(LEVEL+1: ) = '88'
                ELSE
                   LABEL(3:3)=DIGIT(NEST(3)+1:NEST(3)+1)
              ENDIF

          ELSE
*                                           ..generate "exit" label..
              IF  (LEVEL .LT. 3)  THEN
                   LABEL(LEVEL+1: ) = '99'
                ELSE
                   LABEL(3:3) = DIGIT(NEST(3)+2:NEST(3)+2)
              ENDIF
      ENDIF
      END
=========================================================================
```

8.7 Summary

The function and subroutine features of Fortran have now been described in considerable detail. These are among the most useful tools for constructing programs, and systems of programs, in Fortran. The programmer should know them well.

Subroutines are the principal means of modularizing a program and should be used as modules whenever more than one value is to be returned to the calling program. Subroutines are separate programs that begin with a SUBROUTINE statement rather than a PROGRAM statement. The main difference between a SUBROUTINE statement and a PROGRAM statement is that the former (usually) has a (dummy) argument list to communicate information between the subroutine and its calling program, whereas the PROGRAM statement has no argument list. The form of a SUBROUTINE statement is

SUBROUTINE <subroutine name> [([<dummy argument list>])]

A PROGRAM is always a main program, which can only be executed directly, whereas a SUBROUTINE is a subprogram that is executed only when CALLed by another program. A (calling) program calls a subroutine with a CALL statement, which is an executable statement and has the form:

CALL <subroutine name> [([<actual argument list>])]

When a program calls a subroutine, execution of the program is suspended while the subroutine is executed in its entirety. Upon completion of execution of the subroutine, control "returns" to the point of call in the calling program, and execution resumes with the statement following the CALL.

External functions are similar to subroutines in that they are separate program units. The principal difference between functions and subroutines is that a value is associated with a function name, but not with a subroutine name. Therefore every function has a data type, and this type must be specified when defining the function and in programs calling the function. A function is called by using its name (and actual parameter list) as an operand in an expression in the calling program. When this operand is to be evaluated execution of the program is suspended while the specified function is executed. Upon completion of execution of the function, control returns to the calling operand, whose value is then the value of the function just executed, and evaluation of the expression continues.

There are three kinds of functions in Fortran: intrinsic functions, external functions, and statement functions. All are called and used in precisely the same way. Intrinsic and external functions are separate programs that can be called from any program unit, whereas statement functions are one liners that represent expressions in a program unit and are local to that program unit. Intrinsic functions are prewritten routines for making common computations and may be used by the programmer simply by making proper calls. External functions are most like subroutines in that they are separate programs written by the programmer, and begin with FUNCTION statements. The form of the FUNCTION statement is:

[<type>] FUNCTION <function name> ([<dummy argument list>])

Intrinsic and statement functions do not have possible side effects (at least presumably the implementor does not allow side effects with any of the intrinsic functions!) but the programmer must guard against side effects in external functions.

A function normally should be used for a program module whenever that module is to return precisely one value to the calling program, and that value should be the function value. As a rule functions should not change any of the values of actual arguments.

It is important to realize that local variables become undefined between executions of a program unit, unless preserved with a SAVE statement. SAVE statements may be used in both subroutines and external functions. The storage used by local variables not SAVEd may be shared by local variables in other program units.

The ENTRY statement, whose form is very much like the form of the SUBROUTINE statement, except the word ENTRY is used instead of SUBROUTINE, allows execution of a procedure to begin at an executable statement other than the first executable statement. This is sometimes useful where two or more very similar procedures must be provided. ENTRY statements may be used in both subroutines and external functions, and in functions the type of the ENTRY names are declared in type statements.

Programming Exercises

8.1 Write a Fortran function that returns a uniform real random number between X and Y, where X and Y are any real numbers (including negative values).

8.2 Suppose that A, B, and C are any integer numbers (including negative ones), with A<B<C. A Fortran function is desired that returns a random integer in the range A. .C (inclusive), but with each integer in the range B. .C (inclusive) twice as likely as those in the range A. .B−1. Write such a Fortran function.

8.3 Write a one-argument logical function named
(a) ODD7, whose argument is an integer, and whose value is .TRUE. if (and only if) the argument value is an odd integer (either positive or negative) divisible by 7;
(b) FORLET, whose argument is a string, and whose value is .TRUE. if (and only if) the argument value is a four-letter word (first four characters are letters, the rest blanks).

8.4 Write a Fortran function that has a single string as an argument, and returns the first (leftmost) substring bounded (on both ends) by blanks. The returned string should contain no blanks, other than trailing blanks.

8.5 Write a Fortran function, ROUND, that "rounds" a specified real value to an indicated decimal position. ROUND has two arguments, say X and N, one real and the other an integer. N specifies the position in which rounding is to take place, with N=0 meaning round to an integer, N=1 to the tens place, N=2 to the hundreds place, etc. N may be negative, which specifies the fractional position in which to round. ROUND should return the properly rounded value of X, but should not change the value of X itself. Examples of the use of ROUND:

```
ROUND(124.527,1) == 120.0
ROUND(124.527,-2) == 124.53
```

8.6 Rewrite subroutine SQUEEZ of Chapter 6 as a function. The function should return the squeezed (deblanked) string, and leave the original string unchanged. Repeat for the depunctuating routine of the palindrome-checking program PDROME.

8.7 Rewrite program MCMESS of Chapter 5 as a function, so that program DECODE could be re-structured as

```
 do
     READ '(A)', MCLINE
     IF (MCLINE .EQ. 'DONE') exit
     PRINT '(A,A/A)', MCMESS(MCLINE),
:           'is the clear for', MCLINE
repeat
```

8.8 In Chapter 10 the pair of statements

```
do
    IF (<exit condition>) exit
```

at the top of a loop is, for the purposes of the analysis in that chapter, replaced by the single, more lucid, statement

```
do until (<exit condition>)
```

Write a Fortran function that accepts two strings as arguments, and returns the corresponding do until statement string if the two argument strings are do and IF . . . exit, respectively. Otherwise the function returns a single blank.

8.9 Rewrite the external functions STIME and IATIME as statement functions local to PROGRAM QUESIM.

8.10 In a certain application it may be suitable to approximate the exponential function for IATIME, as shown in Figure 8.4a, with a linear function such as shown below. In this case no interarrival times exceed a certain maximum, MAXIAT. Write a Fortran function which, given AVEIAT, returns a random interarrival time based on this distribution. (Hint: the formula 3*AVEIAT*(1−SQRT(1−RANDU())) is one way to convert the uniform random number range 0..1 to the distribution shown.)

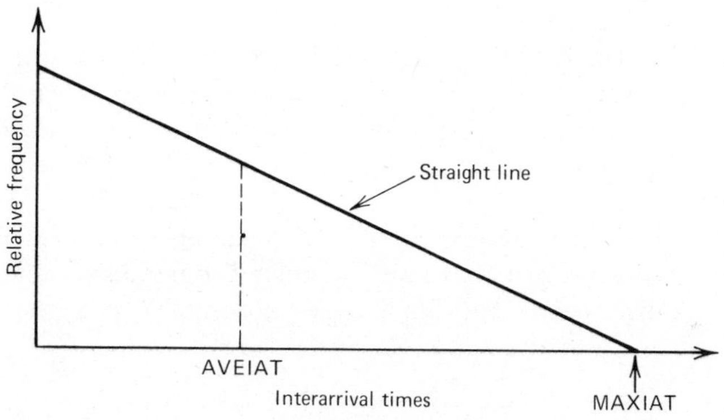

Chapter 9 Control Structures

Since Chapter 4 it has been obvious that few interesting programs can be written without the programmer having the ability to modify the normal pattern of simple sequential execution of processing (input, output, and assignment) statements. The IF-ENDIFand do-repeat structures are sufficient control mechanisms for implementing arbitrarily complex algorithms. These mechanisms are "good" control structures and, when mastered, are easy to use. What makes a control structure "good" is examined in this chapter, and some guidelines are presented for using these mechanisms correctly.

The IF-ENDIF and do-repeat control structures may be sufficient to write any program, but they are not the only means by which execution control may be achieved in Fortran. Nor does it mean that other features should not be occasionally used in Fortran programs. In practice two additional classes of control mechanisms are indispensable: modularization and "abnormal exits." Modularization has been discussed in detail in the preceding three chapters, and so will be mentioned only briefly here. Abnormal exits have not yet been discussed in detail, so Section 9.4 is devoted to such a discussion. And finally, the survey of Fortran's provisions for execution control is completed in Section 9.5.

9.1 Modularization

All of the important Fortran techniques for achieving modularization have been described in detail in Chapters 6, 7, and 8. This section summarizes the guidelines governing effective design and implementation of modularization.

The first step in program design, after problem definition and together with identifying the major data elements involved, is to determine the module structure of the system. Each relatively separate or distinct part of the problem normally should be a separate module. The mainline program normally should do little more than call the main modules in the proper order and under the proper conditions. The structure of the mainline should reflect only the "highest level" of logical structure of the problem.

In general no module should be unduly long or complex; long or complex algorithms should normally be further modularized. A typical rule of thumb concerning module size is that a module should not exceed a page or two (50–100 lines) of Fortran program code.

Modules are often implemented in Fortran as subroutines. This allows any number of results, including entire array values, to be returned to the calling program. The mainline program is therefore usually composed largely of CALL statements. However, when the purpose of a module is to return a single numeric or string value then (and only then) should that module be implemented as a function. The values of actual arguments should not be changed by function calls.

For the remaining portion of this chapter, and indeed the rest of the book, the term "program" will be used for mainline program or any of the subprograms of a system of programs, with the assumption that appropriate modularization has already taken place.

9.2 Selection

Selection control refers to the control of execution so that a group (sequence) of statements may be conditionally executed. In the discussion to follow <S1>, <S2>, and so on, will be used as "shorthand" to denote specific sequences of statements (i.e., <S1> represents some specific sequence of statements). The basic forms of selection, as introduced in Chapter 4 and used in virtually all program examples since then, are summarized in Figure 9.1.

```
if   <condition> then
          <S1>
endif
```

(a)

```
if   <condition> then
          <S1>
     else
          <S2>
endif
```

(b)

```
if   <condition-1> then
          <S1>
     elseif <condition-2> then
          <S2>
     elseif <condition-3> then
          <S3>
     .
     .
     .
     elseif <condition-n> then
          <Sn>
     else
          <Sn+1>
endif
```

(c)

Figure 9.1. The basic forms of selection, using IF-ENDIF. (*a*) Conditional execution of a group of statements (if-then). (*b*) Executing one or the other of two statement groups—two-way selection (if-then-else). (*c*) Selection (for execution) of one from among several groups of statements—*n* way selection.

Figure 9.1*c* is logically equivalent to a series of nested if-then-else structures:

```
if <condition 1> then
      <S1>
   else
      if <condition 2> then
            <S2>
         else
            if <condition 3> then
                  <S3>
                  .
                  .
                  .
               else
                  if <condition-n> then
                        <Sn>
                     else
                        <Sn+1>
                  endif
                  .
                  .
                  .
            endif
      endif
endif
```

(And one can immediately see why the elseif feature is provided.)

The discussion of Chapter 4, and the subsequent program examples, should have made the various uses of if-endif clear, and it should be evident that this is quite a powerful structure and capable of handling, relatively conveniently, virtually any selection situation that might arise. Certainly the simple if-then (Figure 9.1*a*) requires no further elaboration. In the case of if-then-else (Figure 9.1*b*) certain situations can (and therefore assuredly will) arise, such as the following:

```
if <condition> then
        <S1>
        <S2>
    else
        <S2>
        <S3>
endif
```

There is no question about the intended processing here, but the programmer may object to having to write the statements for <S2> twice. Of course, <S2> could be made into a procedure and then each <S2> in the above example would be just a single statement—a call to the procedure. If <S2> is merely a few statements perhaps the objection to supplying them twice will not be too great, although such duplication of code is "inelegant" no matter how short it is.

A third approach is the following:

```
if <condition> then
      <S1>
endif
<S2>
if not<condition> then
    <S3>
endif
```

This involves writing the statements of <S2> only once, without resorting to a procedure and its attendant overhead of designing argument lists, etc. However, duplicating the <condition> (negated at that) is also inelegant, and suffers from two additional drawbacks. The first is that two logical expression evaluations must be made during execution of the program, whereas previously only one such evaluation was performed. The other is that the readability of this last version is definitely inferior to that of the original version.

Consider another example:

```
if <condition> then
          <S1>
          <S2>
    else
          <S2>
          <S1>
endif
```

The first two of the above strategies [i.e., (a) leave it as is, (b) use procedures for <S1> and <S2>] are still possible strategies here, but the third (restructuring) is more difficult in this case. Fortran allows arbitrary control of execution flow using the GOTO statement (see Section 9.5), and therefore two different ways in which the above program can be written with only one appearance each.of <S1> and <S2> are as follows (REVERS and AGAIN are LOGICAL variables):

```
   REVERS = not<condition>
   if REVERS goto 2
1  <S1>
   if REVERS goto 3
2  <S2>
   if REVERS goto 1
3  continue
```

```
AGAIN = false
do
  if AGAIN or <condition> then
      <S1>
  endif
  if AGAIN exit
  <S2>
  if <condition> exit
  AGAIN = true
repeat
```

In the first of these two versions the value of REVERS must be tested three times in executing this program; the do-repeat version involves even more such computation. And the readability of both of these last structures is very poor—the logic of the original version is obvious at a glance, the logic of the other versions is quite obscure.

These two examples involving if-then-else illustrate that there are instances involving selection in which the "best" solution is not immediately obvious. Many other examples, including much larger and/or more complex ones, could illustrate additional "pathological" situations which complicate the design of selection control. Such situations involve trade-offs concerning things such as program efficiency, readability, and the programmer's concerns about elegance and related matters. Despite this confusion (or perhaps because of it) the following two-step guideline is offered as the best approach.

1 Use the if-endif structure that best reflects the logical structure of the algorithm—don't obscure this logical structure in an attempt to prevent the duplication of statements.

2 When it is desired to avoid writing a duplicate statement group, use a procedure (e.g., subroutine) for that group, and issue calls to the procedure as needed.

When used with those two guidelines the Fortran IF-ENDIF structure is extremely effective for implementing selection control, and is sufficiently powerful to achieve any selection control needed. Another selection control structure, the *case* structure, is occasionally more convenient than if-endif, although it does not provide any additional capability over if-endif. Fortran does not have a CASE statement, but in many instances case is easily constructed in Fortran. Section 9.5 and the problems at the end of this chapter describe the nature of the case structure and the Fortran facilities for implementing it.

9.3 Repetition

The if-endif structure owes much of its attractiveness to its "one-in, one-out" nature; that is, no matter how complex the selection is within an if-endif, initially control enters at the point defined by IF and ultimately emerges at the point defined by ENDIF. Such one-in, one-out structures have become recognized as important programming concepts—important because used wisely they tend to make programs easier to construct, easier to read, easier to verify, and easier to modify. These concepts are especially important in repetition structures since the prospects of volumes of incorrect processing, computing time wasted, and programming time wasted are particularly great with loops. In this section the advantages of one-in, one-out control structures are examined, especially as they apply to loops.

The do-repeat structure for loops, as described in Chapter 5, is a one-in, one-out structure. In a do-repeat loop, control enters at the do and emerges, at the end of repetition, at the repeat. The body of the loop, between do and repeat, may be arbitrarily complex, involving selection, nested loops, etc., but unless overridden by

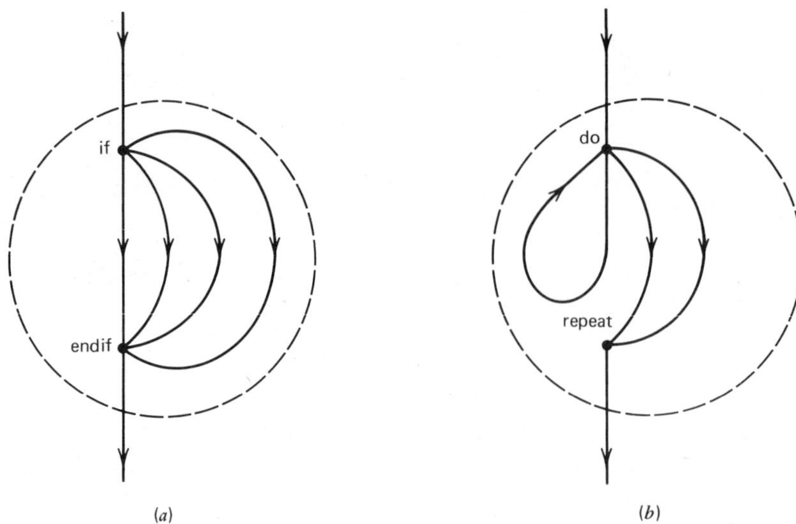

Figure 9.2. Schematic representation of selection and repetition structures. (*a*) Selection (four alternatives shown). (*b*) Repetition (two exits shown).

GOTO statements (or the loop is executed without end), control ultimately emerges at the repeat. Figure 9.2*b* schematically represents such a structure. For comparison, the structure of an if-endif is depicted in (*a*) of Figure 9.2. Figure 9.2*a* is an example of four selection alternatives (perhaps three conditions and an ELSE)—each branch of the diagram representing the condition and processing of an alternative. The dotted line enclosing the structure has only one path in and one path out.

Figure 9.2*b* is an analogous diagram for do-repeat. Here the entire body of the loop is represented by the branch that loops back to the do, whereas the branches between do and (the node below) repeat represent loop exits. Each loop exit branch represents the corresponding exit condition and end-of-the-loop processing (if any). Again, the dotted line enclosing the structure has exactly one path in and one path out.

The key point about one-in, one-out structures is that any of the lines of Figure 9.2 can be "cut" and the "in" and "out" points of any other one-in, one-out structure can be attached to these cut ends. In this manner simple one-in, one-out selection and repetition structures may be used as building blocks to systematically construct a program having any logical structure. Figure 9.3 illustrates such "composite" structures.

Since the one-in, one-out principle has been observed almost exclusively in the preceding chapters, one might well ask "What is an example of a situation that doesn't have this character?" Subroutine SPLIT of the last example (TWOWAY) in Chapter 6 is a case in point. Figure 9.4 shows the structure of that program—two nested loops, in which the exit conditions for both loops occur inside the inner loop. Figure 9.4*a* shows how the auxiliary logical variable DONE was used in SPLIT to allow the double-level exit (where C1 is true) to be done as a sequence of two single-level exits. Figure 9.4*b* shows the direct exiting of both levels of looping (a GOTO could be used to do this) when C1 is true. The structures of Figure 9.4 are recast in Figure 9.5, using the style introduced in Figure 9.3.

Clearly the algorithm of Figure 9.4*b* involves less computation than that of Figure 9.4*a*. This efficiency is achieved, however, at the expense of losing the one-in, one-out nature of the structure. Whereas Figures 9.4*a* and 9.5*a* exhibit the one-in, one-out character, Figures 9.4*b* and 9.5*b* exhibit a one-in, two-out structure. There are generally two serious consequences of using a one-in, two-out structure. The first is that the human reader of the program must be aware of two possible destinations for resumption of execution on exiting from a loop, instead of just one. In general this adversely affects the ease with which the program can be read and comprehended. The second consequence is more serious. The "three-part" nature of the one-in, two-out structure

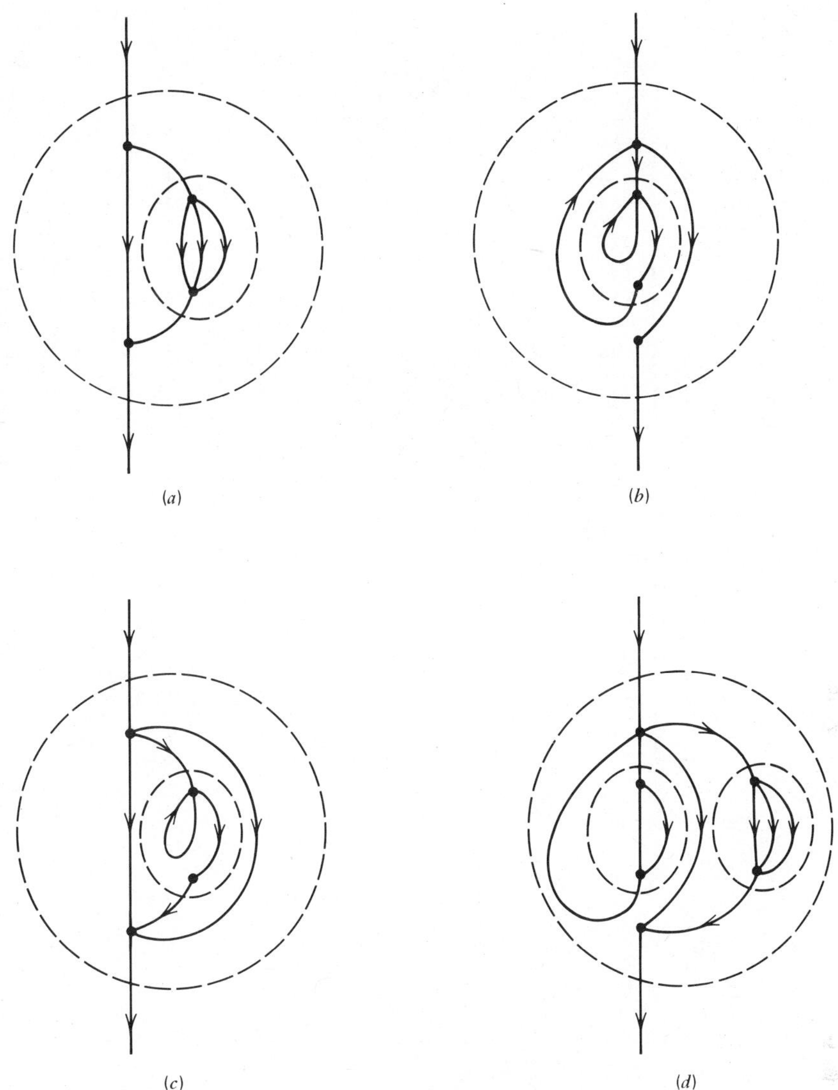

Figure 9.3. Examples of the composition (nesting) of one-in, one-out control structures. (*a*) Nested selection. (*b*) Nested repetition. (*c*) A loop in one branch of selection. (*d*) Selection within a loop, and at an exit of the loop.

means that such a structure is not simply a component in a single path of execution—it must be part of at least two different such paths. Thus modification of such structures may cause changes in more than one execution path. If the modification is undertaken in order to correct an error in one path, an error may inadvertently be introduced into another path. Thus successful modification of non-one-in, one-out structures is typically much more difficult than with one-in, one-out structures.

This example illustrates the major difficulty with repetition—the occasional need for multilevel exits. This should not be confused with multiple (single-level) exits. Any number of single-level exits may occur in a loop without changing the one-in, one-out nature of the structure. As used in this book the exit statement is a single-level loop exit; that is, it causes an exit only from the innermost loop containing the exit. On the other hand a multilevel exit (i.e., the simultaneous termination of two or more levels of looping) always destroys the one-in, one-out nature of the structure. This is so because every loop having a multilevel exit must also contain a single-level exit (otherwise there is no need for, and hence no justification for, the innermost loop). The occurrence of both a single-level exit and a two-level exit means that there are at least two possible destination points on loop termination, and implies therefore (at least) a

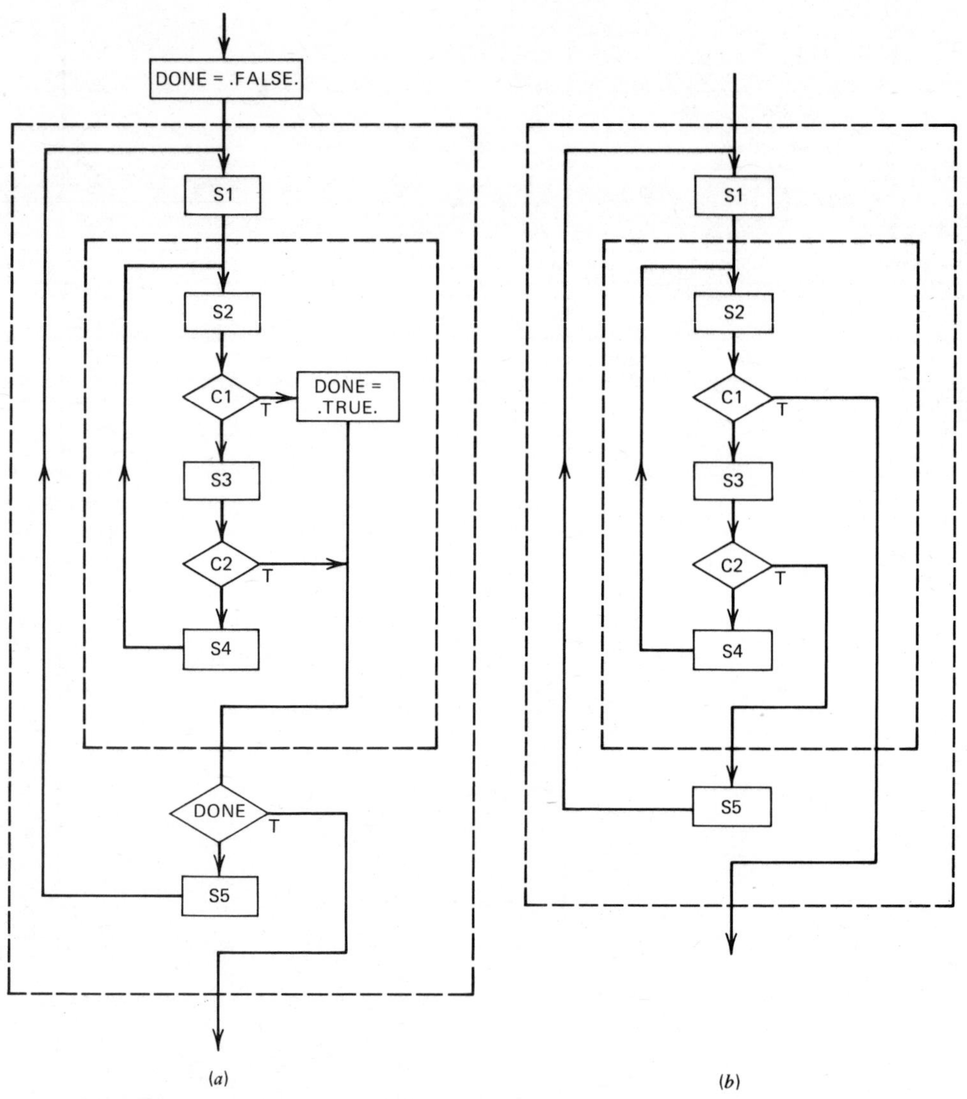

Figure 9.4. The structure of subrouting SPLIT. (*a*) As it appeared in Chapter 6, using the auxiliary variable DONE. (*b*) Without the auxiliary variable DONE.

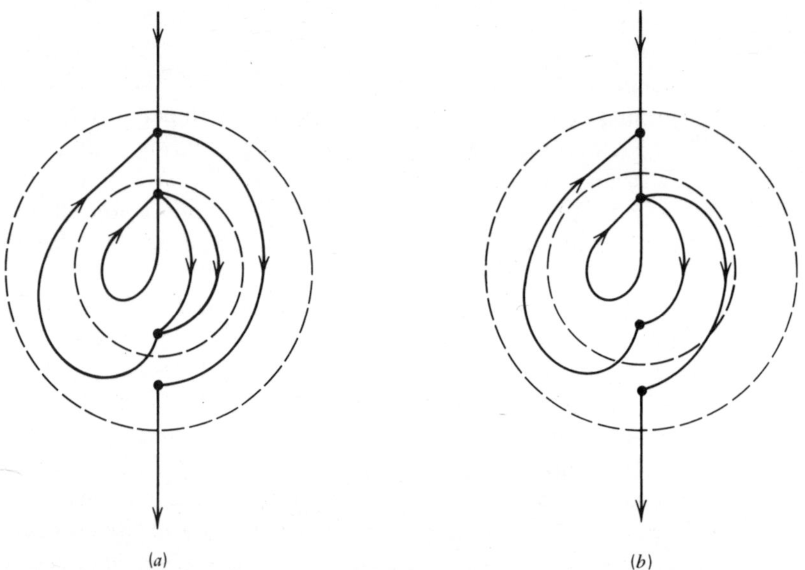

Figure 9.5. Structure diagrams for Figure 9.4. (*a*) The structure of Figure 9.4*a*. (*b*) The structure of Figure 9.4*b*.

two-out structure. This discussion can be taken as "proof" (adequate for the purposes here) of the following "theorem":

"A do-repeat repetition structure has the one-in, one-out property if, and only if, it contains no multilevel exits."

Any multilevel exit (of say N levels) may be replaced by N single-level exits in the manner illustrated by subroutine SPLIT (and Figures 9.4, 9.5). The technique is simple:

1 Introduce a logical variable (DONE, say) initialized to .FALSE. prior to the outermost loop involved in the multilevel exit.

2 When the condition for the multilevel exit is found to be true then execute

```
DONE = .TRUE.
exit
```

3 And then insert the statement

```
IF (DONE) exit
```

after the repeat of each inner loop involved in the multilevel exit. If each multilevel exit is transformed in this manner to a sequence of single-level exits then all loops will exhibit the one-in, one-out property. The transformation of multilevel exits to a cascade of single-level exits involves introduction of logical variables, and the assignment of values and the repetitive testing of such variables. This not only introduces execution inefficiency but in some cases may also detract from program readability—for example, if many levels are exited (implying a long cascade of "IF (DONE) exit"s) and/or if simultaneous multilevel exits are involved. In such cases direct implementation of multilevel exits may be appropriate, and may be achieved by the use of GOTO statements as described in the next section.

A final situation involves indexed loops with one (or more) additional (single-level) exits, with unique end-of-the-loop processing required at the index-satisfied exit. (Chapter 5 described in great detail how unique end-of-the-loop processing may be achieved at each exit for nonindexed loops, and such situations have been illustrated in a number of the example programs.) However, indexed loops have no direct provision for unique end-of-the-loop processing when the "normal" (indexing controlled) exit is taken. This situation can be handled in a number of ways, and one of these ways which is relatively straightforward is to "flag" normal indexed loop termination, and to use this flag as the basis for selecting the desired processing after the loop. This technique is illustrated as follows (IDXEND is a logical variable):

```
IDXEND = .TRUE.
do <indexing>
    ----
    ----
    IF (<exit-condition>) THEN
        ----
        ----
        IDXEND = .FALSE.
        exit
    ENDIF
    ----
    ----
repeat
IF (IDXEND) THEN
      ----
      ----
ENDIF
```

9.4 Abnormal Exits

The "normal" structure for selection or repetition is the one-in, one-out form. Thus single-level exits are normal exits and multilevel exits are *abnormal*. This terminology developed partially from the fact that the detection of an "abnormal condition" during program execution (e.g., an employee of age 417) often requires "getting out quick" from the processing routine, which may well involve "jumping out" of several levels of looping. Although careful program design can minimize the need for abnormal exits, the programmer can be sure that abnormal exits will occasionally arise and must be dealt with.

An abnormal exit represents a failure, a failure on the part of the algorithm design and/or computer language to provide the exact control structures needed to accommodate well the particular problem situation. Fortran is a general-purpose programming language, with general-purpose control structures that do nicely in most situations. But abnormal situations arise in which these structures are inferior—hence the occasional abnormal exit. There often is no elegant way out of an abnormal exit situation. Therefore, escape in the quickest manner possible may be defensible. Such an escape may be achieved in Fortran with the GOTO statement. Moreover, if do, repeat, and exit are used consistently in loop design, then the use of GOTO statements can be limited to the implementation of abnormal exits. This has tremendous advantages for program readability, since abnormal exits are then easily spotted and the programmer is thereby painlessly alerted to the existence of an abnormal situation.

The point to which an abnormal exit is to be made is given a label. Then a GOTO <that label> is placed where the abnormal exit is to be made from. Thus the abnormal (multilevel) exit will appear in the Fortran program, after all single-levels exits have been converted to their corresponding GOTOs, in exactly the same form as the normal (single-level) exit. However, in the preconverted program each single-level exit will appear as exit, and each abnormal exit will appear as GOTO <label>. Both the source and destination points of an abnormal exit could be appropriately "flagged" with comments to further alert the reader to the fact that the one-in, one-out normal control flow has been destroyed.

Program PRIME contains an example of the direct implementation of an abnormal exit by using a GOTO rather than by cascading single-level exits. PRIME computes a

```
*....:-----------------------------------------------------------------
      PROGRAM  PRIME
*                      ..this program computes the first NP primes,
*                      where NP is supplied as input data.  A multi-
*                      level (abnormal) exit occurs when the next
*                      prime number is found..

*     ....variables....
      INTEGER  N, P, NP, K, PRIMES(1:1000)
      DATA  N , PRIMES(1)  /
     :      1 ,     2      /

*     ....execute....
      READ *, NP
      do  P = 2,NP
*                  ..N is the next candidate for the Pth prime..
         do
            N = N+2
            PRIMES(P) = N
            K = 1
*                      ..now, if N is not a prime it must be a
*                       multiple of some smaller prime..
            do
               IF  (PRIMES(K)**2 .GT. N)  GOTO 1234
               IF  (MOD(N,PRIMES(K)) .EQ. 0)  exit
               K = K+1
            repeat
         repeat
1234     CONTINUE
      repeat
      PRINT '(T2,I10/)', (PRIMES(P), P=1,NP)
      END
=====================================================================
```

list of prime integers, and a double loop is used to determine the next prime value. In order that the program be highly efficient, the test for primeness is made in the inner loop, and when a prime is discovered both loops must be terminated. (Thus the abnormal exit is guaranteed to be ultimately taken in this program, which makes the term abnormal seem abnormal in this case.)

Abnormal exits may be envisioned in contexts other than loops. The normal mode of program execution is complete execution from the first executable statement through execution of the END statement. An abnormal condition may require terminating program execution prior to the normal encountering of the END statement. To accommodate this the END statement may be labeled, and a GOTO <END label> placed at the point of abnormal exit from the program. Alternatively Fortran has a STOP statement

```
STOP
```

which is logically equivalent to GOTO <END label> and does not require that the END statement be labeled.

Similarly the normal execution of a subprogram is from beginning to END. A premature return to the calling program may be achieved by a GOTO <END label> statement, or equivalently by a RETURN statement:

```
RETURN
```

RETURN is not a legal statement in a mainline program, but STOP is a legal statement in either a mainline or a subprogram. In a subprogram RETURN serves to terminate execution of the subprogram and return control to the calling program, however STOP in a subprogram has the same effect as STOP in a mainline—execution of the entire system of programs is terminated.

The relationships of called and calling programs exhibit the one-in, one-out nature (as long as the alternate return feature of subroutines is not used). But STOP in a subprogram is truly a "multilevel" (and hence abnormal) exit, in that it results in termination of more than one level of program units. Moreover in practice RETURN and STOP, when used, are usually found internal to some repetition or selection structure in the program unit and thus represent abnormal exits from those structures. Like GOTO abnormal exits, the use of RETURN and STOP should be flagged and explained with comments. In well-structured programs these features would be rarely used. (Note, however, that some Fortran programmers feel that every main program should contain a STOP statement, immediately preceding the END statement, that is executed rather than executing the END statement, and that every subprogram should contain a RETURN statement, immediately preceding the END statement, that is executed instead of executing the END statement. While this view is not taken here, there is nothing wrong with such a practice if it is consistently observed.)

A possible application of RETURN would be in subroutine SPLIT, considered above. In that subroutine each of the two-level exits completes the processing of the subroutine, and after the execution of either of these exits execution returns to the calling program. Therefore the statement

```
IF (N .GT. SIZE) RETURN
```

```
IF  (<exit-condition>) exit             IF  (<exit-condition>) RETURN
        or                                       or
IF  (<exit-condition>) THEN             IF  (<exit-condition>) THEN
        ----}                                    ----}
        ----} pre-exit                           ----} pre-exit
        ----} processing                         ----} processing
        ----}                                    ----}
        exit                                     RETURN
ENDIF                                   ENDIF
            (a)                                      (b)
```

Figure 9.6. Implementation of normal and abnormal exits. (*a*) Normal (single-level) exits using exit. (*b*) Abnormal (multilevel) exits (using RETURN).

```
*....:------------------------------------------------------------------
      PROGRAM  PRIME2
*                        ..a modification of program PRIME that
*                        uses RETURN for the abnormal exit.  The
*                        double loop for determining the next prime
*                        becomes subroutine NXPRIM.  (Note that N
*                        is local to NXPRIM, as is K)..

*     ....variables....
      INTEGER  P, NP, PRIMES(1:1000)
      DATA  PRIMES(1)  /  2  /

*     ....execute....
      READ *, NP
      do  P = 2,NP
         CALL  NXPRIM (PRIMES,P)
      repeat
      PRINT '(T2,I10/)', (PRIMES(P), P=1,NP)
      END
========================================================================

*....:------------------------------------------------------------------
      SUBROUTINE  NXPRIM (PRIMES,P)
                             INTEGER  P, PRIMES(1:*)

*                  ..this program contains the inner double loop
*                  of program PRIME for determining the next
*                  prime.  The multi-level exit is achieved with
*                  the RETURN statement..

*     ....variables....
      INTEGER  N, K
      SAVE  N
      DATA  N  /  1  /

*     ....execute....
      do
*                  ..N is the candidate for the next prime..
         N = N+2
         PRIMES(P) = N
         K = 1
         do
            IF  (PRIMES(K)**2 .GT. N)  RETURN
            IF  (MOD(N,PRIMES(K)) .EQ. 0)  exit
            K = K+1
         repeat
      repeat
*                  ..note that PRIMES(P) has the value of the
*                  next prime upon return to PRIME2..
      END
========================================================================
```

could be used for both of these exits to achieve the same control without the need for the auxiliary variable DONE.

In principle a program requiring an abnormal exit can be structured so that the abnormal exit may be achieved with a RETURN statement. This involves making that part of the program encompassing the abnormal exit into a module (subroutine), which usually is quite compatible with the logical structure of the problem anyway. (And, in fact, subroutine SPLIT is already structured this way.) A good programming style therefore is to design the modular structure of the program so that any multilevel exit not implemented by a cascade of single-level exits is implemented with RETURN, and RETURN is used only for such abnormal exits. With this scheme any appearance of a RETURN statement immediately signifies the presence of an abnormal exit in the program, and the absence of a RETURN guarantees that all control has the one-in, one-out structure. Figure 9.6 summarizes the use of exit and RETURN for single-level and multilevel exits, respectively. And program PRIME2 is a modification of PRIME that implements the abnormal exit with RETURN.

9.5 Arbitrary Branching

Any problem can be programmed in Fortran using IF-ENDIF for selection, do-repeat for repetition, exit for normal exits, and RETURN for abnormal exits. No labels or GOTO statements are necessary, except for the special ones used in the conversion of do, repeat, and exit. The great advantage of these features is, except for abnormal exits, the one-in, one-out nature of control that they provide. It is difficult to overemphasize the benefits that this has for program development and maintenance. It is possible, however, to achieve any desired control using only labels and GOTO statements. In this section the uses, and some implications of the use, of GOTO statements to achieve execution control are described.

In the preceding sections and chapters, labels were used primarily on CONTINUE statements. However Fortran allows any statement to be labeled. And GOTO <any label> is allowed, either as a stand-alone statement or as the action part of a logical-IF statement:

```
IF (<logical expression>) GOTO <any label>
```

These two uses of GOTO are called, respectively, unconditional and conditional branches, and their execution causes unconditional or conditional transfer of execution control to the statement with the specified label. This target statement may be either above or below the branch statement in the program. Thus branching may be (almost) arbitrary; the exceptions are: branches into either an IF-ENDIF or indexed-DO structure from outside the structure are prohibited. Together labels and branches (conditional and unconditional) constitute a fairly "simple" set of programming features that allow arbitrary control of execution. They may be used to achieve looping (see Section 5.5 for realizing do, repeat, and exit), selection (see the problems at the end of this chapter), abnormal exits (see the preceding section), and any other execution control conceivable. The use of GOTOs to control program statement execution is easy to learn and gives the programmer great power for the construction of compact, efficient programs.

Fortran also has several other branching statements, that have more specialized purposes and extend further the Fortran branching facilities. These are summarized in Figure 9.7. While the computed-GOTO has several useful applications (see, for example, the implementation of case in the problems at the end of this chapter, and the application in Chapter 11), the arithmetic-IF and assigned-GOTO are much less useful

GOTO (<label1>,<label2>,. . .<labeln>), <integer-variable>

(meaning: branch to <labeli>, where i
is the value of <integer-variable>.)

(a)

IF (<arithmetic-expression>) <label1>, <label2> [, <label3>]

(Note: if <label3> is omitted it is assumed to be the same as <label2>)

(Meaning: branch to <label1> if the value
of <arithmetic-expression> is negative --
<label2> if value is zero --
<label3> if value is positive.)

(b)

ASSIGN <label-value> TO <integer-variable>

.
.
.

GOTO <integer-variable>

(Note: this form of GOTO is valid only if an ASSIGN
statement involving <integer-variable> has
been previously executed, without any
intervening arithmetic on <integer-variable>)

(c)

Figure 9.7. Additional provisions for arbitrary branching in Fortran. (*a*) The computed GOTO. (*b*) The arithmetic IF. (*c*) The assigned GOTO.

and are not recommended. Branching may also be specified in Fortran by use of alternate return points in subroutine argument lists.

Clearly the arbitrary branching facilities in Fortran are very extensive, and additional control structures (such as IF-ENDIF and do-repeat) are not needed. So why are more sophisticated control structures provided? Because of the one-in, one-out nature of these more sophisticated control structures. Diagrams similar to those in Figure 9.4 can be constructed to show the flow of execution control in a program using GOTO statements; such diagrams are commonly called *flowcharts* and have been popular as aids to program development and documentation. Since a GOTO can easily be used to construct a branch between any two points in a program (and hence in the flowchart), programs containing GOTOs almost certainly violate the one-in, one-out principle unless the programmer has been very careful to prevent such violation. The use of the GOTO statement must be highly disciplined if the resulting program is to have the one-in, one-out structure.

The disadvantages of not having one-in, one-out control structures throughout the program have already been noted—decreased program readability and increased complexity for program development and modification. In reading a program with GOTO statements one is continually distracted from the logic of the program by the hunting for labels. Moreover if GOTOs are used with abandon, with numerous arbitrary branches up and down in the program, the flow of execution control tends to be complex and unstructured, and generally is quite difficult for humans to follow.

The poor readability of a GOTO-strewn program is a potential source of errors. But the more serious source of errors in such programs is that of intertwining two paths of execution. Modifying such a structure, perhaps to eliminate a bug from one path, is analogous to removing a fishhook—the fishhook may be difficult to remove (the bug may be difficult to correct) without the barb (influence on another execution path) adversely affecting some other part of the fish (the other, perhaps correct, path of execution). GOTO statements, like fishhooks, must be handled with care, lest the programmer get seriously stuck. Nevertheless, GOTO statements are advantageous in a number of circumstances, as the previous discussions and examples have demonstrated. Further uses of the GOTO statement are illustrated in the programming exercises at the end of this chapter.

9.6 Summary

This chapter has summarized all of the features that Fortran has for controlling the path of execution in programs, and has discussed many of the particularly troublesome situations that might be encountered in practice. One-in, one-out control structures are consistently observed to offer significant advantages to the programming process, and, after modularization and data element selection, achieving one-in, one-out structures should be the primary consideration in program design. Such structure may be achieved with GOTO statements, but the IF-ENDIF and do-repeat structures are much "safer" and normally result in more readable programs. Only abnormal exits require the use of GOTO statements and even these GOTOs may be eliminated by appropriate modularization and use of the RETURN statement.

The readability benefits of one-in, one-out structures can be enhanced by judicious physical alignment in the program listing. In the listings of all of the examples, each structure in-point (IF or do) is vertically aligned with its corresponding out-point (ENDIF or repeat). Everything in between is internal to the structure and is indented several positions to the right of the in-point and out-point statements. This means that there is no hunting for any structure endpoints, which in turn means that the reader of the program can concentrate on following its logic, with a minimum of distraction from its mechanical form.

(The December 1974 issue of *ACM Computing Surveys* is a special issue on programming, and contains several articles addressing in detail the topics of this chapter. This issue also contains almost 200 other references, many of which deal with these topics.)

Programming Exercises

9.1 Draw a structure diagram, in the style of Figure 9.2*a*, for the selection of program LOT of Chapter 4.

9.2 Show the composition of one-in, one-out control structures, in the style of Figure 9.3, for program QUESIM of Chapter 8.

9.3 Repeat Problem 9.2, but for program BASE of Chapter 5.

9.4 Using the results of Problem 9.3 as the starting point, insert an appropriate one-in, one-out control structure to detect illegal base values (e.g., negative ones, or ones greater than 20) and to "scale" (using MOD, for example) such iliegal values into a corresponding value in the 2..20 range.

9.5 In program BASE (Chapter 5) it was assumed that the digit values supplied as input are valid for the base specified. Extend that program to include a check for an illegal digit, and to take an appropriate abnormal exit if one is found.

9.6 Devise a systematic scheme for achieving IF-ENDIF control, but by using only the control statements:
GOTO <label>
IF (<condition>) GOTO <label>

9.7 A popular contemporary selection control structure is the case structure:

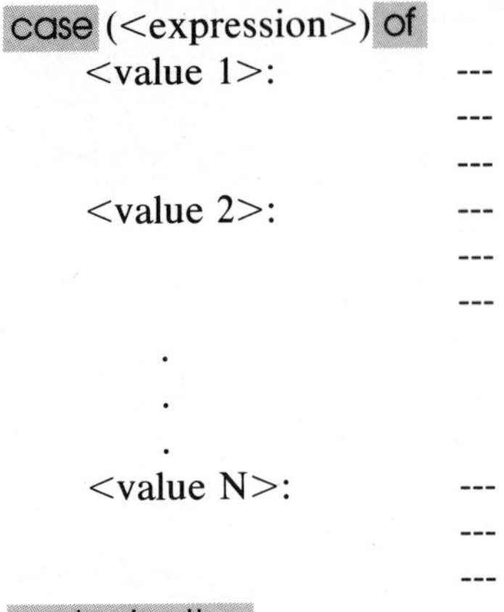

```
case (<expression>) of
    <value 1>:        ---
                      ---
                      ---
    <value 2>:        ---
                      ---
                      ---
        .
        .
        .
    <value N>:        ---
                      ---
                      ---
end selection
```

In this structure each <value> is a legal value for <expression>. When the case statement is encountered during execution, <expression> is evaluated, a direct branch is made to the corresponding <value>, that group of statements is executed, and then control leaves the structure. In general, the <expression>, and the <value>s, could be any data type, as long as for a particular case structure they are all the same. Show how an IF-ENDIF structure can be used to achieve (although not as efficiently, or quite as readably) control equivalent to case control.

9.8 If the <expression> and <value> of the case structure (see Problem 9.7) are of type INTEGER, then the computed GOTO can possibly be used to efficiently implement the case construct in Fortran. For example, if the <value>s are 1,2,3,4,. . ., then the construct could begin with

```
*  case (I) of
   GOTO (1,2,3,4,. . .), I
      .
      .
      .
*  end selection
```

Complete this implementation by inserting the necessary labels and GOTO statements.

9.9 As a modification of Problem 9.8, suppose that the <expression> and <value>s are single-character quantities—for example, 'A', 'B', 'C', . . . etc. Show how case can be implemented using

```
*  case (CHAR) of
   I = INDEX('ABC. . .',CHAR)
   GOTO (1,2,3,. . .), I
      .
      .
      .
   end selection
```

9.10 Extend the technique of Problem 9.9 to arbitrary character string values of length L.

Chapter 10 Program Correctness

A computer program is written in order to specify the performance of some processing function—to achieve some intended results. In practice much effort is expended in attempts to verify that programs do indeed perform as intended, and to "correct" (debug) programs that don't. In fact, it is generally accepted that more time and money is spent on program verification and correction than on program development.

There are several levels of program correctness (or incorrectness), which include the categories shown in Figure 10.1. Category 1 is of no concern here; the compiler identifies such errors so that they may be promptly corrected. Similarly, category 2 is not very interesting, since a single test execution identifies that there is a problem and a systematic debugging process can then be initiated. Categories 3 and 4, however, are interesting, and are the cases of concern in this chapter.

The history of the evolution of programming languages has several interesting aspects. One is the evolution of control structures, another is the introduction of data types that are especially useful with new classes of problems to be solved. Yet another aspect involves the methods used for generating and verifying correct programs. Three rather distinct, albeit somewhat overlapping, chronological phases ("generations") can be identified concerning such correctness concerns. In the first generation, beginning approximately in the early 1950s with the first widespread use of high-level programming languages such as Fortran, and lasting about 20 years, the dominant approach to program verification was extensive experimental testing by executing the program many times with carefully designed input test data. In this generation the initial programming process itself was of no concern to the verification of the resulting program, with the burden of proof for program verification resting entirely with the testing process.

In the second generation, beginning around 1970, concern for program correctness was extended to program design, and is now an important part of program development. In this generation various programming techniques and methodology in "structured programming" were (are being) developed with the intent of maximizing the chances of getting the program correct initially. A primary characteristic of this generation is the emphasis on program readability; the reasoning is that the more apparent

1 Syntactic errors exist—program cannot be successfully compiled, and cannot be executed (so that no results are obtained).

2 The program compiles successfully, but none of the results of execution are correct.

3 Execution results are sometimes correct and sometimes incorrect.

4 Execution results are always correct.

Figure 10.1. Categories of program correctness.

Generation I ------------> Program Testing

Generation II -----------> Structured Programming + Program Testing

Generation III ----------> Structured Programming + Correctness Proofs

Figure 10.2. The generations of program correctness methodologies.

the functioning of the program is on inspection, the greater are the chances that the program will perform the intended processing. Program testing is still used in the second generation as the final indicator of program correctness.

The third generation of program correctness is only beginning to arrive, but its general character is apparent: programs are proved correct by analytical means. When such techniques are perfected then program testing will become much less important. Programs likely will be developed by structured programming, with correctness proofs largely replacing program testing. As correctness proof techniques become more highly developed they are more likely to become an integral part of the programming process itself. The ultimate point in this generation is a set of programming techniques in which every program produced belongs to category 4 of Figure 10.1.

The three identifiable generations of program correctness are characterized by their association with the three methodologies, summarized in Figure 10.2:

Program testing

Structured programming

Correctness proofs

The next three sections discuss each of these three methodologies in greater detail.

10.1 Program Testing

The basic idea behind program testing is to execute the finished program using input data for which the results are known, or for which the program results can be determined to be correct or incorrect. If this process can be repeated many times, for different input values each time, then the correctness properties of the program for a wide range of input values can be identified. If errors are detected then appropriate debugging activities can be undertaken. When errors are no longer detected the programmer may feel satisfied that the program functions correctly, at least for the desired ranges of input data. The number of tests and range of test data depend largely on the nature of the problem and the level of confidence the programmer wishes with regard to the correctness of the program.

Testing the program with the kinds of data expected in actual use of the program is, of course, important. Another important principle of program testing is that a variety of data is used, sufficient to adequately test each possible path of execution in the program. Additional principles of program testing may be found in the references (1) at the end of this chapter.

Program testing is expensive, time consuming, and intellectually unexciting. But its really serious shortcoming is that in general no amount of testing can guarantee that a program is completely error free; it cannot be used to show conclusively that a program is in category 4 of Figure 10.1. Program testing can demonstrate the presence of bugs, but not their absence. A comprehensive set of program tests may reveal no errors, but some pattern in input data not included in the test set may lead to an error. Exhaustive testing may convince the programmer that the program is indeed error free—but the possibility always exists that the testing has simply missed uncovering a bug.

Practical programs are usually fairly complex, with many, many cases and combinations of input data, and even diligent testing can leave many bugs undiscovered. Many payroll systems, compilers, inventory systems, and the like, have been delivered as "working" after thorough testing, only shortly to be found to have serious, amusing, expensive, embarrassing, and/or annoying bugs. The fundamental inability of program testing to guarantee error-free programs has contributed significantly to the interest in techniques for avoiding errors in program development, and hence in structured programming. Because of this fundamental deficiency of program testing, this topic will not be further discussed here. It is, however, currently an important practical aspect of program development, much work has been done in this area, and many fine references exist which discuss it in detail.

10.2 Structured Programming

A great deal could be written in this section, since the term *structured programming* currently connotes a sizable body of knowledge about programming and programming techniques. However, this entire book describes and illustrates structured programming, and there is no point in reproducing much of it here. Therefore, this section simply summarizes the objectives and principal features of structured programming.

The main objective of structured programming is to facilitate the design and writing of error-free programs. A number of programming "styles" or techniques appear to contribute to this facility. These styles will be familiar to the reader of the preceding chapters as the "normal" way to program in Fortran. Figure 10.3 summarizes the four principal features of structured programming. All have been described in previous chapters. The use of structured programming tends to minimize the number of errors introduced into programs because the programmer's understanding of the exact behavior of a program tends to be maximized.

1 Careful problem definition and program modularization.

2 Data types and structures of the problem's data elements similar to the data elements of the problem.

3 Use of one-in, one-out control structures to implement an algorithm closely resembling the logical structure of the problem.

4 Careful program layout—meaningful names for data elements and procedures; effective use of indentation and statement placement; effective use of comments.

Figure 10.3. Features of structured programming.

The best structured programs are short and simple, with straightforward use of data elements. Complex logic is rarely necessary (modularize instead) and "tricky" use of data elements should be avoided. Side effects should not occur. These are important considerations, not only for structured programming but for correctness proofs as well.

10.3 Correctness Proofs

Careful structuring of a program typically results in the programmer being highly confident that the program is correct. This confidence is based on intuitive and informal analysis of the program. Because the well-structured program is easy to understand, the alert programmer tends to mentally verify the program's correctness. Correctness proofs involve putting such informal analysis in a formal and rigorous form. Most elements in a correctness proof are simply formal (i.e., "mathematical") versions of intuitive concepts of the "state" of the program or of the effect of executing a statement. This section describes some elementary methods of constructing correctness proofs, and could serve as an introduction to this topic.

Logical expressions may be used to make assertions about the state of the program (i.e., about the values of data elements). For example at some point in the program the assertion

```
N gt 0          (the value of N is greater than zero)
```

may be made (assume N is an integer variable), and it may be either true or false. Suppose this assertion has been shown to be true at this point in the program, and the next statement to be executed is

```
K = N/2-1
```

After execution of this assignment statement the following assertion is true:

```
N gt 0  and  K eq N/2-1
```

These pre- and post-assertions associated with the statement may be presented as follows (the assertions are preceded by ==>):

```
          ==> N gt 0
K = N/2-1
              ==> N gt 0  and  K eq N/2-1
```

Thus in rigorous terms some facts about the state of the program, and the effects of executing a statement, have been described.

One can imagine a sequence of program statements, with valid assertions intervening and supplying descriptions of the state of execution of the program. The object is to be able to end the program with a valid assertion that demonstrates that the program performs the intended processing. Consider the very simple program SWITCH, which switches the two numerical values of X and Y, if necessary, so that the value of X is the smaller of the two. The assertions are included as comments.

The assertion following the ENDIF in program SWITCH is the "or" composition of the assertions resulting from each possible selection path. This example conforms to the general form for the assertion following selection, as shown in Figure 10.4. In program SWITCH the programmer's intuitive feelings about the behavior of the program have been formalized in the assertions, and the final assertion shows that the program is correct. (Actually the assertions of program SWITCH do not include evidence that the final values of X and Y are the same pair of values as in the beginning. Although this is "obvious" in this program, correctness proofs normally must verify even the obvious. Extending the proof in program SWITCH to include the fact that the final two values for X and Y are the same as the two values input is left for Problem 10.1 at the end of this chapter.)

As long as the statements to be executed appear in the program in the order they are to be executed—for statement sequences involving no execution control or just selection control—the techniques illustrated in program SWITCH can be used to construct correctness proofs. The situation becomes more complicated, however, when statements may be executed again (i.e., for loops). The reason is that the assertion at the *bottom* of the loop is the one that must be used at the *top* of the loop for the next

```
*....:---------------------------------------------------------------------
      PROGRAM  SWITCH

*                   ..A simple example of a correctness proof.  At
*                   the end of the program the value of X is smaller
*                   than (or equal to) the value of Y, and the pair
*                   of values are the same values as given..

*     ....variables....
      REAL  X, Y, T

*     ....execute....
      READ *, X, Y
*                                 ==>  X and Y are defined
      IF  (X .GT. Y)  THEN
*                                 ==>  X gt Y
         T = X
*                                 ==>  X gt Y  and  T eq X  ==>  T gt Y
         X = Y
*                                 ==>  T gt Y  and  X eq Y  ==>  T gt X
         Y = T
*                                 ==>  T gt X  and  Y eq T  ==>  Y gt X
      ENDIF
*                                 ==>  X le Y  or  Y gt X  ==>  X le Y
      PRINT *, X, Y
      END
=====================================================================
```

execution of the loop body. A valid assertion, A1, after the first execution of the loop may produce a different assertion, A2, after the second execution of the loop, and so on until the loop terminates (assuming it does) with assertion An (illustrated in Figure 10.5).

In principle it is possible to construct the sequence A0, A1, A2, A3, . . ., An as part of the correctness proof. This is not very practical, however, since each step in this sequence may be nontrivial, and there may be many thousands of such steps. A "short-cut" method is necessary. Certainly it would simplify matters if perchance A0 = A1 = A2 = A3 = . . . = An. Then one need only determine A0 in the first place, and show that an execution of the loop does not change it. Usually the "tricky" part here is determining an appropriate A0 in the first place, since it not only must remain invariant but must demonstrate that the loop in fact does what it is supposed to do.

Before discussing loop invariant assertions further, an example may help to make the concept more palatable. Program MEAN is a very simple one: it computes the average (AVE) of a set of values (V1, V2, . . ., Vn). The mean (average) is defined to be

$$AVE = (V1 + V2 + \ldots + Vn)/N \qquad \text{(for N gt 0)}$$

The main feature of program MEAN is a loop to generate the sum (SUM) of the V's.

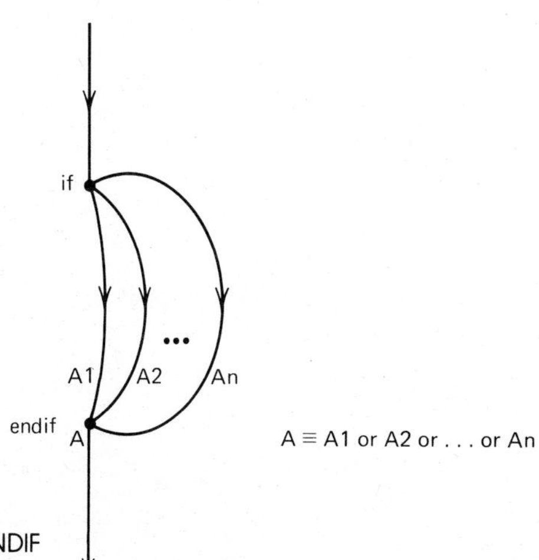

Figure 10.4. The assertion following execution of an IF-ENDIF structure (the A's stand for Assertions).

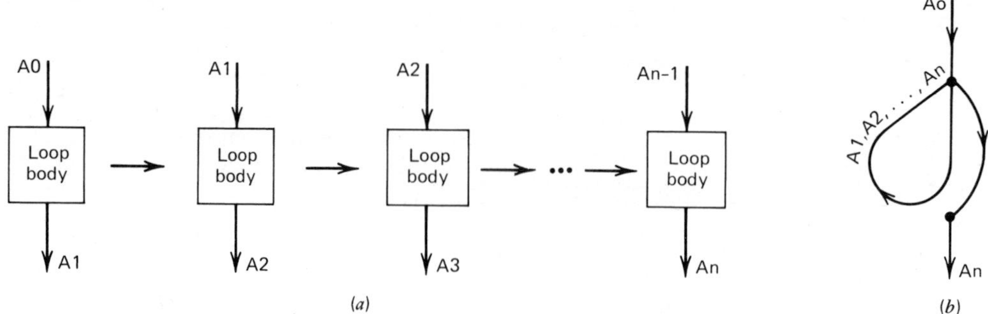

Figure 10.5. The pattern of assertions in a looping context. (*a*) Individual loop executions. (*b*) In the schematic do-repeat framework.

Notice in program MEAN that the loop invariant formally describes the very essence of the loop. Loop invariant assertions, to be useful in correctness proofs, nearly always have that property—they reflect the purpose of the loop. Thus in devising the loop invariant, careful consideration should be given as to how the purpose of the loop can be put in suitable general assertion form.

The loop of program MEAN has one single-level exit, located at the top of the loop, as shown in Figure 10.6. Just prior to the loop body of Figure 10.6, the loop invariant (LI) is true (assuming no side effects in evaluation of the exit condition) and the exit condition (<EC>) is false. Since the loop body leaves LI unchanged, LI is true at the end of execution of the loop body. Upon exit from the loop both LI and EC are true. Therefore LI should be chosen so that together with EC the loop is proved correct (i.e., shown to function as intended).

```
*....:-----------------------------------------------------------------
      PROGRAM  MEAN

*                    ..This program illustrates the use of a loop invariant
*                    assertion to prove the correctness of a loop.  In this
*                    case the loop sums a set of numbers..

*     ....variables....
      INTEGER  K, N
      REAL  AVE, SUM, V(1:10000)

*     ....execute....
      CALL INPUT(N,V)
*                          ..assume INPUT supplies valid values for
*                                 N and V1, V2, V3, ..., Vn
*                                 with N ge 1 and N le 10000..

*                                   ==>  N, V1, V2, ... Vn defined
      SUM = V(1)
      K = 1
*                         loop invariant  ==>  SUM eq V1 + V2 + ... + Vk
      do
         IF  (K .EQ. N)  exit
*                                   ==>  K lt N  and  SUM eq V1+V2+...+Vk
         K = K+1
*                                   ==>  SUM eq V1+V2+...+Vk-1  and  K le N
         SUM = SUM + V(K)
*                                   ==>  SUM eq V1+V2+...+Vk-1+Vk
      repeat
*                                   ==>  K eq N  and  SUM eq V1+V2+...+Vk
*                                   ==>  SUM eq V1+V2+...+Vn
      AVE = SUM/N
*                     ==>  AVE eq SUM/N  ==>  AVE eq (V1+V2+...+Vn)/N
      PRINT *, AVE
      END
=======================================================================
```

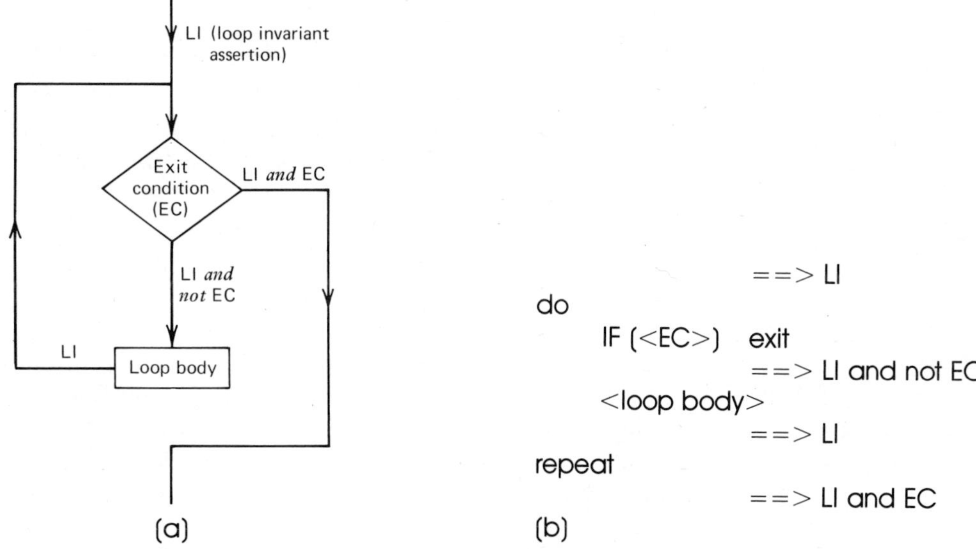

Figure 10.6. Looping structure with exit-at-the-top exhibiting the loop-invariant LI. (*a*) Schematic structure. (*b*) In correctness proof form.

The entire process, which is valid for any loop having the form shown in Figure 10.6*a*, can be summarized as a three-step procedure:

1 Devise a suitable loop invariant LI (requires some creative thinking).

2 Show that LI is initially true and that (LI and EC) implies the desired result.

3 Show that starting with (LI and not EC) true the loop body leaves LI true (requires the step-by-step process illustrated in programs SWITCH and MEAN).

In addition the loop should be shown ultimately to terminate, an important consideration ignored in the above example. Note that in this invariant method only one execution of the loop body is considered during the proof, and that the proof is valid regardless of the number of times the loop body is executed.

Loops with the form shown in Figure 10.6 are the easiest to prove correct, loops with multiple exits are the hardest. Loops with single exits other than at the top, or with abnormal (multilevel) exits, also complicate correctness proofs. For the purpose of correctness proofs, abnormal exits may be converted to the equivalent cascade of single-level exits. Figure 10.7 illustrates how a loop whose (single) exit is not at the top may be converted to an equivalent loop whose exit is at the top. In that figure <S1> and <S2> are any groups of statements.

```
                              <S1>
   do                         do
      <S1>                       IF (<EC>) exit
      IF (<EC>) exit             <S2>
      <S2>                       <S1>
   repeat                     repeat
(a)                        (b)
```

Figure 10.7. Conversion of exit-in-middle to equivalent exit-at-top. (*a*) Original loop with arbitrary exit location. (*b*) Equivalent loop with exit at the top.

Figure 10.7*b* may in fact be used to apply the loop invariant method of proof to any loop having the form shown in Figure 10.7*a*. In this case the three steps given above are modified as follows:

1 Devise a suitable loop invariant LI to be used on the loop of Figure 10.7*b*.

2 Show that LI is true following the initial execution of <S1>, and that (LI and EC) implies the desired result.

3 Show that starting with (LI and not EC) true, execution of <S2> followed by execution of <S1> leaves LI true, that is, this must hold:

```
        ==> (LI and not EC)
<S2>
<S1>
        ==> LI
```

Note that the original three steps are a special case of those just given, in the event that <S1> is empty (has no statements), in which case the loop is already in exit-at-the-top form.

Multiple exits are more difficult to handle. Figure 10.8 illustrates how a two-exit loop may be converted to a one-exit (at the top) loop for purposes of applying a loop invariant correctness proof. Additional exits may be accommodated by further selection nesting below <S2>. Note that the first exit of the multiple exit loop may be assumed at the top of the loop, because the technique of Figure 10.7**b** can always be used to achieve this.

If the loop invariant method is to work for the loop in Figure 10.8**b** then the following must hold:

```
        ==> LI and not EC1
<S1>
        ==> (LI and EC2) or not EC2
```

Furthermore when (not EC) results on execution of <S1>, then the following must subsequently hold:

```
        ==> not EC2
<S2>
        ==> LI
```

Therefore two-exit loops may be proven correct with the same three-step process as above, but with the proof sequence of the third step replaced by the two proof sequences just given. Corresponding extensions can be used for loops with even more exits.

```
do
    IF (<EC1>)
    <S1>
    IF <EC2> exit
    <S2>
repeat
```

(a)

```
DONE = .FALSE.
do
        IF (<EC1> .OR. DONE) exit
        <S1>
        IF (<EC2>) THEN
                    DONE = .TRUE.
            ELSE
                    <S2>
        ENDIF
repeat
```

(b)

Figure 10.8. Conversion of multiple exits to an equivalent single exit. (*a*) Original loop with two exits. (*b*) Equivalent loop with a single exit at the top.

The SPLIT subroutine of the TWOWAY merge program of chapter 6 contains an example of a short, simple loop with two exits. This loop, treating the two-level exit as just a single-level one, has the form shown in Figure 10.9.

```
do
        N1 = N1 + 1
        AUX1(N1) = NEXT
        N = N + 1
        IF (N .GT. SIZE) exit
        LAST = NEXT
        NEXT = FILE(N)
        IF (NEXT .LT. LAST) exit
repeat
```

(a)

```
do      <SA>
        IF (N .GT. SIZE) exit
        <SB>
        IF (NEXT .LT. LAST) exit
repeat
```

(b)

```
<SA>
do
        IF (N .GT. SIZE) exit
        <SB>
IF      (NEXT .LT. LAST) exit
        <SA>
repeat
```

(c)

```
<SA>: N1 = N1 + 1
      AUX1(N1) = NEXT
      N = N + 1

<SB>: LAST = NEXT
      NEXT = FILE(N)
```

(d)

Figure 10.9. One of the loops of subroutine SPLIT (Chapter 6). (Note that <SA> corresponds to <S2> in Figure 10.8, and <SB> corresponds to <S1> in Figure 10.8.) (*a*) The original loop. (*b*) Structural form of original loop. (*c*) Loop equivalent to that in (*b*), but having the form of Figure 10.9*a*. (*d*) The components of <SA> and <SB>.

The purpose of the loop in Figure 10.9 is to transfer the next run from array FILE to array AUX1; the new run is to start in position N1+1 of AUX1 (call this position NS) and the first element of the new run is in FILE(N) with a copy in NEXT. There are SIZE elements in FILE, and N is initially not greater than SIZE. This loop will now be proven correct, using the techniques described above.

The first step is to devise a suitable loop invariant LI, which is usually closely related to the purpose of the loop. Since the purpose of the loop is to transfer a run, a possible candidate for LI is a formal statement of the fact that what has been transferred into AUX1 thus far by the loop constitutes a run. N1 increases by one each time through the loop, so a reasonable candidate for LI is

AUX1(N1) ge AUX1(N1−1) ge AUX1(N1−2) ge . . . ge AUX1(NS)

(This is not a valid form for a Fortran logical expression, but it does clearly and conveniently, and rigorously, express the relationships among the elements of a run.) This assertion may in fact be sufficient for LI, but it would be nice if LI also includes evidence that the AUX1 elements are those transferred from FILE. Therefore let the candidate for LI be:

AUX1(N1) eq FILE(N−1) and AUX1(N1) ge AUX1(N1−1) ge AUX1(N1−2) ge . . . ge AUX1(NS).

Does this LI, combined with the exit conditions, imply that the loop has indeed accomplished its mission? The mission is to transfer the entire next run of FILE, including the case that the run extends to the end of the file. Upon exit from the loop the assertion

==> LI and (N gt SIZE or NEXT lt LAST)

is true. If (N gt SIZE) is true then N eq SIZE+1 (since N increases by one each time through the loop), AUX1(N1) eq FILE(SIZE), and the run has extended to the end of FILE and has been completely transferred. If (NEXT lt LAST) is true then, since LAST eq FILE(N−1) and NEXT eq FILE(N), FILE(N) lt FILE(N−1), and since the last element transferred is AUX1(N1) eq FILE(N−1), the entire next run has been transferred. Thus LI, combined with the exit condition, does indeed mean mission accomplished.

It remains to show that LI is true on entry into the loop, and that an execution of the loop does in fact leave LI unchanged. These proofs follow, in the "program form" used in programs SWITCH and MEAN. The loop itself is that of Figure 10.9*c* transformed to the form of Figure 10.8*b*. Since in this form there is only a single exit point, at the top of the loop, the do and the exit are combined into a single, more esthetic, construct: do until <exit condition> (see Problem 8.8). Proving that the loop terminates has been left as an exercise (Problem 10.2), but it is simple since initially (N le SIZE) and N increases by one each time through the loop.

```
*....:-----------------------------------------------------------------
      RUNDUN = .FALSE.
*                      ==>  NS eq N1+1  (the starting location in AUX1,
*                                           for the next run)
*                      ==>  NEXT eq FILE(N)   (the first element of the
*                                                         next run)
                       ==>  N lt SIZE
      N1 = N1+1
*                      ==>  NS eq N1
      AUX(N1) = NEXT
*                      ==>  AUX1(N1) eq FILE(N) and NS eq N1
      N = N+1
*                      ==>  AUX1(N1) eq FILE(N-1) and N1 eq NS  ==>  LI
*                 LI   ==>  AUX1(N1) eq FILE(N-1) and AUX1(N1) ge
*                             AUX1(N1-1) ge AUX1(N1-2) ge...ge AUX1(NS)

      do until  ((N .GT. SIZE)  .OR. RUNDUN)
*                        ==>  LI and (N le SIZE)
         LAST = NEXT
*                        ==>  LAST eq AUX1(N1) eq FILE(N-1)
         NEXT = FILE(N)
*                        ==>  (LI and NEXT lt LAST) or (LI and NEXT ge LAST)
*                        ==>  (LI and EC2) or (not EC2)
         IF (NEXT .LT. LAST) THEN
               RUNDUN = .TRUE.
*                              ==>  (LI and EC2)
            ELSE
*                              ==>  LI and (not EC2)
*                              ==>  NEXT eq FILE(N) and NEXT ge LAST
*                              ==>  FILE(N) ge AUX1(N1)
               N1 = N1+1
*                              ==>  FILE(N) ge AUX1(N1-1)
               AUX1(N1) = NEXT
*                              ==>  AUX1(N1) eq FILE(N)
*                              ==>  AUX1(N1) ge AUX1(n1-1) ge...ge AUX1(NS)
               N = N+1
*                              ==>  AUX1(N1) eq FILE(N-1)  ==>  LI
         ENDIF
*                        ==>  (LI and RUNDUN) or LI  ==>  LI
      repeat
*                        ==>  LI and (N gt SIZE  or  NEXT lt LAST)
*                        ==>  program correct
=======================================================================
```

In the above examples correctness proofs were used to demonstrate the correctness of programs. A final example will use a correctness proof to find and correct a programming error. Program BASE of chapter 5 had two subtle errors in it (which were uncovered in that chapter using program testing). One of the errors was in the loop

```
K = SIZE
do
    Q = INT(VALUE/BASE2)
    D = VALUE-Q*BASE2
    NUM2(K:K) = DIGITS(D:D)
    VALUE = Q
    IF (VALUE .EQ. 0) exit
    K = K-1
repeat
```

The purpose of this loop was to generate the BASE2 digits that represent a given integer VALUE. The generated digits are placed in the string variable NUM2 (which is initially all blanks). BASE2 is an integer between 2 and 20, and Q, D, and K are auxiliary integer variables. DIGITS is a string holding all of the possible digit characters: DIGITS = '0123456789ABCDEFGHIJ'.

Applying a correctness proof to this loop is nontrivial because of the tricky business of representing a numerical value with a (nonnumerical) string of digits. In formally analyzing the behavior of the loop, great care must be taken that the transformation from digit characters to numerical values is done rigorously. The essence of the loop is that after an execution of the loop body part of the original VALUE is represented by the digits of NUM2 and the rest by the current VALUE. When stated rigorously this could be an appropriate candidate for the loop invariant. Figure 10.10 is a "picture" of NUM2 after several executions of the loop body; the normal positional scheme is used for representing integers—C0 is the least significant digit, C1 is the next least significant, and so on. The Cs are the digit characters; if N0, N1, N2, . . . Ni are the numerical value of C0, C1, C2, . . . Ci, respectively, then the digits in NUM2 represent the numerical value N0 + N1*BASE2 + N2*BASE2**2 + . . . + Ni*BASE2**i. The proper relation between a C and its corresponding N can be expressed by the INDEX function: N = INDEX('123456789ABCDEFGHIJ', C); note that this is valid for C = '0' also.

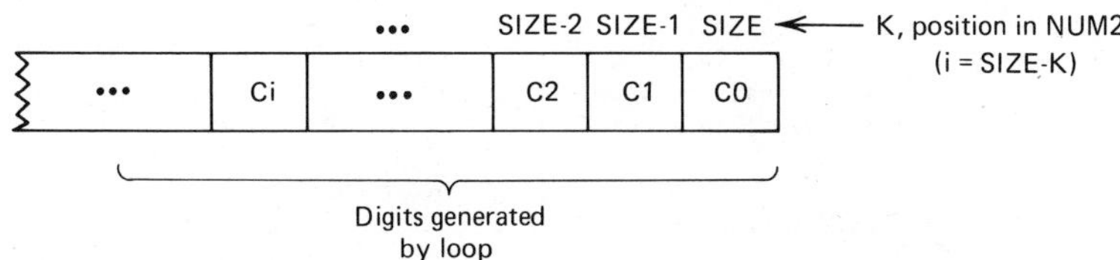

Figure 10.10. The arrangement of digits in NUM2.

The loop invariant is then:

N0+N1*BASE2+N2*BASE2**2+. . .+Ni*BASE2**i + VALUE*BASE2**(i+1) eq constant (the constant is the original VALUE)

Note that this assertion, together with the exit condition (VALUE eq 0), describes the intended function of the loop—for the resulting value of NUM2 to correctly represent the originally given numeric VALUE. The remaining steps of the proof are carried out with the loop in the form (using Figure 10.7*b*))

```
K = SIZE
Q = INT(VALUE/BASE2)
D = VALUE-Q*BASE2
NUM2(K:K) = DIGITS(D:D)
VALUE = Q
do until (VALUE .EQ. 0)
    K = K-1
    Q = INT(VALUE/BASE2)
    D = VALUE-Q*BASE2
    NUM2(K:K) = DIGITS(D:D)
    VALUE = Q
repeat
```

Now for the correctness proof.

```
*....:-----------------------------------------------------------------
*     initial conditions:
      ORIG = VALUE
*               ..ORIG will be the initial value of VALUE, and the
*                 following assertions are assumed to be initially true..
*                       ==>  VALUE ge 0 and VALUE lt BASE2**SIZE and SIZE gt 0
*                       ==>  BASE2 gt 1 and BASE2 lt 21
*                       ==>  NUM2 eq ' ' and DIGITS eq '0123456789ABCDEFGHIJ'
*                       ==>  Ni eq INDEX('123456789ABCDEFGHIJ',Ci) and i eq SIZE-K
*                  LI  ==>  N0+N1*BASE2+N2*BASE2**2+...+Ni*BASE2**i +
*                                 VALUE*BASE2**(i+1) eq ORIG
      K = SIZE
*                       ==>  (i eq 0) and (VALUE eq ORIG)
      Q = INT(VALUE/BASE2)
      D = VALUE-Q*BASE2
*                       ==>  (ORIG eq Q*BASE2+D) and (Q ge 0) and
*                                (D ge 0) and (Q lt VALUE) and (D lt BASE2)
      NUM2(K:K) = DIGITS(D:D)
*                       ==>  (D gt 0 and C0 eq DIGITS(D:D)) or (D eq 0)
*                       ==>  (N0 eq D-1) or (invalid substring reference)
      VALUE = Q
*                       ==>  (ORIG eq VALUE*BASE2+N0+1) and (i eq 0)
*                       ==>  not LI

*     Therefore LI is not true just before the loop.
*     This means that either LI is not an appropriate loop invariant
*     here, or that there is an error in the program.  Since the
*     invariant assertion seems OK, the error might be apparent in the
*     last assertion (actually the last two assertion  lines above.)
*     N0 is too small by one which suggests that something is wrong
*     with the expression DIGITS(D:D).  Moreover the possibility of
*     D eq 0 detected in the proof also suggests trouble with
*     DIGITS(D:D).  This knowledge leads to formulation of the
*     correct expression :  DIGITS(D+1:D+1).  With this change
*     LI is true at this point, and the proof continues.

*                            ==>  (i eq 0) and LI
      do until (VALUE .EQ. 0)
*                            ==>  (VALUE gt 0) and LI
*         K = K-1
*                            ==>  increase i by 1
*                            ==>  N0+N1*BASE2+N2*BASE2**2+...+Ni-1*BASE2**(i-1) +
*                                      VALUE*BASE2**i eq ORIG
          Q = INT(VALUE/BASE2)
          D = VALUE-Q*BASE2
*                            ==>  (D lt BASE2) and (D ge 0) and (VALUE eq D+Q*BASE2)
*                            ==>  VALUE*BASE2**i eq D*BASE2**i+Q*BASE2(i+1)
          NUM2(K:K) = DIGITS(D+1:D+1)
*                            ==>  Ci eq DIGITS(D+1:D+1)  ==>  Ni eq D
*                            ==>  N0+N1*BASE2+N2*BASE2**2+...+Ni*BASE2**i +
*                                      Q*BASE2**(i+1) eq ORIG
          VALUE = Q
*                            ==>  N0+N1*BASE2+N2*BASE2**2+...+Ni*BASE2**i +
*                                      VALUE*BASE2**(i+1) eq ORIG
*                            ==>  LI
      repeat
*               ==>  (VALUE eq 0) and LI
*               ==>  loop is correct
=====================================================================
```

Thus the correctness proof was responsible for identifying the error, and after the error was fixed the correctness proof verified the correctness of the loop.

A correctness proof on a loop is really not complete until the loop also is shown to ultimately terminate, because the invariant assertion together with the exit condition implies that the loop correctly performs its intended function. Usually showing termination is considerably easier than performing the analysis with the loop invariant. In the above example all of the essential facts are included to prove termination. These are that Q (and hence VALUE) must be greater than or equal to zero, and its value each time through the loop is less than the last time. Since VALUE is an integer it therefore must ultimately have the value zero, at which point the loop terminates.

The above examples should serve to illustrate the current "state-of-the-art" with respect to proving programs correct. The techniques described involve making certain assertions about the state of the program at various points (e.g., after each statement) and then demonstrating the veracity of those assertions. The assertions are simply formal forms (usually in the form of logical expressions) of the programmer's informal and intuitive notions about the program. Often the assertions are rigorous statements about what the program is supposed to do. Certainly the programmer who attempts to prove a program correct using these techniques is rewarded with a deep understanding of the program, and with additional insights into the programming process itself.

Currently there are two thorny problems with respect to widespread practical use of correctness proofs. The first is related to "assertion design." There does not yet exist much in the way of practical guidelines concerning which assertions to use where. How detailed should assertions be? An assertion can be extremely detailed (and correspondingly long), describing all conceivable aspects of the state of the program. Normally assertions don't need to be so detailed. On the other hand the assertions have to be general enough so that the proof is rigorous and complete. Although the science of correctness proofs does have some guidelines for conducting proofs (such as the use of loop invariants), assertion formation is still something of a "black art," where individual programmers must rely largely on their own ingenuity to devise a satisfactory proof. This situation will change, of course, as the science of correctness proofs matures.

The second problem is that a correctness proof may itself contain an error, thus a "proof" that appears to verify a program may convince the programmer that the program is correct, when in fact an unsuspected error in the proof itself makes the proof invalid. There are two obvious sources of such errors. The first is a "mechanical" error in the train of logical implications, and the second is a "faulty" initial assertion. As long as humans are doing correctness proofs, mechanical errors will occasionally be made. Some research has been done on automatic proving systems that perform most of the mechanics of the proof on being given the key assertions. Should such systems prove practical, then mechanical errors in correctness proofs will not be a serious problem. Errors associated with initial assertion formulation are a different matter, however, and together with arbitrary assertion design constitute the "weak links" in the use of correctness proofs for verifying programs.

Despite the problems with correctness proofs such proofs can be extremely useful, and are sure to become more and more an important aspect of programming. Probably the era will come in which the major assertions are formulated during the problem definition stage and before any of the program itself has been written, and then much of the proof will be conducted during development of the program. In this manner programs will tend to be constructed as correct, more so than with just structured programming alone, and program testing will decrease in importance.

The correctness proof techniques described above do allow some general observations to be made relative to the use of control structures. Control structures for which proofs are easiest are to be preferred, first because the easier the proof the less likely an error will be made in it, and second because such control structures are the easiest for the programmer to understand. One-in, one-out structures are certainly to be preferred because a proof step can be limited to one execution path. Abnormal exits and arbitrary branching create departures from the one-in, one-out principle, and complicate correctness proofs enormously because parts of the proof then have to deal simultaneously with two or more execution paths. Not surprisingly, loops with single exits are more easily proved correct than loops with more than one exit, and (perhaps a bit surprisingly) loops with the exit at the top are the easiest of all loops to prove correct. For a program consisting of a number of modules, correctness proofs may be applied to each module independently. Therefore, the simpler each module, the simpler will be the corresponding correctness proofs. The programmer who develops a programming style that maximizes the use of programming techniques most compatible with correctness proofs will be in good shape as correctness proofs become an increasingly important aspect of programming.

10.4 Summary

Since the early 1950s computer programming has developed from a "black art", full of tricks and mysterious maneuvers, to a more systematic discipline. Symptomatic of this evolution is the replacement of total reliance on program testing for verifying programs with a combination of structured programming and program testing. With structured programming the program is more likely to be error free than with more undisciplined programming methods, and easier to modify. Therefore structured programming not only eliminates much debugging, but also gives the programmer more confidence in the correctness of the program since program testing can only identify certain errors and cannot guarantee program correctness.

As the discipline of computer programming continues to develop and mature, techniques for proving programs correct (i.e., free of errors) are developing. Common programming practice in the future is likely to include correctness proofs as part of the programming process. Current correctness proof methods typically involve stating the programmer's intuitive notions about the function and state of the program in formal, rigorous terms, called assertions. When the effects of the program's statements are determined on properly designed assertions the results can show that the program performs precisely the intended processing.

The following references may be consulted for further details on these matters.

1 Program testing: Huang, J. C., "An Approach to Program Testing," *Computing Surveys*, 1975.
Hetzel, W. C., *Program Test Methods*, Prentice-Hall (1972).

2 Structured programming: December 1974 issue of *Computing Surveys* (special issue on Programming). This is the same reference as given for the preceding chapter, and it contains many additional references to structured programming.
Wirth, N., *Systematic Programming*, Prentice-Hall (1973).

3 Correctness proofs: Hantler, S. L., and King, J. C., "An Introduction to Proving the Correctness of Programs," *Computing Surveys*, Sept. 1976.
Dijkstra, E. W., *A Discipline of Programming*, Prentice-Hall (1976).
Elspas, B. et al. "An Assessment of Techniques for Proving Program Correctness," *Computing Surveys*, June 1972.

Programming Exercises

10.1 Extend the proof of program SWITCH to include verification of the fact that the final two values (for X and Y) are the same as the two input values.

10.2 Prove that the loop of subroutine SPLIT is guaranteed to terminate.

10.3 Design a comprehensive program testing process to test the correctness of program MCMESS of Chapter 5.

10.4 Prove that program LOT of Chapter 4 is correct.

10.5 Prove that the palindrome-checking program of Chapter 5 is correct.

10.6 Devise a suitable loop-invariant assertion for the loop in program FACT (Chapter 5) which computes the digits of the next factorial value. Use this loop-invariant to prove that the loop functions as intended.

10.7 Devise a suitable loop-invariant assertion, and construct a detailed proof for the following program. (Hint: change the indexed do to an equivalent nonindexed do.)

```
F1 = 1
F2 = 1
do K = 1,10
    F = F1 + F2
    F1 = F2
    F2 = F
repeat
            ==> F = sum of first 10 Fibonacci numbers plus 1
                    (1+1+2+3+5+8+13+21+34+55) +1
```

10.8 Prove that subroutine NXPRIM (Chapter 9), for finding the next prime integer, is correct.

Chapter 11 Recursion

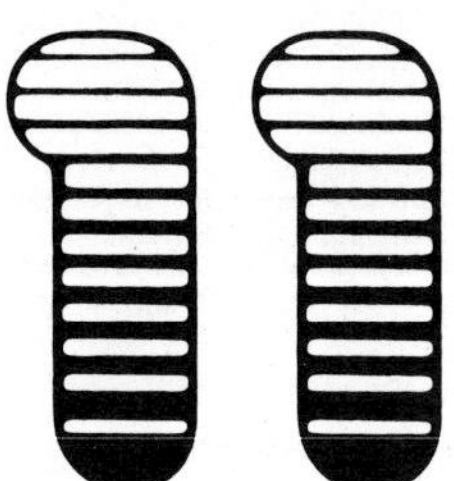

In several of the preceding chapters it has been recommended that, in general, program structure should closely parallel the logical structure of the problem being solved. It occasionally happens that a problem is most simply stated in terms of itself or, more accurately, in terms of the same problem on a smaller scale. An example of such a "recursive" definition is (to take a familiar problem) the following reformulation of the linear search algorithm (see Section 5.2). In this problem an array, TABLE(1:N), is to be searched for a value X, with MATCH having the index of TABLE where a match is found or zero if no match is found. Consider the following informal definition of LSERCH for accomplishing this:

```
LSERCH (X,TABLE(1:N))
    if N lt 1 then
            MATCH = 0
        elseif X ne TABLE(N) then
            call LSERCH (X,TABLE(1:N−1))
        else
            MATCH = N
    endif
end LSERCH
```

The meaning of the statement call LSERCH(X,TABLE(1:N−1)) is that the LSERCH program is repeated using only N−1 elements of TABLE. In other words, the above definition of LSERCH says "check the last (Nth) element of TABLE for a match—if this element doesn't match, and this is not the only element in TABLE, then search the first N−1 elements of TABLE for a match". Notice in this example how searching an array of N elements has been described in terms of the two basic steps:

1 Checking one of the array elements.

2 Searching an array of the other N−1 elements.

Thus the linear search of an array has been described in terms of a linear search of a smaller array. The call statement is called a *recursive call*, and represents the part where the problem is defined in terms of (a smaller part of) itself. The technique of using recursive calls in the description of an algorithm is called *recursion*, and constitutes a repetition mechanism.

As will be seen in this chapter, some problems are recursive by nature, in the sense that a recursive definition is by far the simplest way to describe the problem (although this is not true for the linear search). Recursion is a quite general technique, however, and can be used to describe any repetitive situation. Figure 11.1 illustrates how any do-repeat loop with a single exit (located anywhere within the loop) may be

```
do                                  LOOP
    <S1>                                <S1>
    if <EC> exit                        if not <EC> then
    <S2>                                  <S2>
repeat                                    call LOOP
                                        endif
                                    end LOOP

(a)                                 (b)
```

Figure 11.1. A general single-exit loop. (*a*) do-repeat form.(*b*) Equivalent recursive form.

reformulated with recursion. Conversely any algorithm expressed recursively can be converted to an equivalent do-repeat loop. Since Fortran does not provide for direct implementation of recursion (i.e., does not allow the CALL statement to be used recursively) the main purpose of this chapter is to describe techniques that may be used to simulate recursion in Fortran. In the examples recursive calls will use a lower-case call to emphasize the nonstandard nature of such usage in Fortran.

The key to understanding a recursive algorithm, and indeed to devising recursive algorithms, is to consider a recursive call as a call on a module of the program (forgetting, for the moment, that it is this module that you are currently analyzing). That is, assume that the recursive call "does its job properly", regardless of how it functions; don't analyze the details of the functioning of the recursive call—just assume that it does what it is supposed to do. With this attitude the behavior of the algorithm containing the recursive call is usually easy to understand. In terms of the preceding chapter, assume (don't try to prove) that the recursive call is correct, then with this assumption show that the algorithm containing the recursive call is correct. With this done, showing that the algorithm works for one special case—usually some simple, limiting case—is sufficient to conclude that the recursive algorithm "works."

Consider again the linear search algorithm described above. There are three possibilities:

1 There are no more elements to check.

2 A match occurs in the Nth element.

3 The first N−1 elements must be searched for a match.

Intuitively it is clear that, assuming the recursive call correctly handles possibility (3), the algorithm given above correctly implements the linear search. Now consider the special case for N = 1: here MATCH is set equal to 1 or zero, depending on whether X matches TABLE(1) or not, and the algorithm produces the correct result. For N = 2 it works correctly since the recursive call is for N−1 = 1, which works. Similarly for N = 3 it will work since N−1 = 2 for which the algorithm is now known to work. Progressing in this manner it is clear that the algorithm will work correctly for any value for N. In the next section several other problems are presented, each of which is nicely described by recursion, and each of which is more appropriate for describing recursively than is the linear search.

11.1 Inherently Recursive Problems

A much more efficient searching algorithm than the linear search, for large TABLEs (i.e., large N), is the *binary search*. This algorithm requires that the values in TABLE be sorted (in ascending order, say), as shown in Figure 11.2. The value in the middle of the table is checked and, because the table is sorted, the subsequent search can be confined to either one half of the table or the other half. A recursive call can be used to search the appropriate half.

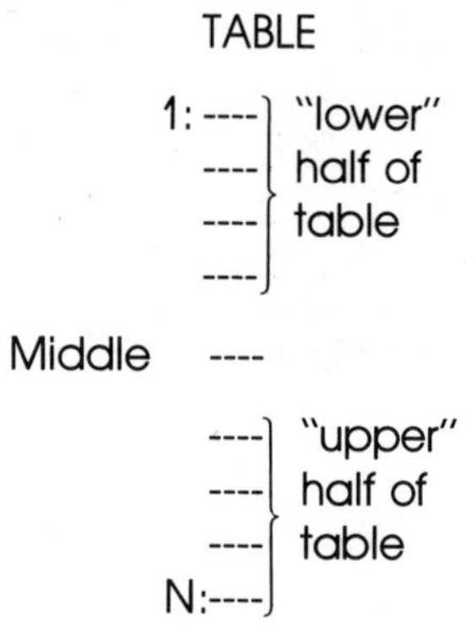

```
         TABLE

       1: ----) "lower"
          ----| half of
          ----| table
          ----)

Middle    ----

          ----) "upper"
          ----| half of
          ----| table
       N: ----)
```

Figure 11.2. A sorted array is used for the binary search algorithm. Assume TABLE is sorted, with TABLE(1) being the smallest value and TABLE(N) being the largest. Then if the searched-for value is less than the middle TABLE value, the subsequent search can be confined to the "lower" half of TABLE.

The algorithm is as follows (as in LSERCH, MATCH is zero or the index of the MATCHed location in TABLE):

```
L = 1              ! note—informally (it's not standard Fortran)
U = N              ! let ! initiate an "end-of-line" comment
BSERCH (X,TABLE(L:U))
    M = int((L+U)/2)        ! M is TABLE midpoint
    if  M lt L then         ! no elements left to check
            MATCH = 0
        elseif X lt TABLE(M) then              ! search lower half of table
            call BSERCH (X,TABLE(L:M-1))
        elseif X gt TABLE(M) then              ! search upper half of table
            call BSERCH (X,TABLE(M+1:U))
        else
            MATCH = M                          ! match found with TABLE(M)
    endif
end BSERCH
```

Here L and U have been used as "generalized" lower and upper limits on the portion of TABLE to search, since both of these limits are likely to vary during the course of execution of BSERCH. The recursive calls tend to systematically squeeze these limits together in such a manner that the searched for value stays bracketed between the two corresponding TABLE values. The great efficiency of the algorithm comes from the fact that half of the remaining "active" part of TABLE may be discarded after each comparison with a TABLE value. In BSERCH there are four possibilities to consider:

1 No active part of TABLE remains (no MATCH in TABLE).

2 Match is found with TABLE(M).

3 Search lower half of TABLE.

4 Search upper half of TABLE.

Again it is (intuitively) clear that the recursive algorithm correctly performs its intended function if it is assumed that the recursive calls, for searching the appropriate halves of the table, correctly perform their functions. In the next section BSERCH will be converted to an equivalent Fortran do-repeat loop.

The binary search algorithm is a much more efficient searching algorithm than the linear search, but it requires that the array be sorted, whereas for the linear search the array need not be sorted. The bubble sort (see Section 5.4) may be used to sort the array, but this sorting algorithm is quite slow. A much faster sorting algorithm (comparable in speed to the two-way merge sort of Chapter 6, but not requiring auxiliary arrays) is the *quicksort* algorithm, which is best described recursively. (Although the

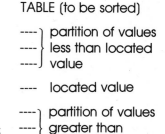

TABLE (to be sorted)

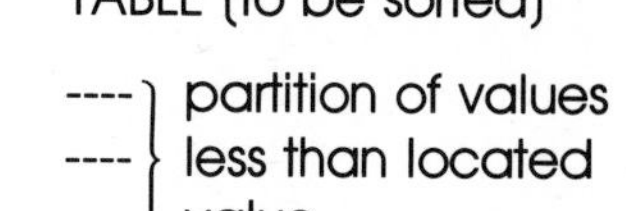

---- located value

---- partition of values
---- greater than
---- located value

Figure 11.3. The basic concept of the quicksort algorithm: partition the array into two unsorted groups separated by a value placed in its correct final sorted location.

quicksort algorithm is best *described* recursively, unfortunately it is not most efficiently *implemented* recursively.) The basic elements of the quicksort are sketched in Figure 11.3. One pass through the array to be sorted is sufficient to place one of the array values (say the first one) in its final location in the sorted array, and at the same time leave all of the values less than this value on one side (but unsorted) and all of the greater values unsorted on the other side. Then recursive calls may be used to sort each of these two "partitions." The speed of the quicksort is due to the fact that each partition has fewer elements than (ideally half as many as) the entire array, and therefore typically requires far fewer comparisons than does the bubble sort. The basic quicksort algorithm therefore is:

1 Locate the (final) position of the first value, partitioning the values in so doing.

2 Sort the first partition.

3 Sort the second partition.

Let PARTIT be a module (subroutine) to perform step 1—for the array of values TABLE(L:U) it determines the proper location PL of TABLE(L), places this value in this location (i.e., TABLE(PL) is set equal to TABLE(L)), places all values less than TABLE(PL) in TABLE(L:PL−1), and places all values greater than TABLE(PL) in TABLE (PL+1:U). The quicksort algorithm is then:

```
L = 1
U = N
QSORT (TABLE(L:U))
    if  U gt L then
        CALL PARTIT (TABLE,L,U,PL)
        call QSORT (TABLE(L:PL-1))
        call QSORT (TABLE(PL+1:U))
    endif
end QSORT
```

Assuming that PARTIT and the recursive calls all do their jobs correctly, informal analysis of the correctness of QSORT could proceed as follows. If U is not greater than L then there is only one element (or none) in TABLE(L:U), and hence TABLE(L:U) is already in its final form. If U is greater than L then (by assumption) PARTIT correctly partitions TABLE(L:U) with element TABLE(PL) having the correct value for the final sorted TABLE(L:U). Separately sorting the two partitions (by assumption performed correctly by the recursive calls) completes the sorting of TABLE(L:U).

For the purposes of a recursive example, QSORT could be left in the above form. For the sake of completeness, however, and because the program is rather short and neat, subroutine PARTIT is given below, including the key steps of a correctness proof (in the spirit of the preceding chapter). Figure 11.4 graphically shows the function of PARTIT, part (*a*) before the main loop has been terminated, and part (*b*) after the loop has been terminated. Basically, J, starting at value L+1, is "slid" to the right until a

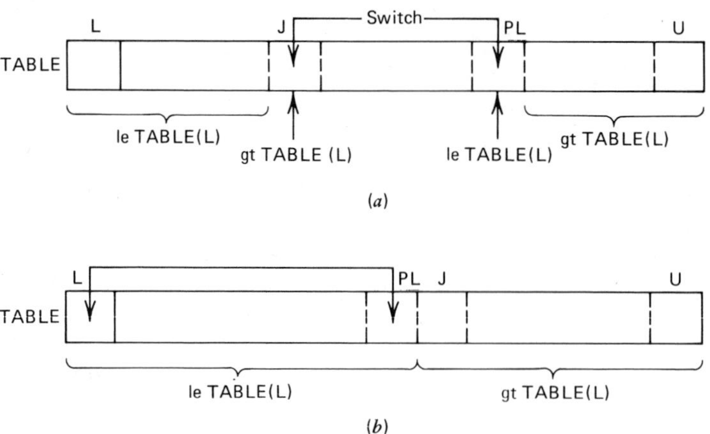

Figure 11.4. The functioning of subroutine PARTIT. (*a*) Before termination of the main loop. (*b*) After termination of the loop.

table element greater than TABLE(L) is found, then PL, starting at U, is "slid" left until a table element less than (or equal to) TABLE(L) is found. These values are exchanged, and the sliding resumes. This continues until J and PL "meet", at which point TABLE is partitioned, as shown in Figure 11.4*b*, and PL is the location for value TABLE(L).

```
*....:------------------------------------------------------------------
      SUBROUTINE  PARTIT (T,L,U,PL)
                          INTEGER  L,U,PL,T(L:U)

*                  ..this subroutine performs the "partitioning" phase
*                    of the quicksort algorithm. This routine places the
*                    first element (subscript L) of array T in its
*                    proper sorted location..

*     ....variables....
      INTEGER  J,TEMP

*     ....execute....     ==>  L lt U     (initial assumption)
      J = L+1
      PL = U
*                         ==>  J eq L+1  and  J le PL
*                    LI   ==>  T(L:J-1) le T(L) and T(PL+1:U) gt TL and T(PL) le T(L)
      do
*        ..slide J right..
         do
            IF  (T(J) .GT. T(L)  .OR.  J .GE. PL)  exit
            J = J+1
         repeat
*                         ==>  T(L:J-1) le T(L) and (T(J) gt T(L) or J ge PL)
*        ..slide PL left..
         do
            IF  (T(PL) .LE. T(L))  exit
            PL = PL-1
         repeat
*                         ==>  T(PL+1:U) gt T(L)  and  T(PL) le T(L)  ==>  LI
*        ..now exit main loop if T fully partitioned..
         IF  (PL .LE. J)  exit
*                         ==>  PL gt J  ==>  T(J) gt T(L)
         TEMP = T(J)
         T(J) = T(PL)
         T(PL) = TEMP
*                         ==>  T(PL) gt T(L)  and  T(J) le T(L)
         J = J+1
         PL = PL-1
*                         ==>  T(L:J-1) le T(L)  and  T(PL+1:U) gt T(L)
      repeat
*                 ..T is now partitioned at PL with value T(L)..
      TEMP = T(L)
      T(L) = T(PL)
      T(PL) = TEMP
*                 ..value T(L) put in proper location, PL..
      END
=====================================================================
```

QSORT is a more interesting example of a recursive algorithm than BSERCH, because the definition of QSORT involves "back-to-back" recursive calls, whereas BSERCH does not.

Another example of an algorithm whose definition is simple using back-to-back recursive calls is HANOI. This algorithm produces the correct sequence of moves to transfer the rings in the problem known as *the towers of Hanoi* from one post to another. The situation is illustrated in Figure 11.5*a*. A board has three identical posts on it, and one post contains N rings, all of different diameters (each ring has a hole in its center so that it can be moved from post to post). The object is to move all of the rings onto one of the other two posts, observing just the following two rules:

1 Only one ring at a time is to be moved.

2 At no time may a ring be placed above a smaller ring on the same post.

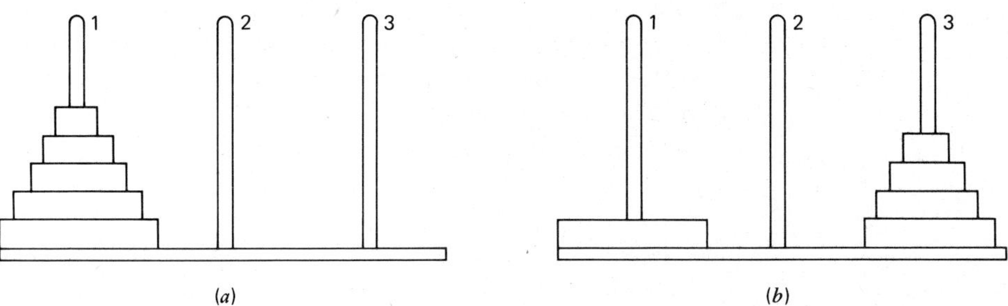

Figure 11.5 Towers of Hanoi, with N rings. (*a*) Original configuration. (*b*) After moving N-1 rings.

In Figure 11.5*a* the rings are shown on post 1; suppose that they are to be moved to post 2. Suppose further that the top N−1 rings from post 1 are somehow successfully moved (observing the rules, of course) to post 3, as shown in Figure 11.5*b*. Then the Nth (largest) ring can be moved to post 2, and the N−1 pile of rings on post 3 moved again, this time to post 2 and on top of the large ring just moved there. A recursive definition of this algorithm is as follows (if the posts are numbered 1, 2, and 3, and P1 and P2 are the number of the "from" and "to" posts, then 6−P1−P2 will always be the number of the third post):

```
HANOI (N,P1,P2)
    if  N gt 0 then
        call HANOI (N−1,P1,6−P1−P2)
        PRINT '(3(A,I3))', ' Move ring', N, ' from post', P1, ' to post', P2
        call HANOI (N−1,6−P1−P2,P2)
    endif
end HANOI
```

This algorithm is even simpler than QSORT, since there is just a single statement (the print statement) in addition to the recursive calls, rather than an entire subroutine that has to be developed and verified. The correctness of HANOI should be intuitively apparent if the recursive calls are assumed to function properly, and ignoring the details of how the recursive calls work.

If N is less than 1 in HANOI then execution of the algorithm does nothing, as it should since this means that there are no rings to move. If N is 1, the statements in the if-endif are executed, but neither of the recursive calls "does anything" since N−1 is zero. Therefore in this case (N eq 1, and assuming P1 eq 1 and P2 eq 2) the results are simply

```
Move ring 1 from post 1 to post 2
```

which is correct for an initial stack consisting of only one ring. Now the algorithm can be seen to work correctly if N is 2. The first recursive call moves one ring (N–1 eq 1) to post 3 (again assuming P1 eq 1 and P2 eq 2) which is now known to work correctly. The print statement is executed (ring 2 is moved to post 2), and then the second recursive call moves ring 1 from post 3 to post 2. The output consists of three lines:

Move ring 1 from post 1 to post 3
Move ring 2 from post 1 to post 2
Move ring 1 from post 3 to post 2

Now that HANOI is known to work correctly for a pile of two rings a similar analysis can be used to show that it works for three rings, then four, then five, and so on, for any value of N.

HANOI and QSORT are examples of algorithms whose descriptions are "natural" using recursion. Nonrecursive descriptions of these algorithms are, of course, possible but are not as simple and straightforward as the recursive descriptions. Many problems are inherently recursive, in that their descriptions are far simpler using recursion than by not using recursion. For example, to describe HANOI without using recursion is possible, but the resulting algorithm is considerably longer, more complex, and much harder to understand.

Before turning to a discussion of how recursion works, and how it can be achieved in Fortran, one additional example of a naturally recursive problem is described. This problem also is relatively simple to describe recursively, but quite hard if recursion is not used. Its algorithm is somewhat more difficult than QSORT and HANOI, however, because it contains a recursive call in a loop.

The problem is to generate all possible permutations of the characters of a string. For example the string 'PQR' has six permutations:

PQR
QPR
PRQ
RPQ
RQP
QRP

For a string of an arbitrary number of characters, this is not a simple problem to solve if recursion is not used. However a relatively simple recursive algorithm exists to solve this problem. Figure 11.6 illustrates the general idea. Figure 11.6*a* shows that if there are N characters in the string then some of the permutations are obtained by holding the Nth character "fixed" and generating all permutations of the first N–1 characters. Figure 11.6*b* shows that then the Nth character may be exchanged with one of the first N – 1 characters, and then (*a*) is repeated. This is continued until each of the original N characters has been used in the Nth position.

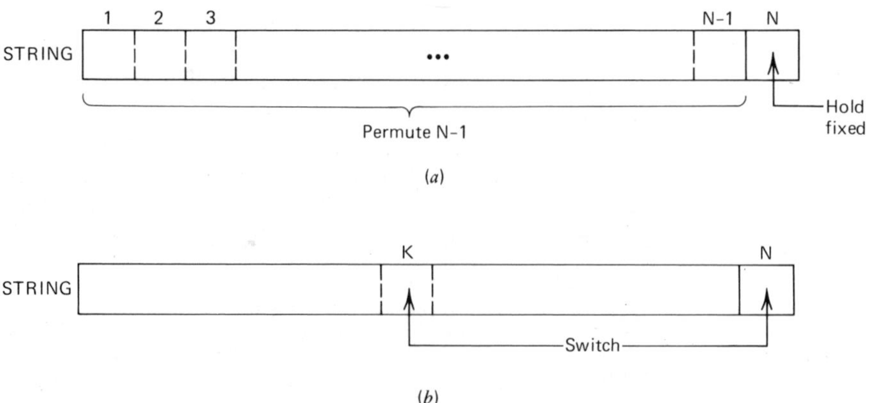

Figure 11.6. Using recursion to generate all permutations of N characters. (*a*) Permute the first N-1 characters, holding the Nth character fixed. (*b*) Exchange the Nth and Kth characters.

More rigorously, the algorithm is as follows (let A<=>B denote the interchanging of the values of A and B):

```
PERMUT (STRING(1:N))
    if N gt 1 then
            do  K = N,1,-1
                STRING(K:K) <=> STRING(N:N)   ! switch these two
                call PERMUT (STRING(1:N-1))
                STRING(K:K) <=> STRING(N:N)   ! switch them back
            repeat
        else
            PRINT *, STRING
    endif
end PERMUT
```

Because of the print statement, executing this algorithm will result in the printing of all possible permutations of the N characters. The analysis of PERMUT, which is a bit more difficult than QSORT or HANOI, is again based on the assumption that the recursive call performs its intended function. Suppose that initially N is equal to 1—then there is only one permutation (the character itself), and PERMUT simply prints the string in this case and then terminates, thus PERMUT works correctly for N eq 1. For N equal to 2 there are two permutations, and PERMUT should print out both. For N eq 2 the do-repeat loop body is executed twice, once for K eq 2 and then for K eq 1. Each time PERMUT is recursively called with N–1 eq 1, which results simply in the string being printed. The first time the two characters are in their original order (say 'XY') and the second time the two characters are switched ('YX'). Note that the second switch results in the string being left in its original form ('XY') at the termination of the algorithm. Thus PERMUT works correctly for N eq 2. For N eq 3 the do-repeat loop is executed three times, each time with N–1 eq 2 in the recursive call. Since a call on PERMUT with 2 characters correctly results in two permutations being printed, PERMUT with N eq 3 results in 3*2, or 6 permutations being printed. This is the correct number of possible permutations for N eq 3, and since a different character is in the third position for each of the three executions of the recursive call all six printouts are different permutations (and, again, afterwards the string is left in its original form). Continuing the analysis in this manner, PERMUT can be seen to work correctly for any value of N.

In all of the above examples of recursion each recursive call is contained in a selection structure, and hence is conditionally executed. This must be the case if infinite recursion (which is analogous to infinite looping) is to be avoided. Consider, for example, the algorithm

```
N = 1
CRAZY (N)
    PRINT *, N
    call CRAZY (1-N)
end CRAZY
```

whose execution results in

```
1
0
1
0
1
0
1
0
:
:
forever
```

Execution of CRAZY always causes another execution of CRAZY, which causes yet another execution of CRAZY, and so on forever. In a practical situation recursive calls are used only on a subset of the problem, and when this subset becomes small enough the recursive process terminates. Thus, in practice, recursive calls are always conditionally executed, the condition most typically being related to limiting cases for performing the recursion. In the next section how recursion works is described in greater detail.

11.2 Data Stacks

Ideally a recursively defined algorithm would be programmed as a subroutine, with the recursive calls being simply CALL statements to the subroutine itself; that is, subroutines would be allowed to call themselves. The mechanisms necessary to handle such recursive calls are not complicated and are described in this section. Unfortunately Fortran does not have these mechanisms as built-in features of the language, and hence Fortran does not allow recursive calls in subroutines. The programmer can however explicitly simulate these mechanisms and fairly easily convert most recursive algorithms to valid Fortran programs.

Recursion is essentially a repetitive execution of an algorithm. It is conceivable, therefore, that a recursive algorithm may be converted to an equivalent loop that contains no recursive calls, and such is indeed the case. In such a conversion the loop encompasses the entire algorithm, and the recursive calls are replaced by suitable changes in variable values and selection of (branching to) the appropriate portions of the algorithm. The result may be written as a Fortran program, and in particular as a Fortran subroutine. Subroutine BSERCH is identical in function to recursive BSERCH, and is an example of converting a recursive algorithm to a Fortran program.

Note that the structure of subroutine BSERCH is very similar to that of recursive BSERCH. A do-repeat brackets the entire recursive BSERCH algorithm, and exits are

```
*....:------------------------------------------------------------------
      SUBROUTINE  BSERCH (X,TABLE,LOWER,UPPER,MATCH)
                          INTEGER  X,LOWER,UPPER,MATCH,TABLE(LOWER:UPPER)

*              ..this subroutine replaces the recursive calls
*                in BSERCH with a loop..

*     ....variables....
      INTEGER  L,U,M

*     ....execute....
      L = LOWER
      U = UPPER
*              ..this corresponds to the beginning of recursive BSERCH
      do
         M = INT((L+U)/2)
         IF  (M .LT. L)  THEN
*                      ..X not in TABLE..
             MATCH = 0
             exit

         ELSEIF  (X .LT. TABLE(M))  THEN
*                                ..search lower half..
             U = M-1

         ELSEIF  (X .GT. TABLE(M))  THEN
*                                ..search upper half..
             L = M+1

         ELSE
*                      ..match found with TABLE(M)..
             MATCH = M
             exit
        ENDIF
      repeat
      END
========================================================================
```

added to those execution paths that don't include a recursive call. The recursive calls themselves are replaced by the associated changes in argument values. This conversion technique is extremely simple and straightforward, and can be used for a certain class of recursive algorithms (of which BSERCH is, of course, a member). The characteristic feature of this class is that any execution path through the recursive algorithm contains (at most) a single recursive call, and this recursive call is the last statement in that path. Thus a recursive algorithm in this class is easy to spot, and it can be converted into Fortran by straightforward application of the following three steps:

1. Make the entire algorithm the body of a do-repeat structure.
2. Insert an exit statement at the end of each execution path through the algorithm that does not end with a recursive call.
3. Replace all recursive calls with assignments that change the arguments as specified in the recursive calls.

Many (possibly most) inherently recursive algorithms do not belong to the class whose members can be converted to Fortran with these three simple steps. Algorithms QSORT, HANOI, and PERMUT, for example, all involve multiple executions of recursive calls (the single recursive call of PERMUT is in a loop, and thus is repetitively executed), which excludes them from the above class. The key point is that such algorithms involve some additional processing (i.e., are not yet completed) after the execution of a recursive call. This means that the values of arguments, and some other data elements in the algorithm, must be restored to their prerecursive call values in order that this additional processing be done correctly. For example in HANOI the variable N must have the same value at execution of the PRINT statement that it had in the execution of the if-then statement, that is, the first recursive call must leave N unchanged. Similarly, in PERMUT, execution of the recursive call must not change the value of K. However the recursive calls must use different values for these variables, and hence must change these values. Therefore—and this is the key aspect in the general implementation of recursion—variable values needed for later computations must be saved prior to executing a recursive call, and restored to the saved values after completion of the recursive call. A built-in recursion facility would include automatic saving and restoring of such values as part of the functioning of the recursive call.

For the special class of recursive algorithms to which BSERCH belongs, the saving of data values is not necessary since no processing is done in the algorithm after a recursive call. Thus for this class conversion to Fortran is simple, without any need for saving and restoring values. For other recursive algorithms, however, such as QSORT, HANOI, and PERMUT, conversion to Fortran requires that the programmer explicitly save the necessary data values, and explicitly restore them after the recursive call. When this is done properly, conversion of recursive algorithms into Fortran is relatively straightforward.

Executing a recursive call can (and usually does) result in another execution of that recursive call before completion of the previous call. In general, data values must be saved and restored at each call, and therefore many saved values of the same variable may exist at a given instant. Thus some provision must be made, such as an array, to save a sequence of values to be restored to a variable. The sequencing of operations in executing recursive calls is such that the last value saved for a variable is the first value to be restored. Thus saved values of a variable may be thought of as being "stacked up", one at a time, as they are being saved, as shown in Figure 11.7*a*. Then as values are restored they are simply taken, one at a time, off the top of the stack, as shown in Figure 11.7*b*. In general the saving and restoring of values can take place as needed, with saved values always placed on top of the stack and restored values taken from the top of the stack. Thus the stack can grow as saved values are added to it, and can shrink when restored values are removed from it.

Data stacks are easy to implement in Fortran with arrays, as shown in Figure 11.8.

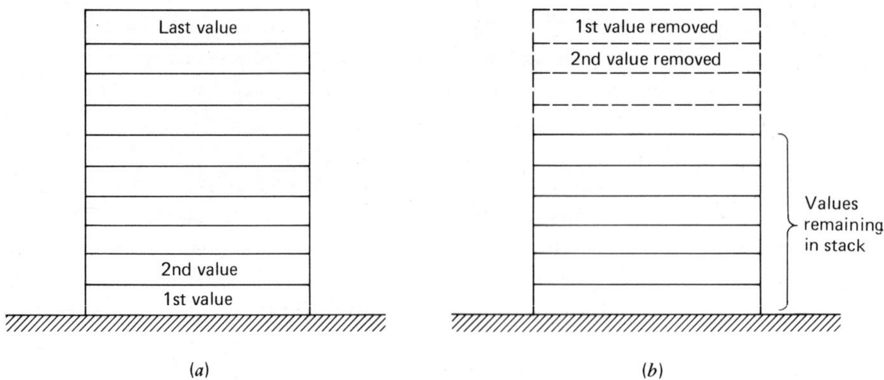

Figure 11.7. The data stack. (*a*) The stacking of saved values. (*b*) The removing of saved values.

An integer variable SP, called the stack pointer, keeps track of the top of the stack as the stack grows and shrinks during execution of a recursive algorithm. (In Figure 11.8, MSH—maximum stack height—is the size of the array, and hence the largest value that SP can have.) Each variable needing values to be saved has its own stack. Suppose that V is such a variable, and SAVEV is the name of the array used for stacking the values of V. Then just before a recursive call the value of V is saved by

```
SP = SP+1
SAVEV(SP) = V
```

and just after a recursive call the value of V is restored by

```
V = SAVEV(SP)
SP = SP-1
```

A data stack must be used for each variable whose values must be saved during recursive calls. In addition one other stack is necessary—the *return* stack. If an algorithm contains more than one recursive call, such as QSORT or HANOI, then some means must be provided to identify the point at which to resume execution after completion of a recursive call. This will be illustrated shortly. A stack may be used for this, in which at each execution of a recursive call information is saved which identifies the return point for that call. In addition to locations of recursive calls, two other "critical points" in every recursive algorithm are (1) the beginning of the algorithm, where recursive calls branch to, and (2) the end of the algorithm, where value restoration and return point identification are performed.

These ideas are all illustrated in subroutine HANOI, which is a conversion of recursive HANOI into Fortran. Figure 11.9 shows the four critical points in HANOI: 'RECUR', 'HANOIA', 'HANOIB', and 'RESTORE'. Points 'HANOIB' and 'RESTORE' are essentially equivalent, so 'HANOIB' could be eliminated from subroutine HANOI. Each critical point is the beginning of an execution sequence. [The selection among critical

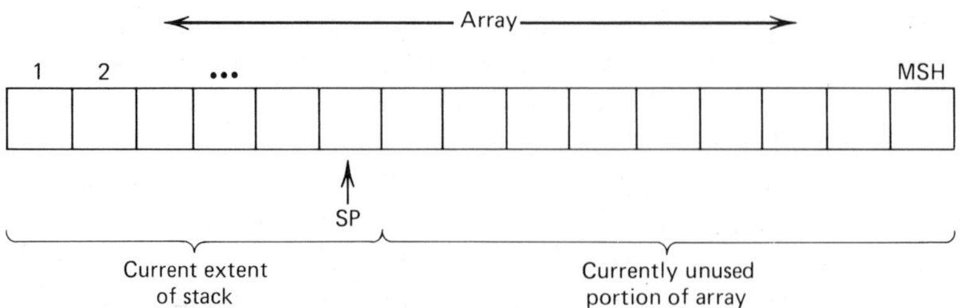

Figure 11.8. The use of an array to implement a data stack.

```
*....:-----------------------------------------------------------------
      SUBROUTINE  HANOI (NRINGS,FROM,TO)
                       INTEGER  NRINGS, FROM, TO

*                 ..this subroutine is a Fortran version of HANOI
*                 that is organized around the identification of
*                 "critical points". The string variable CP always
*                 has a value equal to one of the critcal points:
*                 'RECUR', 'HANOIA', HANOIB', 'RESTORE'.
*                 Before this program can be compiled and
*                 executed, the "case-end selection" and
*                 "do until" constructs must be converted
*                 to standard Fortran, as described in
*                 chapters 8, 9, and 10..

*     ....constant....(maximum stack height)
      INTEGER  MSH
      PARAMETER  ( MSH = 40 )

*     ....variables....
      INTEGER  N, P1, P2, SP
     :         SAVEN(1:MSH), SAVEP1(1:MSH), SAVEP2(1:MSH)
      CHARACTER*8  CP, SAVER(1:MSH)
      DATA  SP /0/

*     .....execute....
      N = NRINGS
      P1 = FROM
      P2 = TO
      SP = SP+1
      SAVEN(SP) = N
      SAVEP1(SP) = P1
      SAVEP2(SP) = P2
      SAVER(SP) = 'DONE'
      CP = 'RECUR'
      do until (CP .EQ. 'DONE')
          case (CP) of
*                                 ..begin executing recursive call..
              'RECUR':
                      IF  (N .GT. 0)  THEN
*                         ..perform stacking..
                              SP = SP+1
                              SAVEN(SP) = N
                              SAVEP1(SP) = P1
                              SAVEP2(SP) = P2
                              SAVER(SP) = 'HANOIA'
*                         ..and make first recursive call
                              N = N-1
                              P2 = 6-P1-P2
                              CP = 'RECUR'
                          ELSE
*                                         ..return from this call..
                              CP = 'RESTORE'
                      ENDIF

*                                   ..return from first recursive call..
              'HANOIA':
                      PRINT '(3(A,I2))','Move ring',N,'  from post',P1,
     :                                                ' to post',P2
*                 ..now perform stacking..
                      SP = SP+1
                      SAVEN(SP) = N
                      SAVEP1(SP) = P1
                      SAVEP2(SP) = P2
                      SAVER(SP) = 'HANOIB'
*                 ..and make second recursive call..
                      N = N-1
                      P1 = 6-P1-P2
                      CP = 'RECUR'

*                                  ..return from second recursive call..
              'HANOIB':
                      CP = 'RESTORE'

*                                  ..restore values and critical point..
              'RESTORE':
                      N = SAVEN(SP)
                      P1 = SAVEP1(SP)
                      P2 = SAVEP2(SP)
                      CP = SAVER(SP)
                      SP = SP-1

          end selection
      repeat
      END
=======================================================================
```

```
HANOI (N,P1,P2)
                                              <---critical point 'RECUR'
   if N gt 0 then
      call HANOI (N-1,P1,6-P1-P2)
                                              <---return point 'HANOIA'

      PRINT '(3(A,I2))', ' Move ring', N, ' from post', P1, to post', P2
      call HANOI (N-1,6-P1-P2,Ps)
                                              <---return point 'HANOIB'
   endif
                                              <---critical point 'RESTORE'
end HANOI
```

Figure 11.9. The four critical points in HANOI.

```
*....:-----------------------------------------------------------------
      SUBROUTINE  HANOI2 (NRINGS,FROM,TO)
                      INTEGER  NRINGS, FROM, TO

*                 ..same as subroutine HANOI, except that all
*                 stacking and restoring of data values is
*                 done by calling subroutines PUSH and POP..

*     ....variables....
      INTEGER  N, P1, P2
      CHARACTER*8  CP

*     .....execute....
      N = NRINGS
      P1 = FROM
      P2 = TO
      CALL  PUSH (N,P1,P2,'DONE')
      CP = 'RECUR'
      do until  (CP .EQ. 'DONE')
          case  (CP)  of
*                             ..begin executing recursive call..
              'RECUR':
                      IF  (N .GT. 0)  THEN
                            CALL  PUSH (N,P1,P2,'HANOIA')
                            N = N-1
                            P2 = 6-P1-P2
                            CP = 'RECUR'
                         ELSE
*                                     ..return from this call..
                            CP = 'RESTORE'
                      ENDIF

*                                ..return from first recursive call..
              'HANOIA':
                      PRINT '(3(A,I2))',' Move ring',N,'  from post',P1,
     :                                               '  to post',P2
                      CALL  PUSH (N,P1,P2,'HANOIB')
                      N = N-1
                      P1 = 6-P1-P2
                      CP = 'RECUR'

*                               ..return from second recursive call..
              'HANOIB':
                      CP = 'RESTORE'

*                               ..restore values and critical point..
              'RESTORE':
                      CALL  POP (N,P1,P2,CP)

          end selection
      repeat
      END
=======================================================================
```

points in HANOI is an ideal application of the case structure described in Chapter 9 (see especially Problem 9.10), and so case has been used in HANOI to describe this selection.] Four stacks are needed in HANOI—data stacks for N, P1, and P2 (respectively SAVEN, SAVEP1, and SAVEP2) and the return stack SAVER. Subroutine HANOI assumes that the stack heights will never exceed 40.

The three conversion steps used for the BSERCH class of algorithms also are used in the conversion of more general recursive algorithms such as HANOI. In addition, three other steps are necessary:

4 Stack data values and return points prior to each recursive call.

5 Restore (unstack) values at the end of the algorithm.

6 Identify all critical points in the recursive algorithm and place the statements between critical points into different selection groups.

Approximately half of the statements in subroutine HANOI are associated with the stacking and unstacking operations, making this program much longer than the corresponding recursive version. These operations could be relegated to a subroutine, making the Fortran implementation of HANOI much "cleaner", as a modification of subroutine HANOI, called HANOI2, illustrates. Adding to a stack is normally called "pushing", and removing from a stack called "popping", which is the reason for calling PUSH and POP in HANOI2. PUSH and POP could be different entry points into the same stack-handling subroutine, as illustrated in subroutine HSTACK following HANOI2.

```
*....:-----------------------------------------------------------------
      SUBROUTINE  HSTACK (N,P1,P2,CP)
                         INTEGER  N,P1,P2
                         CHARACTER CP*8

*                 ..subroutine to perform all of the
*                 stacking and unstacking for HANOI2..

*     ....constant....(maximum stack height)
      INTEGER  MSH
      PARAMETER  ( MSH = 40 )

*     ....variables....
      INTEGER  SP,SAVEN(1:MSH),SAVEP1(1:MSH),SAVEP2(1:MSH)
      CHARACTER  SAVER(1:MSH)*8
      SAVE
*           ..this SAVEs all local variables (i.e., all stacks and SP)..
      DATA  SP /0/

*     ....PUSH entry point....
      ENTRY PUSH (N,P1,P2,CP)
          SP = SP+1
          IF  (SP .GT. MSH)  THEN
                  PRINT *, 'STACK OVERFLOW'
                  STOP
          ENDIF
          SAVEN(SP) = N
          SAVEP1(SP) = P1
          SAVEP2(SP) = P2
          SAVER(SP) = CP
          RETURN

*     ....POP entry point....
      ENTRY POP(N,P1,P2,CP)
          N = SAVEN(SP)
          P1 = SAVEP1(SP)
          P2 = SAVEP2(SP)
          CP = SAVER(SP)
          SP = SP-1
      END
=======================================================================
```

Subroutine HANOI2 is considerably easier to read than subroutine HANOI because it is not cluttered up with the details of pushing and popping the stacks. The basic structure of the recursive algorithm is discernible, although the critical point divisions tend to dominate the program. The critical points are points where execution control enters and leaves the statement sequence because of the effects of the recursive calls. These "points of branching", and the use of variable CP to identify critical points, emphasize the executionally distinct groupings of the recursive algorithm statements. With practice such critical point groupings are relatively easy to read and relate to the original recursive algorithm. In addition, the do-repeat emphasizes the repetitive nature of recursion.

However, HANOI2 can be written in even a shorter and more efficient form by replacing both the do-repeat and the case selection structures by GOTO statements. This is illustrated in subroutine HANOI3. Although HANOI3 is more "primitive" Fortran than HANOI2, that is the price that must be paid in order to implement recursion efficiently in Fortran. HANOI3 could even be considered more elegant than HANOI2 because the structure of HANOI3 is much closer to the structure of recursive HANOI. Moreover the conversion techniques used in HANOI3 are easily generalized, as described in the next section, into a practical method for efficient and reasonably convenient implementation of recursion in Fortran.

```
*....:------------------------------------------------------------------
      SUBROUTINE  HANOI3 (NRINGS,FROM,TO)
                            INTEGER  NRINGS, FROM, TO

*                    ..a "GOTO" version of HANOI2;
*                    labels 10, 11, 12, and 13 correspond
*                    respectively, to critical points
*                    'RECUR', HANOIA', 'HANOIB', and 'RESTORE'..

*     ....variables....
      INTEGER  N, P1, P2, RP
*                           ..the return stack is now an integer stack..
*     ....execute....
      N = NRINGS
      P1 = FROM
      P2 = TO
                            CALL PUSH (N,P1,P2,3)
10                          CONTINUE
                            IF  (N .LE. 0)  GOTO 13
*     if  N gt 0  then
*                           ..the next 4 statements represent
*                             the first recursive call..
         CALL  PUSH (N,P1,P2,1)
         N = N-1
         P2 = 6-P1-P2
         GOTO 10
11                          CONTINUE
         PRINT '(3(A,I2))', ' Move ring', N, '  from post', P1,
     :                                          '  to post', P2
*                           ..now for the second recursive call..
         CALL  PUSH (N,P1,P2,2)
         N = N-1
         P1 = 6-P1-P2
         GOTO 10
12                          CONTINUE
*     endif
13                          CONTINUE
                            CALL  POP (N,P1,P2,RP)
                            GOTO (11,12,19), RP
19    END
=======================================================================
```

Unfortunately (for the sake of implementing recursion) Fortran does not allow branching into any block of statements in an IF-ENDIF structure from outside that block. Since normally all recursive calls appear within such structures, the control represented by such if-endifs must be replaced by more primitive control mechanisms. Subroutine HANOI3 illustrates such modification. In the following examples the if-endif structures will be used, as appropriate, in the description of the recursive algorithms, and retained as comments in the Fortran programs, but are replaced by the equivalent IF (. . .), GOTO . . .s, and labels.

For example,

```
if  <log-expr> then                      IF (.NOT.(<log-expr>)) GOTO <label>
        ----                                    ----
        ----        becomes                     ----
        ----                                    ----
endif                           <label>         CONTINUE
```

and

```
if  <log-expr> then                      IF (.NOT.(<log-expr>)) GOTO <label1>
        ----                                    ----
        ----        becomes                     ----
        ----                                    ----
    else                                        GOTO <label2>
        ----                    <label1>        CONTINUE
        ----                                    ----
        ----                                    ----
endif                                           ----
                                <label2>        CONTINUE
```

The alternative to "abandoning" IF-ENDIF in implementing recursion is to use the techniques illustrated in subroutines HANOI and HANOI2.

In the next section these introductory concepts concerning conversion of recursive algorithms to Fortran programs are completed, and conversions for QSORT and PERMUT given. The examples of this section—BSERCH and HANOI, and especially HANOI—should be thoroughly understood before progressing to the next section. A useful approach to understanding HANOI is to execute subroutine HANOI (with CALL HANOI(5,1,2), for example) after inserting print statements in the loop to provide a running display of the contents of the stacks and the values of the important variables (N, P1, P2, CP, and SP).

11.3 Simulating Recursion in Fortran

Efficient conversion of a recursive algorithm into Fortran requires addition of stack manipulations and branching as follows:

1 Prior to beginning execution of the recursive algorithm: save all appropriate values on stacks and save a value in the return stack that specifies completion of the algorithm.

2 At the end of the algorithm: restore saved values (pop stacks), and branch to the point specified by the return stack value.

3 At each recursive call: push all values to be saved onto the stacks, push the return stack with a value specifying the return point for this call, and then branch to the beginning of the algorithm after adjusting argument values as specified in the recursive call.

As it turns out, each of these three items can be put into systematic Fortran terms that are quite short and convenient, yet do not deform the structure of the recursive algorithm.

Assuming that suitable PUSH and POP subroutines are available (such as in the preceding section—and see also below), and that the recursive algorithm contains n recursive calls, Figure 11.10 shows the Fortran form for each of the above three items.

```
          recursive  ALG (<arguments>)
               ----
               ----
               ----
               ----
               call  ALG (<arguments>)
               ----
               ----
               ----
               ----
          end recursive ALG
```

(a)

```
                            CALL PUSH (<saved-variables>,n+1)
<recur>                     CONTINUE
*         recursive      ALG (<arguments>)
```

(b)

```
*         end recursive ALG
               CALL POP (<saved-variables>,RP)
               GOTO(<ret.1>,<ret.2>,. . .<ret.i>,. . .<ret.n>,<done>),RP
<done> END
```

(c)

```
*         call ALG (<arguments>)
               CALL PUSH (<saved-variables>,i)
                    } argument
                    } changes
               GOTO <recur>
<ret.i>        CONTINUE
```

(d)

Figure 11.10. Elements of converting recursion to Fortran. (*a*) Typical recursive algorithm, showing ith of n recursive calls. (*b*) The initial stacking and branch point preceding the body of the recursive algorithm. (*c*) The restoring of values and return point branching at the end of the recursive algorithm. (*d*) The stacking, branching, and return point associated with the ith recursive call.

In Figure 11.10 it is assumed that the recursive call shown is the ith one of the n recursive calls, and <recur>, <ret.1>, <ret.2>,. . .,<ret.i>,. . .,<ret.n>, and <done> are Fortran statement labels. Thus the recursive heading is replaced by three lines of Fortran (including the comment line); the recursive ending is replaced by four lines of Fortran; and each recursive call is replaced by four lines of Fortran plus however many lines the argument changes require. The complete Fortran program (subroutine) corresponding to Figure 11.10*a* is given in Figure 11.11.

The scheme of Figure 11.11 is perfectly general and can be used with any recursive algorithm having any number of recursive calls. The structure of the recursive algorithm remains intact, especially if the Fortran details of each call are indented as shown in Figure 11.11. Note that auxiliary variables for the arguments, as used in the examples of the preceding section, are not needed in this general scheme (if the actual arguments of the initial CALL are passed by address), since the initial push saves the argument values to be restored upon termination of the algorithm.

Thus any recursive algorithm may be converted to a Fortran subroutine in a straightforward manner. This does require the existence of PUSH and POP subroutines,

```
          SUBROUTINE ALG (<arguments>)
                      } specification
                      } statements
*         . . . .execute. . . .
                                CALL PUSH (<saved-variables>,n+1)
<recur>                         CONTINUE
*           recursive ALG  (<arguments>)
                      ----
                      ----
                      ----
                      ----
*                 call ALG (<arguments>)    . .ith recursive call. .
                                CALL PUSH (<saved-variable>,i)
                                      } argument
                                      } changes
                                GOTO <recur>
<ret.i>                         CONTINUE
                      ----
                      ----
                      ----
                      ----
*         end recursive ALG
                                CALL POP (<saved-variables>,RP)
                                GOTO (<ret.1>,<ret.2>,. . .,<ret.i>,. . .,<ret.n>,<done>), RP
<done> END
```

Figure 11.11. General method for converting recursion into Fortran.

however, which are different for each recursive algorithm since the set of <saved variables> will in general be different for each recursive algorithm. But such subroutines are easy to supply. Figure 11.12 gives a general form for these subroutines, which is very much like subroutine HSTACK of the preceding section. The only things that change in subroutine STACK from application to application are the number of arguments of type INTEGER, number of type REAL, number of type CHARACTER, etc., and the value of MSH. (Also it may be desirable to change the subroutine name and push and pop entry point names if several Fortran programs implementing recursive algorithms are to be in the system library simultaneously.) Thus it would be easy to write a program to create the stacking subroutine, with inputs to this creating program being the above information about numbers of arguments of the various types and the value of MSH (and perhaps the desired subroutine and entry point names). Henceforth in the examples PUSH and POP will be called with the assumption that suitable programs, such as STACK, are available.

Subroutine HANOI4 is an application of the method of Figure 11.11 to the HANOI algorithm. To review, HANOI is recursively defined as

```
recursive HANOI (N,P1,P2)
    if  N gt 0 then
        call HANOI (N-1,P1,6-P1-P2)
        PRINT '(3(A,I3))', ' Move ring', N, ' from post', P1, ' to post', P2
        call HANOI (N-1,6-P1-P2,P2)
    endif
end recursive HANOI
```

In this case n eq 2 (there are two recursive calls) and the labels used are 10, 11, 12, and 19 for <recur>, <ret.1>, <ret.2>, and <done>, respectively.

```
      SUBROUTINE STACK (V1,V2,. . ., Vm, RP)
                                  } argument
                                  } typing
                            INTEGER RP
*     . . . .constant. . . .(maximum stack heights)
      INTEGER MSH
      PARAMETER ( MSH = 40 )
*     . . . .the stacks. . . .
      INTEGER SP
      <type> SAVE1(1:MSH)
      <type> SAVE2(1:MSH)
      .
      .
      .
      <type> SAVEm(1:MSH)
      INTEGER SAVER(1:MSH)
      SAVE
      DATA SP /0/
*     . . . .PUSH entry point. . . .
      ENTRY PUSH (V1,V2,. . .,Vm,RP)
         SP = SP + 1
         IF (SP .GT. MSH) THEN
               PRINT *, 'STACK OVERFLOW'
               STOP
         ENDIF
         SAVE1(SP) = V1
         SAVE2(SP) = V2
         .
         .
         .
         SAVEm(SP) = Vm
         SAVER(SP)  = RP
      RETURN
*     . . . .POP entry point. . . .
      ENTRY POP (V1,V2, . . . . ,Vm,RP)
         V1 = SAVE 1(SP)
         V2 = SAVE2(SP)
         .
         .
         .
         Vm = SAVEm(SP)
         RP = SAVER(SP)
         SP = SP-1
      END
```

Figure 11.12. General structure for the PUSH and POP subroutines.

```
*....:-----------------------------------------------------------------
     SUBROUTINE  HANOI4 (N,P1,P2)
                         INTEGER  N,P1,P2

*    ....local variable....
     INTEGER  RP

*    ....execute....
                    CALL  PUSH (N,P1,P2,3)
 10                 CONTINUE
*    recursive  HANOI (N,P1,P2)
*        if  N gt 0  then
                    IF  (N .LE. 0)  GOTO 12
*            call  HANOI (N-1,P1,6-P1-P2)
                    CALL  PUSH (N,P1,P2,1)
                    N = N-1
                    P2 = 6-P1-P2
                    GOTO 10
 11                 CONTINUE
             PRINT '(3(A,I2))', ' Move ring', N, '  from post', P1,
    :                                        '  to post', P2
*            call  HANOI (N-1,P1,6-P1-P2)
                    CALL  PUSH (N,P1,P2,2)
                    N = N-1
                    P1 = 6-P1-P2
                    GOTO 10
 12                 CONTINUE
*        endif
*    end recursive HANOI
                    CALL POP(N,P1,P2,RP)
                    GOTO (11,12,19), RP
 19  END
=======================================================================
```

```
recursive QSORT (TABLE(L:U))
    if  U gt L then
        CALL PARTIT (TABLE(L:U),PL)
        call QSORT (TABLE(L:PL−1))
        call QSORT (TABLE(PL+1:U))
    endif
end recursive QSORT
```

```
*....:-----------------------------------------------------------------
     SUBROUTINE  QSORT (TABLE,L,U)
                        INTEGER  L,U,TABLE(L:U)

*    ....local variables....
     INTEGER  RP,PL

*    ....execute....
                    CALL  PUSH (L,U,0,3)
 10                 CONTINUE
*    recursive  QSORT (TABLE(L:U))
*        if  U gt L  then
                    IF  (U .LE. L)  GOTO 12
             CALL  PARTIT (TABLE,L,U,PL)
*            call  QSORT (TABLE(L:PL-1))
                    CALL  PUSH (L,U,PL,1)
                    U = PL-1
                    GOTO 10
 11                 CONTINUE
*            call  QSORT (TABLE(PL+1:U))
                    CALL  PUSH (L,U,PL,2)
                    L = PL+1
                    GOTO 10
 12                 CONTINUE
*        endif
*    end recursive QSORT
                    CALL POP(L,U,PL,RP)
                    GOTO (11,12,19),RP
 19  END
=======================================================================
```

In this algorithm the array TABLE is continually being sorted as execution of the algorithm progresses, so this array need not be saved at each recursive call. What needs to be saved are the values of L, U, and PL. PL is a local variable, whose value is undefined before the first call to PARTIT, and therefore any value can be used in the initial PUSH (the value zero is used in subroutine QSORT).

In algorithm PERMUT there is just one recursive call (n eq 1), but this call is inside a loop. Therefore a branch point (critical point) is inside a loop, which requires that branches be made to a point in the interior of the loop from some point outside the loop. As with the IF-ENDIF structure, the Fortran indexed DO-loop does not allow such "into" branching, so the loop must be configured as a nonindexed do-repeat structure in order to permit the application of the general conversion technique. This is easy to do, of course, and then recursive PERMUT takes the form:

```
recursive PERMUT (STRING(1:N))
    if  N gt 1  then
            K = N
            do
                IF (K .LT. 1) exit
                TEMP = STRING(K:K)
                STRING(K:K) = STRING(N:N)
                STRING(N:N) = TEMP
                call PERMUT (STRING(1:N-1))
                TEMP = STRING(K:K)
                STRING(K:K) = STRING(N:N)
                STRING(N:N) = TEMP
                K = K-1
            repeat
        else
            PRINT *, STRING
    endif
end recursive PERMUT
```

The string variables STRING and TEMP need not be saved at each call (although it wouldn't hurt to save them), but both K and N do need to be saved.

These examples (HANOI, QSORT, and PERMUT) demonstrate the generality and relative convenience (given that Fortran does not have built-in recursion) of the conversion method described in this section. For a problem that is inherently recursive, writing it in recursive form and then converting it to Fortran using this method is far simpler than undertaking a nonrecursive solution to the problem. This method will work for any directly recursive algorithm where the recursion is specified in the form of the call recursive calls. Direct recursion is where the recursive calls are directly to the algorithm being defined, as in all of the examples of this chapter.

Recursion can be indirect—algorithm A calls algorithm B, and algorithm B calls algorithm A. The method described here can be used in this case also if both algorithms are placed in the same Fortran subroutine. Functions may also be recursively defined. However, in order to convert these into Fortran, they must be converted to the recursive (subroutine) type call so that the necessary stacking may be done. Thus the method described here is very general and practical, but is simplest in those cases of subroutine-type direct recursion.

The techniques of this section are intended only for algorithms (such as HANOI, QSORT, and PERMUT) that are not in the special class that contains BSERCH. The algorithms in that class do not require any stacking, and the simple do-repeat loop conversion is adequate, and preferable, in these cases. However, the method of this section will work for this class also, without the stacking (although the use of stacking here will not hurt anything, other than execution efficiency). Figure 11.13 shows the

```
*....:-----------------------------------------------------------------
      SUBROUTINE  PERMUT (STRING,N)
                           INTEGER  N
                           CHARACTER  STRING*(*)

*     ....local variables....
      INTEGER  K,RP
      CHARACTER  TEMP

*     ....execute....
                           CALL  PUSH (N,0,2)
 10                        CONTINUE
*     recursive  PERMUT (STRING(1:N))
*         if  N gt 1  then
                           IF  (N .LE. 1)  GOTO 200
              K = N
              do
                  IF  (K .LT. 1)  exit
                  TEMP = STRING(K:K)
                  STRING(K:K) = STRING(N:N)
                  STRING(N:N) = TEMP
*                 call  PERMUT (STRING(1:N-1))
                      CALL  PUSH (N,K,1)
                      N = N-1
                      GOTO 10
 11                   CONTINUE
                  TEMP = STRING(K:K)
                  STRING(K:K) = STRING(N:N)
                  STRING(N:N) = TEMP
                  K = K-1
              repeat
                      GOTO 300
 200                  CONTINUE
*            else
                 PRINT *, STRING
*         endif
 300                  CONTINUE
*     end recursive PERMUT
                      CALL  POP (N,K,RP)
                      GOTO (11,19),RP
 19   END
=======================================================================
```

conversion steps, using this method, for this class; parts (*a*), (*b*), and (*c*) of Figure 11.13 correspond to parts (*b*), (*c*), and (*d*) of Figure 11.10, respectively.

So, for a certain class of recursive algorithms, the conversion to Fortran is rather trivial, since stacking is not required. When stacking is required the question arises as to how high the stacks may be expected to get, and hence how large to make MSH in subroutine STACK. The stack height at any instant is equal to the number of recursive calls executed, minus the number of returns from recursive calls. If a limit can be found for this quantity then a suitable value for MSH has been found. Usually a quick analysis of the nature of the problem will yield such a bound. For example in HANOI the value of N decreases by 1 for each recursive call, and recursion stops when N reaches zero. Thus no more than N+1 recursive calls can be active, which makes the maximum stack height equal to N+1. For QSORT the worst case is when the values of TABLE are precisely in reverse order, which always makes the first recursive call involve one less element in TABLE than the current TABLE size. Thus the maximum stack height is equal to the original size of (number of elements in) TABLE (which is why implementing QSORT recursively is impractical). And finally, in PERMUT, as in HANOI, N decreases by one at each recursive call and recursion stops at N eq 1—therefore the maximum stack height in this case is N (the number of characters to be permuted). (Note, however, that the total number of permutations of N characters is N factorial.) This type of analysis is usually sufficient to quickly estimate the likely maximum stack height needed to execute the program for a given set of data.

One of the questions in implementing recursion is what variable values must be saved on making a recursive call. The answer can vary all the way from none (for the BSERCH class of algorithms) to all of the arguments and local variables in the program.

```
------------------------------------------------------------------------

<recur>                   CONTINUE
*         recursive  ALG (<arguments>)

(a) at the beginning of the algorithm

- - - - - - - - - - - - - - - - - - - - - - - -

*         end recursive ALG
          END

(b) at the end of the algorithm

- - - - - - - - - - - - - - - - - - - - - - - -

*              perform  ALG (<arguments>)
                     }argument
                     }changes
                   GOTO <recur>

(c) at each recursive call

- - - - - - - - - - - - - - - - - - - - - - - -

(d) example -- the above applied to BSERCH

*....:------------------------------------------------------------------
      SUBROUTINE  BSRCH2 (X,TABLE,L,U,MATCH)
                        INTEGER  X,L,U,TABLE(L:U),MATCH

*     ....local variable....
      INTEGER  M

*     ....execute....
 10                      CONTINUE
*     recursive  BSERCH (X,TABLE(L:U))
          M = INT((L+U)/2)
          IF  (M .LT. L)  THEN
                  MATCH = 0

              ELSEIF  (X .LT. TABLE(M))  THEN
*                 call  BSERCH (X,TABLE(L:M-1))
                            U = M-1
                            GOTO 10

              ELSEIF  (X .GT. TABLE(M))  THEN
*                 perform  BSERCH (X,TABLE(M+1:U))
                            L = M+1
                            GOTO 10
              ELSE
                  MATCH = M
          ENDIF
*     end recursive BSERCH
      END
========================================================================
```

Figure 11.13 -- Conversion for the BSERCH class of recursive algorithms.

This latter approach (saving all data elements) is used by built-in recursion facilities. Since data elements may be arrays (such as TABLE in QSORT) the storage requirements of recursion can be very high because a stack is needed for each array element. And if a given array in fact need not be saved at recursive calls, then doing so constitutes a needless inefficiency. This is the price one pays for the convenience of having built-in recursion. In Fortran, where the programmer must explicitly supply the stacking, this inconvenience is (partially) offset by the opportunity to specify stacking of only those quantities that really need it. Stacking is needed only by those quantities that are altered by recursive calls, and whose original values must be restored for the processing following the recursive calls. Normally data elements whose value it is the purpose of the algorithm to change, such as TABLE in QSORT and STRING in PERMUT, should not be stacked. Also, of course, data elements whose values do not change (such as X and TABLE in BSERCH) need not be stacked. Usually the values needing stacking are the parameters and auxiliary variables used in making the computations of the algorithm—sizes, limits, indices, etc. Careful consideration of the role of a data element in the algorithm will usually indicate whether or not stacking is necessary for that data element. In all cases, except for the BSERCH class of algorithms, a return point stack is needed.

11.4 Summary

In this chapter the concept of recursion has been introduced, along with the notion that some problems, by nature, are inherently recursive. That is, the solution to those problems are by far most easily stated in recursive terms. In the typical such case, the solution to a problem is stated in terms of a solution to a subset of the problem. An intuitive analysis of the correctness of a recursive algorithm is typically simple—in some instances almost trivial—if the subset solution (recursive call) is assumed correct. On the other hand, nonrecursive solutions to the same problem are likely to be complex and much more difficult to analyze or construct. Thus recursion is a useful programming tool for such situations.

Fortran does not have built-in provision for supporting recursion; therefore the programmer must simulate recursion by explicitly supplying certain things necessary for the implementation of recursion. The main thing, in general, is the use of data stacks to save, and then restore, the values of variables during the processing of recursive calls. In addition return points must be saved in a stack. A method for programming an inherently recursive problem in Fortran involves the following steps:

1 Develop a recursive algorithm for the problem.

2 Determine which values must be stacked, and the maximum stack height expected, and then write a program to perform the stacking operations—Figure 11.12 may be used as the model for this program.

3 Convert the recursive algorithm to a Fortran program using Figure 11.11 as a model, this involves the following:
(a) Inserting two statements before the recursive algorithm (see Figure 11.10*b*).
(b) Inserting three statements after the recursive algorithm (see Figure 11.10*c*).
(c) Inserting three + statements at the point of each recursive call (see Figure 11.10*d*).

In addition IF-ENDIF and indexed-DO structures must be replaced by the equivalent control using logical-IFs, GOTOs, and labels.

Steps 2 and 3 above represent the extra effort that the Fortran programmer must expend because Fortran does not have a built-in provision for recursion. However, this effort is typically less than that required to solve an inherently recursive problem nonrecursively. And having the programmer supply steps 2 and 3, rather than a built-in recursion facility supplying them, can result in elimination of significant stacking inefficiencies.

There is a class of recursive algorithms whose conversion to Fortran requires no stacking and hence is particularly simple. These are the recursive algorithms that have, at most, a single recursive call in any execution path through the algorithm, and this call is the last statement executed in the path. These algorithms may be implemented as a simple loop (e.g., subroutine BSERCH of Section 11.2, and using the three steps following that program), or using steps 1 and 3 above (e.g., subroutine BSRCH2 of Section 11.3) but with Figure 11.13 used in step 3.

Programming Exercises

11.1 Sometimes QSORT is written so that the smallest of the two partitions is sorted first. Rewrite recursive QSORT so that this is done.

11.2 Convert your algorithm for the preceding problem into a Fortran program.

11.3 The recursive example CRAZY of Section 11.1, whose execution never terminates, is in which class of recursive algorithm—the BSERCH class or the HANOI class? If implemented in Fortran using stacking for N, what would be the maximum stack height?

11.4 Any single-exit loop can be written as a recursive algorithm, of the BSERCH class, that involves no loops (see Figure 11.1). Rewrite the main (outer) loop of subroutine PARTIT (of Section 11.2) as such an algorithm.

11.5 An interesting sorting algorithm, that is in some sense the "opposite" of QSORT, is one which has the following three steps:
(a) Sort the first half of the array.
(b) Sort the second half of the array.
(c) Merge the runs resulting from steps (a) and (b)
into a single run, thereby completing the sort.
(QSORT "partitions," then sorts the parts; this algorithm sorts two parts and then "merges" them together.) Write a recursive algorithm to correctly perform this sort.

11.6 Convert your algorithm for the preceding problem into a Fortran program.

11.7 Program PAL in Chapter 5 checked a string to see if it was a palindrome. Devise a recursive solution to this problem.

11.8 A famous recursively defined function, and an interesting one because of the rapidity with which it grows, is the Ackerman function, whose definition is:

```
ACK(M,N): if M eq 0 then
                  V = N+1
              elseif N eq 0 then
                  V = ACK(M-1,1)
              else
                  V = ACK(M-1,ACK(M,N-1))
          endif
```

Here M and N are the integer arguments of the function (greater than or equal to zero), and V is the value of ACK(M,N). Functions may be converted to subroutines by adding an additional argument for representing the function value. Thus

```
recursive ACK (M,N,V)
    if M eq 0  then
            V = N+1
        elseif N eq 0  then
            call ACK (M-1,1,V)
        else
            call ACK (M,N-1,V)
            call ACK (M-1,V,V)
    endif
end ACK
```

Which variables need stacking in implementing this algorithm? What stack height is necessary?

11.9 Convert ACK of the preceding problem into a Fortran program and use it to compute ACK(0,0), ACK(1,1), ACK(2,2), ACK(3,3), etc. What is the largest value of K such that ACK(K,K) does not exceed the capacity of an integer variable on your computer?

11.10 Figure 11.14 shows four orders of the intriguing "Hilbert curves," for N = 1, 2, 3, and 4, respectively. These figures are made by connecting many three-sided "boxes," with various orientations, together in an appropriate manner. The connections may be described recursively with these four algorithms:

(Up-Right-Down -- URD)	RUL 'up' URD 'right' URD 'down' LDR
(Down-Left-Up -- DLU)	LDR 'down' DLU 'left' DLU 'up' RUL
(Left-Down-Right -- LDR)	DLU 'left' LDR 'down' LDR 'right' URD
(Right-Up-Left -- RUL)	URD 'right' RUL 'up' RUL 'left' DLU

Thus an URD of order N is a RUL of order N−1, followed by an 'up' segment, followed by an URD or order N−1, followed by a 'right' segment, followed by another URD of order N−1, followed by a 'down' segment, followed by an LDR of order N−1. This is illustrated in part (*b*) of Figure 11.14. Similarly DLU, LDR, and RUL are defined in terms of itself and the other algorithms of order one less. A more formal definition of URD is:

```
recursive URD (N)
    if  N gt 0  then
        call RUL (N−1)
        PRINT *, 'up'
        call URD (N−1)
        PRINT *, 'right'
        call URD (N−1)
        PRINT *, 'down'
        call LDR (N−1)
    endif
end URD
```

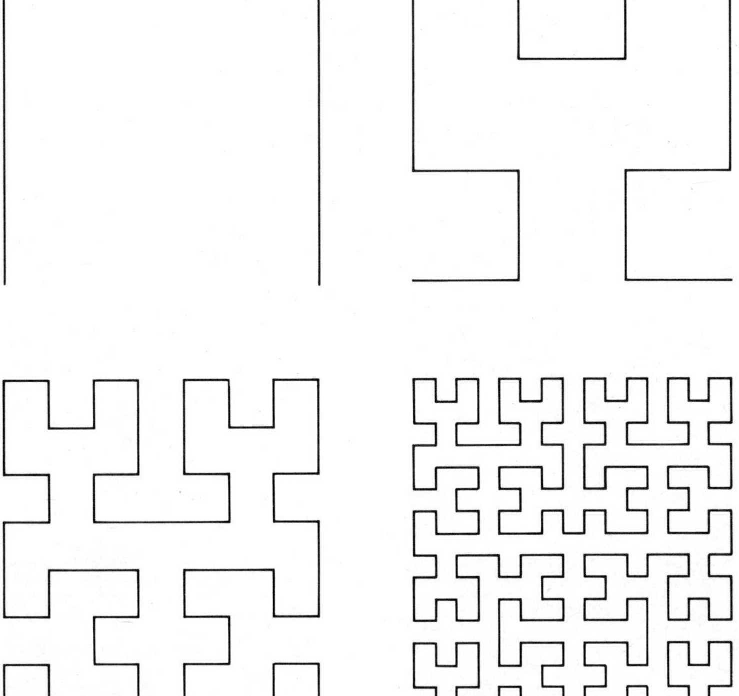

Figure 11.14. Hilbert curves (order 1 . . 4).

Write DLU, LDR, and RUL as recursive algorithms also. Note that each of these four algorithms is both directly and indirectly recursive (for example URD calls RUL, and RUL calls URD).

11.11 Combine the four recursive algorithms URD, DLU, LDR, and RUL into a Fortran subroutine named HILBRT (SUBROUTINE HILBRT(N)), and use it to produce a sequence of 'up', 'down', 'right', 'left' that will allow you to draw the next higher order Hilbert curve (N=5) than shown in Figure 11.14. Note that only two stacks are needed—one for N and the return stack. At each recursive call be sure and branch to the beginning of the proper algorithm, and at the end of each algorithm the stacks must be popped and a branch made to the indicated return point.

Part

Data Structure

Early in Part 1 (Fortran Fundamentals) the concept of data element was introduced along with the most commonly used Fortran data types. Throughout Part 1 the importance of good choices of data elements was stressed, and an important part of each example program was the careful choice and systematic declaration of each data element. The nature, and success, of every program depends vitally on the data elements employed.

Toward the end of Part 1 the emphasis shifted toward control of execution, and the importance of data elements, while always there, left the spotlight. This trend increased in Part 2 (Program Structure), which concentrated on developing concepts, analysis, and techniques related to program execution. Again the importance of the data elements was there, but in general did not receive focused attention. In Part 3, the spotlight returns to the data elements, and they are as thoroughly scrutinized as algorithm execution was in Part 2.

The primary purpose of this part is to present a comprehensive discussion of the various provisions that Fortran has for representing data, and to show how these features may be used in programs. Where Fortran is deficient in important areas of data representation, techniques are presented to achieve the desired effects. (In some instances these techniques are analogous to the use of do-repeat looping and the methods described earlier for implementing recursion, which are techniques to accommodate deficiences in Fortran's control structures.)

To accomplish the goal of a complete discussion of data representation/data processing techniques, this part is organized into four chapters. The first three of these chapters (12, 13, and 14) discuss data representation, starting with the most elementary concept, that of data type, and progressing to the most general and a highly practical data facility, the data file. Then the final chapter, Chapter 15, discusses in detail the Fortran features for using data files.

In Chapter 12, Data Types, the familiar data types INTEGER, REAL, CHARACTER, and LOGICAL are reviewed. Then much of the chapter is devoted to a discussion of types DOUBLEPRECISION and COMPLEX, with example applications to make scientific/engineering type numerical calculations. Finally, bit string data types, and operations on bit strings, are discussed.

A data structure is a *composite* data element made up of two or more elementary data elements; the component data elements may be of different data types. The important data structures are described in Chapter 13, Data Structures. First arrays are described as homogeneous data structures (all components having the same data type), and the array concept is extended to multidimensional arrays. Then lists and trees are described as simple heterogeneous data structures having important applications. Records are presented as general heterogeneous data structures, and the basic data element of the most general data structures, files. And finally, files are described as arrays of records, with universal applicability in computing.

Chapter 14, Data Files, discusses data files primarily in the context of files residing on secondary storage media (usually because they typically are quite large, that is, they have many records and contain much data). This chapter is devoted largely to the Fortran provisions for the organization, access, and control of such files. Chapter 15, File I/O, completes the discussion of data files with a comprehensive presentation of the Fortran provisions for data file input and output, and examples of file use.

Chapter 12 Data Types

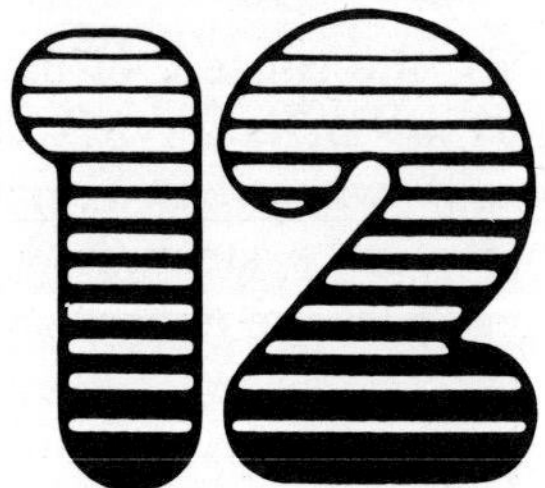

Each data element has a data type, which indicates the "nature", or "class", of the value of the data element. Thus data elements of type INTEGER have integer numeric values, data elements of type REAL have real numeric values, data elements of type LOGICAL have the logical values .TRUE. and .FALSE., and so on. Conceptually, there are an unlimited number of data types. For example a data type MARKS (see Section 4.5) might have values

.NOMARK.
.SPARE.
.STRIKE.

A data type COLOR might have values

.BLACK.
.BROWN.
.RED.
.ORANGE.
.YELLOW.
.GREEN.
.BLUE.
.VIOLET.
.GRAY.
.WHITE.

A data type SEX would have values .MALE. and .FEMALE., and a data type CRITICALPOINTS (see Section 11.2) might have values

.RECUR.
.HANOIA.
.HANOIB.
.RESTORE.

It is clear that the possibilities for data types are unlimited, and, as the example programs have shown, many programs, at least conceptually, involve an "unusual" data type.

Since the number of data types is unlimited, it is not possible to have them all intrinsically defined in a programming language such as Fortran. Fortran provides intrinsically only six of the most commonly needed data types, including INTEGER, REAL, CHARACTER, LOGICAL and two additional types that are useful in making scientific calculations. Other types not directly provided by Fortran must be "simulated" with the types provided, and thus the types provided form the basic "building blocks" for constructing data elements.

The following sections review types INTEGER, REAL, CHARACTER, and LOGICAL, describe how types INTEGER and CHARACTER can be used to simulate the "unusual" data types, and introduce the notions and some applications of types DOUBLEPRECISION and COMPLEX. The final section of this chapter shows how a useful data type not provided directly by Fortran, bit strings, may be simulated.

12.1 Data Types in Fortran

These involve the familiar types, described and used at length in the preceding chapters. For each of these types there may be constants, variables, arrays, expressions, and functions of that type. Chapter 2 describes the declaration of data elements of types INTEGER, REAL, and CHARACTER, and Section 4.3 describes LOGICAL data elements.

While explicit declaration of data elements is strongly recommended, Fortran does provide for implicit typing (see Section 2.4). An IMPLICIT statement at the beginning of the specifications establishes a correspondence between types and first letters of (undeclared) data elements. The form of the IMPLICIT statement is

```
IMPLICIT <list of implicit declarations>
```

where the <list of implicit declarations> has one or more elements, each of the form

```
<type> (<list of letters>)
```

The <list of letters> is any desired list of capital letters, separated by commas; a sequence of consecutive letters may be specified by <first>–<last> rather than listing each letter of the sequence individually. The <type> may be any Fortran <type>: INTEGER, REAL, CHARACTER[*<length>], LOGICAL (or DOUBLEPRECISION or COMPLEX). If the IMPLICIT statement is omitted then

```
IMPLICIT INTEGER(I-N), REAL(A-H,O-Z)
```

is assumed. Of course type statements may (and should!) be used to override implicit typing.

Data elements of any of these types involve physical memory storage to accommodate those data elements. The following subsection discusses the nature of this storage in detail.

12.1.1 Fortran Storage Units

Fortran specifies that two kinds of *storage unit* be defined for each Fortran implementation—a *numerical* storage unit and a *nonnumerical* storage unit. Each constant, variable, and array element of type INTEGER utilizes one numerical storage unit. Similarly, each constant, variable, and array element of type REAL or LOGICAL takes one numerical storage unit. For data elements of type CHARACTER each character requires one nonnumerical storage unit; for example the declaration CHARACTER STRING*20 results in STRING being allocated 20 nonnumerical storage units.

There is no specified relation between numerical and nonnumerical storage units, and the size (number of bits) of each kind of storage unit is implementation dependent. Thus implementors are free to utilize their computers' word sizes most conveniently in establishing the sizes of each storage unit. For example, 32 bits may be used for numerical storage units and 8 bits for nonnumerical storage units. With this implementation of storage units a CHARACTER data element of four characters takes the same physical storage space as an INTEGER, REAL, or LOGICAL value.

Given these facts about Fortran's use of storage units for data elements, several conclusions can be made about the use of such data elements in programs. (1) The largest integer value on one computer may be different from the largest integer value on another computer, because the numerical storage units may be different sizes in the two implementations. Thus a Fortran program may function differently in two different standard-conforming implementations. (And therefore a program might not be fully "portable".) Similarly, the largest (and smallest) REAL values may differ from computer to computer. (2) EQUIVALENCEing (see Section 7.6) elements of type INTEGER, REAL, and/or LOGICAL always results in a one-to-one relationship since these types all use the same kind of storage unit. Such EQUIVALENCEing is allowed in Fortran in order that efficiencies in the use of storage space may be realized. However since the representation of integers and reals is usually different (see Appendix C), equivalenced integer and real variables are usually interpreted as having different values for a given contents of the storage unit. (3) Although two CHARACTER data elements may be EQUIVALENCEd, a CHARACTER data element may not be EQUIVALENCEd with a data element having a numerical storage unit. The reason for this is that the relationship between the size of numerical and nonnumerical storage units is undefined (and is implementation dependent), and therefore prohibiting such equivalencing should increase program portability. (4) Logical variables, and especially logical arrays, in Fortran are wasteful of space since many bits (32, for example) are used to represent a logical value, whereas 1 bit would be sufficient. (5) Simulation of arbitrary data types is normally done with either INTEGER or CHARACTER data types. The fact that these two types have different storage units may affect the choice of which to use.

12.1.2 Arbitrary Data Type Simulation

Each data type has a set of associated values, which are the constants of that type. Thus the values associated with type INTEGER are

0, 1, −1, 2, −2, 3, −3, . . ., etc.,

the values associated with type CHARACTER are

'a', 'b', 'c', . . ., 'aa', 'ab', 'ac', . . ., 'ba', 'bb', . . ., etc.,

and the values associated with type LOGICAL are .TRUE. and .FALSE.. These values are built-in with the Fortran provisions for types INTEGER, CHARACTER, and LOGICAL, and the values of type REAL are similarly built-in. The values of some other, arbitrary, data type are not automatically known to the Fortran system, however, and must be supplied by the programmer. Supplying such values normally involves a listing, or an enumeration, of them, and thus they are easily associated with a corresponding set of integer or character values. Consider, for example, type MARKS given above. As was done in programs ROLL and SCORE of Section 4.5, integer data element names can be used to represent the type values, and unique corresponding integer values assigned to these names via the PARAMETER statement. Therefore the values, once assigned, are constant and cannot change, and so these names can be considered the values of the new type. Similarly character names could be used, with the values "mapped" into a set of character values. Figure 12.1 illustrates how the values associated with type MARKS can be provided.

```
      INTEGER      NOMARK,SPARE,STRIKE
      PARAMETER (
*                  type   MARKS
     :                    NOMARK  = 0,
     :                    SPARE   = 1,
     :                    STRIKE  = 2 )
*                  end    MARKS
```
(a)

```
      CHARACTER NOMARK,SPARE,STRIKE
      PARAMETER (
*                  type   MARKS
     :                    NOMARK  = 'a',
     :                    SPARE   = 'b',
     :                    STRIKE  = 'c' )
*                  end    MARKS
```
(b)

Figure 12.1. Simulation of data type MARKS. (*a*) Using type INTEGER. (*b*) Using type CHARACTER.

In part (*a*) of Figure 12.1 each value of MARKS requires one numerical storage unit, and in part (*b*) each value of MARKS requires one nonnumerical storage unit. Since numerical storage units are typically several times larger than nonnumerical storage units, using type CHARACTER to simulate arbitrary data types can require less storage than using type INTEGER. However this factor is significant only if storage is in short supply, and a large number of data type values are being defined. A possibly more significant factor, on computers with small word sizes (such as 8 or 16 bits—see Section 12.4) is that two or more words are required for a numerical storage unit, whereas rarely would more than one word be required for a nonnumerical storage unit. Thus fewer memory accesses need be required for a reference to a character-based type value than for a reference to an integer-based type value, making execution more efficient for character-based type simulation. On the other hand, if several characters were used for each character-based value (e.g., STRIKE = 'strike') then character-based simulation could be less efficient than for integer based. Generally speaking, either integer- or character-based type simulation is usually satisfactory.

Now that a Fortran technique for defining type values is available, a method of simulating variables, and arrays, of those types is needed. If integer values were associated with the type values then integer variables will be used for such variables; otherwise character variables should be used. For example, declaring variables MARKP and MARKP2 of types MARKS could be simulated as follows:

```
      INTEGER
*                ..really type MARKS, conceptually, instead of INTEGER..
     :           MARKP, MARKP2
```

It has been a bit of work to provide the values and variables of a new data type with the above sort of specifications, but the payoff for this work comes in the executable part of the program. Because now the values and variables of the new type may be used as if they had been built-in. Thus statements like

```
MARKP = SPARE                                  and
IF (MARKP2 .EQ. STRIKE) THEN
```

are legal and may be freely used as statements involving variables and constants of the new type. The value of SPARE may be thought of as "spare", and the fact that this value is really implemented as 1 (or 'b') is immaterial. The great advantage of using new data types in this manner is that it allows the programmer to think more in the terms of the problem being solved, rather than continually mentally converting these concepts of the problem into the integers (or characters) that Fortran supports. Instead the conversion is made once, at the outset, and thereafter the programmer can think in the more pleasant, and less error-prone natural terms of the problem. Therefore the implementation of arbitrary data types is an important application of Fortran's PARAMETER statement.

When new data types are implemented in Fortran in this manner, they have many of the properties of the built-in data types. These new types have constants (which cannot be changed in the program), variables, and arrays. They may be used in systems of programs as long as the type values are identically defined in each program unit in which that type is used. They may be passed as subprogram arguments, and functions of the new type may be constructed. The main limitation is that expressions of the new type are restricted to constants, variables, array elements, and function calls. The reason for this is that operators do not exist for new data types and hence meaningful expressions involving more than one operand cannot be formed. However any operations on or involving the new data types may easily be provided by writing subroutines and/or functions to perform such operations. Some nontrivial examples of such operations are given in Section 12.4.

When integers are used to implement a new type, an ordering is then imposed on the values of the new type, and this ordering may easily be the order in which the values are listed in the PARAMETER statement. Such ordering can be used, if appropriate, in the executable statements; for example,

```
IF (MARKP .GT. NOMARK) THEN
```

If a new type is implemented with characters, an ordering is then also imposed on the new type values, but (except for the usual ordering among the letters and digits) this ordering is, in general, unknown and different from computer to computer because of the implementation dependency of the character collating sequence. Normally, therefore, ordered types should be implemented with integers, but if the ordering property is not needed, then implementation with characters is just as satisfactory.

A final matter concerning new data types is whether or not the type values must be input or output. For I/O operations the underlying values (integer or character) are used, not the names representing the type values. However, a modification of the character implementation of new types described above may be used to make these underlying values the same as the new type values. If type MARKS, for example, is defined as

```
      CHARACTER*6 NOMARK, SPARE, STRIKE
      PARAMETER (
*           type MARKS
     :                NOMARK = 'NOMARK',
     :                SPARE = 'SPARE',
     :                STRIKE = 'STRIKE')
*           end MARKS
```

then "A" formatted I/O (or PRINT*) would make the I/O values identical to the new type values. The disadvantages of this approach are that each new type value (and variable) requires six nonnumerical storage units, and for all practical purposes the type must be considered unordered. By using such character values, of course, many of the same advantages of introducing a new data type can be realized by using these values directly in the executable statements, without the additional step of defining type values with the parameter statement. An example of this is in subroutines HANOI and HANOI2 of Section 11.2.

If the values associated with the critical points of HANOI2 were considered to comprise a new data type, however, called CRITICALPOINTS, simulated with type

CHARACTER, the type declarations could contain:

```
*      ....definition of type CRITICALPOINTS....
       CHARACTER    RECUR, HANOIA, HANOIB, RESTOR
       PARAMETER    (
*                   type CRITICALPOINTS
                               RECUR = 'H',
                               HANOIA = 'A',
                               HANOIB = 'B',
                               RESTOR = 'R')
*                   end CRITICALPOINTS
*      ....declaration of a CRITICALPOINTS variable named CP....
       CHARACTER    CP
```

Then the case structure of that program would have the form

```
case (CP) of
    RECUR:    ---
              ---
              ---
    HANOIA:   ---
              ---
              ---
    HANOIB:   ---
              ---
              ---
    RESTOR:   ---
              ---
              ---
end selection
```

and the first recursive call, for example, would include the statements

```
PUSH (N,P1,P2,HANOIA)
  .
  .
CP = RECUR
```

Note that the names RECUR, HANOIA, HANOIB, and RESTOR appear in the executable statements as the constants of type CRITICALPOINTS, and the underlying values 'H', 'A', 'B', and 'R', are immaterial and are ignored. Thus, after the simulation of CRITICALPOINTS in the declarations, the programmer can, in the executable part of the program, think in terms of the new data type, and hence think more directly in the conceptual terms of the problem. A second advantage of the above implementation of critical points is that only one nonnumerical storage unit is utilized for data elements of type CRITICALPOINTS, which contributes to both storage and execution efficiency.

Thus a number of options are available to the Fortran programmer to create data elements of types that are suitable for the problem being programmed. These techniques may be used to develop the program in terms that closely reflect the nature of the problem, and thus to minimize the chances of introducing errors into the program. The kinds of problems that Fortran was originally designed to solve, and for which it is still a premier language, are those involving scientific and engineering numerical calculations. Fortran has two additional built-in data types that are especially useful for these kinds of problems. These two data types, and example applications, are described in the next two sections.

12.2. Type DOUBLEPRECISION

For general-purpose numerical calculations type REAL data elements are normally used. In the case of 32-bit numerical storage units, for example, 23 or 24 bits are typically used for the mantissa of real values (see Appendix C), which is equivalent to about seven decimal digits of precision in the real values. This is adequate for most general-purpose calculations, but it is not enough precision for many scientific calculations. Arbitrary precision arithmetic may be achieved in Fortran with the technique used in program FACT of Section 5.4, and the libraries of many computing centers have subroutine packages that perform addition, multiplication, etc. on arrays representing arbitrary precision real values. The main disadvantage of such arbitrary precision facilities is that typically such arithmetic operations are quite slow, making programs using such facilities expensive.

Fortunately, few scientific calculations require greater precision than perhaps double the 7 decimal digits. Fortran therefore provides a data type, called DOUBLEPRECISION, that has approximately twice the precision of type REAL. Each DOUBLEPRECISION data element utilizes two numeric storage units, but otherwise is identical to type REAL. In implementations using 32-bit numeric storage units the precision of DOUBLEPRECISION data elements is typically approximately 17 decimal digits. Of course the real and double precisions may be quite different from 7 and 17 on a given computer because of the implementation dependency of the size of numerical storage units. For example, on a computer using 60 bits for a numeric storage unit, types REAL and DOUBLEPRECISION typically respectively have approximately 15 and 33 decimal digits of precision.

DOUBLEPRECISION quantities may appear anywhere in the executable statements that REAL quantities may, and in fact in a statement such as

```
A = B*C
```

it is not possible to tell the difference between REAL and DOUBLEPRECISION (and INTEGER, for that matter) variables without inspecting the specification statements to see which are declared as DOUBLEPRECISION. In an arithmetic operation in which one of the operands is double precision, the other operand is converted to the equivalent double precision value (if it isn't double precision already) prior to performing the operation, and the result of the operation is double precision. If a double precision value is assigned to a REAL variable then the extra digits of precision in the value are truncated and the result assigned as the value of the variable.

Variables and arrays may be declared as type DOUBLEPRECISION by the DOUBLEPRECISION specification statement. This statement is structured, and functions, precisely like the REAL statement, except that the word DOUBLEPRECISION is used in place of REAL:

> DOUBLEPRECISION <list of variable names and array declarations>

Double precision constants have exactly the same form as real constants with an exponent part, but with the "E" replaced by a "D". Thus

```
4.7113598247D3   (=4711.3598247)
         -8D-2   (=-0.08)
```

are examples of double precision constants.

Virtually all of the intrinsic functions that accept real arguments, and return real values, can be used with double precision. In the function call SQRT(X), for example, X may be a DOUBLEPRECISION variable. In this case the value returned will be the double precision square-root value. Functions INT and REAL may have double precision arguments, which cause truncation of the double precision value, just as do assignment of a double precision value to integer and real variables. Functions MAX and MIN may have double precision arguments. In addition Fortran has two intrinsic functions, besides those listed in Section 3.4, that involve double precision quantities. Function DBLE takes either a real or integer argument and returns the equivalent double precision value. Function DPROD has two real arguments, and returns the double precision product of these argument values.

Double precision data elements are most useful in calculations involving a long sequence of arithmetic operations. All noninteger arithmetic operations on a computer involve round-off error, and in a succession of such operations round-off error tends to accumulate, making the result less and less precise. The round-off error in double precision quantities is much less than in ordinary real quantities, and therefore round-off error accumulations in calculations involving double precision quantities are usually much smaller than the same calculations with real quantities. A very simple but striking example of this is illustrated in program ERROR. Here the identical calculation is made

```
*....:-----------------------------------------------------------------------
      PROGRAM  ERROR
*                       ..this program illustrates the use of double
*                       precision data elements in calculations in
*                       which round-off error could be a problem. The same
*                       calculation is performed with Fortran's REAL and
*                       DOUBLEPRECISION data elements, and the results
*                       are compared..
*     ....variables....
      INTEGER  I,N
      REAL  R3,RT,RS
      DOUBLEPRECISION  D3,DS,DT

*     ....execute....
      PRINT *, ' N', '     REAL Result', '     DOUBLEPRECISION Result'
      PRINT *
      R3 = 3.0
      D3 = 3.0
      do  N = 1,20
         RS = 0.0
         DS = 0.0
         RT = 1.0
         DT = 1.0
         do  I = 1,N
            RT = RT/R3
            DT = DT/D3
            RS = RS+RT
            DS = DS+DT
         repeat
         PRINT '(I3,F15.6,F15.6)',
     :          N, (1.0-RS*(R3-1.0))/RT, REAL((1.0-DS*(D3-1.0))/DT)
      repeat
      END
=============================================================================
.EXECUTE  ERROR

 N     REAL Result     DOUBLEPRECISION Result

 1       1.000000        1.000000
 2       1.000000        1.000000
 3       1.000003        1.000000
 4       1.000009        1.000000
 5       1.000029        1.000000
 6       1.000087        1.000000
 7       1.000347        1.000000
 8       1.001130        1.000000
 9       1.004258        1.000000
10       1.013644        1.000000
11       1.055879        1.000000
12       1.203702        1.000000
13       1.710525        1.000000
14       3.421050        1.000000
15       8.552624        1.000001
16      25.657875        1.000002
17      76.973633        1.000007
18     230.920898        1.000022
19     692.762695        1.000088
20    2078.288086        1.000220

=============================================================================
```

twice, the only difference being that in one case "real arithmetic" is used and in the other case "double precision arithmetic" is used (hence the only difference in the two cases is the size of the round-off error involved). The correct result in each case, and for each value of N, is 1.0. The cumulative effects of round-off error can be dramatic and disastrous, and the use of double precision can be extremely effective in combating these effects.

Program ERROR was, of course, contrived (with the formula chosen) to dramatically exhibit disastrous round-off error behavior. The calculation is actually summing the terms of

```
1/3 + (1/3)**2 + (1/3)**3 + . . . + (1/3)**N
```

however, and comparing the result with the theoretically expected value of (1−(1/3)**N)/2. A series of additions and multiplications takes place in this calculation, with round-off error effects growing with each operation. The nature of the comparison then further magnifies the resulting net error. (Actually the above formula is related to the way bank account interest is calculated—which means that one must be careful when using a computer to calculate interest!)

Whenever a calculation is made involving a sequence of arithmetic operations, such as in program ERROR, one can be sure that round-off error will exist, and must be expected to accumulate and cause the final result to be in error. The amount of this error varies from problem to problem, but can be so large as to make the final results totally erroneous, and thus meaningless. Usually careful organization of the calculation can do much to minimize the effects of round-off error—the formula in program ERROR could be reorganized, for example, in such a way that the round-off error effect would have been much less. After careful construction of the calculation, however, the programmer's most expedient defense against such round-off error is to use double precision when making calculations. This will greatly reduce the effects of round-off error, but some round-off error is still present, and can occasionally be intolerable even with double precision. Thus on occasion, resort still must be made to arbitrary precision routines.

Numerous books on numerical analysis and numerical methods treat in detail the types of problems commonly encountered in scientific work, and for which Fortran's double precision data types are applicable. For this class of problems reference is hereby made to these books, some of which are listed at the end of this chapter. One generally useful application of double precision data elements is in the determination of least-squares approximations to experimental data; a Fortran program for this application is given in Section 13.1.

12.3 Type COMPLEX

Another Fortran data type for making certain numerical calculations is type COMPLEX. Complex numbers are those having two components each—a "real" component and an "imaginary" component. The value of each of these components is an ordinary real number. In standard mathematical notation a complex number is written

$$a + ib$$

where a is the "real" component and is a real number, and ib is the "imaginary" component and b is a real number. (Mathematically i stands for SQRT(−1).) There are certain rules for addition, multiplication, and other arithmetic operations involving complex numbers. Complex numbers occur frequently in problems of science and engineering, especially in physics and electrical engineering.

A complex number is essentially an "ordered pair" of real numbers, and another mathematical representation is

(a,b)

where a and b are both real numbers, the first, a, being considered the "real" part of the complex number and the second, b, being the "imaginary" part. Fortran uses this ordered pair form for representing a complex number. Two (consecutive) numerical storage units are used for one complex data element, as shown in Figure 12.2. Both storage units contain an ordinary Fortran real number.

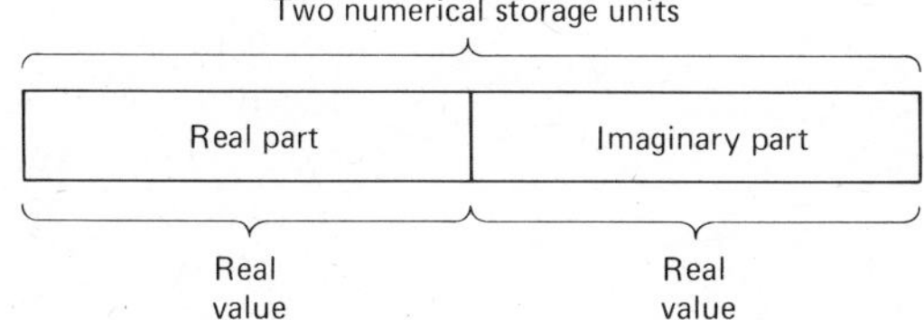

Figure 12.2. Fortran representation of a COMPLEX data element.

On output, the value of a complex data element is displayed in ordered pair form, with the two real values separated by a comma and enclosed in parentheses. On input, the ordered pair form must be used—two real values separated by a comma and enclosed in parentheses. Note that each of the two parts of a complex data element is a Fortran real value, not a double precision value.

Complex data elements are declared with a COMPLEX declaration statement:

COMPLEX <list of variable names and array declarations>

Complex constants are simply any two real constants written in ordered pair form. Examples of valid complex constants are:

(3.0, −4.5)

(16.25, 0.0)

(0.0, 5.61)

(−0.92, 29.0)

The Fortran arithmetic operators (+, −, *, /, **) are used to form arithmetic expressions with complex quantities. Such expressions appear exactly like arithmetic expressions involving integer, real, or double precision quantities, except for complex constants, and in fact may be indistinguishable from integer, real, or doubleprecision expressions without noting the typing in a COMPLEX specification. Normally if an arithmetic operation contains a complex operand the other operand is complex also—but the other operand may be integer or real (double precision is prohibited). If the other operand is integer or real then it is converted to a complex value whose "real" part is equivalent to the integer or real value and whose "imaginary" part has value zero, then complex arithmetic is performed and the result is a complex value. If an integer, real, or double precision value is assigned to a complex variable (note here that double precision is not prohibited) the resulting complex value has a "real" part equivalent to the integer, real or double precision value (or as close as possible) and an "imaginary" part whose value is zero. If a complex value is assigned to an integer, real, or double precision value the result is the same as if just the "real" part of the complex value were the assigned value.

Several intrinsic functions are available for use with complex quantities. The argument for INT, REAL, or DBLE may be complex, in which case the result is the same as if just the "real" part of the complex value were the argument. In particular REAL (<cv>), where <cv> is an argument having a complex value, returns the "real" part of the complex value. Another intrinsic function AIMAG, performs the corresponding function of returning the imaginary part of a complex value. The form of AIMAG is

AIMAG (<cv>)

where <cv> is any expression having a complex value. The value returned by AIMAG is of type real, and has value equal to the "imaginary" part of <cv>. Another intrinsic function, CMPLX, may be used with either 1 or 2 arguments and returns a complex value. These arguments may be of type integer, real, or double precision, but if there are two they must be of the same type. A call on COMPLX of the form

COMPLX (<arg1>,<arg2>)

returns the complex value (REAL (<arg1>), REAL (<arg2>)) and a call of the form

COMPLX (<arg1>)

returns the complex value (REAL (<arg1>), 0.0). If a call on CMPLX has only one argument then that argument may itself be of type complex, in which case the function value is just the argument value; that is,

CMPLX (<cv>)

where <cv> has a complex value, returns (REAL(<cv>), AIMAG(<cv>)). A final intrinsic function returning a complex value is CONJG, which has a single, complex argument. CONJG returns the complex conjugate of its argument. The conjugate of a complex value (a,b) is defined to be (a,−b)—that is, the "imaginary" part is negated. Therefore the call

CONJG (<cv>)

returns the value (REAL(<cv>), −AIMAG(<cv>). In addition the mathematical functions for real arguments, which are also defined for complex arguments—ABS, SQRT, EXP, LOG, SIN, and COS—may be called with complex arguments. The returned values are all the appropriate complex values, except for ABS(<cv>) which is real (the absolute value of a complex number (a,b) is defined to be SQRT(a*a+b*b)—that is, ABS((a,b)) eq SQRT(a*a+b*b).

Program NEWTON is a simple application of the use of type COMPLEX. This program uses "Newton's method" to systematically search for a root of a polynomial equation. Newton's method is a famous root-finding method in which an initial guess is made to the root, and then this guess is used in the Newton's method formula to generate the next (and hopefully much better) approximation to the root. The method is very simple, and is completely described by the algorithm

```
X = <initial-guess>
do
    ROOT = X-F(X)/DF(X)
    X = ROOT
repeat
```

```
*....:-----------------------------------------------------------------
      PROGRAM  NEWTON.
*                     ..this program uses Newton's method to extract a
*                     root of a fourth-degree polynomial. Such a root
*                     may be complex, so COMPLEX data elements are
*                     employed. Thus this program constitutes an appli-
*                     cation of Fortran's COMPLEX data element facility.
*     ....variables....
      INTEGER  N
      REAL  A, B, C, D, E
      COMPLEX  X, ROOT, F, DF
      DATA  N,      X       /
     :      1, (1.0,1.0)  /
*                     (or, initial value of X could be input)

*     ....execute....
      PRINT *, 'Input values for A, B, C, D, E (the coefficients).'
      READ *, A, B, C, D, E
      PRINT '(T2,A,5F8.2)','polynomial coefficients are',A,B,C,D,E
      do
         F = (((A*X+B)*X+C)*X+D)*X+E
         DF = ((4*A*X+3*B)*X+2*C)*X+D
         IF  (ABS(DF) .LT. 0.001)  THEN
               PRINT *, 'derivative too small -- terminate search'
               exit
         ENDIF
         ROOT = X-F/DF
         PRINT *, ROOT
         IF  (ABS(ROOT-X)/ABS(ROOT) .LT. 0.00001)  THEN
               PRINT *, 'root found'
               exit
         ENDIF
         X = ROOT
         N = N+1
         IF  (N .GT. 40)  THEN
               PRINT *, 'too many iterations -- terminate search '
               exit
         ENDIF
      repeat
      END
=====================================================================
.EXECUTE  NEWTON

Input values for A, B, C, D, E (the coefficients).
> 1.0  1.0  1.0  1.0  1.0
polynomial coefficients are      1.00     1.00     1.00     1.00     1.00
    (  0.644128,  0.861210)
    (  0.388321,  0.844367)
    (  0.287305,  0.931895)
    (  0.310216,  0.951910)
    (  0.309020,  0.951058)
    (  0.309017,  0.951057)
root found
=====================================================================


=====================================================================
.EXECUTE  NEWTON

Input values for A, B, C, D, E (the coefficients).
> 1.0  0.0  1.0  0.0 -1.0
polynomial coefficients are      1.00     0.00     1.00     0.00    -1.00
    (  0.632353,  0.720588)
    (  0.243255,  0.341959)
    (  0.412649, -1.024474)
    ( -0.037905, -0.885168)
    (  0.309499, -1.975126)
    (  0.200804, -1.581830)
    (  0.100300, -1.350151)
    (  0.021197, -1.270285)
    ( -0.000085, -1.271331)
    (  0.000000, -1.272020)
    (  0.000000, -1.272020)
root found
=====================================================================


=====================================================================
.EXECUTE  NEWTON

Input values for A, B, C, D, E (the coefficients).
> 1.0  0.0  0.0  0.0 -1.0
polynomial coefficients are      1.00     0.00     0.00     0.00    -1.00
    (  0.687500,  0.687500)
    (  0.323288,  0.323288)
    ( -1.607270, -1.607270)
    ( -1.190399, -1.190400)
    ( -0.855748, -0.855748)
    ( -0.542077, -0.542078)
    ( -0.014188, -0.014188)
derivative too small -- terminate search
=====================================================================


=====================================================================
.EXECUTE  NEWTON

Input values for A, B, C, D, E (the coefficients).
> 0.0  0.0  1.0 -3.0  2.0
polynomial coefficients are      0.00     0.00     1.00    -3.00     2.00
    (  1.200000,  0.400000)
    (  1.200000, -0.000000)
    (  0.933333,  0.000000)
    (  0.996078,  0.000000)
    (  0.999984,  0.000000)
    (  1.000000,  0.000000)
    (  1.000000, -0.000000)
root found
=====================================================================
```

F is the function (polynomial equation in program NEWTON) for which the root is being found and DF is the "derivative" function for F (which is easily determined if F is a polynomial).

The above algorithm for Newton's method is an infinite loop, and a practical program, such as NEWTON, would include provisions for termination. In fact program NEWTON has three conditions for termination, which make the loop seem longer and more complicated than it fundamentally is. One termination condition is if ROOT is "close enough" to the correct value—that is, if the "next approximation" (ROOT) is not very much different from the last one (X). Since the method involves a division it will fail if the divisor (DF) is zero (or close to it)—therefore another termination condition checks for this situation. And finally the sequence of approximations could possibly not converge to a root, and therefore a limit is imposed on the number of iterations.

Program NEWTON is designed for polynomials of degree four, with real coefficients:

```
F(X) = A*X**4 + B*X**3 + C*X**2 + D*X + E
```

where A, B, C, D, and E are real constants; by making A zero, however, the program can also be used to find roots of cubic equations. It will also work for quadratic equations (both A and B zero), and for linear equations (A, B, and C all zero). The initial guess is always (1.0, 1.0), and the value of ROOT for each iteration is printed. Note that this particular program finds only one of the roots.

Actually Newton's method is quite general, and can be used for finding roots of functions other than polynomials. More details can be found in the numerical analysis and numerical methods books listed at the end of this chapter.

12.4 Bit Strings

Each *memory cell*, or word, of a computer is really a set of *bits*—each bit being a "1" or a "0". Typical word sizes are 8 bits, 16 bits, 24 bits, 32 bits, 36 bits, 48 bits, 60 bits, and others. All data in the computer, no matter what type it represents, is ultimately realized as a set of these bits. Appendix C, for example, shows how Fortran's numerical storage units may be implemented in a group of 32 bits. In order to perform a simple Fortran operation, such as multiplying two real values, which is specified simply in Fortran as

```
A * B
```

a large number of operations on the bit groups representing A and B must in fact take place. Each Fortran implementation has routines that perform the needed operations on groups of bits to achieve the Fortran operations. More generally, virtually any system that makes computing facilities available to computer users must manipulate the bit values representing the data elements in ways that achieve the desired processing. In addition many applications programs need to be able to manipulate data on the "bit level", either because of special data requirements or to increase execution speeds.

A group or sequence of bits is sometimes called a "bit string", and it is the purpose of this section to identify some of the most important operations on bit strings and show how to perform these operations in Fortran. Fortran does not have a built-in bit string data type, so bit strings will have to be implemented in terms of those data types Fortran does have—and again integer and character types are the best ones.

Ideally a bit string facility should be able to manipulate bit strings having any arbitrary number of bits. This can be simulated with data elements of type CHARACTER in Fortran, since such data elements may be of any size (number of characters). The idea here is that a character variable of the desired size is declared, and then each character is limited to be a "1" or a "0". For example a "byte" (bit string with eight bits) can be simulated and initialized to all zeros by

```
CHARACTER BYTE*8
DATA BYTE /'00000000'/
```

The individual bits of BYTE are directly accessible. For example

BYTE(4:5) = '11'	sets the middle two bits to ones (regardless of what they were before), and
IF (BYTE(8:8) .EQ. '0') THEN	tests the rightmost bit for the value zero.

It is clear that any desired bit manipulation in BYTE is quite straightforward.

There are two (related) disadvantages of using character data elements for bit strings. The first is that this is merely a simulation of bit strings, and the '1's and '0's are just simulated bits and do not correspond to actual individual bits. In fact, and this is the second disadvantage, each simulated bit requires one nonnumerical storage unit, which typically is implemented in 8 actual bits (and if the ASCII character set is used—see Appendix B—a '1' is really 00110001 and a '0' is 00110000). Thus BYTE, which simulates 8 bits, actually involves 64 "real" bits. Despite these disadvantages, if simulated bits are satisfactory, and "8-for-1" inefficiency isn't a problem, then the use of character data elements to represent bit strings is very simple and flexible, and the common bit string operations (described below) are correspondingly simple to perform.

Using integer variables to represent bit strings has a different set of advantages and disadvantages. The great advantage is that each "simulated" bit is really a "real" bit, so that "real" bit string operations can be performed. (Thus with such a bit string facility Fortran can be used for those systems and applications programs that actually require bit manipulation.) There are two main disadvantages to using integer data elements for bit strings. The first is that each bit string has the same number of bits, namely the number of bits in a numerical storage unit (32 bits, for example). The second is that bit string operations on integer-based bit strings are more difficult to perform, using standard Fortran, than the same operations on character-based bit strings, and in fact are somewhat dependent on the way in which integer values are implemented in a numerical storage unit. However, the vast majority of implementations (if not all) have the following characteristics (see also Appendix C), which is sufficient to allow arbitrary bit string operations: positive integer numbers are stored as true binary numbers in the n−1 least significant ("rightmost") bits of a numerical storage unit, where n is the number of bits in a numerical storage unit (such as 32). The structure of a numerical storage unit of 32 bits is shown in Figure 12.3. Note that the *sign bit* is in the position corresponding to the most significant (leftmost) bit of the sequence of binary digits.

The largest positive integer value that the storage unit of Figure 12.3 can have is 2**31−1; this is when bits 0 through 30 are all 1's (i.e., 1+2+4+8+. . .+2**29+2**30 = 2**31−1). If bit position 30 (i.e., the position just to the right of the sign bit) contains a zero, then the integer value is less than 2**30, and can be doubled without "overflow". Conversely, if bit position 30 contains a one, then the integer value is at least 2**30 and it cannot be doubled without causing overflow. Suppose that in integer variable, WORD, using a 32-bit storage unit, has a nonnegative value less than 2**30; then the statement

```
WORD = WORD + WORD
```

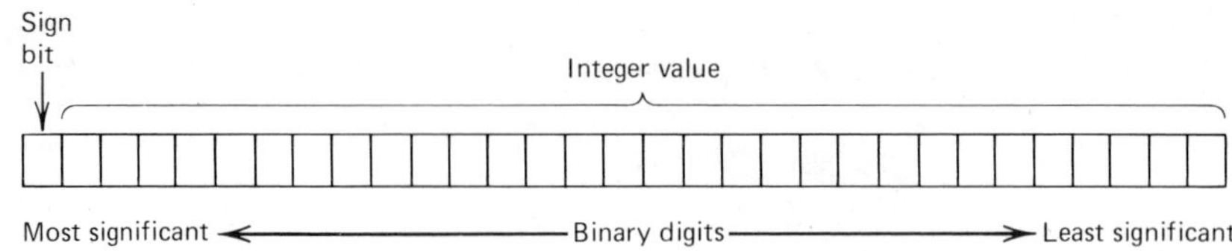

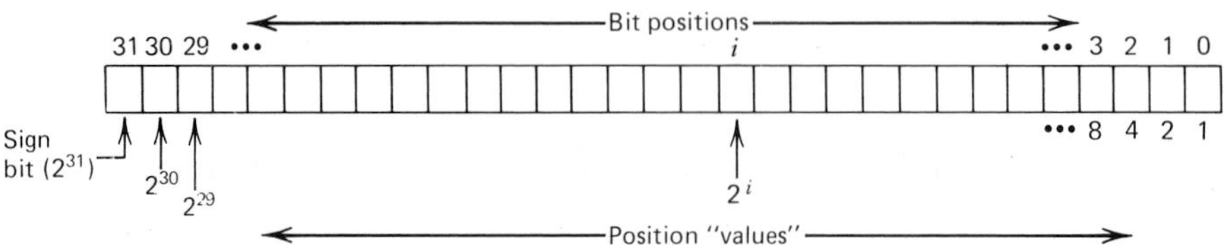

Figure 12.3. A (32-bit) numerical storage unit used as an integer.

(i.e., doubling the value of WORD) causes the entire original bit pattern in positions 0..29 of WORD to "shift" one place to the left (in Figure 12.3), with 0 filling in at bit position 0. The simple operation

```
WORD = 0
```

causes all 31 bits in positions 0..30 of WORD to become 0, and if bit position 0 contains a zero then the operation

```
WORD = WORD + 1
```

results in a one being placed in position 0 with the contents of all other positions unaffected.

In the rest of this section integer variables are used to represent bit strings. The associated routines for bit string operations constitute a practical set of tools for writing programs that perform actual bit manipulations. (The simpler algorithms for performing bit string operations on character-based bit strings are left for the problems.) While the examples of this chapter use 32-bit numerical storage units, any size could be used and all of the program examples will work for any such size simply by changing the PARAMETER value of WORDSZ. The sign bit is not used (and can be ignored) in the techniques described here, so that each integer variable will represent a 31-bit (WORDSZ−1 bits in general) bit string.

If an integer value is input or output, Fortran assumes that it is represented as the decimal value. With bit strings it is the 1's and 0's that should appear, however, so it would be handy to have routines that will make bit string I/O simple and convenient. An intermediate character string CBITS, of 31 characters, (declared as CHARACTER CBITS*31) can be used for this purpose. Thus

READ '(A)', CBITS	allows the 31 1's and 0's to be conveniently input, while
PRINT *, CBITS	will output them.

Moreover CBITS = '<31 bit values>' could appear within the program as another means of establishing a desired bit pattern. Two functions, PACK and UNPACK, will convert between the character string CBITS of bits to the equivalent bit string in the integer WORD. The statement

WORD = PACK (CBITS)

will convert CBITS into WORD, and the statement

CBITS = UNPACK (WORD)

will convert in the opposite direction. In fact the bit pattern of WORD can now be displayed by the statement

PRINT *, UNPACK(WORD)

```
*....:-----------------------------------------------------------------------
      INTEGER FUNCTION  PACK (CBITS)
                                 CHARACTER  CBITS*(*)

*                ..this program provides for converting a
*                bit-string of character '1's and '0's to the
*                corresponding integer-based bit string. (Mainly
*                for purposes of inputting the bit string value.)

*     ....constants....(number of bits in bit string)
      INTEGER  WORDSZ
      PARAMETER  ( WORDSZ = 32 )

*     ....local variable....(loop index)
      INTEGER  N

*     ....execute....
      PACK = 0
      do  N = 1,WORDSZ-1
           PACK = PACK+PACK+INDEX(CBITS(N:N),'1')
      repeat
      END
=============================================================================
*....:-----------------------------------------------------------------------
      CHARACTER*(*) FUNCTION  UNPACK (WORD)
                                          INTEGER  WORD

*                ..this program provides for converting an integer-
*                based bit-string to the corresponding bit characters.
*                (Mainly for purposes of outputting the bit string.)

*     ....constants....(number of bits in bit string)
      INTEGER  WORDSZ, MAXPOS
      PARAMETER  ( WORDSZ = 32, MAXPOS = 2**(WORDSZ-2) )
      CHARACTER  BIT*2
      DATA    BIT / '01' /

*     ....local variables....
      INTEGER  N, TEMP, CARRY

*     ....execute....
      TEMP = WORD
      do  N = 1,WORDSZ-1
           CARRY = 0
           IF  (TEMP .GE. MAXPOS)  THEN
                  CARRY = 1
                  TEMP = TEMP - MAXPOS
           ENDIF
           UNPACK(N:N) = BIT(CARRY+1:CARRY+1)
           TEMP = TEMP+TEMP
      repeat
      END
=============================================================================
```

The important bit string operations fall into three major categories:

1 Shifting and rotating (function SHIFT below).

2 Logical operations (function LOGIC below).

3 Bit extraction and isolation.

These three categories are described in the following four subsections. The fifth subsection presents a simple application of bit strings and operations on bit strings.

Fortran does not have intrinsic functions to provide the bit string operations, so externally provided functions must be used. There are at least three sources of such functions.

1 Assembly (machine) language routines provided on the computing system and callable from Fortran. Many computing systems have such a set of routines available for performing bit-string operations. These are invariably the most efficient bit-string operations available to the Fortran programmer using that computing system.

2 A set of Fortran library routines, made available to all Fortran programmers. Many computing systems have such library routines, and in fact a rather complete set of such routines has been designed, standardized, and is available in many system libraries. The ISA reference at the end of this chapter describes these standard bit-string routines.

3 The Fortran programmer can provide his/her own set of bit-string functions.

If bit-string routines are provided by the computing system then normally they should be used since they are almost certainly more efficient than programmer-supplied ones. In this chapter, however, source 3 is used, and a set of routines are provided that the programmer can use in the absence of sources 1 and 2. The names used here for these routines are the same as the names used in the corresponding ISA routines.

12.4.1 Shifting and Rotating

A group of operations that are useful to have with bit strings involve *shifting* the bit pattern left or right a certain number of positions. Figure 12.4 illustrates the two most important forms of shifting left (nine positions, as an example):

1 Shifting—the leftmost nine bits are lost, with zeros filled in on the right.

2 Rotating—the leftmost nine bits are "rotated" around to the right.

In general a bit pattern can be shifted (or rotated) left any number of positions and, of course, corresponding shifts and rotates can take place to the right.

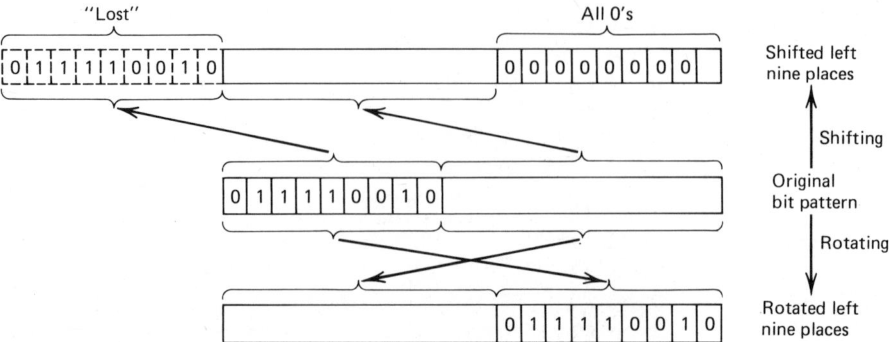

Figure 12.4. Left shifting and rotating a bit string nine positions.

```
*....:-----------------------------------------------------------------
      INTEGER FUNCTION  SHIFT (WORD,N)
                              INTEGER  WORD,N

*                   ..this program is for left and right shifting and
*                   rotating of WORD. If N is positive then the
*                   shift (or rotate) will be left, if negative then
*                   right. The magnitude of N should not be greater
*                   than WORDSZ (the total number of bits in WORD)..

*     ....entry points....
      INTEGER  ISHFT, ISHFC

*     ....external functions called....(both used as arguments)
      EXTERNAL  SHL, ROL
      INTEGER   SHL, ROL

*     ....constant....
      INTEGER  WORDSZ
      PARAMETER  ( WORDSZ = 32 )


*     ....ISHFT entry point....
      ENTRY  ISHFT (WORD,N)
          IF  (N .GE. 0)  THEN
                    ISHFT = SHL(WORD,N)
              ELSE
                 ISHFT = ROL(SHL(ROL(WORD,WORDSZ-1+N),-N),WORDSZ-1+N)
          ENDIF
*                      ..shifting left is more efficient, in Fortran,
*                       than shifting right -- therefore shift right by
*                       rotating left, shifting left, then rotating left
*                       again the appropriate number of places..
      RETURN

*     ....ISHFC entry point....
      ENTRY  ISHFC (WORD,N)
          IF  (N .GE. 0)  THEN
                 ISHFC = ROL(WORD,N)
              ELSE
                 ISHFC = ROL(WORD,WORDSZ-1+N)
*                       ..rotate -N right by rotating WORDSZ-1+N left
          ENDIF
      END
=================================================================
*....:-----------------------------------------------------------------
      INTEGER FUNCTION  SHL (WORD,N)
                            INTEGER  WORD,N

*      SHL shifts WORD N places left
*      ROL rotates WORD N places left

*     ....entry point....
      INTEGER  ROL

*     ....constants....
      INTEGER WORDSZ, MAXPOS
      PARAMETER  (  WORDSZ = 32,
     :              MAXPOS = 2**(WORDSZ-2) )


*     ....local variables....
      INTEGER  K, CARRY

*     ....execute....
      SHL = WORD
      do  K = 1,N
          IF  (SHL .GE. MAXPOS)  THEN
                 SHL = SHL - MAXPOS
          ENDIF
          SHL = SHL + SHL
      repeat
      RETURN

*     ....ROL entry point....
      ENTRY  ROL (WORD,N)
      ROL = WORD
      do  K = 1,N
          CARRY = 0
          IF  (ROL .GE. MAXPOS)  THEN
                 CARRY = 1
                 ROL = ROL-MAXPOS
          ENDIF
          ROL = ROL+ROL+CARRY
      repeat
      END
=================================================================
```

In shifting, the bits ''fall off the end,'' with zeros being inserted on the other end. In rotating (or ''circular''shifting, as it is also called) as a bit ''falls off'' it is not lost, but is inserted into the vacated spot on the other end.

Function SHIFT has two entry points:

ISHFT (WORD,N) for shifting (left or right)
ISHFC (WORD,N) for rotating (left or right)

In each case WORD is the bit string (integer) to be shifted and N is an integer specifying the number of positions WORD is to be shifted. If N is positive then the shift (rotate) is to the left, if N is negative the shift (rotate) is to the right (if N is zero no movement occurs). The value returned by the function is the shifted (or rotated) bit string, and the arguments (WORD and N) are left unchanged.

12.4.2 Logical Operations

Shifting involves only a single bit string. Another class of useful bit string operations involves ''combining'' two bit strings to form a third bit string. The logical operations combine two bit strings, on a bit-by-corresponding-bit basis; that is, the resulting bit value in position P is determined completely by the bits in position P of the two bit strings being combined. There are three common combinations: the IAND, IOR, and IEOR operations. In addition a fourth operation, NOT, which involves only a single initial bit string, ''reverses'' (flips) each bit. (NOT is equivalent to IEORing with a bit string of all 1's.) Figure 12.5 shows, using four-bit-long bit strings, the effects of IAND, IOR, IEOR, and NOT, and includes all possible combinations of two bits.

0	1	0	1	WORD1
0	0	1	1	WORD2
0	0	0	1	IAND(WORD1,WORD2)
0	1	1	1	IOR(WORD1,WORD2)
0	1	1	0	IEOR(WORD1,WORD2)
1	0	1	0	NOT(WORD1)

Figure 12.5. The effects of IAND, IOR, IEOR, and NOT bit string operations.

If a bit value of 0 is thought of as ''false'', and 1 as ''true'', then IAND, IOR, and NOT are analogous to the .AND., .OR., and .NOT. operators in logical expressions, and IEOR is analogous to .NEQV.. However in the bit-string operation, 31 (WORDSZ−1 in general) resulting bits are produced—that is, 31 of these individual bit operations are performed ''simultaneously''. Function LOGIC implements the bit-string operations of IAND, IOR, IEOR, and NOT for integer-based bit strings. In each case the function value is the resulting bit string, and in each case the arguments remain unchanged.

The usefulness of these logical operations will be demonstrated in the following three subsections. Note an interesting property of the NOT function, however: since 0 is a bit string of all zeros, NOT(0) is a bit string of all ones.

12.4.3 Bit Extraction and Isolation

In performing bit string manipulations it is often necessary to check the value of a particular bit, say in position P, as in Figure 12.6.

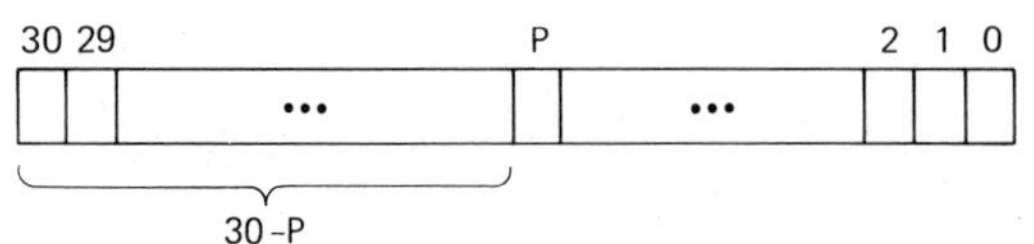

Figure 12.6. Bit position P is 30-P positions from sign bit.

```
*....:--------------------------------------------------------------
      INTEGER FUNCTION  LOGIC (WORD1,WORD2)
                                INTEGER  WORD1, WORD2

*                  ..This program implements the bit string operations
*                  of IAND, IOR, IEOR, and NOT. The two argument bit
*                  strings, WORD1 and WORD2, are left unchanged, and
*                  the function value returned is the desired value
*                  of the operation. The call to CARRYS sets C1 to true
*                  if the leftmost bit of W1 is a one, sets C2 to
*                  true if the leftmost bit of W2 is a one, and shifts
*                  W1 and W2 each one place left..


*     ....entry points....
      INTEGER  IAND, IOR, IEOR, NOT

*     ....constant....(bits for numerical storage unit)
      INTEGER  WORDSZ, MAXPOS
      PARAMETER  (WORDSZ = 32, MAXPOS = 2**(WORDSZ-2) )

*     ....local variables....
      INTEGER  K, W1, W2
      LOGICAL  C1, C2

*     ....IAND entry point....
      ENTRY  IAND (WORD1,WORD2)
          W1 = WORD1
          W2 = WORD2
          IAND = 0
          do  K = 1,WORDSZ-1
              CALL CARRYS (W1,C1,W2,C2)
              IAND = IAND+IAND
              IF  (C1 .AND. C2)  IAND = IAND+1
          repeat
      RETURN

*     ....IOR entry point....
      ENTRY  IOR (WORD1,WORD2)
          W1 = WORD1
          W2 = WORD2
          IOR = 0
          do  K = 1,WORDSZ-1
              CALL CARRYS (W1,C1,W2,C2)
              IOR = IOR+IOR
              IF  (C1 .OR. C2)  IOR = IOR+1
          repeat
      RETURN

*     ....IEOR entry point....
      ENTRY  IEOR (WORD1,WORD2)
          W1 = WORD1
          W2 = WORD2
          IEOR = 0
          do  K = 1,WORDSZ-1
              CALL CARRYS (W1,C1,W2,C2)
              IEOR = IEOR+IEOR
              IF  (C1 .NEQV. C2)  IOR = IOR+1
          repeat
      RETURN

*     ....NOT entry point....
      ENTRY  NOT (WORD1)
          W1 = WORD1
          W2 = 0
          NOT = 0
          do  K = 1,WORDSZ-1
              CALL CARRYS (W1,C1,W2,C2)
              NOT = NOT+NOT
              IF  (.NOT. C1)  NOT = NOT+1
          repeat
      END
====================================================================
```

```
*....:-----------------------------------------------------------------------
      SUBROUTINE CARRYS (W1,C1,W2,C2)
                             INTEGER W1,W2
                             LOGICAL C1,C2
*
                             ..routine to determine the status of
*                            left-most bits of W1 and W2, and to
*                            shift W1 and W2 left..

*     ....constants....
      INTEGER  WORDSZ, MAXPOS
      PARAMETER  (WORDSZ = 32, MAXPOS = 2**(WORDSZ-2) )

*     ....execute....
      C1 = .FALSE.
      IF  (W1 .GE. MAXPOS)  THEN
              C1 = .TRUE.
              W1 = W1-MAXPOS
      ENDIF
      W1 = W1+W1

      C2 = .FALSE.
      IF  (W2 .GE. MAXPOS)  THEN
              C2 = .TRUE.
              W2 = W2-MAXPOS
      ENDIF
      W2 = W2+W2
      END
=============================================================================
```

One way to check the bit in position P is to shift it into the leftmost position. Using 32 for WORDSZ this could be done as follows:

```
      IF (ISHFT(WORD,30-P).GE.2**30) THEN
*                                  . .bit in position P is a 1. .
                    ----
                    ----
                    ----
              ELSE
*                                  . .bit in position P is a 0. .
                    ----
                    ----
                    ----
      ENDIF
```

This leaves WORD unchanged (since all of the SHIFT, and the LOGIC, functions leave the arguments unchanged), and the desired processing in each of the two cases (bit is 1, bit is 0) can be specified in the IF-ENDIF structure.

The shifting operations can also be used to "isolate" a group of one or more bits within a bit string. Figure 12.7 shows the situation (assuming PL greater than or equal to PR). A group of bits, specified by the leftmost bit position of the group PL and the rightmost bit position of the group PR, is to remain unchanged, and all bits to the left and right are to be set to zero. Three successive operations, a shift to the left 30-PL places (again using 32 for WORDSZ), followed by a left rotate PL−PR+1 places, followed by a shift left PR places, will achieved the desired result:

WORD = ISHFT(ISHFC(ISHFT(WORD,30−PL),PL−PR+1),PR)

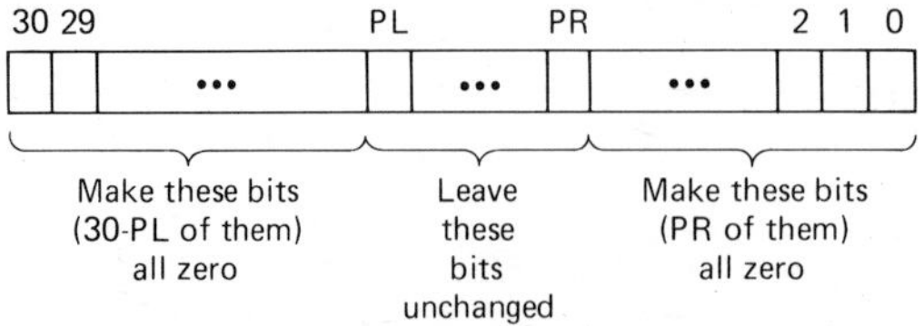

Figure 12.7. Isolating the group of bits between positions PL and PR (inclusive).

If WORD is to remain unchanged, the result of the shifting could be assigned to another integer variable, say WORD2. The effect of the first shift (ISHFT(WORD,30−PL)) is to slide the PL. .PR group clear to the left of the bit string, with 30−PL zeros coming in on the right. Then the ISHFC slides the PL. .PR group, unchanged, around to the right end, preceded by the 30−PL zeros. And finally the last ISHFT puts the PL. .PR group back in its original position with the 30−PL zeros on the left and PR zeros on the right. The "opposite" effect—zeroing the PL. .PR group of bits, leaving all other bits unchanged—may be achieved by interchanging ISHFT and ISHFC in these three operations:

```
WORD = ISHFC(ISHFT(ISHFC(WORD,30-PL),PL-PR+1),PR)
```

These two bit isolation operations may be combined to construct a bit string (WORD) by taking bits from two other bit strings (WORD1 and WORD2). For example, WORD is to be identical to WORD1, except for the PL. .PR group, which is to come from the PL. .PR positions of WORD2:

```
WORD = IOR(ISHFC(ISHFT(ISHFC(WORD1,30-PL),PL-PR+1),PR),
           ISHFT(ISHFC(ISHFT(WORD2,30-PL),PL-PR+1),PR))
```

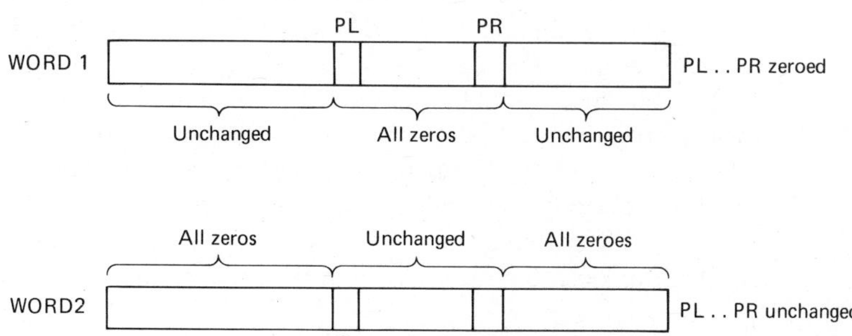

Figure 12.8. The operands for the IOR construction of WORD.

Both WORD1 and WORD2 remain unchanged. Figure 12.8 shows the situation. Note that the IOR operation properly "combines" the two isolated bit groups (since after this isolation no position contains ones from both WORD1 and WORD2, IEOR would have the same result as IOR in this example).

From these examples it is clear that shifting and rotating, together with the logical operations, are very powerful operations for manipulating bit-string values. Additional examples are given in the following subsections.

12.4.4 Masking

Zeroing a group of bits, as in the preceding subsection, is called *masking*, with the PL..PR group of bits set equal to 0 being called the masked group. Masking is even simpler for the programmer than in the preceding subsection, if an auxiliary bit string, called a *mask* is available as shown in Figure 12.9. If this bit string is called MASK, then bits PL..PR of bit-string WORD are masked by the following statement:

```
WORD = IAND(WORD,MASK)
```

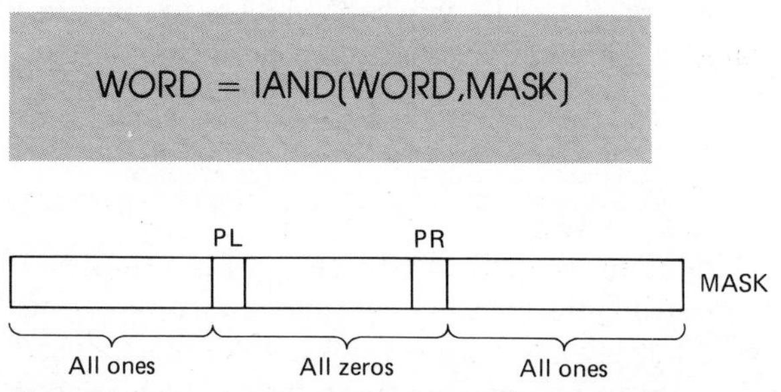

Figure 12.9. An auxiliary bit string, used for masking.

A mask may be created in either one of two ways:

1 Shift and rotate a bit-string of initially all 1's:
MASK = ISHC(ISHFT(ISHFC(NOT(0),30–PL),PL–PR+1),PR)
(Note that NOT(0) is a bit-string consisting of all 1's.)

2 Specify the desired mask explicitly as a PACKed character string of 1's and 0's:
MASK = PACK('<the 31 ones and zeros of the desired mask>')

The second of these two ways is especially convenient if the mask is to contain two or more disjoint mask groups, as shown in Figure 12.10.

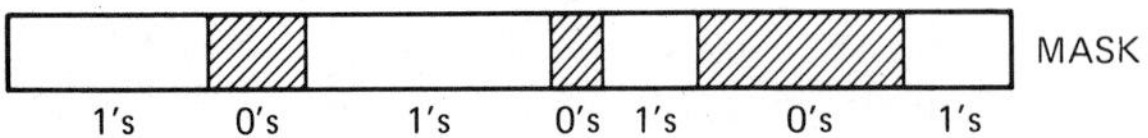

Figure 12.10. A mask containing several disjoint mask groups.

If a WORD is masked using the IAND function and a MASK such as shown in Figure 12.10, then the one operation (IAND) causes the "simultaneous" masking in WORD of all mask groups contained in MASK. Therefore if an application requires several uses of the same mask, and/or if the mask is a complicated bit pattern, then it is convenient for the programmer to establish the appropriate auxiliary bit string MASK at the outset, and then use the IAND function to perform each masking operation.

Occasionally the opposite masking effect is needed—namely setting a group of bits to all 1's, instead of all 0's, leaving the other bits unchanged. The same mask can be used for both operations. Whereas the operation

```
IAND (WORD,MASK)
```

makes the masked bits all 0, the operation

```
IOR (WORD,NOT(MASK))
```

makes the masked bits all 1. In either case the unmasked bits are left unchanged. The result of NOT(MASK) is to flip the 0's and 1's of MASK—all 1's are changed to 0's and all 0's are changed to 1's as the function's value (but MASK itself is not changed). Thus this "negative" mask has 1's where WORD is to contain 1's, and 0's where WORD is to be unchanged. The IOR function then performs the desired operation since

IOR(<bit>, 0) --> <bit>
IOR(<bit>, 1) --> 1

If IOR masking is to be performed a lot, in a given program, with a given mask, then it might be worthwhile having a permanent copy of the IOR mask so that the NOT function need not always be used. Of course masks used with IORing may have any pattern of 1's in it to be imposed upon the WORD being masked.

12.4.5 An Application of Bit Strings

This brief introduction to bit strings will conclude with a simple application. Bit strings are used in general to represent data, and in particular to efficiently (i.e., with a minimum number of bits) represent data. Often bit-string operations are used to "streamline" and "pack" data; large data files can often be compressed in this manner, with great savings in storage space. Such techniques are used also to make the computing facilities (i.e., the "systems" programs) more efficient, and hence provide better service to the computer users. The example of this subsection is much more frivolous than either of these major applications, but illustrates the usefulness of bit strings.

A poker hand (5-card draw, no wild cards) has 5 cards (from an ordinary deck of 52 playing cards), each of which has a suit (spades, diamonds, hearts, clubs) and a rank (2–10, jack, queen, king, ace). Thus a poker hand has 10 "pieces" of data—the suits and ranks of each of the 5 cards. If integer data elements are used to represent this data then 10 numeric storage elements are likely to be used, although it is simple to represent both the rank and suit of a card with a single integer value (e.g., 109 is the 9 of clubs, 209 is the 9 of hearts, etc.). Representing the poker hand conveniently with a character string requires 10 characters (10 nonnumerical storage units). Thus typically 32*5=160 bits (for integers) or 8*10=80 bits (for character strings) would be used to represent a poker hand.

However, since there are only four suits only 2 bits are needed to represent a suit; and the 13 ranks can be accommodated with 4 bits. In principle, therefore, only 6 bits are needed to represent a card, making a total of only 30 bits for the entire poker hand. Thus only one integer-based bit string (having 31 bits) is needed to represent a poker hand. Figure 12.11 illustrates how the bits could be allocated—the shaded positions are used for the suits and the unshaded for the ranks.

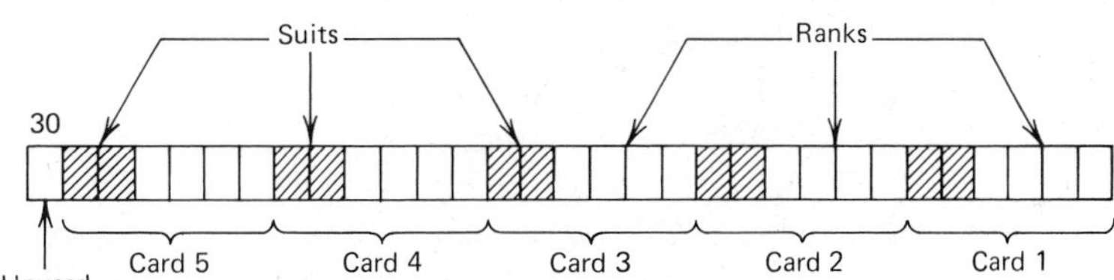

Figure 12.11. Using a bit string to represent a poker hand.

As an example of how the bit-string operations may be used in a "practical" problem, function POKER accepts a bit-string poker hand (HAND) organized as in Figure 12.11 and returns a bit string representing a poker analysis of that hand. That is, POKER determines which of the ranks in HAND occur once, which twice, which three times and which four times. If no rank occurs more than once then HAND is checked to see if it is a "flush" (all cards have the same suit). Figure 12.12 shows how the bit string that POKER returns is organized. Figure 12.13 shows the bit pattern used for the rank values, suit values, and rank counts, although the algorithm of POKER is dependent only upon the fact that none of the ranks are represented by 0000.

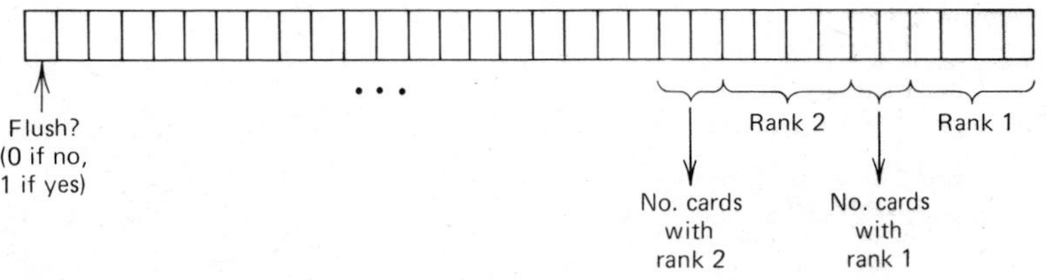

Figure 12.12. Bit string returned by function POKER.

Suit Values		Rank Values				Rank Counts	
Clubs	00	2	0010	8	1000	1	01
Hearts	01	3	0011	9	1001	2	10
Diamonds	10	4	0100	10	1010	3	11
Spades	11	5	0101	Jack	1011	4	00
		6	0110	Queen	1100		
		7	0111	King	1101		
				Ace	1111		

Figure 12.13. Bit patterns used in poker hand and function POKER.

In Figure 12.12 the number of rank-rank count pairs contained in the bit string will be two to five, depending on the amount of rank duplication among the cards in HAND. Any bits "not used" are set to (left at) 0.

The basic idea for making the rank counts is to first isolate the rank of the first card of HAND and then to compare this rank with that of the other four cards. If an identical rank is found then the rank count is incremented, and then this card is "blanked out" (rank bits all set to 0) to indicate that this card has already been tallied. After the ranks of the last four cards have been compared with the rank of the first card then the rank of the next "nonblanked" card is compared with the ranks of the remaining nonblanked cards. And this is continued until the ranks of all five cards of HAND have been categorized. Informally, the algorithm is:

1 initializations

2 do five times (once for each card)
  2.1 shift MASK to next card rank position
  2.2 isolate RANK, and initialize COUNT to 1
  2.3 if RANK ne 0000 then
    2.3.1 do for all remaining cards
      2.3.1.1 shift MASK and RANK to next card
      2.3.1.2 if ranks match then COUNT=COUNT+1 and blank card
    repeat
    2.3.2 tally COUNT and RANK in POKER
  repeat

3 if five different ranks, check for flush

Figure 12.14 shows the relative "position" of MASK, RANK, and the poker hand when the first card (a jack) is being compared with the third card.

The bit-string techniques of this section allow the programmer to use bit strings for efficient representation of data fairly conveniently. Moreover, the various operations are reasonably efficient because addition and comparison are typically very fast for integer data elements. This execution efficiency is not as great, however, as can be achieved at the assembly language level where most of these operations can be performed with fewer memory references.

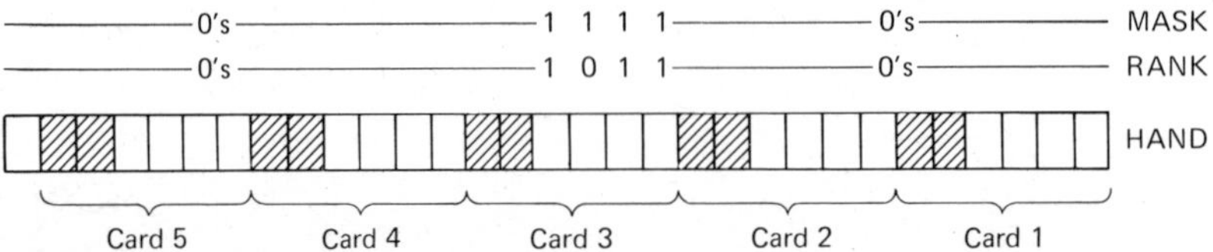

Figure 12.14. Comparing the rank of the third card with the rank of the first card of HAND.

```
*....:-------------------------------------------------------------------
      INTEGER FUNCTION  POKER (HAND)
                              INTEGER  HAND

*           ..this program analyzes a 5-card poker hand.
*           Hand represents the five cards, as described in figure 12.11
*           POKER returns a bit string after the fashion of
*           figure 12.12, that constitutes an analysis of HAND..

*     ....external functions called....(ISHFT,IOR,NOT used as arguments)
      EXTERNAL  ISHFT, IOR, NOT
      INTEGER ISHFL, ISHFL, ISHFT, IAND, IOR, NOT

*     ....local variables....
      INTEGER  MASK, RANK, COUNT, H, CARD, NEXT, SUIT

*     ....execute....(a copy of HAND is made, H, so that HAND
*                    need not be changed)
      POKER = 0
      H = HAND
*                ..analyze each card, in turn..

      do  CARD = 1,5
          MASK = ISHFC(ISHFT(NOT(0),-27),6*(CARD-1))
*                ..MASK is four 1's, positioned over CARD rank..
          RANK = IAND(MASK,H)
*                ..see figure 12.14..
          COUNT = ISHFT(NOT(0),-30)
          IF  (RANK .NE. 0)  THEN
*                ..if this card not "blanked", compare with others..
                do  NEXT = CARD+1,5
                    MASK = ISHFT(MASK,6)
                    RANK = ISHFT(RANK,6)
*                   ..now make comparison..
                    IF  (RANK .EQ. IAND(MASK,H))  THEN
*                   ..ranks are the same -- adjust COUNT (fig.12.13)..
                            IF  (ISHFT(COUNT,-1).EQ.0)  THEN
                                    COUNT = ISHFT(COUNT,1)
                                ELSEIF  (ISHFT(COUNT,30).EQ.0)  THEN
                                    COUNT = ISHFT(NOT(0),-29)
                                ELSE
                                    COUNT = 0
                            ENDIF
                            H = IAND(H,NOT(MASK))
*                           ..this "blanks" NEXT rank in H..
                    ENDIF
                repeat
*                       ..now tally rank and count in POKER
                MASK = ISHFC(MASK,7)
*               ..four 1's are now right-justified..
                RANK = ISHFC(RANK,7)
                COUNT = ISHFT(COUNT,4)
*                       ..find first "empty slot" in POKER..
                do
                    IF  (IAND(MASK,POKER) .EQ. 0)  exit
*                                                ..."slot" found..
                    MASK = ISHFT(MASK,6)
                    RANK = ISHFT(RANK,6)
                    COUNT = ISHFT(COUNT,6)
                repeat
                POKER = IOR(POKER,IOR(RANK,COUNT))
          ENDIF
      repeat
*                ..the rank counts are now complete;
*                  if five different ranks then check for flush..

      MASK = ISHFT(ISHFT(NOT(0),27),-4)
*                ..the 4 1's in MASK positioned over fifth rank..

      IF  (IAND(MASK,POKER) .NE. 0)  THEN
*                                        ..check for flush..
              POKER = IOR(POKER,ISHFT(NOT(0),30))
              MASK = ISHFC(ISHFT(NOT(0),29),6)
              SUIT = IAND(MASK,H)
              do  NEXT = 2,5
                  MASK = ISHFT(MASK,6)
                  SUIT = ISHFT(SUIT,6)
                  IF  (SUIT .NE. IAND(MASK,H))  THEN
*                                                   ..not a flush..
                          POKER = ISHFT(ISHFT(POKER,1),-1)
                          exit
                  ENDIF
              repeat
      ENDIF
      END
=====================================================================
```

12.5 Summary

In this chapter the general concept of data type has been explored, and techniques presented for the simulation of arbitrary data types in Fortran. The Fortran types of INTEGER and CHARACTER are especially useful for such simulation. INTEGER and CHARACTER data elements may also be used to represent bit strings, a data type for the efficient storage of information. A few simple operations defined for bit strings allow any sort of data processing to be specified on bit-string data.

Fortran was originally designed for making scientific and engineering numerical calculations. Type REAL is not sufficiently precise (i.e., not enough significant digits) for many of these calculations, largely because of the cumulative effects of round-off error in calculations involving many arithmetic operations. Therefore to enhance Fortran's usefulness in making such calculations type DOUBLEPRECISION is provided. This data type is precisely like REAL, except that each such data element has approximately twice the number of significant decimal digits as does a REAL data element. Each DOUBLEPRECISION constant, variable, and array element requires two numerical storage units, whereas a REAL (like INTEGER and LOGICAL) takes one numerical storage unit.

Scientific calculations also occasionally involve complex numbers. Fortran provides a type COMPLEX to facilitate such calculations, where a COMPLEX data element is a pair of ordinary real values—the first being the "real" part of the complex number and the second being the "imaginary" part. Each COMPLEX constant, variable, and array element requires two numerical storage units, one for each of the two real parts. Fortran also has several intrinsic functions that make convenient certain manipulations involving complex numbers.

References

1 Data types: Wirth, "Data Types," Chapter 8 of *Systematic Programming*, Prentice-Hall (1973).

2 Numerical analysis and numerical methods: Carnahan, Luther, and Wilkes, *Applied Numerical Methods*, Wiley (1969).
Conte and deBoor, *Elementary Numerical Analysis*, Second Edition, Addison-Wesley (1970).
Gerald, *Applied Numerical Analysis*, Addison-Wesley (1970).

3 Bit string facilities: ISA draft standard S61.1 (also an ANSI standard) for Industrial Computer System Fortran, Instrument Society of America, 400 Stanwix St., Pittsburgh, PA.
PE TC 1, 1978, "Industrial Real-Time Fortran," Purdue Laboratory for Applied Industrial Control, Purdue University, West Lafayette, IN.

Programming Exercises

12.1 Using the techniques of Section 12.1, simulate an ordered data type SUITS for representing the four suits of ordinary playing cards (clubs, hearts, diamonds, spades).

12.2 Suppose that an array of five elements of the type in the preceding program represents the suits of a hand of five cards. Write a program to determine if this hand is a "flush" (all cards of the same suit).

12.3 Write a Fortran program that repeatedly adds 0.01 to SUM (i.e., SUM = SUM+0.01 is in a loop).
The value of SUM should be initially zero, and the program should print out the value of SUM after each 1000 additions. Terminate after about 20 printouts. Do this for two cases, and compare results:
Case 1—SUM and 0.01 are type REAL
Case 2—SUM and 0.01 are type DOUBLEPRECISION

12.4 What is the square root of 43.766429531? Write any Fortran program that correctly computes this value to 16 decimal places.

12.5 Using NOT and IEOR as defined in Section 12.4.2, what is the effect of NOT (IEOR(WORD1,WORD2))?

12.6 Show that, for N>0 ISHFT(WORD,−N) is equivalent to ISHFC(ISHFT(ISHFC (WORD,WORDSZ−1−N),N),WORDSZ−1−N), for bit-strings with WORDSZ−1 bits.

12.7 Modify function POKER so that a 1 is placed in bit position 30 if the poker HAND is a "straight": five consecutive ranks in the sequence 2, 3, 4, 5, 6, 7, 8, 9, 10, jack, queen, king, ace.

12.8 Write a Fortran program that takes the value returned by function POKER and determines if that hand was a "full house" (three cards of one rank and two cards of another rank).

12.9 How many numerical and nonnumerical storage units are used by the data elements of program FACT of Section 5.4? On a minicomputer having 16-bit words, with 32 bits for each numerical storage unit and 8 bits for each nonnumerical storage unit, how many words would be used for these data elements?

12.10 Multiple Precision Division. Program FACT of Section 5.4 performed arbitrary precision multiplication by using elements of an array to represent the decimal digits of a many digit number. Let N and R be two such arrays of digits, of 200 digits each, but with a decimal point assumed to be between some two digits of each. Write a Fortran program that performs the arbitrary precision division N/R using the following technique:

(a) "Position" R as far "left" as possible under N so that N still appears larger than R (for example if N=24963 and R=57, then position

```
N   24963
R    57
```

(b) Subtract the digits of R from the digits of N (borrowing where necessary), repeat this subtraction as long as N remains "bigger than" R; the number of subtractions is a digit of the quotient.

(c) "Shift" the digits of R one place to the right, relative to N, and repeat step (b) to get the next digit of the quotient.
The program should determine many digits of the quotient, perhaps 100, and should determine the proper location of the decimal point.

12.11 Multiple Precision Square Roots. If Newton's method is applied to the specific quadratic equation X**2 − N (N>0) then the root found is N**(.5) (and is real).
Using R for the root value of X, the formula in Newton's method becomes
R = R−(R*R−N)/(2*R) = (R+N/R)*.5
In other words, the next approximation to the root is the average of the current approximation and N divided by the current approximation. Use your multiple precision division program, developed in the preceding problem, to compute N/R with any desired precision so that square roots can be computed to any desired precision. Use your program to compute SQRT(2.) to 40 decimal places. (And you can use the old-fashioned "hand" method of computing square roots to check the results of your program.)

Chapter 13 Data Structures

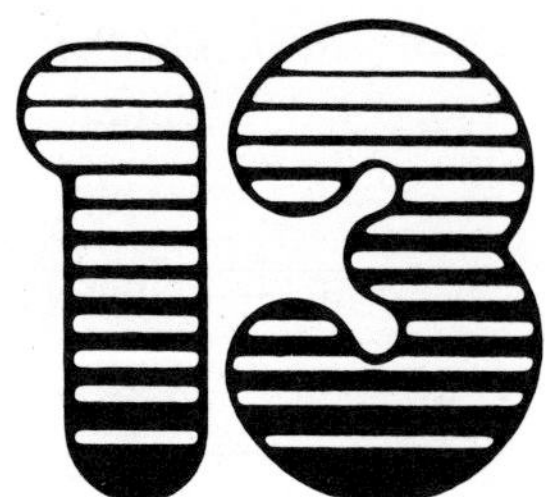

Variables of types INTEGER and REAL are examples of simple, or elementary, data elements. Such data elements contain single "individible" data values—these values are not "combinations" of two or more other (simple) data element values. Variables of types DOUBLEPRECISION and LOGICAL are also simple data elements. On the other hand variables of type COMPLEX are not simple data elements; but are "compound" data elements, each COMPLEX value is composed of two separate REAL values. Arrays may be considered as compound data elements, made up of arbitrarily many "parts" (the individual array elements). Similarly, a character string may be considered to be a compound data element, composed of a set of individual character data elements. Compound data elements are called *data structures*. The simple data elements are elemental and cannot be "broken down" into constituent parts; data structures are constructed as combinations of other data elements, the fundamental building blocks of which are the simple data elements.

Data structures may be arbitrarily complex—limited only by the imagination and/or needs of the programmer. The most commonly used data structures tend to be explicitly provided in a programming language, and Fortran makes three such provisions: arrays, character strings, and type COMPLEX. Other data structures must be indirectly provided by the programmer, or simulated. This chapter discusses briefly the fundamental data structures concepts, identifies the most commonly useful data structures, and presents example applications involving these data structures.

The data structuring facilities provided explicitly in Fortran all involve *homogeneous* data structures, that is, compound data elements whose constituent parts are all of the same data type. These have all been thoroughly discussed in earlier chapters, except for *multidimensioned* arrays. The arrays discussed thus far have all been *one-dimensional* arrays, and Fortran provides for considerably more general array data structures. These additional array features are described in the first section below. Data structures need not be homogeneous, constituent parts need not be all of the same data type, and many important data structures are constructed of parts with different data types. Some simple but very useful such data structures are described in Section 13.2 below. A *record* is a rather general data structure, having arbitrarily many parts of arbitrary data type. Records are extremely important data elements in all large systems and data processing applications of computing, and record concepts are introduced in Section 13.3. And finally, in Section 13.4, files are introduced as essentially arrays of records, and the universal form in which large amounts of data are organized and stored.

13.1 Multidimensional Arrays

Figure 13.1 pictorially compares one-, two-, and three-dimensional arrays. Multidimensional arrays have array elements extending in more than one dimension (direction). A two-dimensional array may be thought of as a table with rows and columns. Often two-dimensional arrays are used and referred to as *matrices*, which are extremely important computational devices. Somewhat more generally, a two-dimensional array may be considered to be a one-dimensional array of one-dimensional arrays (i.e., an array whose array elements are themselves arrays). Thus each column in Figure 13.1*b* is an array of *n* elements, and there are *m* such columns—therefore A2 may be thought of as an array of *m* elements (columns), each such element being a one-dimensional array of *n* elements. Similarly a three-dimensional array may be considered to be a one-dimensional array whose elements are two-dimensional arrays. In Figure 13.1*c*, A3 may be thought of as an array of *k* "planes", each plane being a two-dimensional array of *m* columns and *n* rows.

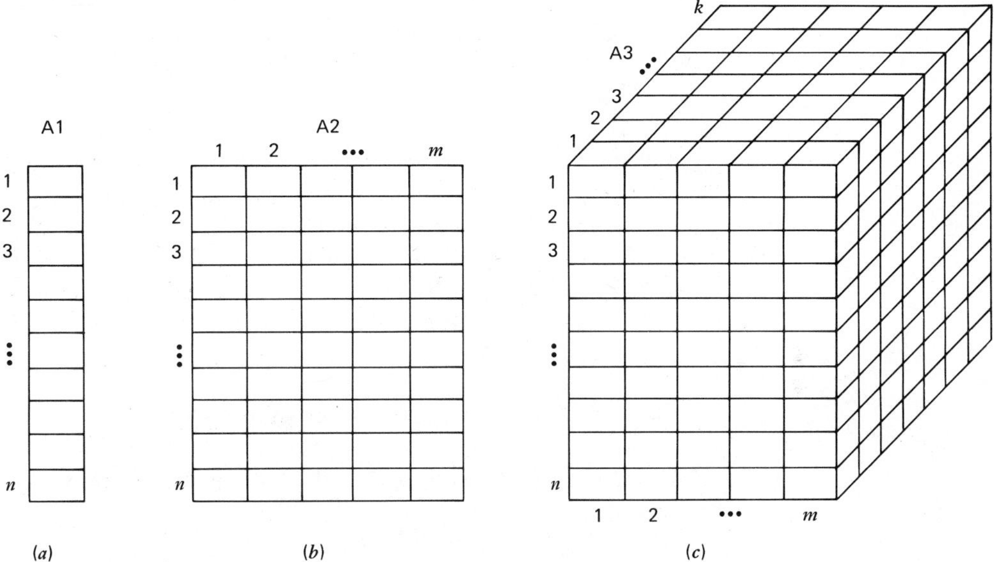

Figure 13.1. Comparison of one-, two-, and three-dimensional arrays. (*a*) One-dimensional array. (*b*) Two-dimensional array. (*c*) Three-dimensional array.

In this manner an N-dimensional array is described as a one-dimensional array of (N−1)-dimensional arrays. Fortran arrays may be dimensioned as high as seven, although drawing arrays for more than three dimensions becomes difficult (to say the least!).

The declaration and manipulation of arrays and array elements for multidimensional arrays in Fortran are straightforward extensions of those for one-dimensional arrays. Declaring multidimensional arrays requires specifying the array name and type, and the bounds for each dimension. This is easily done in an ordinary type specification statement, and has exactly the same form as the declaration of a one-dimensional array except that bounds on the other dimensions are included. Suppose, for example, that an integer matrix named PICTUR with 10 rows and 20 columns is to be declared. Then the statement

```
INTEGER PICTUR(1:10,1:20)
```

will do the job. Note that two sets of bounds specifications, separated by a comma, are enclosed in parentheses; for arrays with three or more dimensions the list of bounds specifications is simply extended with the additional information. The general form is

<type> <array name> (<list of bounds specifications>)

where the <list of bounds specifications> is a sequence of <bounds specification>s separated by commas. Each <bound specification> has the form

<lower bound>:<upper bound>

and <lower bound> need not be 1—it may be any integer value (including negative values) not greater than <upper bound>. And if the <lower bound>: part of any <bound specification> is omitted, then Fortran assumes that the <lower bound> is 1. Thus the above example (declaration of PICTUR) has the equivalent form

```
INTEGER PICTUR(10,20)
```

and the compiler will assume that 1 is the <lower bound> for each dimension. Multidimensional arrays may be declared in the same declaration statement with other variables and arrays of that type.

(Fortran has an additional specification statement for dimensioning arrays, the DIMENSION statement, that can be used to dimension arrays having implicit type. The form of the DIMENSION statement is precisely that of a type statement, with <type> replaced by DIMENSION:

DIMENSION <list of array declarations>

where each element in the <list of array declarations> is

<array name>(<list of bounds specifications>)

If all data elements are explicitly typed, and arrays are dimensioned in the type statements, as is strongly recommended, the DIMENSION statement cannot be used. The DIMENSION statement does not give Fortran any additional functionality.)

When referencing an array element in the executable statements, a subscript must be supplied for each dimension. To do this, the form for one-dimensional array elements is simply extended by using a list of subscripts in place of the single subscript. Thus the element in the sixth row and third column of PICTUR is specified by PICTUR(6,3). The general form is

<array name>(<list of subscripts>)

where each <subscript> in the <list of subscripts> is an integer expression, and <subscript>s are separated from each other by commas. The number of <subscript>s in the <list of subscripts> must be the same as the number of dimensions specified in the declaration of the array, and each subscript value must be within the declared bounds for the corresponding dimension.

Thus declaring and referencing multidimensional arrays are rather trivial extensions of these operations for one-dimensional arrays. Slightly more complex is the matter of inputting or outputting all of the values of a multidimensional array. With a one-dimensional array the "first" and "last" elements are pretty obvious, and the statement

```
PRINT *, ARRAY
```

where ARRAY is a one-dimensional array, fairly clearly means "print out all of the values of the array, in order, beginning with the first one, and ending with the last one". This statement still means the same thing if ARRAY is a multidimensional array, but, while it may still be as clear which is the "first" element and which is the "last", it is not at all clear what the "order" of the elements might be in between. The safest thing to do here is to explicitly specify the order desired by using implied-do's (see Section 5.3). Implied-do's may be nested, so that the programmer can specify any desired input or output order for the array elements. Suppose, for example, that array PICTUR is to be output row by row. Then the statement

```
PRINT *, ((PICTUR(I,J), J=1,20), I=1,10)
```

specifies this order for the array elements. Notice that the range specification on J is nested inside the range specification on I. Therefore for I=1, J will range from 1 to 20, then for I=2, J will again range from 1 to 20, and so on, until for I=10, J will once more range from 1 to 20. Thus the order of the output is

```
PICTUR(1,1)
PICTUR(1,2)
PICTUR(1,3)
    .
    .
PICTUR(1,20)
PICTUR(2,1)
PICTUR(2,2)
PICTUR(2,3)
    .
    .
PICTUR(2,20)
PICTUR(3,1)
PICTUR(3,2)
    .
    .
PICTUR(10,20)
```

If the order of the output is to be column by column, rather than row by row, then the statement

```
PRINT *, ((PICTUR(I,J), I=1,10), J=1,20)
```

specifies this order. Here the loop on I is nested inside the loop on J, and the output order is

```
PICTUR(1,1)
PICTUR(2,1)
PICTUR(3,1)
    .
    .
PICTUR(10,1)
PICTUR(1,2)
PICTUR(2,2)
PICTUR(3,2)
    .
    .
PICTUR(10,20)
```

If the order is not specified by the programmer then Fortran assumes the column-by-column order. (Ironically when a matrix is to be input or output the row-by-row order is usually desired—therefore the programmer is normally "forced" into using implied-do loops for array I/O.) Actually using implied do loops for array I/O isn't too inconvenient; the implied-do's are compact and sensible, and their use gives the programmer the comfortable feeling that the I/O order is definitely known.

Multidimensional arrays may be used as procedure arguments. When used as actual arguments just the array name is used and the entire array is passed (for two-dimensional arrays) in column-by-column order. There is no problem with this as long as the dummy argument array is dimensioned exactly the same as the corresponding actual argument array (same number of dimensions and same bounds on corresponding dimensions). One way to insure proper dimensioning is to pass all array bounds as arguments also, and to use adjustable dimensioning on the dummy array. Assumed-size dimensioning may be used, but only the upper bound of the last dimension may be the asterisk; therefore adjustable dimensioning is safer. If fixed dimensioning is used on the dummy arrays, and this does not match the dimensioning of the actual array, then the intended correspondence between the dummy and actual array elements may not occur. An association between the actual and dummy arrays exists, however, and the association is that which occurs when the actual array, in column order, is overlaid by the dummy array, in column order.

Problems are often of a two-dimensional (or higher-order) nature. Consider a picture drawn on a two-dimensional surface (this is the character of most pictures). The picture (a black-and-white one, for this example) can be approximately represented in a computer by superimposing a two-dimensional "mesh" over the picture, as shown in Figure 13.2, and representing the mesh in Fortran as a two-dimensional integer array. Wherever a mesh square is mostly dark, the corresponding array element is assigned the value 1; the other array elements have the value zero. The finer the mesh (a finer mesh corresponds to a greater number of array elements) the better will be the approximation of the picture.

Space probe pictures of other planets, for example, may be transmitted to earth as a string of electrical pulses, each pulse (or absence of a pulse) representing a one or zero in a two-dimensional array approximation to the picture. (Actually, several gray levels, representing various shades of gray between white and black or different colors, are used in such applications. While the example presented here uses only two—black and white—the technique illustrated need be changed only very little to accommodate any number of shades of gray or colors. See Problem 13.17 at the end of this chapter.)  Pictures sent as pulses through space tend to be "noisy" because of interaction with cosmic rays and dust particles—some pulses are missing and spurious pulses are introduced. Computer "refinement" of the picture usually can correct at least a portion of the erroneous data. Program PLANET is a Fortran program that performs a simple, yet very effective, picture refining process. Figure 13.3 illustrates the fundamental aspect of the refinement process—the scanning of a small "neighborhood" around each point (array element) of the picture. The idea is that if the neigh-

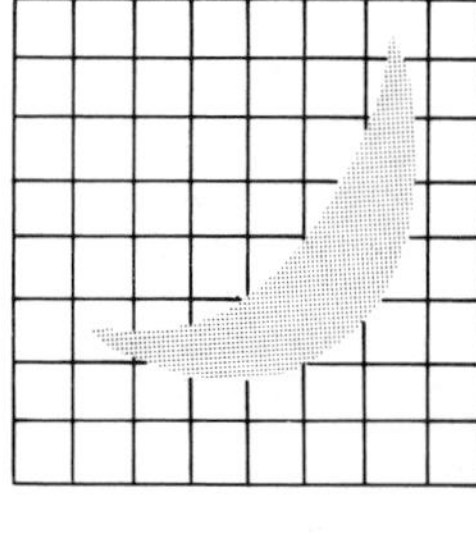

(*a*)

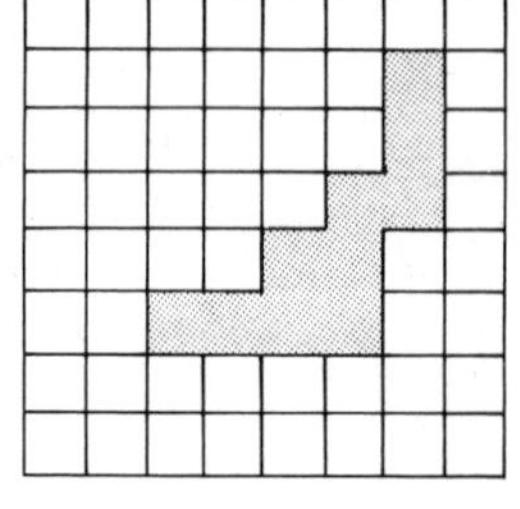

(*b*)

Figure 13.2. Picture approximation with a two-dimensional array. (*a*) Picture, overlaid with a two-dimensional array. (*b*) Array approximation to the picture.

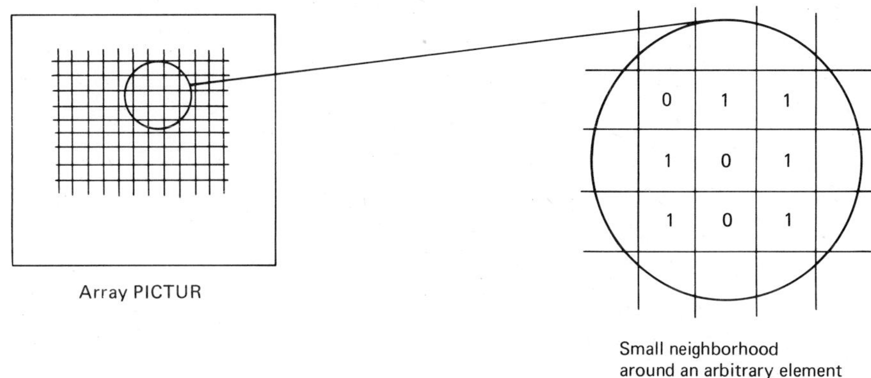

Figure 13.3. The nine-element neighborhood of a given element.

borhood is predominantly 1's (dark), then the central point of that neighborhood should most likely be 1 (dark); if the neighborhood is predominantly 0's (light) then the central point of that neighborhood should most likely be 0 (light). For the particular case shown in Figure 13.3 the neighborhood contains six 1's, and therefore the central element should be a one. Since it currently is a zero, it was probably received incorrectly.

Program PLANET (on page 284) systematically performs this refinement process on every element of the PICTUR array (except the "edge" elements, which remain as received). A one-dimensional character array, REFPIC, is used for the refined picture, and the original values of PICTUR are not changed. In REFPIC blanks are used in place of zeros and '#' in place of ones.

The original picture data for the above execution of PLANET had a "noise level" amounting to a 40 percent loss of information. As the output shows, the picture restoration with one refinement pass over the PICTUR matrix is quite impressive (even if the grinning space creature isn't too attractive!). Additional refinement passes would "clean up" the picture even more.

Another practical application of two-dimensional arrays involves the fitting of linear functions to experimental data. Suppose, for example, that scientists for the EPA (Environmental Protection Agency) are investigating the concentrations of PCP (PentaChloroPhenol), a highly toxic and carcinogenic substance that concentrates in fish, in the waters of the Great Lakes. In particular the effects of water temperature (TEMP), pressure (DEPTH), and illumination levels (LIGHT) on PCP concentrations (PCP) are of interest. Therefore, after a two-year period of data gathering, 20,000 measurements have been made, of the form shown in Figure 13.4: each measurement includes data for TEMP, DEPTH, and LIGHT, and the corresponding value of PCP.

Measurement	TEMP value	DEPTH value	LIGHT value	PCP value
1	–	–	–	–
2	–	–	–	–
3	–	–	–	–
⋮	⋮	⋮	⋮	⋮
20,000	–	–	–	–

Figure 13.4. The form of the "raw data" for the PCP study.

```
*....:----------------------------------------------------------------
      PROGRAM  PLANET
*                 ..program to refine a picture (two-dimensional
*                 array PICTUR) of ones and zeros using the dominant
*                 neighborhood technique. The character array REFPIC
*                 is used to print out the refined picture, with
*                 blanks for the zeros and '#' for the ones..

*     ....constants....(picture size)
      INTEGER  NR, NC
      PARAMETER  (NR=30, NC=72)

*     ....variables....I,J are index variables;NB the neighborhood count
      INTEGER  I, J, NB, PICTUR(1:NR, 1:NC)
      CHARACTER  REFPIC(1:NR)*(NC)
      DATA  REFPIC /NR*' '/

*     ....execute....first input PICTUR data
      READ *, ((PICTUR(I,J), J=1,NC), I=1,NR)
*                  ..then refine..
      do  I = 2,NR-1
          do  J = 2,NC-1
*                 ..now determine the number of 1's in the
*                   neighborhood of element PICTUR(I,J)..
              NB = PICTUR(I-1,J-1) + PICTUR(I-1,J) + PICTUR(I-1,J+1)
     :           + PICTUR(I,J-1) + PICTUR(I,J) + PICTUR(I,J+1)
     :           + PICTUR(I+1,J-1) + PICTUR(I+1,J) + PICTUR(I+1,J+1)
              IF  (NB .GT. 4)  THEN
                  REFPIC(I)(J:J) = '#'
              ENDIF
          repeat
      repeat
      PRINT '(T2,72I1/)', ((PICTUR(I,J), J=1,NC), I=1,NR)
      PRINT '(T2,A/)', (REFPIC(I), I=1,NR)
      END
======================================================================
```

```
.EXECUTE  PLANET
     ....input not shown, except as echoed at end of program as output of PICTUR....
```

```
000000100001010001010000010001000000000100000100000000011001010010100001
011000110010000000000000010000000001000000010010101000101000010000000000
000000000000000000000111111110010000001011011001110000001000000000010000
000010000010001001000111111111100001010001111101110000100000000100101000
000100001000001100000011111101100000000000111111001001100100111000000000
101001000010000000000001011101110010001001111111111100000010000001000000
000000000000000000000100101111101000000101111101111101000010000101000000
010000000010010000000101110111101000000011111111111100000000101000100001
010110100000000000000111101101111100010000011111111101000000000000001000
001100100110110111000111010001010000010101110001111101100000100000001100
000011110100010001001111111001000000110000111111111100000011011111100010
000101101100001000000111101011110010000000111101101111000000101111000000
000000101110101011000110111011100000000011111110111000100000010111100000
011101110101000000000000011000001000001000000100000100010000001111100000
000000111100010100000010000101000101000000100010000000000100000011110000
100100110100000010110001100100000000000000001000000000010000000101010100
100000111110000000000000000000000000001000000000000010000000110011100111
001001111111000000000100000100010010000000000000001000010100100011011100
000001101100100000001000010000011000000100000010000000000000000011100100
010010011110000001010010000100000000000101000100000100010010000111110000
010001110110000000000000000000000000011010000000100000010000010111110100
001001101010000000100000000100100000000010001000000100000000100001111110
000011011100000010101101000000000000000100010010001100010000100011111101
000001111110100000011001001101101110000000101110110000010100001001111101
000011111111001111110111010110111011011111100101110011111111111111100000
011011111111111011110111011011101111110111010111111011111111111101101111
000101111110111111111110101111010100111110111011111111111111011111101110
000000100000000000111000010110000000000000001100000100000100000010000010
000000000000000000000100001001010000000100001010001010000010001000000000
000001000000000011001010010100001011000110010000000000000000001000000000
```

```
                      ###
                    #########           ###### ##
                    #########          ####### ##
                    #########          ##########
                     ########         ###########
                     #########        ############
                   ###########         ###########
#                  ###### ####         ###########
 ####             #######  ##          ###########
  ######          ####### ###          ###########        ######
   #####          ###########          ###########        #######
   ######          ## ######           ######  ###         ######
    #####              ##                 ##                #####
    ###                                                     #####
    ####                                                   ######
    #####                                                 ### ###
   ######                                                  ### ##
   ######                                                  ######
   ######                           #                      ######
   ######                           #                      #######
   #####                                                   #######
   #####        #                        #   #             #######
  #######     #######        ##      #####  ###     # #   ########
  #########  ####################   ############  ################
  ################################################################
   ################# ######     ##### #######################  ###
               ###     ###             ##     ###         ##
                       #
```

==

In order to estimate the individual effects (if any) that TEMP, DEPTH, and LIGHT have on PCP concentration it is useful to express PCP as a linear combination of the other three values:

PCP = BC + TF*TEMP + DF*DEPTH + LF*LIGHT

where BC is some "base concentration" independent of TEMP, DEPTH, and LIGHT, and TF, DF, and LF are "temperature factor", "depth factor", and "light factor", respectively, which reflect the extent to which PCP is dependent upon TEMP, DEPTH, and LIGHT. If TF turns out to be large, for example, and LF is small, or nearly zero, then it is apparent that PCP concentration is heavily dependent on water temperature, but essentially unaffected by illumination levels. Moreover, if the values of BC, TF, DF, and LF can be determined, then the temperature, depth and light levels for which PCP concentrations would have minimum or maximum values can be estimated. Moreover, the PCP value could then be predicted for any given combination of TEMP, DEPTH, and LIGHT.

The formula in the preceding paragraph expresses PCP as a linear function of TEMP, DEPTH, and LIGHT. The problem is to find values for BC, TF, DF, and LF that make this formula "best fit" the data, as given in Figure 13.4. Figure 13.5 illustrates this "fitting", assuming that PCP is just a function of TEMP (drawing a picture for the general case is too difficult). The job is to find BC and TF, in Figure 13.5, so that the straight line PCP=BC+TF*TEMP is "most representative" of the entire collection of individual data points.

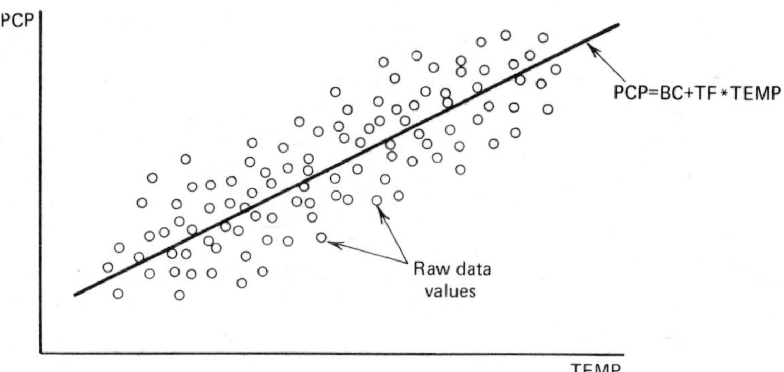

Figure 13.5. Fitting a linear function to experimental data.

The line should be constructed (i.e., BC and TF determined) so that the totality of data point distances from the line is in some sense minimized.

The almost universal way of determining such a line is known as the method of *least squares*. Generating least-squares fits involves making certain numerical calculations with the raw data values, but the resulting lines are the "best" fits possible. ("Best" in this case is defined as "minimize the sum of the squares—hence the term "least squares"—of the vertical distances between all data points and the line.") The actual calculations needed to make such fits are fairly straightforward. If n values are to be determined by the least squares method then a matrix of n rows and n+1 columns is needed. In the PCP problem there are four values to be determined (BC, TF, DF, and LF) and so the least-squares method requires a matrix of four rows and five columns for this problem. If this matrix is named LSM (for Least Squares Matrix), Figure 13.6 shows the "layout" of the elements of this four-by-five matrix.

```
-----------------------------------------------------------------------
LSM(1,1)     LSM(1,2)     LSM(1,3)     LSM(1,4)     LSM(1,5)
LSM(2,1)     LSM(2,2)     LSM(2,3)     LSM(2,4)     LSM(2,5)
LSM(3,1)     LSM(3,2)     LSM(3,3)     LSM(3,4)     LSM(3,5)
LSM(4,1)     LSM(4,2)     LSM(4,3)     LSM(4,4)     LSM(4,5)
-----------------------------------------------------------------------
```

Figure 13.6. The least-squares matrix for four unknowns.

The initial value for each element of LSM is determined from the raw data values. Suppose that there are N (20,000 in the discussion above) measurements of raw data values, and that the sum of all N measured temperature values is represented as sum(TEMP). Similarly sum(DEPTH), sum(LIGHT), sum(PCP) represent the sum of all N of the other measured quantities. And finally imagine that the table of Figure 13.4 is augmented with nine additional columns, for TEMP*TEMP, TEMP*DEPTH, TEMP*LIGHT, TEMP*PCP, DEPTH*DEPTH, DEPTH*LIGHT, DEPTH*PCP, LIGHT*LIGHT,and LIGHT*PCP. Then these columns could be filled in by computing the appropriate nine products in each row. (This is a lot of repetitive calculating, but that's what the computer does best!) And then finally the sums are computed for these nine extra columns. Figure 13.7 shows the resulting table, and all of the sums (with T, D, L, and P used as abbreviations for TEMP, DEPTH, LIGHT, and PCP).

Meas.	T	D	L	P	T*T	T*D	T*L	T*P	D*D	D*L	D*P	L*L	L*P
1													
2													
3													
•													
•													
•													
20,000													
sums →	(T)	(D)	(L)	(P)	(T*T)	(T*D)	(T*L)	(T*P)	(D*D)	(D*L)	(D*P)	(L*L)	(L*P)

Figure 13.7. Augmented table of raw data, containing columns of computed products and the sums of each column.

Of course a Fortran program will do all of the work of performing the multiplications on the measured values, and computing all of the sums. These sums, in the bottom row of Figure 13.7, are the initial values for the elements of matrix LSM, as shown in Figure 13.8.

Now comes the heart of the least-squares method. After the elements of LSM have been initialized to the values shown in Figure 13.8, the matrix is systematically modified until it has the values shown in Figure 13.9—all of the values in the first four columns are zeros, except for the ones on the "diagonal". This is called "reducing"

N	sum(T)	sum(D)	sum(L)	sum(P)
sum(T)	sum(T*T)	sum(T*D)	sum(T*L)	sum(T*P)
sum(D)	sum(D*T)	sum(D*D)	sum(D*L)	sum(D*P)
sum(L)	sum(L*T)	sum(L*D)	sum(L*L)	sum(L*P)

Figure 13.8. The initial values of the elements of LSM.

```
1 0 0 0 BC
0 1 0 0 TF
0 0 1 0 DF
0 0 0 1 LF
```

Figure 13.9. The reduced LSM.

the matrix, and after the matrix is thus reduced the desired values are in the fifth column, as shown in Figure 13.9.

There are only two simple operations that are allowed in reducing the matrix from its initial form as given in Figure 13.8 to its final form of Figure 13.9. These two operations are:

1 Any row may be multiplied by any numerical value, other than zero. In such an operation each of the five elements in the row is individually multiplied by that value.

2 Any row may be "added" to any other row; that is, if row P is added to row Q then the (new) value of LSM(Q,1) becomes equal to LSM(Q,1)+LSM(P,1), (the new) LSM(Q,2) becomes equal to LSM(Q,2)+LSM(P,2), and so on for each column. Thus row Q is changed but row P isn't.

These two operations may be performed in any sequence, and any number of times until the matrix is in its final reduced form. [A good intellectual exercise, for those not already familiar with matrix reduction, is to devise a sequence of these two operations—before looking at program LSFIT—that will result in a properly reduced matrix. Since the order of such operations is crucial, this exercise is somewhat analogous to that of devising (nonrecursively) a suitable sequence of moves in the "Towers of Hanoi"—see Chapter 11.] The numerical analysis references given at the end of Chapter 12 contain additional information about least-squares fits, and a great deal about reducing matrices. There are many reduction algorithms, varying from very simple ones to quite sophisticated ones tailored to reduce the effects of round-off error. Since a large number of arithmetic operations must be performed during the reduction process, round-off error accumulation can be a problem, especially with large matrices. When round-off error is (or might be) a problem, the best defense is to employ a reduction algorithm that tends to minimize such effects. Second, this is a good application for the use of DOUBLEPRECISION data elements. In example program LSFIT (actually in subroutine REDLSM, which LSFIT calls) given below only the simplest reduction algorithm is used, but the calculations are made in double precision. Problem 13.8 at the end of this chapter involves replacing the algorithm of REDLSM with a significantly superior one.

Thus there are two main steps in solving the given PCP problem: those of initializing the matrix with the proper values, and then reducing the matrix so that the results may be extracted. Program LSFIT is the main program that calls subroutines to perform each of these steps. Thus LSFIT also illustrates the use of multidimensional arrays as procedure arguments. Although LSFIT has been somewhat specialized for the PCP problem, only very slight modification is necessary to allow its use for many other applications of the least-squares method (see the numerical methods references at the end of Chapter 12).

13.2 Lists and Trees

Compound data elements need not be homogeneous. Figure 13.10*a* shows a simple two-part data structure whose basic constituent parts are a character string and an integer. Two-part data elements where one part is any arbitrary data type (including INTEGER), and the other part is always (in Fortran) of type INTEGER, are the basic data elements in a very useful type of application—those involving *linked lists*. The form of such a data element is given in Figure 13.10*b* where the name of the arbitrary type

```
*....:-----------------------------------------------------------------
      PROGRAM  LSFIT
*                 ..this program performs the least squares fit
*                 to supplied raw data.  It is somewhat specialized
*                 for the PCP problem described above.  This
*                 program calls ESTLSM to establish the initial
*                 values of the least-squares matrix, and then
*                 calls REDLSM to reduce the least-squares
*                 matrix to the "diagonal" form.  Double
*                 precision data elements are used to minimize
*                 the effects of round-off error due to the
*                 large number of arithmetic operations in REDLSM..

*     ....variables....
      INTEGER  NR, NC
      PARAMETER  ( NR = 4, NC = 5)
*           ..these values of NR and NC are for the PCP problem..
      DOUBLEPRECISION  LSM(1:NR,1:NC)
      DATA  LSM /NR*NC*0.0/

*     ....execute....

      CALL ESTLSM (LSM,NR,NC)
      CALL REDLSM (LSM,NR,NC)

*     ....output results....
      PRINT *, 'BC =', LSM(1,5)
      PRINT *, 'TF =', LSM(2,5)
      PRINT *, 'DF =', LSM(3,5)
      PRINT *, 'LF =', LSM(4,5)
      END
=================================================================
*....:-----------------------------------------------------------------
      SUBROUTINE  ESTLSM (LSM,NR,NC)
                          INTEGER  NR, NC
                          DOUBLEPRECISION  LSM(1:NR,1:NC)

*                 ..procedure to establish the initial values
*                 of LSM (see figures 13.5, 13.6, and 13.7)

*     ....local variables....
      INTEGER  I, J, K, N
      DOUBLEPRECISION  TEMP, DEPTH, LIGHT, PCP

*     ....execute....
      N = 20000
*                 ..N is the special value for the PCP problem
      do  K = 1,N
         READ *, TEMP, DEPTH, LIGHT, PCP
         LSM(1,2) = LSM(1,2) + TEMP
         LSM(1,3) = LSM(1,3) + DEPTH
         LSM(1,4) = LSM(1,4) + LIGHT
         LSM(1,5) = LSM(1,5) + PCP
         LSM(2,2) = LSM(2,2) + TEMP*TEMP
         LSM(2,3) = LSM(2,3) + TEMP*DEPTH
         LSM(2,4) = LSM(2,4) + TEMP*LIGHT
         LSM(2,5) = LSM(2,5) + TEMP*PCP
         LSM(3,3) = LSM(3,3) + DEPTH*DEPTH
         LSM(3,4) = LSM(3,4) + DEPTH*LIGHT
         LSM(3,5) = LSM(3,5) + DEPTH*PCP
         LSM(4,4) = LSM(4,4) + LIGHT*LIGHT
         LSM(4,5) = LSM(4,5) + LIGHT*PCP
      repeat
      LSM(1,1) = N
      LSM(2,1) = LSM(1,2)
      LSM(3,1) = LSM(1,3)
      LSM(3,2) = LSM(2,3)
      LSM(4,1) = LSM(1,4)
      LSM(4,2) = LSM(2,4)
      LSM(4,3) = LSM(3,4)
      END
=================================================================
```

```
*....:-----------------------------------------------------------------
      SUBROUTINE  REDLSM (LSM,NR,NC)
                          INTEGER  NR, NC
                          DOUBLEPRECISION  LSM(1:NR, 1:NC)

*                 ..procedure for reducing the least squares
*                 matrix.  Note that of the two allowable
*                 operations on the matrix, operation (1)
*                 appears twice, and operation (2) appears
*                 once in the program.  However two of these
*                 3 appearances are inside a triply nested
*                 loop, so are actually performed many times.
*                 In the loops the column bounds go from I
*                 to NC, rather than 1 to NC, because at
*                 those points all row I elements to the left
*                 of column I are zero..

*     ....local variables....I, J, K are loop indices,
*                             P is storage for a multiplier
      INTEGER  I, J, K
      DOUBLEPRECISION  P

*     ....execute....the basic loop is to put column I in reduced form
      do  I = 1,NR
*                 ..first make LSM(I,I)=1 by using operation (1)
          P = 1/LSM(I,I)
          do  J = I,NC
              LSM(I,J) = P*LSM(I,J)
          repeat
*                 ..now, zero the rest of the Ith column..
*                 for each row K, except for K=I, make
*                 LSM(K,I)=0; do this by adding to row K (operation (2))
*                 -LSM(K,I)*row I (operation(1))
          do  K = 1,NR
              IF  (K .NE. I)  THEN
                  P = -LSM(K,I)
                  do  J = I,NC
                      LSM(K,J) = LSM(K,J)+P*LSM(I,J)
                  repeat
              ENDIF
          repeat
      repeat
      END
=======================================================================
```

part is INFO and the name of the integer part is LINK. The parts of a compound data element are normally called *fields*—thus the element of Figure 13.10*b* has two fields, one of arbitrary type named INFO and one of type INTEGER named LINK. In a specific application, of course, the INFO field would have some specific type, such as CHARACTER.

A linked list involves a set of elements of the form shown in Figure 13.10*b*. The data contained in this set is entirely contained in the INFO fields of the elements. The LINK fields are used to *link* the elements together in any desired sequence. The simplest way to implement such a set in Fortran is with (one-dimensional) arrays. Actually the set of elements can be thought of as an array, with each array element having the two fields INFO and LINK as shown in Figure 13.11*a*. However the implementation in Fortran requires two "parallel" arrays, as shown in Figure 13.11*b*, with each compound INFO–LINK data element being implemented by the corresponding (same index) elements of the INFO and LINK arrays.

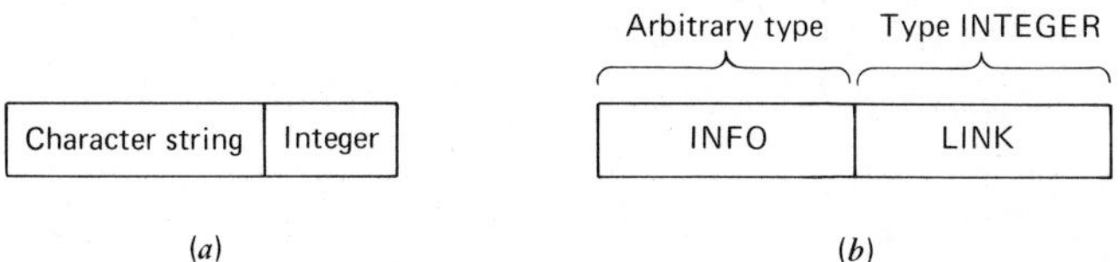

Figure 13.10. Two-part data element, with the parts having different types. (*a*) A specific example. (*b*) General list element.

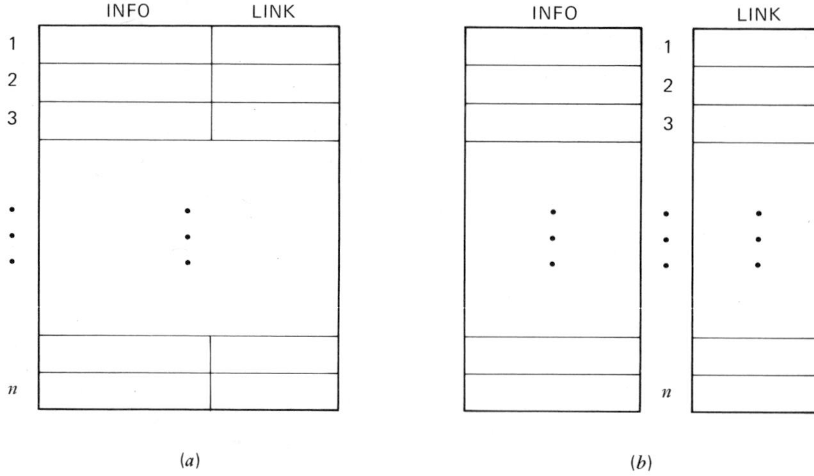

Figure 13.11. An array of list elements. (*a*) As a single array of compound elements. (*b*) As two "parallel" arrays of simple Fortran elements.

The arrays, and array indices, of Figure 13.11*b* establish a "physical" order for the list data elements. The LINK fields may be used to establish any desired "logical" order for these data elements, irrespective of and without changing the physical order. Figure 13.12 illustrates such linking among a set of eight list elements. An integer variable FIRST identifies the (array index of the) initial element of the desired (logical) ordering (this is the fourth array element in Figure 13.12); then the link field "points to" (contains the array index of) the next element of the list. This linking continues, with each element pointing to its logical successor, until the end of the list is reached, which is identified by a special link value, such as −1. (This special value is often given the name NIL, thus NIL could be an integer constant having the value −1.) As illustrated by Figure 13.12, the (logical) order of elements of a linked list has in general no relationship to the physical order of the array elements.

Suppose that THIS is an integer variable containing the value of an array index of an element in a linked list. Then the array index of the (logical) successor of THIS element is always given by

```
LINK(THIS)
```

A listing of the contents of INFO in a linked list is readily given by

```
THIS = FIRST
do
    IF (THIS .EQ. NIL) exit
    PRINT *, INFO(THIS)
    THIS = LINK(THIS)
repeat
```

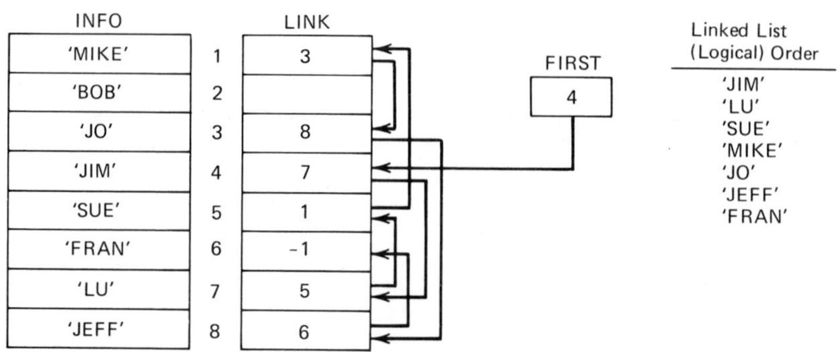

Figure 13.12. A linked list.

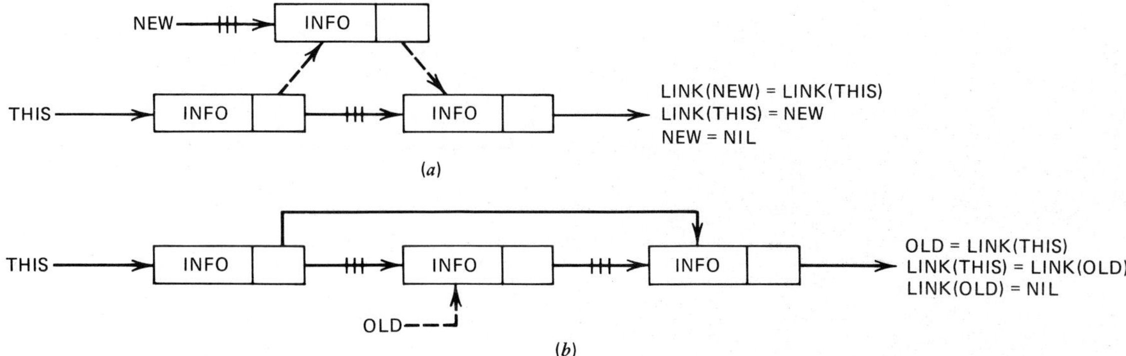

Figure 13.13. Linked list order modifications. (*a*) Inserting an element into a linked list (assuming NEW and THIS are not NIL). (*b*) Removing an element from a linked list (assuming THIS and LINK(THIS) are not NIL).

The PRINT statement of this algorithm could be replaced by any desired processing of THIS element, and the elements of the linked list will be processed in their linked logical order.

The separation of logical and physical ordering is a powerful programming tool. In many applications the use of linked lists can drastically reduce the necessity of moving of data in array INFO. Any ordering can be achieved by simply changing the link values appropriately. If INFO is an array of long strings, for example, then the integer operations on the links are much more efficient than moving the INFO data around. In addition, inserting new elements into a linked list, or removing list elements, is much simpler and more efficient than inserting or removing elements in an (unlinked) array. Figure 13.13 shows how insertions and deletions in a linked list are accomplished by merely adjusting three link values. In this figure list elements are shown in their logical order, with the solid lines representing the original links and the dotted lines the final links.

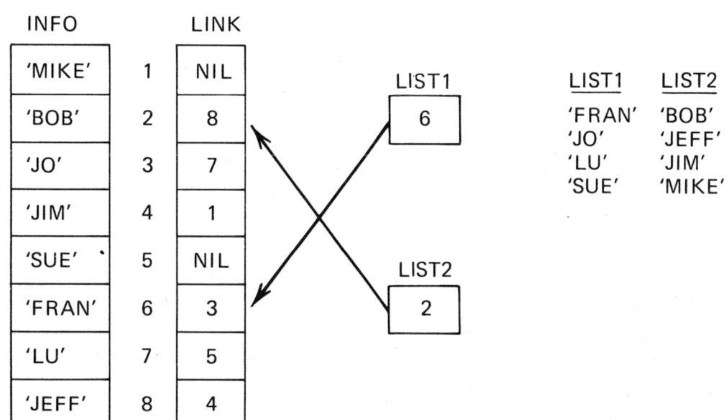

Figure 13.14. Two lists in a single array.

Several lists may simultaneously reside in the same array, as shown in Figure 13.14. Even though the physical order of the two (or more) such lists may be "all mixed up", the links specify the proper logical ordering and keep the lists logically separate. Linked lists tend to be dynamic structures; that is, the number of elements of each list grows and shrinks during program execution. If an individual array is used for a given list then the array must be as large as the maximum list size. If several lists use the same array then the array may not have to be as large as the total of separate arrays; this will be the case if not all of the lists reach their maximum size simultaneously. Suppose, for example, that an array of 500 elements is used to represent the students' names in a large service-course class. The names are divided into three lists, one for lower-division students, one for upper-division students, and the third for graduate students.

The number of students in any of the three categories may be anything from 0 to 500, but the total is not more than 500. If separate arrays were used for each of the three categories then each array would need to have 500 elements, thus (almost) tripling the allocated storage space. [Almost, because with three arrays the links may not be needed, in which case the storage for the link fields could be saved. For this application (500 students' names) the INFO field would be typically about 40 characters, and hence the storage for INFO is typically ten times that for the links. Thus the storage overhead for links is small compared to the storage required for INFO.]

Data stacks (see Section 11.2) are dynamic structures that can be nicely implemented as linked lists. Several such stacks may be "housed" in one array, and thus each may, in a more real sense, be thought of as a stack rather than as a special application of an array. When the stack is a linked list then the stack pointer points to the first element of the list, PUSHing the stack means inserting a new element at the front of the list (top of the stack), and POPping the stack means deleting the first element. Figure 13.15 illustrates these concepts. Subroutine LIST is a program that provides the PUSHing and POPping operations for up to 10 stacks, all implemented in a single array of list elements. In this example the values to be stacked are assumed to be of type CHARACTER. Each operation (PUSH and POP) has two arguments—the first (VALUE) is the character value to be stacked (PUSH) or returned (POP), and the second (STKNUM) is an integer between 1 and 10 specifying which stack is involved. LIST assumes that enough space for the stacks is provided (i.e., that overflow on stack space will not occur), that the stack number is valid (i.e., between 1 and 10), and that POP is not called on an empty stack.

An interesting feature of subroutine LIST is that it maintains an additional stack, whose top is pointed to by SPACE. This is a stack of *available space*, from which the next list element is taken for a PUSH operation and to which is added the list element from a POP operation. (Therefore, a PUSH operation pops the available space stack, and a POP operation pushes the available space stack.) Thus any space released by a POP operation becomes immediately available for subsequent PUSHing. The contents of any particular stack could easily be accessed if this were desired, by simply following the links from the top of the stack to its bottom, even though the individual stack

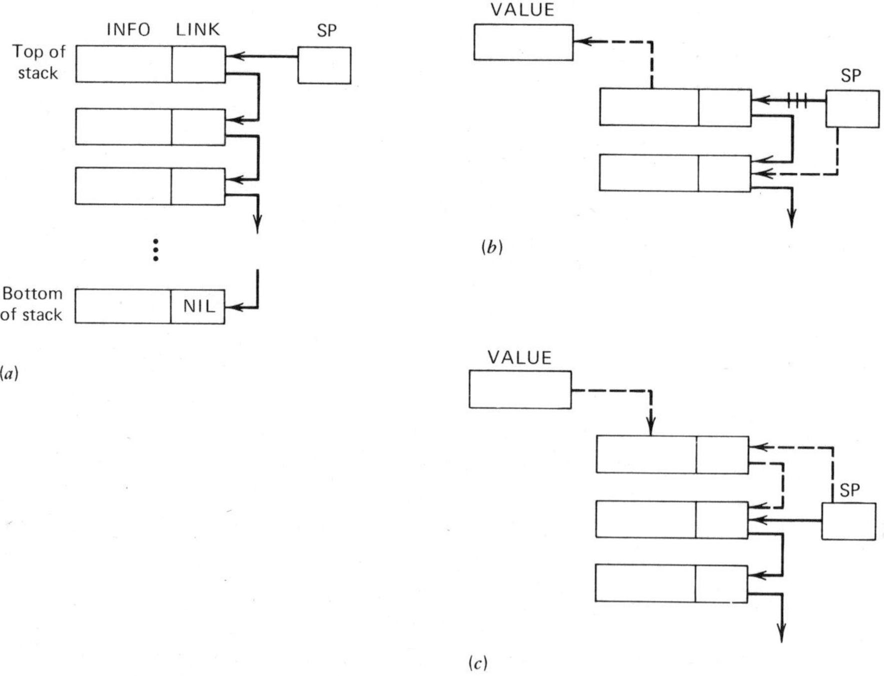

Figure 13.15. Implementing a stack as a linked list. (*a*) The (logical) structure of the stack. (*b*) POPing the stack. (*c*) PUSHing the stack.

```
*....:-----------------------------------------------------------------
      SUBROUTINE  LIST (VALUE,STKNUM)
                        INTEGER  STKNUM
                        CHARACTER  VALUE*(*)
*                 ..this program uses a list structure to
*                 implement several (10 in this example)
*                 stacks. Each stack pointer (SP) points to
*                 the head of a list.  SPACE points to the top
*                 of the available SPACE stack.

*     ....constants....maximum number of stacks (NS),
*                      stack space limit (NLE),
*                      number of characters in strings (NC)
      INTEGER  NS, NLE, NC, NIL
      PARAMETER  (NS=10, NLE=1000, NC=100, NIL=-1)

*     ....local variables....
*         list element declaration
      CHARACTER  INFO(1:NLE)*(NC)
      INTEGER  LINK(1:NLE)
*         end list element declaration

      INTEGER SP(1:NS), SPACE, TOP
      SAVE
      DATA  SP /NS*-1/
     :      LINK /NLE*-1/
*                 ..initialize all stack pointers and links to NIL
     :     SPACE /1/

*     ....PUSH entry point....
      ENTRY  PUSH (VALUE,STKNUM)
          TOP  =  SPACE
          IF  (LINK(SPACE) .EQ. NIL)  THEN
                  SPACE = SPACE + 1
              ELSE
                  SPACE = LINK(SPACE)
          ENDIF
          INFO(TOP) = VALUE
          LINK(TOP) = SP(STKNUM)
          SP(STKNUM) = TOP
      RETURN

*     ....POP entry point....
      ENTRY  POP (VALUE,STKNUM)
          TOP = SP(STKNUM)
          VALUE = INFO(TOP)
          SP(STKNUM) = LINK(TOP)
          LINK(TOP) = SPACE
          SPACE = TOP
      END
=======================================================================
```

elements are scattered throughout the array of list elements. Note that at any particular instant it is not possible to ascertain, by simply inspecting a list element and the set of stack pointers, to which stack (including the available space stack) the list element currently belongs. Subroutine LIST is an especially good way to implement stacks if during program execution some stacks are growing while others are shrinking, or if there are many stacks of the same INFO data type.

Another very useful compound data element is similar to a list element, but has an additional link field. The two link fields, LEFT and RIGHT, and the INFO field, are shown in Figure 13.16 for this data element (which is often called a *tree* element). Whereas a list element could point to only one other list element, a tree element can point to two other tree elements. Thus the interconnection of tree elements can be quite complex, compared to the simple linear nature of a linked list. As with lists,

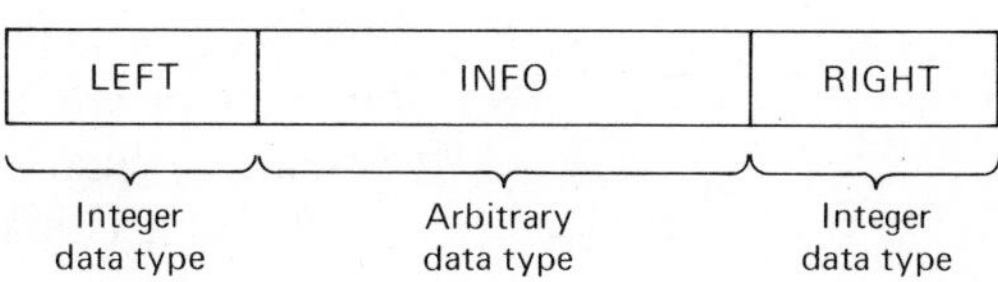

Figure 13.16. The structure of a tree element.

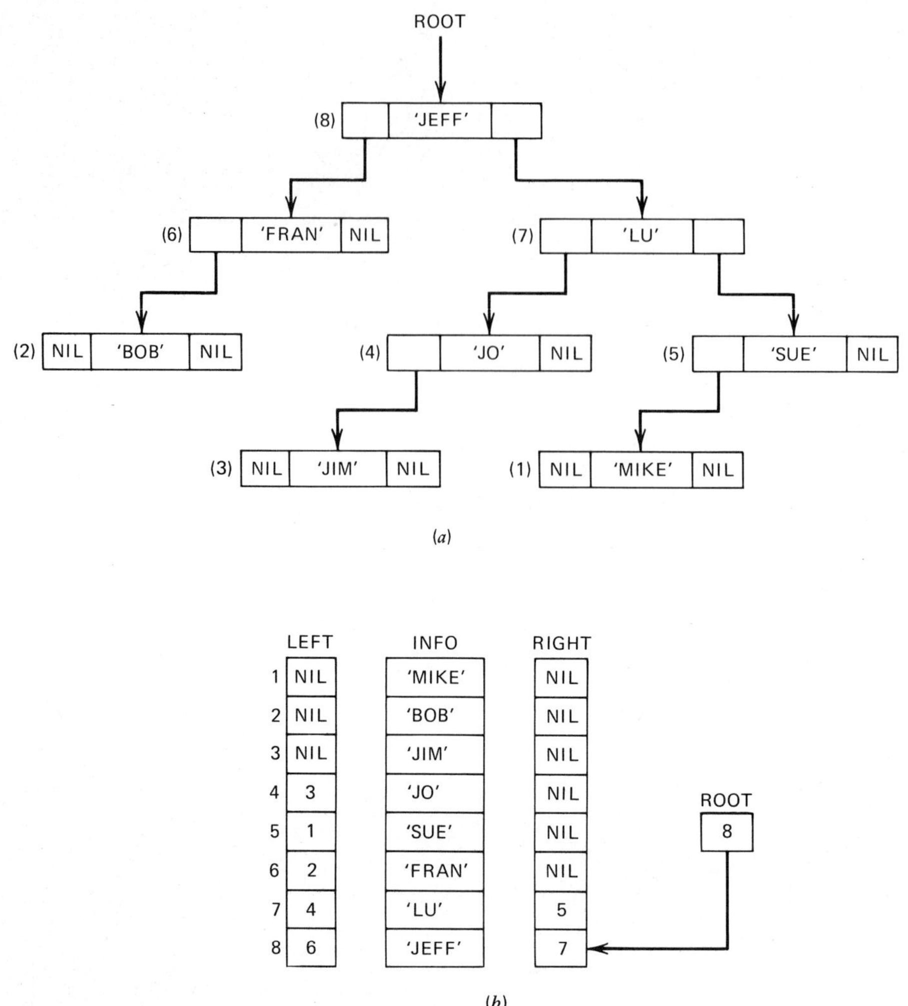

Figure 13.17. A set of tree elements linked together. (*a*) Logical structure of the tree elements. (*b*) Physical structure of the tree elements.

parallel arrays are used to implement a set of tree elements in Fortran. Figure 13.17 illustrates such a set, together with the logical structure for the given linking.

The links in Figure 13.17 have been constructed so that in part (*b*) of the figure all of the INFO values of elements "reachable" through the LEFT link of an element are less (i.e., earlier in alphabetical order) than the INFO value of that element, and all values reachable through the RIGHT link are greater. In this figure there is a unique sequence of links, starting from the ROOT, to get to a particular element.

A structure having the form illustrated in Figure 13.17 is called a *tree*, and the "starting" element is called the *root* (computer trees usually grow upside down!). Characteristic of trees is the fact that, starting from the root, there is only one path of links that lead to any particular element (sometimes called *node*) of the tree—that is, each node of a tree has exactly one link leading into it, except the root which has no links pointing to it. While the form of Figure 13.17 is characteristic of all trees, the alphabetic ordering illustrated in that figure is not a requirement for tree structures.

Trees exhibiting the ordering shown in Figure 13.17 are sometimes called "dictionary trees". Dictionary trees can be very useful in efficient processing of textual material. In making word counts of textual material, for example, it is not known before hand which words appear in the text; that is, a listing of the words is not initially available—such a listing must be compiled as the text is being scanned. Of course the word count is made at the same time. When the next word is encountered in such a scan it must be determined if it is the same as one already processed (in which case its count is incremented by 1) or must be added as a newly acquired word and its count initialized to 1. If an ordinary (unlinked) array is used for this application then the following two approaches are obviously available:

1 Don't order the words in the array—in which case adding a new word is easy, but an inefficient linear search through the array must be made to see if the next word is already present.

2 Keep the array of words sorted—in which case an efficient binary search may be used, but adding a new word requires moving a large number (half, on the average) of the array.

Although the second of these options is the better of the two, especially for long texts, the continual sorting of the array constitutes a major source of inefficiency. The use of a dictionary tree for this application, while perhaps not as obvious an approach as the two listed above, allows the search to proceed at speeds often approaching that of a binary search. Insertion of a new word into the tree is almost as efficient as in the first method above.

Subroutine TREE builds a dictionary tree for a supplied TEXT, and counts the number of times each word appears in TEXT. TEXT itself is an array of strings, each array element representing one line of text. TREE calls subroutine GET, which provides the next word (NXWORD) from TEXT to be processed. And finally subroutine TRPRNT prints the words, and word counts, from the tree in alphabetical word order. Note that in subroutine TREE the INFO field is really two data fields—a character field (WORD) to contain the word value and an integer field (COUNT) to contain the count for that word. Thus the array of tree elements is really four parallel arrays. The basic operation of TREE is to compare NXWORD with the WORD value in the current tree element, starting with the root element. If the two match, the search is finished and the word COUNT is incremented. If NXWORD is (alphabetically) less than WORD then the next tree element for comparison is that accessed by the LEFT link; if NXWORD is greater than WORD then the RIGHT link is followed. And if a NIL link is encountered then NXWORD has not been previously encountered, and so must be added as a new tree element. In greater detail, but still informally, the TREE algorithm is

1 establish ROOT element (first word in TEXT)

2 do
   2.1 get next word (NXWORD)
   2.2 if not end-of-TEXT then search tree

   repeat

The algorithm for searching the tree also increments word counts and inserts new tree elements as may be appropriate:

```
if at end of path then
        NXWORD is a new word,
        so add new tree element
            (and terminate search)
    elseif NXWORD lt tree WORD
        go left and search
    elseif NXWORD gt tree WORD
        go right and search
    else match found, increment count
        (and terminate search)
endif
```

```
*....:---------------------------------------------------------------
      SUBROUTINE  TREE (TEXT)
                      CHARACTER  TEXT(1:*)*(*)

*          ..this program builds a dictionary tree
*          from the array of words TEXT. In
*          building the tree this program calls subroutine
*          GET (not supplied) that obtains the next word
*          from TEXT. After the tree is built, subroutine
*          TRPRNT (also not supplied) is called to print
*          the words and word-counts from the dictionary tree..
*

*     ....constants....(maximum word size and number of words)
      INTEGER  MWS, MNW, NIL
      CHARACTER  ENDTEX*2
      PARAMETER  ( MWS  =  40, MNW = 2000, NIL = -1, ENDTEX = '/$' )

*     ....local variables....
*     tree element declarations
          INTEGER    LEFT(1:MNW)
          CHARACTER  WORD(1:MNW)*(MWS)
          INTEGER    COUNT(1:MNW)
          INTEGER    RIGHT(1:MNW)
*     end tree element declarations
      CHARACTER  NXWORD*(MWS)
      INTEGER  ROOT, NODE, SPACE
      DATA  ROOT, SPACE /1,2/

*     ....execute....insert first word into tree
*                 then loop on remaining words
      CALL  GET (NXWORD,TEXT)
      LEFT(ROOT) = NIL
      WORD(ROOT) = NXWORD
      COUNT(ROOT) = 1
      RIGHT(ROOT) = NIL
*                ..process next word..
      do
          CALL GET (NXWORD,TEXT)
          IF  (NXWORD .EQ. ENDTEX)  exit

*                ..search tree, beginning at root
*                NODE is the current tree element..
          NODE = ROOT
          do
              IF  (NODE .EQ. NIL)  THEN
*                                  ..add NXWORD to tree and exit
                  NODE = SPACE
                  SPACE = SPACE+1
                  LEFT(NODE) = NIL
                  WORD(NODE) = NXWORD
                  COUNT(NODE) = 1
                  RIGHT(NODE) = NIL
                  exit

              ELSEIF  (NXWORD .LT. WORD(NODE))  THEN
*                                                 ..go left
                  IF  (LEFT(NODE) .NE. NIL)  THEN
*                                            ..if left node exists
                          NODE = LEFT(NODE)
                      ELSE
*                                        ..otherwise add left node
                          LEFT(NODE) = SPACE
                          NODE = NIL
                  ENDIF

              ELSEIF  (NXWORD .GT. WORD(NODE))  THEN
*                                                 ..go right
                  IF  (RIGHT(NODE) .NE. NIL)  THEN
*                                            ..if right node exists
                          NODE = RIGHT(NODE)
                      ELSE
*                                     ..otherwise add right node
                          RIGHT(NODE) = SPACE
                          NODE = NIL
                  ENDIF
              ELSE
*                     ..words match -- increment COUNT and exit..
                  COUNT(NODE) = COUNT(NODE) + 1
                  exit
              ENDIF
          repeat
      repeat
      CALL  TRPRNT (ROOT,LEFT,WORD,COUNT,RIGHT)
      END
=====================================================================
```

(Note that this informal algorithm for the tree-searching process is very nearly recursive in nature. Algorithms involving trees are often good candidates for recursion and TREE is such a candidate. However the recursive version of TREE is in the class that doesn't need stacking, and thus the nonrecursive form is no more complex.)

The speed of the tree search approaches that of the binary search if the tree happens to be *balanced*. A balanced tree is one that is as completely "filled in" as possible (all nodes, except possibly one which points to a single terminal node, are either terminal nodes or point to two other nodes). In such a tree the maximum number of links in a path is approximately the base 2 logarithm of N, where N is the number of elements in the tree. Thus for N=2000 no more than 11 comparisons are needed to search the tree for NXWORD. The likelihood that subroutine TREE will produce a perfectly balanced tree, however, is small. Because of the random nature of the order in which new words are encountered by subroutine TREE, there is a good chance that paths significantly longer than the maximum in a balanced tree will be produced, and this adversely affects the search speed. By the same token, however, a great many short paths are likely to exist. Thus in practice the search process of subroutine TREE is likely to be considerably faster than the linear search, but not quite as fast as the binary search.

A final example in this section is the use of a tree data structure for the principal data element in a Morse Code decoding algorithm (see the corresponding examples in Chapters 4, 5, and 6). Here the Morse code and corresponding clear letters are contained in a (balanced) tree, as shown in Figure 13.18. Decoding a Morse code character involves searching the tree for the Morse code pattern, and extracting the corresponding clear character. This tree search is very fast—much faster than the linear searches used in the previous solutions to this problem, and comparable in speed to the binary search (see Chapter 11)—if a '.' means "go left" in the tree and a '–' means "go right".

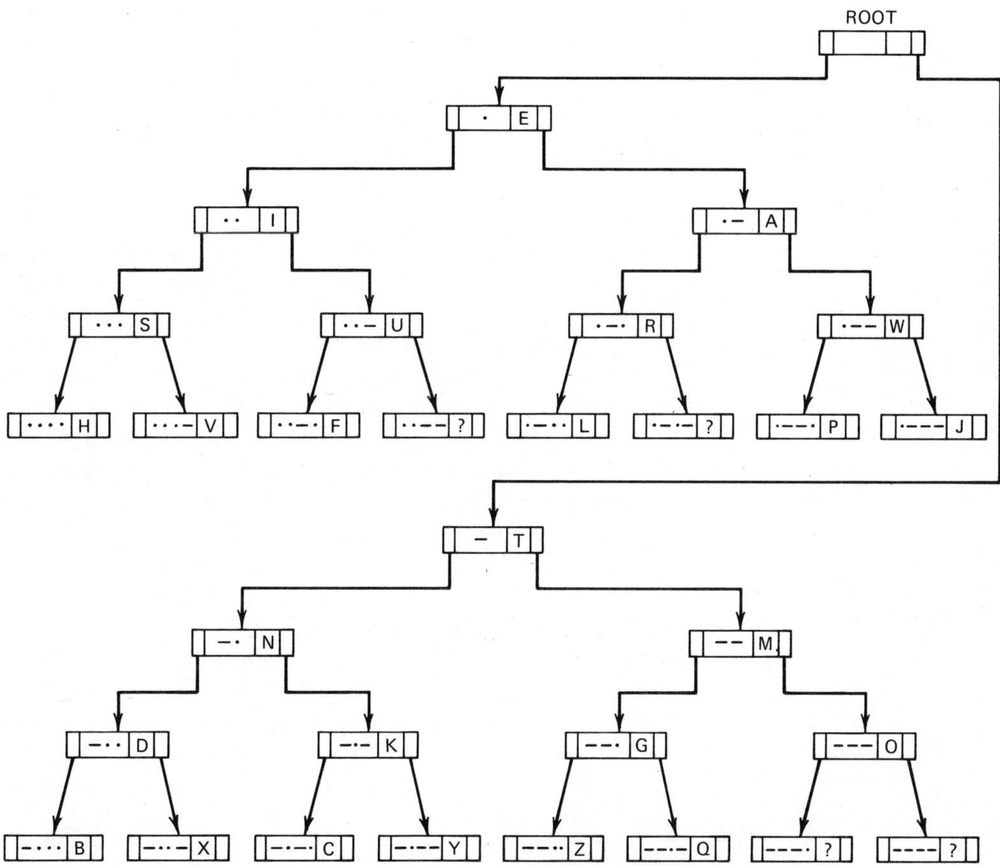

Figure 13.18. Tree for Morse code, left links → dots; right links → dashes.

	LEFT	CLEAR	RIGHT	
1	2		3	
2	4	E	5	•
3	6	T	7	–
4	9	I	10	••
5	12	A	15	•–
6	13	N	11	–•
7	14	M	8	––
8	30	O	31	–––
9	18	U	28	••–
10	16	S	20	•••
11	22	K	23	–•–
12	17	R	29	•–•
13	21	D	26	–••
14	27	G	25	––•
15	19	W	24	•––
16	NIL	H	NIL	••••
17	NIL	L	NIL	•–••
18	NIL	F	NIL	••–•
19	NIL	P	NIL	•––•
20	NIL	V	NIL	•••–
21	NIL	B	NIL	–•••
22	NIL	C	NIL	–•–•
23	NIL	Y	NIL	–•––
24	NIL	J	NIL	•–––
25	NIL	Q	NIL	––•–
26	NIL	X	NIL	–••–
27	NIL	Z	NIL	––••
28	NIL	?	NIL	••––
29	NIL	?	NIL	•–•–
30	NIL	?	NIL	–––•
31	NIL	?	NIL	––––

Figure 13.19. Fortran implementation of the tree structure of Figure 13.18. LEFT and RIGHT are integer arrays; CLEAR is an array of (single) characters.

The Morse code tree of Figure 13.18 may be established in Fortran as shown in Figure 13.19. As in the previous examples, if the Morse code pattern is all blanks then the clear is a blank; if the Morse code pattern is too long then the clear is a '!'; and if some other error occurs then the clear is a '?'. Function MCTREE accepts the Morse code pattern and returns the appropriate clear character, using the tree data structure of Figures 13.18 and 13.19 for the decoding. Function MCTREE illustrates that wise use of data structuring can result in simpler and more efficient programs.

Both list elements and tree elements involve link fields. Nonhomogeneous compound data elements need not include any link fields, however, and you should not get the idea that linking and link fields are always a part of such data structures. Lists and trees were not chosen in this section primarily to illustrate linking, but because the elements of these data structures are quite simple (about the simplest possible!) examples of nonhomogeneous compound data elements that have interesting, practical applications. A compound data element can, in general, have any number of fields of any data type. Any of the integer fields may be used for linking, but none have to be so used. Arbitrary compound data elements are normally called "records", and introducing some additional concepts pertaining to records is the topic of the next section.

13.3 Records

A record is a data element composed of any set of fields. Thus even a simple data element is a record, but usually a record is a compound data element. Conversely, a compound data element is a record—that is, "record" is simply the common name for

```
*....:-----------------------------------------------------------------
      CHARACTER FUNCTION  MCTREE (CODE)
                                     CHARACTER*(*)  CODE

*                       ..uses tree structure of
*                       figures 13.18 and 13.19
*                       to decode a Morse Code character..

*     ....constants....
      INTEGER  NIL
      PARAMETER  ( NIL = -1 )
      INTEGER  LEFT(1:31), RIGHT(1:31)
      CHARACTER  CLEAR*31
      DATA  LEFT /2,4,6,9,12,13,14,30,18,16,22,17,21,27,19,16*-1/,
     :      RIGHT /3,5,7,10,15,11,8,31,28,20,23,29,26,25,24,16*-1/,
     :      CLEAR /' ETIANMOUSKRDGWHLFPVBCYJQXZ????'/

*     ....variables....
      INTEGER  NODE, N

*     ....execute....
      NODE = 1
      N = 1
      do
          IF  (NODE .EQ. NIL)  THEN
              MCTREE = '!'
              exit

          ELSEIF  (CODE(N:N) .EQ. ' ')  THEN
              MCTREE = CLEAR(NODE:NODE)
              exit

          ELSEIF  (CODE(N:N) .EQ. '.')  THEN
              NODE = LEFT(NODE)

          ELSEIF  (CODE(N:N) .EQ. '-')  THEN
              NODE = RIGHT(NODE)

          ELSE
              MCTREE = '?'
              exit
          ENDIF
          N = N+1
      repeat
      END
=====================================================================
```

a compound data element. Although data elements of type COMPLEX, and even arrays, may be considered to be records, normally the term record is used for a programmer-defined compound data element. Thus the term *record* may perhaps most practically be used to refer to a programmer-defined set of fields, where each field is a data element (either simple, or itself compound). Records are extremely important in computing, finding extensive use in virtually every major systems program or large data processing application. This section contains a brief examination of record concepts and their implementation in Fortran.

Records are involved whenever data comes in "groups". The group may be composed of individual fields of integers, character strings, real values, etc., but these fields exist together and have meaning only in the context of the group. Examples are the list and tree elements of the preceding section, both of which are records. The structure of each of these records is reproduced in Figure 13.20. In the tree record, for example, the COUNT field really has no meaning without the WORD field. Each of the fields of the tree element is useful only to the extent of its contribution to the group of four values composing the tree element. Moreover each field is a vital part of the record, at least for the two records in Figure 13.20. No field can be missing without destroying the usefulness of all of the other fields, that is, without destroying the meaning of the record itself.

Other examples of records come readily to mind. For instance, consider a computer application for generating a company's paychecks. For each paycheck an important piece of information is the employee's name. But of course this is not enough since the monthly salary is also needed, or, if the employee is hourly, the number of

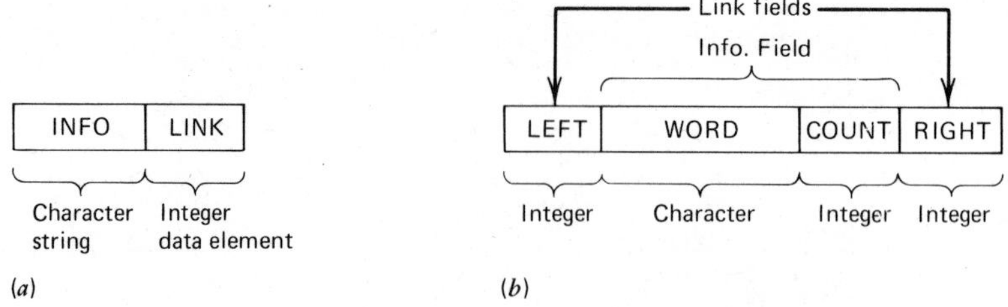

Figure 13.20. Examples of records (from Section 13.2). (*a*) List element. (*b*) Tree element.

hours and the hourly pay rate are needed. This is still not enough information for a payroll system, because withholding taxes must be computed, which requires the number of the employee's dependents. And in order to determine correctly the deduction for social security the yearly wages to date must be known. Thus, as an absolute minimum (if the employee is hourly), all of the fields of information shown in Figure 13.21 must be provided before a paycheck can be generated. For the purposes of payroll, therefore, these fields would always be supplied as a group, since a paycheck could not be generated if any one value were missing. Thus the payroll application would involve a record with these fields. (Actually, in practice payroll records typically have these fields and more. Additional fields are needed to specify other items that usually affect paycheck amounts, such as retirement plan, health plan, community chest contributions, and other deductions.)

A program for maintaining inventory information would need several pieces of data for each item in the inventory:

Stock number	(character)
Description	(character)
Retail price	(real)
Number in stock	(integer)
Number on order	(integer)
Date of last order	(character)
Supplier	(character)

Such an inventory record would have seven fields, four of type CHARACTER, two INTEGER, and one REAL. Another example is that of submitting a job (program) to be run on a large computing system. Among other things, and depending on the specific computer, the following information typically must be available for successful processing of the program:

Compiler to be used

Location of input

Destination of output

User's account

Job priority

CPU time limit

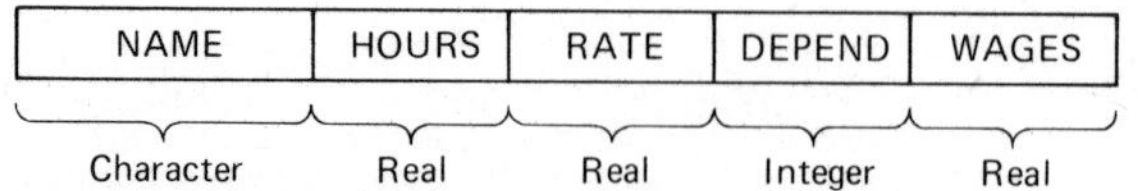

Figure 13.21. Required fields for a payroll record.

FIELD1	FIELD2	FIELD3	•••		FIELDn

Figure 13.22. The general structure of a record. There are *n* individual fields, each having some arbitrary data type.

Some of this information may be automatically supplied by the system itself, although these defaults usually can be changed by the user, and some of this information (i.e., user's account, compiler to be used) must be supplied by the user. In any event the systems program handling the job management would deal with a record (or several records) containing this and other necessary information.

This list of examples could go on, but the point should be clear that often data logically comes in groups, and all individual data elements of the group must be present before any of the data can be used. In such instances it is convenient, and logically natural, to consider such a group as a record—then reference to a record constitutes a reference to the entire group of data. Figure 13.22 illustrates the general structure of a record. There may be arbitrarily many fields in the record, of arbitrary data types. Any given field may itself be compound—that is, consist of two or more "sub"-fields—but in the more common case, each field is a simple data element. In the remainder of this book a record will be a programmer-defined set of simple data elements; the picture in Figure 13.22 is a good general representation of such a structure.

Ideally, the programmer should be able to define a record in the specification statements, give it a name (such as PAYREC, for the payroll application), and then use that name in the executable statements to refer to the entire group of data. For example the statement

```
READ *, PAYREC
```

would mean "input a data value for each field of the record PAYREC". Unfortunately, Fortran does not provide for the formal naming of records. Records in Fortran are represented directly as groups of ordinary Fortran variables, each representing a field of the record. The PAYREC record, for example, would consist of the variables NAME, HOURS, RATE, DEPEND, and WAGES—each of which is the name of the variable of the appropriate type representing the corresponding field of PAYREC—and the Fortran READ statement for inputting PAYREC is

```
READ *, NAME, HOURS, RATE, DEPEND, WAGES
```

Therefore, for reading a record in Fortran, the list of field names for the record is used in the READ statement, rather than the record name. The same is true of outputting a record, or passing a record to a procedure: the list of field names, rather than the record name, is used. The input (or output, or procedure call) statement can be conveniently documented as a transfer of data for a record, however, by using a comment such as the following:

```
*     . . read record PAYREC. .
      READ *, NAME, HOURS, RATE, DEPEND, WAGES
```

Using just the comment statement for record input makes the development of the program easier, and the actual READ statement can be inserted after the development is complete and before the program is submitted for compilation.

Although records cannot be formally named in Fortran, there is no reason why record structures cannot be clearly identified, and informally named, in the specification statements. Wise use of comments and individual field declarations can be very effective in this regard, as shown in Figure 13.23.

```
*    ----record       PAYREC
     CHARACTER    NAME*20
     REAL         HOURS
     REAL         RATE
     INTEGER      DEPEND
     REAL         WAGES
*    ===end       PAYREC
```

(a)

```
*    ----record  <record-name>
     <type 1>    <field 1>
     <type 2>    <field2>
     <type 3>    <field 3>
        .           .
        .           .
        .           .
     <type n>    <field n>
*    ===end  <record-name>
```

(b)

Figure 13.23. A style for Fortran record declarations. (*a*) Declaration of the payroll record of Figure 13.21. (*b*) General form.

If records are declared in the manner shown in Figure 13.23 then the program development technique mentioned at the end of the previous paragraph becomes quite practical, since inserting the correct field list for each record READ involves simply copying the field list from the appropriate record declaration list. Such declarations not only benefit program development, but also constitute effective documentation of the program's data elements; additional documentation can be included in the two comment lines, if desired.

13.4 Files

One inventory record does not an inventory make. An entire inventory would be represented by many (typically many thousands of) records, each record representing the data for a certain item in the inventory. Each record has the same field structure, but of course the values in the fields are in general different for the different inventory items. Similarly, in a payroll system there would be a record for each employee. Applications involving records typically deal with a *data base* consisting of large numbers of identically structured records of data. Such a data base may be considered to be (organized into) a sequence of records, each record having the same field structure.

A sequence of (like-structured) records is called a *file*, or *data file*. A file is essentially a one-dimensional array of records, as shown in Figure 13.24.

Each record in a file may involve hundreds, or thousands, of storage units, and a file may contain tens or hundreds of thousands of records, or more—thus data files may be enormous in terms of the storage space they require. Even modestly sized files usually require surprisingly large amounts of storage space, and the users of a computing system collectively have many thousands of files in their accounts. All of this requires many millions, and often billions, of storage units, far surpassing the primary storage capacity (main memory) of any present-day computer. For this reason files are actually stored on secondary storage devices such as magnetic disks and tapes, and must be transferred to main memory for processing. Usually a small group of records

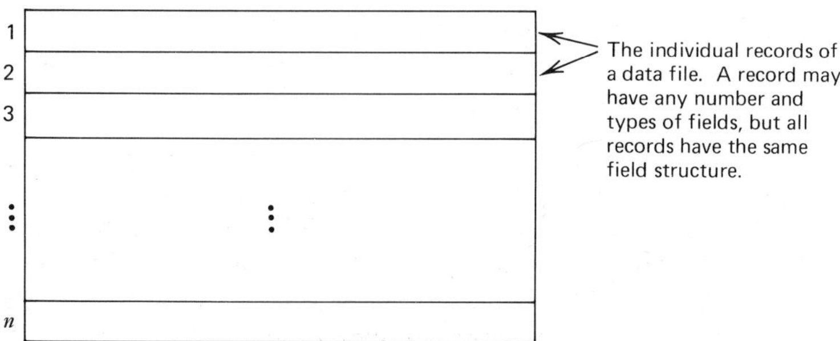

Figure 13.24. A data file as a sequence of n records.

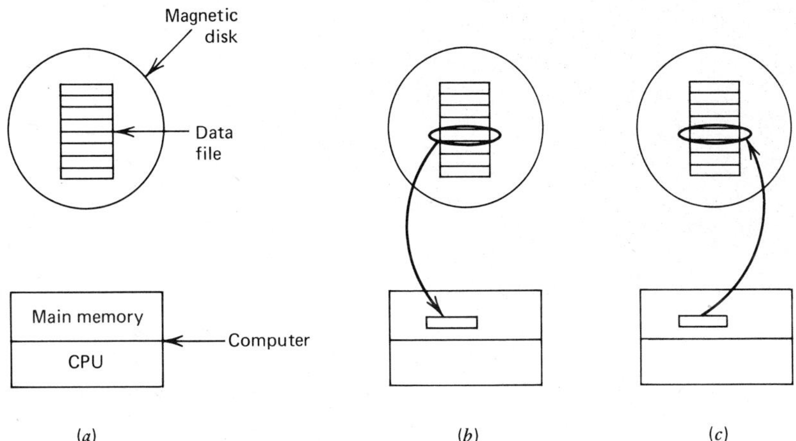

Figure 13.25. Processing a record of a data file. (*a*) The components of the system, showing the data file residing on disk storage. (*b*) Reading (a copy of) a record into main memory for processing. (*c*) Writing (a copy of) the (modified) record back into the file.

(often just one) is transferred at a time, processed, and returned to the file before processing the next group. Thus the file will not actually be an array (which is a sequence of data elements in main memory), but the analogy with an array is useful, and the sequence numbers are important in some aspects of file processing. Figure 13.25 illustrates the concept of processing a single file record at a time.

The fact that data files reside in secondary storage (are "external"), and that processing the data in such files requires transferring the data to and from main memory, means that the programmer must have provisions available for accessing external files. Moreover, it must be possible to simultaneously access several external files. Fortran has a comprehensive set of features for accessing external files, which are both powerful and convenient to use. The next two chapters are devoted to describing these features in detail.

13.5 Summary

This chapter has presented an introduction to the principal data structures concepts of modern computing, and has described Fortran's provisions pertaining to each of these concepts. Effective use of data structuring nearly always simplifies the programming process, and often contributes significantly to program efficiency.

Data structures are composite data elements. The constituent parts of a data structure are, ultimately, individual simple data elements such as integer, real, character, etc. A homogeneous data structure is one in which all of its component parts are of the same data type. An array is such a structure, and arrays may be two-dimensional, three-dimensional, and even higher-dimensional (up to seven) structures, in addition to the familiar one-dimensional array introduced as early as Chapter 2. While applications involving one-dimensional arrays are by far the most common, occasionally higher-order arrays are extremely useful. Two important application areas in which this is particularly true are (1) certain classes of numerical calculations, and (2) graphic information processing. Arrays are declared by giving their names, types, and array bounds for each dimension.

Heterogeneous data structures are composite data elements in which the constituent parts are not necessarily all of the same data type. A "record" is such a structure, and is (usually) simply an arbitrary set of individual simple data elements. These constituent parts are called fields, and in Fortran records are defined and referenced only by defining and referencing the individual fields. Thus printing a record in Fortran would take the form

PRINT *, <field list>

Each field is an ordinary Fortran data element, and hence each has its own unique name. Therefore <field list> is just a list of Fortran data element names.

A data file is a data structure, and is essentially an array of records. Usually a file is a large collection of data, with each record of the file being one of many identically structured sets of data. For example, each record of a payroll file would normally contain payroll data for one employee, with the individual fields being such things as employee name, pay rate, social security number, annual wages to date, etc. Data files are typically so large that they must be stored not in main memory but on secondary storage media such as magnetic tape and disk. Processing such data files involves reading each record into main memory for processing.

One or more fields of a record may be a "link" field. The values of link fields are locations of other records. Link fields allow records to be "tied together" in arbitrarily logical order, and may be used to build arbitrarily complex data structures. Such linked structures may be very useful, as illustrated by the foregoing examples involving linked lists and trees. In Fortran, link fields are implemented by integer variables, with the values being array indices.

Thus the important concepts of this chapter are:

1 A data structure as a composite data element.

2 Homogeneous and nonhomogeneous data structures.

3 Multidimensional arrays, and corresponding Fortran provisions.

4 Records and fields, and corresponding Fortran provisions.

5 Data files.

6 Link fields and linked data structures, and corresponding Fortran provisions.

Programming Exercises

13.1 Write a Fortran program that prints the contents of an array dimensioned as CHARACTER . . . (1:10,−4:4,101:105)*4, so that each "plane", with indices 101, 102, 103, 104, 105, respectively, is printed as a 10 (rows) by 9 (columns) matrix.

13.2 Pass a singly dimensioned (say 1:1000) array as an actual argument in a CALL statement.

(a) In the subroutine dimension the dummy argument as (1:100) and, by using suitable PRINT statements, output the dummy argument values in order to "see" the association between the actual and dummy arguments.
(b) Repeat for the dummy argument dimensioned at (1:10,1:20).
(c) Repeat for the dummy argument dimensioned at (1:20,1:10).
(d) Repeat for the dummy argument being a three-dimensional array.
(e) Experiment further in this vein, as may be warranted.

13.3 A "page buffer" is a two-dimensional array whose elements represent the print positions on a printed page. Page buffers are useful for piece-by-piece construction of graphic data—the page buffer conveniently allows the data to be acquired in any arbitrary order prior to being printed. Suppose that two one-dimensional arrays, X and Y, specify the row and column respectively of the page buffer into which a character is to be placed. C is a one-dimensional character array containing the actual characters to be inserted into the buffer. Thus C(i) is the character to be placed in row X(i), column Y(i) of the page buffer. Write a Fortran program to establish the contents of the buffer from X, Y, and C, putting blank characters in the "unused" spaces of the buffer. Assume that arrays X, Y, and C have been supplied, together with the number of elements they specify.

13.4 The game of "life" is a simple but interesting exercise in "population dynamics" involving a two-dimensional array. Actually "life" is exactly like the picture refinement example, except the rules for changing a 0 to a 1 ("birth") and a 1 to a 0 ("death") are somewhat different. Each "refinement pass" over the life array constitutes one "generation" of life. It is interesting to establish an initial population distribution, and then observe the population patterns of succeeding generations. The rules for life are: (1) the occupant of a cell "dies" from isolation if it has less than two immediate neighbors (of the eight possible), and from overcrowding if it has more than four neighbors, (b) a "birth" occurs for an unoccupied cell if that cell has two or three immediate neighbors (an interesting biology!). Write a Fortran program that "plays" the game of life, printing out the population pattern of each generation. Use a two-dimensional logical array for the life matrix.

13.5 Repeat Problem 13.4, but use a one-dimensional array of (integer-based) bit strings for the principal life data elements, rather than a two-dimensional logical array.

13.6 Modify the picture refinement example (and/or the game of life in the preceding two problems) so that the picture is represented by a one-dimensional array of character strings rather than a two-dimensional array involving numeric storage units.

13.7 (a) Modify the picture refinement example so that the "edge" elements are refined also. (b) Modify the picture refinement example so that an arbitrary number of refinement passes are performed.

13.8 Generalize the least-squares algorithm so that is can be used with a problem involving any number of independent variables (there were three independent variables in the PCP example: TEMP, DEPTH, and LIGHT). If n is the number of independent variables then the required matrix is n+1 rows by n+2 columns, and element (i+1,j+1) of this matrix is sum(variable-i * variable-j). Element (1,1) is N (number of new data points), and element (i,j+1) = element (j+1,1) = SUM (variable..j).

13.9 The least-squares algorithm described in this chapter determines the least squares coefficients of the linear function Y = A0 + A1*X1 + A2*X2 + . . . + An*Xn, where Y is the dependent variable and X1, X2, . . ., Xn are the independent variables. Often problems involve a single independent variable, X, but the relationship between the dependent variable, Y, and X is not linear. Whatever the relationship, it can be approximated by the polynomial function Y = A0 + A1*X + A2*X**2 + A3*X**3 + . . . + An*X**n and the larger n is, the closer the approximation normally is. Making polynomial fits of a single X is analogous to making linear fits with many X's, in that the A's are to be computed. In fact, with the least-squares algorithm, making such polynomial fits is identical to making linear fits, if X**2 is used for X2, X**3 for X3, . . ., and X**n for Xn. Thus least-squares polynomial fits involve only the extra step, over linear fits, of computing X**2, X**3, . . ., X**n for each given value of X, and then using these powers as if they were the supplied values of X2, X3, . . ., Xn. Write a Fortran program that accepts N (X,Y) pairs, and performs the least-squares polynomial fit to this data for any given n.

13.10 Modify the program example LIST so that the following errors are detected and an appropriate message printed. (a) Overflow—a PUSH operation attempted when the available space stack is empty. (b) Underflow—a POP operation attempted on an empty stack.

13.11 Write a Fortran program, that can be called at any time, to display the current contents of all of the stacks in the LIST example.

13.12 Write a Fortran program TRPRNT that prints the contents (WORDs and COUNTs) of the dictionary tree (example TREE), such that the words are listed in alphabetical order. (a) Without recursion. (Hint: a stack is useful in this case to "remember" the current path in the tree.) (b) Using recursion (this is easy).

13.13 (a) Write the inner loop of example TREE as a recursive algorithm, TSERCH. (b) Write the entire algorithm of TREE recursively.

13.14 Modify example MCTREE so that the digit characters are also included.

13.15 A linked list is a "doubly linked" list if each element has two link fields, one pointing to the successor element and the other pointing to the predecessor element as shown:

Write two Fortran programs: (a) one to insert a new element between two currently adjacent elements in such a structure, and (b) one to remove a given element from such a structure.

13.16 A hotel chain wishes to establish a central reservation system. In such a system, reservation information must be maintained for several hundred different hotels in the chain, each, potentially, with a different number of rooms in each of the various categories (singles, doubles, suites, etc.). What data elements/structures could be used effectively in such a system? Note that part of such a system is that the names of customers having reservations must be maintained in the system.

13.17 Modify the picture refinement process illustrated in program PLANET so that it may be used to refine a picture containing 16 shades of gray. Each shade, from white to black, is represented as an integer in the range from 0 to 15. Each cell of the refined picture should contain the (nearest integer) average value of its unrefined neighborhood.

13.18 In subroutine REDLSM of the least-squares example, the reduction process used each diagonal element, in turn, as the "pivot" element to zero-out all of the other elements in that column of the matrix. A much better method is to always use, as the next pivot, that element whose magnitude is the largest value remaining in the matrix. Excluded from consideration as the next pivot element, however, are the elements in the rightmost column and all elements in any row or column of a previous pivot element. This technique, called "maximum-pivot", leaves the 1's of the reduced matrix in "random" positions rather than on the main diagonal. The significance of this is that the results in the rightmost column, while being the correct values, are scrambled in order and must be unscrambled. Since implementing maximum-pivot requires keeping track of the row and column numbers of the pivot elements (so that those rows and columns can be excluded from the searches for subsequent pivot elements) adequate information is available to perform the unscrambling. If Ri is the row number of the ith pivot element, Ci is the column number of the ith pivot element, and Xj is the jth element of the unscrambled solution set, then
X(Ci−1) = LSM (Ri, n+2) for i = 1,2,. . .,n,n+1
Modify subroutine REDLSM so that it uses the maximum-pivot technique.

Chapter 14 Data Files

The concepts of a record, and a data file being a sequence of records, were introduced briefly in the last two sections of the previous chapter. This chapter discusses in detail the Fortran provisions for accessing, creating, and deleting files, and other file operations. The concept of a file as an array of records is useful for imagining the basic structure of a file, but since files are stored in secondary memory (e.g., disks, tapes) rather than in main memory they are not true arrays, and methods of accessing a record in a file are somewhat different from accessing an element in an array. Fortran supports two access methods, *sequential* and *direct*, giving rise to the terms SAM (Sequential Access Method) and DAM (Direct Access Method) files. The first two sections below describe these two file access methods. The final two sections describe how lines of communication between data files in secondary storage and the executing program are established.

Processing a data file normally involves transferring the (contents of the) records to be processed, one by one, to the (data elements of the) program for processing, and then transferring the updated records back to the file (see the last section of the previous chapter). The action of transferring a record from the file to the program is called "reading" from the file, or "file input", and constitutes a form of data input to the program. An extended form of the READ statement that includes identification of the file to be read is used for file input. Its simplest version is

```
READ (<file id>,<format specification>) <list of input variables>
```

Here the <format specification> is the same as that introduced in Part 1, and its various options are described in detail in Chapter 15. The <list of input variables> is also constructed as previously, but for file input these variables will normally be those representing the fields of the file record. This READ statement directs that data be transferred from the indicated file to the program variables listed. The means of establishing the <file id> are described in Section 14.3 below.

The action of transferring a record from the program to the file is called "writing" to the file, or "file output", and is analogous to PRINTing output. The statement used is the WRITE statement, which is an extended form of the PRINT statement, and whose simplest form is:

```
WRITE (<file id>,<format specification>) <list of output quantities>
```

Again the <format specification> is the familiar one, as is the <list of output quantities>. The <file id> identifies the file to be written, and the <list of output quantities> normally is the set of field values to be written into the file record.

Before file input or file output can take place for a given file, the file must be made accessible by *opening* it. Opening a file prepares it for access, and is performed at the same time that the <file id> is established. Opening a file is described in Section 14.3.

14.1 Sequential Files

Sequential access of a file means that the processing of the records of the file must proceed in the physical order of the records, beginning with the first record. No records may be skipped, and no departure from the record sequential order is permitted. Opening a file for sequential access automatically "positions" the file so that the first READ or WRITE operation on that file involves the first record of the file. After a READ or WRITE operation on that file has been executed, the file is automatically positioned so that the next READ or WRITE operation takes place on the next record in the sequence. Thus the statements

```
<OPEN inventory file INVEN as a SAM file>
do I=1,100
    READ (INVEN,<format>) STKNUM,DESC,STOCK
    PRINT *, STKNUM,DESC,STOCK
repeat
```

will cause STKNUM, DESC, and STOCK to be read from each of the first 100 records of the file named INVEN, in order, and printed on the user's output terminal. Usually the exact number of records in a file is not known, and all records must be processed. A special *endfile* record may be appended after the last data record, and detected during the file read. Thus

```
<OPEN inventory file INVEN>
do
    READ (INVEN,<format>,IOSTAT=IOS) STKNUM,DESC,STOCK
    IF (IOS .LT. 0) exit
    PRINT *, STKNUM,DESC,STOCK
repeat
```

allows the reading and printing of all of the records of file INVEN, regardless of how many there are, assuming the special "endfile" record has been appended to the end of INVEN. The function of the IOSTAT= feature, which has the form

```
IOSTAT= <integer variable>
```

is to cause the <integer variable> (IOS in the above example) to acquire a value upon execution of the READ statement. If it is not the end of file, then the integer-variable value becomes zero and the input process takes place. If the end of the file has been reached, then the integer variable is given a negative value and the input process does not take place. The value of the IOSTAT variable may be tested after the READ statement, as in the above example, to achieve the desired control on reaching the end of file.

The ENDFILE statement specifies the writing of the special "endfile" record; it has the form:

ENDFILE <SAM file id>

In addition the REWIND statement:

REWIND <SAM file id>

repositions the file back to the first record. Program SAM illustrates all of these features; it causes data records (assumed for simplicity to be strings, and ending with the special string '/$') to be input from a terminal or data cards, written onto a SAM file, and then the entire file is echoed back out.

```
*....:------------------------------------------------------------------
      PROGRAM  SAM

*                 ..illustration of the writing and reading of
*                 SAM files; data is input from a terminal or cards,
*                 written into a file referred to as SAMF, and
*                 then the file is echoed back out.
*                 This program uses the
*                     IOSTAT=
*                     ENDFILE
*                     REWIND
*                 SAM file features of Fortran, in addition to
*                 file READ, and WRITE.  A very restricted, but
*                 valid, example of file OPENing is also
*                 illustrated..

*     ....constant....(the <file-id> -- see section 14.3)
      INTEGER  SAMF
      PARAMETER  ( SAMF = 10 )

*     ....variable....
      INTEGER  IOS
      CHARACTER  RECORD*72

*     ....execute....
      OPEN (SAMF)
      do
          READ '(A)', RECORD
          IF  (RECORD .EQ. '/$')  exit
          WRITE (SAMF,'(A)') RECORD
      repeat
      ENDFILE SAMF
      REWIND SAMF
      do
          READ (SAMF,'(A)',IOSTAT=IOS)  RECORD
          IF  (IOS .LT. 0)  exit
          PRINT *,  RECORD
      repeat
      END
========================================================================
```

Fortran provides one additional operation for use with SAM files—the BACKSPACE statement:

BACKSPACE <SAM file id>

BACKSPACE is like REWIND in that it causes the file to be positioned to an earlier record, but unlike REWIND it causes "backing up" only one record, rather than repositioning back to the beginning of the file. This is useful for sequentially updating a file, as shown in the following statements:

```
OPEN (<SAM file id>)
do
    READ (<SAM file id>,<format>,IOSTAT=IOS) <field list>
    IF (IOS.LT.0) exit
        ----)
        ----| Record
        ----| processing statements
        ----)
    BACKSPACE <SAM file id>
    WRITE (<SAM file id>,<format>)<field list>
repeat
```

The BACKSPACE positions the file to the record just read, so that after the processing of this record the following WRITE will update its field values back in the file.

Sequential files may be used on any storage device, but an important use is for data files stored on magnetic tape, where the only practical method of file processing is to process the records in the order that they appear on the tape. Figure 14.1 illustrates the situation. Data records are read or written by a magnetic read/write head over which the tape is passed. Records are located in linear order along the tape, and this physical order is the order in which the records are processed. Files on magnetic tape must be SAM files.

Because of various physical/mechanical limitations of magnetic tape devices, the read-process-backspace-write technique described above is normally not used with magnetic tape files. More typically the updated records are written onto a second tape file, with the processing proceeding through the original file without any backspacing. Then, after a completely updated file has been created, both files may be rewound and the original file replaced by (overwritten with the records of) the updated file by sequentially passing through the files again.

14.2 Direct Files

A direct access file must be stored on magnetic disk, the most common case, or another storage device (e.g., magnetic drum), which permits "immediate" (or "random") accessing of any portion of the stored data. On magnetic disks, the various records of the file are arranged in essentially arbitrary order on a spinning magnetic platter, as depicted in Figure 14.2*a*. Each record has an associated sequence number, starting with 1, so that there is a logical order (as shown in Figure 14.2*b*). The sequence numbers are called *record numbers*, and are used to identify individual records in a

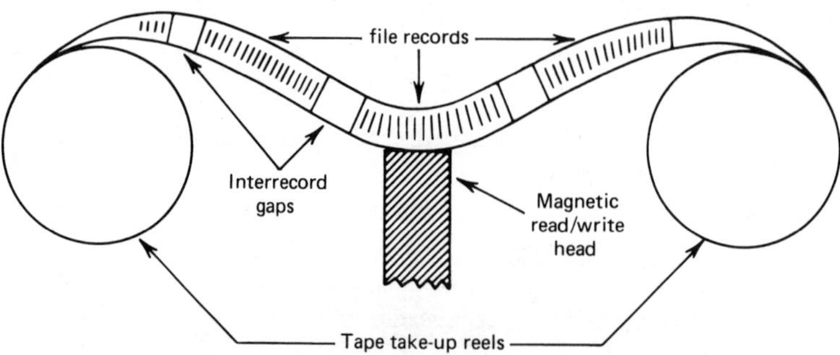

Figure 14.1. Magnetic tape storage for data files.

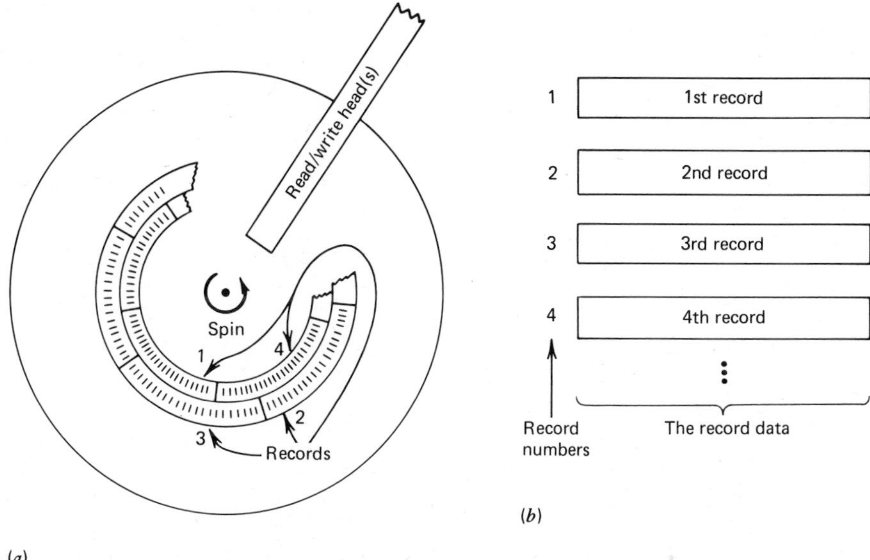

Figure 14.2. A data file on disk. (*a*) Physical organization. (*b*) Logical organization.

Fortran DAM file. Physically the file records are placed in concentric bands around the center of the spinning disk, but not necessarily in the order of the record numbers; a read/write arm, containing one or more magnetic read/write heads, is suspended above the spinning surface. In a movable head disk, the arm normally contains a single read/write head and the arm can move radially in and out to position the read/write head over any of the record-containing bands. In a fixed head disk, there is no arm movement, and a separate read/write head is permanently fixed over each band. Actually most magnetic disk units consist of a stack of several (perhaps a dozen) platters, all spinning around the same axis, and separated just enough to accommodate the read/write heads. Each surface of each platter in such a stack can contain data, and one can imagine concentric cylinders of data, each made up of a stack of 20 or so of the bands ("tracks") shown in Figure 14.2.

DAM file READs and WRITEs are similar to those for SAM files, except that a record number must be supplied for each such operation, and DAM file records may be processed in any desired order. The REC= feature of the Fortran READ and WRITE statements specifies the file record that is to be involved in the direct file operation. The basic form is

```
READ (<DAM file id>,<format>,REC=<record number>) <field list>
WRITE (<DAM file id>,<format>,REC=<record number>) <field list>
```

Since the record number must be explicitly supplied (as an integer expression) for each DAM file READ or WRITE, the REWIND and BACKSPACE features so useful with SAM files are not meaningful, and are not allowed, with DAM files. Similarly the ENDFILE feature is valid only with SAM files. In effect the REC= feature, which is not allowed with SAM files, replaces REWIND, BACKSPACE, and ENDFILE, which are not allowed with DAM files.

A file on a direct access storage device may be processed as a SAM or as a DAM file; for example the file may be created as a DAM file, and then later processed as a SAM file. In such a case the SAM processing causes the records to be processed in the order of the DAM record numbers: 1, 2, 3, 4,. . . . Figure 14.3 illustrates how the first 1000 records of a disk file named (FILE) may be processed using either SAM or DAM modes.

```
<OPEN FILE as sequential>
do RNUM = 1,1000
    READ(FILE,<format>) <field-list>

    <process record>
    BACKSPACE FILE

    WRITE(FILE,<format>) <field-list>
repeat
```

(a)

```
<OPEN FILE as direct>
do RNUM = 1,1000
    READ(FILE,<format>,REC=RNUM)
  :                          <field-list>
    <process record>
    WRITE(FILE,<format>,REC=RNUM)
  :
repeat                       <field-list>
```

(b)

Figure 14.3. Processing the first 1000 records of FILE, in order. (*a*) As a SAM file. (*b*) As a DAM file.

Figure 14.3*b* shows that a disk file may easily be processed in sequential order using the direct access method, and thus DAM is "more general" than SAM for disk files. The special SAM "endfile" record is not legal in a DAM file, however, so if a file of arbitrary (and unknown) length is to be processed in sequential order using DAM then the programmer must supply an appropriate endfile record. This is usually done by using special values in one (or more) fields of the record following the last data record of the file; such a programmer-supplied endfile record is sometimes called a "sentinel record". Using a sentinel record Figure 14.3 would be modified as follows:

```
<OPEN FILE as direct>
RNUM = 1
do
    READ (FILE,<format>,REC=RNUM) <field list>
    IF (<sentinel record>) exit
    <process record>
    WRITE (FILE,<format>,REC=RNUM) <field list>
    RNUM = RNUM+1
repeat
```

Although much data processing is still done directly on files stored on magnetic tape, modern computing facilities increasingly use magnetic disks as the storage medium for files being processed. However, tapes are very important for the storage of "inactive" files, and it is therefore necessary to be able to transfer a file from disk to tape, for inactive storage, and to transfer a file from tape to disk, for processing. Figure 14.4 gives algorithms for performing these two functions. Part (*a*), algorithm TOTAPE, transfers a copy of a disk file to tape, and part (*b*), algorithm TODISK, transfers a copy of a tape file to disk. In these algorithms both RNUM and IOS are integer variables. Both algorithms use DAM for the disk file, although SAM could have been used. In all subsequent examples, unless noted otherwise, all files will be assumed to be on disk and processing will use the direct access method.

14.3 File Connection

Fortran programs communicate with files through *units*. A unit may be imagined as a port through which the program may access external devices such as tape and disk storage devices, card readers, line printers, users' terminals, and other such devices. Units are referred to by integer values, as illustrated in Figure 14.5, and for a given computing system certain unit numbers are associated with certain devices. These

```
*   ....TOTAPE....
    <OPEN file TAPE as sequential>
    <OPEN file DISK as direct>
    RNUM = 1
    do
        READ (DISK,<format>,REC=RNUM) <field-list>
        IF (<sentinel-record>) exit
        WRITE (TAPE,<format>) <field-list>
        RNUM = RNUM+1
    repeat
    ENDFILE TAPE
```

(a)

```
*   ....TODISK....
    <OPEN file TAPE as sequential>
    <OPEN file DISK as direct>
    RNUM = 1
    do
      READ (TAPE,<format>,IOSTAT=IOS) <field-list>
        IF (IOS .LT. 0) exit
        WRITE (DISK,<format>,REC=RNUM) <field-list>
        RNUM = RNUM+1
    repeat
    WRITE (DISK,<format>,REC=RNUM) <sentinel-record>
```

(b)

Figure 14.4. Disk-to-tape and tape-to-disk algorithms. (*a*) Transferring from disk to tape. (*b*) Transferring from tape to disk.

```
unit        device
----        ------
 1          user terminal
 2          paper tape reader/punch
 3          card reader/punch
 4          line printer

 5    }
 6    }
 .    }
 .    }  16 magnetic disk units
 .    }
19    }
20    }

21    }
22    }
 .    }
 .    }  8 magnetic tape units
 .    }
27    }
28    }
```

Figure 14.5. An example of association of Fortran units with computing system devices. (This is the association on one particular computing system. In general, the association will be different for different systems; consult the appropriate manual for the system being used.)

associations are different for different systems (i.e., are implementation dependent) and the manual for each implementation must be consulted for its version of Figure 14.5.

The system of Figure 14.5 has 16 disk units and 8 (magnetic) tape units. This means that up to 16 different disk files, and 8 different tape files, could be simultaneously available to the Fortran program in addition to the terminal, printer, etc. However, there are (typically) thousands of files residing on the disk, and some means must be provided to specify the desired association between a unit and a specific file. This is called *connecting* a file to a unit, and after a file has been connected to a unit all subsequent READing and WRITEing of the file is done by referring to the unit number. Connecting a file is also called *opening* a file on that unit, and is accomplished by the Fortran OPEN statement. The Fortran OPEN and CLOSE statements allow quite flexible control of file connections.

14.3.1 Opening Files

For example, suppose that a file named INVENTORY in the disk's catalogue of files is to be opened on unit 14 for sequential access. Then the statement

```
OPEN (14,FILE='INVENTORY')
```

will cause the desired connection. An equivalent statement is

```
OPEN (UNIT=14,FILE='INVENTORY',ACCESS='SEQUENTIAL')
```

The reason that these two statements are equivalent is that the UNIT= is optional, and sequential access is assumed if the ACCESS= specification is not given. The unit number may be given by an integer constant, as in the above example, but may be any integer expression. In particular it may be the name of an integer data element whose value (established, perhaps, by a PARAMETER statement, as in program SAM) is a valid unit number. Thus the above OPEN statements are equivalent to

```
INVEN = 14
OPEN (UNIT=INVEN,FILE='INVENTORY',ACCESS='SEQUENTIAL')
```

Now the 'INVENTORY' file may be referred to as INVEN and accessed sequentially. Note that <file id> as used in the preceding two sections is really a unit number, and an integer data element name was used for the unit number in all of the examples in those sections.

The OPEN statement has the general form:

```
OPEN (<list of connection specifications>)
```

There must be at least one entry in the <list of connection specifications>, specifying the unit number, and there may be up to seven additional specifications (see Figure 14.6*b*). For opening a file for sequential access two additional specifications are usually sufficient—the FILE= specification and the STATUS= specification. A general form of the OPEN statement with these specifications is

```
OPEN (<unit number>,FILE='<file name>',STATUS=<'OLD' or 'NEW'>)
```

The ACCESS= specification may be omitted since the default is 'SEQUENTIAL'. The order of the specifications in the list is immaterial, except that if the UNIT= is omitted in specifying the <unit number> then <unit number> must be the first specification in the list. (In all subsequent examples the UNIT= will be omitted, and an integer name will be used for the <unit number> specification.) If 'OLD' is specified as the file status then <file name> must be the catalogued name of a file existing on the storage device—it is this file that is then connected to the unit. If STATUS='OLD' is specified and the file does not exist then an error condition exists and a connection is not made. (See the next section for a discussion of error conditions.) If STATUS='NEW' is specified then the file must not exist on the storage device, execution of the OPEN statement creates a new file with the specified name, catalogues it, and then treats it as an OLD file. Such a newly created file initially has no data in it (i.e., is empty).

OPENing a file for direct access typically requires six specifications—in addition to the <unit number>, FILE= and STATUS= specifications, which have the same functions as in opening a SAM file, DAM files need the ACCESS=, RECL=, and FORM= specifications. The forms for these are

ACCESS = 'DIRECT'
RECL = <number of characters in record>
FORM = 'FORMATTED'

The ACCESS='DIRECT' specifies, of course, that the file is being opened for direct access, and thus the REC=<record number> must appear in every READ and WRITE statement involving the file. The FORM='FORMATTED' specifies that a <format specification> is used in each READ and WRITE statement involving the file. This specification may be included in the opening of a SAM file, but it's not needed in this case because the default for SAM files is FORM='FORMATTED'. The other form of this specification, FORM='UNFORMATTED' (which happens to be the default if this specification is omitted in the opening of a DAM file), means that no formatting (not even the "*", for "free-formatting") is to be specified in the READ and WRITE statements involving this file. Unformatted files are discussed in the next chapter.

Since the records of DAM files may be processed in any order, the location on the disk of any record in the file must be determinable. Determining such locations is easiest for the computer system if each record in the file has the same length. For this reason Fortran requires that all of the records of a DAM file be the same length (but of course this length can be different for different DAM files). Consequently, the RECL= specification must be given in the opening of DAM files. (Fortran allows a SAM file to contain records of different lengths, however, and so the RECL= specification must be omitted in the opening of SAM files.) The number of characters in a file record (i.e., the "length" of the record) is the same as the number of print positions the record would take if printed. This is completely determined by the (sum of the) field widths given in the format specification. (For unformatted files the record length is determined differently—see the next chapter.) In the RECL= specification, the record length is given as an integer expression specifying the number of characters (positions) in the record.

On occasion *scratch files* are needed in the processing of one or more data files; a scratch file is a temporary unnamed file used to hold intermediate file data during file processing. A Fortran unit may be used as a scratch file—that it, a new, unnamed file may be created, connected to a unit, and used as an ordinary file. When a scratch file is no longer needed, and is disconnected from the unit, it disappears (i.e., no longer exists). Scratch files may be provided by the OPEN statement, and may be either SAM or DAM files. The FILE='<file name>' must be omitted for scratch files, and STATUS='SCRATCH' must be specified, all other specifications in the OPEN statement are the same as for any other SAM or DAM file. Thus a SAM scratch file is opened by execution of the statement

```
OPEN (<unit number>,STATUS='SCRATCH')
```

and a DAM scratch file is opened by execution of the statement

```
OPEN (<unit number>,STATUS='SCRATCH',ACCESS='DIRECT',
                    RECL=<record length>,FORM='FORMATTED')
```

One or more errors can occur during execution (or attempted execution) of an OPEN statement. These include: (1) a file whose status is given as 'OLD' may not in fact exist, (2) a file whose status is given as 'NEW' may already exist, (3) the file may already be connected to another unit, (4) an invalid specification may be given (e.g., any character expression may be used for the string constants in the example OPEN specification above—these expressions must evaluate during execution of the OPEN statement to one of the allowed values, such as 'NEW', 'OLD', or 'SCRATCH' for the STATUS= specification), and (5) the specified unit may not exist (i.e., an invalid unit number is given). Another specification that may appear in the specifications list of the OPEN statement provides for recovery from such errors. This is the IOSTAT= specification, which has the form

```
IOSTAT=<integer variable name>
```

If this specification is present in the OPEN statement, and no error occurs during execution of the OPEN, then the IOSTAT variable is assigned the value zero, and execution continues in the normal manner after the file connection is established. If an error occurs during execution of the OPEN then a connection is not established, and the IOSTAT variable is given an implementation-dependent positive value which indicates the nature of the error (the implementation manual must be consulted for the meaning of each value). By testing the value of the IOSTAT variable after the OPEN statement, the programmer may specify any desired corrective action to be taken in the event of an error incurred during OPENing. If the IOSTAT= specification is omitted from the OPEN statement, and an error occurs, then execution of the program is terminated.

The set of valid unit numbers is the same for all of the individual programs in a system of programs, and file connection is ''global'' to the system. Thus a file may be opened in the main program or any subprogram, and this connection then exists for all of the programs in the system. Figure 14.6 summarizes the OPEN specification options and the use of the OPEN statement for establishing the connection of files with Fortran units.

The STATUS = specification is shown in every instance in Figure 14.6 and its use is recommended. However it may be omitted, in which case the computing system supplies an implementation-dependent status. In many cases the supplied status will be the same as specified in Figure 14.6. In every instance where a string constant is shown in Figure 14.6, any character expression may be used. The most useful such case is the use of a character variable for '<file name>', which allows the <file name>

OPEN (<unit-number>,<list-of-optional-specifications>)

Table of optional specifications for opening:	SAM files	DAM files
an existing file, catalogued under name '<file-name>' (without error-recovery)	FILE='<file-name>' STATUS='OLD'	FILE='<file-name>' STATUS='OLD' ACCESS='DIRECT' RECL=<record-length> FORM='FORMATTED'
with error-recovery add:	IOSTAT=<integer- variable>	IOSTAT=<integer- variable>
a new file, cataloguing it under name '<file-name>' (without error-recovery)	FILE='<file-name>' STATUS='NEW'	FILE='<file-name>' STATUS='NEW' ACCESS='DIRECT' RECL=<record-length> FORM='FORMATTED'
with error-recovery add:	IOSTAT=<integer- variable>	IOSTAT=<integer- variable>
a scratch file (without error-recovery)	STATUS='SCRATCH'	STATUS='SCRATCH' ACCESS='DIRECT' RECL=<record-length> FORM='FORMATTED'
with error-recovery add:	IOSTAT=<interger- variable>	IOSTAT=<integer- variable>

Part (a) -- above -- Various uses of the OPEN statement

Part (b) -- below -- List of OPEN statement specifications

form	comments
[UNIT=] <integer-expression>	specifies unit-number
FILE= <character-expression>	value is name of file
ACCESS= <character expression>	must evaluate to 'SEQUENTIAL' or 'DIRECT' (default is 'SEQUENTIAL')
STATUS= <character-expression>	must evaluate to 'OLD', 'NEW', or 'SCRATCH' (default is implementation-dependent)
RECL= <integer-expression>	required for 'DIRECT' ACCESS must be omitted for 'SEQUENTIAL' ACCESS
FORM= <character-expression>	must evaluate to 'FORMATTED' or 'UNFORMATTED' (default is 'FORMATTED' for 'SEQUENTIAL' ACCESS, 'UNFORMATTED' for 'DIRECT' ACCESS)
IOSTAT= <integer-variable>	0 assigned to <integer-variable> if no error during execution of OPEN implementation-dependent non-zero positive value assigned if error condition exists

Figure 14.6. The OPEN statement.

to be specified during program execution. (Thus, for example, the desired <file name> may be supplied as input during program execution.) In the RECL= specification, <record length> may be any integer expression; and in the IOSTAT= specification, <integer variable> must be the name of an integer variable. In any opening of a SAM file, ACCESS='SEQUENTIAL' and/or FORM='FORMATTED' may be included if desired. (A final option in the OPEN statement, the BLANK= specification, is discussed in Chapter 15.)

14.3.2 Closing Files

A file connected to a unit may be disconnected from that unit. This is necessary:

1 If the unit is to be connected to another file.

2 If the file is to be connected to another unit.

3 If the file is to be reopened in another form.

4 At the end of program execution.

The CLOSE statement causes disconnection of a file from a unit, and the simplest and most common form of the CLOSE statement is

```
CLOSE (<unit number>)
```

As with the OPEN statement, UNIT= may optionally precede <unit number>. Closing a unit that does not exist, or has no file connected to it, has no effect and causes no error. A unit that has been closed may be subsequently reopened in the same program, to either the same or a different file, and a file that has been disconnected from a unit may be subsequently reconnected, either to the same or a different unit. Closing a file is also global to a system of programs, and may occur in a different program than the one in which the file was opened.

When the above CLOSE statement is used to close a file opened with status 'OLD' or 'NEW' that file is automatically kept as a catalogued file on the storage device, and may be subsequently reopened in any program as an old file. Scratch files are automatcially deleted when closed. The existence status of a file after disconnection, either kept or deleted, may appear explicitly as an optional specification in the CLOSE statement, however. This option takes the form of

STATUS='KEEP'   or   STATUS='DELETE'

and the above CLOSE statement is equivalent to

```
CLOSE(<unit number>,STATUS='KEEP')       for named files; and
CLOSE(<unit number>,STATUS='DELETE')     for scratch files.
```

The status 'DELETE' may be specified for named files if the programmer wants this file deleted upon disconnection; closing any file with a STATUS='DELETE' terminates the existence of the file. On the other hand, scratch files may not be kept after disconnection, and specifying STATUS='KEEP' for such files causes an error condition. The general form of the status specification is STATUS=<character expression>, and any value of <character expression> other than 'KEEP' or 'DELETE' also causes an error. Recovery from such an error may be accomplished by use of the IOSTAT= optional specification, which functions for the CLOSE statement exactly as it does for the OPEN statement. And also as with the OPEN statement, if an error occurs and the IOSTAT= option is not specified then execution of the program terminates.

Thus the list of specifications in the CLOSE statement must include the <unit number> being closed, and may optionally include two additional items: the STATUS= and IOSTAT= specifications. In most instances, however, only the <unit number> is needed, in which case named files are automatically kept and scratch files are deleted. Any file not closed, by execution of a CLOSE statement, is automatically closed upon termination of program execution; the effect is the same as if a

CLOSE(<unit number>)

statement had been executed just prior to termination of program execution.

14.3.3 Preconnected Files

At the beginning of execution of any Fortran program there are two units that are automatically preconnected by the system, and need not be opened in the program. These are the units used by the

READ <format>, <input list>
PRINT <format>, <output list>

(where <format> may be "*") employed since Chapters 1 and 2. The lines of output produced by the PRINT * statement may be considered to be records of a file "on" the printing device. This is a preconnected sequential file, and each execution of a PRINT* statement writes a new record (the next line) on this file. Similarly a sequential file is preconnected "on" an input device, and execution of a READ * statement reads the next record from this file. If the user is at a terminal, for example, this next record is the line of input typed by the user.

The preconnection of units for the normal program input and output is determined and performed by the computing system at the time the program is initiated, and is completely transparent (i.e., unnoticed and of no concern) to the programmer. Which devices are used for these files depends on the user's "location": if the user is at an interactive terminal then both the input and output files are preconnected to that device; if the user submits a program to the batch stream, the input file is normally preconnected to the card reader and the output file is normally preconnected to the line printer.

If the Fortran units are configured on the system as in Figure 14.5, for example, unit 1 is the preconnected unit for both input and output if the job is initiated from a terminal. Then

PRINT <format>, <output list>
is equivalent to WRITE (1,<format>) <output list>

If the asterisk option for formatting is chosen, then

PRINT *, <output list>
is equivalent to WRITE (1,*) <output list>

Similarly,

READ *, <input list>
is equivalent to READ (1,*) <input list>

If the program is submitted to the batch stream then unit 3 is preconnected as the input file and unit 4 is preconnected as the output file (again assuming device configurations as in Figure 14.5), and in this event

PRINT *, <output list>
is equivalent to WRITE (4,*) <output list>

and

READ *, <input list>
is equivalent to READ (3,*), <input list>

In any event Fortran permits the preconnected files to be specified by an "*" for the unit number. Thus

```
                     READ *, <input list>
is equivalent to     READ (*,*) <input list>

and                  PRINT *, <output list>
is equivalent to     WRITE (*,*) <output list>

and                  PRINT <format>, <output list>
is equivalent to     WRITE (*,<format>) <output list>
```

Whenever an "*" is used in place of the unit number in a file READ or WRITE statement the system automatically assumes the preconnected unit number. Thus all of the input/output statements used in the preceding chapters are really convenient special forms of Fortran's powerful file I/O provisions.

14.4 File Inquiry

Fortran has an extensive file inquiry feature that allows the program to ascertain certain properties about any file or unit. Among the questions that can be answered by the inquiry feature are the following:

1 Does a certain file exist?

2 Does a certain unit exist?

3 Is a certain file currently opened?

4 Is a certain unit currently connected to a file?

5 To what unit is a certain file connected, if open?

6 Is the file connected to a given unit a named file or a scratch file?

7 What is the name of the file connected to a certain unit, if the unit is connected?

8 Is a certain connection for SAM or DAM?

9 For a certain file is SAM allowed?

10 For a certain file is DAM allowed?

11 Has a certain file been opened as formatted or unformatted?

12 May a certain file be opened as formatted?

13 May a certain file be opened as unformatted?

14 What is the record length of a file connected for direct access?

15 What is the record number of the last record accessed in an opened DAM file?

File inquiry can be used to prevent errors from occurring during the opening, reading, and writing of files.

A single statement, the INQUIRE statement, provides the Fortran inquiry feature. The INQUIRE statement has two forms, one for inquiry about a certain file and one for inquiry about a certain unit. These two forms are, respectively,

```
INQUIRE (FILE='<file name>', <list of inquiry specifiers>)
INQUIRE ([UNIT=]<unit number>, <list of inquiry specifiers>)
```

One or more elements in any order, from the following set of inquiry specifiers makes up the <list of inquiry specifiers>:

EXIST = <logical variable>

OPENED = <logical variable>

NUMBER = <integer variable>

NAMED = <logical variable>

NAME = <character variable>

ACCESS = <character variable>

SEQUENTIAL = <character variable>

DIRECT = <character variable>

FORM = <character variable>

FORMATTED = <character variable>

UNFORMATTED = <character variable>

RECL = <integer variable>

NEXTREC = <integer variable>

BLANK = <character variable>

IOSTAT = <integer variable>

The IOSTAT= specifier serves the same purpose as in the OPEN and CLOSE statements. Each of the other options specifies a variable (or array element) that is to be defined during execution of the INQUIRE statement with a value that tells something about the file or unit being inquired about, as summarized in Figure 14.7.

As is clear from Figure 14.7, the INQUIRE statement may be used to obtain virtually any relevant information about a file or unit concerning connection properties and valid I/O operations. Suppose, for example, that it is desired to know if a file named 'QUIRK' exists and may be opened for sequential access, the statement

```
INQUIRE (FILE='QUIRK',EXIST=QEX,SEQUENTIAL=QSEQ)
```

where QEX is a logical variable and QSEQ is a character variable, may be used to supply this information. This information could then be used to control opening of 'QUIRK' as follows:

```
if QEX then
        if QSEQ eq 'YES' then
                OPEN (<unit number>,FILE='QUIRK',STATUS='OLD')
            else
                PRINT *, 'File QUIRK can not be a SAM file.'
        endif
    else
        PRINT *, 'File QUIRK does not exist.'
endif
```

As another example, suppose that it is desired to know if unit number 8 is connected to a direct file, and if so what the file name and record length are. Execution of the statement

```
INQUIRE (UNIT=8,OPENED=OP8,NAMED=NMD8,NAME=FNAME,
                                    ACCESS=FACC,RECL=FRL)
```

INQUIRE option	resulting variable value for file inquiry:	resulting variable value for unit inquiry:
EXIST=	.TRUE. if file exists, .FALSE. otherwise	.TRUE. if unit exists, .FALSE. otherwise
OPENED=	.TRUE. if file is currently connected to a unit, .FALSE. otherwise	.TRUE. if unit is currently connected to a file, .FALSE. otherwise
NUMBER=	the unit number of the unit to which the file is currently connected undefined if file is not currently connected	not useful
NAMED=	not useful	.TRUE. if connected file is a named file, .FALSE. if connected file is a scratch file, undefined if no file is currently connected to this unit
NAME=	not useful	the name of the connected file, if the unit is connected to a named file, undefined otherwise
ACCESS=	'SEQUENTIAL' if file is connected as a SAM file, 'DIRECT' if the file is connected as a DAM file undefined otherwise	'SEQUENTIAL' if the unit is connected to a SAM file, 'DIRECT' if the unit is connected to a DAM file undefined otherwise
SEQUENTIAL=	'YES' if the file exists and may be opened as a SAM file, 'NO' if the file exists and may not be opened as a SAM file, 'UNKNOWN' otherwise	not generally useful -- applies to file connected to unit
DIRECT=	'YES' if the file exists and may be opened as a DAM file, 'NO' if the file exists and may not be opened as a DAM file, 'UNKNOWN' otherwise	not generally useful -- applies to file connected to unit
FORM=	'FORMATTED' if the file is connected for formatted I/O, 'UNFORMATTED' if the file is connected for unformatted I/O, undefined otherwise	'FORMATTED' if the unit is connected to a file for formatted I/O, 'UNFORMATTED' if the unit is connected to a file for unformatted I/O, undefined otherwise
FORMATTED=	'YES' if the file exists and may be opened as a formatted file, 'NO' if the file exists and may not be opened as a formatted file, 'UNKNOWN' otherwise	not generally useful -- applies to file connected to unit
UNFORMATTED=	'YES' if the file exists and may be opened as an unformatted file 'NO' if the file exists and may not be opened as an unformatted file, 'UNKNOWN' otherwise	not generally useful -- applies to file connected to unit.

```
-----------------------------------------------------------------------
RECL=             record length, if the        record length if the unit
                     file is connected for        is connected to a DAM
                     direct access,               file,
                  undefined otherwise          undefined otherwise
-----------------------------------------------------------------------
NEXTREC=          n+1, where n is the record   n+1, where n is the record
                     number of the record         number of the record
                     involved in the last         involved in the last
                     I/O operation (n is          I/O operation on the file
                     zero if no I/O               connected to this unit
                     operations have              (n is zero if no I/O
                     occurred since the file      operations have occurred
                     was opened),                 since this unit was
                  undefined if the file is        connected to the file),
                     not connected for         undefined if the unit is
                     direct access                not connected to a
                                                  DAM file.
-----------------------------------------------------------------------
BLANK=            'NULL' if null blank         'NULL' if null blank
                     control is in effect         control is in effect
                     for this file,               for the file connected
(see next chapter 'ZERO' if zero blank            to this unit,
for discussion       control is in             'ZERO' if zero blank control
of blank control)    effect for this file,        is in effect for the file
                     undefined otherwise          connected to this unit,
                                                  undefined otherwise
-----------------------------------------------------------------------
IOSTAT=           Same as in the OPEN and CLOSE statements.
-----------------------------------------------------------------------
```

Figure 14.7. The function of the INQUIRE statement specifier options.

will provide this informaion, and the following statements will print it.

```
if OP8 then
        if FACC eq 'DIRECT' then
            if NMD8 then
                PRINT *, 'DAM File ', FNAME, 'on unit 8,',
                                            ' with record-length ', FRL
              else
                PRINT *, 'DAM scratch file on unit 8,',
                                            ' with record-length ', FRL
            endif
          else
            PRINT *, 'Sequential file opened on unit 8.'
        endif
    else
        PRINT *, 'Unit 8 not connected to a file.'
endif
```

The INQUIRE statement is, of course, an executable statement, and may appear any number of times among the executable statements of any Fortran program.

14.5 Internal Files

The data files described thus far in this chapter exist on storage devices, such as magnetic tapes and disks, external to the program and its main memory data elements. Such files are therefore called "external" data files, and the above described features (OPEN, READ, WRITE, etc.) are used to establish "lines of communication" between the program and external files. Normal processing of such files involves transferring and processing a single record at a time—each record is individually transferred between the external file and the main memory data elements that represent the fields of the record. Thus file processing typically involves a large amount of data transfer between main memory and external devices, with appropriate data conversions taking place during such transfer.

In certain data file situations the record format (field structure) may not be known prior to each file input operation, and thus conversion of the record data to the proper internal form must take place after the record has been transferred to main memory. In addition, file processing may often be expedited by reading and writing records in "blocks" of several records at a time. Both of these situations may be accommodated by *buffering*. Buffering involves an intermediate storage area, called a buffer, in main memory for the (block of) record(s), as shown in Figure 14.8. Records are read from (written to) the external file to (from) the buffer area with little or no conversion. Then another transfer takes place prior to processing the record data, this time from the buffer area to field data elements, with conversion of the data to the appropriate internal forms.

Most computing systems employ some buffering for file I/O in such a way that it is completely transparent to the Fortran programmer. However, Fortran allows the programmer to specify and control any additional buffering operations. In the following discussion on buffering, and in the next chapter, the term "buffering" is used to refer to programmer-controlled buffering.

When using buffering, effectively two "read" operations are required to input a record from an external file—the first to transfer the record data into the buffer and the second to convert and transfer the buffer contents to the field elements for processing. Similarly outputting external record data using buffering involves two "write" operations—the first to convert and transfer the field data into the buffer and the second to transfer the buffer contents to the external file. In Fortran such a buffer area is also called an *internal file*, since it is a data area in main memory upon which file read and write operations are performed. Data transfer between an internal file and the record field elements are internal main memory data transfers and hence very fast compared to data transfers from external files to main memory. Internal files facilitate efficient data transfer from external files to main memory, and make convenient the conversion of data to (from) the desired field structure. A READ statement specifying an internal file, rather than an external file, causes the second transfer illustrated in Figure 14.8; a WRITE statement specifying an internal file causes field data to be transferred from the field elements to the buffer area. READs and WRITEs on internal files must be sequential formatted I/O operations. The OPEN, CLOSE, and INQUIRE operations do not apply, and are not allowed, on internal files. In addition, internal files are always positioned at their "beginnings" and the REWIND, BACKSPACE, and ENDFILE operations may not be used on them.

Internal files are merely CHARACTER data elements—variables, arrays, or array elements of type CHARACTER, or substrings. Any such data element is being used as an internal file when it is specified as the <file id> in a sequential file READ or WRITE operation. There is nothing "special" about such a data element—it is an ordinary

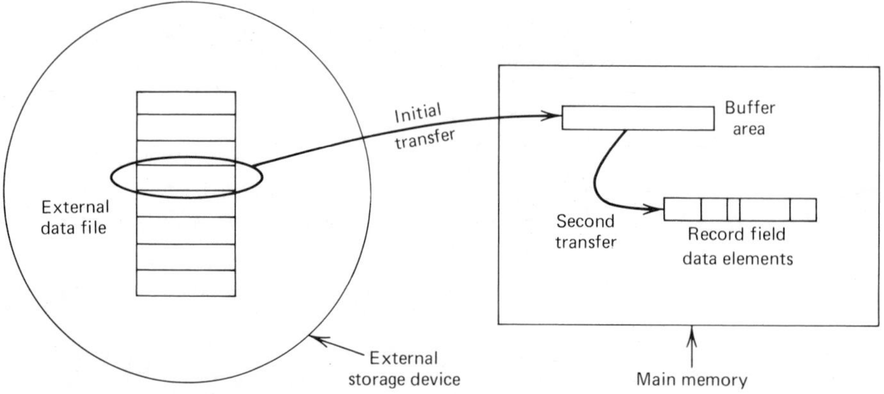

Figure 14.8. Data file input using a buffer area.

CHARACTER data element that can be used freely as such. It's just that any CHARACTER data element may also be used as an internal file. In using input buffering the CHARACTER data element being used as a buffer is an ordinary receiving field in the first READ operation (moving the record data from the external file to main memory). In the second READ the CHARACTER data element is used as the internal file being read. Supposed that BUFFER is declared as

CHARACTER BUFFER*72

and that each record in the external file (having <unit number> FILE) is a formatted DAM file with a record length of 72 characters. Then execution of

```
READ (FILE,'(A)',REC=<record number>) BUFFER
```

will transfer the data from the specified record in FILE into BUFFER. And then execution of

```
READ (BUFFER,<format>) <field list>
```

will transfer the data in BUFFER to the elements of <field list>, with the conversions specified by <format>. The effect of these two READ statements is precisely the same as the single statement

READ (FILE,<format>,REC=<record number>) <field list>

except that in addition BUFFER has a copy of the FILE record contents. Note that in the first READ of the two-READ pair, BUFFER is used as an ordinary CHARACTER variable, but in the second it is used as an internal file. The actual reading of the external file is done in the first READ, and the second READ is merely a conversion of the record characters according to the specified format and transfer of the values into the various field variables. Figure 14.9 summarizes the concept of buffer use in Fortran.

The usefulness of buffering is not readily apparent from the discussion in this section. The intent here is to illustrate the Fortran mechanisms for achieving buffering. The importance and practical applications of buffering are described in the next chapter, in the section entitled "Buffered File I/O".

(a) READ (FILE,'(A)',REC=<record-number>) BUFFER
READ (BUFFER,<format>) <field-list>

equivalent to
READ (FILE,<format>,REC=<record-number>) <field-list>

(b) WRITE (BUFFER,<format>) <field-list>
WRITE (FILE,'(A)',REC=<record-number>) BUFFER

equivalent to:
WRITE (FILE,<format>,REC=<record-number>) <field-list>

Figure 14.9. Examples of buffered I/O. FILE is <unit number> of a formatted DAM file. BUFFER is a CHARACTER data element. (*a*) Typical buffered input. (*b*) Typical buffered output.

14.5 Summary

Large amounts of data used in computer processing are normally organized into data files residing on external storage devices, such as magnetic tapes and disks. Processing such files of data involves the transferring of the data, usually record by record, into the data elements of main memory that represent the individual fields of a file record. The processing is performed on these field elements, and the updated record value, if any, is then transferred back to the storage device. READ statements cause data to be transferred from a file to data elements in main memory; WRITE statements cause data to be transferred from main memory to a file.

In order that the program may successfully access a file, means are provided in Fortran to connect the file to the program. Input/output units are available to which READ and WRITE statements may make reference; the OPEN statement causes an association (connection) between a unit and a data file. The CLOSE statement may be used to disconnect a file from a unit. In order to facilitate the error-free connecting and accessing of data files, Fortran has an INQUIRE statement that can be used to determine the existence, connection, structural, and other properties of a file.

Two forms of access are available for external data files—sequential access and direct access. The records of a sequential file must be processed in sequential order, from the first record to the last one. Records of a direct file may be processed in any order, and each I/O operation on a direct file must specify the sequence number of the record involved in the operation. Limited forms of positioning may be achieved in sequential files with the REWIND and BACKSPACE statement, and an end-of-file record may be written on sequential files with the ENDFILE statement.

CHARACTER data elements may be used as internal files in main memory so that data conversions may be conveniently made with sequential READ and WRITE statements.

The important concepts of this chapter are:

1 External storage of data files.
2 Sequential access of data files.
3 Record Numbers.
4 Direct access of data files.
5 Fortran I/O units.
6 File connection.
7 The global nature of file connection.
8 Preconnected files.
9 File positioning.
10 Reading file records.
11 Writing file records.
12 File and unit inquiry.
13 Buffers and internal files.

The Fortran statements introduced in this chapter are as follows. All are executable statements.

1 READ (for formatted sequential files).
2 READ (for formatted direct files).
3 WRITE (for formatted sequential files).
4 WRITE (for formatted direct files).

5 ENDFILE
6 REWIND
7 BACKSPACE

} all for sequential files.

8 OPEN.
9 CLOSE.
10 INQUIRE.

This chapter introduced the important data file concepts and illustrated the Fortran mechanisms pertaining to these concepts. Chapter 15 details the provisions Fortran has for handling file I/O, and presents a number of example programs involving file processing.

Chapter 15 File I/O

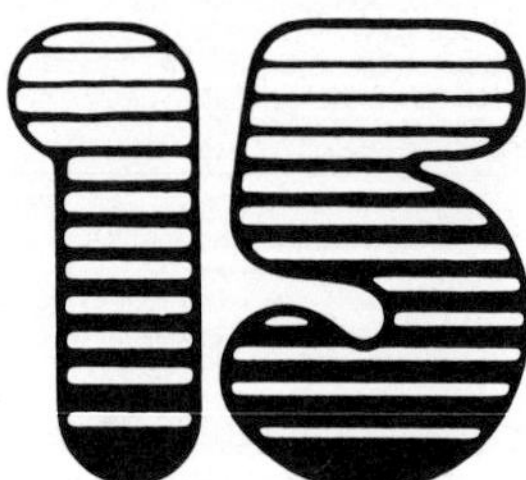

Data files are processed by transferring the data, record by record, into data elements in main memory which represent the file record fields. The data transferred to these fields is then processed in the desired manner by the program (using the Fortran assignment statements and control structures). New records generated by the processing, are then transferred back to the appropriate file(s). The actual processing of the data is done by Fortran programs using the techniques discussed throughout this book. A major aspect of file processing involves no actual processing of the data, but is of critical importance to the correct and efficient processing of the data. This aspect is the necessary transfer—the input/output—of the data between the external storage unit and the program (main memory). It is typically by no means a trivial aspect of processing data files. In fact, often programs dealing with data files are rather dominated by the file I/O considerations, rather than by the actual data processing algorithms, and usually the execution of such programs are heavily "I/O bound" rather than "compute bound" (most of the actual execution time is spent performing the data transfers rather than the data processing).

There are three principal components to the effective transfer of data between external media and the program. The first is data conversion. The external form of the data is in general different from the form used in the numerical and nonnumerical storage units of Fortran's data elements, and the I/O operations must perform the appropriate conversions. There is a wide range of possibilities for the external form of the data, and the programmer must therefore take care to specify the proper conversion for file I/O operations. If the data conversion is incorrect, even in the slightest way, either the processing of the data will be incorrect or file output will not be as intended.

The second principal component of practical file I/O techniques is the efficiency of data transfer between the external media and the program. The speed at which such data transfer can be made is limited by several things, including the following:

1 The amount of conversion needed in the form of the data.

2 The mechanical speed limitations of the external storage devices.

3 The amount of data involved in each I/O operation.

Although the programmer has no control over the second of these items, Fortran provides the programmer almost complete control over the other two. Both of these items can have dramatic effects on file I/O efficiency.

And, finally, the possibility of file I/O errors can be of considerable concern. Without special provision for recovery from such errors, their occurrence, in most cases, causes termination of program execution. This often is highly undesirable in the processing of a large data file, as the processing could terminate at some "random" point, leaving part of the file processed and part unprocessed. In the worst of such cases the file data may, for all practical purposes, be no longer useful. Fortran has provisions to allow the programmer to specify any desired recovery procedures in the event of a file I/O error.

If any of these aspects of file I/O—data conversion, transfer efficiency, or error recovery—is the most important, it would have to be data conversion. This is because no successful file processing can be achieved without the appropriate data conversion during file I/O operations. Therefore most of this chapter concerns matters related to data conversion, and their implementation in Fortran. However, the chapter is devoted to a detailed examination of all of Fortran's features for performing file I/O, which includes those features related to transfer efficiency and file I/O error recovery. The chapter ends with several complete examples of the use of Fortran for processing external data files.

15.1 Formatted I/O

The most common form of file I/O is formatted I/O. In this form of I/O each record in the data file is simply a string of characters—as if the record consisted of only a single field of type CHARACTER having the same length as the record. Reading such a record into a CHARACTER data element would involve minimal, if any, conversion. The string of characters in the record may, however, represent the field values for any desired field structure for the record. Consider, for example, the following string of 32 characters, which could be the data contained in a certain record of a file:

```
M43282REDOAKS,JY0010.5542.7
```

Although this appears as a single string of characters in the record, its meaning may in fact be

M43282RE	DOAKS,JY	10.55	42.7
Employee ID	Employee name	Hourly wage	Hours worked

Thus the string of 27 characters represents the data for four fields: employee J. Y. Doaks has employee number M43282RE, earns $10.55 per hour, and has worked 42.7 hours this week. The single string of 27 characters must be converted into these four fields in order for this record to be processed (e.g., to generate this week's paycheck for J. Y. Doaks). The string of file characters '42.7', for example, must be converted into the proper form for the real value 42.7 in a numeric storage unit in order that the pay rate may be used in calculating the week's wages.

Thus formatted I/O involves converting data from its representation in Fortran's storage units to a corresponding string of characters, and vice versa. For processing by the Fortran program the data must be in the form used by Fortran's numeric and nonnumeric internal storage units. But there is a reason, of paramount importance, why the records in exernal data files should consist simply of strings of characters. This reason is the universality of character strings for communication. Humans can read data, reasonably well, if it is in some suitable character string form. Any program, or any computer, in any language, can read character strings and convert them into any desired internal form. The internal form that the programming language Cobol, say, uses for real numbers is different than the form used by Fortran. Even Fortran's numeric storage units are implementation dependent and the numeric storage unit on one computer may be quite different from that on another computer. If data file records were always in internal form then it would be difficult to process a data file with a program written in another language, or even with a Fortran program on another machine. Character strings are the "common denominator" for data file records, which allows a file to be a rather independent and widely useful collection of data. The price one pays for this flexibility is the need to convert input from data files from a string of characters into the appropriate internal form, and to convert output to files from the internal form to a string of characters. This conversion will, in most implementations, be fairly minimal for Fortran's nonnumeric storage units, since the internal form of character strings will usually be similar, if not identical, to that used in the external file. However, extensive conversion is required between character strings and numeric storage units.

Fortran performs all such conversions automatically when the programmer supplies the information as to what conversions to make. That is, the programmer must indicate which characters from an input record are to be converted to integer values, double precision values, etc., and on output the programmer must specify how many characters are to be used to represent a numeric value, and where these characters are to be placed in the character string comprising the output record. This is all accomplished with the <format specification> in READ and WRITE (and PRINT) statements. The concept of a <format specification> was introduced in Chapter 1, and throughout the book simple examples of <format specification>s have been used. This section summarizes the extensive Fortran features for formatting file I/O. You may find reviewing Section 1.3 worthwhile before proceeding further in this section.

15.1.1 Format Specifications

Format specifications appear in formatted input/output statments, which are the only type of I/O statements discussed thus far. The context in which format specifications appear in these statements is summarized in Figure 15.1 for READs and WRITEs on both SAM and DAM files. Note that FMT= may optionally precede the <format specification>. If the FMT= is used, and the optional UNIT= is also used with the unit number, then the order of the various items, (UNIT=, FMT=, IOSTAT=, REC=) is immaterial. If FMT= is not used, then UNIT= must also not be used, and the order of the items must be as shown in Figure 15.1. In the special forms for input and output on the preconnected units

READ <format>, <input list>
PRINT <format>, <output list>

the FMT= is not allowed. These two statements are equivalent, however, to the sequential file I/O statements

READ (*, <format>) <input list>
WRITE (*, <format>) <output list>

and the FMT= option is permitted in these latter forms. Since there are so many optional forms for file I/O statements, to minimize confusion a consistent convention

SAM file READ (on pre-connected unit)	READ (<unit>,<format>) <input-list> equivalent { READ <format-specification>, <input-list> { READ (*,<format>) <input-list>
SAM file WRITE (on preconnected unit)	WRITE (<unit>,<format>) <output-list> equivalent { PRINT <format-specification>, <output-list> { WRITE (*,<format>) <output-list>
DAM file READ	READ (<unit>,<format>,REC=<number>) <input-list>
DAM file WRITE	WRITE (<unit>,<format>,REC=<number>) <output-list>
<format>	[FMT=] <format-specification>

Figure 15.1. Forms of the formatted file READ and WRITE statements. Any of the above I/O operations may include an IOSTAT= option in the specifications list to provide for error recovery. (In addition, IOSTAT= may be used for end-of-file detection in SAM READs.

is adopted for all following examples. This convention is that the order of items in parentheses following READ and WRITE is that shown in Figure 15.1. The optional UNIT= phrase will not be used, but the FMT= phrase will be used. The "file forms" (with asterisks as unit numbers) of the READ and PRINT will be used for the preconnected units.

The <format specification> can take several forms. The form used the most thus far has been "*", which specifies list-directed formatting and is discussed further in Section 15.2 below. The other common forms are:

1 A string constant.

2 A CHARACTER data element name.

3 The statement label of a FORMAT statement.

In each case a list of format descriptors that describe the nature of the data conversions between the file record and the elements of the field list is specified. In all forms the list of format descriptors is enclosed in parentheses, and thus form (1), string constant, is

'(<list of format descriptors>)'

In form 2, CHARACTER data element name, the value of the data element at the time the statement is executed must begin (except for leading blanks) with "(", end (except for trailing blanks) with ")", and contain the list of format-descriptors in between. If form 3, statement label, is used, then the label must be that of a FORMAT statement:

<label> FORMAT (<list of format descriptors>)

The FORMAT statement is considered to be a specification statement, and not an executable statement, but it may be located anywhere in the program.

Of the above three forms for a <format specification> the second, a CHARACTER data element name, is the most flexible since it allows the format to be determined during program execution. Thus, for example, the first record of a file might contain the format of the file records, rather than any of the principal data of the file; at the beginning of processing of the file this format can be read into a character variable and then used as the format for reading, and/or writing, the rest of the file. Such a variable could also be initialized in a DATA statement, and its value may be changed prior to using it as a format. (If the character data element is a string constant name, whose value is specified in a PARAMETER statement, then of course the value cannot be changed.) Forms of the <format specification> less common than the above three are provided by Fortran. These are (1) a CHARACTER array name, (2) a character expression, and (3) an integer variable whose value (acquired by execution of an ASSIGN statement) is the statement label of a FORMAT statement. Again there are many options, and for the sake of simplicity and consistency option 2 of the above list is used in most of the subsequent examples. Of course, the "*" is used for list-directed formatting.

15.1.2 Data Descriptors

Data descriptors are elements of the <list of format descriptors> and specify the nature of data conversion. There must be one data descriptor for each field in the input or output list, and data descriptors and field elements are associated in the left-to-right manner described in Chapter 1. If there are more data descriptors than fields in the I/O list then the extra descriptors are ignored, if there are more field elements than data descriptors then the format list is reused, starting with the rightmost opening parenthesis that is not encompassed by a repeat number (see below), until the I/O list is satisfied. The different categories of data descriptors, and hence of data conversion, are for:

1 Character data.

2 Logical data.

3 Integer data.

4 Real, double precision, and complex data.

15.1.2.1 Character Data Conversion

Conversion between formatted records and character data fields is usually the simplest, both in terms of the data descriptors needed and the complexity of the conversion. Data descriptors associated with character field I/O have two forms:

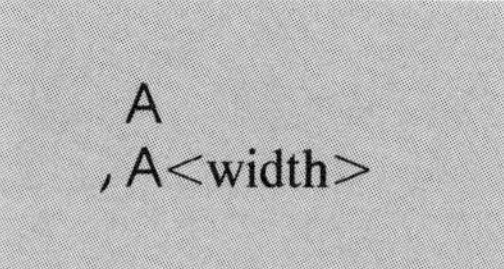

The <width>, which must be an unsigned nonzero integer constant, specifies the number of characters (positions) this field is to occupy in the file record. If the option without <width> is used then a value is assumed for <width> equal to the number of characters in (length of) the associated field element. In formatted I/O each character data element in the field list must be associated with an A-data descriptor.

On input, the A[<width>] data descriptor specifies that the next <width> characters of the record are to be transferred to the associated character field in the input list. This is treated exactly like a character assignment operation, except that any necessary conversion from external character form to internal character form (nonnumerical storage units) is automatically performed. If an explicitly specified <width> is different from the length of the field element, then the extra or missing characters are treated as in a character assignment, from the specified record positions to the field data element.

On output the A[<width>] data descriptor specifies that the value (characters) of the associated output list element is to be transferred to the next <width> positions of the record. If <width> is different from the length of the field element then the result is the same as a character assignment from the field element to the specified record positions.

15.1.2.2 Logical Data Conversion

Conversion between formatted records and logical data fields is also rather simple to specify and perform. Essentially all the programmer need do is to specify the number of positions (characters) the logical value is allocated in the file record. Each logical field element in an I/O list must be associated with an L data descriptor:

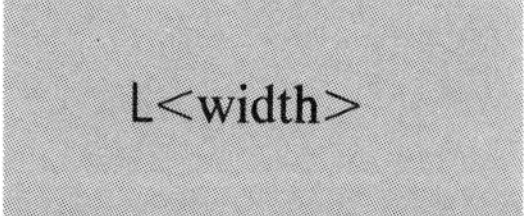

The <width> must be given, and specifies the number of positions this field is allocated in the file record. As with the A-data descriptor, the L-data descriptor <width> is an unsigned nonzero integer constant.

On input the L data descriptor causes a search for the first (leftmost) nonblank characters in the next <width> positions of the file record. If these are "T" or ".T" then the corresponding input list element is assigned the value .TRUE.; if the first (nonblank) characters are "F" or ".F" then the field element is assigned the value .FALSE.; any other initial characters in the record field result in an input error. Any characters may follow T, .T, F, or .F without affecting the value assigned to the element in the input list. Note in particular that this allows T, TRUE, .T., .TRUE. to be used as .TRUE. input values, and F, FALSE, .F., .FALSE. to be used as .FALSE. input values.

On output the L data descriptor causes a "T" or an "F" to be right justified in the next <width> positions of the file record, depending on whether the corresponding field element in the output list has value .TRUE. or .FALSE., respectively. (Blanks are placed in the leftmost <width>-1 positions.) Note that on output the L data descriptor never needs a <width> value greater than 1, and on input a <width> of 1 is also sufficient.

15.1.2.3 Integer Data Conversion

Specifying integer conversion for formatted I/O is similar in form to specifying character and logical conversions. The actual conversion process, however, is more complex since conversion must be made between a string of characters in the record and the internal form for integers in numerical storage units (see Appendix C). All integer field elements in I/O lists must be associated with I data descriptors:

```
I<width>
```

Again <width> is an unsigned positive integer constant, and specifies the number of characters representing the integer value in the file record. These characters are limited to blanks, decimal digits, and signs ("+" or "−"). At most one sign character is allowed, with no digits to the left of it in the record field and at least one digit to the right. The record field may be all blanks, in which case it is interpreted as representing the value zero. Note that a decimal point is not allowed.

On input the I data descriptor specifies that the characters in the next <width> positions of the record are interpreted as an integer value represented in ordinary integer decimal form (without a decimal point). The equivalent internal form value is assigned to the associated integer field element in the input list. Normally the digits in the record representing the value are right justified in the field, with no interspersed blanks. Leading blanks (on the left) are always ignored. If blank characters are interspersed among the digits, or trail the digits, in the record then such blanks may be either ignored or treated as if they were zero digits. The normal rule is that they are ignored, that is, as if they didn't exist and the digits were right justified without intervening blanks. However, if the file had been OPENed with BLANK='ZERO' included with the connection specifications then each interspersed and trailing blank would be treated as if it were a zero.

On output the I data descriptor causes the integer value of the associated output-list element to be converted to the appropriate string of decimal digits and placed right justified in the next <width> character positions of the file record. If the value is negative, a "−" sign is placed in the position just to the left of the string of digits (i.e., in the "normal" position for a sign). If <width> is too small to hold all of the nonblank characters of the integer value then the entire record field is filled with asterisks. Normally an integer output value has all leading zeros replaced by blanks, except that the value zero is represented by a single (right justified) zero. The programmer may optionally specify the minimum number of decimal digits to appear in the record, however, and this can be used to either cause leading zeros to be placed in the record or to cause all blanks to be used for the value zero. The I data descriptor may be extended in the form

```
I<width>.<num digits>
```

where <num digits> is an unsigned integer constant specifying the minimum number of decimal digits to appear in the record. The valid range for <num digits> is 0 to <width>, inclusive. Examples of this form of I data descriptor are:

1. I10.5 will write 34 as 00034
   and −34 as −00034

   (leading blanks complete the field of 10 characters)
2. I4.0 will write 0 as four blanks
3. I6.6 will write 2792 as 002792

Thus the complete description of the I data descriptor is

```
I<width>[.<num digits>]
```

If the optional part is omitted a value of .1 is assumed. The optional part is useful only for output, and has no effect on input operations.

15.1.2.4 Real, Double Precision, and Complex Data Conversions

The most complicated conversions to make are those involving real numeric values, which include elements of type REAL, DOUBLEPRECISION, and COMPLEX. These are also the most difficult to specify since there are many typical ways to represent real numeric values as character strings, and Fortran accommodates several of these. There are two basic data descriptors for real values, and four additional variations of these that are occasionally useful. All apply to the I/O of either real or double precision or complex data, with one such data descriptor being associated with each real or double precision element and two used for each complex element (one for the real part and the second for the imaginary part).

The two basic data descriptors for real values have the forms

```
F<width>.<decimal places>
E<width>.<decimal places>
```

The F descriptor causes real values to be represented in the record by a string of characters in "ordinary decimal" form,

```
[<sign>]<integer part>.<fractional part>
```

whereas the E descriptor causes real values to be represented in the record by a string of characters in "normalized scientific" form,

[<sign>][0].<significant digits>E<sign><exponent>

In both descriptors the <width> is an unsigned integer constant specifying the number of characters the value is to use in the file record. For the F descriptor, <width> must be at least 3 (to accommodate the <sign>, decimal point, and at least one digit), and <width> for the E descriptor must be at least 8 (to accommodate the <sign> of the value, the leading 0, the decimal point, at least one digit, and four characters for the exponent (the E, the <sign>, and two decimal digits)). In the F descriptor, <decimal places> is an unsigned integer constant whose value is between 0 and <width>−3, inclusive; it specifies the number of decimal digits to be used for the <fractional part> of the representation of the real value. The interpretation of <decimal places> is similar in the E descriptor, except that the value is automatically "scaled" so that the decimal point precedes the most significant digit of the value, and the exponent value is adjusted accordingly. Thus, for example, −174.59 (in F7.2 "format") is −0.17459E+03 in E12.5 format. In E format, <decimal places> is effectively the number of significant digits of the value that are to be contained in the file record. The value of <decimal places> in this format should be between 1 and <width>−7, inclusive.

Actually, on input the F and E data descriptors are treated the same. The data on the file record may be in any form that is valid for a Fortran real or double precision value. However, if neither a decimal point nor an exponent part is present then the rightmost <decimal places> digits are assumed to represent the fractional part of the value. In addition an exponent may be represented by a signed integer constant. Thus the following are all equivalent (i.e., convert to the same real or double precision value) for F or E controlled input:

−147.59 (anywhere in the record field)

−14759 (right justified in the record field and descriptor is F7.2)

−14759E−2 (anywhere in the record field)

−1.4759D2 (anywhere in the record field)

−1.4759+2 (anywhere in the record field)

−14759−2 (anywhere in the record field)

On output the F and E descriptors produce character strings as described in the second paragraph of this subsection. These characters are placed right justified in the next <width> character positions of the file record. All fractional parts are rounded in the least-significant digit. If the field <width> is too small then the entire field is filled with asterisks. If the magnitude of the exponent value E format requires three decimal digits to express, then the exponent is represented by the four characters <sign><3 digits> rather than the usual four characters E<sign><2 digits>. Exponents requiring more than three decimal digits cause the entire record field to be filled with asterisks unless a sufficient number of digits is specified for the exponent. This is done with an optional extension of the E data descriptor:

E<width>.<decimal places>E<num exp digits>

The additional E<num exp digits>, where <num exp digits> is an unsigned integer constant, specifies the number of decimal digits to be used in the exponent. If this integer value is n then the form of the exponent is

E<sign><n digits>

and the exponent occupies n+2, rather than 4, characters in the record. (Thus E<width>.<decimal places> is equivalent to E<width>.<decimal places>E2. The extra exponent option has no effect on input.)

Another form of the E descriptor uses D instead of E:

D<width>.<decimal places>

and has the same effect as the E descriptor except that a D is used to denote the exponent rather than an E. The D form gives no extra capability, but may be preferred for double precision values. The extra exponent option is not allowed on the D form.

A rather "general" data descriptor for output of real values is rather like a combination of the F and E descriptors. This is the G data descriptor

G<width>.<decimal places>[E<num exp digits>]

and results in the production of <decimal places> significant digits of the value. If the actual location of the decimal point is within these significant digits then that is where it is placed and n+2 blanks replace the exponent part (where n is the value of <num exp digits>). In this event G format produces a representation similar to what F format would generate (with a different value for <decimal places> and not right justified), otherwise G format has the same effect as E format. On input G format has the same effect as F, E, and D formats.

To summarize, data descriptors for converting real values in file I/O have the following forms:

F<width>.<decimal places>

E<width>.<decimal places>[E<num exp digits>]

D<width>.<decimal places>

G<width>.<decimal places>[E<num exp digits>]

All are equivalent for input, and may be used successfully on record data that is a valid representation of a real, or double precision number. Although each of these data descriptors produces a different style output for real values, all such output is suitable for subsequent input with any of these data descriptors. In all cases the <width> represents the number of characters (field width) of the real value in the record for either input or output. In the E, D, and G descriptors the value of <decimal places> represents the number of significant digits to be output; in the F descriptor <decimal places> is the nummer of decimal digits to the right of the decimal point to be output.

15.1.2.5 Repeating Data Descriptors

The A, L, I, F, E, D, and G data descriptors are all *repeatable* descriptors in the sense that any may be preceded by an unsigned positive *repeat count*:

<repeat count><data descriptor>

The <repeat count> specifies the number of times the <data descriptor> is to appear in succession. Thus, for example, 4F7.2 is equivalent to

F7.2, F7.2, F7.2, F7.2

and 7A10 is equivalent to A10, A10, A10, A10, A10, A10, A10.

In addition to their use with individual data descriptors, <repeat count>s may be used to specify the repetition of a group of descriptors. In such cases the <list of descriptors> to be repeated is enclosed in parentheses, and the resulting "packet" is preceded by the <repeat count>:

<repeat count>(<list of descriptors>)

For example 3(A10,F7.2) is equivalent to

A10, F7.2, A10, F7.2, A10, F7.2

In addition to data descriptors the <list of descriptors> may contain the position and other special descriptors described in the following two sections.

15.1.3 Positional Control in File I/O

As described in Section 1.3, Fortran format specifications may contain descriptors for specifying positioning in the file record, rather than for converting data values. These are the

T<position>	(tabulate to specified position)
TL<num positions>	(tab left specified number of places)
TR<num positions>	(tab right specified number of places)
/	(begin next record)

descriptors, which are completely described in Section 1.3 and summarized in Figure 1.1. These are not repeatable, by themselves, but may appear in a repeated <list of descriptors>. Thus 3(TR9,I15) is equivalent to TR9, I15, TR9, I15, TR9, I15.

In addition to the above position descriptors Fortran allows the position descriptor

<num positions>X

which performs the same function as TR<num positions>. The "TR" form is recommended since it and the "T" and "TL" descriptors form a complete coherent facility for position control within a record.

15.1.4 Special-Purpose Format Descriptors

Fortran provides several other special-purpose descriptors (all of which are nonrepeatable, except in lists) for achieving various effects in data file I/O. The first of these are the "S" descriptors for controlling the appearance of the plus sign on numeric output. If an S, SP, or SS descriptor appears in a <format specification> of a file output operation then the remaining numeric fields (i.e., "to the right" of the S, SP, or SS) are affected as follows:

SP means the "+" sign should appear on subsequent positive numeric values.

SS means the "+" sign should not appear on subsequent positive numeric values.

S restores the option of supplying "+" signs to the processor.

At the beginning of each file output operation (statement) the processor has the option of putting a "+" on positive values, or not. The programmer may override this option with the SP and SS descriptors, and may restore the option with the S descriptor.

The second special-purpose descriptor is for "scaling" real (i.e., noninteger) numeric output, and has the form

<scale factor>P

where <scale factor> is an optionally signed integer constant. At the beginning of each file I/O operation the processor assumes that <scale factor> is zero, and appearance of the "P" descriptor in the <format specification> establishes a new value for <scale factor> until another "P" descriptor occurs in the <format specification>. The rules governing the "P" descriptor are the following:

1 On input:
   (a) The <scale-factor> has no effect if the input data contains an exponent.
   (b) Otherwise the value transferred to main memory is the value represented in the file divided by 10**<scale-factor>.

2 On output:
   (a) With F formatting the value transferred to the file is the value in main memory multiplied by 10**<scale factor>.
   (b) With E and D formatting the value is not changed, but the decimal point is shifted, <scale factor> places right (for positive scale factors) in the output, and the exponent is reduced by the amount <scale-factor>.
   (c) With G formatting the value is not changed, but if exponent form results the exponent and decimal points are adjusted as in (b).

Note that <scale factor> may be positive or negative, so that scaling can be "up" or "down". Actual scaling (i.e., changing) of values occurs only with F-formatted quantities; in other instances scaling has no effect or merely affects the position of the decimal point without changing the value.

The third set of special-purpose descriptors are the "B" descriptors, which allow further control over the interpretation of blanks in numeric input fields (the B descriptors have no effect on output operations). The two forms of these descriptors are:

BN (blanks are ignored)

BZ (blanks are treated as zeros)

The B descriptors may be used at any place in the format specification to control the interpretation of blanks in subsequently processed numeric fields in the input operation.

At the beginning of a file input operation the control in effect is determined by the BLANK= specification in the opening of the file; the default for BLANK= is BLANK='NULL', which is equivalent to the BN descriptor.

And finally Fortran allows <format specification>s to contain literal data that is to be placed in file records during output operations. Such data may be in the form of a string constant or an "H" descriptor. An H descriptor has the form

<num char>H<char string>

where <num char> is an unsigned positive integer specifying the number of characters in the string of characters <char string>. These two provisions are equivalent to placing the string of characters in the <output list>, as a string constant, and using a corresponding "A" in the <format specification>. Thus the following are all equivalent:

```
PRINT '(T2,A,F4.1,A,F7.3)', 'X=',X, 'Y=', Y
PRINT '(T2,' 'X=' ',F4.1,' 'Y=' ',F7.3)',X,Y
PRINT '(T2,2HX=,F4.1,2HY=,F7.3)',X,Y
```

The first form (which is the one used exclusively in preceding chapters) is by far the preferred one, since it is the only one of the three that doesn't "mix" in the <format specification> WHAT is being output with HOW it is being formatted. (Ideally all of the WHATs should be in the <output list>, with the <format specification> containing only the HOWs.) Because such mixes are allowed, however, the "colon descriptor" is also provided to specify termination of formatting when the output list is satisfied. The only practical function of the ":" in the <format specification> is to suppress the outputting of literal data placed in the <format specification> in the event the <output list> is exhausted before the <format specification> is.

15.1.5 Summary of Descriptors for Formatted File I/O

A <format specification> is effectively a list of descriptors that specify the form of the data on a record of a file. There are three general categories of descriptors:

Data descriptors	(which are associated with input/output list items)
Position descriptors	(fairly useful for position control)
Special-purpose descriptors	(occasionally useful)

Each of these is summarized in Figure 15.2.

In each case with the data descriptors, the <width> is the number of characters in the record to be converted for the associated element in the input or output list. One can imagine a "pointer" to a character position in the file record, with the pointer "at" the first position in the record at the beginning of execution of a READ or WRITE statement. On input the next <width> characters from the record, starting with the pointer position, are converted and transferred to main memory. After each such operation (during execution of the READ statement) the pointer is left at the position following the last one used during the operation. On output the next <width> characters of the record are written, starting with the pointer position; the pointer is left in the position following the last one written.

Thus use of each data descriptor indirectly causes positioning in the file record; the position descriptors allow direct positioning in the record so that positions may be skipped, overwritten, or reread. Any positions skipped on input are simply ignored, positions skipped on output are filled with blanks.

	Descriptor	Use
data descriptors	A[<width>]	used with CHARACTER values
	L<width>	used with LOGICAL values
	I<width>[.<num-digits<]	used with INTEGER values
	F<width>.<decimal-places>	used with REAL, DOUBLEPRECISION, and COMPLEX values
	E<width>.<decimal-places>[E<num-digits>]	
	D<width>.<decimal-places>	
	G<width>.<decimal-places>[E<num-digits>]	

	Descriptor	Use
position descriptors	T<position>	tabulate to specified position
	TL<num-positions>	tab left specified number of positions
	TR<num-positions>	tab right specified number of positions
	<num-positions>X	not recommended (but like TR)
	/	begin new record

	Descriptor	Use	
special purpose descriptors	SP	print "+" sign	only for output operations
	SS	suppress "+" signs	
	S	revert to processor sign control	
	<scale-factor>P	scaling (see section 15.1.4)	
	BN	ignore blanks	only for input operations on numbers
	BZ	treat blanks as zeros	
	'<char-string>'	print literal data (only for output operation) — not recommended	
	<num-chars>H<char-string>		
	:	suppress formatting if <output-list> exhausted (not recommended)	

Figure 15.2. Descriptors for use with formatted file I/O.

The programmer constructs <format specification>s by putting together a sequence of descriptors so as to achieve the desired formatting. Any of the descriptors of Figure 15.2 may appear in a <format specification>, in any order. All of the data descriptors are repeatable, that is, any of them may be preceded with a <repeat-count>. None of the position or special-purpose descriptors are repeatable. However, a list (sequence) of descriptors may be enclosed in parentheses and preceded by a <repeat count>; position and special-purpose descriptors may appear in such repeated lists. There must be a data descriptor, of the proper type, for each element in the <input list> or <output list>, these are associated in the normal left-to-right manner. If there are more data descriptors than I/O list elements then the extra descriptors are ignored. If there are more list elements than data descriptors then the data descriptors are "reused", starting with the first one following the rightmost opening (left) parenthesis that is not encompassed by a <repeat count>.

SAM file READ (on pre-connected unit)	READ (<unit>,FMT=*) <input-list> equivalent { READ *, <input-list> READ (*,FMT=*) <input-list>
SAM file WRITE (on pre-connected unit>	WRITE (<unit>,FMT=*) <output-list> equivalent { PRINT *, <output-list> WRITE (*,FMT=*) <output-list>

(note: the 4 characters FMT= are optional)

Figure 15.3. Forms of the list-directed file READ and WRITE statements. IOSTAT= may be used for I/O error recovery and end-of-file for READs. List-directed I/O is allowed only on sequential files.

15.2 List-Directed File I/O

List-directed I/O is formatted I/O in which the processor, rather than the programmer, supplies the formatting. The programmer uses "*" for the <format specification> to indicate list-directed I/O, as summarized in Figure 15.3. List-directed output uses processor-fixed data descriptors for logical and numeric data elements. Strings are output using A descriptors (without the <width>); logicals typically use L1 descriptors, integers use a reasonable I descriptor, and reals (and double precision and complex) use a reasonable G descriptor. The processor may separate individual data values in the record with commas or blanks—blanks are most common—and may begin new records as needed. Strings output by list-directed WRITE statements are not enclosed in quotes, and therefore are not suitable for subsequent list-directed input. For this reason list-directed output is used primarily for conveniently generating printed output for human consumption.

Whereas list-directed output can be quite accurately described as "fixed format", list-directed input is more appropriately described as "format free". The data values may be located in any positions of the record, as long as they are in the proper order for the <input list> and are separated from each other by commas or blanks. (If a comma is used as a separator it may optionally be preceded and/or followed by a blank, and a group of blanks has the same effect as a single blank.) The valid forms for record data values with list-directed I/O are exactly the same as with formatted I/O, except that string values must be enclosed in single quotes. The reason for this is the position-independence of list-directed input, and since blanks and commas are valid string characters the quotes are necessary to delimit character strings.

Neither formatted nor list-directed output causes quotes to be placed around string data on the output record (unless, of course, enclosing quotes are part of the string value). Thus list-directed input/output is not very practical for general file I/O, and finds greatest use for programmer interaction with the executing program—usually via the preconnected units. Numerous examples of such I/O have appeared in the preceding chapters. An exception to this practical limitation on list-directed I/O is if the data contain no strings (e.g., is all numeric), then all sequential file I/O can safely be list directed (list-directed I/O is not permitted for direct files). If programmer-specified formatting is to be avoided, however, a more efficient and less restrictive means of doing this is with unformatted I/O, which is described in the next section.

15.3 Unformatted I/O

Fortran allows file I/O to be completely unformatted, which means that data is transferred between main memory and the file with no conversion whatever—the bit patterns representing the data are transferred completely intact. Unformatted I/O therefore should not be confused with list-directed I/O, although in neither case does the programmer specify a format. List-directed I/O is a special form of formatted I/O, and involves the same kinds of data conversions. Unformatted I/O involves no data con-

SAM file READ	READ (<unit>) <input-list>
SAM file WRITE	WRITE (<unit>) <output-list>
DAM file READ	READ (<unit>,REC=<number>) <input-list>
DAM file WRITE	WRITE (<unit>,REC=<number>) <output-list>

Figure 15.4. Forms of the unformatted file READ and WRITE statements. IOSTAT= may be used, as in Figures 15.1 and 15.3.

version, is therefore more efficient than formatted I/O (including list-directed I/O), but can only be used for files on magnetic tape and disk. Thus, for example, unformatted I/O cannot be specified for I/O on the user's terminal. Moreover, files written with unformatted output statments are not very portable from one computer model to another, since the file data is in the form of Fortran's numeric and nonnumeric storage unit bit patterns (which are implementation dependent).

Nevertheless unformatted I/O is an extremely important facility for files that are not to be transported to other equipment since such I/O is more efficient in terms of execution time, and also usually in terms of file space required. Figure 15.4 summarizes Fortran's unformatted I/O statements—in all cases they are identical to the corresponding formatted I/O statements except that the FMT= specification is omitted.

Unformatted READs and WRITEs cause bit patterns to be transferred between the file and main memory, as illustrated in the example of Figure 15.5. Here CODE is a five-character string element, and X and Y are both numeric elements (each requiring a single numeric storage unit). The statement

```
WRITE (<unit>) CODE,X,Y
```

causes the bit patterns of the five nonnumeric storage units and two numeric storage units to be transferred intact to the file record. If each nonnumeric storage unit is 8 bits, and a numeric storage unit is 32 bits, then execution of this statement causes a total of 104 bits to be copied from main memory to the file. The statement

```
READ (<unit>) CODE,X,Y
```

causes the reverse transfer—the first 40 bits in the record would be transferred to the 5 nonnumeric data elements named CODE, the next 32 would go into X, and the last 32 bits would be copied into the main memory area named Y.

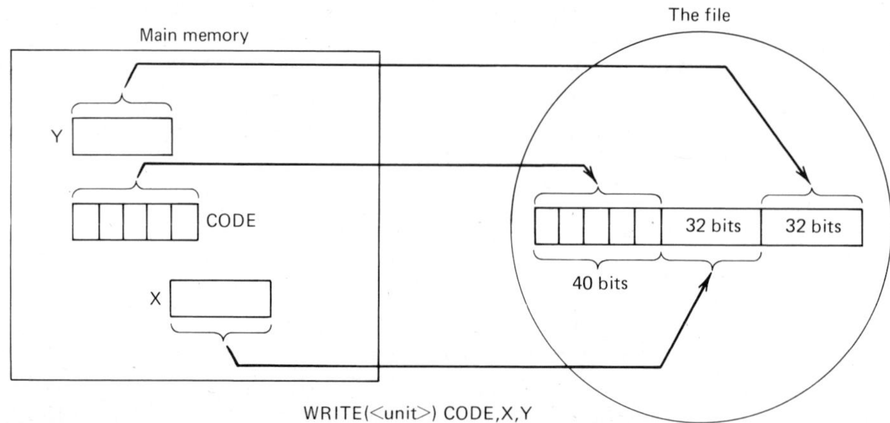

Figure 15.5. An example of unformatted file I/O. [The picture is the same for READ (<unit>) CODE, X, Y—just reverse the three arrows.]

Data written by unformatted WRITEs must be read using unformatted READs. And care must be taken that the order of elements in the <input list> of an unformatted READ is correct so that the proper bits get transferred into the intended storage units in main memory. (See the problems at the end of this chapter, however, for deliberate "mismatching" of output and input quantities in unformatted file I/O in order to investigate the nature of data representation in numeric and nonnumeric storage units.)

The specification of unformatted I/O is identical to that for formatted I/O except for the absence of the <format specification>, and except for two items in file opening. First, when a file is opened it must be specified whether it is opened for formatted I/O or unformatted I/O; this is done with the FORM= option in the OPEN statement. Note (from the preceding chapter) that the default is FORM='FORMATTED' for sequential files and FORM='UNFORMATTED' for direct files. Second, the opening of files for direct access requires that the record length be specified. For formatted files the record length is given in number of characters, but for unformatted files the basic unit is a bit rather than a character. Thus the number of bits must be specified for the record length of unformatted DAM files. Unfortunately, the way in which the number of bits is specified in this regard is implementation dependent, and is normally related to the size (number of bits) of the words and storage units of the implementation. The manuals for each implementation must be consulted for a description of how record lengths are to be specified for unformatted DAM files. This may be a number of words or a number of bytes (each byte is 8 bits, but the number of bits in a word depends on the machine). In the examples of Section 15.6 unformatted record lengths are specified in number of bytes, and in these examples a nonnumeric storage unit is assumed to be 8 bits (1 byte) and a numeric storage unit is assumed to be 32 bits (4 bytes). Thus, for example, the record length in Figure 15.5 is 13 bytes (5+4+4).

15.4 I/O Error Recovery

As mentioned earlier, any of a number of different errors can occur which will cause a file I/O operation to fail and terminate execution of the READ or WRITE statement.

1 The unit does not exist.

2 The unit has not been connected to a file.

3 An attempt has been made to read past the end of a sequential file.

4 An attempt has been made to read more data from a record than the record contains.

5 An attempt has been made to write more data onto a record than the record can contain.

6 A formatted I/O operation has been specified for an unformatted file.

7 An unformatted I/O operation has been specified for an unformatted file.

8 A sequential READ or WRITE statement has been attempted on a direct file.

9 A direct READ or WRITE statement has been attempted on a sequential file.

10 A data descriptor of the wrong type has been specified.

11 In a formatted input operation, the file record contains invalid data.

12 In a direct file an I/O operation has been specified for a nonexistent record.

If one of these errors occurs, and provisions have not been made to recover from it, the execution of the program terminates. Fortran provides for recovery from such errors, however, should the programmer so desire. This is done with either of the

IOSTAT=<integer variable name>
ERR=<statement label>

specification options in the READ and WRITE statements. The form that this may take, for a direct READ for example, is

READ (<unit>,<format>,REC=<number>,IOSTAT=<variable>) <input list>

The use of IOSTAT= is very much like its use in the OPEN and INQUIRE statements.

The IOSTAT= option provides for determination of the exact nature of the error. The integer variable specified in the IOSTAT= option becomes defined with an implementation-dependent nonzero positive value if an I/O error occurs during execution of this statement (the implementation manuals must be consulted for the meaning of each such value). (If no error occurs, nor does end-of-file, then the variable value becomes zero; if no error occurs, but end-of-file does, then the variable assumes an implementation-dependent negative value.)

The ERR=<statement label> option may be used in place of (or in addition to) the IOSTAT= option. The ERR= option specifies the point at which execution is to continue if an error occurs in the execution of the I/O statement containing the ERR= specification. Fortran also has an analogous END=<statement-label> option, which identifies the point at which execution should continue in the event that end-of-file (for sequential file READs) is encountered. At times the END= and ERR= options may be convenient for the programmer, but neither provides any additional capability over the IOSTAT= option. In the examples below, the IOSTAT= feature will be used exclusively. The action taken upon detection of an I/O error may be the printing of an appropriate error message and then either terminating execution or proceeding with the program, retrying the I/O operation (with perhaps some change in it, such as in the <format specification>), or any other action that the programmer may desire.

15.5 Buffered File I/O

As described in Section 14.4 it is often advantageous to perform file I/O in two steps: the first step being a transfer of the data from its source location to a buffer area (internal file) in main memory, with the second step transferring the data from the buffer to its destination location. There are two principal applications of this technique:

1 Reading files having two or more different record formats in an unpredictable mix.

2 "Blocking" individual records into groups in order to decrease the number of file accesses (and increase the file I/O efficiency).

In the first of these applications each record is read from the file into the buffer, which is normally a character variable. One of the fields of the record contains information as to what format applies to this record, and this field is accessible as a substring of the buffer. Testing the value of this field then allows the buffer data to then be transferred to the desired field elements using the appropriate format. In this second transfer, the buffer is used as an internal file for the READ statement. The general structure of the program in this case is shown in Figure 15.6. In that figure it is assumed that positions 7, 8, and 9 of the record contain the "code" for the record format, with CODE1 corresponding to <format1> and <field list 1>, CODE2 corresponding to <format 2>, and <field list 2> and so on. Note that the file is (arbitrarily) assumed to be an unformatted DAM file.

```
READ   (FILE,REC=<number>) BUFFER
CODE   = BUFFER(7:9)
IF     (CODE .EQ. CODE1) THEN
            READ (BUFFER,<format-1>) <field-list-1>
            ----
            ----
            ----
       ELSEIF (CODE .EQ. CODE2) THEN
            READ (BUFFER,<format-2>) <field-list-2>
            ----
            ----
            ----
          .
          .
          .
       ELSEIF (CODE .EQ. CODEn) THEN
            READ (BUFFER,<format-n>) <field-list-n>
            ----
            ----
            ----
       ELSE
            ----error in CODE field----
ENDIF
   .
   .
   .
```

Figure 15.6. Using a buffer for reading a file containing records with different formats in an unpredictable mix.

When buffering is used to "block" records, the buffer is used as the interface between a number of individual records in main memory and their grouping into a single record for purposes of transfer between main memory and the external device. In this case the buffer is usually a character array, with the same number of elements as there are individual records in a block. READing the external file fills the buffer with a block of records (but is considered as only one record as far as the external file is concerned), and then a loop in the program processes each record in the block. If processed records are to be updated and returned to the file, they may be rewritten to the buffer and then returned as a block to the file. Figure 15.7 illustrates the concept. In this figure BLKFAC (for blocking factor) is an integer representing the number of records in a block (and the number of elements in the array BUFFER). Note that the file is (arbitrarily) assumed in this case to be a formatted SAM file.

```
READ (FILE,FMT='(A)') BUFFER
do   RECORD = 1,BLKFAC
     READ (BUFFER(RECORD:RECORD),<format>) <field-list>
     ----
     ----  } process record
     ----
     WRITE (BUFFER(RECORD:RECORD),<format>) <field-list>
repeat
BACKSPACE FILE
WRITE (FILE,FMT='(A)') BUFFER
```

Figure 15.7. Using a buffer for blocking records for file I/O.

Blocking, in the manner illustrated in Figure 15.7, almost always results in improved file I/O efficiency. This is so for magnetic tape files because the number of times the tape must start and stop has been significantly reduced—perhaps by an order of magnitude. (Starting and stopping the tape is usually the most wasteful aspect of magnetic tape I/O.) Similarly with disk I/O one of the greatest sources of inefficiency is the time needed to position the read/write head over the proper track (cylinder) for each I/O operation. Reducing the number of such operations, and transferring more data per access, usually results in significantly increased file I/O efficiency.

READs and WRITEs on internal files must be formatted sequential I/O operations. Such files may be character variables, arrays, array elements, or substrings. Such buffers may be filled from, or emptied to, external files that are either formatted or unformatted, SAM or DAM. An effective technique, when file portability is not important, is to use the efficient unformatted I/O statements to transfer data between the external file and the buffer, and to achieve the desired data conversion with formatted I/O on the internal file.

15.6 Examples of File Use

The preceding section completes the discussion of Fortran's file features. Several examples of file use are now presented to further explain and illustrate these features. These examples range from simple processing of sequential files to applications involving linked records in direct files, and include formatted and unformatted files, scratch files, and file inquiry. Two of the examples are extensions of previous examples to a (more realistic) file environment.

15.6.1 Automatic Conversion of do-repeat to Standard Fortran

Modern computing facilities usually allow the programmer to place the program in a disk file, and this file may be submitted to the Fortran compiler when the program is to be compiled. (On many systems this is the normal method of program submission, since editing a program that is in such a file is typically quite simple and convenient.) With such a facility the conversion of Fortran programs containing the do-repeat structures for looping can be done automatically, making the use of do-repeat quite practical.

The conversion is performed by a program (often called a "preprocessor") that reads the records of the file containing the do-repeat Fortran program (the "source" file), and creates a second file which contains the corresponding standard Fortran program. Each record (of each file) is one line of Fortran program. Each record of the source file that does not contain a do, repeat, or exit is copied by the preprocessor into the second file unchanged. However, whenever the source file record contains a do, repeat, or exit then the preprocessor places the proper standard Fortran statements, according to Figure 5.14, into the second file instead of the do-repeat form. When the source file is entirely processed in this manner then the second file, created by the preprocessor, contains a standard Fortran program that is equivalent to the do-repeat program in the source file, and may be submitted to a standard Fortran compiler.

The following example is the preprocessor program; it calls subroutine DOREPZ, which is essentially the same as DOREPX in Section 8.6, except for the modifications needed to allow the source and standard programs to be disk files.

Program F PLUS may be used to convert any of the example programs in this book to standard Fortran programs. It can also be used to convert any do-repeat Fortran program to standard Fortran as long as do-repeats are not nested more than three levels deep, and as long as the number of loops at each level does not exceed the three-digit number capability (see Figure 5.16). To insure no conflict with preprocessor-generated statement labels, programmer-supplied statement labels (e.g., for FORMAT statements and/or abnormal loop exits) should not be three-digit numbers (use two- or four-digit numbers instead). The "do", "repeat", or "exit" may be in either upper or lower case letters.

```
*....:-----------------------------------------------------------------
      PROGRAM  F PLUS

*                  ..this program converts a (sequential) file
*                  containing a Fortran program in do-repeat
*                  form into a file containing an equivalent
*                  standard Fortran 77 program.  This mainline
*                  primarily opens the two files, and calls
*                  subroutine DOREPZ (similar to subroutine
*                  DOREPX of chapter 8) to perform
*                  the actual conversion.  The user
*                  supplies the names of the two files, so that
*                  this program may be used for the conversion
*                  of any desired file, and the resulting file
*                  can then be submitted for compilation.

*     ....constants....(the unit numbers for the two files)
      INTEGER  F77, F78
      PARAMETER  ( F77 = 7, F78 = 8 )

*     ....variables....(assume file names  -- FNAME
*                      may be up to 16 characters long)
      INTEGER IOS
      LOGICAL  EXIS
      CHARACTER  FNAME*16, STAT*3
      DATA  STAT /'OLD'/

*     ....execute....(error message printed if either OPEN fails)
      PRINT *, 'DO-REPEAT Fortran conversion--input name of source file'
      READ '(A)',  FNAME
      OPEN (F78,FILE=FNAME,STATUS=STAT,IOSTAT=IOS)
      IF  (IOS .GT. 0)  THEN
              PRINT *, 'Opening of ', STAT, ' file  ',FNAME,
     :                 '  unsuccessful -- program terminated.'
              STOP
      ENDIF
      PRINT *, 'Input name of file to hold the standard Fortran program'
      READ '(A)',  FNAME
      INQUIRE (FILE=FNAME,EXIST=EXIS)
      IF  (.NOT.EXIS)  THEN
          STAT = 'NEW'
      ENDIF
      OPEN (F77,FILE=FNAME,STATUS=STAT,IOSTAT=IOS)
      IF  (IOS .GT. 0)  THEN
              PRINT *, 'Opening of ', STAT, ' file ',FNAME,
     :                 '  unsuccessful -- program terminated.'
              STOP
      ENDIF
      PRINT *, 'Begin conversion....'
      CALL  DOREPZ (F77,F78)
      PRINT *, 'Conversion finished.'
      CLOSE (F77,STATUS='KEEP')
      CLOSE (F78,STATUS='KEEP')
      END
=======================================================================
.EXECUTE  F PLUS

DO-REPEAT Fortran conversion--input name of source file
> PROJECT#1
Input name of file to hold the standard Fortran program
> PROJ1
Begin conversion....
Conversion finished.
=======================================================================

              (Now PROJ1 can be compiled and executed)

=======================================================================
.EXECUTE  F PLUS

DO-REPEAT Fortran conversion--input name of source file
> INVENTORY
Opening of OLD file INVENTORY unsuccessful -- program terminated.
=======================================================================
(possibly because INVENTORY was intended, and the file INVENTORY doesn't exist)
```

15.6.2 The Two-Way Merge Sort

The basic two-way merge sort algorithm was presented in Section 6.4. This is a highly efficient sort that is suitable for use with large data files stored on magnetic tape. The two-way merge sort works well on such files as long as three physical tape drives (corresponding to three different Fortran units) are available—one for the file to be sorted (FILE) and one for each of the two split files (SPLIT1 and SPLIT2). All three files are, of course, sequential files, and in the following example the two split files are unformatted scratch files that are not kept after completion of the sort. The data file to be sorted is a formatted file whose format is stored as the first record (thus the actual data begins with the second record); for the purposes of the sort the format is assumed to be of the form

```
(A<rl>,T<kc>,A<kl>)
```

where <rl> is the record length (number of characters in record—all records are assumed to be the same size), <kc> is the column in which the key begins, and <kl> is the key length. With this format, a read statement of the form

```
READ (<unit>,<format>) RECORD, KEY
```

will cause the entire record to be read into RECORD and just the key portion of the record to be read into KEY (both RECORD and KEY are character variables).

Program M2SORT is a mainline program that opens the necessary files and then calls subroutine TWOWAY to perform the actual sorting. Subroutine TWOWAY, and the procedures it calls, are modified from the versions given in Section 6.4 only to the extent necessary to change the environment from arrays to files. Note that M2SORT is quite general, due to the fact that provision is made for the file itself to contain its format (rather than the format being fixed in the program), and because any valid file name can be used. Note also that an error message is generated if the tape containing the specified file is not mounted on the appropriate tape drive.

15.6.3 Blue-Eyed Blondes

This final example requires the use of direct files, since the records are not processed in the order of their record numbers. (Or rather, not all records are processed—processing starts at the beginning of the file, and proceeds to the end, but many records may be "skipped" entirely.) This problem involves the common data file application of searching for records having certain combinations of characteristics. Such searches can be conducted in the straightforward manner of checking each record in the file for the desired characteristics.

If, however, only a small fraction of the records are candidates for meeting the desired criteria, then the search could be made much more efficient if it could be confined to the candidate records, ignoring the rest of the file. In order to accomplish this, some means must exist whereby the candidate records, which may be "sprinkled randomly" throughout the file, can be identified. One way of doing this is to "tie together" records with certain characteristics by using link fields—such a link field could contain the record number of the next record in the file having this same characteristic. For each such characteristic each file record would contain a link field pointing to the next record in the file having that characteristic, and thus there could be many link fields in each record.

```
*....:-----------------------------------------------------------------
      PROGRAM  M2 SORT

*                 ..this program performs the two-way-merge sort on
*                 a formatted magnetic tape data file.  It uses two
*                 auxiliary (unformatted) tape files, on different
*                 tape drive units, for the two "split" files.  The
*                 algorithm is the same as that of TWOWAY (chap 6)
*                 except that files are used for the data instead
*                 of arrays.

*     ....constants....(unit numbers for the magnetic tape files)
      INTEGER  DFILE, SPLIT1, SPLIT2
      PARAMETER  ( DFILE = 22, SPLIT1 = 23, SPLIT2 = 24 )

*     ....variables....
      INTEGER  IOS
      CHARACTER  FNAME*16
      LOGICAL  EXIS

*     ....execute....
      PRINT *, 'Two-way-merge sort -- input name of file to be sorted'
      PRINT *, '(tape containing file should be mounted on drive #1)'
      READ '(A)', FNAME
      INQUIRE (FILE=FNAME, EXIST=EXIS)
      IF  (.NOT.EXIS)  THEN
          PRINT *, 'File  ',FNAME, '  not mounted on tape drive #1.'
          STOP
      ENDIF
      OPEN (DFILE,FILE=FNAME,STATUS='OLD',IOSTAT=IOS)
      IF  (IOS .GT. 0)  THEN
          PRINT *, 'Opening of file  ', FNAME, '  unsuccessful.'
          STOP
      ENDIF
      OPEN (SPLIT1,STATUS='SCRATCH',FORM='UNFORMATTED')
      OPEN (SPLIT2,STATUS='SCRATCH',FORM='UNFORMATTED')
      PRINT *, 'Begin sorting....'
      CALL TWOWAY (DFILE,SPLIT1,SPLIT2)
      PRINT *, 'Sorting finished.'
      END
=======================================================================
```

As an example, consider the simple case of a personnel file, in which each record contains data on one person, and this data includes the person's eye color and hair color. Further suppose that on occasion it is desired to determine the names of all red-haired people, and on another occasion to determine the names of all green-eyed people, and on still another occasion to determine the names of all blue-eyed blondes. One way to do all of these searches efficiently is to organize the file so that each record contains a link field for eye color and a link field for hair color. And then, when the file is first created, all of the green-eyed records are linked together, all of the blue-eyed records are linked together, all of the red-haired records are linked together, all of the blonde-haired records are linked together, and so on, for each eye color and hair color. (In such a structure the actual data—'green', 'blue', 'red', etc.—need not appear in the record at all, although it could, since this information is common to each record of the corresponding linked list. Thus each record linked together by eye color would have the same eye-color value, say 'blue', and thus 'blue' would not have to appear explicitly in each of these records.)

Typically the first record (or first few records) in such a file contain not the principal data (such as personnel data) but the record numbers of the first record in each of the linked lists in the file. In the examples below the first record contains the initial links to the various eye-color lists, and the second record contains the initial links to the various hair-color lists. The actual personnel data begins with the third record. The file is a DAM file, of course, since the link fields specify "the next" record to be accessed and thus (many) records may be skipped in processing the file. (In this application the file could be either formatted or unformatted—unformatted was arbitrarily chosen for example BL BL.) In program BL BL, the links for blue eyes are followed, simultaneously with the links for blonde hair, and when they converge on the same record a blue-eyed blonde has been found.

```
*....:-----------------------------------------------------------------
      PROGRAM  BL BL
*             ..this program searches a personnel data file, and
*             extracts (prints a listing of) all blue-eyed-blondes.
*             The data file is an unformatted direct file, and the
*             eye-color and hair-color fields in each record contain
*             not the actual data but links to the next record in
*             the file of the person with the same characteristics.
*             Thus the records of all blue-eyed people form a linked
*             list, as do all green-eyed people, red-haired people,
*             blonde-haired people, etc. Thus in extracting all
*             blue-eyed-blondes from the file, only the records
*             of blue-eyed people and blonde-haired people need
*             be searched. (This scheme results in extremely
*             efficient data file searches.) The first record of
*             the file contains the first record numbers for the
*             various eye-colors (assume the first is for blue eyes),
*             and the second record contains the first record numbers
*             for the various hair colors (assume blonde is the third
*             such, after black and red).

*     ....constant....(the file unit number)
      INTEGER  PDATA
      PARAMETER  ( PDATA = 11 )

*     ....variables....(used for record numbers)
      INTEGER  BLUE, BLONDE, RED, BLACK

*     ----record PERSON....(EYES and HAIR are link fields)
          CHARACTER  NAME*20
          INTEGER    EYES
          INTEGER    HAIR
*     ----end PERSON....(normally more fields would be present)

*     ....execute....(record length in bytes)
      OPEN (PDATA,FILE='PERSONNEL',STATUS='OLD',ACCESS='DIRECT',RECL=28)
      READ (PDATA,REC=1)  BLUE
      READ (PDATA,REC=2)  BLACK, RED, BLONDE
*         ..now comes the search -- follow links
*         BLUE and BLONDE, printing out when they
*         coincide, and stop at sentinel record '/$'..
      do
          IF  (BLUE .LT. BLONDE)  THEN
*                                     ..get next BLUE link..
                  READ (PDATA,REC=BLUE)  NAME, EYES, HAIR
                  BLUE = EYES

              ELSEIF  (BLUE .GT. BLONDE)  THEN
*                                             ..get next BLONDE link..
                  READ (PDATA,REC=BLONDE)  NAME, EYES, HAIR
                  BLONDE = HAIR

              ELSE
*                 ..this is a blue-eyed-blonde
*                     (if not the end-of-file)..
                  READ (PDATA,REC=BLUE)  NAME, EYES, HAIR
                  IF  (NAME .EQ. '/$')  exit
                  PRINT *, NAME
                  BLUE = EYES
                  BLONDE = HAIR
          ENDIF
      repeat
      CLOSE (PDATA,STATUS='KEEP')
      END
=====================================================================
```

15.7 Summary

A large portion of this chapter has been devoted to extending and completing Fortran's formatting facilities, some simple cases of which were introduced in Chapter 1 and used throughout the book. And the simple uses of READ and PRINT used throughout the book are seen to be special cases of Fortran's powerful file I/O facilities. The general cases are:

READ (<input control list>) <input variable list>
WRITE (<output control list>) <output quantity list>

The <input control list> and <output control list> contain information such as

<file id>	required (may be '*', for preconnected units)
<format>	required for formatted I/O, omitted for unformatted I/O ('*' for list-directed I/O)
<record id>	REC= required for DAM files, omitted for SAM files
<error recovery>	optional IOSTAT= (or ERR=, or END= for SAM input)

A new concept contained in this chapter is that of unformatted file I/O. This is not to be confused with list-directed I/O. List-directed I/O is formatted I/O, but the programmer does not supply the format. In unformatted file I/O bit patterns are transferred directly between the external medium and Fortran's internal storage units, with no conversion. (Formatted I/O always involves a conversion from/to character form on the external storage medium.)

A number of possible error conditions can arise during file I/O operations. The IOSTAT= option in the control-list provides for programmer-specified recovery action in the event of such an error. An implementation of Fortran may distinguish between different kinds of I/O errors, by giving the IOSTAT= variable a unique value for each such error. The programmer may use these values in specifying the desired recovery action. (The implementation manuals must be consulted for the actual IOSTAT values.)

The discussion of buffered I/O, initiated in the previous chapter, is completed in this chapter. The two principal applications of buffering (use of internal files) are (1) processing files with (an unpredictable mix of) records having different formats (field structures), and (2) blocking records on the external device in order to decrease the number of external file accesses needed in processing the file. Buffering is accomplished in Fortran by using a character data element as an intermediate file (buffer) between the external file and the internal record field elements.

The chapter ends with the presentation of three actual program examples using external data files. The first example, a preprocessor for converting do-repeat Fortran programs into standard Fortran, uses two sequential formatted files. The second example, a file version of the two-way merge sort, uses a formatted sequential permanent file and two unformatted sequential scratch files (for the two split files). The third example, an efficient file search for data extraction, uses an unformatted direct file. These three examples illustrate a wide range of file applications, and Fortran's features for accommodating such applications.

Programming Exercises

15.1 A sequential file contains names and addresses, and is to be used for generating mailing labels. Each record in the file contains the 40 characters to be printed on a mailing-label line. However, the record corresponding to the first line of each label contains periods in the first four character positions, to "flag" the start of a new label, and these four periods should not be printed. A label may have up to 8 name/address lines, and a new label starts 10 lines after the (beginning of the) preceding label. Write a Fortran program that will print such a set of mailing labels from the data in the sequential file.

15.2 A sequential file contains the semester grades for the students at the state university. The records are either "student name" records or "grade report" records. For a given student, zero or more grade report records follow the student name record for that student.
The format of each record is as follows:

Student Name		Grade Report	
'N'	A1	'R'	A1
Name	A19	Course name	A19
Soc. sec. #	A11	Section number	A6
Total hours	I3	Credit hours	I1
Grade point average	F6.3	Grade	A1

The total hours and GPA fields in the 'N' records are the "old" (after last semester) values. Write a Fortran program that produces a new file, containing only 'N' style (student name) records, with the total hours and GPA field values updated to reflect the 'R' record values. Use A = 4, B = 3, C = 2, D = 1, E = 0 for the grade values. Note that an internal file could be useful in this problem.

15.3 Write program DOREPZ. That is, modify subroutine DOREPX of Chapter 8 so that program FPLUS works satisfactorily. This requires changing the source of "input" from a character array to a sequential file, and changing the output PRINTs to the appropriate file WRITEs.

15.4 Generalize program BLBL so that it works for an arbitrary number of data fields. Additional (linked) data fields, for example, might be height, weight, age, religion, birthplace, education level, etc. Your program should efficiently extract those records pertaining to any number (one or more) of these attributes, in any mix.

15.5 Program PLANET of Chapter 13 involved a considerable amount of input data. This data came from a file, rather than being input by "hand," and, in fact, the READ statement of that program was actually replaced by a CALL to a subroutine that performed the data input from the file. Design an appropriate file for this application, and the corresponding subroutine and CALL statement for program PLANET.

15.6 Data for a very large index is located in a direct file, with each record corresponding to one index item (A20) and its associated page number (I5). The index items are unsorted. Write a program that sorts this file efficiently, even though the file is too large to be transferred into an array in memory. Convert either the Shell sort (Problem 6.48) or the quick sort (Chapter 11) to perform the sort directly on the file.

15.7 Repeat Problem 15.6, but use a bubble sort (Chapter 5). Compare the speed of the bubble sort to that of Problem 15.6, for file sizes of 100 records, 1,000 records, and 10,000 records. (Note: a random-number generator could be used to generate test data for this problem, if you do not want to make up all that data by hand.)

15.8 Perform the sort desired in Problem 15.6 by copying the index data from the direct file into a new sequential file, and then use program M2SORT to perform the sorting. (Note that this requires that you convert subroutine TWOWAY of Chapter 6 to the appropriate file environment.) How does the speed of this sort compare to the speeds in Problems 15.6 and 15.7?

15.9 Change TWOWAY (as converted in Problem 15.8) to NWAY, with the objective of performing an "n-way sort," The "n" in n-way could be 2, 3, 4, or 5.

15.10 A file contains taxpayers' records, with fields for taxpayer identification and taxable income. Write a Fortran program that uses this file and the tax table in Problem 6.32 to create a new file that contains each taxpayer's income tax. The new file should contain all of the data of the original file, in addition to the calculated tax value.

15.11 Repeat Problem 15.5, but for the least-squares data of the problem LSFIT of Chapter 13.

15.12 A (formatted) data file is to be "secured" by coding the characters of the file. A "simple substitution code is one in which a permutation of the alphabet is substituted for the characters in the clear message. For example, the permutation

ABCDEFGHIJKLMNOPQRSTUVWXYZ
ZAYBXCWDVEUFTGSHRIQJPKOLNM

will code the message

NOW IS THE TIME

into GSOVQ JDXJV TX

Note that, in generating the code, blanks are removed from the clear message and the coded message is blocked into groups of 5 characters. Write a Fortran program that, given the permutation, will code any sequential file. The output file should have records exactly 60 characters long.

15.13 A Vignere tableau is a code that uses a "key word," rather than a permutation (see Problem 15.12), for performing the encoding (and is harder to "break"). The key word is replicated along side the (deblanked) clear message, and the key-word letters specify the "displacement" of a clear letter to its corresponding code. If FORTRAN is the key word, for example, the message

NOWISTHETIME
FORTRANFORTR

becomes

SCNBJ TUJHZ FV

Write Fortran programs to code and decode files using this method. Assume that the key word is known.

15.14 A presidential preference poll is being used to estimate voter preferences among the four leading candidates in a certain political party. The raw data from the poll is placed in a sequential file, each record of which contains a list of the four candidates names (4A20 format) in the order preferred by a respondent to the poll. Write a Fortran program that accesses this file and, without modifying any data in the file, determines the percentage of "first place" and "last place" votes received by each of the four candidates.

15.15 Modify the salesperson data problem (6.10) so that the monthly data, which comes from a file, updates the year-to-date sales data located in another file. The updated year-to-date data should be placed in a third file.

Appendix

Summary of Fortran 77 Statements

Fortran statements are contained in columns 7-72 of the lines comprising a program.
An "*" or "C" in column 1 is used for a comment line.
A non-blank, non-zero character in column 6 causes that line to be a continuation of the preceding line.
A labelled statement has the <label> in columns 1-5.
<....> indicates a programmer-supplied entry.
[....] indicates an optional part of the statement.
{....} indicates a sequence of zero or more elements.
A <list> is a sequence of elements separated by commas.

Statement	Comment	Reference
Form of a Fortran Program		
PROGRAM <program-name> {<specification-statement>} {<executable-statement>} END	the PROGRAM statement is optional	part 1
Specification Statements		
INTEGER <integer-declaration-list>	INTEGER,REAL,CHARACTER,	chapter 2
REAL <real-declaration-list>	LOGICAL,DOUBLEPRECISION,	chapter 2
CHARACTER[*<length>] <character-declaration-list>	and COMPLEX are the Fortran	chapter 2
LOGICAL <logical-declaration-list>	data types	chapter 4
DOUBLEPRECISION <double-precision-declaration-list>		chapter 12
COMPLEX <complex-declaration-list>		chapter 12
IMPLICIT <implicit-declaration-list>	specify default typing	chapters 2,12
PARAMETER (<constant-definition-list>)	define the constants used in program	chapter 2
DATA <variable-name-list> / <constant-value-list> / {[,]<variable-name-list> / <constant-value-list> /}	specify initial variable values	chapter 2
Executable Statements		
<variable-name> = <expression>	assign <expression> value to variable	chapter 3
PRINT *	print a blank line on output device	chapter 1
PRINT *, <output-expression-list>	print values on output device	chapter 1
READ *, <input-variable-name-list>	input data from input device	chapter 2
PRINT <format>, <output-expression-list>	same as PRINT * (READ *), except	chapter 1
READ <format>, <input-variable-name-list>	that programmer explicitly specifies the form of the output (input)	chapter 2

Statement	Comment	Reference
IF (<logical-expression>) THEN {<executable-statement>}	control for selective processing (block-IF)	chapter 4 chapter 4
[ELSEIF (<logical-expression>) THEN {<executable-statement>}]	zero or more ELSEIF-blocks	
[ELSE {<executable-statement>}]	optional ELSE-block	
ENDIF	termination of block-IF	
DO <label>[,] <indexed-range> {<executable-statement>} <label> CONTINUE	indexed loop control -- see chapter 5 for additional loop facilities	chapter 5
CALL <subroutine-name> [(<actual-argument-list>)]	subroutine call	chapters 6,7
GOTO <label>	unconditional branch	chapters 5,9
IF (<logical-expression>) GOTO <label>	conditional branch	chapters 5,9
<label> CONTINUE	the CONTINUE statement has no effect, and is used primarily to label points in the program	chapter 5
Fortran Procedure (Subroutine, Function) Facilities		
SUBROUTINE <subroutine-name> [(<dummy-argument-list>)] {<specification-statement>} {<executable-statement>} END	executed by a CALL statement in another program unit	chapters 6,7
[<type>] FUNCTION <function-name> [(<dummy-argument-list>)] {<specification-statement>} {<executable-statement>} END	called by using the <function-name> as an operand in an expression in another program unit	chapter 8
ENTRY <entry-name> [(<dummy-argument-list>)]	additional entry point specification	chapter 7
SAVE [<local-variable-list>]	a procedure specification statement which specifies that local variables remain defined between calls	chapter 7
File I/O Operations		
WRITE (<control-list>) <output-expression-list> READ (<control-list>) <input-variable-name-list> <label> FORMAT(<format-specification-list>)	same as PRINT (READ) above, except that <control-list> may include file identification, error-recovery, etc, in addition to format specification	chapter 14 chapter 14 chapter 15
OPEN (<unit>,<open-list>)	connect a file to specified I/O unit	chapter 14
CLOSE (<unit>,<close-list>)	disconnect file from specified I/O unit	chapter 14
INQUIRE (<unit>,<inquire-list>)	obtain information about an I/O unit	chapter 14
INQUIRE (<file>,<inquire-list>)	obtain information about a file	chapter 14
BACKSPACE <unit>	position SAM file to preceding record	chapter 14
REWIND <unit>	position SAM file to first record	chapter 14
ENDFILE <unit>	write end-of-file record on SAM file	chapter 14
Global Data Facilities		
COMMON [/<common-block-name>/] <common-variable-list>	specification of global variables	chapter 7
BLOCKDATA [<block-data-name>] {<specification-statement>} END	BLOCK DATA subprogram unit -- used primarily to initialize variables in COMMON, and hence primarily contains COMMON and DATA statements	chapter 7

Statement	Comment	Reference
Miscellaneous Statements		
ASSIGN <label> TO <variable-name>		chapter 9
DIMENSION <array-declaration-list>		chapter 13
EQUIVALENCE <equivalence-list>		chapter 7
EXTERNAL <procedure-name-list>	if being used as actual arguments	chapter 7
GOTO <variable-name>	used with the ASSIGN statement	chapter 9
GOTO (<label-list>)[,] <integer-expression>	the "computed GOTO"	chapter 9
IF (<arithmetic-expression>) <label>,<label>,<label>		chapter 9
IF (<logical-expression>) <executable-statement>	<executable-statement> can't be IF or DO	chapters 5,9
INTRINSIC <intrinsic-function-name-list>	if being used as actual arguments	chapter 7
PAUSE	requires computer operator intervention	
RETURN [<integer-expression>]	[....] for subroutine alternate returns	chapter 7,9
STOP		

Miscellaneous Constructs

<list>	<item> {,<item>}	
<name>	1-6 capital letters and decimal digits, the first of which must be a letter	
<label>	sequence of 1-5 decimal digits	
<expression>	specification of a data value -- see chapters 3,4	
<integer-expression>	an expression involving only integer operands and (possibly) arithmetic operators	
<arithmetic-expression>	an expression involving numeric operands and (possibly) arithmetic operators	
arithmetic operators:	+	addition
	−	subtraction (and unary negation)
	*	multiplication
	/	division
	**	exponentiation
character operator:	//	concatenation
substring:	<character-variable-name>(<integer-expression>:<integer-expression>) left position / right position	
relational operators: (for comparisons)	.EQ.	equal to
	.NE.	not equal to
	.LT.	less than
	.GT.	greater than
	.LE.	less than or equal to
	.GE.	greater than or equal to
logical operators:	.NOT.	complement
	.AND.	true if both operands true
	.OR.	true if either (or both) operands true
	.EQV.	true if operands have the same value
	.NEQV.	true if operands have different values
logical constants:	.TRUE.	
	.FALSE.	
numeric constants:	integer constant	optionally signed sequence of decimal digits
	real constant	see chapter 3
	doubleprecision constant	see chapter 12
	complex constant	see chapter 12
string constant:	'<sequence-of-characters>'	
Hollerinth constant:	<integer>H<sequence-of-characters>	(integer is character sequence length)
<array-declaration>	<array-name>(<dimension-bound-list>)	

<dimension-bound>	<lower-bound>:<upper-bound> or integer (⇒ 1:integer)	
<array-element>	<array-name>(<subscript-list>) (a subscript is an <integer-expression>)	
<implicit-declaration>	<type>(<letter-range-list>) (see chapter 12)	
<constant-definition>	<constant-name> = <constant-value>	
<indexed-range>	<integer-variable-name>=<integer-expression>,<integer-expression>[,<integer-expression>]	
<implied-do-list>	(<expression-list,<indexed-range>) (<expression-list> may contain <implied-do-list>s)	
<equivalence-declaration>	(<variable-name-list>) (see chapter 7)	

File I/O Control

I/O <control-list> options: (see chapter 14)	[UNIT=] <integer-expression>	
	[FMT=] <character-expression>	or [FMT=] <FORMAT-statement-label>
	REC= <integer-expression>	(only with DAM files)
	END= <label>	(only with SAM file reads)
	ERR= <label>	
	IOSTAT= <integer-variable-name>	
<open-list> options: (see chapter 14)	[UNIT=] <integer-expression>	(this is <unit>)
	FILE= <character-expression>	
	ACCESS= <character-expression>	
	STATUS= <character-expression>	
	FORM= <character-expression>	
	RECL= <integer-expression>	
	BLANK= <character-expression>	
	ERR= <label>	
	IOSTAT= <integer-variable-name>	
<close-list> options: (see chapter 14)	[UNIT=] <integer-expression>	(this is <unit>)
	STATUS= <character-expression>	
	ERR= <label>	
	IOSTAT= <integer-variable-name>	
<inquire-list> options: (see chapter 14)	[UNIT=] <integer-expression>	(this is <unit>)
	FILE= <character-expression>	(this is <file>)
	EXIST= <logical-variable-name>	
	OPENED= <logical-variable-name>	
	NUMBER= <integer-variable-name>	
	NAMED= <logical-variable-name>	
	NAME= <character-variable-name>	
	ACCESS= <character-variable-name>	
	SEQUENTIAL= <logical-variable-name>	
	DIRECT= <logical-variable-name>	
	FORM= <character-variable-name>	
	FORMATTED= <logical-variable-name>	
	UNFORMATTED= <logical-variable-name>	
	RECL= <integer-variable-name>	
	NEXTREC= <integer-variable-name>	
	BLANK= <character-variable-name>	
	ERR= <label>	
	IOSTAT= <integer-variable-name>	

<format-specification-list> options (see chapter 15)	(<format-specification-list>) I<width> I<width>.<digits> A A<width> L<width> F<width>.<digits> E<width>.<digits> [E<digits>] D<width>.<digits> G<width>.<digits> [E<digits>]	repeatable -- e.g., 12F7.2 general form: <integer-constant><format-specification>
	<scale-factor>P <string-constant> <Hollerinth-constant> T<column-number> TL<number-of-positions> TR<number-of-positions> <number-of-positions>X S SP SS BN BZ / :	not repeatable, except when included in parentheses

Appendix B Representation of Character Data

Nonnumeric data consists of elements ("characters"), or sequences of characters, from an "alphabet" of nonnumeric values. There are an unlimited number of such possible alphabets. A common such alphabet in computer programming consists of the familiar letters of the English alphabet, the decimal digit characters, punctuation characters, and other special characters. These form the basic set of values for Fortran 77's CHARACTER data type.

All data, including character data, is represented in the computer as a string of bits—0's and 1's. For any given alphabet, there are many ways in which each character can be uniquely coded as a bit string. This appendix describes the two most commonly used such codes, the American Standard Code for Information Interchange (ASCII), and the Extended Binary Coded Decimal Interchange Code (EBCDIC).

The ASCII code employs 7 bits for each character, which provides for an alphabet of 128 characters; the EBCDIC code employs 8 bits and thus can support an alphabet of up to 256 characters. The figure (next page) shows the complete ASCII and EBCDIC codes. Note that some (about one-fourth) of the characters in each code are "control" characters, and do not "print" on output devices.

On a typical "ASCII terminal" the 16 characters in row 000 (first row of the ASCII table) are obtained by depressing the "CONTROL" key simultaneously with depressing the key containing the corresponding row 100 key. For example, CONTROL-G rings the bell on the terminal. The 16 row 001 characters are obtained by CONTROLing the row 101 characters. The control character mnemonics stand for:

NUL	null	DC1	device control 1
SOH	start of heading	DC2	device control 2
STX	start of text	DC3	device control 3
ETX	end of text	DC4	device control 4
EOT	end of transmission	NAK	negative acknowledge
ENQ	enquiry	SYN	synchronous idle
ACK	acknowledge	ETB	end of transmission block
BEL	bell	CAN	cancel
BS	backspace	EM	end of medium
HT	horizontal tab	SUB	substitute
LF	line feed	ESC	escape
VT	vertical tab	FS	file separator
FF	form feed	GS	group separator
CR	carriage return	RS	record separator
SO	shift out	US	unit separator
SI	shift in	DEL	delete
DLF	data link escape		

	Least significant bits →	0000	0001	0010	0011	0100	0101	0110	0111	1000	1001	1010	1011	1100	1101	1110	1111
ASCII	000	NUL	SOH	STX	ETX	EOT	ENQ	ACK	BEL	BS	HT	LF	VT	FF	CR	SO	SI
	001	DLE	DC1	DC2	DC3	DC4	NAK	SYN	ETB	CAN	EM	SUB	ESC	FS	GS	RS	US
	010	space	!	"	#	$	%	&	'	(	)	*	+	,	—	.	/
	011	0	1	2	3	4	5	6	7	8	9	:	;	<	=	>	?
	100	@	A	B	C	D	E	F	G	H	I	J	K	L	M	N	O
	101	P	Q	R	S	T	U	V	W	X	Y	Z	[		]		—
	110	`	a	b	c	d	e	f	g	h	i	j	k	l	m	n	o
	111	p	q	r	s	t	u	v	w	x	y	z	{	|	}	~	DEL

		0000	0001	0010	0011	0100	0101	0110	0111	1000	1001	1010	1011	1100	1101	1110	1111
EBCDIC	0000	NUL	SOH	STX	ETX	PF	HT	LC	DEL			SMM	VT	FF	CR	SO	SI
	0001	DLE	DC1	DC2	TM	RES	NL	BS	IDL	CAN	EM	CC	CUI	IFS	IGS	IRS	IUS
	0010	DS	SGS	FS		BYP	LF	EOB	ESC			SM	CU2		ENQ	ACK	BEL
	0011			SYN		PN	RS	UC	EOT				CU3	DC4	NAK		SUB
	0100	space											.		(	+	|
	0101	&										!	$	*	)	;	
	0110	—	/										,	%	—	>	?
	0111										`		#	@	'	=	"
	1000		a	b	c	d	e	f	g	h	i						
	1001		j	k	l	m	n	o	p	q	r						
	1010		~	s	t	u	v	w	x	y	z						
	1011																
	1100		A	B	C	D	E	F	G	H	I						
	1101		J	K	L	M	N	O	P	Q	R						
	1110			S	T	U	V	W	X	Y	Z						
	1111	0	1	2	3	4	5	6	7	8	9						

Representation of nonnumeric (character) data as bit strings. The 7-bit ASCII and 8-bit EBCDIC codes are the most common character codes. The '$' character, for example, is represented as 0100100 in ASCII, and as 01011011 in EBCDIC. The first two rows of the ASCII code are nonprinting, or "control," characters, and the last 6 rows are the printing, or "graphic," characters. In the EBCDIC code the first 4 rows are control characters, and the last 12 rows are the graphic characters.

Some of the additional EBCDIC control characters are:

PF	punch off
LC	lower case
RES	restore
NL	new line
IDL	idle
BYP	bypass
EOB	end of block
PN	punch on
RS	reader stop (note change from ASCII)
UC	upper case

The Fortran 77 implementor is free to make the nonnumeric storage unit any size (number of bits) desired. If the ASCII code is used this must be at least 7 bits, and if the EBCDIC code is used then at least 8 bits are needed for a nonnumeric storage unit. If some other coding scheme is used then the minimum number of bits per storage unit may be less than or greater than these values. In practice two likely choices for the nonnumeric storage unit are:

8 bits (fits evenly into bit groups of 8, 16, 32 and other common word sizes)

one word, whatever that might be for that computer

If more bits are used for the nonnumeric storage unit than the minimum number needed for the code employed, then the implementor can (optionally) increase the size of the alphabet, and/or use the extra bits for error detection/correction. For example if the ASCII code is used with 8-bit storage units then actually the extended-ASCII code, which is an 8-bit code with more characters than the regular ASCII code, may be used. Or the eighth bit may be used as a *parity bit* for error detection. A parity bit records information as to whether the number of "1" bits in the character is odd or even. For example, if a (leading) parity bit of value 1 is used for an odd number of 1-bits in the character, then an ASCII '$' would be represented as 00100100, and an ASCII 'J' would be represented as 11001010. An error in any single bit would cause the parity bit to be wrong, and hence the fact that an error has occurred can be detected. If more than one bit is available for parity use it may be possible to determine which bit is in error, and hence to correct the error.

Fortran data elements of type LOGICAL may also be considered to be of a non-numerical nature. However, the Fortran standard specifies that numeric storage units, rather than nonnumeric storage units, be used for LOGICAL data elements. Numeric storage units are discussed in Appendix C. Typically specific numeric values, such as 1 and 0, are used to represent the logical values of .TRUE. and .FALSE. Although LOGICAL values are implemented as numeric values, the interpretation in the Fortran program is always as .TRUE. or .FALSE., not as numeric values, and the specific numeric values used for .TRUE. and .FALSE. are immaterial.

Appendix C Representation of Numeric Data

Numeric data, types INTEGER and REAL (and DOUBLEPRECISION and COMPLEX) of Fortran, must be represented in a computer as strings of 1's and 0's. Fortran uses a "numeric storage unit", which is a fixed number of bits for storing numerical data. The implementor is free to choose the number of bits to be used for the numeric storage unit. A popular choice is 32 bits since the word size on most minicomputers is 16 bits (16 bits are not enough for a numeric storage unit, but 32 are usually adequate). Also, many large computers have a 32-bit word size, which suggests a 32-bit numerical storage unit. However, some computers have different word sizes—such as 36, 48, 60 bits—and implementations on these computers would normally use numeric storage units equal to one computer word. The concepts related to storing numeric data in a string of 1's and 0's are not dependent on the number of bits in the numeric storage unit. For the discussion below a 32-bit numeric storage unit is assumed.

There are a number of ways in which a numeric value can be represented in 32 bits. The "two's complement" form is probably the most popular, and so this form will be used here to illustrate the use of numeric storage units. In two's complement representation, positive integer values are stored in ordinary binary number system form. Figure C.1 illustrates the use of 32 bits for representing integers in binary form.

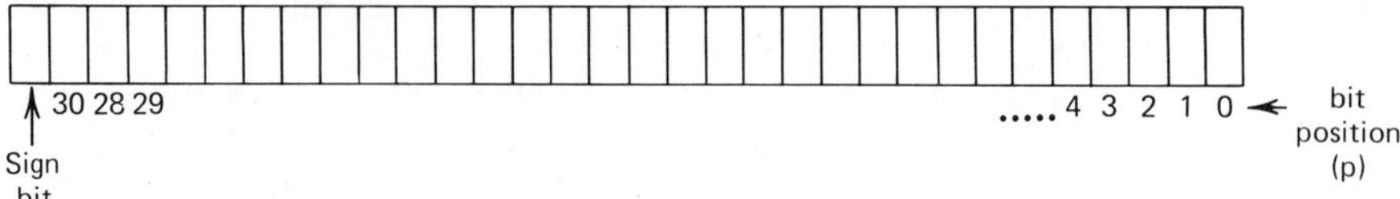

Figure C.1. A typical 32-bit numeric storage unit. Each bit position can have a "0" or a "1". The "weight" (value) of the pth position is 2**p; thus a "1" in the pth position contributes a value of 2**p to the value of the number; a "0" in the pth position contributes nothing to the value. For positive numbers the sign bit is "0" (usually), and for negative numbers the sign bit is "1".

For example, the integer value 6452 (in decimal) has the (32-bit) binary form

00000000000000000001100100110100

Since the leftmost bit is reserved for the sign (and is a "0" for positive numbers), the largest integer that a 32-bit numeric storage unit can represent is

01111111111111111111111111111111

which has the value (2**31)−1 or 2147483647 (decimal). The value of zero is represented with all zero bits (all 32 bits are zero).

Thus for positive integers, and zero, the leftmost bit is "0" and the other 31 bits represent the magnitude of the value in ordinary binary form. The corresponding negative integers could be represented the same way, except for changing the sign bit to a "1" (this is called sign + magnitude representation). A different scheme is used, however, to represent negative values using two's complement form. The rule is as follows: start with the representation of a positive integer, and then, beginning with the rightmost bit and working all the way left, up to and including the first (rightmost) "1", copy the bits as they appear; after the first "1", copy the "opposite" bits ("0" in place of "1", and "1" in place of "0"). For example the value of 6452, as used above, has the two's complement form:

```
00000000000000000001100100110100    (+6452)
11111111111111111110011011001100    (-6452) (two's complement)
```

The two's complement of 2147483647 is

```
01111111111111111111111111111111    (+2147483647)
10000000000000000000000000000001    (-2147483647)  (two's complement)
```

This process is called "taking the two's complement". If the two's complement of a negative number is taken, (i.e., if the two's complement of a two's complement is taken), then the original positive number is obtained. Note that the sign bit has value "1" for all negative integers in two's complement form, but the other 31 bits do not represent the "straight binary" value of the number. In reading a two's complement number, and ascertaining its value, one first looks at the sign bit. If it is a "0", then the number is positive and its value is the straight binary value of the other 31 bits. If the sign bit is a "1" then the number is negative and its two's complement gives its magnitude in binary.

The main reason that two's complement representation is predominantly used, rather than sign + magnitude representation, is that (somewhat surprisingly) the logic and circuitry needed for doing efficient arithmetic is simpler with two's complements.

Each real number effectively involves the storage of two integers—one for the integer part and one for the fractional part. There are other ways to represent real numbers, but all require using two "pieces" of information, equivalent to storing the integer and fractional parts of the value. The most popular form is related to "scientific notation." This is illustrated as follows:

22.375 = 0.22375 * 10**2	(in decimal standard scientific form)
= 10110.011 = 0.10110011 * 2**101	(in binary standard scientific form—note that the binary power of 2 is the decimal value 5)

The standard-form fractional part is called the "mantissa", and the power of the base is called the "exponent". A real number can be represented by storing both its mantissa and its exponent. On a computer the binary form is used, since that involves only 1's and 0's, and the 32 bits of a numeric storage unit are typically allocated as shown in Figure C.2.

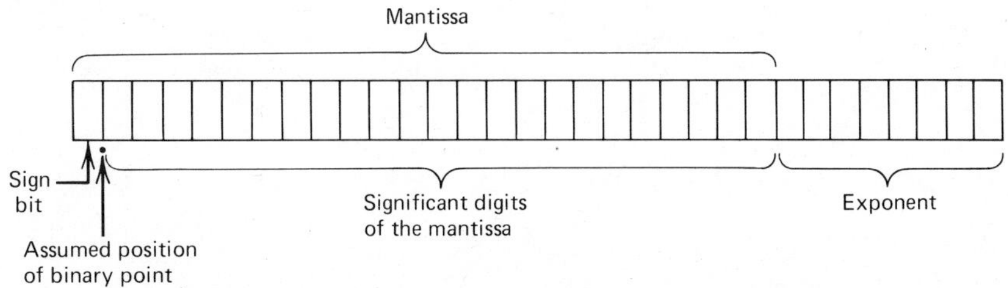

Figure C.2. Allocation of the 32 bits of a numerical storage unit for real numeric values. The value is stored as a mantissa and an exponent. Eight of the 32 bits are used for the exponent.

Thus 22.375 would be stored as

01011001100000000000000000000101

Negative exponents could be represented in 8-bit two's complement form (the rightmost 8 bits). Similarly, negative real numbers could be represented by 24-bit two's complement mantissas. For example −22.375 would be

10100110100000000000000000000101

Note that for −22.375 whereas the mantissa is negative (two's complement) the exponent is positive. The real binary number +0.10110011*2**(−101) would be stored as

01011001100000000000000011111011

that is, with a positive mantissa and a negative (two's complement) exponent.

The fact that real numbers really involve the storing of two pieces of numerical information is the reason that numeric storage units must have in the vicinity of 30 bits or more—16 are simply not enough. With 8-bit binary exponents the largest exponent size is 127, which corresponds to a decimal exponent part of about 10**38. With 24 bits left for the mantissa—one for the sign bit and 23 bits of "precision," the represented real number has about seven decimal digits of precision. If only 16 bits were used for a numeric storage unit, and half of these taken for the exponent, then real numbers could be represented with only about two decimal digits of precision.

The above schemes for representing numeric information, while they may be widely used, are by no means the only forms for numeric storage units and their use. As mentioned above, computers having a word size different from 8, 16, or 32 bits will typically use a numeric storage unit different from 32 bits. And, while two's complement machines may be the most common, sign + magnitude, one's complement, and other forms are used to represent integer data. Even greater diversity exists in the use of a numeric storage unit to represent real data. Exponents may be 9, 10, or 16 bits, for example, and may be in excess representation, powers of 16 (rather than 2), or some other form. Normally the Fortran programmer need not know the form of representation of numeric data, but when this knowledge is desired the documentation for the particular computer being used must be consulted.

INDEX